Leaving the Cave

Evolutionary Naturalism in Social-Scientific Thought

PAT DUFFY HUTCHEON

Thesis ₁₁ 46 5 1976

Wilfrid Laurier University Press

Canadian Cataloguing in Publication Data

Hutcheon, Pat Duffy, 1926-
    Leaving the cave : evolutionary naturalism in
social-scientific thought

Includes bibliographical references and index.
ISBN 0-88920-258-3

1. Social sciences – Philosophy – History.
2. Naturalism.   I. Title.

H61.H87 1996   300'.1   C95-932396-1

Cover design by Leslie Macredie using an illustration created for
this book by Sandra Woolfrey.

Printed in Canada

Leaving the Cave: Evolutionary Naturalism in Social-Scientific Thought has been produced from a manuscript supplied in electronic form by the author.

*To my grandchildren
and all their generation*

The frailty of our reason
and the brevity of our sojourn here
need not deter the inquiring mind.
For by searching out the footsteps
of the giants, we — like they —
can leave the confines of the cave behind.

— Pat Duffy Hutcheon

Contents

Preface

This book was prompted by a question that just would not go away. How can one explain the general failure of social science to accumulate reliable knowledge? It has been around, in its present modern form, for over three centuries, and its seeds have been germinating for much longer. Why, then, the dearth of progress in all but a few isolated areas of scholarship? Why are practitioners in the social realm (such as therapists, politicians, educators and criminologists) still being forced to operate virtually on a "wing and a prayer" while the public continues to suffer the consequences of failed trial-and-error interventions?

As a sociologist of historical, theoretical and interdisciplinary bent, I had become dissatisfied with the excuses of the increasingly beleaguered scientists within these disciplines, and with the popular celebrations of irrationality favoured by the anti-scientists among us. In the end, it was in the justifications of the latter group that I discerned a glimmer of the possible answer.

I began to conjecture that there must be some formidable obstacle to the scientific study of humanity in our culture — if not in human nature, as the non-rationalists believe and even seem to hope. It came to me that the dominant current of thought in every society, in every historical era, has been fundamentally opposed to the very idea of the operation of cause and effect in human behaviour. This led me to ponder on the nature of the world view that *would* encourage social science to flourish, and to marvel that elements of it had continued to survive at all, in an environment so consistently hostile.

For I saw at once that the way of thinking conducive to the development of a scientific approach to human studies has been with us for a long time, although its influence is muted even now, in this so-called age of science. It is a way of thinking usually referred to as *naturalism*, and it has been associated throughout history with the companion idea of *evolution*. It stems from the premise that human beings are continuous with all of nature, and that all of nature is continuously evolving. I recognized, as well, what I had already sensed but not fully understood about this minority stream of thought. It has always posed a threat to the established philosophy in every time and place in history. It could not do otherwise, for its two necessary premises about existence, and of the place of humankind within it, are in direct conflict with prevailing beliefs about human nature.

This dilemma is too often overlooked by practising social scientists. We seldom pause to reflect that the premises of naturalism are also the philosophical prerequisites for any behavioural or social discipline attempting to be *scientific* in fact as well as name. Without a firm grounding in the philosophy of naturalism, social science can be nothing but an empty promise. It is imperative, therefore, that we understand the nature of the necessary premises of this world view.

The first concerns a commonality and consistency among all existing inorganic and organic forms. It implies that humans are an integral part of the "stuff" of the universe, no less natural than any other part. This naturalistic premise requires no injection of — nor interjection by — an unknowable "spirit" from beyond nature at some crucial point in our emergence. Nor does it demand belief in some mysterious access to a consciousness beyond that created by our experience of nature. It implies, simply, that our actions and relationships (regardless of the complexity of the connections involved) are as subject to causality as are those of any other existing entities. It is this crucial conclusion that both justifies and demands the use of the scientific method in studies of human relations.

A recognition of human groundedness within nature has allowed the pioneers of naturalism to focus on its other defining premise. This has to do with the *distinctiveness* of our species as the only animal thus far to have evolved a critical consciousness and culture. It involves the human animal, firstly, in its role as *knower*, and secondly, as *artist and valuer*. Proponents of the naturalistic view have tended to be interested in the evolutionary origin and use of reason — and of language and sense-perception — in the ongoing human task of observing regularities, and of proposing and testing explanations of these. Many have celebrated the worth of our species' imaginative and aesthetic products such as architecture, music, literature and the visual arts. Others have dealt with the significance of humankind's capacity for morality: the propensity to create ideals, and to make choices, which then function to direct and shape individual characters and the very culture which gave them birth.

People with these sorts of abiding interests, commitments and assumptions have been the true social scientists all through history — whether they were known as social philosophers, philosophers of science, humanists, psychologists, sociologists, anthropologists, political economists, or by more esoteric labels. Often they have pursued their chosen path at great risk to their careers, if not, indeed, their very lives. For an insistence on explaining human behaviour in terms of natural evolutionary processes undermines the very foundation of "conventional wisdom." It has been an unpopular practice in every age.

At this point in my thinking, I knew what I must do. I had come to the realization that too often we have been taught to revere the wrong heroes. We have been encouraged to create larger-than-life idols out of the prophets of mysticism, and to cower within the caves of absolutism that their words have conjured up. I decided that it is time for a thorough look at the builders of the naturalistic and evolutionary current within social-scientific thought: one that would consider them in the context of their times, and in all their human fallibility and lonely courage. These are the people who dared to ask, "How did it come to be?" and "How do we know that is true?" and "Is there not a natural explanation for those events?" It was their habit of asking and checking out ideas that was important — not their answers, although we can only marvel at the enduring quality of some of those early insights. These were the ancestors of a *scientific* approach to what we have prematurely called social science, and if that deeply human project is ever fully realized, it will be due, in large part, to the maps they drew.

I discovered that, at times, their answers led us into detours and costly dead-ends. Inevitably, however, the *method* forced succeeding inquirers back to the enduring path that opened up ahead. And the search went on.

The criterion used for selecting my heroes was a universally influential contribution to the origin, survival or enhancement of concepts crucial to the development of any or all of the major components of the naturalistic world view. These are: (1) the idea of evolution as the key to understanding change at all levels of existence; (2) the crucial assumption of cause and effect in human behaviour; (3) the idea of knowledge as humanly devised and verified; and (4) the belief that morality and creativity are grounded in, and restricted to, human experience.

On the whole, my attempt to trace the perseverance of this naturalistic current within social thought throughout twenty-six centuries of cultural evolution has been at once intriguing and profoundly sad. From the perspective of humanity in general I found it to be the story of opportunities lost and possibilities unrealized. All too often the record revealed a painful "rediscovery of the wheel," century after century. The failure of scholars to evaluate and build upon what came before — and even to read seriously the works of their contemporaries operating from competing models and in related disciplines — has been an almost insurmountable obstacle to progress in every era. It is my hope that this book will be a means by which all who enter any of the social sciences may become aware of the common ontological, biological and psychological grounding of the entire field, and of the encompassing conceptual map within which their own particular problem area must be located.

For the major discovery of this study is that, over the centuries, there has indeed been a cumulative build-up and enhancement of certain significant ideas. I have tried to show how these ideas form the outlines of a commanding new conceptual framework: one that is beginning to be recognized as *evolutionary naturalism*. I view this as the source of an emerging paradigm that could provide social science with the type of power given to the life sciences by Darwin's breakthrough, and to the physical sciences by Copernicus, Newton and Einstein. The thinkers whose works are dealt with in the following study have either made profound contributions to this evolving system of ideas or have created uniquely influential roadblocks or detours that had to be surmounted by subsequent pioneers. Sometimes they did both.

This book is not intended to be a compendium of modern social science. Nor is it an exhaustive history of ideas. Rather, it represents an attempt to chart the evolution of those concepts deemed necessary to the success of any scientific study of humanity — through the lives and writings of a relatively few selected thinkers whose works seem to provide the most essential links in that specific evolutionary chain. Crude beginnings of these concepts are to be found in the theories of the Hellenic Greeks and in early Buddhist and Confucian thought. I have attempted to trace their subsequent development through the works of the early pioneers of modern social science to those social theorists of the late nineteenth and twentieth centuries whose ideas have been firmly rooted in the Darwinian and Pavlovian revolutions in biology, genetics and neuropsychology.

In each case, my intent was to locate the individual thinker within the relevant cultural setting — as determined by history, the content of the available community of ideas, and family circumstance. I wanted to show how each person was shaped to some degree by current environmental influences and how each, in turn, was privileged to "stand on the shoulders" of those giants who had gone before. And, as much as possible, I used primary, rather than secondary, sources. I decided, where feasible, to do a comprehensive study of the original words of the theorists dealt with — attempting to organize, condense and explain their ideas for students and educated lay readers. I wanted to avoid the many serious omissions, errors, deliberate distortions and well-intentioned misinterpretations that inevitably creep into the secondary literature and are passed along as authentic aspects of the original works. My sincere hope is that, in taking this route, I have not inserted new misunderstandings of my own.

I discovered that the focus of social theory in every generation kept returning to certain issues, and it was the stand taken on these that identified the incipient evolutionary naturalists. Crucial contributions to the evolution of this current of thought involve the following: (1) a recognition of the universality of cause and effect; (2) confirmation of the premise of order underlying the nature of all things; (3) a recognition of the critical function of language in the process of human knowing; (4) a spelling-out of the conditional nature of scientific knowledge; (5) a resolution of the free will/determinism problem which recognizes the significance of the issue for morality; (6) a response to the question of how humans can determine "the good" that dispenses with the premises of dualism; (7) an emphasis on the continuity of means and ends, and thus of the inevitable contribution of human choices to the course of history; (8) an identification of the experiential sources of moral development; (9) a focus on the social origins of power and structures of authority, and on the enduring conflict between democratic and totalitarian approaches to politics; (10) a recognition of the interactive nature of individual innovation and culture, and the consequent necessary relationships among art, politics and morality; (11) a concern with the nature of biological evolution, and its implications for our understanding of individual and social behaviour as complex products of an inextricably intertwined genetic-social co-evolution; and (12) a corresponding concern with the nature of cultural evolution, and with the role of science in the process.

As a woman, I particularly wanted to include as many female contributors as male. But after a lengthy period of frustrating research, I came to realize that we feminists cannot have it both ways. We cannot, on the one hand, acknowledge the fact that women in the past have seldom enjoyed the leisure or credentials necessary for advanced intellectual pursuits, and, on the other hand, insist that our contribution in this hitherto-male preserve has been equal to that of those more fortunate humans who benefited as well from the support of their female partners. We can only deal with the predictable results of our legacy of limited opportunity, and, by means of our current contributions, ensure that a history of ideas in the twenty-first century will present a vastly different picture.

In writing from a female perspective, I have been able to emphasize relevant but usually overlooked achievements and views of women. Furthermore, I am convinced that the chapter on Harriet Martineau may well accomplish more for the cause of equality of opportunity for my gender than any artificial balancing of female-to-male representation could ever do. It tells the story of how, almost alone — and in the face of a virtually insurmountable wall of cultural sexism — she pioneered a scientific sociological approach to the study of humanity. And how, in that process, she sparked a revolution in world view concerning the role of women in society and of the human species in the nature of things: a fundamental conceptual and behavioural transformation that has yet to reach its culmination.

The other female whose work rated a separate chapter is Hannah Arendt: a mid-twentieth-century theorist whose contributions to social-scientific thought have also been sadly underrated. Arendt's work on the nature of totalitarianism — and on the related concepts of power and authority — ranks with the best ever done on the subject. Her courageous and insightful analyses and her prescient conclusions, departing radically from the opinions of the time, have never been adequately appreciated by the social-science establishment.

Others whose work is often missing from compendiums of social science include Herbert Spencer, whose fundamental and lasting influence on the field has accordingly been overlooked; Ivan Pavlov, whose revolutionary breakthrough has been little understood by subsequent generations of social scientists who should have benefited from it; John Dewey, whose philosophy provides a large part of the necessary epistemological foundation for any scientific approach to the study of humanity; George Santayana, whose attempts to unify social theory comprise an essential link between the ideas of Spencer and those of Jean Piaget and modern cognitive theorists; and Charles Darwin — along with those twentieth-century evolutionists whose contributions are crucial to any possible future progress in the social sciences in general.

It is sadly apparent that the story traced in the following pages has been far from one of uninterrupted progress. I discovered that some of the most influential of the social theorists of the past several centuries have led us into what can aptly be termed "evolutionary dead-ends." These were the people who proposed mystically oriented theories of subjective relativism and romanticism, as well as those who used the social disciplines to promote ideologies of either the Left or Right. I have sought to identify the origins of these currents in certain of the ideas of Jean-Jacques Rousseau, Karl Marx, Herbert Spencer, Henri Bergson and Edmund Husserl, for example.

In the absence of a comprehensive, integrated paradigm for the entire field of study, the above currents have been free to exert great power. They have rendered the social disciplines extremely vulnerable to competing creeds and bandwagons, and to the seductions of technology. The evidence also suggests a further unfortunate consequence of the continuing influence of such currents — and of the encompassing tide of cultural dualism from which they periodically emerge. This has been a premature establishment of boundaries for the field of human behaviour and institutions. Not only have these studies been artificially "fenced off" from biology and the inorganic sciences — and from philosophy and history — but inappropriate internal fences have been erected as well. The result is an incongruous aggregate of theoretically and practically isolated subjects, approaches and schools. It is a compartmentalization that appears neither logically nor empirically warranted; yet it has become firmly institutionalized by the happenstance of history and the demands of university politics.

Finally, my assessment of the mixed legacy of these intellectual giants has led me to a conclusion concerning the necessary future role of social science. It seems clear that, with the achievement of an authentically *scientific* study of individual development and social relations, humankind would for the first time have the capacity to adapt in a disciplined and reasoned way to the problems thrown up by the ever-changing circumstances of our existence. An effective social science — and *only* that — could provide us with an adaptive problem-solving instrument for guiding the course of cultural evolution in the direction determined by our collective values.

Inevitably this has been too large an undertaking for one volume. I have tried to do justice to the subject and to the creators and carriers of the philosophical foundations of evolutionary naturalism. My objective has been to contribute to a recognition of this particular system of ideas as the most powerful ever to evolve in the social studies — and as the most likely source of a guiding paradigm for a more fruitful and reliable science of human behaviour and culture than we have yet achieved. My hope is that this book will inspire today's students of the social scene to begin a lifetime exploration on their own in these magnificent currents of human thought; and to build, in their turn, on the best of what was built before. And I trust that it will spark a renewed appreciation for the remarkable people whose work still casts both light and shadow upon the evolving path that all who would be social scientists must tread.

Acknowledgements

L<i>eaving the Cave</i> is the culmination of a ten-year labour of love, during which I have received aid and counsel from more people than I could possibly acknowledge. I especially would like to express my gratitude to the Humanities and Social Sciences Federation of Canada. This book has been published with the help of a grant from the Humanities and Social Sciences Federation of Canada, using funds provided by the Social Sciences and Humanities Research Council of Canada. Leslie Enid Butters of the Federation and Sandra Woolfrey of Wilfrid Laurier University Press were particularly helpful. The patient and professional copy-editing job performed by Maura Brown deserves special mention as well.

A number of colleagues have read the manuscript — either in part or in its entirety — and I wish to take this opportunity to thank them for their generosity and helpfulness. Richard Dawkins, Professor of Zoology at Oxford, gave me expert criticism and moral support in the project's early days, and Professor Thomas S. Kuhn of the Massachusetts Institute of Technology's Department of Linguistics and Philosophy was generous, as well, in his response to my request for information. Lynn McDonald, Professor of Sociology in the Department of Sociology and Anthropology at the University of Guelph read and commented on the entire manuscript, as did Professor Donald Fisher of the Department of Educational Studies at the University of British Columbia. Both of these readers offered knowledgeable and constructive suggestions which contributed significantly to the strengthening and sharpening of the message throughout. Others whose responses to selected chapters were much appreciated are Professor John Novak of the Faculty of Education at Brock University and Professor Loren H. Houtman of the Department of Educational Foundations at Western Illinois University. Carolyn Hutcheon in the undergraduate science program of the University of British Columbia and Shane Westcott in the undergraduate arts program of the University of Calgary did a superb editing job at one stage. Both provided me with invaluable feedback from the perspective of second-year students — one in the biological and the other in the social sciences.

I also wish to thank the following for permission to quote liberally from their publications: Cambridge University Press (North American branch) for their 1978 publication of W.G. Runciman's superbly edited *Max Weber: Selections in Translation*; the Stanford University Press for Donald M. Frame's 1958 translation of *The Complete Essays of Montaigne*; and MIT

Press for their 1955 edition of George Santayana's *The Life of Reason* and their 1972 edition of George Santayana's *Realms of Being*.

Certain brief sections in this book have been published previously in articles. I would like to acknowledge Gordon and Breach Publishers in the Netherlands who gave me permission to reprint a few paragraphs of "Evolutionary Theory in Freud, Piaget and Skinner" (*World Futures* 44 [1995]: 203-11) and Prometheus Books of Amherst, New York, for the same in the case of "Through a Glass Darkly: The Concept of Love in Freud," in David Goicoechea, ed., *The Nature and Pursuit of Love: The Philosophy of Irving Singer* (1995, pp. 183-95). I should also mention my review essay of Paul J. Hager's 1994 book, *Continuity and Change in the Development of Russell's Philosophy* (in *Studies in Philosophy and Education* 15, 3 [1996]: n.p.), in which can be found a paragraph used in my chapter on Russell. My article, "Popper and Kuhn on the Evolution of Knowledge" (*Brock Review* 4, 1/2 [Spring 1996]: 28-37), also contains some material repeated in *Leaving the Cave*.

No list of acknowledgements would be complete without recognition of the steadfast support and advice of my husband, Sandy, who was an integral part of the creative process throughout. And finally, I wish I could find the words to thank all those teachers, faculty members and students in universities in Canada, the United States and Australia who helped me, over many years, to "stand on the shoulders of giants." I can only express the sincere hope that this book may do the same for the generations who follow after me.

One

Distant Echoes of a Road Not Taken
Undercurrents of Naturalism in the Classical World

Nothing at all is ever born from nothing
By the gods' will. Ah but men's eyes are frightened
Because they see on earth and in the heavens,
Many events whose causes are to them
Impossible to fix; so they suppose
That god's will is the reason. As for us,
Once we have seen that nothing comes from nothing,
We shall perceive with greater clarity
What we are looking for, whence each thing comes,
How things are caused, and no "god's will" about it.
— Lucretius, *De Rerum Natura*

Where did we come from? What sort of creatures are we? What is the nature of this existence of which we are a part, and how did it come to be? How can we distinguish what is real? How can we know the good? What causes people to believe and value and behave as they do? What effect, if any, do human actions have on the scheme of things?

For at least twenty-six centuries, a minority of human beings in each generation have found the courage to express a dissenting viewpoint on these issues. They have risked animosity, ridicule and even personal danger in order to formulate explanations that did not rely on supernatural entities and essentially mysterious forces. They have dared, instead, to look for answers in the observable surroundings: answers involving previous history as well as current conditions and the natural consequences of these. Their answers have been the kind that lead to ever-more-penetrating questions, rather than to the end of inquiry. It is in such answers, as expressed by some of the earliest recorded thinkers, that we find the first stirrings of a philosophy of evolutionary naturalism.

For it seems that Western cultures are the heirs of not one but two currents of philosophical thought: currents co-existing in uneasy and unequal relationship since the sixth century BCE. One has been a powerful tradition, usually

---

References for this chapter are on p. 16-17.

representing the views of the elite and mainstream of every generation. Out of this dominant current has evolved the dualist philosophy of the world view so familiar to all of us. The other is the minor theme that pictures humans and the universe as natural rather than divine. It is an undercurrent, always present, but often unnoticed and uncomprehended by the majority. Yet from it has come the most effective and reliable process of knowledge-building the world has ever seen: the method of modern science. And it has been a major source of the democratic ideal which has never ceased to beckon and inspire humanity. The struggle for survival of this abundantly fruitful stream of thought is a story worth repeating to every generation.

The power of culture

Metaphysical dualism is a powerful force in shaping the way the world's current inhabitants assimilate and interpret their experience. Whether consciously recognized or not, socialization implants in each new generation the culturally prevailing conceptual framework which defines their most private notions of the universe and their own place and relations within it.

For human culture in general the perspective has tended to be one of dualism. This view incorporates two realms of existence: physical and spiritual, or natural and supernatural. Dualism also implies two discrete categories of experience (secular and sacred) and two kinds of knowing (experiential and mystical). Application of the scientific method (disciplined observation, reasoning and public verification) as a means of achieving knowledge or understanding is limited to the first of these. The spiritual realm — laying claim to matters relating to entities such as those called God, soul, mind, consciousness, virtue and wisdom — is reserved for certain essentially mysterious religious or mystical processes. In this domain the scientific mode of inquiry is not welcomed.

So dominant is metaphysical dualism in all cultures that it determines the language available for discussing the human condition as well as the very terms under which that discussion can occur. Abstract constructs having no referents or meaning beyond a dualist world view abound in general discourse. People argue about whether or not the mind can affect the body, a question that makes no sense unless we first assume a mind/body dualism. Most of us distinguish religious systems on the basis of beliefs about what happens to the soul after death, or to the spirit during life, taking body/soul dualism as a given. And there is little acceptance of the need to conform to the rules of logic or of evidence when discussing human thinking, feeling and valuing.

This unfortunate compartmentalization has endured because, according to prevailing cultural definitions, human affairs belong to the intuitive and spiritual: that inherently unknowable realm of being where any one opinion is as valid as any other. And where, at times, the opinions of all must defer to the pronouncements of the religious leader with some special divine access to the supernatural — or to a universal Mind. However, there is another way of viewing reality. Its roots go back to the very beginning of recorded history: to the Buddha and Confucius and their early followers. It can be traced, as well, to the intellectual awakening of the early Greeks in the formative period of Hellenic civilization.

The evolution of naturalism in Hellenic culture

The evolution of Western naturalism began prior to 500 BCE with a group of Ionian thinkers who were descendants of an ancient Greek people living along the shore of Asia Minor. Called the Milesian School, it reached its apex during the flowering of Hellenism from the fifth to the fourth centuries, culminating in the teachings of the Abderan School of atomists, as well as those of the sophists. The atomists taught that humans differ from inorganic and other organic forms solely by the arrangement of the atoms that make them up. Sophists introduced the idea that values, tastes and even ways of perceiving are relative to humanity — rather than being supernaturally ordered.

The naturalistic outlook came under strong attack in the latter half of the fourth century by Plato and his followers. Although Plato's dialogues are ambiguous, certain generalizations are warranted. He appears to have believed that humans differ in essence from any other level of existence, and are not to be understood solely as aspects of nature. He (and the Platonists who came after) thought that humanity has access to an "ideal" realm prior to and encompassing the "material": an essentially true realm of which observable phenomena are the mere shadows on the walls of the cave. Plato viewed reasoning as a pure capacity of the soul; all other aspects of the human being, such as empirical cognition, are "of the body" and quite separate. Authentic understanding is limited to knowledge of the Form, or "essence" of reality, and is not accessible by means of experience.

From Plato's time, dualism was dominant in Greek thought. However, one can trace elements of a materialistic monism as they appear in the few remaining fragments of the teachings of the philosopher Epicurus, who became influential during the late third and early second centuries. In fact, the naturalistic philosophy called Epicureanism managed to survive as a minor philosophical and ethical movement for seven hundred years, until Christianity became the official and all-powerful state religion of the Roman Empire.

The beginning

The Ionians, sometimes called the physical philosophers, were the first Western thinkers to speculate about the origin and nature of the world in other than animistic, supernatural and mystical terms. They looked for causes not in mysterious supernatural forces but within nature itself. Thales of Miletus (600 BCE), usually considered to have been the first scientist, developed systematic theories of astronomy and geometry. He sought elemental substances by which to explain all existence. His successor, Anaximander (570 BCE) continued in this endeavour, theorizing that all of the universe must be made up of a material substance of some kind. Probably the first evolutionist, he originated the idea that early forms of life emerged from moist conditions, and that higher species, including humans, grew out of these in an ongoing developmental process. What the Milesians had in common was the idea that natural forces operate everywhere in a consistent and explainable way, and that nothing is created by arbitrary actions of beings or forces beyond nature. It is difficult to imagine the genius of such men, flowering among the myths and magic and animism of their times!

About a generation later, Heraclitus (540-480 BCE) built upon the ideas of the Milesians, including the notion of the mutability of animal species. A belief that change is the only constant in nature is apparent in his famous comment about not being able to step into the same river twice. For Heraclitus, it was fire that formed the one basic material principle of the universe: a universe of continuous substance in the process of becoming. The fire results in steam, then condenses and fills the oceans and eventually seeps back into the hot bowels of the earth where it returns to fire again in a never-ending cycle of emergence and decay. Perhaps because of this, Heraclitus is credited with the idea of a continuum rather than discrete categories as the ultimate ordering principle in nature. There is no distinction between mind (or spirit) and body in his work.

Heraclitus also emphasized the importance of human reason in any attempt by humans to understand this single, continuous realm of experience. Another early philosophical naturalist, Alcmaeon of Croton (*c*. 500 BCE), is remembered as the first medical scientist. He believed that all animals learn through the senses, but that humans are superior in the power of thought.

Opposing currents

Anaxagoras (500-428) is known as the philosopher of the Periclean Age: a time of revolutionary transition. An Ionian Greek who taught at Athens, he thought that the universe began as a state of perfection which was subsequently organized by a divine Mind into an ongoing mechanism. Anaxagoras is of particular interest because he apparently tried to straddle two irreconcilable positions. On the one hand, he exhibited the scientific curiosity and radical scepticism of the materialists, along with their commitment to the search for rational explanations of all activities. On the other hand, he insisted on the divinity of the sun and moon, and on the omniscience of a supernatural Mind. These teachings signal a retreat from naturalism and a succumbing to the dualist and mystical currents of the time.

The period seems to have witnessed a powerful upsurge of dualism, idealism and mysticism within philosophy. This revolutionary change is seen initially in the ideas of Parmenides of Elia, who had probably influenced Anaxagoras. Parmenides taught that change is apparent rather than real: a mere illusion of the senses masking the eternal essence below the surface of things. His ideas are thought to be an early source of Plato's theory. During the same period, Pythagoras of Samos developed a sort of mysticism of numbers, complete with cosmology and eschatology, which exerted powerful popular appeal.

The sophists

Protagoras of Abdera (484-410), a contemporary of Anaxagoras, seems not to have been tempted by the "new age" mysticism and dualism. He is known as the founder of the sophist movement, a group of professional teachers later reviled by Plato and his followers. He was an honoured teacher in Athens for many years and a friend of the great democratic Athenian leader, Pericles. Protagoras was sceptical of the increasingly speculative philosophy of the period, concluding that it had lost its earlier grounding in human experience. His most famous sentence, "Man [or 'humanity'] is the measure of all things," may well establish him as the first humanist. What he probably intended to express by this was the need to move philosophical discourse from the heavens to humanity, and to understand how human beings can come to "know" anything.

Protagoras introduced the idea that human perception is relative to external and internal conditions — although he also emphasized the reality of the material world which is the object of perception. He rejected the possibility of absolute knowledge of that world, recognizing the built-in limitations on human measurement imposed by the fact that matter is always in flux and differently seen from different perspectives. He was equally sceptical of the concept of the divine as the source of absolute good. For example: "As regards the gods I am not able to know whether they exist or do not exist. . . . There are many things that hinder [such] knowledge — the obscurity of the subject and the shortness of human life" (Boardman:273).

Protagoras' scepticism led him to repudiate the idea that right and wrong are decreed by supernatural forces. He taught, instead, that ethics is a practical matter, governed by the principle of prudence. No doubt it was this radical and sophisticated theory of knowledge and morality that led to the charge of extreme subjectivism and relativism against Protagoras and his followers. It is likely that later dualist philosophers simply could not comprehend any basis for morality or knowledge other than supernatural authority (or the pure "form" or "essence" of Plato) and therefore wrongly assumed that the sophists were preaching moral anarchy and nihilism. We are fortunate that enough of their works escaped destruction to demonstrate that some of them, at least, were not guilty of these charges.

One of Protagoras' few surviving treatises is devoted to the first known systematic treatment of grammar. Other fragments indicate the emphasis he placed on the priority of the individual over the state, his championship of the common person, and his rejection of slavery, chauvinism and war. In general, the sophists taught that laws and institutions are human products which vary from group to group, and are not inherent in the order of things. Contrary to the conventional wisdom of the time, they claimed that no one was ever born to be a slave. On the other hand, they explained, *natural* laws are everywhere the same. And natural laws, unlike social conventions, are indeed compulsory in an absolute and irrevocable sense!

In questioning the morality of slavery (which even democratic Athens took for granted) Protagoras and his followers were being very courageous. These radical ideas were congenial to Pericles, however, and while he led the Assembly at Athens, the sophists were safe. Pericles governed in the tradition of Solon, the great stateman and poet of the sixth century who had democratized Athenian government and established a code of law. But the Athenian Alliance suffered grievous losses in the Great Peloponnesian War against those Greek city-states led by Sparta. This was followed by internal rebellion, wholesale massacres and the ravages of the black plague brought home by soldiers returning from Africa and the Orient in the years from 433 to 430. The people turned against Pericles, blaming him for their misfortunes, and sided with the oligarchs who assumed leadership. With Pericles' death in battle in 429, the sophists fell from favour and were much maligned by Plato, who was propagating a very different message.

The atomists

A contemporary of Protagoras, a little-known philosopher named Leucippus, is remembered as the founder of materialistic atomism. He produced two significant works, *Great World System*, and *On the Mind*, of which only a few sections survive. His theory stated that all is matter, and that all matter is homogeneous in its ultimate nature, although consisting of an infinity of small, indivisible particles called atoms. These atoms are constantly in motion. Through their collisions and regroupings they form various compounds, which in turn at some point must have gathered into a "whirl" that resulted in our universe. He guessed that the earth is drum-shaped, rather than flat, and he placed it in the centre of the universe. What happened to Leucippus or to the bulk of his writings is not known.

Leucippus' student, Democritus of Abdera (460-370) developed and vastly extended his teacher's ideas. He would have grown to manhood just as Periclean Athens was beginning to disintegrate. During most of his adult life the Athenian Alliance to which Abdera belonged was buffeted by the Peloponnesian Wars with their accompanying civil strife. We know little of how Democritus lived and worked, as only a few of his writings survive. The Persian (and then Greek) imperialism of the period would have provided a priceless opportunity for people like him to explore surrounding territories. It is known that Democritus travelled widely in the East, where he may well have encountered early Buddhists and Confucianists, with their message of naturalism.

Democritus' scholarly work involved a considerable elaboration and refinement of the theories of Leucippus. Like his predecessor, Democritus rejected the prevailing view of a dualism of body and mind, along with the commitment to a pluralism of elements typical of much of the previous speculative philosophy. He is recognized as having been the first to formally spell out the monism toward which earlier materialists or naturalists were groping. His ideas are also the first indication of individualism and universalism in Greek thought. The system of knowledge he developed was organized into five categories: ethical, physical, mathematical, aesthetic and technical. Within these he completed comprehensive treatises on cosmology, astronomy, geography, physiology, medicine, sensation, epistemology, geometry, computation, magnetism, musical theory, linguistics, agriculture, painting and more. According to Diogenes Laertius, third-century-BCE author of the world's oldest compendium of philosophy, Democritus produced seventy-three books covering the entire range of knowledge. What little remains of all this gives us an indication of the range and profundity of what seems to have been wantonly destroyed in subsequent years.

The cosmology of Democritus explained the universe in terms of atoms infinite in number, arrangement, position and variability of shape, and infinitesimal in size. He thought of atoms as perpetually in motion within a surrounding vacuum called "the void." He maintained that all existence must be corporeal — composed of atoms which are the elemental "stuff" of nature — though not continuously present everywhere. He seems to have been the first to postulate the notion of a vacuum as a necessary context for the motion of atoms. This condition of motion was a given for Democritus. He saw no logical necessity for a "first cause."

Democritus on causality

The imagination of Democritus reached far beyond the limited knowledge and the animistic and teleological views of his time. For example, his ideas about causality are startlingly modern. He taught that, although there is no need to postulate a first cause, the *course* of all movement is determined, and that, from the human point of view, nature's course seems to reflect both chance and necessity. However, he was defining chance in a very specific sense. He did not mean a randomness inherent in nature, enabling events to have no relation to natural causes. Rather, he seems to have believed that each effect is *necessarily* caused. But he maintained that in many instances the necessary causes involved are so complex and multiple that it is beyond human powers to comprehend them. He also made it clear that when he referred to chance as causal, he meant something that exceeds current human powers of prediction. However, he apparently believed that a condition of complete omniscience (impossible for humans) would allow for complete predictability.

Objectively, then, there is no such thing as randomness, or chance, according to Democritus. All existence is subject to a universally operating necessity. But *within this* it is possible to distinguish what are, for limited human knowledge-seekers with their culturally derived instruments, two different kinds of causation. There is that which necessitates cosmic reality and that which happens when a seed germinates. For Democritus, the latter is predictable for humans, and therefore recognized as "necessary," while the former is not predictable and tends to be viewed subjectively as "random."

To sum up Democritus' views on causality:

1. Every event is determined. There is no such thing as chance when we are using the term in an absolute or objective sense.
2. The notion of chance or randomness has to do with the human subject's ability to predict complex events and is useful when referring to a cause which is likely to remain forever obscure to us.
3. The incomprehensibility of causes which we call random is due to the indefinitely large number of possibilities surrounding the occurrence. Most of these our sensing techniques cannot assimilate nor our thought processes imagine.

The impact of Democritus

Democritus believed that sensation and thought are both alterations of the body, operating as a continuous process. He claimed that sensations result from the impact of images, or physical contact with the environment, and thought acts upon this data from the senses. Perhaps acting on Protagoras' principle of prudence, Democritus did not ever deny the existence of souls and gods. However, he attempted to render them harmless by defining them in corporeal terms. He insisted that gods, like humans, are governed by necessity, and that souls are mortal and perish with the body.

One of the most profound ideas originating with Democritus was his repudiation of the cyclical conception of time that was held by the ancients, whereby all existence was believed to be repeated in endlessly recurring cycles. For him, time was the impression made upon living things of the succession of natural events like light and darkness. Equally remarkable was his suggestion that humans once lived like other animals, in caves, and only slowly and gradually developed social institutions. These may stand with his sophisticated theory of causation and his monist theory of atoms as his most significant and lasting contributions to the evolution of human thought.

In rejecting the demand for a first active agent of motion, beyond nature, Democritus was following Leucippus. And both philosophers were nearer than was Aristotle, writing two generations later, to the views of modern science. Aristotle, like his master, Plato, was a convinced teleologist: one who views all natural processes only in terms of some end toward which an external purpose is propelling them. The fact that Aristotle's system of philosophy survived, rather than that of Democritus, has had profound consequences for humanity.

Thucydides

The historian Thucydides was a contemporary of Democritus. Exiled from Athens in 424 BCE, following Pericles' death during the war between Athens and Sparta, he did not live to complete the famous *History* which was published in 395 BCE. His significance for us is that he might well be considered the first *scientifically* oriented historian — indeed, the first practising social scientist. He originated a disciplined methodology designed to correlate eyewitness accounts and thus ensure the utmost possible objectivity. He also attempted to relate cause to consequence in human behaviour without resort to mysterious governing forces.

Socrates

Like Democritus, Socrates (469-399) lived through much of the period of Athenian greatness and decline known to historians as the Hellenic era of Greek civilization. But the lives of the two men differed greatly. Democritus was distant from the seat of power. He lived in Abdera, a city on the coast of Thrace, off the Thracian Sea north of the Aegean: an area controlled by Persia during his early years. Socrates grew up in Athens, the heart of the Greek world, and seems not to have gone far afield. Democritus was the highly educated son of a wealthy family who supported authoritarian Persian rule, while Socrates was of the working class, a trained sculptor with little formal education. Democritus spent his inheritance in travelling and studying, returning to live out the rest of his long life as a happily penniless scholar. Socrates, on the other hand, rose from social obscurity to a position of great status as the teacher of the offspring of the privileged, until he was condemned to death by the Athenian democracy in 399 for subverting the young.

Democritus was a lifelong democrat; a philosophical materialist concerned with justifying, and guaranteeing a cultural climate conducive to, the pursuit of science. Socrates became an absolutist and idealist; a supporter of oligarchy, whose work as a teacher seems to have been dedicated to undermining democracy and the very possibility of science. Democritus produced seventy-three books encompassing and organizing the entire range of human knowledge. Socrates wrote nothing. Yet, thanks to the subsequent dominance of Plato and his school, and the success of Plato's self-serving reconstruction of history, it is Socrates who is worshipped as the epitome of open inquiry, while Democritus is largely ignored.

The mystical dualism popularized by Parmenides and Pythagoras had wrought a virtual sea-change in Greek culture during the late fifth and early fourth centuries. For the first time the notion of the soul as an entity apart from and in opposition to the body had gained credence. This encouraged the theory that there exist two realms of reality: the one apparent to the senses and the other, essentially unknowable but eternal and absolute. Of these, it was the observable that was considered the least true. This meant that knowledge and virtue could not be learned through experience or teaching and thereby made available to all (as the sophists believed) but could only be discovered through a complicated process of definition and circular logic requiring the guidance of a uniquely inspired guru. There was one man in Athens whose ideas and teaching style almost perfectly reflected this change in the prevailing winds. That man was Socrates.

There are three images of Socrates available, from the plays of Aristophanes, the historical account of Xenophon, and the apologies of Plato. Aristophanes pictured him as a buffoon. Xenophon seems to have considered him as merely the most influential of the sophists, dangerous only in terms of the general sophist tendency to raise disconcerting questions. Plato presented him as an object of worship, whose values and philosophy just happen to mirror those of his pupil and admirer. Winspear (1939) and Stone (1988) indicate that clues to the values and activities of the real person condemned to death by democratic Athens can be unearthed in a critical reading of all three sources, if one is willing and able to go back to contemporary documents and translate afresh the original Greek.

Was Socrates a real threat to the survival of the fragile and increasingly beleaguered Athenian democracy? Winspear and Stone believe that he was. In the first place, any experienced teacher cannot help but question the integrity of the teaching method so admired by Plato. The Socratic dialogue, stripped of its romantic overtones, emerges as manipulative and stultifying to intellectual growth. To read Plato's description of Socrates in action is to witness a chillingly powerful and articulate authoritarian eliciting a predetermined series of responses — to the point where the pupil is forced to accept a similarly predetermined conclusion often contrary to both common sense and empirical evidence. The conclusion inevitably leaves Socrates manning the lifeboat in a nihilistic sea, with the pupil hopelessly adrift in his wake.

The Socratic method seems more a subtle form of indoctrination than education: an indoctrination into strangely Orwellian definitions of equality, justice and democracy. When one realizes that the future leaders of Athens were being closeted with this man, year after year, with no countervailing influences, one begins to appreciate the dilemma of the Athenian government.

Two of Socrates' star pupils were Plato and another young aristocrat named Alcibiades. The latter is chiefly remembered as the leader of a traitorous rebellion against Athens during the Peloponnesian War. It is known as the Uprising of the Thirty. After that infamous event, and the eight years of "black terror" imposed on the population by this group of Socrates' friends and pupils, the returning democrats decided that they could no longer afford to tolerate the viper in their midst.

Stone notes that a puzzling feature of Socrates' trial has always been Socrates' defence — or lack of it. He seems to have deliberately provoked his judges, virtually challenging them to condemn him to death. He threw in their faces a claim to have communicated with Apollo at Delphi. This may have been more significant than is generally recognized. Whereas the goddess Athena represented the personification of democracy and the rule of law, and Hermes was the symbol of working- and merchant-class values, Apollo was worshipped as the guardian of aristocracy. Stone also sees considerable significance in Socrates' mysticism — notably his often articulated belief that only in death could one achieve knowledge and virtue. This seductive vision may have held more attraction than the prospect of disrepute at the hands of the Athenian democrats. He wonders whether Socrates, at the age of seventy and plagued by various ailments, might have actually sought a martyr's death.

Naturalism in Hellenistic times

Epicurus

About a half-century after the deaths of Socrates, Thucydides and Democritus, a young teacher named Epicurus (341-270) began to attract a following. His was a relatively minor movement, struggling to surface against the current of the times. The Greek states had endured a century of intermittent oligarchic revolution, internecine warfare and social and political disintegration, followed by invasion and conquest by Philip of Macedonia. During much of this period, philosophical thought had been dominated by Plato (427-346) and his student, Aristotle (384-322). Plato — assuredly shaped by his powerful mentor, Socrates — was a dualist and idealist in cosmology, an absolutist in epistemology and strongly totalitarian in political theory. Aristotle shared Plato's dualism and built an enduring system of knowledge on that foundation. He differed from Plato in that he was neither totalitarian in politics nor an elitist — except where slaves and women were concerned. "The deliberative faculty," he once explained, "is not present at all in the slave, in the female it is inoperative, in the child undeveloped" (Boardman:215).

The Hellenistic civilization of Epicurus' day was in the throes of social turbulence and cultural breakdown. It was marked by a declining faith in human reason, and an increasing resort to mysticism and all manner of revealed authority, with seers, soothsayers and dream interpreters abounding. There was a revival of old myths and superstitions, along with a growing enthusiasm for astrology and the old polytheisms of the Egyptians and Persians. Most aspects of this eclectic mix were quite compatible with the Platonists who dominated the Hellenistic era, but were anathema to Epicurus. To him these developments represented an appalling cultural regression for humanity.

Epicurus attempted to reformulate and integrate what he understood to be the ideas of Democritus and Socrates. He wanted to derive a practical, ethical theory from the earlier atomism, remaining faithful to the monism of Democritus and what he saw as the humanism of Socrates. He believed that Democritus had successfully summed up over two hundred years of the most fruitful of Greek speculation on the nature of things, and that this accomplishment provided a far more reliable explanation of the cosmos than did that of Plato and Aristotle. He took from this heritage of materialistic monism a belief in the universality of cause and effect, but could not quite bring himself to extend it to all aspects of human life. Epicurus thought that there had to be room for free will, in order for ethical conduct to be possible. It worried him that the atomism of Democritus did not seem to allow for this. He either did not understand, or did not accept, Democritus' explanation of the inevitability of subjectively experienced chance (and therefore the *feeling* of independence of choice) within an objective cosmic necessity. Epicurus tried to improve on the theory of atomism by introducing the idea of objective randomness, hoping to make room for human free will. However, his strange speculation about uncaused "swerves" of atoms is considered the weakest aspect of the Epicurean system of thought.

Epicurus favoured returning from super-nature to human nature in the search for ultimate criteria of "the good" and "the real." He claimed that the arbiter of truth is sensation, acted upon by reason, just as the final criterion of good is the feeling of pleasure or pain and the desire to prolong the first and avoid the second — again, as interpreted by reason.

> You will find
> All knowledge of the truth originates
> Out of the senses, and the senses are
> Quite irrefutable. Find, if you can,
> A standard more acceptable than sense
> To sort out truth from falsehood. . . .
> All is lost
> Not only reason, but our very life,
> Unless we have the courage and the nerve
> To trust the senses. (Lucretius:132)

Epicurus taught that justice is never a thing in itself, as the Platonists viewed it. He explained that it is, rather, a condition which emerges in the dealings of human beings with one another, based on a commitment to be fair to others. An enduring state of trusting friendship was his highest goal for human beings. He envisioned a friendship involving enjoyment of food for thought as well as the senses. It seems that his main aim in teaching ethics was to help people overcome the fear of gods and the fear of death: twin burdens of humanity fed by the myths and mysticism of Hellenistic culture.

Epicurus believed that Platonism represented a mountain of obscurity towering over humankind, and he was committed to lighting candles in the darkening cave. Because his idea of free will contradicted the dualist belief in an external purpose and plan, it was interpreted as a direct attack upon the supernatural sanction that Plato had claimed for the oligarchy. It therefore aroused much hostility. Epicurus also came under virulent attack for his practice of encouraging women and slaves to join his school and become students of philosophy. The principle of equality for women and slaves was so foreign to carriers of the Platonic-Aristotelian world view that it would have been easy to destroy the reputation of anyone brave enough to take such a revolutionary stance. Consequently, Epicurus was reviled as an atheist and corrupter of youth, and many of his writings were destroyed.

The Roman influence

Lucretius

Stoics such as Panaetius and the scientific historian Polybius — who emigrated to Rome during the second century BCE — can be credited with the survival of many naturalistic and evolutionary ideas from Greece. Stoicism was a philosophical school which originated with Zeno in the third century BCE and was later systematized by Chrysippus. An offshoot of Epicureanism, it explicitly rejected the hedonism of which Epicurus has sometimes been accused. Its proponents recommended a virtuous life founded on knowledge which, in turn, was based on materialism, empiricism and reason. Nevertheless, it was a first-century Roman writer whose work had the greatest impact on posterity. It is almost entirely due to the poet Lucretius that the ideas of Epicurus are readily available to us today. Ironically, we know almost nothing about Lucretius himself, other than that he was a remarkably gifted poet and philosopher who died young, leaving his six-book tome on Epicurus uncompleted. He seems to have devoted his brief life (75-51?) to the resurrection and poetical depiction of the works of the man whom he considered to have been a neglected genius among the Greek philosophers.

Since the time of Epicurus a darkness had indeed descended on Greek civilization. Under Alexander the Great, both Macedonia and Greece had become mere provinces in a vast empire, with Asian cities developing as centres of the Hellenistic world. Trade flourished, but the serfs in the Asian parts of the empire and the labourers in Europe had grown increasingly impoverished. Meanwhile, a new power had arisen in the West. During the third century BCE, the Roman city-state completed its expansion and consolidation of all Italy and, by 265 BCE, was set for further conquests. The aspiring new empire confronted two great rivals: Carthage in the West and the far-flung Hellenistic holdings in the East. The Punic Wars, ending in about 200 BCE, eliminated Carthage as a viable contender. During the next half-century, Rome managed to gain supreme control of the entire then-known civilized world. It had evolved from one among a confusion of warring city-states to the vibrant hub of a rapidly growing empire and in the process had begun to assimilate many aspects of the culture of classical Greece. But all this expansion was not without cost. The Roman Republic was beset by political strife. It wavered back and forth between democracy and despotism, with the need for control at its rapidly expanding borders always an overwhelming concern.

Lucretius' lifetime saw the emergence of Julius Caesar as the great conqueror of Gaul and Britain. He also lived to see the subsequent end of the Republic and the founding of the Roman Empire with Caesar in absolute control. Old codes of honour, basic social institutions and sexual morality had broken down. Reason was under attack and Oriental cult-worship was once again in the ascendant. No form of superstition, mysticism or emotionalism was out of bounds. The times must have been extremely unsettling to the thoughtful observer searching back across the centuries for a more enlightened perspective.

On the Nature of Things, Lucretius' epic, comprises six books, each with an extensive introduction. Books 1 and 2 develop the atomic theory of Leucippus and Democritus; Book 3, the structure and mortality of the soul; Book 4, the origin and operation of the universe; Book 5, the evolution of life and human society; and Book 6 (unfinished) deals with the various non-organic materials of the earth and sky.

The poem expresses boundless sympathy for the human race trapped in its cave of ignorance and terror. It attacks those who inculcate fear of gods and death. "Religio" is presented as a monster thrusting its fearful head down from the sky, ultimately to be crushed by the hero, Epicurus.

> When human life, all too conspicuous,
> Lay foully groveling on the earth, weighed down
> By grim Religion, looming from the skies,
> Horribly threatening mortal men, a man,
> A Greek, first raised his mortal eyes
> Bravely against this menace. No report
> Of gods, no lightning-flash, no thunder-peel
> Made this man cower, but drove him all the more
> With passionate manliness of mind and will
> To be the first to spring the tight-barred gates
> Of Nature's hold asunder. (Lucretius:21)

Lucretius also has Epicurus condemn false philosophers such as Plato and Aristotle, along with their ideas about the transmigration of souls, the supernatural sanction of despotism and divine purpose. There was good reason to do this, better than either Epicurus or Lucretius could have ever known. For the premises of Plato and Aristotle about the nature of reality have indeed proven to be major obstacles to the development of the perspective of evolutionary naturalism so essential to progress in the social sciences.

Consequences

It would be difficult to overestimate the influence of Plato and Aristotle on the evolution of Western culture. During the century in which they dominated Greek philosophy, most of the works of Leucippus, Protagoras and Democritus were either lost or deliberately destroyed. Aristotle, in his powerful position in the Macedonian court as the tutor of the future Alexander the Great, produced a complete system of knowledge to replace that of Democritus. This was based on the premise of a "first cause" and universal logic and on the possibility of interference by this extra-natural force in the course of human history. It furnished the framework of ideas defining future Greek and Roman scholarship in every field.

There is no denying that Aristotle made a revolutionary and lasting contribution to human cultural evolution. The value of his thought, however, was not in its ontology, but in his discovery of the syllogism as an intellectual instrument for testing the validity of knowledge-claims. A syllogism is an argument expressed in the form of three propositions. The major premise identifies some attribute common to all members of a class, and the minor premise identifies a particular object or relation as a member of that class. The conclusion demonstrates that the particular instance must necessarily possess the defining attribute of the class. Ironically, it was largely due to the effectiveness of this tool that science persevered during the millennium to follow — in spite of the grievous cultural obstacles thrown up by Hellenistic Platonism and Aristotelianism. Spread throughout the vast Middle-Eastern empire created by Alexander the Great, and ultimately translated to Arabic, this system of ideas — with its powerful tool for logical analysis — provided the foundation for Islamic philosophy and science in the seventh to tenth centuries AD.

Given the logical power of Aristotelian thought, and the dominance of Platonic metaphysics during the lifetime of Epicurus, it is a wonder that the latter's rival approach to philosophy and ethics survived at all. But survive it did, in small pockets throughout the Greek and Roman world, for seven hundred years, until outlawed and persecuted in Christian Rome. It is tempting to imagine what might have happened to the evolution of human culture if Epicureanism had spread throughout the Western world. Science might not have developed within a hostile cultural environment in isolation from ethical thought and the general study of society and culture. It might have been generally assumed that human behaviour and institutions are susceptible to the test and validation of experience and reason — rather than essentially mysterious and unknowable. And the current appalling gap between the level of reliable knowledge about our physical environment and that concerning our sociocultural arrangements might not exist. There *was* an alternative path of cultural evolution to the one staked out by Plato and Aristotle. There was a path that might have led us sooner to that brightly beckoning world framed in the far-off exit from Plato's cave. There was another path, but, tragically for humanity, it was the road not taken!

References for Chapter One

Bailey, Cyril. 1928. *The Greek Atomists and Epicurus: A Study*. London: Oxford University Press.

Boardman, John, et al., eds. 1986. *The Oxford History of the Classical World*. Oxford: Oxford University Press.

Burns, E.M. 1955. *Western Civilizations: Their History and Culture*. New York: W.W. Norton.

Farrington, Benjamin. 1967. *The Faith of Epicurus*. New York: Basic Books.

Guthrie, W.K.C. 1974. *A History of Greek Philosophy*. Vol. 2. London: Cambridge University Press.

Laertius, Diogenes. 1958. *Lives of Eminent Philosophers*. Translated by R.D. Hicks. London: Heinemann.

Lucretius. 1947. *De Rerum Natura*. Translated by Cyril Bailey. London: Oxford Press.

————. 1969. *De Rerum Natura*. Translated by Rolfe Humphries. Bloomington: Indiana University Press.

Plato. 1968. *The Republic*. Translated by Allan Bloom. New York: Basic Books.

Plutarch. 1910. *Plutarch's Lives.* 3 vols. Revised by Arthur Hugh Clough. New York: J.M. Dent and Sons.

Rist, J.M. 1972. *Epicurus.* London: Cambridge University Press.

Stone, I.F. 1988. *The Trial of Socrates.* Toronto: Little, Brown.

Stromberg, R.N. 1963. *A History of Western Civilization.* Homewood, IL: Dorsey Press.

Trever, Albert A. 1936. *A History of Ancient Civilization.* 2 vols. New York: Harcourt, Brace and World.

Winspear, Alban Dewes. 1939. *Who Was Socrates?* New York: S.A. Russell.

_____. 1940. *The Genesis of Plato's Thought.* New York: S.A. Russell.

Two

Erasmus
The Re-emergence of Naturalism

> I see obscurity in all things human. I see how much easier it is
> to start than to assuage a tumult. Those who raise this tumult
> claim to be impelled by the Spirit. This Spirit has never im-
> pelled me.
>
> — Erasmus, quoted in
> *The Reformation of the Sixteenth Century*

Some fifteen hundred years after the death of Lucretius a man was born in western Europe who was to assume the torch so ably carried by the Roman poet. His name was Desiderius Erasmus. To understand his role in the survival of naturalistic thought it is necessary to place him in his own times. Accordingly, a brief summary of those intervening centuries would seem justifiable at this point.

The centuries between

Most of what we now know as the Middle East had been conquered by Alexander by 300 BCE. When the great Hellenistic empire collapsed, a little dependency of great importance to our story was claimed by both the Ptolemies of Egypt and the Seleucids of Syria. This was Judaea. Eventually, by means of the Hasmonean revolt against the Syrians in 168 BCE, it was established as an independent state under the protection of the Roman Empire. In 40 BCE, Herod became king of a Judaea then functioning as a semi-independent Roman province. It is into this political setting that Jesus of Nazareth was born.

No mention of this event is to be found in the *Annale* and *Historae* of the scientifically oriented second-century-AD Roman historian Tacitus. Therefore all we know about Jesus' birth, death and achievements is what was communicated by the early Christians. It is generally accepted that Saul of Tarsus (later known as the apostle Paul) expanded upon the earlier beliefs, producing a religion compatible with Hellenistic dualism. We know, as well, that in 313 AD, the Roman Emperor Constantine ended the persecution of Christians, and that,

---

References for this chapter are on p. 28-29.

only seventy years later, Emperor Theodoseus commanded all Roman subjects to become Christian.

We also know that two important developments changed the shape of Christianity during the early medieval period. The first was the growth of orthodoxy which inevitably followed its acceptance as a state religion. The second was the emergence of authoritarian organization. What started out as the establishment of a professional priesthood at the parish level gradually proceeded to the elevation of bishops, then to the distinctions of rank among these which culminated in the primacy of the Bishop of Rome.

In fact, during the two confused, transitional centuries following the final collapse of Rome in 476 AD, three religion-based civilizations emerged. In addition to early medieval western Europe, there were the Byzantines organized from Constantinople and the Saracens, or followers of Mohammed. The Byzantine Empire was populated by Hellenized Southern Europeans and Central Asians: Greeks, Syrians, Jews, Armenians, Egyptians and Persians. By the sheer fact of its existence, in those first cruel centuries after the fall of Rome, it performed a crucial holding action for human culture. Within it were preserved many of the achievements of the classical world.

By the seventh century, however, the emergence of a new religion among the Arabs and Bedouins to the south sparked a civilization which eventually encompassed and surpassed much of Byzantine achievement. Mohammed, the founder of Islam, became at the same time the founder of a new Arabian state with its capital in Medina. In the century after his death, the Islamic rulers — called Caliphs, or successors to the Prophet — expanded their jurisdiction from the Arabian Peninsula west to Morocco, north to Spain and Armenia and eastward to Persia, Palestine, Syria and even to the borders of India.

By the middle of the tenth century the greater part of the civilized world was under the rule of Islam. With western Europe still struggling to emerge from its Dark Age, and the Byzantines "treading water," a Golden Age burst forth within Islamic culture. Mecca was its spiritual centre and Baghdad its political, cultural and creative heart. Paper-making had been imported from China. Translation was revolutionized, with Arabic superseding Greek and Latin as the universal language of civilized discourse. Poetry, science and philosophy flourished.

One of the many geniuses of the age was Avicenna (980-1037). He produced at least sixteen medical works plus about a hundred on theology, philosophy and astronomy. His elaboration of Platonic-Aristotelian thought was subsequently refined by Averroës of Cordoba, and ultimately inherited by Aquinas. Another great civilizing influence was the prolific astronomer, mathematician and poet: Omar Khayyam. It was largely through his poetry that remnants of Epicurean thought survived the Crusaders and Mongols to reach the Moors in Cordoba (a group of Islamic Arabs and Berbers who had invaded

Spain four centuries earlier). From this community wandering Jewish scholars distributed their precious legacy of classical and Arabic-Persian thought among the far-flung monasteries of western Europe.

The three hundred years following the early thirteenth-century Mongol conquest of Oriental Islamic civilization had witnessed a gradual reawakening of the West. The institution of monasticism was the crucial vehicle for this process. Imitating an old Egyptian custom, it had begun long before as a few scattered establishments in which devout and practical Christians were able to retreat from the savagery around them and create a condition that made learning possible. The most isolated and least doctrinaire of these were the Benedictines of Ireland; and of all the "heretical" monks nourished there perhaps the boldest was John Scotus Erigena, who had travelled in the East and knew Greek. He was a forerunner of scholasticism: a system of thought based on the work of the Saracen Averroës, and developed in the thirteenth century by Albertus Magnus and Thomas Aquinas. Its roots had been planted by the African monk Constantine who translated Arab texts and introduced the "new" learning to the Benedictine monastery at Monte Cassino in Spain. Another Benedictine, Adelhard of Bath, brought Arabian/classical materials from Cordoba in the early twelfth century and did much to disseminate these ideas through France and England. Jews who followed William of Normandy to England were chiefly responsible for setting up the first School of Science at Oxford, where Roger Bacon subsequently studied. Bacon (1214-94) was perhaps the first western European to maintain that the experimental inquiry method is the only way to true knowledge. Meanwhile, the Holy Roman Emperor Frederick II — one of the most committed sceptical inquirers of all time — was busy establishing pioneering universities at Naples (where Thomas Aquinas was an early and able student) and at Messina and Padua. Into these centres of learning Frederick gathered learned Jewish and Arab scholars who completed the translation of the bulk of Arabian scholarship.

In its time the scholastic philosophy systematized by Aquinas was a great step forward because it emphasized the primacy of human reason and the importance of precision in the use of language. It therefore gave an impetus to science, even though the rationalism it promoted was based on a logic that ignored empirical causes and relationships in favour of *a priori* premises and "essential" attributes.

A movement called "nominalism," expounded by an English Franciscan, William of Occam, became popular in the fourteenth century. It both laid the ground for subsequent scientific progress and anticipated Kant's arguments three centuries later about the impossibility of proving religious claims by the use of logic. Also, as in the case of Kant's transcendentalism, this movement had the further consequence of encouraging a revival of mysticism.

So long as feudalism remained the dominant form of government, the Christian monasteries, and the scholars within their walls, were able to survive and flourish. In a setting where all political power was exercised by private barons and lords of the manor, the institution of the clergy and that of monasticism were the only large-scale organizations. The monks gained control of most of the good farming land and grew powerful and aggressive in defence of their territory. In time, however, the very economic and political success of monasticism led to its corruption and eventual demise.

Tumultuous times

The recognition of the Carolingian dynasty by the Franks during the eighth century — and especially the unifying rule of Charlemagne which ended in 814 — had provided an early example of what would become a new form of centralized power in western Europe: the nation-state. In the following centuries, as national monarchies gradually emerged from the old feudal institutions, these newly centralized political systems began to pose a serious challenge to the Church's power and monopoly on property. The Christian establishment tried to justify its continued dominance by claiming that it was God's wish. However, by the end of the fifteenth century it was becoming obvious that a majority of both clergy and monks had long since lost their commitment to poverty and good works. Even the papacy had grown warlike and decadent. The increasingly powerful national monarchs could scarcely wait to be rid of the great international structure standing between them and their own personal form of despotism.

During the same period, momentous events were occurring that began to direct the attention of many western Europeans outward. By the late thirteenth century, the voyages of Marco Polo and advances in sailing technology — along with a growing suspicion that the earth was spherical — had given an impetus to trade with distant and exotic lands. By the time two more centuries had passed, the zeal of the Portuguese and Spaniards to break the Italian monopoly on trade was motivating an intensive search for new routes to the Orient. Ultimately, this activity resulted in an awareness by the western Europeans of the existence of great civilizations other than that nourished in their own Indo-European and North African heartland. And perhaps, even other worlds! By 1543, when Copernicus' *On the Revolutions of the Heavenly Spheres* was published posthumously, it had even become possible for a few courageous thinkers to contemplate humankind's infinitesimal role within a universe of infinite space.

Meanwhile, the world into which Desiderius Erasmus was born, in 1466 at Goude in the Netherlands, was still the church-ridden and strife-torn reality of Renaissance Europe. By the time he reached adulthood, however, a temporary lull had settled over Christendom. The Wars of the Roses were over in England; new wars convulsing all of Europe were yet to begin. The heresies of the Middle Ages had been suppressed. The Albigenses, Waldenses, Fraticelli, Hussites and Wycliffes who had threatened to disrupt the Church were being stamped out by the Inquisition. In Spain the long struggle to subjugate the Moors was winding down, and the expulsion of the Jews had not begun. The Ottoman Turks had yet to initiate their ultimate push into western Europe. All was relatively quiet, but the potential danger to any sceptic with an inquiring mind must have hovered like a tangible and terrifying presence.

Discovering the classical heritage

Erasmus began life as an outsider, the illegitimate child of a priest and his servant. At the age of fifteen, following recovery from a year-long attack of the plague, he was placed in a monastery. There he chose the classics rather than Christian studies as his focus. He was often rebuked for his "profane" rather than "sacred" interests. These rebukes were no doubt one of the sources of his later disenchantment with monasticism, which he concluded had grown negligent in its appointed task of cultivating human learning.

In 1492, after being ordained as a priest, Erasmus left the monastery to become Latin secretary to a nearby bishop. In 1495, with the bishop's blessing, he enrolled in the University of Paris. He soon became disillusioned with the wrangling among various theological factions. He also encountered discord between the traditional scholasticism as it had evolved from its Aristotelian, early Islamic and Christian roots, and certain re-emerging ideas of classical Greece and Rome referred to as neo-Platonism. In later life Erasmus was to claim that his professors were overly fond of infinite debates about infinity and vacuous speculation about vacuums. In Erasmus' opinion such discussion contributed nothing to either the edification or the morality of the students — thereby failing his personal criteria for worthwhile education. He found himself agreeing with the fellow student who said that to graduate from the University of Paris at that time was to emerge from Stygian darkness.

There *was* one source of authentic educational opportunity at the university, however. Erasmus found himself part of a lively group of young classicists, most of them Italian. He tutored some of them as well. In 1499 one of his pupils, an English nobleman, invited him to visit the family's ancestral home in England. There Erasmus was introduced to a circle of the foremost men of letters, scholars and classical revivalists of the day: the Oxford Reformers. One of these was Thomas More, a brilliant law student. This was the beginning of a close lifelong friendship between the two. More introduced Erasmus to the royal family, including the boy, Prince Henry — later to become Henry VIII. As a result of this visit to England, Erasmus realized that he wanted to be a serious theologian: someone capable of reconciling the most fruitful of ancient Greek and Roman learning with the best of the early Christian tradition.

Erasmus discovered that his newfound English friends were dedicated to a somewhat different goal: the wholesale revival of neo-Platonism, which involved discrediting the rationalism and science supported by scholasticism. He was not able to accept their enthusiasms uncritically, preferring to select only those elements of the classics that met his own test of reason and morality. Erasmus disliked neo-Platonic idealism, for he found all aspects of Oriental occultism repugnant. And he was particularly suspicious of claims about experiences of religious ecstasy. On the other hand, he was no blind supporter of scholasticism. He found great value in the Hellenic assumption that truth is discovered by inquiring human minds in collaboration, and not revealed from above to human reasoning faculties by the supernatural — as the scholastics seemed to believe.

By this stage Erasmus was already widely and deeply versed in the classics. Interestingly, he appears to have charted an independent course by choosing as his intellectual heroes neither the neo-Aristotelian scholastics nor the popular neo-Platonists — but Thales, Democritus, Socrates, Epicurus and the Roman poets Lucretius and Lucan.

Of more contemporary thinkers, Erasmus was most profoundly influenced by an Italian, Lorenzo Valla (1406-57) who was a secretary to Pope Nicholas V. Valla is considered to be the father of historical criticism because of his *Annotations on the New Testament*: a scholarly attack on many of the hitherto-accepted Christian documents. His work challenged the authenticity of the "Donation of Constantin" justifying papal supremacy, and the so-called Apostles' Creed, formulated in Nicea. Valla also pointed out many errors in Jerome's Vulgate version of the Bible, as compared to the original Greek. He even went so far as to repudiate the supernatural basis for morality and to challenge the equally sacred idea that to die for one's country is the ultimate moral good.

Valla fearlessly announced himself to be a follower of Epicurus, and devoted much of his life to correcting popular misconceptions concerning the teachings of the great Greek moral leader. He explained to readers like Erasmus that the "eat, drink and be merry" connotation was unwarranted; and that the "hedone" of Epicurus' ideal was closer to the meaning of "felicity" than to what had come to be associated with hedonism. Consequently, Erasmus came to the conclusion that monasticism, as it had been practised in earlier times before becoming corrupted, was, in fact, an example of the true Epicureanism.

Discovering the printing press

Erasmus returned to Europe to study in earnest, without any means of support. He was forty years old by the time he completed the requirements for his doctorate in theology from the University of Torino. During his time in Italy he had witnessed Pope Julius and his entourage, in all their ceremonial splendour, waging a bloody battle to capture the Christian city of Bologna. He had realized that Julius — not unlike the other warlords along the Italian peninsula — thought nothing of resorting to violence in his effort to extend the power of his papal states. From that day, the former monk became a lifelong pacifist and church reformer. He endured desperate poverty until he turned to the new invention, the printing press, and thereby contributed to one of the most fundamental cultural revolutions the world has ever known.

Erasmus moved to Venice and began an association with the Aldine Press and Academy which was to last for many years. He published his own original essays and poems as well as numerous translations of the classics that had been unavailable to the public until then. With the possible exception of Martin Luther, he became the most widely read author of his generation. He continued the work begun a generation before by Lorenzo Valla, printing the entire New Testament in Greek and then translating it into Latin. During this process he made the earthshaking discovery that the verse in the Vulgate version traditionally used to support the idea of the Trinity was nowhere to be found in the original Greek. It was eventually to inspire Sebastian Castellio's courageous defence of Servetus and other sceptics: a book entitled *Concerning Heretics*. And it provided the theological justification for the religious movement called Unitarianism which developed during the following two centuries.

Meanwhile, in 1509, after the death of Henry VII, Erasmus had gone to England where he was promised a living under Henry VIII. His most famous book, *The Praise of Folly*, was written at this time.

Searching for compromise

Having established a reputation as one of the leading scholars of all Christendom, Erasmus returned to the Netherlands in 1516 to accept the position of Counsellor to the Archduke. The following year he became aware of Martin Luther, with the "great indulgences scandal" and the *Ninety-five Theses*. He sent a copy of the latter to his closest confidant, Sir Thomas More. (More was subsequently appointed Lord Chancellor of England — only to be beheaded in 1534 for refusing to acknowledge Henry VIII as Head of the Church of England.) Meanwhile, through the gathering storm of the Lutheran controversy Erasmus tried to spell out a middle ground between the violence and dogmatic excesses of both sides. He, too, opposed the corruption and power-mongering of the church establishment. But he believed that Luther had replaced the veneration of saints and foolish selling of indulgences with an even greater evil: the idea that only the pre-ordained would be granted salvation.

Erasmus wanted to believe in an element of free will, claiming that human depravity was environmentally conditioned, not innate, as Luther would have it. However, as the storm broke all over Europe, Erasmus was left increasingly isolated in his moderate, reasoning stance. Besieged from both directions, he wrote in a letter, "I do not know whether either side can be suppressed without grave fear of ruin. No one can deny that Luther calls for many reforms which brook of no delay. . . . Each side pushes me and each reproaches me. My silence against Luther is interpreted as consent, while the Lutherans charge that I have deserted the gospel out of timidity" (Bainton 1969:175).

Erasmus had no patience for fruitless speculative argument with its inevitable potential for devastatingly violent consequences. Concerning what happened after death he said that since the matter cannot be resolved until the day of judgement, why not suspend judgement until then? Once he referred to at least two hundred examples of unprofitable questions habitually discussed by the scholastics. Of some of Luther's key arguments, he wrote, "These are subjects for scholastic disputation. Over such matters I would not take away any man's life nor do I propose to lay down my own. I would hope to be a martyr for Christ if I have the strength. I am not willing to be a martyr for Luther. . . . The world is full of rage, hate and wars. What will the end be if we employ only bulls and the stake? . . . It is no great feat to burn a little man. It is a great achievement to persuade him" (ibid.:178).

The rush to violence was more heartbreaking to Erasmus than any theological issue could ever be. In one of his works he has Peace complain:

> Surely men are mad to reject me since I am the fount of every blessing and war the greatest bane. . . . Man depends for his very existence upon cooperation. He comes into the world physically helpless and cannot survive without other's existence. Why, then, should man prey upon man? . . . This mortal life is beset by calamities which concord can alleviate and with joys which harmony can enhance. But how trivial are the objects of our strife! . . . What tumults a little animalcule incites who will himself soon be wafted away like a whiff of vapour! At the door is eternity. Why wrack ourselves to be possessed of shadows, as if life would last forever? (Ibid.:123-24)

A lonely doubter in a tumult of true belief

Erasmus was a scholar of great integrity, tolerance and moral vision, caught in the eye of the storm in an era of extreme danger for the free thinker. That he survived to die a natural death in 1536 was no doubt due to a wisdom and prudence born of a careful reading of the lessons of the classics. The terrible fate of his dearest companion, Sir Thomas More, and a number of other English friends at the hand of Henry VIII must have confirmed his awareness of the limits on freedom of belief throughout Christendom. An examination of his written works shows increasing moderation and meticulousness in choice of topics, words and genre as the confrontation of "true believers" raged around him.

In fact, Erasmus was always clever about his choice of genre and terminology. From his ancient Greek and Roman mentors struggling to express their insights in similar periods of despotism and doctrinaire ideology he had learned the sophisticated use of innuendo, double entendre and allegory. Merely to take Erasmus' words at their face value is to fail to comprehend the message that he tried to impart to humanity. *The Praise of Folly* (written as a satire) gave him an opportunity in his earlier, relatively secure years, to express criticisms of Christianity, and indeed of religion in general.

Because the comments purportedly came from the mouth of the goddess of foolishness, who could attribute them to the author? For example, "The Christian religion on the whole seems to have a kinship with some sort of folly, while it has no alliance whatever with wisdom . . . you will notice that the original founders of religion . . . were the bitterest foes of literary learning. Lastly, no fools seem to act more foolishly than do the people whom zeal for Christian piety has got possession of " (Erasmus:118). And, "the whole life of Christian folk everywhere is full of fanaticisms of this kind" (ibid.:58).

Concerning the larger issues of creative gods and the divine nature of humanity, Folly exclaims, "Jupiter put in — how much more of passion than of reason? Well the proportions run to about one pound to one half ounce. Besides, he imprisoned reason in a cramped corner of the head, and turned over all the rest of the body to the emotions. After that he instated two most violent tyrants in opposition to reason: anger, which holds the citadel of the breast, and consequently the very spring of life, the heart; and lust, which rules a broad empire lower down, even to the privy parts" (ibid.:23). And later, Folly asks, "For what offenses have men deserved these things? What angry god compelled them to be born to such miseries. . . . You will observe, I am sure, what would happen if men generally became wise; there would be need for some fresh clay and for another potter like Prometheus" (ibid.:41).

A naturalist in theological clothing

It seems that many biographers of Erasmus have failed to note the significance of his choice of genre and of what he chose to select and reject from the classical tradition. A generally ignored but intriguing pattern throughout his work indicates a strong preference for the minor theme of naturalism over the dominant meld of neo-Platonism and scholastic Aristotelianism. Luther recognized it, for, at the height of the controversy between the two men, he called

Erasmus a sceptic, a Lucian, or "some other hog from the Epicurean sty" (Phillips:198).

Clearly, Thales and Democritus were deeply revered by Erasmus. This is indicated by numerous references in his works such as his appreciative comments to Thomas More, "and through our common course of mortality you move as a sort of Democritis" (Erasmus:2). In reference to the scholastics, he has Folly say, "in fact they are most foolish, and yet are eager to seem wise men and veritable Thaleses; shall we not with entire justice dub them 'foolosophers'?" (ibid.:10). Other examples in the same publication are: "One Democritis cannot suffice" (ibid.:35) and "But I should be foolish myself and worthy of the manifold laughter of Democritis if . . ." (ibid.:70).

The influence of the Roman, Lucan, on Erasmus in his formative years has been similarly overlooked—but not by Luther, as his derogatory label of "Lucian" indicates. Lucan was a youthful poet of prolific output and great genius who lived during the rule of Nero in the first century AD. His only surviving work is an unfinished ten-volume epic poem called *Pharsalia*, a powerfully compelling indictment of Caesarism. Either for this, or for an even more direct attack on Nero entitled, *De Incendio Urbis*, Lucan was banned from writing and from reciting his works. About a year later he became the symbol and possibly the leader of an unsuccessful conspiracy to depose Nero, and was forced to commit suicide at the age of twenty-six.

Pharsalia has a philosophical message as well as a political one. Politically it is a lament for the death of democratic Republicanism and of freedom in Rome, which occurred with the advent of Julius Caesar: "the day when crime became law." Philosophically it is an attempt to replace Virgil's *Aeneid* (which provided a religious legitimation for the rule of the Caesars) with a vastly different view of Roman history. It is a largely factual account with a focus on human morality and an implied denial of supernatural intervention: all this accomplished within the form and metaphor of the great classical tradition of Homer and Virgil. Knowledgeable commentators have concluded that Lucan's work could have revolutionized Roman literature, but that it proved too dangerous a route, and instead, marked the dividing line between Roman literary greatness and the decadence that followed.

Fourteen centuries later, Lucan and Lucretius became the intellectual and literary heroes of the young Erasmus. It is impossible to understand this great Renaissance thinker without an awareness of his beloved cultural predecessors, and the beliefs for which they lived and died. In one of his *Colloquies, The Godly Feast*, Erasmus seems to be expressing very similar philosophical ideals as clearly as it was possible to do in his own treacherous times. He wrote of a group of friends visiting a hospitable comrade in an estate set in beautiful "Epicurean" gardens. The host explains, "This entire place is intended for pleasure—honest pleasure, that is: to feast the eyes, refresh the nostrils, restore the soul" (Thompson:135). And later a guest says, "I behold an Epicurean luncheon" (ibid.:150). The colloquy is devoted to demonstrating to the reader the ideal of true friendship espoused by Epicurus. The friends spend the afternoon in deep conversation about issues of substance, attempting to search out, together, insights into the human condition and moral guidance for humanity.

This is the ultimate in Epicurean pleasure. For the most part the issues are clothed in the Christian metaphor of the day, but it is the practical ethics of Christianity that are involved, rather than the theology. The setting, approach and content of the colloquy illustrate the twin principles guiding the life and work of Erasmus: his *humanitas* (love and respect for the dignity and reasoning capacity of the human being) and his *pietas* (simple Christian morality, compassion and humility).

No doubt Desiderius Erasmus remained nominally Christian in doctrine, but the evidence of his intellectual preferences and his writings seems to indicate that he steered a radically independent course. It is probable that Erasmus was only as orthodox in theology as he had to be to survive. He had no choice but to live *in* his cultural epoch; but he was not *of* it. He devoted his life to an attempt at expanding the narrow doctrinaire world of his contemporaries, in the hope that if people could be exposed to the civilizing tradition of the past — and to the variety of human perspectives possible in their own time — they would learn to live in peace with their fellows.

He has been described as a doubter in an age of absolutism; a man of compromise in an age of confrontation; and an internationalist in an age of nationalism. Increasingly out of step with his times, he seemed to stand alone, without followers. But more important than any failure to influence his contemporaries is the contribution to humanity that resulted from a lifetime of reviving and making universally available the long-lost tradition of classical naturalism.

The legacy of Erasmus lies in the enduring impact of his work on the world views that guide humanity. His contribution was not, like Luther's, a violent dislocation in the politics of Christendom. It went much deeper than that. Erasmus sowed the seeds of a profound cultural revolution: one that would stimulate an evolution of ideas for centuries to come.

References for Chapter Two

Ahl, Frederick M. 1976. *Lucan*. Ithaca: Cornell University Press.
Bainton, Roland H. 1952. *The Reformation of the Sixteenth Century.* Boston: Beacon Press.
————. 1969. *Erasmus and Christendom.* New York: Charles Scribner's Sons.
Briffault, Robert. 1930. *Rational Evolution: The Making of Humanity.* New York: Macmillan.

Burns, E.M. 1995. *Western Civilizations*. New York: W.W. Norton.

Erasmus, Desiderius. 1941. *The Praise of Folly*. New York: Random House.

Lavender, E., and N. Sheffe, eds. 1964. *A Sourcebook of Ancient and Medieval History*. Toronto: McGraw-Hill.

Phillips, Margaret Mann. 1949. *Erasmus and the Northern Renaissance*. London: English Universities Press.

Sowards, J.K. 1975. *Desiderius Erasmus*. Boston: Twayne.

Thompson, Craig R., trans. 1957. *Ten Colloquies of Erasmus*. New York: Liberal Arts Press.

Trever, Albert A. 1939. *History of Ancient Civilization*. Vol. 2. New York: Harcourt, Brace and World.

Three
Pioneers of Modern Social Science
Montaigne, Hobbes and Hume

Michel de Montaigne (1533-92)

This is an excellent foppery of the world that, when we are
sick in fortune — often the surfeit of our own behaviour — we
make guilty of our disasters the sun, the moon, and the stars;
as if we were villains by necessity, fools by heavenly compulsion . . . and all that we are evil in, by a divine thrusting on.
— William Shakespeare, *King Lear*

Erasmus had been right in feeling pessimistic about his world, for he died
on the eve of one of the grimmest periods in European history. With
Henry VIII's Act of Supremacy, and his consequent purging of loyal Catholics like Thomas More, England officially broke with the Church of Rome. Yet
the new religion seemed Protestant in little more than name, for its rituals were
largely unaltered, and reading the Bible was still forbidden. Meantime, across
the channel, King Francis I of France remained with Rome. So, too, did that
other great power, the Holy Roman Emperor Charles V. However, Francis, in
his ongoing war with Charles, took advantage of the growing schism in Christendom by manoeuvering for aid from Protestants as well as from the Turks
who were threatening central Europe from the south.

The war for political supremacy between these two Catholic monarchs
(Charles, a last vestige of the old order, and Francis, a harbinger of the new)
was to last for almost forty years. Massive social destruction was its legacy. It
was followed almost immediately by the onset of the Huguenot religious wars
within France. This civil strife took the form of ferocious outbreaks between
Catholics and Protestants that were to continue sporadically for another thirty
years. The worst of these was the Saint Bartholomew's Day Massacre of 1572,
when two thousand Protestant Huguenots were slain by a Paris mob.

Outside of France religious strife was similarly endemic. No sooner had
Protestantism been established in Scandinavia and the northern German states
than it began to disintegrate into warring factions, each with its own doctrinal
interpretations "writ in stone." Although Lutheranism prevailed in the north,

---

References for this chapter are on p. 55-56.

John Calvin of Geneva emerged as the dominant systematizer and enforcer of the new theology in Central Europe. His methods soon rivalled in ruthlessness the Catholic Inquisition in Spain and the barbarous persecution of Anabaptists by the Lutherans in the northeasterly German states. Political as well as religious enemies of Calvin were punished mercilessly, with burning at the stake a likely fate for dissenters. Under Luther, heresy and witchcraft cases had already mushroomed, and the mad hysteria of brutal persecutions for these alleged crimes spread throughout Europe. In 1545 in Geneva alone, Calvin ordered thirty-five women to be burned or quartered as witches.

Living in dangerous times

It seems an understatement to say that the cultural climate of sixteenth-century Europe had become one of extreme hostility to reason. Clearly, to express disagreement or even doubt concerning prevailing dogma was to risk one's life. Yet there were a few who dared to do so, and who even managed to record their sceptical inquiries and sentiments for posterity. One of the greatest of these was Michel de Montaigne, whose life spanned the most depraved years of this dark time.

Montaigne was born in France into a prosperous family, as the eldest of eight children. Although schooled in his father's Catholic faith, he was influenced by his mother, a converted Protestant of Jewish origin. He was educated intensively, graduating from university while still an adolescent. He then trained as a soldier. At the age of thirty-five he inherited his father's estate and retired there to raise a family and to study and write.

Montaigne managed to maintain this detached life until his death, with only a few interruptions for public service of various kinds. One of these was a tour of duty in the war against Charles V; another involved a period in civil government. In politics and religion Montaigne accomplished the amazing feat of acting as advisor to Henry of Navarre (Huguenot contender for the throne of France) while remaining loyal to Henry III, the Catholic incumbent. His *Essays*, which reveal much more than he would have dared to speak, were not published in their entirety until a few years before his death.

A message surreptitiously expressed

Who was this man and what did he really think and believe? Montaigne was a clever survivor and his essays must be read in full awareness of the oppressive cultural milieu in which they were written. This means that, as with Erasmus, accurate interpretation requires close attention to clues, for there is much that he could not have risked declaring directly. Where, then, can the knowledgeable reader of a later, freer time, look for indications of the world view of Michel de Montaigne?

One ploy is to infer his ideals and principles by identifying the people whom he most admired. Interestingly, the hero of his youth was Cato the Younger, whose courageous but ill-fated opposition to Julius Caesar was immortalized by the Roman poet Lucan in his first-century epic, *Pharsalia*. It is clear from his essays that Montaigne loved the writer as well as his subject. Not because he was the most gifted poet of antiquity (Montaigne reserved that honour for Virgil and Lucretius) but because of Lucan's nobility of character. "I love him for his worth and the truth of his opinions and judgements" (Montaigne:298). Another lifelong hero was Socrates, whose legendary character Montaigne considered the ideal to be sought by less perfect human beings. Lastly, and most profoundly, there was his admiration for the ideas of Epicurus, as viewed through the medium of Lucretius' poetry.

A person can also be known by the great men whom he chooses to despise. Montaigne referred to Aristotle as the prince of the dogmatists, "yet covering himself with such thick and inextricable obscurity that we cannot pick out anything of his opinion" (ibid.:376). And elsewhere, "The god of scholastic knowledge is Aristotle; it is a religious matter to discuss any of his ordinances . . . his doctrine serves as magisterial law, when it is preadventure as false as any other" (ibid.:403). References to Plato throughout his writings are similarly negative.

The method most favoured by Montaigne to convey thoughts too dangerous for direct expression was quotation — especially of poetry. His writings are sprinkled liberally with verses from the works of the ancient Greeks and Romans. In the three books comprising his complete essays there are over 130 selections from Lucretius, and about a third as many from Lucan. Cicero and Virgil are other sources used extensively to communicate criticism of absolutist ideologies.

Montaigne explained that when he first attempted to express his own world view, "to make it appear in public a little more decently, I set myself to support it with reasons and examples, it was a marvel to myself to find it . . . in conformity with so many . . . [early philosophers]. What rule my life belonged to I did not learn until after it was completed and spent" (ibid.:409). It is clear that he learned a certain prudence of technique from his ancient forebears. "By profession they do not always present their opinion openly and apparently; they have hidden it now in the fabulous shades of poetry, now under some other masks. For . . . raw meat is not always for our stomach; it must be altered. . . . They do the same; they sometimes obscure their natural opinions and judgements and falsify them to accommodate the public usage" (ibid.: 408).

Another signpost designed to alert the reader to the obstacles to honest expression of ideas is offered through the mouth of Cicero: "But now men all go at one pace — who are addicted and devoted to certain set and fixed opinions, so that they are forced to defend even those things which they do not approve" (ibid.:420).

A third technique employed gleefully throughout the essays is irony. For instance: "Christians have a particular knowledge of the extent to which curiosity is a natural and original evil in men" (ibid.:368). And, in referring to strange foreign customs, "Where they live in the belief, so rare and uncivilized, of the mortality of souls" (ibid.:81). His own opinion of the soul was made clear in countless ways throughout his writings. He quoted Cicero regarding yearnings for the soul's immortality. "They are dreams, not of a teacher, but of a wisher" (ibid.:414). And Lucretius, on the idea of the soul as non-corporeal:

> For surely it is utter madness to combine
> A mortal thing with an eternal, and opine
> That both can feel and act as one, what more detached
> Can we imagine, more repugnant, more ill-matched,
> Than an immortal and a mortal thing together
> Trying to stay united through the fiercest weather? (Ibid.:413)

Elsewhere, we can almost hear Lucretius and Montaigne chuckling across the centuries, as Lucretius is quoted again tackling the same theme.

> Lastly, it seems absurd that souls should stand
> Beside the marriage bed, ready at hand
> And at the birth of beasts; that without end
> For mortal husks, immortals should contend
> As in a race, to beat the others in. (Ibid.:416)

A fourth ploy resorted to by Montaigne has puzzled scholars for centuries, although it should really not be troublesome for thoughtful readers. As many have done since, he simply used the excuse of an ostensible book review to drive home his own ideas. Under the guise of a defence of a writer called Ramond Sebond, whose book, *Natural Theology*, he had translated as a last gift to his dying father, Montaigne grasped the opportunity to express his own philosophy. Although he must have disagreed strongly with Sebond, he was probably constrained both by his father's sensitivities and the very real danger facing any would-be critic of religious orthodoxy. So Montaigne pretended to praise Sebond's arguments while actually holding them up to ridicule. His use of irony here is delicious, but too subtle, it seems, for those readers who have insisted on taking his statements at face value, and then railing at his inconsistencies.

For example, in commenting upon Sebond's attempt to harness human reason to the service of Christian faith — rather than to doubt — he showed the reader how vulnerable to reasonable doubt such religious doctrines must inevitably be:

In this he was well advised, rightly foreseeing . . . that this incipient malady [doubt] would easily degenerate into execrable atheism. For the common herd, not having the faculty of judging things for themselves, let themselves be carried away . . . when once they have been given the temerity to despise and judge the opinions that they have held in extreme reverence. . . . And when some articles of their religion have been set in doubt . . . they will soon after cast easily into like uncertainty all the other parts of their belief, which had no more authority or foundation in them . . . and they shake off as a tyrannical yoke all the impressions they had once received from the authority of the laws or the reverence of ancient usage . . . determined from then on to accept nothing to which they have not applied their judgement and granted their personal assent. (Ibid.:320)

Later, in a discussion of Sebond's reliance on reason as the pathway to Christian faith, Montaigne wrote, "Just as the virtuous actions of Socrates and Cato remain vain and useless because they did not direct them toward the end of loving and obeying the true creator of all things, and because they did not know God: so it is with our ideas and reasonings" (ibid.:326-27). The very notion that Montaigne would be serious in castigating his two most revered examples of human piety and integrity because they were not Christian theists is laughable, and those readers who knew the author would have been aware of this and have realized what he was really saying.

He had gambled on discernment in his readers. Because his works had already been condemned by the papal censors, he knew he had to be careful. So he was forced to dissimulate somewhat and to resort to scattering clues. Typically, he let Lucan say it for him:

But if you have a penetrating mind
These little tracks will serve the rest to find. (Ibid.:751)

A focus on the human

So we come to the question of what Montaigne hoped we would find in his three books of essays. In his oblique, ironic and always colourful style he did indeed manage to convey a great deal. And he had much to communicate, for his lifetime of study was unparalleled at that time in its depth and breadth of focus. Not only had he covered the entire range of human history and literature with a remarkable thoroughness, but his familiarity with the nature and variety of existing world cultures was truly astounding for a European of his day. In fact, this aspect of his knowledge and the comparative analysis of human behaviour made possible by it qualifies him to be remembered as the father of anthropology.

Above all, Montaigne was a student of the human condition — in all its aspects. He recognized humans as one of the animal species with no unique claim to divinity and no means of attaining knowledge other than by their senses, supplemented (but not superseded) by reason. His essays amount to an impassioned plea for people to stop squabbling and destroying one another over supernatural forces and non-corporeal entities: all these being nothing more than elaborate fictions which, by the very nature of the human condition, can never be known by human beings. And always his message is expressed in a conversational tone, coloured with an unfailingly wry humour. "Between ourselves," he remarked, "there are two things that I have always observed to be in singular accord: supercelestial thoughts and subterranean conduct" (ibid.:856).

For Montaigne, humanity's greatest failing was the ever-popular desire to be something other than human. As he expressed it, "They want to get out of themselves and escape from the man" (ibid.:856). He recognized as particularly pernicious the religious theme illustrated by the typical comment: " 'Oh what a vile and abject thing is man if he does not raise himself above humanity!' How absurd!" he exclaimed, "to make the handful bigger than the hand . . . is impossible and unnatural. Nor can man raise himself above himself . . . ; for he can see only with his own eyes, and seize only with his own grasp" (ibid.:457).

Most worrying to Montaigne was humanity's lack of interest in learning about the nature of the human condition, and the consequent dearth of knowledge in that area. "He who understands nothing about himself, what can he understand? As if he could really take the measure of anything, who knows not his own!" (ibid.:418). And again, "Man can only be what he is, and imagine only within his reach" (ibid.:387).

The senses as crucial

Hoping to contribute to a much-needed understanding of the human being, he tried to establish that the senses are the windows on experience, and that reason and imagination are necessarily circumscribed by what can enter those windows. He quoted Lucretius:

> Our senses, then, you will find, did first provide
> The idea of truth, they cannot be denied . . .
> In what, then, should we place a greater trust? (Ibid.:444)

If the senses are the sole source of our awareness of what is real, so too, Montaigne reasoned, must they be the source of our ideas of "the good." A pleasurable sensation, then, must be the primary indication that an action is moving in the right direction, just as pain must alert us to the opposite conclusion.

On religion

Inevitably, Montaigne recognized the mystical and superstitious world view of gullible, tradition-ridden humanity as the greatest enemy to free inquiry into the reality of the human condition. His writings abound with astringently sceptical comments regarding these foibles. He tried to explain the all-too-human sources of all religion; sometimes directly, as in the following: "Our religion has no surer human foundation than contempt for life" (ibid.:65); "Miracles arise from our ignorance of nature, not from the essence of nature" (ibid.:80); "If this ray of divinity touched us at all, it would appear all over; not only in our words but in our works" (ibid.:322); and again,

> There is no hostility that exceeds Christian hostility. . . . Our religion is made to extirpate vices; it covers them, fosters them, incites them. . . . we receive our religion in our own way and with our own hands, and not otherwise than other religions are received. We happen to have been born into a country where it was in practice; or we regard its antiquity, or the authority of the men who maintained it; or we fear the threats it fastens upon unbelievers, or pursue its promises. . . . Another region, other witnesses, similar promises and threats might imprint upon us in the same way another belief. (Ibid.:324)

Elsewhere, he commented: "Man is certainly crazy. He could not make a mite, but he makes gods by the dozens. . . . In short, the construction and destruction of the deity, and its conditions, are wrought by man, on a basis of a relationship to himself" (ibid.:395). And, finally,

> It must be noted that to every creature there is nothing dearer or more estimable than its own being . . . and each relates the qualities of other things to its own qualities . . . for beyond this relation and this principle our imaginations cannot go. . . . For why should a gosling not say thus: "All parts of the universe have me in view: the earth serves for me to walk on, the sun to give me light, the stars to breathe their influence into me. . . . I am the darling of nature." . . . Now then, by this same reasoning, . . . we are the end and the goal of which the universality of things arise. (Ibid.:397)

Montaigne believed that the fear of death is a major impetus to supernaturally based religion. He attacked this fear vehemently. "What stupidity to torment ourselves about passing into exemption from all torment! As our birth brought us the birth of all things, so will our death bring us the death of all things. . . . Nothing can be grievous that happens only once" (ibid.:65). He believed that the aim of all philosophy is to learn not to fear death. He quoted Lucretius:

> Then none shall mourn their person or their life. . . .
> And all regret of self shall cease to be. . . .
> For us, far less a thing must death be thought,
> If aught there be that can be less than nought. (Ibid.:66)

A sound and brave beginning

In his lifetime Montaigne was a force for reform in France. He fought incessantly against the superstition of witchcraft, and its horrifying consequences of torture and burning of innocent people. A recurring message in his volumes of *Essays* is a plea for moderation, tolerance and scepticism of claims concerning abstractions not amenable to the test of human experience. These three books, in their richness of historical perspective and their immense scope — incorporating cross-cultural comparisons of diverse and far-flung human societies — were clearly an attempt to provide the groundwork for a disciplined approach to the study of human behaviour.

Montaigne's goal was objective knowledge of those aspects common to all humanity, regardless of differing customs. "Truth must have one face, the same and universal" (ibid.:436). He yearned to live to witness the beginning of this task. "How I wish that while I am alive . . . some man . . . might have the will and the health and the leisure to compile a register, according to their divisions and classes, as honestly and carefully as we can understand them, of the opinions of ancient philosophy on our being and conduct" (ibid.). Clearly he saw this as the essential first step for a future science of humanity. We will now turn our attention to a man who tried to follow Montaigne in lighting a pathway for humankind toward the exit of the cave.

Thomas Hobbes (1588-1679)

Our lives we borrow from each other
And men, like runners, pass along the torch of life.
— Lucretius, *De Rerum Natura*

The man who was to carry the torch of social-scientific inquiry was born across the channel in England just as Montaigne approached the end of his journey in France. Elizabeth's English church, though less doctrinaire than those of the Pope and Calvin, had originally managed to rival them in authoritarianism. However, by the time of Hobbes' birth, it had become a relatively tolerant institution, and — in spite of periodic and arbitrary executions of dissidents — had avoided the general climate of religious strife plaguing continental Europe.

Thomas Hobbes grew to manhood just as the old European order changed forever, with the nation-state in ascendancy everywhere. The civil strife in France, the successful Dutch revolt against the Spanish remnants of the old Holy Roman Empire and the English-Spanish wars all ebbed away with the dying of the century. Riches from the New World conquests flowed into a Europe now obsessed with trade. With the death of the Tudor queen, the institution of Parliament as an arm of the monarch's government became firmly established in England. However, in the absence of Elizabeth's control over church and state, Puritanism and anti-Catholicism began to surface. Meanwhile, the religious-political issue of the day throughout the developing nation-states of Europe had become a struggle between religious absolutism and the divine right of the newly powerful monarchs. The controversy reached a crisis in England in 1618, just as the devastating Thirty Years War between Catholic and Protestant states began in Europe.

James I had experienced an increasingly difficult time with a Parliament which controlled the finances. A number of the nobles had begun to justify their claim to power on religious grounds. They were Protestant Dissenters who disagreed with the concept of "divine right." James' absolutist son and successor, Charles I, who viewed the equally absolutist Puritan members as the source of his troubles with Parliament, sought to purge them from the official Church of England by making that institution more doctrinaire. This had the unintended consequence of antagonizing the Scottish Presbyterians, while isolating the Catholics as well.

Although Charles' policies did clear out the more intransigent of the Puritans (who were happy to migrate to Massachusetts with a generous charter) this did not solve his problems. He was soon embroiled in a war in Scotland over the religious issue. At the same time, he found himself deserted financially by a Parliament demanding governing supremacy for itself. In August of 1642 he tried unsuccessfully to arrest the leaders of Parliament, and the civil war between the Royalists and Roundheads was begun.

The Civil War was really an internal power struggle within the ruling gentry. Although it has subsequently been recognized as the defining struggle between limited and absolute monarchy in England, it was not generally seen in that light at the time. To the degree that an overriding principle motivated those involved, it concerned the two competing absolutisms of the day: *religious*, as symbolized by Calvin and the Pope, and *secular*, as expressed by the Stuart king's claim to divine right.

Living in a time of troubles

More by accident than design, Thomas Hobbes became affiliated with the Royalist side early in life. However, his scepticism would no doubt have made the Puritan cause abhorrent in any case. Although of humble birth, he had attended Oxford University by means of an uncle's support. His studies had included Greek and Latin and the full range of available classical thought. He was later to express vehement criticism of the narrow scholastic emphasis at Oxford. In referring to Plato's philosophy with its Pythagorean overtones, he wrote, "The natural philosophy of those Schooles was a Dream rather than Science, and set forth in senseless and insignificant language" (Hobbes 1951:686). He considered Aristotle's work an obstacle to overcoming belief in supernaturalism, and "so far from the possibility of being understood, and so repugnant to naturall Reason, that whosoever thinketh there is anything to be understood by it, must needs be supernatural" (ibid.:689).

Hobbes was intensely critical of the university establishment of his time. He accused the academics of using their monopoly position to spread false and fruitless ideas. He was all too aware of their power. "For seeing the Universities are the fountains of Civill and Morall Doctrine, from whence the Preacher and the Gentry, drawing such water as they find, use to sprinkle the same . . . upon the People, there ought certainly to be great care taken to have it pure, both from the Venime of Heathen Politicians, and from the Incantations of Deceiving Spirits" (ibid.:728). His own long and scholarly life was spent as a tutor or companion in leading Royalist households. He must have chafed at his lack of financial independence, but there was no alternative for someone who desired to express opinions that did not conform to the "conventional wisdom" of the scholastic academy.

Hobbes' first publication was a translation of Thucydides. He was attracted by the Greek historian's concept of causality arising out of the historical events themselves. According to a biographer, this early choice "indicates that his outlook was already more secular than that of his contemporaries; his arguments for history are practical and logical, Hobbes nowhere repeating the popular refrain that history supports religion by showing the hand of God in the events of man" (Reik:50).

Another influence on Hobbes must surely have been *The Prince* by Niccolò Machiavelli, first published in 1511. Machiavelli, who described the evolution of the Florentine Republic, had also followed Thucydides in his approach to history. Like the latter, he explained events in terms of natural laws, and was perhaps the first Renaissance humanist to approach the study of politics realistically. Machiavelli — living in a place and time in which the nation-state was evolving from feudalism — quite predictably emphasized the necessity of absolute authority for the ruler. He saw the evolving state as an end in itself, and the state's survival and interest as the ultimate "good." In describing everyday political behaviour in humans as he actually observed it rather than in terms of abstract ideals, Machiavelli had broken new ground. He had sought to wrest politics from the supernaturally based sanctions which had defined it during medieval times. However, in failing to recognize an alternative basis for ethics, he had ended by defining the pursuit and maintenance of political power in completely amoral terms.

When the Civil War broke out Hobbes fled to France where he remained for eleven years. Early in his career he had noted that Anaxagoras' opinions earned him a reputation as an atheist, and eventually cost him his life. Hobbes could not then have known with what relevance he was writing of himself, for he was to escape a similar fate only by virtue of his consistent preference for prudence over heroism.

Yet Hobbes had remarkable courage. He could have chosen no path more loaded with potential pitfalls than his actual life's work: a pioneering study of the human being in all its facets — including its power relationships. What more dangerous pursuit can be imagined than initiating a scientific study of political power in the age of political absolutism that had followed Machiavelli! There was only one more perilous undertaking, and Hobbes dared to take that on as well. He decided to include a scathing critique of Catholicism and Puritanism: the religious absolutisms of his day.

No sooner was his *Leviathan* published in 1651 than Hobbes was abruptly excluded from the French court, at that time understandably uneasy about the future of the boy king Louis XIV. Hobbes may not have expected this, for his conclusions supported monarchy in preference to the then-available alternatives. He had been able to identify no credible source of natural rights of man that could ensure protection against tyranny. He concluded that history taught otherwise. He thought that it demonstrated, instead, three major natural *sources* of tyranny: (1) the struggle of all against all in a brutish state of nature; (2) the temporary enslavement of the conquered by the conqueror by means of the constant civil wars that he believed were the inevitable fruits of attempts at democracy; and (3) the self-proclaimed Puritanical Kingdom of God on Earth. So Hobbes opted for a monarchy — legitimized by the people in a social compact — believing it more likely than authority based on conquest or religious absolutism to prove benevolent and just over the long term.

However, Hobbes, unlike Machiavelli, was not a supporter of royal absolutism *on principle*. Also, Hobbes' frank conclusion about the all-too-human sources of *all* power and authority may have displeased both the French royalty and Charles II, who was restored to power in England in 1660. And it is just possible that Charles (whose brother, James II, later sought to take England back to Catholicism) was offended by Hobbes' comparison of the papacy with the Kingdom of the Fairies. Whatever the precise reason, Hobbes was never again welcome in court circles in either country.

On the implications of dualism

In Paris, during the years of Cromwell's dictatorship, Hobbes was able to think and write in relative freedom. He engaged in a continuing verbal duel with René Descartes (1596-1650), a French scientist who had formulated a sophisticated philosophy based on the Platonic assumption that reality is made up of two separate and distinct realms. He viewed the physical world as deterministic and subject to mechanical laws: a form of existence different in innate "essence" from the spiritual realm governing human actions. Although the two scholars shared a love for Euclidian geometrical reasoning, Hobbes saw mathematics as an *aid* to empiricism while, for Descartes, it was an *alternative* means of arriving at knowledge. Descarte's rationalism accepted certain universal, or *a priori* premises and sought to deduce from these the precise nature of particular effects. Hobbes respected the scientific accomplishments of Descartes, especially his explanation of inertia, but he disagreed with his doctrine of innate essences and the dualism supported by a mathematical rationalism.

Hobbes referred to such dualism as the Error of Separated Essences and claimed that it resulted from trying to imagine the Infinite, which, by definition, is that which is beyond human (or finite) conception. "The Universe . . . the whole Masse of all things that are, is Corporeall, that is to say, Body . . . and consequently . . . that which is not Body is no part of the Universe: And because the Universe is All, that which is no part of it is Nothing, and consequently, Nowhere" (Hobbes 1951:689).

It was Descartes' philosophy that gave the incipient dualism of earlier times a sophisticated, logical base. In order to keep God in the picture of a material world then emerging from the findings of "natural philosophy," Descartes had offered the concept of a formal separation of mind and matter. This left scientists free to regard the physical world as subject to cause and effect while the mind remained the ever-mysterious seat of innate, spiritual essences, amenable to non-natural influences. It was a contribution that gave a huge spur to what was to become known as the physical sciences, for it freed them from the strictures of supernatural religion. But its effect on social science has been disastrous to this day. It is to Hobbes' credit that he recognized at once the harmful implications of a wholesale acceptance of Descartes' theories for the development of knowledge about the human condition.

On the laws of nature

Hobbes' approach to the study of politics and its role in the world was very different from the idealistic stance of the following generation. Like most of them, he believed in a "first cause," but his approach to the concepts of natural rights and natural law was unique. He recognized only one form of natural justice among human beings that would actually operate if culture and civilization were absent: the equality of their insatiable demands on available resources. Hobbes thought that this condition would produce an inconceivable "state of nature" marked by continuous war of all against all. However, he was concerned about the need for morality in politics, as Machiavelli was not. Hobbes identified, in place of a natural moral order necessarily prevailing in the universe, a number of Laws of Nature — those humanly structured rules which, given the nature of humanity, are a prerequisite for the maintenance of peaceful group life.

Hobbes' Laws of Nature are as follows: (1) to resort to violence only when unavoidable for the purpose of self-defence; (2) to be content with only the degree of liberty that one is willing to allow others; (3) to do that for which one has covenanted; (4) to be grateful for benefits received from others; (5) to accommodate one's desires and needs to those of others; (6) to pardon offenders; (7) in setting punishment, to be concerned with results rather than the offence; (8) to abstain from expressions of hatred and contempt for other people; (9) to acknowledge the equality of all human beings; (10) to refrain from reserving to oneself any right not available to all; (11) to apply the standard of equity to all one's dealings and judgements; (12) to enjoy in common those goods that cannot be divided; (13) to determine by lot those things that can neither be divided nor shared without destroying them; (14) to follow the rule of primogeniture where property is concerned; (15) to guarantee safe conduct for peacemakers; (16) to submit the settlement of controversies to an arbitrator; (17) to refrain from arbitrating one's own cause; (18) to refrain from arbitrating if there is a possible cause of partiality; (19) to insist on more than one witness to any controversial matter of fact; and (20) to be willing to protect in war that civil authority by which one is protected in peace.

A science of humanity

Hobbes was more scientifically oriented than many of the later Enlightenment thinkers. He was well aware of the Copernican model of astronomy and of the religious opposition to it. He was familiar, too, with the more recent confirmation of Copernicus' theory provided by Galileo's telescopes which had led, in turn, to the latter's discovery of the laws of gravity and to Kepler's updated model of the solar system. All this, it seemed, provided compelling evidence from nature for the arguments of the ancient monists against dualism. It clearly demonstrated that no external force is needed in the rotation and revolution of the planets.

Science, or natural philosophy as it was then called, was very much a part of Hobbes' life. He knew Pierre Gassendi, a scientist who published a revival of Epicurean atomic theory in 1649. And for a time he was employed by Francis Bacon, who also disagreed with Descartes' method of rationalism as a way to knowledge. The first of the great philosophers of empiricism, Bacon insisted that the road to reliable knowledge begins with disciplined observation and testing, rather than with *a priori* premises. General laws explaining reality must be derived from experience, he said, not from supernatural beliefs. What better preparation for an inquirer into the nature of human behaviour than the unique combination of classical thought and contemporary science to which Hobbes had been exposed! It is not surprising that out of this background should come a determination to develop the foundations of a scientific study of humankind.

On the need for precise definition

Hobbes began what was to be the major scholarly concern of his life by attempting a rigorous definition of each of the terms commonly used in describing the human condition of "being." His goal was to connect each term to direct human sensory experience. This theory, later known as "sensationalism," was subsequently refined and formalized by John Locke. In some ways Hobbes' approach was also a harbinger of the twentieth-century school of analytic philosophy, as well as the operational definitions applied in much of modern social science. Recognizing that all terms used to describe "being" must inevitably represent phenomena of extreme complexity, Hobbes believed that the scientific study of these phenomena was possible *only* if the excess baggage of abstract, uncheckable ideas that had become attached to the terms could be pared away, and direct ties to sensory experience isolated.

Precise use of language was essential to Hobbes:

> It appears necessary for any man that aspires to true knowledge to examine the definitions of former authors; either to correct them . . . or to make them himself. For the errors of definitions multiply themselves according as the reckoning proceeds, and lead men into absurdities. . . . Nature itself cannot err; and as men abound in copiousness of language, so they become more wise, or more mad, than ordinary. (Hobbes 1910:339-40)

On thought and imagination

Hobbes began with the concept of thought, which he considered the source of understanding. He maintained that "a man can have no thought representing anything not subject to sense" (ibid.:335) and, therefore, no *real understanding* of such abstractions as the infinite. For him a thought is a representation, within the thinker, of some quality or impact of an external object resulting from sensory messages. Thoughts, imaginings and memory all have the same sensory origin. "But memory," he wrote, "or memory of many things, is called experience" (ibid.:326).

Imagination uses the raw materials of thought to create abstractions and fictions, some of which may represent possibilities not yet realized. Imaginings occurring in sleep are called dreams:

> And these also, as all other imaginations, have been before, either totally or by parcels, in the sense. And because in sense, the brain and nerves, which are necessary organs of sense, are so benumbed in sleep as not easily to be moved by the action of external objects, there can happen in sleep no imagination and no dream but what proceeds from the agitation of the inward parts of man's body. (Ibid.:327)

Hobbes believed that other animals share the human ability to think. Yet "peculiar to man is the understanding not only of his will, but his conceptions and thoughts, by [the use of] speech" (ibid.:330). He devoted considerable space in his writing to a careful treatment of the uses and abuses of speech. Among the latter, he cited metaphorical language designed to confuse and deceive.

On reason and the nature of science

Reason was a crucial concept for Hobbes. He referred to two mental activities: the sensing-naming operation leading to the categorizing of experience; and reasoning, or making connections among these.

> The use and the end of reason is not the finding of the sum and truth of one or a few consequences remote from the first definitions and settled significance of names, but to begin at these and proceed from one consequence to another. For there can be no certainty of the last conclusion without a certainty of all those affirmations and negations on which it was grounded and inferred. (Ibid.:345)

Logical contradictions he considered not errors but absurdities, and he felt that the philosophy of his day was ridden with these. He noted that factual errors, on the other hand, result from faults in the sensing-naming process.

Hobbes claimed that reason is not born in us, nor inevitably gained through experience,

> but attained by industry, first in the appropriate posing of names, secondly by getting a good and ordered method of proceeding from the elements, which are names, to assertions made by connecting one with another, 'til we come to a knowledge of all the consequences of . . . [the relations pertaining] to the subject at hand. And that is what men call science. (Ibid.:347)

For Hobbes, it meant that scientific knowledge is always *conditional* on established preconditions, and *public* or shared by means of precise identification of the expected consequences. However, he recognized two kinds of public knowledge: (1) of fact; and (2) of the relationships among facts along with the logical implications of these. History is the recorder of the first; science of the second.

Hobbes went on to distinguish between public knowledge and opinion, or belief, which he defined as a private contemplation about something. For him, belief comprised two opinions: (1) about the veracity of the source; and (2) about the reliability of the content. This implies that a belief in any proposition not directly verifiable by the senses must inevitably demand a corresponding faith in the person communicating the proposition. He applied this to the abstract messages of prophets, scriptures, philosophers and poets alike. He pointed out that, although people may attribute their religious beliefs to faith in God, such beliefs invariably represent, instead, faith in the *men* who gave them voice at some time in history.

On morality

Pleasure, for Hobbes, is the appearance of a sensation of the good, and displeasure, the sensation of evil. Of these, "some arise from a sense of the objects present . . . [sensual experiences], others from the expectation of the consequences of things [such as pleasures of the mind, or joy]" (ibid.:353). He viewed all morality as based upon this capacity of the senses, just as knowledge is founded upon a corresponding capacity to sense and create images of experienced objects and events. However, humans desire not only momentary sensual pleasure, but contentment and continuation of the conditions that sustain it:

> Therefore the voluntary actions and inclinations of all men tend not only to the procuring, but also to the assuring, of a contented life and differ only in the way; which ariseth partly from the diversity of passions in divers men, and partly from the differences of knowledge or opinion each has of the causes which produce the effect desired. (Ibid.:384)

On religion

Hobbes even dared to propose an explanation for the universality of religion:

> And they that make little or no inquiry into the natural causes of things, yet from the fear that proceeds from the ignorance itself of what it is that hath the power to do them good or harm, are inclined to suppose . . . several kinds of power invisible and to stand in awe of their own imaginings, and in time of distress to invoke them, . . . [and] to give them thanks, making the creatures of their own fancy their gods. . . . And this force of things invisible is the natural seed of that which everyone in himself calleth religion, and in them that worship or fear that power otherwise than they do, superstition. (Ibid.:390)

On the causes of war

Hobbes tackled, as well, the issue of the pervasiveness of war. He wrote that inherent in the human condition is a desire for power and glory and fear of the unknown. These drive us to attempt to conquer others for gain, or exploitation, or reputation, or to ensure safety against others so driven. Without some sort of shared political power established through a mutual transferring of rights — a social compact — there will be no possibility of justice and therefore no peace. He concluded his treatise on moral philosophy with a plea for the Golden Rule: " Do not that to another which thou wouldst not have done to thyself" (ibid.:428).

Keeping the flame alive

Hobbes has often been attacked for his dark view of human nature. However, he never claimed that humans are born evil — merely that *goodness is not innate*, but has its source in those civilizing influences created by humans. And the evidence of history both before and since his time would seem to justify his pessimistic conclusions, rather than the beliefs concerning natural piety and natural justice that became so popular after his death. He would have considered those beliefs mere delusions based on wishful thinking rather than experience. He had hoped to provide the groundwork for a social science that would penetrate just such myths about human behaviour and institutions so that knowledgeable reform might be effected. It was an almost impossible task in the prevailing cultural climate and, inevitably, he made mistakes.

Hobbes has been accused of favouring despotism, but his reading and direct experience would have shown him few successful models of functioning democracy. The terrors of the Civil War in his homeland seemed to indicate the overriding need for a living symbol and legitimation of authority in terms understandable to the common people: in other words, a monarch. In fact, *Leviathan* can only be adequately understood in the context of the chaotic era in which it was written.

Hobbes has been accused, as well, of being overly obsequious to the aristocracy and insufficiently critical of the premises of their official Church of England. But certain members of this elite group were his sole sources of employment, and only they seem to have appreciated his abilities. We should remember that his dissenting ideas were anathema to another powerful establishment — the university — and that he never enjoyed the security of his counterparts in academia.

He has been accused of arrogance, but he probably could not have persevered without it. All his life he was without an independent source of income, sustained by few friends and virtually no disciples, attacked by his contemporaries, and living in fear of persecution for heresy. Occasionally, he made mistakes, as when, in *Leviathan*, he developed a justification of absolute monarchy at the very time that the rise of the British merchant and trading class was rendering that institution obsolete.

Clearly Thomas Hobbes was a man out of step with his times. Yet he stood his ground and managed to bequeath to posterity some highly significant signposts for those who tried, in later centuries, to continue his quest for an honest science of human behaviour.

David Hume (1711-76)

Know then thyself, presume not God to scan,
The proper study of mankind is man.
— Alexander Pope, *An Essay on Man*

David Hume was born in Scotland two generations after the publication of *Leviathan*. In the decade following the death of Hobbes, England had experienced a second political uprising, known as The Glorious Revolution because of its effect on the subsequent development of democracy. Charles II had been succeeded in 1685 by his brother, James II, a Catholic who showed signs of returning the country to papal rule. In a bloodless coup, James' Protestant daughter and son-in-law (Mary and William of Orange) were brought from Holland to assume the throne. Under them, Parliament passed the Toleration Act, granting religious freedom to all but Catholics and Unitarians. That was accompanied by a Bill of Rights limiting the power of the monarchy. This revolutionary legislation marked the end of absolute monarchy in England. It was to serve as an example for the French and Americans a century later.

On the continent, however, the opposite trend obtained. Royal despotism was becoming more firmly entrenched than ever, under such rulers as Louis XIV of France, Frederick the Great of Prussia, Maria Theresa and Joseph of Austria and (late in the eighteenth century) Catherine the Great of Russia. The Europe of Hume's century was dominated by a competition between two powerful dynasties: the French Bourbons and the Austrian Hapsburgs. This power struggle had its roots in the Thirty Years War which had begun as a confrontation between Protestantism and Catholicism. The bloody war had devastated the people and countryside of Germany and Bohemia, leaving a legacy of untenable national boundaries in its wake. Conflicting claims to the political entities involved provided grist for the mills of war for years to come.

With the ascension of William and Mary to the Stuart throne, England was drawn into the continental power struggle on the side of the Hapsburg Alliance. The result was decades of intermittent warfare between England and France, intensified by their competition in the New World and culminating in the Seven Years War of 1756-63, which marked the triumph of England and Prussia and the beginning of their subsequent domination of the European scene.

Living in exciting times

David Hume's life straddled the years of British political and colonial ascendancy. It was at the same time a period of remarkable intellectual ferment in England and France. The works of Isaac Newton and John Locke were available to the young scholar. Newton (1642-1727) had built on Galileo's observations concerning gravity and Kepler's discovery of the elliptical orbits of the planets to produce a powerful theory capable of explaining the operation of the entire universe in precise, mechanical terms. Locke (1632-1704) had tried to devise a new discipline of psychology based on the mechanistic theory of his friend, Newton, and Hobbes' sensationalism. Locke is generally known for his concept of *tabula rasa*: the idea that the child is born with a mind completely open to shaping by incoming sensations. He also sought to refine Hobbes' concept of a social contract between the governed and their rulers.

Voltaire, Montesquieu, Diderot and Rousseau were David Hume's contemporaries, and he died just as Adam Smith and Goethe rose to prominence. What the free thinkers of the time shared was an emancipation from Christian orthodoxy. For this, the majority had substituted deism and rationalism: faith in a god of nature demonstrable by pure logic. Unlike Hobbes, they tended to believe in natural rights and natural justice and to consider customary aspects of human culture to be inherent in nature in the form of natural laws similar to those of physics.

There were, of course, exceptions. Montesquieu's *Spirit of Laws* had an empirical rather than a speculative and deductive base. It introduced the idea of separation of powers and checks and balances, which represented an advance over Hobbes' works on politics. In France the Encyclopedists, of whom Denis Diderot is the best known, collected and published seventeen volumes of what they considered the most enlightened thought then available. Diderot is remembered most for his conclusion that "Men will never be free until the last king is strangled with the entrails of the last priest" (Burns:478). However, it is his comment on the means of knowing that marks him as an intellectual heir to Hobbes:

> We have three principal means: the observation of nature, thought, and experiment. Observation collects the facts, thought combines them, and experiment verifies the results of the combination. The observation . . . must be assiduous, the thinking must be profound, and the experiment must be exact. One rarely sees these methods combined. (Setton:337-38).

Hume, continuing in the tradition of sceptical naturalism, was closer to Diderot than to most of the philosophers of his day. He was as critical of the rationalistic deist world view as of the simpler dogmas of Christianity. Aware that he was out of step with even his liberal contemporaries, and recognizing the limits to free thought even in the best of times, he wrote carefully. An early biographer noted the "gradual and most observable increase of caution in his expression . . . [over the years]" (Hume 1955:iv). Yet his century must have seemed to Hume like the dawning of an era of opportunity: an age when human culture could at long last emerge from the darkness of superstition. He could not have guessed that his era was to be remembered in later, darker times as the Age of Enlightenment, and that he would be viewed as its most singular and brightest star.

Shedding light

The second son of an aristocratic Scottish family, Hume had a small inheritance with which he struggled to support a frugal life entirely devoted to study and writing. Steeped in the classics but, like Montaigne and Hobbes, not a follower of the popular neo-Aristotelianism, he must have decided early to devote his life to an attempt to establish the conceptual basis for a science of human nature on the foundation laid by Hobbes and Locke. At the age of twenty-seven he published his major *Treatise of Human Nature*, but "It fell dead born from the press" (ibid.:4). Well aware that he was challenging the prevailing assumptions of his culture, Hume soldiered on. A decade later he republished the first part of the *Treatise*, this time in simpler language and entitled, *An Inquiry into Human Understanding*. This was followed a few years later by *Political Discourses* and *An Inquiry Concerning the Principles of Morals*: the latter being, in his opinion, his most important work. Hume also wrote a remarkably objective series on the history of England, seeking to correct earlier biases in the record. It has been said that his history was more reviled than read. Unappreciated, intellectually lonely, yet confident of the worth of his contribution to posterity, Hume approached a lingering and painful death at the age of fifty-nine with an acceptance rivalling that of Epicurus.

What was the world view that Hume found so complete and satisfying in the waning days of his life? Building on the ideas of those who had gone before, he had developed a theory of the human being as a functioning aspect of nature: a theory that contained no internal contradictions and was supported by the evidence of human experience. It has stood the test of time.

On understanding and reasoning

We should begin where Hume did, with the nature of human understanding. His basis of understanding is *belief* — a steady, forcible concept within a person of some external object or effect. All understanding consists of ideas arising from either (1) the relationships among beliefs, or (2) the feeling produced by the belief itself — and has its ultimate origin in sense impressions. However, imagination is always part of the process, mixing, conjoining, extending and subtracting sense impressions into beliefs which expand into unlimited elaborations of fiction and vision. Reason, in *producing* ideas, makes connections among these imaginings as well as among beliefs stemming from immediate sensation. Reason also *relates* ideas. It does both these things according to three principles of association: similarity and contrariety (the same and opposite); contiguity (occurring together); and causation (antecedent and consequent). These principles operate both *demonstrably* (as when relationships among ideas are established) and *according to probability* (as when the ideas are generalized from sensory inputs). The first employs mathematical logic; the second, inferential.

Hume explained that, because reasoning on the basis of inference from experience is probabilistic, it can never achieve the certainty claimed by beliefs deduced logically or mathematically from taken-for-granted assumptions. If the original experience has been inadequate or the reasoning process faulty, errors can arise. This means that empiricism can never guarantee absolute knowledge. On the other hand, rationalism (reasoning based on demonstrable relationships among ideas) if faulty, results in contradictions or absurdities. And even where the logic is faultless, the conclusions of rationalism are only as reliable as the original premise has been precisely defined and in accordance with sense impressions rather than imaginings.

Hume noted that, as scientifically sound premises seldom form the basis of philosophical systems, we tend to end up with elaborate rationalist fictions that create the false appearance of certainty. On the other hand, when we stick to matters of fact, we realize that in human experience there can only be degree of probability, and never certain truth. Although he did not use modern terminology, Hume was providing here the first clear distinction between deductive and inductive reasoning.

Hume presented one of the best cases ever made for reliance on the empirical source of inference, as opposed to the strictly rational, or *a priori*, source. He explained that all inference from experience is based on two powerful expectations in the sensory system: (1) that the future will resemble the past, and (2) that similar objects or events will have similar effects. This sensation may well be instinctive, for the newborn child begins to act upon it immediately, as do all animals. Survival cannot wait for the infant to acquire experience and judgement. It must rely on the inference of like results from like precedents. And experienced regularities soon become habitual. "Custom, then, is the great guide of human life" (ibid.:58). If there were no regularities in nature, there could be no assumption of cause and effect built into the nervous system by instinct and experience.

Hume concluded that there is

> a pre-established harmony between the course of nature and the succession
> of our ideas, though the powers and forces by which the former is governed
> be wholly unknown to us, yet our thoughts and conceptions have still gone
> on in the same train as other works of nature. Custom is that principle by
> which the correspondence has been effected, so necessary . . . [for our exist-
> ence as a species]. (Ibid.:67-68)

It operates as do our limbs and other organs, without consciousness or volition. He explained that, wherever the past has been entirely uniform, we expect familiar effects with great assurance; therefore the probability of the particular cause-effect relationship is high, and our behaviour habitual. But where different effects have followed similar-appearing causes, we learn to weigh the probability of the connection. Here reason must operate.

Application to the social studies

This theory of the nature of understanding applies to all aspects of existence. Hume was not a dualist. He believed that we unconsciously make cause-effect inferences as readily in connecting motives and character attributes to human actions as we do regarding the physical environment, and that they are justified in precisely the same way. Humans experience these regularities in their fellows from birth onwards. When we say we "know" someone, we really mean that we feel confident that the character and motives with which we are familiar will allow us to predict what that person is likely to do in most circumstances. Group life would be impossible without the assumption of causation concerning human behaviour. It is so much a part of the reality of our existence that we do not recognize it, just as a fish would not be aware of the water in which it swims. For example, Hume noted that "The prisoner, when conducted to the scaffold, foresees his death as certainly from the . . . [obstinacy] of the guards as from the action of the axe or wheel. The prisoner, after testing the attitudes of his guards, may regard the iron stone of his prison as more amenable to his efforts to escape" (ibid.:100).

This assumption of causation in human behaviour does not mean an acceptance of the idea of cosmic "necessity" or "purpose." Hume saw no justification for believing that humanity is preordained to evolve according to a set of natural laws toward some predetermined end, and even less reason to believe that humans could achieve knowledge of such a "necessary" development in the remote possibility that it did exist. He said that, although each individual act is really the *effect* of the acting person's motive and character, the person can always choose not to act in any given situation. All legal and ethical systems are founded on this premise. Hume claimed that ordinary people are aware of this element of freedom. Only philosophers — lost in their abstractions — doubt it. Hume left the matter at this point, putting aside the question of the nature and origin of individual character and motives.

Like Hobbes, Hume was a nominalist in the modern sense, in that he rejected the Platonic idea of "essences": the innate, immutable potentialities of a thing, presumably revealed and represented by its name. Questions like "What is justice?" and "What is the essential nature of the state?" he considered fruitless. For him, words are merely instruments of description which have evolved through use, and should be employed with precision and clarity, as the initial step in communicating, recording and comparing human experiences.

On morality and ethics

Hume's model of morality is entirely consistent with his model of understanding. He viewed all morals as derived from the human valuing sentiment. He saw no need to invent a supernatural source. Neither did he recognize a phenomenon of good or evil apart from human relationships. Value, he declared, is not, like belief, a reflection of the nature of things. "Truth is disputable; not taste; what exists in the nature of things is the standard of judgement; what each man feels within himself is the standard of sentiment" (Hume 1975:171).

This did not lead him to conclude that morality must therefore be totally relative, or totally irrelevant. Far from it! Hume realized that moral rules or standards are essential for humans to survive in any form of group life. But, precisely because they are not innate, they can never be assumed — as they are by those who believe in natural piety and justice. Rather, morality must be assiduously taught by the adult community, from infancy on:

> The end of all philosophical moral speculation must be to teach humanity its moral duty . . . and, by proper representations of the deformity of vice and the beauty of virtue, beget corresponding habits, and engage us to avoid the one and embrace the other. [If we were to] extinguish all warm feelings and predispositions in favour of virtue, and all disgust and aversion to vice . . . morality . . . [would no longer have] any tendency to regulate our lives and actions. (Ibid.:172)

Hume sought a foundation for ethics in a universal human principle from which all censure and approbation are derived:

> As this is a question of fact . . . we can only expect success by following the experimental method and deducing general maxims from particular instances. The other . . . method, where a general abstract principle is first established and is afterwards branched out into a variety of inferences and conclusions, may be more perfect in itself, but suits less the imperfections of human nature, and is a common source of illusion and mistake, in this as well as in other subjects. Men are now cured of their passion for hypothetical systems in natural philosophy [physical science] and will hearken to no arguments but those derived from experience. *It is full time they should attempt a like reformation in all moral disquisitions*. (Ibid.:174)

On benevolence and justice

Hume proceeded to marshal evidence that, of all the social virtues, benevolence and justice are most necessary to human life. He considered it obvious that justice "derives its existence entirely from its necessary *use* to the intercourse and social state of mankind" (ibid.:186), and he believed that at least part of the merit of benevolence is its necessary role in promoting the survival of the species and the general happiness of human society. Hence he concluded that public utility, viewed as whatever contributes to the health and happiness of society in the long term (as distinct from an exclusive self-love) is the one universal criterion of virtue and worth. He asked, "What need we seek for abstruse and remote systems when there occurs one so obvious and natural?" (ibid.:219).

Hume accepted no sharp distinction between means and ends, realizing that the former must of necessity produce effects that shape the latter. And he saw no essential conflict between the long-term good of the individual and that of the species. But here, he emphasized the important role of reason in instructing us on the probable tendencies of actions and the nature of their consequences, over time and place. He was convinced that "humanity . . . makes a distinction in favour of those which are useful and beneficial" (ibid.:286). (The term, "humanity," is used by Hume as an expression of reflective sympathy or empathy.) He believed that the human being "has a tendency to project himself into the situation of persons around him and to imagine how he would feel under similar circumstances . . . and to experience vicariously the pleasure or suffering involved" (Burns:501). He considered this proclivity to be the source of benevolence and a prerequisite for morality.

On necessity

Hume seems to have considered the Christianity then under attack by his scholarly contemporaries to be a doctrine unworthy of serious criticism. He reserved his fire for a telling indictment of the popular deism and rationalism espoused by the intellectual establishment of his day. He challenged the concept of necessary cause: the idea of a great causal Chain of Being originating with a first cause beyond nature. He maintained that we believe such things because all that we can *feel* are immediate effects of action, and we therefore imagine that there must be an inherent difference between the momentary cause-effect connections which humans experience and those rules governing the universal nature of things. But he wanted us to recognize that nothing more can be known about *any* causation than the constant conjunction of experienced events and the inferences we humans make about their connections. There is no justification for speculating that the cause of the one is any more "necessary" or supernaturally based than the cause of the other.

Morality is a meaningful concept and desirable goal for humans only in the *absence* of belief in a "first cause," natural law and natural justice, according to Hume. If there were an established moral order in nature, what would human choices matter? But the facts indicate something quite different. History teaches that injustice and tyranny are more likely than their opposites to be characteristic of nature; precisely *because* this is the case, he declared, humans must work at developing virtue and liberty.

On religion

The frankest discussion of Hume's position on religion is contained in his *Dialogue with Epicurus*, in which he put his most sceptical ideas into the mouth of that Ancient, and, as the protagonist, presented the opposing argument. Hume referred to "the bigoted jealousy, with which the present age is so much infested" (Hume 1955:142). He had Epicurus argue that we cannot infer a cause (the Deity) from an effect (nature). It is not logically justifiable, explained Epicurus, to ascribe to the cause any qualities that are not exactly sufficient to produce the effect (and therefore natural) nor can we turn back to the cause and assign other effects to it, such as a future, perfect state. As he pointed out, "You find certain phenomena in nature. You seek a cause, or author. You imagine you have found him. You afterwards become so enamored of this offspring of your brain that you imagine it impossible but he must produce something greater and more perfect than the present state of things, which is so full of ill and disorder" (ibid.:147).

The flickering torch

Hume deplored the dominance of Aristotle and Plato in the academies and general intellectual culture. He recommended a return to the ideas of the Hellenic philosophers who had held that there is no possibility of absolutely conclusive knowledge about the consequences of human choices. Thinkers such as Democritus were among the significant historical sources nourishing Hume's ideas on the nature of scientific inference and the necessity to act in the absence of proven truth. True to his intellectual forebears, he was a sceptical naturalist: what we would currently call a "neutral monist" (although the term "monism" was not used until Haeckel introduced it a century later). In other words, Hume assumed neither that existence is ultimately ideal nor ultimately material in content; nor that it is divided between spirit and substance. The nature of which we are an integral part is not substance, he implied, but cause-effect relations. Our knowledge comes solely from what we experience of these, but even that we cannot claim with certainty.

Hume's compelling insight concerning the probability of a correspondence between the order of nature and cause-effect linkages in the human nervous system was overlooked until revived a century later by John Stuart Mill — and, subsequently, by Bertrand Russell and Jean Piaget. Like Hobbes, Hume focused on the need for precise definition of those terms symbolizing the basic elements of understanding and morality. And, like Hobbes, he was deeply critical of most of the philosophy of his day, believing that the chief obstacle to improving the human ("philosophical") sciences was "the obscurity of the ideas and the ambiguity of the terms" (ibid.:73).

A biographer wrote that, in ethics, Hume "produced one of the first completely and consciously secular systems in the modern era" (Flew:272). Unfortunately, however, the subtleties of his model of morality were lost on subsequent generations of rationalists and empiricists alike. So, too, was his careful distinction between the premise of the universality of cause and effect required for the pursuit of social science, and the belief in metaphysical necessity which assumes a first cause and a purposeful plan or irrevocable cosmic pattern for human history. He was the first modern thinker to point out that the former premise makes possible a degree of scientific prediction, while the latter leads only to a religious type of ideological prophecy.

It is due largely to the contributions of Montaigne, Hobbes and Hume that the legacy of classical naturalism, which Erasmus and others had resurrected, was reformulated in modern terms. Montaigne's remarkable grasp of past insights and current information concerning the human condition sparked a torch that began to shed light in a superstitious darkness where no light had shone for centuries. Hobbes fuelled the torch with his recognition of the conditional nature of scientific knowledge and the key function of the senses and of language in the process of knowing. Also enlightening was his courageously unsentimental appraisal of human nature which made apparent the impossibility of group life in the absence of some sort of humanly inspired and mutually accepted covenant and system of laws. His ideas, combined with Hume's, were the source of subsequent movements known as "utilitarianism" and "associationism" — both of which represented a considerable reinterpretation of the original theories, however.

Throughout his working life David Hume had concentrated on refining the basic concepts involved in human understanding and values. In that process, he built a philosophical foundation for the study of knowledge and morality that has never been surpassed. Regrettably, however, the torch so ably carried by these great pioneers of social-scientific thought flickered and faded in the hands of subsequent generations. Their warnings about the fruitlessness of abstract and untestable speculation went unheeded by many who followed, and the would-be social sciences floundered for the next two hundred years.

References for Chapter Three

Burns, E.N. 1955. *Western Civilizations: Their History and Culture*. New York: W.W. Norton.

Flew, Antony. 1961. *Hume's Philosophy of Belief*. London: Routledge and Kegan Paul.

Hobbes, Thomas. 1910. Of Man. In *The Harvard Classics*. Vol. 24. Edited by Charles W. Elliot. New York: P.F. Collier and Son, p. 323-434.

———. 1951. *Leviathan*. Edited by C.B. MacPherson. Baltimore, MD: Penguin Books. (First published in 1651.)

Hume, David. 1955. *An Inquiry Concerning Human Understanding*. With a supplement: An Abstract of a Treatise on Human Nature. Edited by Charles W. Hendel. New York: The Liberal Arts Press.

_____. 1975. *An Inquiry Concerning the Principles of Morals*. Reprinted from the posthumous edition of 1777 by L.A. Selby-Bigge. Oxford: Clarendon Press.

Lucan. 1992. *The Civil War* (or *Pharsalia*). Translated by S.H. Braund. Oxford: Oxford University Press.

de Montaigne, Michel. 1958. *The Complete Essays of de Montaigne*. Translated by Donald M. Frame. Stanford: Stanford University Press.

Reik, Miriam M. 1977. *The Golden Lands of Thomas Hobbes*. Detroit: Wayne State University Press.

Setton, Kenneth M., and Henry R. Winkler., eds. *Great Problems of European Civilization*. Englewood Cliffs, NJ: Prentice-Hall.

Stromberg, R.H. 1963. *A History of Western Civilization*. Homewood, IL: Dorsey Press.

Four

The Political and Educational Theories of Jean-Jacques Rousseau

I am very fond of truth, but not at all of martyrdom.
— Voltaire, *Letter to d'Alembert*

David Hume represented the radical extreme of a continuum of ideas referred to by historians as the eighteenth-century Enlightenment. His philosophy of naturalism was based on three assumptions, all vital to the continued development of a social science. The first of these concerned the unity of science: the recognition of its validity as a mode of knowing for the human as well as the physical realm. The second was a nominalist belief in the function of language and its relation to mental conceptions of reality. To a nominalist, words are merely symbols devised and used by fallible humans to represent things; they contain within them no "essence" of the things themselves. This means that precise definition is a prerequisite for study. Hume's third assumption involved a rejection of the prevailing idea of cosmic necessity, or of a predetermined direction and goal, as applied to either human history or physical change.

Not only did these assumptions pose a challenge to the Christianity of the time; they were also in conflict with the deism and pantheism of most Enlightenment thinkers. The ideas of Newton and Locke in England — and of Voltaire, Diderot and d'Alembert in France — contained remnants of metaphysical thought unacceptable to Hume. They were committed to a teleological form of materialism which allowed for the rule of immutable natural law originating in a force beyond matter and aiming at the progress and ultimate perfection of humanity. Their other vital commitment was to a rationalism that seemed to ignore the complexity of human motivation and the continuity between humans and the other animals in the evolutionary process. Both beliefs were ultimately to become obstacles to the progress of a science of humanity.

This is not to minimize the magnificent contributions of those who represented the mainstream of Enlightenment thought. Voltaire (1694-1778) — who, more than any other person, epitomized its core of rationality — was

---

References for this chapter are on p. 69.

responsible for disseminating the ideas of Newton and Locke throughout Europe. He was perhaps best known for his support of individual liberty and tolerance of diversity, as exemplified by his famous comment about defending to the death the right of someone to express ideas with which he himself disagreed. Voltaire devoted his life to promoting the idea that the world is governed by natural laws and that humans can only know what they are able to experience and order through the use of reason. However, he was to see almost all of these ideas challenged by Jean-Jacques Rousseau: the man who in many ways represented the conservative or even reactionary wave in the Enlightenment spectrum.

Making his way in the world

Rousseau was a theist who found himself at odds with the Enlightenment philosophers on the one hand and with traditional Christianity on the other. Cast in a very different mold from David Hume, his sentiments have nevertheless influenced succeeding generations no less powerfully than have the ideas of that other lone dissident. Jean-Jacques, as he was universally known, has been referred to as one of the most explosive mixtures of genius and deluded sensibility the world has ever seen. Where Hume's ideas formed an integrated world view which guided his behaviour, Jean-Jacques was torn by conflict. Nonetheless, the latter's obsession with the human problems of politics and morality gave his ambiguous and emotive prose a lasting significance for social science.

Rousseau seems to have lived two lives. Along with the life he actually experienced, which is documented in the correspondence and other sources of that very literate period, there is the partly imaginary one described in his *Confessions* and *Reveries*. These two lives seem to have produced two people: an embittered, scheming, self-serving sycophant and a simple saint seeking only virtue and truth while beleaguered on all sides by the forces of an evil civilization conspiring against him. Sympathetic biographers have tried to fit these discordant parts together and to reconcile the logical and factual contradictions within Jean-Jacques' philosophical works with the occasional flashes of insight flickering there. However, even describing his serious writing as philosophical invites controversy. Voltaire claimed that Rousseau resembled a philosopher "only as a monkey resembles a man" (Lamont:56).

To summarize a life so embroidered by its subject and reviled by its witnesses is no easy task. However, certain facts seem indisputable. Jean-Jacques' mother died at his birth in Geneva in 1712. His childhood was dominated by an irascible father. Isaac Rousseau was a watchmaker of peasant origins, with a taste for grandeur. He had another son who seems to have been ignored while Jean-Jacques, who displayed a precocious propensity for reading the classics to his father, was doted upon.

Then, suddenly, Isaac was forced to flee Switzerland due to a minor scandal. Jean-Jacques was left with the family of his mother's brother, where he enjoyed the privileges of an upper-class rearing. This idyllic existence ended abruptly when, at the age of thirteen, he saw his cousin (and bosom companion) go on to higher things while he was rudely thrust into a pursuit considered appropriate to his station in life. He became the apprentice of a craftsman who treated him with the abusive discipline common to the times.

Jean-Jacques afterwards claimed that he was brutalized by this experience of apprenticeship. Certainly it scarred him for life, imbuing him with a fierce drive for upward mobility — coupled with a jealous resentment of those above him in the social structure and a scorn of those below. At the age of sixteen he ran away, determined to seek the fortune merited by his talents.

The story of the metamorphosis of the homeless wayfarer into a confidant of Diderot and d'Alembert, a contributor to their famous *Encyclopedia* and a favourite of the Court of France is both magnificent and sordid. That spectacular rise owed as much to his disturbingly handsome appearance and emotional and moral crippling as to his intellectual brilliance. For he had learned rapidly that people (especially women) could be used to achieve the rewards of which he had been so cruelly cheated by fate.

For Jean-Jacques, women were a species apart. Throughout his life he relied on the patronage of wives or mistresses of the powerful, with whom he invariably persuaded himself that he was in love. Not all responded in kind, however, and he soon found that orgies of idealized and unrequited love were hardly sufficient for the passions aroused within him. At a low point in his fortunes he began a liaison with Thérèse Le Vasseur: a simple-minded maid in his hotel. She meant little to him as a person, but was loyal and provided the required sexual and housekeeping services. The liaison endured as an underground relationship with no connection whatever to his social and intellectual life.

Five times in the ensuing years Thérèse became pregnant, and five times Jean-Jacques had the infants placed in a foundling home. Ashamed of the maternal bloodlines that he had imposed upon his offspring, he recognized the impossibility of acknowledging them without also acknowledging Thérèse's true role in his life. But this he could not do and remain the protégé of prestigious women.

Discoursing on the evils of civilization

After a number of attempts at composing music and writing plays, Jean-Jacques was encouraged by Diderot to try his hand at serious writing. He won an essay competition with what is now known as the first of his *Discourses*: a paper claiming that the effect of the development of the arts and sciences on civilization has been more harmful than advantageous. He argued that dissolution of morals and advance in the arts and sciences have always occurred together; therefore the latter must have caused the former. He explained it as follows: "Astronomy was born from superstition . . . geometry from avarice; physics from vain curiosity; all, even moral philosophy, from human pride. Thus the sciences and arts owe their birth to our vices. . . . If our sciences are vain in the subjects they have in view, they are even more dangerous in the effects they produce. Born in idleness, they nourish it in turn" (Rousseau 1964:48-49). On reading the prize-winning essay, Voltaire remarked, "I saw here a man who started by hating the abuse of the arts and came in the end to hate the arts themselves" (Havens:56).

However, not all science is bad, declared Jean-Jacques; only *popular* enlightenment! Science should be restricted to the "true" wise men; "It is for these few to raise monuments to the glory of the human intellect" (Rousseau 1964:63). These should be the advisers of princes. "Only then will one see what can be done by virtue, science and authority . . . working together for the felicity of the human race" (ibid.:64).

Jean-Jacques published his second *Discourse*, on the sources of human inequality, when he was forty-three. He identified two sorts of inequality: that based on physical differences and the moral and political form established by humankind. The second, harmful form of inequality began only when humans moved away from their original "state of nature." He denied any supernatural legitimacy for social-political systems. Indeed, he declared, society — far from being divinely inspired — is the source of all evil.

Rousseau described the human as a natural species, part of the "animal system," and as amenable to scientific analysis as any other part of nature. He even suggested that human beings might be related to the apes, and have evolved over a time-span immeasurably longer than that indicated by the Bible. Like Montaigne, he recommended the development of a science of primitive humans and their origins. Having also rejected the idea that human rationality had a divine source that set us apart from the other animals, Jean-Jacques attacked the other sacred cow of the Enlightenment. In an echo of Hobbes, he maintained that the only natural right guaranteed by nature is that of the strong to impose their will on the weak.

However, Jean-Jacques disagreed with Hobbes' negative assessment of the state of nature. He saw it, instead, as superbly desirable: a sort of Arcadian Utopia. In his imagination, primitive men had roamed about in isolated freedom, sporadically coupling with females, then wandering on. They had obeyed only an impulse to further their own welfare and an urge to pity the suffering of others. They were one with nature. Then they began to gather together in herds for cooperation, and that marked the beginning of their "fall from Eden."

These human herds in time began to acquire property, seek the esteem of their fellows and to prey on one another for valued resources, eventually forcing their members to form crude societies by giving up individual freedom in return for mutual protection. Jean-Jacques believed that it was only in the resulting more restricted setting that families began to evolve. "Such was, or must have been, the origin of society and laws, which gave new fetters to the weak and new forces to the rich, destroyed natural freedom for all time, established forever the law of property and inequality, changed a clever usurpation into an irrevocable right, and for the profit of a few ambitious men henceforth subjected the whole human race to work, servitude and misery" (ibid.:160).

Rousseau argued that, as all political societies are but imperfect human institutions, their members must have the right to renounce them in favour of something better. The ideal goal would be to return to the idyllic primitive condition, for "The example of savages . . . seems to confirm that the human race was made to remain in it always; that this state is the veritable prime of the world; that all subsequent progress has been in appearance so many steps toward the perfection of the individual, and in fact toward the decrepitude of the species" (ibid.:151).

Voltaire, in responding to the copy of the essay sent him by the author, commented, "One feels like walking on all fours after reading your work" (Havens:65).

Returning to nature

With this essay Jean-Jacques was immediately propelled to fame. Convinced by his own eloquence, he decided to live the simple life that he was extolling. He would become the first "natural" modern man! A friend, Mme. d'Épinay, offered him a cottage on her estate, called L'Ermitage. From this time on he began to assume the role of prophet for all France, if not the world. He was convinced that his name was "destined to live and be known to posterity" (Guehenno 1967a:337).

During the next two years Jean-Jacques wrote *La Nouvelle Héloise*: a romantic fantasy of the ideal love affair that he believed should have been his. Meanwhile, at L'Ermitage the winters were long and cold and living even that close to a state of nature was not proving to be easy. Jean-Jacques was still a poor man, but he had never lived on what he earned. He simply did not know how to begin.

He had always accepted favours from his various benefactors, while resenting their beneficence and refusing to accept even the smallest obligation of gratitude or even politeness. Invariably this attitude led, on his part, to accusations of interference and of attempts to limit his freedom, and on theirs, to hurt feelings, frustration and eventual withdrawal of support. To complicate matters this time, he had been carrying on a heavy flirtation with Mme. d'Épinay's sister-in-law, Mme. d'Houdetot, and had probably aroused the jealousy of both his benefactor and the long-suffering Thérèse.

It is possible that Thérèse had a hand in creating some of the enmity that began to erupt between the prophet and his friends, and which finally isolated him as completely as in any state of nature that he could have imagined. For one with her simple mind and insecure position, every grand acquaintance must have posed a threat. In his *Confessions* Jean-Jacques relates an incident concerning a breach of trust by Mme. d'Épinay, supposedly witnessed by Thérèse and her mother. In the course of an appalling showdown Thérèse's mother denied the story. There is also the opinion expressed by Boswell in the account of his visits at the writer's home, that Thérèse resented him as well. To Jean-Jacques, Thérèse was a non-person, but the author of the revolutionary *Discourse on Inequality* should have known that the downtrodden and disparaged can be a powerful force in human affairs.

In 1758 Rousseau moved into lodgings at Montmorency, in France. Here he wrote the strange pamphlet attacking the proposed establishment of a theatre in Geneva. By now he was viewing himself as the guardian of public virtue and in a special relationship with God. In fact, the God with whom he was conversing daily, in his isolation from men, existed only within. God and his personal conscience had become one! He wrote of his own work, "never has nature created anything so beautiful. I have surpassed the work of the Gods!" (Guehenno 1967b:127). This marked the end of his relationship with Diderot and the French literary establishment. Voltaire asked a friend, "What's this about Jean-Jacques writing a book against the theatre? Has he become a father of the church?" (ibid.:7).

At this point in his life Rousseau seems to have been so haunted by his past moral failings that he could not face accepting responsibility for them. Others *must* have been to blame. He convinced himself of his own essential purity and of the heavenly rewards due him. "I believe in God, and God would be less than just if my soul were not immortal" (Guehenno 1967a:444). The disgust that he ought to have felt for his own behaviour, he transferred to society. A former friend asked him how it was that the self-professed friend of humanity was not on friendly terms with any of his fellows. Rousseau replied, "I am the friend of the human race and men can be found anywhere" (Guehenno 1967b:11).

Discoursing on education

The following spring the Maréchal de Luxembourg came to visit Jean-Jacques and persuaded him to move to the Petit Chateau until his home at Montmorency was upgraded. Here he completed *Émile*, a treatise on education. "All that we lack at birth," he wrote, "all that we need when we come to man's estate, is the gift of education. This education comes to us from nature, from men, or from things. . . . Thus we are really taught by three masters" (Rousseau 1967:6). When the teacher's lesson is inconsistent with the child's level of maturation or ignores the need to handle things in the natural environment, then the child is in trouble. There is nothing more important than the education of one's children. "Poverty, pressure of business, mistaken social prejudices, none of these can excuse a man from his duty, which is to support and educate his own children. If a man . . . neglects these sacred duties he will repent it with bitter tears and will never be comforted" (ibid.:17). (Jean-Jacques' treatment of his own children was still a well-kept secret!)

Rousseau was far ahead of his time in recognizing that a child's education begins at birth. "Education precedes instruction; before he can speak or understand anything he is learning" (ibid.:29). He condemned the popular custom of swathing babies. "It is only by movement that we learn the difference between self and non-self; it is only by our own movements that we gain the idea of space" (ibid.:31).

He explained that the cries of infants are essential first attempts to communicate and control their environment. "Here is forged the first link in the long chain of social order" (ibid.:32). These cries should not be needlessly ignored nor punished, for such responses will offend the infant's innate sense of justice. However, he reminded the reader that, in caring for children, "it is one thing to refrain from thwarting them, but quite another to obey them . . . [the child] begins by asking for aid, he ends by demanding service" (ibid.:33). He warned against allowing children to think of people as tools to be used. Dependence on things is natural; dependence on people is one of the chief sources of immorality. Where possible, he advised, let nature instruct — especially in her first law of accepting limits. "That man is truly free who desires what he is able to perform, and does what he desires. This is my fundamental maxim. Apply it to childhood and all the rules of education spring from it" (ibid.:48).

The first requirement for Émile's education is total isolation from "society" and immersion in "nature." An understanding of what is meant by these two key concepts would seem to be imperative, yet nowhere in Rousseau's works are they clearly explained. We only know that society represents all that is bad and nature all that is good. This failure to define his terms is one of the greatest sources of the confusion of radically conflicting messages conveyed by his books.

It is not that the author of *Émile* was unaware of the power of language, nor even of the process by which it is acquired. He knew that it does not come from nature, but from society. Concerning Émile's language development Rousseau recommended good example rather than correction, and a rule of simply not responding to the child who mumbles or speaks faintly. He noted that teachers should adjust their vocabulary to the children's level of understanding, avoiding abstract and general terms, as a young child is incapable of thinking beyond immediate, concrete experience. He exclaimed, "What dangerous prejudices are you implanting in them when you teach them to accept as knowledge, words that have no meaning for them!" (ibid.:76). He emphasized that words are merely meaningless sounds "without the idea of the things symbolized" (ibid.:73). He recognized that the young child "receives images, not ideas; . . . images are merely the pictures of external objects, while ideas are notions about those objects determined by their relations. . . . Our sensations are merely passive . . . ideas spring from an active principle which judges" (ibid.:71-72).

Too early an introduction to reading and books is dangerous. "I hate books. They only teach us to talk of things we know nothing about" (ibid.: 147). Children should be allowed to remain in ignorance of matters beyond their grasp. "Ignorance never did anyone any harm, error alone is fatal" (ibid.:129). The business of the educator is to arouse curiosity, and to instil the question, "What is the *use* of that?" (ibid.:142). Geography should begin where the child lives. Sciences should not be taught for the answers they provide, "but to give . . . [the child] a taste for them and methods of learning them" (ibid.:135). History should comprise facts, not opinions. And all adolescents should be taught a trade.

In *Émile* Rousseau acknowledged the importance of reason to an extent not found in his other works. "Reason alone teaches us to know good and evil. Therefore conscience, which makes us love the one and hate the other, though it is independent of reason, cannot develop without it" (ibid.:34). However, the ability to reason develops with maturation. Attempting to reason with the young child *about* right and wrong is futile. Instead, "All the reasons you give him, while he is still too young to reason, are so many pretences in his eyes . . . he resents all opposition" (ibid.:51). You are merely training the child "to be argumentative and rebellious" (ibid.:52). At this point in the book Rousseau's description of a miseducated child grown to egocentric adulthood is an eerily apt description of himself!

Rousseau recognized the necessity of controlling the environment of children so that, as much as possible, they can be made to experience the natural consequences of their actions. They must be made to suffer at times, otherwise they will grow up unable to feel pity. They must be encouraged to imitate the deeds the teacher wishes to establish as habits. (This in spite of the fact that elsewhere he maintained that Émile must be taught no habits!) To learn about justice children must first be taught the idea of property. (But in an earlier work he had claimed that property is the source of all evil!)

There is no advice about how to develop religious faith in *Émile*. "The obligation of faith," Rousseau wrote, "assumes the possibility of belief" (ibid.: 220). Religious dogma refers to that which is beyond any possible experience of a child; therefore it could only be taught as illusion. He concluded, "It is in matters of religion more than anything else that prejudice is triumphant" (ibid.:223).

Inserted in the book we find a long conversation with an imaginary Savoyard priest, obviously used by Rousseau to spell out his own religious beliefs, lest he be accused of teaching atheism. These beliefs constitute what he called "natural religion": a theism that rejected all doctrines except for that of a just, personal God and immortality of the soul. In addition the book includes numerous lengthy diversions into political theory, and, near the end, a treatise on the "desirable role" of the female of the species.

Rousseau's true opinion of women is revealed in this latter part of *Émile*, as he described the attributes of Sophie, the ideal mate for his pupil grown to manhood. She is a creature of superior cunning and wit, but little capacity for reason. Education for her must aim at developing docility and industry, and the *appearance* of virtue. "A woman's honour does not depend upon her conduct alone, but on her reputation, and no woman who permits herself to be considered vile is really virtuous" (ibid.:328). From childhood she must be accustomed to restraint and be taught to accept religious practices and dogma early and strictly on the basis of authority. There is no use postponing this, as one must for males, for she will never be capable of comprehending religious mysteries. "The search for abstract and speculative truths, for principles and axioms in science, for all that tends to wide generalization, is beyond a woman's grasp; their studies should be thoroughly practical" (ibid.:349). So much for equality!

Discoursing on politics

Following closely upon *La Nouvelle Héloise* and *Émile* came *Le Contrat Social*. In the latter Rousseau attempted to encapsulate all his thinking on moral and political matters. By now he had moved closer to Hobbes. He explained the social order as necessary and fundamental to human welfare even though it is not natural in origin. He maintained that it is founded on human conventions that have evolved over time out of a state where only the natural law of physical inequality ruled human relationships. As existing social orders are thus not based on natural law they are not irrevocable, nor can they bestow on their members natural rights that are immutable.

Like Hobbes, Rousseau compared the state to a living organism. "As nature gives each man an absolute power over all his members, the social compact gives the body politic an absolute power over all its [members]; and it is this very power which . . . has the name of sovereignty" (Masters:318). However, he charted a course very different from that of Hobbes when he set out to establish the preconditions for an ideal social order: "a form of association which defends and protects the person and the goods of each associate with the common force, and by which each one, being united with all, only obeys himself and remains as free as before" (ibid.:314). In order to accomplish this paradoxical goal Rousseau came up with the concept of the General Will, representing some sort of mystical consensus or unity with the "whole," rather than a reasoned compromise among all the individual wills.

According to Rousseau, the General Will is by definition always right, while individual wills are subject to error. Only duty to God and honour (undefined) can countermand the sovereign authority representing the General Will. Therefore the social contract will require that the members first relinquish *all* their rights to the sovereign state. This will ensure the good of all, for virtue can be no more than the conformity of all the private wills to the General Will. "Someone who dares to undertake the institution of a people should feel capable of changing human nature, so to speak: of transforming each individual into a part of a larger whole from which this individual receives in some way his life and being" (ibid.:354). Education under rules prescribed by the government will be necessary, as will censorship. "Censorship maintains morals by preventing opinions from being corrupted" (ibid.:384).

Rousseau was scornful of England's pragmatic progress toward democracy. "The English people think they are free," he wrote, "but they are very much mistaken. They are free only during the election of members of parliament. Once these members are elected the people are slaves, they are nothing" (Havens:91). In Rousseau's scheme there is no such regular opportunity for a corrective process, in the event that the sovereign misreads the General Will, or that the conditions justifying the consensus change. Instead, in extending the analogy of the state as a living organism, he mentions the possibility of a violent revolution (like a cataclysmic personal trauma causing memory loss) whereby "the state, having been set aflame by civil wars, is so to speak, reborn from the ashes" (Masters:358).

The chapter on religion in *Le Contrat Social* puzzled even Rousseau's most enthusiastic supporters. Whereas in *Émile* he had argued for freedom of religious belief (at least for men) here he recommended the exact opposite. Under the proposed social contract, the sovereign power would impose a civil religion on all members of society, and any citizens who failed to obey and uphold the chosen dogma would be banished. Of this, Voltaire wrote, "All dogma is ridiculous, harmful. All constraint on dogma, abominable. Ordering anyone to believe is absurd. Limit yourself to ordering people to behave themselves rightly" (Havens:92).

Rousseau lives with the consequences of his actions

All in all, Rousseau managed to offend just about everybody. His explosive prose seemed aimed at provoking religious anarchy and revolution against the established political order, while at the same time, justifying the most absolute authoritarianisms in a future state. Not surprisingly, *Émile* and *Le Contrat Social* caused a violent reaction in the religious and political establishments of France and Geneva. Rousseau was forced to flee, first to the protection of Frederick of Prussia, and later, with the help of David Hume, to the safety of the hated English.

In England, things went from bad to worse. Jean-Jacques began to turn against the kindly, gentle man who had rescued him. He imagined that he had been tricked into leaving France for one purpose only: to be ensnared in the power of David Hume and his fellow conspirators so that the prophetic voice could be silenced. He was trapped, surrounded by enemies. And as usual, Thérèse complained of being ridiculed and patronized by the servants. Hume was baffled by the strange behaviour of his guests. Thinking the problem was financial insecurity, he arranged a pension from the King of England. Ostentatiously and insultingly, Jean-Jacques refused it, only to accept it quietly later. Secretly, he began to write what he considered to be his most revealing and dangerous book: *The Confessions*. In it he penned his version of his life and times.

In 1767 Rousseau returned to France, believing that he had given his jailers the slip. He performed a do-it-yourself marriage ceremony with Thérèse. For the next few years the two moved about, ignored by the authorities, who no doubt believed that Rousseau's influence was waning. Wherever the couple went, troubles with "surly, disrespectful servants" and "thieving peasant neighbors" invariably followed. *The Dialogues*, a strange three-way conversation intended to portray Jean-Jacques in his true and virtuous light, was written and distributed personally on the streets of Paris, after a failed attempt to submit it to God at a church altar. More than ever the prophet was obsessed with the need to prove himself worthy of the rewards of both heaven and posterity.

The last two years of Jean-Jacques' life were more peaceful. He had given up on the world and was concerned only with justifying himself to God. He was pursuing his hobby of botany and writing *The Reveries of a Solitary Walker*. "I am now alone on earth, no longer having any brother, neighbour, friend or society other than myself" (Rousseau 1979:1). As usual, the loyal Thérèse was ignored. He had now come to the conclusion that his lifetime of undeserved persecution had been ordained by God. He was being tested, like Job, but divine justice would be his.

A note of honest regret pervades *The Reveries*. The writer seemed to realize that he was afraid to entertain new ideas, in case they undermined the religious convictions that he needed so badly. "Confined thus within the narrow sphere of my former knowledge, I do not share with Solon the happiness of being able to learn each day as I am growing old" (ibid.:39).

He bragged of having lived according to chance, without the guidance of reason. He had trusted to "the truth of his moral instinct" and dared to follow the impulses of his native temperament. "To act against my natural inclinations was always impossible for me" (ibid.:77). Always his intentions had been unassailable; how, then, could he be held responsible for the evil consequences inevitable in a corrupt society? Until the day of his death in 1778 (the year in which Voltaire also died) Jean-Jacques was busy convincing his God-within of his "natural" virtue. The judgement of posterity would have to wait.

The world lives with the consequences of Rousseau

Two hundred years later, the jury is still out. The sentiments and ideas of Jean-Jacques Rousseau have blasted down the currents of history like a torpedo, propelling people to the extremities of Right and Left and leaving in its wake a blood-soaked trail of shattered hopes and dreams. More than any one man, he inspired the French Revolution. Robespierre — the extremist leader of the second, and most violent, stage of the revolution — was a devoted disciple. He was the last to see the philosopher alive and had accepted the latter's beliefs as sacred doctrine. Both the admirable goals and the appalling excesses of that period owed much to the theory of Jean-Jacques. (Ironically, one of the many innocent victims of the conflagration was the scholarly Marquis de Condorcet, who is thought to have coined the term, "social science.")

In the troubled century to follow, Rousseau's poorly defined dreams of freedom, equality and a "brotherhood of Will" were the hope and battle cry of all who struggled against oppression. "Man was born free and is everywhere in chains!"; "The poor have nothing to lose but their fetters!"; and "Property is the root of all evil!": all were expressed first by Rousseau.

Certainly he contributed to a great push for equality in Europe. And some of his insights furthered the progress made by Montaigne, Hobbes, Hume and others toward a science of humanity. His understanding of the immense time involved in human evolution and of the possible connection of humankind with the ape family was prescient. His shrewd comments on the harmfulness of social inequality are still valid. Some of his ideas about the educational process were remarkably acute. They helped to inspire the sophisticated theory of John Dewey and the fruitful research of Jean Piaget. But *Émile* spawned as well the "nativist" model that views children as the sole authors of their own educational development: a pedagogical dead-end resulting only in the cult of permissiveness.

For there is indeed a dark side to the influence of Rousseau. Because his works were so ambiguous and emotive, they held the potential for great harm.

He had a way of expounding totally contradictory opinions on the same subject, while remaining blissfully unaware of any problem. And he was utterly unable to follow an argument to its logical conclusion. His key concepts remain vague. His cult of nature, incorporating as it did the worship of an erroneous vision of an idyllic primitivism, has been a major obstacle to solving human problems. It is a chief source of the reactionary, escapist form of romanticism that plagues us to this day. His exaltation of feeling over reason and knowledge and his faith in intuition have fed a dangerous but psychologically appealing anti-intellectualism and moral irresponsibility. And his mystical General Will has proven to be an all-too-tempting tool for the totalitarian impulse — whether of left or right.

There is no denying that Rousseau had a major impact on the development of modern social philosophy. On the one hand his writings furthered the evolution of a science of humanity. On the other hand, they nourished within philosophical thought a strain of romanticism considered by many to be antithetical to any lasting progress in social science. It is no wonder that, more than two centuries later, his contradictions plague us still.

References for Chapter Four

Babbitt, Irving. 1919. *Rousseau and Romanticism*. New York: World Publishing.

Boswell, James. 1947. Dialogue with Rousseau. In *The Portable Johnson and Boswell*. Edited by Louis Kronenberger. New York: Viking Press, p. 414-37.

Guehenno, Jean. 1967. *Jean-Jacques Rousseau*. 2 vols. London: Routledge and Kegan Paul.

Havens, George R. 1978. *Jean-Jacques Rousseau*. Boston: Twayne Publishers.

Lamont, Corliss. 1949. *The Philosophy of Humanism*. New York: Philosophical Library.

Masters, Roger D. 1968. *The Political Philosophy of Rousseau*. Princeton: Princeton University Press.

Naves, Raymond. 1968. Voltaire's Wisdom. In *Voltaire: Twentieth-Century Views*. Edited by William Bottiglia. Englewood Cliffs, NJ: Prentice-Hall, p. 150-65.

Rousseau, Jean-Jacques. 1947. *Social Contract*. Edited by Charles Frankel. New York: Hafner.

_____. 1953. *The Confessions*. Translated by J.M. Cohen. New York: Penguin Books.

_____. 1964. *The First and Second Discourses*. Edited and translated by Roger D. and Judith Masters. New York: St. Martin's Press.

_____. 1967. *Émile*. Translated by Barbara Foxley. London: Dent, Everyman's Library.

_____. 1979. *The Reveries of the Solitary Walker*. Translated by Charles Butterworth. New York: New York University Press.

Five

Harriet Martineau and the Quiet Revolution

> I found myself, with the last link of my chain snapped —
> a free rover
> in the broad breezy common of the universe . . .
> I felt the fresh air of nature, after imprisonment
> in the ghost-peopled cavern of superstition.
> — Harriet Martineau, *Autobiography*

Two generations separated the productive years of Hume and Rousseau and the coming of age of Harriet Martineau. Those generations had witnessed the American War of Independence and the heady days of the French Revolution when, for a brief time, people believed that democracy and social justice for all were realizable in their lifetimes. But this was not to be — at least not in the "old world." The bloody aftermath of the revolution and Napoleon's subsequent dictatorship and wars of aggression resulted in a period of social crisis throughout Europe. With Napoleon's downfall, nationalism began to emerge as a powerful new religion, with numerous regional and cultural groupings seeking political unification into nation-states. At the same time, the Industrial Revolution in Britain, and to a lesser degree on the continent, was rapidly destroying the old social patterns and creating a new impoverished urban class.

Meanwhile, at least five identifiable schools of moral philosophy had evolved out of the formulations of the pioneers of social-scientific thought. The sensationalism of Hobbes and Locke was most apparent in the ideas of the French materialists such as Claude Helvetius, Étienne de Condillac and Baron d'Holbach. They, too, viewed the human being as a thoroughly material organism operating in a Newtonian universe of mechanistic cause and effect. And they held that all mental faculties and moral strivings are rooted in the senses.

A somewhat related strand of thought had originated with Adam Smith, who was also greatly influenced by the Newtonian world view and by Hume's

---

References for this chapter are on p. 96.

insights concerning the origin of moral feelings in the sensations of pleasure and pain. In his *Theory of Moral Sentiments*, published in 1758, he expanded on Hume's theory, explaining the role of *empathy* in human morality. In the year of Hume's death, Smith published his famous book, *Inquiry into the Nature and Causes of the Wealth of Nations*. To a considerable extent this book marked the beginning of a disciplined approach to what became known as political economy. In it Smith defined labour rather than primary resources (such as land, minerals and forests) as the major source of wealth, along with the capital required for utilizing both. He introduced the idea of an economic order operating according to natural law. This implied doing away with all existing mercantilist restrictions on the free flow of trade, as well as special privileges for business, and monopolies. It also implied no government intervention in internal economic affairs, except where necessary for the prevention of injustice and oppression, the advancement of education, protection of public health and maintenance of any other necessary services unlikely to be provided by private enterprise. Smith was concerned chiefly for the working poor, who invariably suffered the most from protectionist trade policies.

Among those who carried on Adam Smith's legacy of general social-scientific thought was Thomas Malthus. A remarkably original thinker, Malthus added the idea that populations invariably outgrow their food supply — if not limited by other natural disasters such as war or pestilence — unless rational means are utilized by the group members to control fecundity.

A third identifiable strand of thought — this one growing out of a need to refute Hume — was what became known as the Scottish school of moral philosophers. It originated with Thomas Reid, a contemporary of Hume, who sought a way around what he saw as the latter's radical scepticism. Reid favoured what he called a "philosophy of common sense." He defined perception in terms of an internal projection of objects *suggested* by sensations, rather than in terms of the sensations themselves. He claimed that all forms of behaviour and language necessarily reflect, and thereby demonstrate the existence of, the external world. A younger disciple, Dugald Stewart, was the chief exponent of this school during the early nineteenth century.

David Hartley combined many of the ideas of the Scottish moral philosophers with those of the French materialists as he attempted to work out the principles of a deterministic psychology based on associationism. Joseph Priestley (a scientist and Unitarian minister) took over Hartley's theories and accommodated them to the pre-Hume Enlightenment concepts of necessary cause and argument from design. The result of all this was a movement known as "necessarianism." It became an influential — although minority — current within the world view of early nineteenth-century Unitarianism.

Yet another aspect of the intellectual culture of Harriet Martineau's England was the utilitarianism of Jeremy Bentham. He had published *Principles of*

Morals and Legislation in 1789. He taught that the interest of the community is necessarily the sum of the interests of its members. Based on the principle of "the greatest good for the greatest number" and the "pleasure/pain" origin of moral sentiment, he attempted to design a kind of moral calculus by means of which it would be possible, theoretically, to measure the social usefulness of any practice or institution. Utilitarianism was subsequently taken up by James Mill.

Martineau's life as a girl-child

Such was the nature of the minority current of naturalistic thought that struggled for existence at the turn of the century within a majority culture still firmly shaped by dualism and ritualized supernaturalism. All of these ideas defined the intellectual legacy available to the children born at the time of Harriet Martineau's childhood. Available to boy-children, that is. As a girl-child, born in 1802, Harriet could only rattle the bars of her gender-defined cage and rage against its strictures. She was caged in as well by a congenital lack of the senses of taste and smell, and a steadily developing deafness. Ironically, however, it was those handicaps, plus two factors in her immediate subcultural environment, that ultimately were to provide her with an advantage not generally available to females.

Harriet was the sixth of eight children born to a manufacturer and his wife in the city of Norwich. Her father's business failed in the depression of the 1820s and he died not long after. He was of Huguenot descent, his ancestors having emigrated from France after the revocation of the Edict of Nantes in 1685. Harriet's mother was descended from a Dissenting vicar who had been ejected from his living after the passing of the Act of Uniformity in England in 1662, which excluded all non-Anglican Protestants or "Nonconformers" from public office. The Martineaus belonged to the most notorious of the Dissenters: the Unitarians. A unique intellectual culture resulting from the theological "looseness" of Unitarianism was to prove a fruitful seedbed for radical thought during the entire century, and Harriet no doubt benefited from this. In addition, the intimate knowledge of manufacturing and commerce provided by her family environment, along with her early propulsion into a situation of severe financial hardship, gave Harriet an experience of "the real world" rare in the life of an intellectual. She was grateful, she said later, for the "loss of gentility" — which, in fact, allowed for some loosening of the bars of the gender-cage. And the Unitarian connection, with its preponderance of members who belonged to the established intellectual elite both in England and the United States, was to open doors for her for many years.

What this particular girl-child gained from the physical and environmental contingencies of her growing-up was a marginality that provided her with an abiding curiosity about how people operate, along with the observer status and detached, objective stance that were to serve her all her life. She was *necessarily* different, so she felt less fettered by the cage of sex- and work-role expectations than did her fellow females. This is possibly the explanation for Harriet Martineau's remarkable — albeit sadly ignored and underrated — accomplishments as a social reformer, educator, social scientist, novelist and children's writer, journalist, historian, philosopher, pioneering feminist and environmentalist. She was one of the greatest Renaissance figures of the nineteenth century, yet we scarcely know her name!

As an early feminist

All her life Harriet Martineau fought for equality of opportunity for women. It is a measure of the durability of the very bias against which she struggled that she is seldom recognized for this. When she was growing up, women in England (as elsewhere) had no political rights. Universities had never even thought to provide for the possibility that Fellows might have wives; the very idea of a female graduate was to provoke horrified response some fifty years later. Martineau experienced this injustice early, in the matter of her own all-too-typical exclusion from formal schooling — except for a fortuitous combination of circumstances that allowed her to attend a Unitarian boys' school for a year-and-a-half. There she encountered Tacitus and was to read him all her life. But even self-education had its difficulties. "When I was young," she wrote, "it was not thought proper for young ladies to study very conspicuously . . . thus my first studies in philosophy were carried on with care and reserve" (Martineau 1983b:100-101).

Her first article, published in 1823 in the Unitarian *Monthly Repository*, was on the subject of lack of educational opportunity for females. She noted that "The boy goes on to continuously increase his stock of information . . . while the girl is probably confined to low pursuits . . . and thus before she is sensible of her powers, they are checked in their growth, chained down to mean objects, to rise no more; and when the natural consequences of this mode of treatment arise, all mankind agrees that the abilities of women are far inferior to those of men" (Martineau 1983a:ix). She was convinced that the *objectives* of female education were at the root of the problem. "Girls will never make a single effort," she suggested, "for such an object as being companions to men, and mothers to heroes. The boys are not encouraged for such a reason as becoming intelligent companions to somebody thereafter, or being the fathers of great men" (Sanders:174).

Martineau slipped her ideas into her novel, *Deerbrook* — as when she described a woman as "sensible, as she is a woman; if she were a man she would be called philosophical" (Martineau 1983a:49) and when she referred to the common custom of fathers not leaving any of their estate to daughters, because of the widespread belief that "women have little occasion for money, and do not know how to manage it" (ibid.:75). The novel gave her a vehicle for pointing out the contradictions in these customs and their devastating consequences. For example, she put the following words into the mouth of a female character: "A woman from the uneducated classes can get a subsistence by washing and cooking, by milking cows and going into service, and, in some parts of the kingdom, by working in a cotton mill, or burnishing plate.... But, for an educated woman ... there is in all England no chance of subsistence but by teaching" (ibid.:448).

In a subsequent book of fiction, *Sketches from Life*, she pointed out the dead-end nature of that sole employment opportunity: "No young woman who has been engaged in education," she had a character say, "can ever again move in society like one who has not" (Martineau 1856:5). In another story about an aging governess who had been left behind when her employers emigrated to Canada, Martineau told how the family received a last letter written by the woman as she lay dying in a poorhouse. "There was so much in her letter as rather surprised them about her hope and expectation that the time would come when early work in the vigorous season of life should secure its easy close; and when a greater variety of employment would be open to women" (ibid.:52). A story entitled "The Despised Woman" reveals the author's own faith in the strength of females. The tale of the subject's quiet heroism in the face of her husband's scorn and ill-treatment concludes with the comment that "for many years she must have had a strong sense of power within herself" (ibid.:63).

Martineau "escaped" marriage by what proved to be, for her at least, another fortuitous circumstance. Her fiancé committed suicide. She said later, "The older I have grown the more serious and irremediable have seemed to me the disadvantages of married life, as it exists among us at this time.... My business in life is to think and learn, and to speak out with absolute freedom what I have thought and learned" (Martineau 1983b:133). She was right in believing that she could not have done so as a married woman. She had only to look around her to see how the typical attitude of women in that state at that time was shaped in response to male expectations. It is with apparent shame that she recorded the behaviour of women who had been invited to a learned conference. They had been referred to by a speaker as "the fair sex." "That same fair sex, meantime, was there to sketch the *savans* ... or to pass the time by watching and quizzing the members. Scarcely any of the ladies sat still for half an hour" (Martineau 1983b:137).

Thinking and speaking out, on this subject as on others, were what Martineau did. She begged women not to encumber themselves in the clothing styles dictated by men. When, as a girl, she read Shakespeare's *The Taming of the Shrew*, her response was one of grief and anger. "Such a monstrous infringement of all rights, leading to such an abominable submission, makes one's blood boil!" (Webb:180). She criticized the literary lions of her time for their portrayal of her gender. She said that Thackeray must never have known a good and sensible woman; that Dickens saw the function of women as being solely to adorn the houses of men, and seemed unaware that most poor women held down jobs of some kind; that Charlotte Bronte and other popular women writers presented women as mindless creatures mired in a sea of sentimentality. She blamed such novelists for their complicity in perpetuating "this corrupted 'patriarchal' system" (Martineau 1983b:452). She thought that they also fed another male prejudice. "I had heard all my life," she said, "of the vanity of women as a subject of pity to men: but when I went to London, lo! I saw vanity in high places which was never transcended by that of women in their lowlier rank" (Martineau 1983b:350). However, she mentioned two eminent men of her acquaintance who were neither vain nor sexist: the geographer, Charles Lyell, and his friend, "the simple, childlike, painstaking Charles Darwin" (ibid.:355).

Martineau painted a grim picture of women's situation merely by quoting the two foremost liberal thinkers of the time. According to Jefferson, she said, democracy *must exclude* "(1) infants; (2) women, who, to prevent depravation of morals, and ambiguity of issue, could not mix promiscuously in the public meetings of men; and (3) slaves, from whom the unfortunate state of things with us takes away the rights of will and of property" (Martineau 1962:126). And, according to James Mill, "one thing is pretty clear, that all those individuals whose interests are involved in those of other individuals may be struck off without inconvenience. . . . In this light women may be regarded" (ibid.).

Martineau believed that the test of any civilization has to be the condition of that half of society over which the other half has power. She was horrified at the unconcern in the political arena about the injustice suffered by women — even in the United States where the new revolutionary constitution proclaimed that "all are endowed by their Creator with certain inalienable rights: that among these are life, liberty and the pursuit of happiness" (ibid.:308). Indulgence, she said, is everywhere provided as a palliative. She observed in America (as she had learned early in her own life) how "the whole apparatus of public opinion is brought to bear offensively upon individuals among women who exercise freedom of mind" (ibid.:293). It is not surprising that, while writing about the United States, she shed new light on the Salem witchcraft trials — citing the event as a tragic example of superstition, pious fraud and the subjugation of women.

The conclusion of one of her female biographers was that Martineau "will be remembered for all time as one of the women — perhaps the first among them — who made the nineteenth century the dawn of freedom for half the human race" (Courtney:263). She was a member of the fledgling Women's Suffrage movement and numerous other organizations for the advancement of women. In later life she wrote: "I have no role in elections . . . and I regard the disability as an absurdity, seeing that I have for a long course of years influenced public affairs to an extent not professed or attempted by many men" (Martineau 1983b:402).

She was always particularly incensed at attempts to define an appropriate role for women as distinct from that of men. "Let a hundred women," she said, "be educated up to the highest point that education can reach, and it would soon be clear what would be the sphere of that hundred" (Webb:181). She believed that the solution to women's unequal status "consists simply in giving their faculties fair play. I repudiate all abstract doctrines of rights — all *a priori* arrangements for giving a position — a position being a thing that must be earned" (Wheatley:363). This was consistent with her general philosophical stance on what she considered the regressive notion of inherent natural rights.

As a philosopher

Martineau was critical not only of Enlightenment premises concerning natural rights, but also of the romantic idealism so popular among German philosophers of the time. The comment of a character in *Deerbrook* compares her own world view to theirs. "There is a pleasure in making one's way about a grotto in a garden; but I think there is a much higher one in exploring a cave on the seashore . . . where you never know that you have come to the end — a much higher pleasure in exploring a life than in living out an allegory" (Martineau 1983a:60). Her entire life was one of intellectual exploration and growth. The world view revealed in her early fictional works is very far from the place at which she arrived in her mature years. Only the open-ended *method*, as expressed in the above quotation, remained the same.

In her autobiography Martineau traced what she considered her progression from Unitarianism to secular enlightenment. She described how, in her early twenties, she had moved out of the Unitarian brand of theism which rejected the divinity of Jesus but retained a liberal Christian form and identity. She became committed to Priestley's necessarianism, with its assumption of first cause and teleological purpose. It was not until her trip to the Middle East during the following decade — in which she conducted a comparative study of religions — that she arrived at a different approach to the lawfulness of nature. She concluded that, although a cosmic plan and purpose cannot be assumed, "all the world is *practically* Necessarian. All human action proceeds on the supposition that all the workings of nature are governed by laws that cannot be broken by human will. . . . The very smallest amount of science is enough to enable any rational person to see that the constitution and action of the human faculty of Will are determined by influences beyond the control of the possessor of that faculty" (Martineau 1983b:110). She then made the same distinction as had Duns Scotus between the "volition" and the "will." And she referred to the notion of free will as "that monstrous remnant of old superstition" (ibid.:111) which does great harm.

She once mused that "it is possible, that human beings, with our mere human faculty, may not understand the scheme . . . of the universe . . . any more than the minnow in the creek . . . can understand the perturbations caused in his world by the existence of the tides" (Martineau 1983b:185). She described how she came to the realization that "the philosophical atheists were the most humble-minded in the face of the mysteries of the universe . . . the most devout in their contemplation of the unknown, and the most disinterested in their management of themselves and their expectations for the human being; in short, the moral advantages of knowledge (however limited) and of freedom . . . over superstition" (ibid.:189).

By this time Martineau had moved far from both the Christian theism of her family's Unitarianism, and the transcendentalist variety which had been popularized in the United states by Ralph Waldo Emerson. Emerson remained a valued personal friend, however. He once wrote to her, "Joy that you exist. Honour to your spirit, which is so true and brave" (Wheatley:157). She was not so fond of another well-known American transcendentalist, Margaret Fuller. Of her she wrote, "While she was living and moving in an ideal world, . . . discoursing in public about the most fanciful and shallow conceits which the transcendentalists of Boston took for philosophy, she looked down upon persons who acted" (Martineau 1983b:71). Her opinion of all forms of American pantheistic deism was not much better. "All these claim to be philosophers, and scientific . . . while . . . wandering wide of the central point of knowledge . . . each in his own balloon, wafting in complacency by whatever current he may be caught by, and all crossing each other . . . hopeless of finding a common centre" (ibid.:331). Romanticism had no appeal for her. A woman in America probed her feelings at seeing Niagara Falls. "Did you not long to throw yourself down and mingle with Mother Earth?" she rhapsodized. "No" said Martineau (Sanders:133).

Martineau was criticized for asking her personal correspondents to destroy her letters. Her explanation of this request reveals much about her philosophy. "How could human beings open their hearts and minds to each other," she asked, "if there were no privacy guaranteed by principles and feelings of honour?" (Martineau 1983b:3). She wanted to maintain a boundary between the public and private realms, convinced that "If, by what I have done, I have fixed attention upon the morality of the case, this will be a greater social benefit than the publication of any letters written by me" (ibid.:7). She took her principles seriously. Although her financial situation was always precarious, she refused three offers of a government pension. "It is only by taking our stand on principle," she said, "and keeping ourselves free to act, untrammelled by authority, that we can retain any power of resolving and working as rational human beings" (Webb:32). This infuriated a leading politician. "Harriet Martineau!" he said, "I hate her. I hate a woman who has opinions. She has refused a pension — making herself out to be better than other people" (Wheatley:224).

A much louder chorus of castigation resulted from Martineau's recovery from a lengthy incapacitating illness by means of what was then known as "mesmerism": a treatment routinely accepted today as the effective procedure of hypnosis. Because mesmerism was then so universally associated with the grotesque claims and magical explanations of spiritualism, it seemed to the rationalists of Martineau's acquaintance (including many family members) that she had gone over to the other side. Martineau knew simply that it worked, and she expected that the reasons would someday be found to be quite natural ones. She was also quick to acquire the procedures and to use them to help other sufferers. She later observed: "I had more than my share of persecution for the offence of recovery from a hopeless illness by a new method" (Martineau 1983b:199), and she went on to cite "the despicable treatment medical men inflict on women . . . who have recourse to mesmerism" (ibid.:201). Always the observer, she offered the following explanation for the outrage and general abuse. "Human pride and prejudice cannot brook discoveries which innovate upon old associations and expose human ignorance; and, as long as anything in the laws of the universe remain to be revealed, there is a tolerable certainty that someone will be persecuted" (ibid.:199).

In her mature years Martineau concluded that the Scottish moral philosophers had got hold of something important in their "postulate of a fundamental complete faculty [of 'common-sense reasoning'] which could serve as a basis for the mind's operations — whereas Hartley lays down simply a principle of association" (Martineau 1983b:106). She recognized that the flaw in utilitarianism was Bentham's calculus of feelings, because of its underlying premise of the equality of pleasures. She deplored her youthful inability to "distinguish between a conception and a conviction" (ibid.:107). She commented on the handicap of having been self-educated and receiving no guidance in her search for understanding. She recognized how she could have benefited from a teacher "to show me the boundary line between the knowable and the unknowable, as I see it now, and to indicate to me that the purely human view of the universe derived solely from within, and proceeding on the assumption that Man and his affairs and his world are the centre and crown of the universe, could not possibly be a true one" (ibid.).

She felt her biggest breakthrough had been her realization of the ultimate connection between the physical and the "moral" sciences (as the social disciplines were then called) resulting from the discovery that "no action fails to produce effects, and no effort can be lost" (ibid.:111-12). She explained that human actions and rational choices are just as much links in the chain of cause and effect as are physical reactions.

It seems clear that Martineau was an evolutionary naturalist for some time before Darwin's *The Origin of Species* came out in 1858. She was one of the few who read the book with great enthusiasm and an immediate understanding of its significance for philosophy. Sometime earlier, she had sought to explain the evolution of culture in terms of the development of religious belief systems, and to relate this to individual development. "Every child, and every childish tribe of people, transfers its own consciousness, by a supposition so necessary as to be an instinct, to all external objects, so as to conclude them all to be alive like itself; and passes through this stage of belief to a more reasonable view; and, in like manner, more advanced nations and individuals suppose a whole pantheon of Gods first — and then a trinity — and then a single deity: all the divine being exaggerated men, regarding the universe from the human point of view, and under the influence of human notions and affections. . . . [Ultimately] the conceptions of . . . divine government become abstract and indefinite, till the indistinguishable line is reached which is . . . not seen to separate the highest order of . . . [theology] from the philosophical atheist" (Martineau 1983b:280). She thought that all the great religions, at their best, contain the same noble insights which arise naturally out of individual minds and then become part of the general "group mind," or cultural legacy. And she felt that her own era was an infant stage of the evolution of that culture.

During a later debilitating bout of illness she expressed a tranquil acceptance of the fact of death. "The laying down of our own life, to yield our place to our successors, and simply ceasing to be, seems to me to admit of no fear or regret, except through the corruption introduced by false and superstitious associations" (ibid.:206). She added, presciently, that "the very conception of *self* and *other* is, in truth, merely human, and when the self ceases to be, the distinction expires" (ibid.:207). Similarly, of the argument from design, she said that the very conception of design is a human one.

She agreed with her favourite correspondent, Henry Atkinson, when he wrote "We may sign ourselves Naturalists, as having no knowledge, and no means of knowing anything, beyond nature. . . . The power of knowledge is the knowledge of causes; that is, of the material conditions and circumstances under which any effect takes place" (ibid.:398). She suspected, however, that it might be essential to human nature to feel that there is something above and beyond that which can be known. "If that something were God," she wrote, " (and I am confident it is not) he would consider those of us the noblest who must have evidence in order to believe" (ibid.:290). She viewed philosophy as the legitimate offspring of science and deplored the fact that so few people have "the remotest conception of the indispensableness of science as the only source, of not only enlightenment, but wisdom, goodness and happiness" (ibid.:330). Her own philosophy had been the joy of her life, "harmonizing, animating all its details, and making life itself a festival" (ibid.:445).

As an educator

One of Martineau's biographers accused her of being "an incurable teacher" as if it were a fatal flaw of character. It is true that one cannot understand her without a firm grasp of the centrality of education in her philosophy. "Wisdom may spring, full-formed, from the head of a god," she liked to say, "but not from the brains of men" (Martineau 1962:67). Long before "socialization" was ever conceived, she saw education in the broadest cultural terms. In her novel, *Deerbrook*, the governess exclaims, "If I had them to myself, to spend their whole time with me, so that I could educate, rather than merely teaching them" (Martineau 1983a:21). From the point of view of society, Martineau suggested, "The prudent speak of the benefits of education as a matter of policy, while the philanthropic promote it as a matter of justice" (Martineau 1962:70). She saw it in both senses. She remarked on the sad social consequences of the lack of education in the American frontier communities which she visited on her trip to the United States in 1832-34. "The result is a society which is a punishment for its members to live in. There is pedantry in those who read; prejudice in those who do not . . . and an absence of all reference to the higher . . . objects of life" (ibid.:154).

However, she appreciated the independence and fearlessness of the American children. She had a great love for all children. She was anticipating later discoveries concerning moral education when she once exclaimed, "It is a beautiful spectacle to watch the expansion of affections in the mind of a child; to see how, by pleasurable association, his interests are gradually transferred from himself to others" (Webb:111). She never believed that the poor in either the United States or England were less educable than the upper classes. In fact, she wrote in 1832 that she had always found poor children to be superior to the progeny of aristocrats, because they possessed a common-sense knowledge of reality lacking in the more privileged children. In the 1840s she lobbied for a national system of education in England, and for the ensuing two decades she worked on the improvement of school curricula, believing that vocational as well as intellectual education was vital. She supported legislation that would have provided schooling for factory children, although the bill (which was defeated) required that they be taught by the Anglican church. "Better that they be raised as Mohammedans or even pagans," she said, "than deserted and left to chance" (Webb:320).

In her own childhood, Harriet seems to have had the rare ability to observe the learning process while it was occurring. She described her early fascination with a sundial. "There did I watch and ponder, day by day, painfully forming my first clear conceptions of Time, amidst a bright confusion of notions of day and night, and of the seasons and of the weather" (Martineau 1983b:30). She remembered going through the Bible methodically, listing the moral rules, and, in the process, discovering that, "whereas Judaism was a preceptive religion, Christianity was mainly a religion of principles" (ibid.: 36). When she was nine years old, she welcomed the birth of her little sister with delight, telling a relative that "I should now see the growth of a human mind from the very beginning" (ibid.:52). She recalled the enthusiasm with which she encountered school for the short time that it was available to her. Lant Carpenter, the Unitarian minister who taught her, had a profound influence on her — turning her into a religious fanatic, as she afterward concluded. She thought of him later as an example of what a teacher should *not* be.

Martineau's educational role began with her writing career. Her first published article (about education) was noticed by her eldest brother, who seems to have been the only member of her family to take her interests and abilities seriously. He said, "Now, dear, leave it to other women to make shirts and darn stockings; and do you devote yourself to this" (ibid.:120). Although she was not free to follow his advice, she began writing in earnest whenever she could snatch the time from household chores. Among these was the never-ending task of mending and sewing clothes for the entire family. Because of a series of family tragedies (including the deaths of her father and this same brother) she was soon faced with the imperative of making a living for her mother and younger sister. So she *had* to write, although, for some time, her earnings came largely from proofreading.

Martineau's stories and articles were invariably planned with the objective of teaching a lesson. A voracious reader, she had become interested in political economy as a youth. This led her, in 1827, to what was to be a momentous decision. She surmised that the main principles of the discipline could be taught to relatively unsophisticated readers through simple stories about believable people. She proposed a series of small books that would deal with economic issues as they actually affected the working poor. Her struggle to find a publisher is a long, sad story. In the end she succeeded, in every sense of the word. *The Illustrations of the Political Economy* (thirty-four volumes in all) was a best seller — read even by the young Princess Victoria. And it propelled her into notoriety.

John Stuart Mill was scornful of her project. He wrote it off as a mere reiteration of the work of others — simplified to the extent that her stories reduced utilitarianism, with its principle of absolute rights and individual self-interest, to absurdity, by "carrying it out to all its consequences" (Webb:107). But she was not pretending to contribute anything original — just simplifying and explaining for the ordinary person, and pointing out the often-unintended results of the kinds of ideas promulgated by theorists like Mill. She considered John Stuart Mill greatly overrated as a philosopher, in that, although his intellect was admirable his judgement was unsound. She was considered prudish and censorious by Mill and others because she objected to explicit sensual detail and imagery in fiction unless a positive moral point was being made. But she was aware, as they were not, that all literature is educational — in spite of an author's intentions. Her approach to journalism and history was similarly educational in nature. It was the educational *uses* of history that fascinated her. She planned hundreds of tales to illustrate the rise of the world's great civilizations. She saw history as the best possible source of lessons for humanity.

In the years before her final illness Martineau taught working-class children in the Lake District — and their parents as well. She also wrote a secular burial service. In 1847, she produced another series, called *Household Education*, aimed at "secularists." She had identified a need for juvenile literature which could be a source of moral education for parents who did not want their children exposed to orthodox religion. She viewed the persistence of beliefs in the supernatural as the result of faulty childhood education and ignorance of the causes of human behaviour. She was convinced that the more ignorant we are of human nature, the greater is our tendency to attribute to the external world aspects of our own consciousness.

She could no more stop educating than she could stop breathing. A biographer notes that she saw her work as an effective alternative to both preceptive teaching and political action, as ways of improving society (Martineau 1983b:460). She tried to explain that "individuals could be formed so as to allow natural laws to produce a happy . . . society; if they were not so formed the laws would operate anyhow, but the society would not be a happy one" (Webb:110). She was sadly misinterpreted in her own time because there was no place in the prevailing world views for the crucial role of what we now recognize as the socialization process.

As a novelist and writer of children's stories

In spite of her proven record at the time, Martineau's publisher refused her novel, *Deerbrook*, because it dealt with middle-and lower-class people in "the familiar life of everyday." In the early decades of the nineteenth century, the "silver fork" school had governed the writing of novels. It was thought that people would only buy books that romanticized the doings of the gentry. *Deerbrook* was published in 1839 and it sold well, but, in later years, Martineau expressed her own dissatisfaction with it. "The laborious portions of meditation, obtruded at intervals, are wholly objectionable," she wrote in her autobiography (Martineau 1983b:116). Literary historians judge it less harshly, however. She is credited with having established the middle-class domestic love story as a valid genre: one that was subsequently followed by Charlotte Bronte, Mrs. Gaskell, George Eliot, Trollope, Dickens and Thackeray.

Her only other novel was quite different. *The Hour and the Man* dealt with the exploits of the black Haitian hero Toussaint L'Ouverture. It was written during her long first illness, and reprinted many times. She also wrote numerous short stories, beginning in 1825 with "The Machine Breakers," "The Rioters" and "The Turnout." In 1829 she published *The Traditions of Palestine*, a book of three stories, and one called *Sketches from Life*, in 1856.

Martineau's output of children's literature was also considerable. She published *Five Years of Youth* in 1831, and the *Playfellow Series* in 1841, while confined to her bed. Her *Household Education* series has already been mentioned. All in all, her distinctive characteristics as a writer of fiction were her precise use of language and convincing portrayal of the poor. Unlike Dickens, however, she showed the positive effects of industrialization in their lives as well as the dark side. She once referred dubiously to "life of any rank, presented by Dickens in his peculiar artistic light, which is very unlike the broad daylight of actual existence" (Wheatley:213). She regretted the influence of the romantic movement in poetry and fiction. "How much utter nonsense is cried up as fine poetry, because dressed in words which awaken pleasant associations as they pass over the ear!" she said (Sanders:6).

As a social reformer

Martineau departed from the utilitarians most radically in the priority she gave to justice over individual liberty. As a child, she had suffered from injustice at the hands of her own family, and ever after she felt the suffering of others with a passion. One of her earliest sources of dissatisfaction with the church of her youth was the fact that "not a word was ever preached about the justice due the weaker from the stronger" (Martineau 1983b:21). She was involved in the struggle for justice all her life. She did not believe that this could be merely assumed as the natural result of individuals freely pursuing their interests. "What is everybody's business is nobody's business," she said. "No man stirs against an abuse that is no more his than other people's. The abuse goes on until it begins to overbear law and liberty. Then the multitude rises, in the strength of the law, and crushes the abuse" (Martineau 1962:72). She felt that this applied to the slavery issue. While travelling in the United States from 1832-34 she became convinced that the harm being done to the entire moral/social fabric of the country was such that the time had arrived when people would begin to act in concert against it. And she was prepared to lead the anti-slavery movement rather than follow reluctantly in its wake.

Martineau's abhorrence of slavery was already well known to the Americans. Her book, *Demarara*, dealing with the issue, was one of the earliest in her series on political economy and was considered by many to be less exaggerated and sentimental — and, accordingly, more influential — than *Uncle Tom's Cabin*. What she saw on her travels in the young country confirmed her earlier judgement. She described the situation as follows: "As long as the slave remains ignorant, docile, and contented, he is taken care of, humoured, and spoken of with contemptuous, compassionate kindness. But from the minute he exhibits the attitudes of a rational being — from the moment his intellect seems likely to come into the most distant competition with that of the whites, the most deadly hatred springs up — not in the black, but in his oppressors" (ibid.:208). Martineau showed an acute ability for accurate observation and analysis of the problem requiring solution. "The best argument for Negro emancipation lies in the vices and subservience of the slaves" she once wrote, and "the best argument for female emancipation lies in the folly and contentedness of women under the present system" (Sanders:119).

During a meeting of abolitionists she made the courageous choice of taking a public stand with them against the colonization scheme then being pushed by liberal reformers — including most of the American Unitarians with whom she visited. This was a dangerous position for a famous visitor to take at the time, although, within twenty years, most liberals had come to the same conclusion. At that time the issue of slavery had never once been raised in Congress. Martineau was subsequently pursued by death threats and was forced to abort a planned trip because of information concerning a conspiracy to lynch her.

This was to be far from the last time that she took the side of the underdog on political issues. And it was not the first time that Martineau had aroused the fury of the establishment. After her series on political economy came out she was barred from entry into France, Russia and Austria. And her volume on population aroused the righteous anger of women and men alike. Influenced by Malthus, who had long been the object of similar attacks, she dared to suggest openly what Malthus had implied: that prolific childbearing should be curbed.

She was concerned with the health of the environment long before most people had ever thought of such a thing. She went so far as to develop a self-sustaining farm on her property, after she had moved to Ambleside, and wrote an agricultural pamphlet based on the project. She learned all the hiking trails in the area, became expert on the local flora and fauna, and published a book on the walks in the Lake District that is still popular today.

Martineau maintained a lifelong antipathy to prejudice and unwarranted discrimination. When asked by an American acquaintance what she thought of the idea of a black person marrying a white, she replied that if two people loved each other she didn't really see what their complexions had to do with it. In 1849 Martineau refused to write anything more for Charles Dickens' *Household Words* because of his refusal to print an article she had written which seemed to him to have presented too favourable a picture of Catholics. "The last thing I am likely to do," she told him, "is to write for an anti-Catholic publication; and least of all when it is anti-Catholic on the sly" (Martineau 1983b:422).

She was never able to comprehend the burgeoning nationalism all about her, saying, "I have no distinctive national feelings at all — having to do with a good many nations, [I] am without any belief in . . . [the notion of] distinctive nationality" (Webb:335).

Martineau deplored the living conditions of the poor in England, and her writing demonstrates remarkable empathy for them. A biographer noted her ability to "translate great events into human terms; to show how a particular piece of legislation, or a specific social abuse, might be an integral part of a man or woman's daily life" (Sanders:108). She did not think mere tinkering would be sufficient to correct the wrongs. "A social idea or system that compels such a state of things must be worn out," she wrote in her history of England. "In ours it is clear that some renovation is wanted, and must be found" (ibid.:56). However, she was optimistic that major reform would come. While still a girl she had encountered the ideas of Saint Simon, and his faith in the inevitability of progress stayed with her. An early story, "Life in the Wild," demonstrated what she saw as the essential common sense involved in everyone working according to their abilities for the good of all.

In spite of her intimate knowledge of the problems of employers (gained from her father's business failure) she took a firm stand in favour of the union movement as a corrective to the power imbalance of the period. Distressed about the widespread incidence of child labour, she was convinced that only when workers were adequately paid would they be persuaded to keep their children at home. Hers was a long-term view. In her *History of England*, she analyzed the conflict between employed and employer in England as an extension of the old Saxon-Norman feud. But she felt that, in the end, the interests of the two groups is the same, in that both depend for their prosperity on the accumulation of capital.

While quite young, Martineau told a friend in a letter that she was convinced "of the paramount duty of society to provide for the support, comfort, and enlightenment of every member born into it. All that I write is now with . . . the hope of pressing upon the rich a conviction of their obligation and of inducing the poor to urge their claims with moderation and forebearance and . . . intelligence" (Webb:123). A fundamental concern for creating the good society pervades all her writing. An editor once remarked of her, "I have never before met — and I do not hope again to meet — one so earnest to promote progress and so practical in the means to arrive at it" (Wheatley:358).

She was always interested in new possibilities for the ownership and management of property, but she approached such proposed schemes in a sceptical, rather than an ideological, manner. While in the United States she visited communities of Shakers and Rappites. They were groups who held property in common and enforced celibacy among their members. She concluded that the experiment was successful from an economic standpoint, but that "The interest which would be felt by the whole of society in watching the results of a community of property is utterly destroyed by the presence of the other distinction; . . . the ignorance and superstition of which it is a sign" (Martineau 1962:175).

Martineau later wrote, "What I witnessed in America considerably modified my views on the subject of property" (Martineau 1983b:232). She became acquainted with Robert Owen, who was the sole apostle of communal ownership in England at that time. She acknowledged the benefits of "economy of association," but rejected his theory "that man is a creature of circumstances — his notion of 'circumstance' being literally, *surroundings*; no allowance being made for constitutional structures and differences. His certainty that we might make life a heaven, and his hallucination that we are going to do so immediately under his guidance" (ibid.).

She supported consumer's cooperatives, and developed a Building Society for workers in her home district. And she remained hopeful that a fairer arrangement of property ownership would someday emerge. "What forms of society may arise as features of this new growth, neither you nor I can say," she wrote in a letter. "We can only ask each other whether, witnessing as we do the spread of Communist ideas in every free nation of Europe . . . the result is not likely to be a wholly new social state" (Martineau 1983b:453).

As a pioneering social scientist

Martineau's major contributions to scholarship were as follows: a thirty-four-volume series, *Illustrations of Political Economy*; a two-volume *Society in America*; *Eastern Life: Past and Present* (a study of the evolution of religion in the Middle East); a three-volume *History of England During the Thirty Years' Peace: 1816-1846*; and *The Positive Philosophy of Auguste Comte*, which was a translation and condensation of the latter's six-volume work. These were published in 1827, 1962, 1847, 1849 and 1854 respectively. Other less weighty works, such as *How to Observe Manners and Morals* and her *Essays on the Art of Thinking*, could be included here as well.

For the long series on political economy, Martineau devised a comprehensive logical framework, organized into the four major areas of production, distribution, exchange and consumption. Within each of these categories she identified topics or themes around which stories could be told. Each character represented some aspect of a general principle, and the working out of these principles in the lives of the characters provided the plot. Her approach was uniquely sociological and educational, and was consequently misunderstood by most intellectuals of the time, for whom such disciplines did not exist. What she sought to emphasize throughout was the *consequences* of legislation as well as failure to legislate, in the actual world of social beings, rather than the *intent* of lawmakers and of theorists.

Seymour Martin Lipset said that Martineau's *How to Observe* (published in 1838) was the first book to spell out a methodology for what would become the infant disciplines of sociology and anthropology. She called her chosen field of study "the science of morals and manners." Her book made the point that "Every prevalent virtue or vice is a result of the particular circumstances amidst which the society exists" (Martineau 1838:27). She recommended a comparative approach to the evolution of institutions—identifying the major organized functions operating within a society. One should begin with the written constitution defining the form that these societal functions were intended to take, she suggested, and assess the consequences of their actual operation in the behaviours and attitudes of the people. "The Institutions of a nation—political, religious and social—put evidence into the observer's hands as to its capabilities and wants which the study of individuals could not yield in a lifetime" (ibid.:64).

Two major objectives guided her two-year study of the United States: (1) to compare existing conditions with the principles stated in the nation's founding constitution; and (2) to record in detail the circumstances of her observations, and her means of gathering information (Martineau 1962:48-49). Here she was expressing a then-unheard-of concern for replicability in social research! In her approach she also demonstrated an understanding of social change unusual for the time. "Institutions are rarely sudden and complete inventions," she wrote. "They have usually an historic origin, even when renovated by revolution" (ibid.:76).

She was not surprised to find that the United States was not the classless society represented in its myths. In her opinion, "there is rank, and tenacity of rank, wherever there is society" (ibid.:259). But she considered the aristocracy of wealth that she found in Boston a particularly vulgar form of the phenomenon. "Wealth is power; and large amounts of wealth ought not to rest in the hands of individuals," she said (ibid.:263). However, she noted approvingly that the absence of primogeniture served as an indirect way to distribute wealth. Still, her own belief was that "there is no way of securing perfect social liberty on democratic principles but by a community of property" (ibid.:264).

Martineau had an acute understanding of politics as well. "Politics are morals, all the world over; that is, politics universally implicate the duty and happiness of Man" (ibid.:59). She had an abiding faith in the concept of majority rule as enshrined by the Americans. "The majority eventually wills the best," she said, "but . . . the ultimate demonstration often crowns a series of mistakes and failures" (ibid.:70-71). She identified several potential sources of trouble, however. "The great theory presumes that the majority not only will be the best measure, but will choose the best men. This is far from true in practice" (ibid.:71). She noted a marked subservience to the opinion of others everywhere she travelled — encouraged by a scandal-mongering press — and she surmised that the lack of principled people in leadership roles might be related to this. "In a country where the will of the majority decides all political affairs," she said, "there is a temptation to belong to the majority" (ibid.: 248). She was clearly disillusioned by the dishonesty and flattery directed at the people by their politicians. Another concern was the widespread political apathy that she observed among the ordinary people. And she was worried about the confused and contradictory nature of the constitutional clause designating state versus federal jurisdiction on the subject of residual power. Another disappointment for Martineau was the discovery that American philosophical fashions were primarily reflections of German romantic idealism and transcendentalism, with little interest expressed in an experimental approach to "the complex science of humanity." She thought that, taken together, these things did not bode well for the future of the new nation.

A journey to the Middle East in the early 1840s resulted in one of Martineau's best works, a comparative study in which she traced the evolution of the early Egyptian, Judaic, Christian and Islamic religions. In it she demonstrated the very human origin of all of these systems of belief. She spoke of Moses as a man with an important political objective, but quite uninspired by any divine mission. In fact, she pointed out the danger involved in myths of divine inspiration and origin. She dared to say of Christianity, "That which has drawn the Christians into their excesses is the dogma which they profess of the divinity of a creature" (Wheatley:265). Her first publisher thought these passages so offensive that he withdrew from his contract with her. She was able to find someone who would risk bringing out that book, however, as well as her next major project, *History of England*. The latter surprised many with its depth of scholarship, and demonstrated to all her critics that she was an accomplished historian. The book was reprinted in 1863, and widely acknowledged as one of the best accounts available of English society during the three decades following the end of the Napoleonic Wars.

In 1851 Martineau decided to attempt a translation and condensation of Auguste Comte's six-volume *Philosophie Positif*. Comte, inspired by the pioneering work of Condorcet, had spent twelve years writing the book. However, the calumny and persecution that had followed its publication in France caused him to have a nervous breakdown. Martineau must have read Comte's work with the joy of having found a long-sought kindred spirit. One can only imagine what it must have meant to her to discover a name ("sociology") for what she had been absorbed in all her life! In fact, many of Comte's ideas had been expressed earlier in her own writings — as when she outlined three stages of civilization in an 1834 article.

Francis Bacon had been an important influence on the mature Martineau, as he was on Comte. She once referred approvingly to Bacon's method of accumulating all the possible facts relevant to an issue and inferring from them a principle which then may be applied to the observation and explanation of new facts. She claimed that "ideas are classed in the order of Cause and Effect. In this manner alone can the true relations of things be ascertained: by this method alone can our experience be made useful to us, or our present circumstances become conducive to our future good. . . . We can only reason from the fact that certain antecedents have invariable consequents; it is plain that without a distinct apprehension of this truth there can be no real knowledge" (Webb:73).

She had retained from her earlier necessarianism the belief that all human actions stem from motives which are themselves determined by impressions of events outside the individual: events resulting from the playing out of natural laws. And she believed that these laws operate as mechanically as do those governing the movements of the planets. "How?" she maintained, is the question to be asked by the social scientist; not "why?" (ibid.:294). All this she would have found in Comte's work as well, along with the belief in cosmically necessary laws of historical development and the hope for a religion of humanity.

Comte spelled out a philosophy of science to update that of Francis Bacon and attempted to define the nature and role of sociology in that context. He explained that no one can discover the "essence" of things: that all we can hope to know is how things happen and the laws that govern their occurrence. He said that the scientific approach is simply the generalization and systematization of common-sense reasoning — "practical wisdom having been unquestionably the agency by which the old speculative methods have been converted into sound ones" (Martineau 1854:425). Comte explained that his "positivism" was to be distinguished from older philosophies by its rejection of first and final causes and by its exclusive focus on the goal of observing and identifying the invariable relations constituting natural laws. He repudiated the notion that scientific knowledge consists of a collection of disparate facts; claiming that it is, instead, a body of laws — or hypotheses of laws — by means of which facts are connected with one another. It is the knowledge of these connections that makes prediction possible. "To see in order to foresee is the business of science: to foresee everything without having seen anything is only an absurd metaphysical Utopia," he said (ibid.:429).

All our knowledge is necessarily relative to the external conditions obtaining, and to the organism doing the observing, according to Comte, and this applies no less to the physical sciences than to the social. He saw his proposed discipline of "sociology" as somewhat analogous to physics. It would deal with the essential relations among all of the other social sciences and among all of the "social facts" comprising these. The other social sciences would be dependent on the findings of sociology, just as it would, in turn, be subordinate to biology.

In her introduction to her two-volume *The Positive Philosophy of Auguste Comte*, Martineau identified what was lacking in her chosen field. She recognized that the study of humanity was still too crude and confused to be established as a science. She said that, so long as it "is split up into arbitrary divisions; while abstract and concrete ... [studies] are confounded together, and even mixed up with their applications in the arts and with natural history; and while researches of the scientific world are presented as mere accretions to a heterogeneous mass of facts, there can be no hope of scientific progress" (ibid.:v). She noted that Comte's theory should not be seen as the final answer: that the inevitable evolution of moral philosophy and the resulting growth of knowledge would provide amplifications which could not yet be conceived. She explained the significance of the picture he had painted as follows: "We find ourselves suddenly living and moving in the midst of the universe — as a part of it and not as its aim and object. We find ourselves living, not under capricious and arbitrary conditions, unconnected with the constitution and movements of the whole, but under great, general, invariable laws that operate on us as a part of the whole" (ibid.:x).

Martineau seized the opportunity to respond to critics who had accused Comte (and by inference, herself) of arrogance. That response is perhaps the best summary possible of her approach to knowing. "Pride of intellect," she said, "surely abides with those who insist on belief without evidence, and on a philosophy derived from their own intellectual action, without material [support] and corroboration from without, and not with those who are too scrupulous and too humble to transcend evidence" (ibid.:xi).

As a journalist

All her life Martineau made her living mainly from journalism. The first objective indication of her talent in this direction came when she won all three prizes in an essay contest as a youth. Her single most profitable writing enterprise was the best-selling series on political economy, from which she netted ten thousand pounds — prudently invested in a small lifetime annuity. Because of the absence of laws to protect intellectual property she never received a cent from the vast sales of her books in the United States. At the onset of her final illness friends and appreciative supporters collected funds to establish another annuity. But always, journalism was her chief source of income and her major professional involvement. And she was good at it. During the entire period leading up to and during the American Civil War, a leading Liberal politician credited Martineau, alone, with keeping England informed on that issue. A female biographer described Martineau as "an incomparable journalist, the first, perhaps, of all women journalists" (Courtney:224). George Eliot said that Martineau was "the only Englishwoman that possesses thoroughly the art of writing" (Wheatley:336). She once tried to explain to a friend that it was not desire for money or fame that drove her. "I told her that I wrote because I could not help it. There was something that I wanted to say and I said it. That was all" (Martineau 1962:33).

Sometime in the late 1830s, she was offered the editorship of a major economics periodical. Although she decided against it because of ill health and the desire for time to write a novel, she was sorely tempted. "The possibility is open before me," she wrote at the time, "of showing what a periodical with a perfect temper might be — also of setting women forward at once into the ranks of men of business" (Martineau 1983b:110). When she became confined to her bed she immediately turned her journalistic focus inward and produced *Life in a Sickroom: Essays by an Invalid*. She had begun her career by writing regularly for the Unitarian journal, *The Monthly Repository* — publishing fifty-two articles there altogether. She moved on to such distinguished periodicals as *The London and Westminster Review* (in spite of John Stuart Mill's frequent criticism of her contributions) and Charles Dickens' *Household Words* (until she quit on the issue of his anti-Catholicism). Her second book on the United States, was entitled, *Retrospect of Western Travel*. In 1852 she began a job which lasted for most of the rest of her life: that of writing lead editorials for *The Daily News*. She published 1,600 pieces between 1856 and 1866. In the face of all this, a male academic who is credited with producing *the* definitive biography on Harriet Martineau reluctantly admitted that "she was a supremely competent journalist" (Webb:42).

As a victim of institutionalized sexism

The most puzzling aspect of Harriet Martineau's achievement is the response of others to it. During her lifetime she was liked, admired, and even adulated by many — although the radical nature of her plainly articulated ideas aroused intermittent abuse and created numerous enemies. The odds against any woman rising to the heights of her obvious accomplishment was no doubt generally recognized in that male-dominated era. After her death, however, the chorus of calumny directed at her work and reputation rose to fever pitch, continuing unabated until — with the passage of time — her name and contributions to knowledge were buried almost as deeply as the pain-wracked body.

What was going on here? We should perhaps begin at the beginning, with the obstacles faced by Martineau in her early years. She spoke insightfully of the socialization to which she was subjected (although the term itself was yet to be coined). "I had no self respect," she recalled later, "and an unbounded need for approbation and affection. My capacity for jealousy was something frightful" (Martineau 1983b:29). At the age of eighteen she had to get up at five a.m. in order to have time to study. When the family finances crumbled no one (least of all, Harriet) questioned the expectation that she, as the single daughter, would be the one to assume responsibility for the mother and crippled younger sister — as well as an alcoholic older brother. No one thought to chastise the mother for insisting that Harriet take on the routines and daily chores of a dutiful housekeeper and daughter, even though it meant that she could write only at night. No one wondered at the mother's refusal to allow her mature daughter to move to London, where she had a chance for regular proofreading.

During the early period of her career she had to deal with her mother's demands to live in circumstances more "fitting to their status." But there was no suggestion that the son, James, a Unitarian minister, or the two daughters married to doctors, should share expenses. Martineau's later comment on this trying time when others were influencing her mother to pressure her into conformity was "It was my fixed resolution never to mortgage my brains" (Martineau 1983b:249). She felt compelled to write to her mother sometime later, "I fully expect that both you and I shall increasingly feel as if I did not discharge a daughter's duty, but we shall both remind ourselves that I am now as much a citizen of the world as any professional *son* of yours could be" (Wheatley:94).

And what about Martineau's treatment by the publishing establishment? One of her earliest encounters was with a religious publisher who appropriated her early stories and altered and used them with neither acknowledgement nor payment (Martineau 1983b:135). This treatment was, in fact, sadly typical. She was also to discover that she would invariably be resented and criticized for insisting on the same treatment as male writers. And there was much worse. When she finally found a publisher who expressed interest in her first major project, James Mill took it upon himself to advise strongly against it, claiming that her proposed method of explaining political economy could not possibly succeed (Wheatley:78). Later, when her story on the approaching population problem was published, the reviews took the form of personal attacks involving her feminine attributes (Martineau 1983b:200). And, when she began to write *Society in America*, her publisher presumed that he had the right to insist that she not mention the position of women. Later, a publisher refused to publish *Deerbrook* when he found its characters and setting were merely middle class (Sanders:58). And the same man who subsequently brought out Darwin's revolutionary *Origin of the Species* broke his promise to publish Martineau's *Eastern Life* because of its unorthodoxy! (Wheatley:264).

The contemptuous attitude of certain particularly influential males must have been galling to an independent and proud spirit like Martineau. She met James Mill after her thirty-four-book series on political economy had become a best seller. It was just before her departure to the United States. He asked, patronizingly, if she intended to become an expert on that country in two years

(Martineau 1983b:1). The personally abusive outburst following her resort to mesmerism was probably also motivated largely by sexism, as it was chiefly menopausal women who were using the treatment.

Like the poet Elizabeth Barrett Browning and the female activist Florence Nightingale (whose major work was published without her name on it), Martineau wrote from her bed for many years. In fact, she was an invalid for one third of her life. This raises questions about the seriousness with which female illnesses were dealt. It also forces one to consider the possibility that, for women, retiring to one's room may well have been the only way to ensure the kind of time and privacy required for concerted creative work.

Probably no autobiography before or since aroused the depth of outrage that greeted the publication of Martineau's two volumes on her life and work. She had meant it to be taken seriously, and exhibited neither false modesty nor a sufficiently "ladylike" reluctance to express strong opinions. She had also dared to write with authority on subjects thought to be the sole preserve of men. Her contemporaries' comments are revealing. Her publisher, John Murray, intending to commend her, said that she was masculine in a feminine way. John Stuart Mill, in rejecting one of her articles, criticized the style as being what one would expect of a woman writer who had "learnt to put good women's feelings into men's words, and to make small things look like great ones" (Sanders:182). (This represents a remarkable gap between precept and practice on the part of the author of *The Subjection of Women*.)

Martineau was scolded for her assertiveness, which was invariably read as conceit and arrogance. Yet, when she once tried writing under a male pseudonym she was accused of odd subterfuges that could only indicate a lack of self-confidence and an unwarranted belief that women were not taken seriously. Ralph Waldo Emerson thought her a masculine woman. Elizabeth Barrett Browning called her "the most manlike woman in three kingdoms" (ibid.: 167). William Howett referred to her as "one of the finest examples of a masculine intellect in a female form which have distinguished the present age" (ibid.). Mrs. Oliphant considered her not much of a woman at all. Yet Charles Darwin was obviously entranced with her, and described how she tended to attract the brightest men in the country (Webb:175).

By far the worst outrage committed against Martineau during her lifetime, however, occurred after the publication of a collaborative book entitled *The Atkinson Letters*, consisting of the correspondence between herself and a close friend, Henry Atkinson. The response from reviewers was overwhelmingly negative. The content was, of course, part of the problem, as it was the first time she frankly admitted to being an atheist. An amusing response was a letter to Atkinson (a virtually unknown figure compared to Martineau) advising him to publish something of his own at once "to repair the disadvantage of having let a woman speak under the same cover" (Martineau 1983b:360).

Leading the attackers was her favourite brother, James — by then, a widely respected theologian — who rushed into print with a personally insulting review. He wrote that "we remember nothing in literary history more melancholy than that Harriet Martineau should be prostrated at the feet of such a master, and should lay down at his bidding her early faith" (Wheatley:310). This ignorance on the part of her most beloved brother of his accomplished sister's long-held ideas — plus the implication that she could not possibly have come to any radical conclusion on her own — seems unforgivable. A biographer simply noted, "Whatever the motive for his attack he did it superbly" (Webb:300).

The extremity and extent of the abuse heaped on Harriet Martineau seems inexplicable. She believed, along with John Stuart Mill, that a thinker must follow reason and evidence wherever it might lead. Yet she was almost universally condemned for demonstrating the very quality for which Mill was honoured as a man of great intellectual integrity. Both John Stuart Mill and Martineau were inheritors of certain aspects of Hume's legacy, and they lived and wrote during the same period. Both rejected Bentham's physics of morality. Mill sought to build a philosophical system based on a combination of his father's utilitarianism, Hume's epistemology and Voltaire's idea of the sovereign individual. Martineau, while retaining the older Enlightenment notion of natural law, adopted Hume's premises about the *social* sources of morality and the significance of both biology and society for human behaviour — along with Hume's emphasis on the universality of cause and effect. Most of Martineau's insights survived to become the foundation-stones of sociology, while Mill's concept of the supreme rights of the free-floating individual lies at the roots of modern libertarianism. On the face of it, there seems little reason for Martineau to have been ignored for over a century, while Mill was uncritically idolized. It seems we must look elsewhere for the real source and extent of the prejudice that she faced.

The problem may well be that the opinion-setters and gatekeepers of her time were all men. People like her friend Thomas Carlyle could have a devastating influence by dropping comments such as "I admire this good lady's integrity and sincerity; her quick, sharp discernment *to the depth it goes*" (ibid.:1 emphasis added). It was assumed that she could only spout the opinions of her betters. For example, merely because Henry Atkinson supported the popular theory of phrenology it was widely believed that she did too, even though she wrote carefully of her scepticism about it (Martineau 1983b:393).

Her project on the political economy was derided by male intellectuals in spite of its overwhelmingly enthusiastic acceptance and use by politicians and ordinary citizens. Her pro-democracy study of the United States was ignored by academics who came after, while a contemporary book far less accurate and acute in its analyses — the pro-autocracy *Democracy in America* of de

Tocqueville — has become a classic. Her *History of England* was only grudgingly acknowledged. In a typical response to her work, a commentator wrote that "the major reviews tracked her progress with their usual mixture of respect tempered with amusement" (Martineau 1983a:xi). A biographer, in noting her unmarried status, makes the strange statement that "she was far too self-centred to have made another person happy" (Courtney:212). How many single male intellectuals have been characterized this way?

Even her support of women's rights was damned with faint praise — this time by a woman. "And though women might have wished the forerunner of their freedom to appear in a more gracious guise" she wrote (ibid.:236). How many of the men who stood for human rights have had their contribution denigrated because they were lacking in grace? "Harriet Martineau," concluded another biographer, "was the perfect example of a limited intellect secure enough in its convictions to challenge its betters" (Webb:23). This appears as a weird non sequitur, following quotations that would seem to indicate quite the opposite. A similarly incongruous comment (and one equally unwarranted by the context) was that, as always, her ideas were "not less fervent for being over-simple and parochial" (ibid.:74). The same prestigious biographer claimed that her writings represented an "oversimplified near-travesty of the best thought of the Enlightenment" (ibid.:90), while all of his references to her actual work would seem to prove otherwise. Pejorative expressions like "underlying the jargon" and "she sneered" (by letter!!!) abound in this influential biography.

In describing her translation of Comte's work, the above biographer admits that "Miss Martineau's style was admirably adapted to that task, whatever the deficiencies of her mind" (ibid.:303). And he concludes that "within her purpose . . . the book was adequate, no more" (ibid.:305). This seems doubly strange given the fact that Comte was so impressed with her condensation of his theories that he had it translated back into French and substituted for his own original work in the Positivist Library.

Some have said that Martineau paved the way for Marx. Certainly a passion for justice and a commitment to the possibility of discovering immutable laws governing human nature and social change were common to both. But Martineau sought means of dispersing, rather than centralizing, economic and political power. She favoured local cooperatives for ownership of property and for managing consumption, and thought that economic production and exchange should be freer rather than more centrally controlled. In fact, the cultural transformation that she inspired was to be slower and deeper than a mere surface disruption in the ownership of the means of production. Hers was a revolution not only in the values and attitudes determining our innermost expectations about gender-and work-roles, but in the very way we perceive reality. And it was to be a long time in the making.

Interestingly, Martineau also predicted a prolonged struggle between the forces of despotism and democracy, with Russian and Asian cultures aligned against the West. However, as life ran down for her in Ambleside in 1876, it is highly unlikely that she would have associated that future conflict with the ideas of the intense German intellectual who was perhaps at that very moment burrowing away in the library of the British Museum.

References for Chapter Five

Courtney, Janet E. 1920. Harriet Martineau. In *Freethinkers of the Nineteenth Century*. London: Chapman and Hall, p. 198-239.

Hoecker-Drysdale, Susan. 1992. *Harriet Martineau: First Woman Sociologist*. Oxford: St. Martin's Press.

Martineau, Harriet. 1838. *How to Observe Manners and Morals*. London: Charles Knight.

_____. 1856. *Sketches From Life*. London: Whittaker.

_____, ed. and trans. 1893. *The Positive Philosophy of Auguste Comte*. 2 vols. London: Kegan Paul, Trench, Troebner. (First published 1854.)

_____. 1962. *Society in America*. Edited by Martin Seymour Lipset. New York: Anchor Books. (First published 1835.)

_____. 1974. *A Description of the English Lakes*. Wakefield: E.P. Publishing. (First published 1858.)

_____. 1983a. *Deerbrook*. London: Virago Press. (First published 1837.)

_____. 1983b. *Autobiography*. 2 vols. London: Virago Press. (First published 1877.)

Sanders, Valerie. 1986. *Reason over Passion: Harriet Martineau and the Victorian Novel*. New York: St. Martin's Press.

Webb, R.K. 1960. *Harriet Martineau: A Radical Victorian*. New York: Columbia University Press.

Wheatley, Vera. 1957. *The Life and Work of Harriet Martineau*. London: Jecker and Warburg.

Six

The Dialectical Materialism of Karl Marx

> Oh masters, lords and rulers in all lands,
> How will the future reckon with this man?
> How answer his brute questions in that hour
> When whirlwinds of rebellion shake all shores?
> How will it be with kingdoms and with kings —
> With those who shaped him to the thing he is —
> When this dumb terror shall rise to judge the world,
> After the silence of the centuries?
>   — Edwin Markham, *The Man with the Hoe*

With the end of the Napoleonic Wars, an undercurrent of conservative reaction had welled up and begun spilling over Europe in response to the tidal wave of real and threatened change. People everywhere sought refuge in the imagined certainties of an unchanging metaphysical order. Or, like Prince Metternich of Austria, they retreated to the remembered certainties of a past political order, to be perpetuated by the allies who had engineered Napoleon's defeat. But history could not be undone. The pace of social change continued to accelerate. In Britain this was furthered by liberal legislation such as the 1832 Reform Bill (which enfranchised the middle and upper working classes) and in France, by the July Revolution of 1830, replacing the previously reinstated Bourbons with another — albeit constitutionally controlled — Napoleon.

One casualty of the turmoil of the times was the possibility of steady progress toward a scientific study of humanity. Two initially appealing detours that have since been recognized as dead-ends were substituted for the slow, difficult trail staked out by the pioneers. One of these involved distortions of the scientific approach; the other, a rejection of it — at least where the social studies were concerned. The first had two features: (1) a premature emphasis on quantification that may have been encouraged by Jeremy Bentham's utilitarianism; and (2) a continuing focus on the discovery of immutable laws of hu-

---

References for this chapter are on p. 113.

man history, to some extent fuelled by the positivism of Martineau and Comte. Both ultimately led to forms of "scientism" that were to become obstacles to the scientific approach to the study of humanity. The second detour, with its anti-science orientation, had its roots in the romanticism of Rousseau and was nourished by the transcendentalism of Immanuel Kant.

Changing currents

The seductive power of the second detour meant that the most influential thinkers of the early nineteenth century were to be neither positivists labouring under a generally shared misapprehension of the nature of social science, nor the heirs of Enlightenment rationalism. They were the German followers of a far different drummer. It was the reactionary elements in Rousseau's romanticism that inspired them, the insistent drumbeat of Hegel's dialectic that propelled them, and the mystical transcendentalism of Immanuel Kant that gave them shape and direction.

A new philosophy of transcendentalism

Immanuel Kant (1724-1804) set out to complete Hume's undermining of rationalism as a source of ultimate truth but, in the process, elevated his own concept of transcendental reason. He began by rejecting the older metaphysics of the Enlightenment which had maintained that the entire chain of cause and effect (and thus the very possibility of science) is meaningless if it cannot be attached to a "first cause." Kant repudiated this "pure rationalism" but wanted to replace it with the proposition that certainty of physical knowledge of a *part* is compatible with total ignorance of the *whole*. He determined that demonstrative ("pure") logic could not legitimately be used to prove metaphysical ("supersensual") truths. He showed that contradictory beliefs can be deduced from the same ontological premise, and that no conclusions about the nature of ultimate reality (no matter how mutually incompatible) can ever be disproved. He went on to explain that the type of logical contradiction identified by Aristotle, which allows humans to arrive at definitive conclusions, can never be possible in the case of metaphysical entities. What results instead "is merely dialectical, and an illusory conflict originating in the application of the idea of absolute totality to appearance" (Kant 1949:161). Humans must give up the demand for rational knowledge of the supersensual, he concluded, and be content with faith in matters such as the nature of God.

Kant could not follow Hume the rest of the way, however. He simply could not live without the possibility of certainty concerning "the real" and "the good" — at least in what he considered the observable or sensual realm. At the same time, he was unable to deny the logic of Hume's conclusion that inferential ("practical") reason is no more able than the "pure" variety to provide absolute truth. He decided that what Hume had shown to be rationally and empirically impossible could be revealed as philosophically possible *if* — and *only* if — humans can assume the *a priori* existence of inferentially derived generalizations from the sensual realm ("synthetic judgements").

Kant had to assume this, for he began with two absolutely non-negotiable beliefs. These were (1) that intuition as a source of true knowledge of the sensual realm is not derived from experience; and (2) that human beings are morally autonomous; that is, moral judgements, like intuitions, are unconditioned by experience.

To solve his dilemma Kant retreated through the door opened by Descartes. In addition to an assumed dualism of supersensual and sensual existence, he would posit a dualism of *method* within the latter. He postulated that the sensual realm involving humanity must have two aspects: what is externally observable and conditioned by experience (the mechanical level with which science deals) and a second, uncaused aspect open to intuition and accessible only to the understanding. He claimed that the first of these involves "phenomena," and the second, "noumena." He saw the latter as the autonomous "things in themselves" existing outside of time and independent of the laws of nature: an aspect of existence exclusive to the human being.

What had made the impossible possible, for Kant, was the notion that all objects capable of being sensed by humans must conform to the structure and activity of the mind of the knower and valuer. He concluded that the mind, therefore, is the ultimate and defining aspect of the realm of noumena. Humans come into the world, he declared, equipped with the logical forms and mental operations necessary for discovering knowledge of the essential nature of social reality — including the imperatives of the moral order. This implanted reason has the innate capacity to speculate *beyond any possible experience* in order to locate the unconditioned (therefore certain) knowledge.

Science is limited to that which is conditioned by previous events. Here, as Hume had demonstrated, knowledge is uncertain. But Kant was convinced that there must be a second form of causality applicable only to the realm of noumena. His *a priori* premises of unconditioned intuition and moral autonomy necessitated this. He thought that human beings represent "intelligence with a will" and are thus "endowed with causality." "Freedom of Will is autonomy, i.e., that property of will by which it determines its own causality, and gives itself its own law" (Kant 1871:57). "Heteronomy," on the other hand, is the condition of "necessary cause" moving the merely phenomenal.

According to Kant the mechanistic causality governing phenomena and the cosmically purposive design of noumena function without interfering with each other. Humans are both bound by physical necessity and free to become "the final end toward which all nature is teleologically subordinated" (Kant 1949:39). For him, the history of matter represented an inexorable development toward the creation of those political-social conditions necessary for the blossoming of humanity's hidden nature.

Kant claimed that, with this theory, he had achieved a second Copernican revolution. But, in fact, it could be argued that his was a counter-revolution! Where Hume had viewed the knower as the sensor, selector and interpreter of an external reality, Kant's philosophy defined this minuscule human entity as the very microcosm of the superior and defining realm of a two-stage reality. Kant's entire life's work was devoted to placing humans once more at the centre of things. The material world in which science seemed to have rendered the human being so insignificant was indeed real for Kant, but it was a lower order of reality than that reflected in the logical structures of the mind of humankind!

Although he had not intended it to do so, Kant's dualist philosophy opened the door to a wave of abstract metaphysical speculation with built-in immunity to critical assessment based on either reason or experience. Followers of the powerful new romantic idealism, such as Fichte, Schelling and von Schegel, went so far as to claim that the *only* reality is the realm of noumena. Here a universal Intelligence is thought to hold sway. The only hope for humanity is to free itself from the chains of sense and reason that tie it to the lower, surface realm of phenomena, and to put its faith in intuition as the sole guide to understanding the sublime perfection of this higher reality.

George Wilhelm Hegel was the most influential of the German romantic idealists. He appropriated Kant's conclusion concerning the inevitability of contradiction whenever one tries to apply reason to metaphysics — and subverted it. Hegel maintained that contradiction is a necessary and desirable aspect of all reality. He also borrowed from Kant the principle of a teleological unfolding of historical conditions. He developed from these premises the idea of a purposeful evolution of history, fuelled by the "dialectic" (a term which Kant had used pejoratively). Hegel taught that all is in flux, tending toward two opposing directions, then coming together in a synthesis out of which emerges a new contradiction. Each stage of synthesis represents an advance upon the previous one. This is inevitable, because the entire process is guided by Universal Reason — a new definition of God. The earthly representation of that divine idea is the state. Therefore the highest liberty possible for humanity is the subjection of the self to the state. To oppose the state is to oppose God. There is no place to hide.

It is all too easy to see how modern totalitarianism had its source in the romanticism of Rousseau and the mystical ideologies of the nineteenth century. Not so well understood, however, is the long-term effect of the "scientism" unwittingly invoked by the empiricists. Both strands of thought met in the fertile mind of Karl Marx, who considered himself a scientific naturalist, and the resulting explosion is still affecting the course of human history.

The making of a revolutionary

Out of the political ferment of revolution and reaction — out of the cultural clash of competing ideologies — new social movements and visions for humanity were bound to emerge. The instigator of what was to become one of the most influential of these epitomized the contradictions and ideological certainties of his times. Born in Trier in 1818, Karl Marx grew up in the French border area that had become a part of Prussia, due to post-Napoleonic border settlements. The grandson of two Jewish rabbis, he was raised a Christian due to his lawyer father's conversion. And somewhere along the way he developed an antipathy to the Judaism of his ancestors.

Introduced by his father to Kant, and immersed in the Hegelianism of the University of Berlin during his student years, Karl nevertheless sought out the works of Democritus and Epicurus for his dissertation topic and became fascinated with the idea of creating a new version of materialism. Although an offspring of upper-middle-class parents and married to the cosseted daughter of an equally affluent family, he allied himself with the working class and developed an uncompromising hatred for the members of all other social groupings. An individualist himself, he willingly sacrificed the claims of family, career and friends to his own beliefs and propagated one of the most anti-individualistic doctrines the world has ever known.

It is not surprising that this man of contradictions originated a theory of historical change founded upon the necessity and inevitability of conflict. However, this was still in the future when he obtained his first job, at the age of twenty-four, as editor of a liberal newspaper in Prussia. Later that year, his career as a political journalist apparently launched, he married Jenny, his long-time fiancée. But the job did not last, and the next few years witnessed a number of moves for the little family: from Prussia to Paris (for a short but intellectually and politically momentous period) then to Brussels, then over to Manchester (for a brief tour of factory conditions with Friedrich Engels) and back to Brussels for a second stint in newspaper editing. This ended with the arrest of Marx and Jenny following the printing of *The Communist Manifesto* (a publication scarcely intended to reassure his host government) and their deportation back to Prussia. Soon after, Prussia moved to expel Marx from his homeland for life. He and Jenny were forced to flee to a Paris then engulfed in misery and reaction in the aftermath of the failed revolution of 1848. After a fruitless and necessarily brief stay in that unfriendly city, his supporters settled the family in London. There, Marx was to spend the remainder of his life in exile.

Forging the lightning bolt

Marx's early writings indicate that the foundation and general outline of his theory were already in place by the time he was thirty. It was an eclectic mix of disparate ideas then prevalent in the surrounding culture. The young philosopher, introduced by his father-in-law to the works of Saint Simon, began with a fierce commitment to improving the lot of the exploited and impoverished. From the British and French materialists he took a belief in the senses as the sole source of experience; in enlightened self-interest as the guiding principle of morality; and in equality and fraternity as ultimate ideals. He reformulated Kant's premise concerning freedom, maintaining that it can only apply to the innate human capacity to assert "true individuality" within an ideal society — one in which the "correct historical conditions" have been achieved.

Marx shared Rousseau's scorn of liberal democracy, considering it merely a ploy for deluding the working class into thinking that they are free. Freedom cannot apply to those individuals shaped by the conditions of industrialization, he said. As for the major defining principle of the Enlightenment, Marx wrote, "the so-called rights of man, as distinguished from the right of the citizen, are nothing else than the rights of the member of bourgeois society, that is, of the egoistic individual, of man separated from man and the community" (Marx 1926:73).

Rousseau's notion of the necessity of violent revolution, and that of the originally good "natural man" having been alienated by society, became the pillars of Marx's conceptual structure. He also adopted Rousseau's belief in an infallible General Will, which he made the prerogative of one class only within bourgeois society. This was the class of exploited workers, or proletariat. Marx saw this class as the sole remaining representative of the "hidden nature of man" which had been sought by Kant. However, he concluded that these essentially good qualities of humanity had been alienated by the demands of industrialization.

Marx took from Kant the premise of a purposeful movement of history toward the political system most conducive to the ultimate perfection of the human being. His unique application of Kant's concept of "pragmatic anthropology" saw the human as an active agent through which the forces of history realize this inexorable progress. He referred to his new concept as "praxis." All this he incorporated into Hegel's dialectic, declaring that historical progress is thus accomplished by the dialectic working through matter, rather than spirit. For Marx, the manifestation of the dialectic is revealed by means of the inevitable conflict between classes in industrializing societies. The proletariat is the negation of the bourgeois class, and the ultimate synthesis — forged by revolution — will be the classless and stateless Communist society.

Meanwhile, there was work to be done. "In order that the revolution of a people should coincide with the emancipation of a special class of bourgeois society, it is necessary for a class to stand out as a class representing the whole of society. This further involves, on the obverse side, the concentration of all defects of society on another class, and this particular class must be the embodiment of the general social obstacles and impediments" (ibid.:33). If the proletariat were not already recognized as the epitome of the good, and the bourgeois as the source of all evil, Marx, as a journalist, would do his best to make this happen!

One seldom-noted aspect of Marx's original theory is his identification of Judaism with the hated bourgeois society. He claimed that the secular impact of Judaism had been the furthering of egoism, hucksterism and the worship of money. "Very well. Emancipation from huckstering and from money, and therefore from practical, real Judaism, would be the self-emancipation of our epoch" (ibid.:88). This statement was followed by a prediction which has been rendered eerily sinister by subsequent German history. "As soon as a society succeeds in abolishing the empirical essence of Judaism, the huckster, and the conditions which produce him, the Jew will become impossible" (ibid.:97). Of course Marx was calling for the destruction of a *system* presumed to be the source of the problem — not the destruction of a *people*!

A philosophy of materialism grounded in dualism

It was not only the Judaism of his day that provoked the ire of the young revolutionary. With each forced move Marx had become more critical of all the social institutions and religious belief systems dominating Europe and more determined to bring about fundamental changes in both. While in Paris in 1843-44, he had studied the works of the English school of economists, and had become acquainted with British and French history. It was in this period that he finalized his materialist interpretation of history, a theory that was to become famous in the decades following his death. It identified economic factors as the causes of all historical change. Profoundly influenced by Hegel's dialectical version of romantic idealism, Marx nevertheless rejected its supernaturalism. He was convinced that anti-materialist assumptions concerning reality serve to provide justification for all manner of superstitious beliefs which then function as obstacles to human progress. He included in his list of harmful beliefs deism, Judaism and Christianity.

Marx considered himself a naturalist — a follower of Democritus, Epicurus and the eighteenth-century materialists — and there is no indication in his writings of an awareness that his acceptance of Hegel's historical determinism was bound to take him in an entirely different direction from that of previous materialistic philosophers. For his unique brand of materialism was founded, not just on an assumption of order in nature, but on an unshakeable commitment to a particular pattern in which that order was to be expressed: to an immutable dialectic of history acting upon a world of matter. The specific mate-

rial relations fuelling the process he identified as the technologies of production — which determine the nature of the economic relationships. These, in
turn, he said, shape all other socio-cultural institutions, including science and
religion. He concluded that alterations in individual beliefs concerning matters
of fact and value are therefore the *results* rather than the causes of social
change, as the empiricists and other Enlightenment liberals would have it. "It
is not the consciousness of men that determines their being, but, on the contrary, their social being that determines their consciousness" (Marx
1958:363).

There is no doubt that Marx believed himself to be following in the tradition of scientific naturalism. The scientific philosophy of Martineau and
Comte was indeed compatible with Marx's desire for an all-encompassing,
absolute answer to the complexities of human history. For their model had
held out the possibility of discovering social laws capable of predicting, not
just observable regularities in human behaviour, but a successive development
of cultural systems. It probably encouraged Marx to assume a scientific justification for positing an unchanging pattern of historical evolution. Along with
this he accepted the Enlightenment faith in progress and in the perfectibility of
humankind. His theory was also consistent with many of the premises of the
prevailing Hegelian world view, involving as it did both an inevitable pattern
and predictable culmination of human evolution and a repudiation of individualism and worship of the state as an abstraction. All these ideas were part of
the cultural stream which had shaped the thinking of the young political philosopher.

The Hegelians and other German romantic idealists proclaimed the necessity of subordinating the individual to the *current* state because it was the
earthly manifestation of "divine intelligence." Marx, on the other hand, believed in the necessity of individual subordination to a *future* Communist state
because it would emerge as the ultimate realization of the forces of history. In
more ways than one he turned Hegel on his head. For the romantic idealist the
individual could either remain enslaved to sensory experience and reason, and
thereby separated from the divine and bereft of the power and benevolence of
the state, or he could, through mystical intuition, become "one with the divine" and accept the state as the sole legitimate expression of selfhood. With
Marx, individuals got equally short shrift, but it was material reality that
would shape and control them. They were powerless to thwart the dialectic of
matter, and similarly powerless to hasten its progress. They could act as
midwives to history; no more.

Working for the revolution

These were the ideas being mulled over by Marx during the exciting months of his first stay in Paris, a period that proved to be a turning point in his intellectual and political development. Friedrich Engels, whom he had met earlier, came for a two-week stay. The visit was decisive for both men. It established a guru-follower relationship between the two able intellectuals that was to survive Marx's death. Another interesting visitor was Pierre-Joseph Proudhon, founder of the non-violent anarchist strain of European socialism. Also, here in Paris, Marx was introduced for the first time to a sort of working-class movement, although its members were artisans, rather than the unskilled labourers whom he was idolizing as the proletariat. However, he had learned about the latter from Engels, who had just completed a historical study of working conditions in the early factories of Manchester, England. A six-week visit to Manchester with Engels convinced Marx that his theory was accurate and that it represented the only true socialism. He moved to Brussels and set about establishing the Organization of International Socialism, based on his newfound "dialectical materialism."

During this period Marx wrote to Europe's leading socialist writers, requesting them to join his movement. He made it clear that they would be required to accept *his* ideas alone as the official doctrine. Proudhon, who believed that violent revolution had never been effective as a means of lasting social reform, replied with a note so prophetic that it is well worth quoting.

> Our proletarians have such a thirst for understanding that we would get a very bad reception from them if we gave them nothing to drink but blood. . . . Let us by all means collaborate in trying to discover the laws of society, the way in which these laws work out, the best method to set about investigating them; but for God's sake, after we have demolished all the dogmatisms *a priori*, let us not of all things attempt in our turn to instil another kind of dogma in the people. Let us not fall into the contradiction of your compatriot, Martin Luther, who, after overthrowing the Catholic theology, addressed himself to the task of building up . . . a Protestant one. For three whole centuries Germany has been doing nothing but pull down the plaster work of Martin Luther. Let us not, by contriving any more restrictions, leave any more such tasks for the human race. (Jackson:63-64)

On the basis of this response Marx relegated Proudhon forever to the role of enemy, believing that anyone who was not wholeheartedly for him was against him. He began a series of virulent attacks on Proudhon and the other socialists who had disagreed with him, in effect, excommunicating them as heretics from the future community of Communists. From that time on, Proudhon and other socialists who did not accept the "dialectic of history" were labelled "utopian" in Marxist writings. By this Marx and Engels meant that their opponents were naive in their understanding of society and out of step with the inevitable tide of history.

The communist manifesto

In 1848 Marx and Engels published *The Communist Manifesto*: a document intended to establish the nature and direction of the new movement. As Engels indicated in a subsequently written preface, "Communism meant henceforward an understanding of the nature, conditions, and the general aims arising therefrom, of the struggle into which the proletariat had entered" (Marx 1963:9). *The Manifesto* reads like the call to arms that it was meant to be. It reduces all human history to the convolutions of class struggle. Each phase of social evolution is viewed as a new synthesis arising from the ruins produced in the explosion of class warfare precipitated by the contradictions of the previous one. The European industrialized society of the day is identified as the hateful Bourgeois State which has "destroyed all feudal, patriarchal and idyllic relationships . . . it has left no other bond betwixt man and man but crude self interest and unfeeling cash payment . . . it has degraded personal dignity to the level of exchange value" (ibid.:28).

However, bourgeois society is seen as the first inherently revolutionary one in that it "cannot exist without incessantly revolutionizing the institutions of production and therefore the totality of social relations" (ibid.:9). It is also inherently urbanizing and internationalist, yet centrist in its thrust, in that it "drags all nations, even the most barbarian, into the orbit of civilization . . . and . . . has brought huge cities into being . . . [with the inevitable result of] . . . centralized ownership . . . and . . . political centralization" (ibid.:30).

The workers in bourgeois society are forced to sell themselves like commodities, becoming increasingly "emiserated" as wages are forced down to the lowest possible level that allows them to subsist and thereby fulfil the capitalist's need for labour. They form a group with no stake in the economic system, for their lot worsens as the system progresses. Hence they are the only truly revolutionary class: the force destined by history for that express function. They have "nothing to lose but their chains" (ibid.:68), whereas the peasants, merchants and artisans are involved to some extent in the ownership of private property and are consequently conservative in their politics. The slum proletariat are even more "apt to become the venal tools of the forces of reaction" (ibid.:39) and cannot be expected to help in the coming revolution.

Ironically, the bourgeoisie, whose capitalization and mechanization of the means of production has created the propertyless condition of the wage-earning class, in effect, "produces its own gravediggers. Its downfall and the victory of the Proletariat are equally inevitable" (ibid.:42). The bourgeoisie tries to justify its exploitation of workers by appeals to religion, morality and philosophy, but this appears to carry no weight with Marx and Engels, who address these "exploiters" as follows: "your ideas are themselves the outcome of Bourgeois methods of production and Bougeois property relations; just as your 'right' is only the will of your class writ large as law . . . (ibid.:46).

The authors proclaim that, as with all other forms of human output, "mental production changes concomitantly with economic production" (ibid.:50). Family structures are likewise the products of economic relationships. In the Communist society controlled by the proletariat, bourgeois family forms will disappear, along with prostitution and the exploitation of children, for matings will be love-inspired and offspring will be accepted fully as the responsibility of the state.

All other versions of socialism are attacked as, at best, conservative (Proudhon's anarchism) or, at worst, feudal-reactionary (all Christian socialist reform movements). Only Marx's revolutionary Communist form is the true socialism, for it alone correctly expresses the forces of history. The aim of workers' organizations must never be viewed as the amelioration of conditions or economic progress for the workers; their sole aim is the violent overthrow of existing institutions. For even apparently effective reforms in working conditions and social justice are merely illusionary because "social reform remains a utopia until the Proletarian revolution and the feudalistic counter-revolution measure swords in a *world war*" (Black:97).

Following publication of the *Manifesto* and their subsequent arrest and expulsion from Belgium, Karl and Jenny went to Paris to see what they could do for the revolution that had already begun there. They established a new headquarters for the Communist League in Paris, then returned to Prussia, upon hearing of prospects for an uprising back home. Marx began to edit another newspaper. In it he supported the Prussian drive for German unification. He also advocated Prussian attacks on Russia and Denmark and war with Britain — all in the hope that the resulting social chaos would precipitate a revolution. Although Marx's championship of nationalist aggression must have been agreeable to the Prussian establishment, his continued focus on the inevitability of revolution was not. He suffered his second expulsion, this time from his homeland, and for life.

After the failed revolutions of 1848, Marx settled into what was to be a wretched and unproductive decade in London. He and Jenny lived in poverty in a two-room flat. In all they had seven children, four of whom died in those years. Marx was isolated, except for the faithful friendship and financial support of Engels, whose father conveniently owned a factory in Prussia. Marx spent long days in the library of the British Museum, writing intermittently for publication and submitting regular columns to *The New York Tribune*. Two of his journalistic pieces from this period are well known: "The Civil War in France" and "The Eighteenth Brumaire of Louis Bonaparte."

The critique of political economy

In 1859 Marx published *A Contribution to the Critique of Political Economy*.
It is clear that his goal was to reveal the "essence" behind the "phenomenal
appearance" of market relations. He explained that individuals and their ideas
are the inevitable products of these particular relations, and of nothing else.
Their social existence evolves according to a necessary process of periodic
revolutionary cataclysms in which each new order arises from the ashes of the
old. However, the time must be ripe, if the revolution is to succeed, for "no
social order is ever destroyed before all the productive forces for which it is
sufficient have been developed, and new superior relations of production never
replace older ones before the material conditions of their existence have matured within the framework of their old society" (Marx 1970:21).

The book presents a detailed elaboration of Marx's emerging economic
theory. For him, the exchange value of a commodity was determined by the
labour-time contained in it — either in its immediate production or in the previously produced machinery required for it. It is immaterial whose labour-
time it is. Ultimately, all commodities are no more than congealed labour-
time; individuals are defined merely as its vehicles, or as "the conscious representatives of the economic exchange process involving the products of labour
and its receipt of a subsistence wage" (ibid.:41).

The concept of labour-time is similar to that of horse-power in its disregard for the varying motivations, interests and dependability of the individuals
who produce it. Skilled labour, however, is calculated as some sort of multiple
of basic labour-time. The capitalist will always pay only the minimal wage for
a basic unit of labour-time — that being the lowest possible amount required
to ensure the workers' subsistence and reproduction. This concept of minimal
wage is likewise unrelated to any variations in the individual capitalist's business ethics or goals, or to a worker's attitude or initiative, or even to the demand for (or price of) commodities. Like labour-time, it is an absolute "essence." Thus, for Marx, the concrete and observable disappear, while abstractions become the only reality!

The *Critique* was intended primarily as just that: a criticism of the theories
of dominant classical economists such as Adam Smith and David Ricardo, as
well as those of their traditional socialist opponents. Marx repudiated the idea
that there are regularities in economic behaviour that hold across cultures or
over time — such as the conditions necessary for production. He held that it is
useless to define production, consumption and distribution separately, for purpose of analysis — declaring that they are all phases of one "wholistic" economic process, with distribution acting as the engine directing all the rest. In
the industrialized capitalist society that engine is fuelled by capital, and it
operates to appropriate both labour power and natural resources in the inter-

ests of the bourgeoisie. Communism would, instead, distribute goods for the benefit of the proletariat.

Nowhere did Marx deal with the consequences for freedom and equality, of arbitrary control of distribution by a bureaucracy not limited by the rule of law. This focus in Marxist theory on command-distribution as an abstract causal force — isolated from the demands of production and consumption — was to have significant consequences for socialist countries.

Das Kapital

With the mid-1860s came a revival of socialism. In 1864, The International Working Men's Association was formed in London and a general council and drafting committee for rules of operation were established. Marx was named to both these bodies. From that time on his financial troubles eased as well, for two reasons: an inheritance from Jenny's family and an improvement in Engel's fortunes as a result of his becoming a partner in his father's manufacturing business. Over a two-year period Marx managed to achieve total control over The International with few being aware of what was happening. He wrote to Engels in triumph, "We . . . have this powerful engine in our hands" (Jackson:156). One of the few who had noticed, however, was Michael Bakunin, the Russian anarchist. He wrote of Marx, "as a German Jew he is an authoritarian from head to heels" (ibid.:159).

In 1867, the first edition of *Das Kapital* was ready. The publication of Marx's major economic work was well timed, for the social evils attending industrialization were spreading throughout Europe, and socialist hopes and activities were on the rise. But it was an impossibly difficult book: poorly organized and abstruse in its theoretical sections; selective, repetitious and tedious in its historical detail. However, that did not prevent the book's widespread distribution, and its increasing influence in the decades to follow. In all of history, probably only the Bible has been quoted and interpreted by so many, yet read by so few.

As the editor of one edition points out, this is puzzling only if one fails to recognize the two simple premises on which Marx's entire edifice is built: (1) the idea that the rich get richer on the backs of the increasingly impoverished poor, and (2) the belief that there is one law for the poor and another for the rich. Most of us who have suffered economic injustice resonate to these statements, and there is invariably some truth in them.

Marxism proclaims both beliefs as fact, and sets out to explain how the conditions they describe have come about. Theoretical justification for the first premise is provided by the Doctrine of Surplus Value, whereby the capitalist is seen to appropriate the productivity earned by all the labour power not required for maintaining an ever-decreasing level of worker subsistence. The second is explained by the proposition that the state is no more than the executive committee for the ruling bourgeois class. These two premises created a powerful revolutionary brew which required, not the critical understanding gained from careful reading, but merely belief in a simple thesis that felt too good not to be true.

The power of the myth

Still hoping to encourage the onset of violence, Marx wrote, in reference to the Franco-Prussian War of 1870, "The French need a thrashing" (ibid.:161). The Paris Commune incident of 1871 provided him with a vicarious experience of conflict which he later used to great effect. He mythologized a violent street fight resulting in a few Communist deaths into a watershed of great historical significance. Such was the newfound power of political journalism! The following year, at the gathering of The International, Marx made an attempt to further centralize control. However, this time he encountered opposition from the Proudhonists and others. The result was a general breakaway and the eventual disintegration of the organization. Marx published nothing in the last decade of his life, but seems to have spent the time amassing notes and documents in support of his theory. After his death in 1883, Engels used these as the basis for two additional volumes of *Das Kapital*.

What remained was a powerful myth based largely on the first volume of *Das Kapital*. For Marx thought that he had discovered a universal law determining not only the process of historical change, but its final culmination. He maintained that the relentless movement of history is toward one particular social order and no other: a society in which all class distinctions and conflicts (so essential to previous social change) have disappeared completely. Of all the exploited classes of earlier times, the proletariat is destined to be the final one. It is the sole instrument by which will be achieved the "perfect human society": the worldwide dictatorship of the proletariat. This time there will be no temporary synthesis providing the seedbed for new classes destined to engage in a renewed struggle for dominance. This time the universal historical process grinds to a stop with the attainment of the end goal of all human history: Communism. The laws of history no longer operate. Human consciousness has been transformed. Conflicting interests — even differing perspectives and goals — no longer exist.

Marx claimed that bourgeois society was the first truly revolutionary one; that, in its encouragement of technological innovation, it produced the progressive "emiseration" of the proletariat and hence the seeds of its own destruction. No other form of society had been revolutionary in that sense. One assumes that he considered historical change prior to this period as evolutionary. So his life and writings were to form the watershed of history! It was his destiny not only to live in the world's first truly revolutionary era and country (he thought that Britain was ripe for proletarian revolution) but to be the one thinker able to understand and foresee the total process!

But the Communist society representing the ideal end of socio-cultural change was to be the opposite of a revolutionary society. There would no longer be any need or possible source of revolution — or even of evolution. *There could be no more social change.* Technological innovation and the scientific individuals who created it would be counter-revolutionary in the perverted sense that they would be subversive of the Communist status quo. A new consciousness would have to be inculcated through a controlled socialization process. Could this task be left to the now-dispirited and motionless forces of history, or would the proletarian midwives be forced to adopt an eternal vigilance and permanent state of authoritarian control?

Marx gave no indication in his writings of having recognized where his own logic was leading. In fact, his works include no concrete suggestions whatever for structuring or operating the classless society. However, all that we know about him affirms an impression of authoritarianism, and of willingness to manipulate human beings. A biographer says of him: " What persisted among Communists was the temper as well as the teaching of Marx. . . . The authoritarianism and intolerance which had been characteristic of Marx himself continued to characterize the Party and government officials who were to act in his name" (ibid.:182).

Assessments

The harm visited upon humanity by Marxist dogma is as apparent today as are the horrific consequences of the fascist form of totalitarianism, and needs no further emphasizing. But what about the valuable insights contained in the theory of Karl Marx? What aspects of his theory should be considered lasting contributions to social science?

It could be said that Marx was far ahead of his time in his understanding of the socio-cultural sources of human beliefs and values. He failed to develop this idea beyond a simplistic and extreme economic determinism, but because of his writings the insight was widely distributed. Certainly his work provided a powerful impetus to the growth of sociology: a discipline founded upon that very premise. And his concept of "praxis" — shedding new light on the nature of the relationship between the knower and the known — contributed to the subsequent development of the scientific philosophy of pragmatism. In addition, his work hastened recognition of the significance of technological innovation for socio-cultural change. Lastly, there is no doubt that he inadvertently forced the world to face up to the detrimental effects on workers of rapid and uncontrolled industrialization and to accept the necessity of union organization as a means of achieving a more just balance of power in developing economies.

But was he a legitimate heir to the naturalistic monism and scientific tradition of Democritus and Epicurus? Here the answer must be no. In the first

..ce, his misunderstanding and misuse of science was too grievous. In his preface to the first German edition of *Das Kapital*, Marx tried to explain his methodology and objective. His justification of the abstract nature of his theorizing was that "when we come to an analysis of economic forms we have neither microscopes nor chemical reagents to help us out. The power of abstraction has to take the place of both these expedients" (Marx 1957:xlvii). And he cited his primary concern as the discovery of "the laws themselves, the tendencies which work with an iron necessity towards an inevitable goal" (ibid.: xlix). Later, he revealed his dualism in a reference to wages as merely the phenomenal form of the essential relation or hidden substratum which is labour-power. " The phenomenal forms show themselves spontaneously and directly, as current forms of thought; the actual substrata must be discovered by scientific inquiry" (ibid.:591). Taken together, these three statements shed considerable light on Marx's peculiar perspective on the nature of science.

There is no place in Marx's epistemology for the process of disciplined observation of experienced regularities that is crucial to honest scientific inquiry. For him, the only justifiable method was abstract speculation. The other core component of science is surely the rule that theoretical models, however abstract, must be capable of yielding predictions that are testable — or capable of being falsified. Marx's predictions take the form of large-scale historical prophecies concerning total transformations of the *essence* of social relations; not of their so-called *appearances*, which would at least have the merit of being observable.

Historical prophecy — even when it deals with experienced realities — is by nature not amenable to testing. The claim can always be made that the time-frame was underestimated, and the evidence not complete. Comparisons can never be made. Controls are impossible. And prophecies expressed in abstractions unrealizable through direct human experience are even less subject to scientific verification. It is not surprising that Marx's mind proved to be singularly closed to the evidence of events in the later years of his life that did not support his thesis.

To a certain extent he was a naturalist. He was a strong supporter of Darwin and was no doubt influenced by the new evolutionary theory. He believed that "the ideal is nothing other than the material when it has been transposed and translated inside the human head" (ibid.:lix). An ideal or divine Intelligence or a Consciousness beyond human beings did not represent reality for Marx. But, then, neither did observable events and behaviours! His ultimate assumptions were Kantian as well as Hegelian. He was a committed dualist in the tradition of Descartes; a believer in the reality of "essences" behind the "appearances" of phenomena in the tradition of Plato and Kant, and, like Hegel, a mystic convinced of the possibility of absolute knowledge of the future course of history.

Marx took something else from his early socialization. He assimilated the totalitarian vision of the German romantic idealists. For him it was always true that "the One is more real than the Many" (ibid.:xxxi). He referred to the social product as an unanalyzable "whole"; to labour-power as a "whole." And he sought the essential "oneness underlying the phenomenal multiplicity of the capitalist world" (ibid.:xxxii). A reviewer of *Das Kapital* commented on the prevalence in Marx's doctrines of his "belief in the 'masses' as somehow more real than the individual. . . . In history he sees classes as the essential realities and agents of social change; and in his Theory of Surplus Value the whole capitalist class ranks as the power which extracts the surplus" (ibid.: xxxiii).

Marx's commitment to the priority of an abstract state over the individual person places him in Plato's current of thought, rather than in that of Democritus and Epicurus. And the instigation and legitimation of violence as the sole vehicle of social change is a doctrine foreign to his intellectual heroes. Perhaps on these grounds alone we would have to conclude that Karl Marx has forfeited membership in the tradition of those ancient worthies who were the focus of his student dissertation.

References for Chapter Six

Black, Eugene C., ed. 1964. *Posture of Europe, 1815-1940: Readings in European Intellectual History*. Homewood IL: Dorsey Press.

Jackson, Hampden J. 1958. *Marx, Proudhon, and European Socialism*. London: English Universities Press.

Kant, Immanuel. 1871. *The Metaphysics of Ethics*. Edinburgh: T.&T. Clark.

_____. 1949. *Critique of Practical Reason*. Translated and edited by Lewis White Beck. Chicago: University of Chicago Press.

_____. 1974. *Anthropology from a Pragmatic Point of View*. Translated by Mary J. Gregor. The Hague: Martinus Nijhoff.

_____. 1982. *Critique of Pure Reason*. Translated by Wolfgang Schwarz. Aalen, West Germany: Scientia.

Lefèbre, Henri. 1968. *The Sociology of Marx*. New York: Vintage Books.

Marx, Karl. 1926. *Selected Essays*. Translated by H.J. Stenning. Freeport, NJ: Books for Libraries Press.

_____. 1957. *Capital*. New York: Dutton (Everyman's Library).

_____ and Friedrich Engels. 1958. *Selected Works*. Vols. 1 and 2. Moscow: Foreign Languages Publishing House.

_____. 1963. *The Communist Manifesto*. New York: Russell and Russell.

_____. 1970. *A Contribution to the Critique of Political Economy*. New York: International Publishers.

Meyer, Alfred G. 1961. *Marxism since the Communist Manifesto*. Washington: American Historical Association.

Seven

Charles Darwin
The Reluctant Revolutionary

There is grandeur in this view of life . . .
From so simple a beginning
Endless forms most beautiful
And most wonderful
Have been and are being
Evolved.
> — Charles Darwin,
> *On the Origin of Species*

Karl Marx was not the only revolutionary of his generation. Nor was the tidal wave of political upheaval that he inspired the only current of change to challenge the conservative bulwarks of the age. There was another man and another idea: an idea so radical and momentous that it would alter irrevocably the culture's most cherished beliefs about what it means to be human. And in that process, it would totally undercut the empirical and rational grounding of the *a priori* premises required for Kant's transcendentalism. The man was Charles Darwin and the idea was the theory of the evolution of life by means of natural selection.

The making of a scientist

Darwin (born nine years before Marx, in 1809) was almost the polar opposite of his German contemporary. A product of upper-class Victorian England, there was little in his upbringing to inspire rebellion. Like Martineau, he came from a Unitarian background. He seems to have imbibed the cautiously liberal religious values of his family like the oxygen of the air he breathed — without questioning or even conscious examination. His heritage had ensured him a safe place to grow and a firm identity, a far cry from the cultural conflicts and insecurities of Marx's childhood. Charles' maternal grandfather was Josiah Wedgewood, the famous British pottery maker. On the paternal side, he was the grandson of Erasmus Darwin, a well-known natural historian and physi-

References for this chapter are on p. 126-27.

cian. Very early in life he must have been able to assume the freedom to pursue personal interests that both Martineau and Marx had been forced to wrestle from their social environment.

Charles was not an inspired nor a particularly conscientious student. Neither was he attracted to grand schemes of abstract thought. His family were intensely practical people, so habits of careful observation and methodical recording were probably learned early on. Pebbles interested him, and beetles, and always his question was "How did that come to be?" However, in the unscientific, metaphysical intellectual milieu of the time, such a mindset was not highly valued in educational institutions. Charles first entered medical studies at the University of Edinburgh because that was what was expected of him. There he became interested in natural history, finally confessing to his father that he had no wish to become a doctor.

Dr. Darwin decided that the clergy would be the best place for his seemingly non-intellectual son. Charles acquiesced, but with little enthusiasm. He wrote later: "I asked for some time to reconsider, as from what little I had heard and thought about the subject I had scruples about declaring my belief in all the dogmas of the Church of England, though otherwise I liked the thought of becoming a country clergyman. . . . [However] it never struck me how illogical it was to say that I believed in what I could not understand and, in fact, what is unintelligible" (Clark:12). All in all, his chief doubt seems to have concerned his lack of any inward encounter with "the Holy Spirit."

Charles' subsequent years at Cambridge gave him the opportunity to become acquainted with geology as well as to continue his interest in natural history. The possibility that his growing fascination with scientific pursuits might some day conflict with the religious career for which he was supposedly being prepared seems not to have occurred to him. As a biographer noted, all the scientists he knew seemed to have successfully reconciled the metaphysical assumptions of their science with church dogma. Why should he be different?

Darwin said later that his student experiences at this time left him with a burning zeal to make a contribution to "the noble structure of science." They probably left him with something else as well. Once, on a tour with Sedgwick, the noted geologist, he discussed a tropical mollusk found near his home in Shrewsbury. Rather than the expected curiosity and enthusiasm, Sedgwick responded with disinterest and foreboding. He replied that such a find would be most unfortunate, as it would upset "all that we know." Numerous such instances over the years must have taught Darwin that the scientific community of his day, with its vested interest in established "truths," could be as hostile as any other group to the challenge of new and anomalous evidence.

Setting out on a voyage of discovery

Just after graduation a remarkable opportunity was presented to the young student. In 1828, Robert Fitzroy, the captain of the H.M.S. *Beagle*, had been commissioned to do a hydrographic survey of the coast of South America and was looking for a self-supporting biologist to accompany him on an extended ocean voyage. Charles' botanist friend and professor, J. S. Henslow, recommended him for the job.

The trip began well, with Darwin seemingly as earnestly religious as the orthodox Fitzroy, and even quoting Scriptures. The youthful biologist was not doctrinaire, however, for he had been well socialized into liberalism, and flexibility of thought came naturally to him. Although generally accepting some of prevailing Grand Design assumptions about the origin of the universe, he was probably ahead of most of his contemporaries in having a vague belief that life had evolved. After all, his grandfather Erasmus had been an evolutionist, and had published a poem on the subject in 1803. In fact, "by the 1750's cosmic evolution was openly discussed; geological change, timidly; the evolution of life in subdued and sporadic whispers" (Eiseley:16). But, according to a biographer, if Charles had a scientifically inspired problem spurring him on as the voyage proceeded, it was that of traditional taxonomic biology — "What is a species?" The more radical question of "How did the different species come to be?" — one which would upset the biological as well as religious orthodoxies of his day — had not yet occurred to him.

It has often been said of Darwin that his inward (conceptual) voyage was to prove even more magnificently impressive than the remarkable outward (geographical) one that spanned five years and half the globe. He had taken with him the first volume of Charles Lyell's *Principles of Geology* in which Lyell presented a truly revolutionary theory of the earth's formation. Reading it, Darwin came to see the earth as incredibly ancient. He saw as well, that nature has an inherent order, comprising regularities recurring over long periods of time — all capable of being explained naturally. And he must have begun to recognize that his early mania for documenting such observed regularities was not just a strange childish hobby, but the very factual foundation required for any scientific explanation of the nature of things.

Geology was the ideal study to develop an evolutionary — as well as a broadly scientific — viewpoint. The story of cumulative development was there, in the rocks, even though Lyell himself had not fully understood it. From then on, it is likely that Darwin began to observe the new and startling surroundings to which the trip exposed him from a perspective that was equally new and startling. It is also likely that he was not at all aware of what was happening.

At that time biological thinking was dominated at the practical level by taxonomy (the attempt to define discrete categories of species) and, at the theoretical level, by the ideas of Georges Cuvier of France. His "Grand Design" envisioned a discontinuous series of ever-improving holistic "creations," modelled upon Aristotle's system: a view that allowed a comfortable compromise with Old Testament mythologies. Darwin must very soon have begun to suspect that his observations directly contradicted Cuvier's theory.

Discovering the unexpected

On the five-year voyage there were many opportunities for extended excursions on shore. Everywhere, Darwin collected specimens, sending them back to Cambridge whenever he connected with homeward-bound British ships. He filled countless notebooks with careful accounts of everything he saw. The mammals, birds and insects, as well as the geology of each region, were minutely described and, where possible, fitted into gaps in the existing taxonomical record. Then Darwin began to note facts suggesting that certain species might have changed almost beyond recognition over the millennia. For example, there were three birds whose wings clearly had evolved for use in flight but now had other functions. These were the penguin, with wings now employed as fins for swimming; the "steamer" duck which used its wings for paddling; and the ostrich, which used them for sails.

On September 17, 1835, the *Beagle* anchored off the most easterly of the Galapagos Islands. There, Darwin began to notice that the huge tortoises seen everywhere differed substantially from island to island. However, he seems not then to have registered the full significance of this. The situation was the same for the finches. Thirteen varieties could be traced to the same source, but the present inhabitants of each island were in many ways unique. The range of variation, especially in the beaks, was remarkable. While still on the island Darwin noted that his data would seem to undermine current assumptions concerning the stability of the species. From that moment on, the problem apparently puzzled and haunted him.

By this time relations between Captain Fitzroy and his biologist had grown tense. The two men grappled intellectually over their increasingly polarized convictions regarding creation, the Bible, species immutability, ethics, God and nature. Rather than quoting the Scriptures, Darwin was now openly challenging their reliability as a source of historical fact.

Solving the puzzle

On arriving home, considerably diminished in health, Darwin went to work immediately on his collection of species. He also married his cousin Emma and established a home for the family which was eventually to include eleven children. His notebooks of that period show that he set about immediately organizing and interpreting his findings. An interdisciplinary scholar by nature and necessity (he knew that the implications of his evidence extended far beyond biology) his reading ranged far and wide. As a friend of Martineau's, he is likely to have read her work — indeed, it may have been she who introduced him to Thomas Malthus. Malthus, who recognized the inherent capacity of animal species to overpopulate their environments, seems to have supplied the missing piece for the puzzle. Suddenly, all of Darwin's observations were leading him inexorably to a new and exciting explanation of how nature must have been operating over the millennia to produce the variations in species that he had found in such abundance.

The facts seemed to permit only one conclusion: that organic species are indeed mutable — not fixed, as was then popularly held — and that they have undergone continuous modification as a result of a process by which the variations of each generation were either selected or destroyed by environmental demands. Only those modifications that proved advantageous to the survival of the individual members of the species have persevered over time. Others failed to survive because their carriers did not live to reproduce; that is they were selected out by nature. Darwin recognized an inescapable logic in the idea that such a gradual accumulation of advantageous changes could eventually produce all of the complex structures of even the highest mammals of the present day.

The conclusion was revolutionary, and Darwin knew it, for he was no single-minded, socially alienated technician, burrowing away in his own narrow scientific niche. He had studied philosophy and theology. A Unitarian by birth and temperament, he was immersed in the cultural climate of his era. He knew that the prevailing religious view was orthodox in the extreme, and although he could no longer share it, he was well aware of the depth of its roots, even among scientists. His grandfather's ideas on evolution had been tolerated rather than admired by his own family. His wife's belief in the Bible and a personal God was literal and central to her emotional wellbeing, and Darwin was deeply concerned about her feelings. His lengthy arguments with Captain Fitzroy had been enough to convince him of the depth of fear and loathing that his ideas would arouse in the general populace. And he knew from experience that the scientific community would be little more receptive to a theory bound to challenge the very foundations of their enterprise.

The following comment in a letter to a colleague shows how tentative was his approach, even with trusted friends: "I am almost convinced (quite contrary to the opinion I started with) that species are not (it is like confessing to a murder) immutable . . . I think I have found out (here's presumption!) the simple way by which species have become exquisitely adapted to various ends" (ibid.:84).

Shaking the foundations

Darwin must have known that his theory would pose a grievous challenge to religion on two crucial counts. First, the concept of mutability of the species left no room for a God as the creator of each, and for a soul as an entity apart from nature and reserved for humans. Secondly, the idea of a guiding design and purpose in the earth's affairs could not reasonably survive an acceptance of natural selection as the energizing force in evolution.

Charles Darwin was an unlikely revolutionary. As Martineau had noted, he was a gentle, unassuming and thoroughly decent man: scarcely the type to have purposely set out to destroy the philosophical and theological foundations of his world. But his biographers agree that there was something in his makeup which made his course, if not inevitable, at least predictable — given the opportunities that became available to him. For he was an honest, dogged, meticulous inquirer into the nature of things, bound to follow where observation and reason dictated. No doubt he was as appalled as any of his contemporaries at where his relentless journey led him. But unlike many of them, he could not detour around the logic of the evidence in his desire to learn the truth. As one biographer put it, "frequently to discover kingdoms while searching for asses, he was always cautiously following his nose to the most bizarre and extravagant destinies.... In short, Darwin muddled into genius and greatness like a true Englishman" (Irvine:43-44).

Documenting his theory

No wonder, having arrived at his unexpected destination, Darwin hesitated. His biographers are all intrigued by his activities during the next twenty years. He wrote out a sketch of his theory with the supporting evidence, but then put it away, with directions to Emma to publish it at his death. He then devoted himself to minute biological research. Such work was his passion, but he may have been motivated as well by the need to achieve credibility as a scientist by lengthy, in-depth immersion in his field. He also judged correctly that the painstaking documentation of confirming data was absolutely necessary if he were to gain worldwide support for his theory. In 1854 he published the fruits of these years of labour: four volumes on the subject of hereditary modification in barnacles, which were well received in the scientific community.

Darwin might well have devoted the rest of his life to the task of collecting confirming evidence for his theory of "descent with modification" (and preparing the discipline of natural history for the publication of his bombshell) if it had not been for a young biologist named Alfred Russel Wallace. In 1858, Wallace arrived at the same answer concerning natural selection as the vehicle of evolution and informed Darwin that he was about to publish. With the aid of Thomas Huxley and Charles Lyell — and considerable trepidation on Dar-

win's part — arrangements were made for the two papers to be presented together.

The origin of species

On the Origin of Species presented a wealth of evidence for Darwin's claim
that descent with modification was a fact and natural selection the explanation
for it. The analogy of changes in domesticated species wrought by humans
was applied to the course of evolution in nature. The performance standards of
breeders were compared to the natural environmental demands operating to
select variations advantageous to survival in changing circumstances. In each
case there were pressures exerted from outside the organism that tended to
favour certain variations over others in the long run. Darwin thought that one
of the most effective selective pressures operating in nature could be sexual at-
tractiveness. He suggested that many of the seemingly useless appendages and
colours might possibly function to attract the opposite sex and thereby ensure
procreation and survival of the most attractive and strongest members of the
species.

Darwin admitted ignorance as to the *cause* of variations in organisms, but
assumed that, when discovered, it would confirm his theory. In fact, he went
so far as to imagine invisible characters in the blood that unite in each fertil-
ized egg and "lie ready to be evolved whenever the organism is disturbed by
certain . . . [newly challenging] conditions" (Weiner:214). He made a similar
and equally well-warranted assumption about the then-sparse and spotty fossil
record. He was later to write: "I look at the geological record as a history of
the world imperfectly kept, and written in a changing dialect; of this history
we possess the last volume alone, relating only to two or three countries. Of
this volume only here and there a short chapter has been preserved; and of
each page only here and there a few lines. Each word of the slowly changing
language . . . may represent the forms of life which are entombed in our con-
secutive formations, and which falsely appear to us to have been abruptly
introduced" (Leakey:165).

The Origin avoided the potentially explosive issue of humanity's place in
the scheme of things. The only reference was a sentence promising that "light
would be shed" on the subject. The book concluded as follows: "Thus, from
the war of nature, from famine and death, the most exalted object which we
are capable of conceiving, namely the production of the higher animals, directly follows. . . . There is a simple grandeur in the view of life with its
powers of assimilation and reproduction having been originally breathed into
matter under a few forms . . . that from so simple an origin, through the selection of infinitesimal varieties, endless forms most beautiful and most wonderful have evolved" (ibid.:223). In later editions, trying to lessen the shock of
his message, he added, "by the Creator" after "breathed."

And the world trembled

The controversy and vilification following publication probably exceeded all expectations. Ill health, family concerns and a non-confrontational temperament forced Darwin to remain aloof from the fray. He relied on the vigorous and intelligent Thomas Huxley to do public battle in the cause. (Huxley is known by non-scientists today chiefly as the originator of the term, "agnosticism" — for the scientific attitude of holding only those beliefs that are warranted by evidence.) Meanwhile, Darwin continued his life's work: producing a long list of studies documenting and elaborating upon various aspects of natural selection in evolution. Ironically, he overlooked the melanic moth in his own locality, whose wings were then in the very process of taking on an increasingly smoky colouration to match the pollution-darkened buildings of industrial Britain!

Darwin's approach throughout the storm that followed the publication of *The Origin* was to ignore the fact that many religious beliefs were contradicted by his findings. In response to a letter from Karl Marx, who criticized him for this, he wrote: "though I am a strong advocate for free speech on all subjects, yet it appears to me ... that direct arguments against Christianity and Theism produce hardly any effect on the public; and freedom of thought is best promoted by the gradual illumination of men's minds which follows from the advance of science. It has therefore always been my objective to avoid writing on religion, and I have confined myself to science. I may, however, have been unduly biassed by the pain it would give some members of my family if I aided in any way direct attacks on religion" (Clark:212).

His eye was on the long term, and for that he relied on the perspective of history. At one point he commented that "by far the greater part of the opposition is just the same as that made when the sun was first said to stand still and the earth go round" (ibid.:149). He also noted that the law of gravity had been attacked by the seventeenth-century mathematician Gottfried Leibniz as "subversive of natural, and inferentially of, revealed religion" (Leakey:216). All in all Darwin was far from naive about the difficulty of altering world views or even the paradigms of fellow scientists, as the following indicates: "I by no means expect to convince experienced naturalists whose minds are stocked with a multitude of facts all viewed, during a long course of years, from a point of view directly opposite to mine. ... A few ... endowed with much flexibility of mind, and who have already begun to doubt the immutability of the species, may be influenced by this volume; but I look with confidence to the future, to young and rising naturalists who will be able to view both sides of the question with impartiality" (ibid.:217).

Attempting to influence personal friends was another matter, however. He wrote to Asa Gray (the noted American natural historian) that there was too much misery in the world for the concept of an omnipotent and beneficent

God to be credible. He noted that no such entity would have designed the *ichneumonidae* with the express intention of their feeding within the living bodies of their hosts (ibid.:143).

The descent of man

By the 1860s, Darwin felt sufficiently prepared for a detailed look at the origin and development of humanity. *The Descent of Man* was published in 1871. In the introduction he acknowledged his great debt to the German biologist, Ernst Haeckel (1834-1919), who had arrived at many of the same conclusions and had supported him steadfastly throughout the years of controversy. Haeckel is important to our story for a number of reasons. Thirty years before the first transitional fossils were discovered he offered a hypothesis of the lineage of human evolution that has stood the test of time and evidence. He suggested a remote ancestor, *Pithecanthropus alalus*, an ape-like primate with a relatively small brain who walked upright and used simple language. Haeckel also coined the phrase, "ontogeny recapitulates phylogeny" — although he recognized numerous exceptions to the rule that the developing human fetus progresses through the stages of species evolution. The name of "ecology" for a science of the diversity of life came from him as well. Another important contribution was his term "monism" which, unfortunately, was taken up by some romantic idealists and applied to the notion of the ideal (or a cosmic spirit or consciousness) as the essential, defining reality. Haeckel was referring, instead, to the seamless web of nature in all its emergent forms, including that of humankind.

Darwin, now in full agreement with Haeckel, tried to prepare his readers with the observation that, "It has often and confidently been asserted that man's origin can never be known; but ignorance more frequently begets confidence than does knowledge; it is those who know little ... who so positively assert that this or that will never be known by science" (Darwin 1874:19). He went on to provide chapter after chapter of compelling evidence pointing to "the conclusion that man is the co-descendant with other mammals of a common progenitor" (ibid.:631). He described this remote ancestor as a hairy, tailed quadruped, probably arboreal in habits, but surmised that in the dim obscurity of the past the progenitor of all vertebra may have been aquatic.

Darwin conceded that, on the surface, the relatively high level of our intellectual and moral capacities would seem to argue for a discontinuity of descent between humanity and other animals. But he then presented a surprisingly modern discussion of the interdependent development of intellect and language and of the influence of these upon the gradual evolution of the moral sense from the social instincts shared by many animals. He even confronted the issues of God and soul. "I am aware that an assumed instinctive belief in God has been used by many persons as an argument for his existence. But this is a rash argument as we should then be compelled to believe in the existence of many cruel and malignant spirits only a little more powerful than Man; for belief in them is far more general than in a beneficent deity" (Darwin 1845:637).

In a notebook Darwin went even further, musing about "the probability of the constant inculcation of a belief in God in the minds of children producing so strong and perhaps an inherited effect on their brains not as yet fully developed that it would be as difficult for them to throw off their belief in God, as for a monkey to throw off its instinctive fear and hatred of a snake" (Burrow:181). Concerning the soul, he reminded his readers that many primitive peoples have no such beliefs; therefore the common argument that universal awareness of a personal soul proves its existence simply does not hold. And he added that there seems no accountable way or specific point in evolution that such an entity could possible appear.

After *The Descent* came out, Darwin's religious attackers were joined by most of the general public, and the press had a field day. A number of his previous supporters fell away. Even Wallace could not make the step that the logic of his own evidence and reasoning clearly demanded. He was unable to give up the idea of a spiritual essence distinguishing human beings from other animals in kind as well as in degree. Lyell, Darwin's inspiration in earlier days, drew back as well. So much so, in fact, that Darwin was forced to remark regretfully that his former mentor had slipped into old age and transcendentalism. But there remained powerful defenders in the British scientific establishment — notably Thomas Huxley — who successfully engaged in debate on the subject whenever the occasion arose.

Paradigm-shifts and after-shocks

Reception of Darwin's theory varied from country to country. In the United States, as in Britain, the majority of commentators agreed either with Agassiz of Harvard, who was convinced that he would outlive "this mania of evolution" or with Henry Ward Beecher, who accepted it enthusiastically as "the Divine method in creation." In Germany, Ernst Haeckel continued as an influential supporter, maintaining the heretical proposition that psychology was by rights a department of physiology and that the study of mental processes would also someday be fitted into the scheme of evolution. Support came also from Japan, where a popular writer agreed that the story of Genesis is absurd, and that the Shintoist and Buddhist classics are entirely consistent with Darwinism.

As with his lifetime voyage of discovery, Darwin faced the inevitable end with an acceptance of nature's way and a quiet concern for his family. "I am not in the least afraid of death," he told them as his life drew to a close in April of 1882 (Irvine:227). He died confident that posterity would confirm his theory, but even he would probably have been astounded at the extent to which this has indeed been the case.

Discovering the missing pieces

By 1918, Darwin's theory of descent by modification was supported by a vast body of research in genetics built upon Mendel's discoveries of the laws of heredity, the mutation hypothesis of Hugo De Vries and by new discoveries and carbon-dating techniques in geology and natural history. Natural selection had become the prevailing organizing paradigm in the rapidly growing disciplines of paleontology, biology, archeology and anthropology. And it had been grossly misunderstood and *misapplied* to sociology and political economy — but that is another story.

Darwin's guess that selection might possibly operate for the survival of family groupings has now been extended and substantiated by theorists and researchers in the area of "kin selection." And his musings about the crucial implications of his theory for moral education were followed up to great advantage by Jean Piaget. More recent developments in biochemistry have explained the almost unlimited capacity for variation in organisms that had been hypothesized by Darwin and required by his theory. Most significant was the discovery by James D. Watson and Francis Crick of the structure of DNA or deoxyribonucleic acid, the material that passes genetic information from one generation to the next. Subsequent research has indicated that every living thing carries its genetic code in the same four bases ("letters") of DNA, variously arranged in groups of three. It has also been found that there is surprisingly little variation in order from species to species of animal, and that modern chimps and modern humans share 99 percent identity in their genetic makeup. Some researchers hypothesize that *homo sapiens* shares a single ancestor, located in Africa less than 100,000 years ago. On the other hand, recent evidence in conjunction with the advanced mathematical analysis now made possible by computers seems to indicate that human ancestry extends much further back in time, and that the migration out of Africa may have occurred earlier than had been assumed. Regardless of the outcome of this particular controversy, however, current knowledge provides strong confirmation of Darwin's claim that all organic life evolved from one source.

New light is also being shone daily on problems such as the origin of species — demonstrating how both of Darwin's processes of selection (natural and sexual) intertwine in nature to create those invisible boundaries which result, over time, in the biological separation of one group of organisms from another. Studies have also found that, although *Darwin's essential selection processes operate throughout*, under rapidly changing environmental conditions, speciation can occur at much faster rates than he had ever dreamed possible.

Darwin's idea of sexual selection, largely ignored by subsequent generations of biologists, has now been given substantial support by the work of Stephen Jay Gould, Peter and Rosemary Grant and many others. Recent geological and paleontological discoveries as to the great age of the earth (and of the possible six-million-year lifespan of homo erectus) now demonstrate that there was indeed sufficient time for the non-random accumulation of the type of trial-and-error modifications predicted by the theory of evolution. The old argument that the "missing link" between human and ape has never been found has been decisively put to rest by several momentous fossil discoveries. The first was that of the 3.6 million-year-old Lucy (*Australopithecus afarensis*), a member of the australopithecine species which had an ape-like brain and upright posture and is considered to be the common root of the human family tree. This was followed in 1992-93 by the discovery of *Australopithecus ramidus*, a chimp-sized creature that roamed the forested areas of northern Africa about 4.4 million years ago. Then, in 1995, Ronald Clarke discovered in caves near Johannesburg 3.5 million-year-old fossilized footbones (dubbed "Little Foot") which seem to be from an upright-walking hominid. The use of statistics and computer-modelling by theorists such as Richard Dawkins further supports and clarifies the basic theory of evolution by natural selection.

Although a wave of anti-Darwinism and of "post-Darwinist" conjecturing among evolutionary theorists gained headway around the mid-period of the twentieth century, the tide is now rapidly moving back to a renewed appreciation of Darwinian theory. A flood of research during the eighties and early nineties has provided newly convincing "hard" evidence — not only of the central role of natural selection in evolution, but of its ongoing operation within our present ecology. The powerful shaping influence of the human race on the process is now being recognized, as research increasingly unearths the far-reaching consequences for natural selection of humankind's proliferation and behaviour. Examples of this are the role of our use of insecticides and antibiotics in the evolution of resistant species, and the effects on host species of our thoughtless introduction of plants and animals into new habitats.

Amazingly, only one of Darwin's ideas does not seem to have stood the test of time. This was the small opening that he left for the Lamarckian theory of inheritance of learned characteristics. Back in 1809 the French naturalist J.P.B. Lamarck had published the first great treatise on evolution, *Philosophie Zoologique*. His theory was that individual organisms respond creatively to perceived needs and the attributes thus acquired are inherited by succeeding generations. Darwin thought that there might be some way that deeply ingrained habitual behaviour could enter the realm of heritable instinct, and that organs might appear or disappear with countless generations of use or disuse. Recent work on DNA, which shows conclusively that genetic instructions follow a one-way street only, seems to allow no possibility for messages from an individual's life experience to penetrate the code transmitted by the sex cells.

However, molecular biologists have discovered that the *mutation rate* is considerably increased under environmentally induced stress, making the potential for rapid and varied change much greater than usual in these situations. Also, they are more aware than before of the profusion of unused genetic instructions carried in every germ cell, which, under extreme conditions, may come into play to shape newly effective adaptations. They have also found that a very small change in genetic instructions can result in a very large alteration in the form and functioning of an organism. They now understand, as well, how organisms exhibiting behaviours conducive to survival tend to reproduce and nourish their young more successfully than do those who do not, so that, in effect, the web of uniquely workable reciprocal behaviours resulting within a group over time amounts to an "extended phenotype" typical of the particular species. Because of all these factors the actual outcome can sometimes give the *appearance* of learned behaviours having been inherited.

Thus, in the end, it is the power of the evidence discovered by means of Darwin's insightful explanations of previously mysterious and irresolvable anomalies that has won the day. As a result, our view of nature and of our origin and place within it has been changed forever — even though few of us yet recognize the significance of the Darwinian revolution for our understanding of behaviour. And all this was effected by a gentle English biologist remarkable only for a certain methodical persistence in observation; an intellectual integrity that allowed no wavering in the face of logic and evidence; and the humility to "sit down before the *fact* as a little child, be prepared to give up every preconceived notion, and follow to whatever abysses nature leads" (Irvine:129).

References for Chapter Seven

Berry, R.J. 1990. Industrial Melanism and Peppered Moths. *Biological Journal of the Linnean Society* 39: 302-303.

Burrow, J.W. 1966. Charles Darwin. *Horizon*. Autumn: 40-47.

Carson, H.L. 1978. Speciation and Sexual Selection in Hawaiian Drosophilia. In *Ecological Genetics: The Interface*. Edited by Peter F. Brussard. New York: Springer-Verlag, p. 93-107.

Clark, Ronald W. 1984. *The Survival of Charles Darwin*. New York: Random House.

Darwin, Charles. 1845. *Naturalist's Voyage in H.M.S.* Beagle. London: J.M. Dent.

———. 1874. *The Descent of Man and Selection in Relation to Sex*. New York: P.F. Collier and Son.

———. 1962. *On the Origin of Species*. Edited by Ernst Mayr. Cambridge, MA: Harvard University Press. (Facsimile of 1859 edition).

Dawkins, Richard. 1986. *The Blind Watchmaker*. New York: W.W. Norton.

Eiseley, Loren. 1972. *The Firmament of Time*. New York: Atheneum.

Endler, John A. 1983. Natural and Sexual Selection on Color Patterns in Poeciliid Fishes. *Environmental Biology of Fishes* 9: 173-90.

Gibbs, H. Lisle. 1988. Heritability and Selection on Clutch Size in Darwin's Medium Ground Finches. *Evolution* 42: 750-62.

Gould, James L., and Carol Grant Gould. 1989. *Sexual Selection*. New York: Scientific American Library.

Gould, Stephen Jay. 1973. *Ever Since Darwin*. New York: W.W. Norton.

————. 1980. *The Panda's Thumb*. New York: W.W. Norton.

————. 1985. *The Flamingo's Smile*. New York: W.W. Norton.

Grant, B. Rosemary, and Peter Grant. 1989. Natural Selection in a Population of Darwin's Finches. *American Naturalist* 133:377-93.

Grant, Peter R., and B. Rosemary Grant. 1992. Hybridization of Bird Species. *Science* 256:193-97.

Huxley, Thomas. 1910. *Lectures and Lay Sermons*. London: J.M. Dent.

Irvine, William. 1962. *Apes, Angels and Victorians*. New York: Meridian.

Leakey, Richard, ed. 1979. *The Illustrated Origin of Species by Charles Darwin*. Boston: Faber and Faber.

Price, Trevor D. 1984. Sexual Selection on Body Size, Territory, and Plumage Variables in a Population of Darwin's Finches. *Evolution* 38: 327-41.

Reznick, David, and John A. Endler. 1982. The Impact of Predation on Life History Evolution in Trinidadian Guppies. *Evolution* 36: 160-77.

Stone, Irving. 1980. *The Origin*. New York: Doubleday.

Weiner, Jonathon. 1994. *The Beak of the Finch: The Story of Evolution in Our Time*. New York: Alfred A. Knopf.

Eight

Herbert Spencer
Setting the Stage for a Unified Study of Humanity

Hail to the steadfast soul,
Who, unflinching and keen,
Wrought to erase from its depth
Mist and illusion and fear!
Hail to the spirit who dared
Trust . . . [his] own thoughts, before yet
Echoed them back by the crowd.
— Matthew Arnold,
"Haworth Churchyard"

By the time Darwin began publishing his findings, acceptance of the *fact* of evolution was widespread among the "Renaissance thinkers" of the period. Most of these, however, were Lamarckian in terms of their understanding of the *process*. They were convinced that characteristics acquired through experience by one generation are inherited by the next, in the shape of either more complex mental "forms" or some kind of race memory. Darwin's younger cousin Herbert Spencer was just such a thinker. His detailed grasp of information from every field of scholarship was equalled only by his zeal and profound wisdom and his ability to integrate facts into comprehensive and presumably universal bodies of knowledge. Spencer devoted his life to this task, as had Democritus, Aristotle and Avicenna so long before. He produced ten massive volumes, rich in anthropological and historical detail and elaborate deductions. These constitute a magnificent organization of all available knowledge concerning organic and psycho-social life, along with an attempt to identify the laws shaping that life. But they were tragic as well, for Spencer's remarkable synthesis was fatally flawed at its very core. He had founded it all on a premise which his cousin's discovery had already rendered obsolete: a Lamarckian belief that hereditary "form" in the species is directly affected by the "functioning" of individuals.

References for this chapter are on p. 148.

Survival of the fittest

Like most of his contemporaries, Spencer never really comprehended the theory of natural selection and its implications for causation, especially in the psycho-social realm. He clung, instead, to the notion that even moral and intellectual achievements are somehow biologically inherited. For Darwin, species survival was evidence of increasingly viable adaptation between environment and organism resulting from the operation of environmental contingencies upon accidental variations of organismic forms. This was a new kind of cumulative and after-the-fact causation — the effects of which could only be assessed over thousands of generations. It meant that the *consequences* of the individual organism's activities within its environment feed back to become, in turn, the *causes* of subsequent species change. These consequences include both the impact of the organism on its surroundings and the degree to which it is successful in producing offspring. Spencer either did not understand or chose not to accept this explanation of the vehicle of evolution.

He made another mistake as well. In applying Darwin's theory to psychological and moral development and the evolution of society, Spencer focused on the differential survival of individuals rather than on that of ideas, norms and ultimately, of culture. In spite of Darwin's emphasis on the survival of *species*, Spencer seemed to think that, with both cultural and biological evolution, *individual* survival was the issue.

For Spencer, fitness to survive depended on the total mix of attributes belonging to individuals — whether these had resulted from their biological legacy, or the history of the race, or personal life experience. All were heritable, in his view. This confusion of the racial, cultural and experiential cast a sinister shadow over Spencer's ultimate evolutionary principle of "survival of the fittest." It represented a profound subversion of Darwin's fruitful scientific model and had the long-term effect of maligning the scientist's reputation as well. For it produced, in other hands, the politically persuasive theory of Social Darwinism: a ruthlessly racist ideology that Spencer's own value system would never have countenanced.

The life of a lonely scholar

Perhaps the saddest aspect of the story of this essentially kind, committed and intelligent man is that the image of the magnificent edifice with the flawed foundation is a fitting metaphor for his life as well as for his life's work. Although devoted to expanding public understanding of humanity in general, he seemed singularly unable to achieve satisfying human relationships in private life.

Herbert Spencer was born in 1820, the son of a Dissenting schoolmaster. He was a brilliant but lonely child and youth, and although an uncle offered to send him to Cambridge, he preferred to remain at home and study on his own. He tried his hand at teaching, and then at civil engineering, but was satisfied with neither pursuit. Then one day, while working as an engineer for the London and Birmingham Railway, he began to find fossils in the railway cuts. His discoveries intrigued him, starting a train of thought that was to become a lifelong obsession. The message that he took from the fossils was that organic life has an inherent tendency toward progress, and that the apex of evolutionary advance — humanity — is indeed perfectible, so long as we discover the laws of nature and refrain from obstructing them. He recognized immediately what his own life's work must be. He would identify the laws directing individual and social development and would discover, as well, the political and economic conditions most conducive to their successful operation.

It seems clear that Spencer was profoundly influenced not only by his cousin Charles Darwin, but by two other great thinkers of the preceding generation: John Stuart Mill and Harriet Martineau. He told of having learned a great deal by reading Martineau's series on political economy as a youth. Certainly his mature work shows evidence of familiarity with her translation of Comte. And Mill's emphasis on individual liberty was to be his guiding star throughout his years of scholarship.

By 1842 Spencer had a promising start on a literary and scholarly career. He had begun by producing letters and pamphlets for *The Nonconformist* on the proper sphere of government. In 1848 he was hired by *The Economist* and by 1851 was working on his first book, *Social Statics*. In 1852 he published an essay in *The Leader* entitled "The Developmental Hypothesis," followed somewhat later by "Progress: Its Law and Cause." In 1853 he received a sizeable legacy from his uncle and was able to resign from his job at *The Economist*. From then on he devoted himself full-time to the study of biology, philosophy, psychology, history, anthropology, and to what, since Comte, had become known as sociology.

The task that Spencer had set himself was no less than the establishment of philosophical and scientific foundations for a comprehensive evolutionary sociology. This was to incorporate humanity's biological base and its psychological structures and functions (as well as the manifestations of these in social institutions) and conclude with the implications of all this for the eventual evolution of a "natural" system of ethics. By this he meant ethics having a source and justification in the natural world rather than in the supernatural. His specific master plan was to complete a total synthesis of human knowledge of all aspects of organic life, beginning at the simplest level with its biological underpinnings and limitations, and moving to the more complex social relations. From 1855 until well past his death, the various sections of his vast system entered the public forum in a steady stream of publications.

By the 1880s and 1890s Spencer's *Principle of Biology* was the standard source in that subject at Oxford and Harvard. His *Principles of Psychology* was a major reference throughout the Western world. His *Principles of Sociology* was the sole textbook for the first course in sociology ever offered at any university. It was taught at Yale University in 1876 by William Graham Sumner and was responsible for establishing sociology as an identifiable academic discipline. Spencer's works also nurtured the historians of the period and came to dominate late-nineteenth-century American social philosophy.

All this occurred before the author's death in 1903, but it was not enough to allow him to die a happy man. For there was that bitter irony to his life, that flaw similar to the crumbling mortar at the base of his philosophical system. Although his entire life was spent in the service of an obsession with the genesis and nature of social relations in the general and abstract, it was extraordinarily devoid of social relations in the particular and concrete. He had a number of acquaintances, including Thomas Huxley and Andrew Carnegie, but few friends. Marian Evans (better known as George Eliot, the novelist) was in love with him for years, but he was unable to reciprocate. Near the end of his life he admitted to Beatrice Webb (the Fabian-socialist daughter of a long-time acquaintance) that he had never really loved anyone. She reported: "He has sometimes told me sadly that he has wondered at the weakness of his feelings, even of friendship . . . that he thought it came from his mind being constantly busied with the perfection of his one idea" (Webb:31). Although a darkening depression haunted his last years, Spencer died never doubting the value of that one idea, nor of the validity and ultimate beneficence of the world view that it had spawned.

The philosophy of transfigured realism

Spencer referred to the idea on which he based his work as the philosophy of "transfigured realism." His position was one of naturalism, although he rejected the materialism of his day. He accepted not only the existence of an objective reality beyond human consciousness, but the objective reality of consciousness itself. He believed that there is an antithesis of subject and object that cannot be transcended while consciousness lasts, although both are aspects of the same reality. The subject can never be one with its surroundings to the extent of achieving total objectivity, because the very fact of human consciousness establishes an unbridgeable gap between subject and object. This means that consciousness can never acquire knowledge of the ultimate reality uniting the two; here, said Spencer, agnosticism is the only justifiable stance.

For Spencer, as for Hume, internal and external reality — although clearly demarcated by the fact of human consciousness — are nonetheless organically related. "The belief in an external world is the outcome of reflexive intelligent actions established, like all those others which entail forms of thought, during that moulding of the organism to the environment which has been going on for countless millions of years" (Spencer 1899c:505). He believed that changes in consciousness can be traced to the effects of changing external conditions, but that the beliefs within consciousness produced by these effects cannot constitute knowledge of their *cause,* but only of regularities in the patterns encountered.

Spencer called the patterns of these effects, as registered within the organism, "representations" of thought, a concept he borrowed from Hobbes. The term had been used, as well, by Arthur Schopenhauer, a Kantian scholar of the early nineteenth century who had tried to improve and build upon Kant's theories. Spencer departed drastically from Schopenhauer's dualist definition of "mental representations," however. For Spencer, these internally structured impacts of external effects inevitably depend upon the particular conditions obtaining between subject and object, so that the subject's knowledge of them can only be relative to those conditions. Therefore "representations" in human consciousness can never be final nor absolute. However, he noted that it is impossible even to conceive of relative knowledge of something without assuming the existence of a non-relative (objective) reality to which the knowledge refers. Hence his premise: "There is some ontological order whence arises the phenomenological order we know as Space; there is some ontological order whence arises the phenomenological order we know as Time; and there is some ontological nexus whence arises the phenomenological relation we know as Difference" (Spencer 1899b:227).

Spencer believed that evolution of the species, with its corresponding development of the individual from infancy to maturity, has resulted in great progress in the general representativeness of human thought. This has brought with it "conceptions more general and abstract, which opens the way to uniformity and law, which simultaneously raises up ideas of exact and ascertained fact, which so makes possible the practice of deliberate examination and verification, and which helps to change belief which is sudden and fixed to belief less quickly formed and modifiable, [all of which] is a development of what we commonly call imagination" (Spencer 1899c:537).

The illusion of free will

Along with imagination, and its fruits in the form of representative thought, came a consciousness of free will. According to Spencer, this "subjective illusion" survives, with its implication of an inevitable and mysterious break in the continuity of organismic-environmental mutual adjustment, in spite of steady progress towards cause-and-effect thinking in studies of the non-human realm. He explained that the sensation of free will probably came into being during evolution as a result of the increase in complexity of the conditions affecting organisms, which rendered automatic actions increasingly inadequate and therefore subject to a series of groping readjustments. A feeling of spontaneity no doubt accompanied the beginning of crude representativeness of thought within the individual, as the external world slowly became differentiated from the internal as a result of these gropings. In an echo of Democritus, he concluded that the illusion of free will perseveres because wherever causes and effects are so numerous and varied as to seem incalculable, they are not readily seen as subject to law.

The relation of function to form in evolution

Spencer began his synthesis of knowledge with a study of biology, looking for the source and vehicle of evolution. He concluded that "the direct action of the medium was the primordial factor in organic evolution" (Spencer 1887:39) but that its surroundings would have affected different aspects of the organism in varying degrees. This meant that the parts would have gradually begun to *function* somewhat differently in response to each environmental impact, and thereby the organism's *form* would have altered over time, "for inevitably the unlikenesses produced among the units had effects on their lives: there was survival of some among the modified forms rather than others" (ibid.:39). The state of "homogeneity" in which Spencer assumed that all minute life forms must have begun was thus rendered inherently unstable by the effects of its milieu. It is this that caused evolution, he said.

In Spencer's model natural selection does indeed operate, but he was trying to go beyond Darwin to explain the *source* of the variation favourable to adaptation. He thought that it was differential function (and consequent form) resulting from the uneven distribution of environmental forces over the surface of the organism. He explained that this would cause a tendency towards "heterogeneity." In the absence of our modern knowledge of genetics, this seemed a more plausible explanation than Darwin's then-unexplainable mutations.

Spencer maintained that life is a combination of heterogeneous changes, both simultaneous and successive. It is marked by a certain *definiteness* of combination, so that it is actually the coordination of these changes that distinguishes living things from the non-living. Between the coordinating operations occurring within the organism and those without, there is an invariable and necessary conformity. Life, therefore, amounts to an ongoing coordination process; that is, "*the continuous adjustment of internal relations to external relations*" (Spencer 1898:99). A biological individual is "any concrete whole having a structure which enables it, when placed in appropriate conditions, to continuously adjust its internal relations, so as to maintain the equilibrium of its functions" (ibid.:250). Spencer used the term "equilibration" for the tendency towards establishment of a balance between inner and outer changes.

In Spencer's view, all this means that the spur to action, or the creative urge, is inherent in the very nature of organic matter. It is not necessary to posit an exterior, supernatural source. He was particularly scornful of vitalism (the belief that the source and spur of life is an essentially mysterious and nonnatural "vital" entity). In Spencer's opinion this doctrine could be "not even a figment of the imagination, for that implies something imaginable, but the supposed vital principle cannot even be imagined" (ibid.:117).

Spencer remained absolutely convinced that living *structures* are permanently altered, in the species as a whole, by changes in *function* during the lifetime of the individual. His entire theory of human knowledge was based on contemplation of the relation between morphology and physiology, or structure and function. "Everywhere structures in great measure determine functions; and everywhere functions are incessantly modifying structures" (Spencer 1899a:4). This applies for plants as well as animals, the distinction between the two having arisen from differences in the conditions favouring nutrition. Although the food source of plants is universally present, it cannot be utilized without light. Therefore the structures crucial for survival would have been whatever served to enable the plant to get light. In the case of animals, because the food is scattered, structures facilitating locomotion would have been favoured by evolutionary pressures. Every increase in the locomotive power of animals would have increased both the multiplicity and multiformity of the actions of the environment upon them, and similarly, of their action upon the environment. Spencer saw this as the critical factor which set animal life into the particular progressive evolutionary spiral not shared by sedentary plant life.

Evolution as increasing complexity

Spencer concluded that each advance in the complexity of organic organization becomes an added source of complexity in the totality of environmental forces. Minute alterations of structure and function accumulate rapidly according to the principle of "multiplication of effects" as "one part which has a fresh force impressed upon it must go on changing and communicating secondary changes, until the whole of the impressed force has been used up in generating equivalent reactive forces" (ibid.:392). Every increased multiplication of effects promotes further differentiation and consequent integration at a higher level of temporary equilibrium within the organism and between it and the surroundings. "So that we may recognize something like a growing life of the entire aggregate of organisms — an exchange of services among parts enhancing the life of the whole" (ibid.:408).

Spencer saw science as necessarily progressive in the same sense. He explained that it involves both analysis and synthesis, with each new synthesis (in the form of a hypothesis or theory) yielding more appropriate direction for analysis and finer units to analyze. For, he wrote, "Nature everywhere presents us with complexities within complexities, which go on revealing themselves as we investigate smaller and smaller objects" (Spencer 1898:252).

He pointed out that, although the evolutionary *process* is inherently progressive, it does not mean that progress is inevitable for any particular species. He was aware that the history of evolution is one of extinction as well as survival. Those individuals whose functions are most out of balance with the continuously modified aggregate of external forces will be the first to die, and thereby fail to propagate their kind. "Survival of the fittest implies multiplication of the fittest" (ibid.:430). Eventually there will emerge an altered type in closer equilibrium with the altered conditions. Or possibly the entire species will be gradually superseded by one which is more viable.

Spencer recognized a necessary inverse relationship between a species' power to preserve individual life and its power to propagate additional individuals. The frenetic egg production of short-lived insects makes abundant sense in the scheme of evolution. Whenever the relations between a species and its environment become altered to the extent that self-preservation is virtually guaranteed, Spencer claimed, then the birth rate goes down to bare replacement level. He was convinced that this was already happening for humans in the civilized world of his time, and that, in due course, the process would work itself out in developing countries.

The development of the nervous system

In turning from biological to psychological functioning, Spencer began with the nervous system. He explained that all action of organic beings is discernible as motion, and the initiator of all motion is the nervous system. There are certain chemical/physical prerequisites for the nervous activity which results in organic movement. Specifically: ongoing decomposition within the system must be facilitated; absorption must be possible; perpetual repair must be carried on; and there must be contact-continuity of nerve fibre plus molecular continuity in the form of heat. Spencer considered all these to be the subject matter of physical science — empirically observable, at least in theory.

However, he recognized much greater difficulty in proceeding from a study of the workings of the nervous system, and the movements initiated by it, to an assessment of the effects of this motion on subjective feelings; in other words, to a study of psychology. He believed that, while there may be a role for introspection in the search for psychological knowledge, it is not sufficient for the task. Feelings, whether of sensations or emotions, are directly experienced by persons solely within their own consciousness. They can only assume that others feel similarly in similar circumstances. "That feelings exist in a world beyond consciousness is a belief reached only through an involved combination of inferences" (Spencer 1899b:127).

Spencer concluded that there is no possibility of a scientific analysis of consciousness unless one accepts the premise that the mental and nervous systems are opposite sides of the same coin, and that both sets of structures somehow correspond to *structures in the surrounding milieu*. The fact that psychology has to deal with all three systems (nervous, mental and environmental) makes it a science like no other. "That which distinguishes Psychology from the sciences on which it rests is that each of its propositions takes account both of the connected internal phenomena and the connected external phenomena to which they refer. . . . *It is the connections between these two connections*" (ibid.:132).

Accordingly, the fundamental premise on which Spencer based his entire Synthetic Psychology was that connections among nervous and mental activities within the individual continuously form structures which correspond, either directly or indirectly, to patterned connections among motions in the surroundings. He saw this as the source of all logic. It is very different from Kant's transcendental logical forms, however. Spencer's logical structures evolve with experience, as they approximate, more and more closely, the logic of external relations. He believed that there is an increasing adjustment of inner and outer relations in the course of psychological development of the individual parallel to that found in evolution in general — from the lowest to the highest forms of life. He referred to this idea of progress in terms of an increasingly accurate internal mirroring of the structure of an increasingly complex external reality as his General Synthesis.

The development of intelligence

Spencer's Special Synthesis had to do with the corresponding Law of Intelligence. He considered human intelligence to be simply the most advanced of a series of organically developed tools for enhancing the possibilities for adjustment, the most elementary being a propensity to sense disjunction on contact as painful and a semblance of comfortable "fit" as pleasurable. The innate ability to distinguish between these two feelings is the organism's guiding mechanism that makes individual survival possible at all. In other words, "pleasures are the incentives to life-supporting acts and pains the deterrents from life-destroying acts" (Spencer 1899b:284). All this represents a considerable refinement of the sensationalism, associationism and utilitarianism of the previous century. Spencer concluded that the highly evolved instrument of human intelligence has been built on this foundation. It involves "the establishment of correspondences between relations in the organism and relations in the environment; and the entire development of intelligence may be formulated as the progress of such correspondences in Space, in Time, in Speciality, in Generality, and in Complexity" (ibid.:385).

According to Spencer, the early stages of intelligence are found in reflex action: that simplest of organic responses to environmental stimulation. "From that lowest kind of reflex action in which a single impression produces a single contraction, the ascent is to complications in the stimuli and in the acts resulting from them" (ibid.:430). Spencer described instincts as patterns of compound reflex action. In keeping with his belief in the heritability of acquired characteristics, he drew no line between instinctive and habitual complexes of action. Clearly, for him, habits merge into instincts as the species progresses.

Spencer explained that memory, although simpler in constitution, is the crucial link between reflexive response and intelligent functioning. It has to do with the revivability of feelings evoked by environmental stimulation. Strong external pressures generate feelings that are readily revived. He claimed that each incoming sensation aggregates, in one continuous process of assimilation, with the memory of its like from past experience, for "recognition and . . . association are two aspects of the same act" (ibid.:270). There is no other law of association. Hume's three principles of "similarity/contrariety," "contiguity" and "causation" do not, in fact, describe separate mental operations. Spencer claimed that the one process of assimilation is sufficient to explain all human acquisition and recall of experience. In order for memories to be utilized by the organism they must be instantly assimilated into organized, automatic units of action, or instinctive complexes. Instinct is organized memory, and memory is incipient instinct. Reason, in turn, is built upon instinct, in that "rational action arises out of instinctive action when this grows too complex to be perfectly automatic" (ibid.:458). At the same time, "rational actions pass, by constant repetition, into automatic or instinctive actions" (ibid.:459).

Spencer explained that, eventually, there develops a cohesion among psychological states in direct proportion to the frequency with which the corresponding external relations have been repeated in experience. This produces "forms of intuition" which are built up within the individual's nervous system and gradually rendered heritable. He was convinced that "habitual psychic successions entail some hereditary tendency to such successions, which, under persistent conditions, will become cumulative from generation to generation" (ibid.:466).

This led to Spencer's belief that structures of thought and feeling, previously organized through the experience of the race, lie latent in newborn infants, to be disclosed initially in vague and crude forms with the beginning of individual experience. He noted that the one form which is absolutely antecedent to any life experience whatever is the amatory passion. Whether organized during the individual's lifetime, or inherited at birth, all intuitive forms have but one ultimate source, according to Spencer: the ever-changing conditions of the physical, organic and social surroundings. "Since all modes of consciousness can be nothing else than incidents of the correspondence between the organism and its environment, they must all be different sides of, or different phases of, the coordinated groups of exchanges whereby internal relations are adjusted to external relations" (ibid.:495-96).

Spencer's entire second volume of *Principles of Psychology* was devoted to his special synthesis concerning the development of intelligence. It was built upon the premise of a continuity and unity of composition among all mental coordinations between organism and environment. "When regarded in its fundamental aspect, the highest reasoning is seen to be one with all the lower forms of human thought, and one with instinct and reflex action. . . . The universal process of intelligence is the *assimilation* of impressions" (Spencer 1899c:297). For Spencer all mental activity is explainable as the continuous differentiation and integration of states of consciousness. He disagreed vehemently with earlier philosophers who separated understanding and reason from the process of sensing.

He particularly disagreed with Kant's idea of cosmic reason as an aspect of a reality inherently transcending experience. Spencer saw logic as existing both within consciousness and throughout the external world. In his view, external logic is the expression of general laws of correlation existing apart from humanity, "while an account of the process of [human] Reasoning formulates the most general laws of correlation among the ideas corresponding to these existences" (ibid.:87). He also distinguished between perception and the beliefs resulting from it. He insisted that, while perception is the source of the external data by means of which special relations among states of consciousness are established (i.e., the initiator of the process of assimilation and coordination) these resulting states in no way simply mirror perceived images.

The stages of intellectual development

Spencer's detailed exposition of the development of intelligence deals with both quantitative and qualitative reasoning, beginning with the development of internal representations of time and space relations and object permanence. His theory involves four hierarchically ordered, increasingly abstract, internally specialized and functionally integrated classes of mental organization. Each is dependent on the achievement of the previous one and, in its turn, achieves a functional co-existence with all the others. He called these classes the *presentative*, *presentative-representative*, *representative* and *re-representative*. In other words, mental development involves a cumulative increase in "the degree of representativeness in the states of consciousness" (Spencer 1885:55).

The presentative form of mental functioning has to do with simple localization and response to an incoming sensation, such as withdrawing the hand that has been bitten. The second form involves recognition and association into functioning patterns on the basis of similarity, proximity in time and space and continuity. The third advance (the representative) makes possible the building of further mental relations or ideas among these intuitive patterns: ideas concerning imagined experience not directly traceable to immediately perceived sensations. The thinker is thus released from the confines of the concrete and immediate and is able to operate from the perspective of other people, places and times. At the re-representative level the thinker is able to go further; it becomes possible to manipulate *symbolic representations* of relations expressed in representative thought and reapply them to the mental re-ordering of experience. Algebra is a good example of this. The assumption here is that something approaching the actual logic of external reality has been coordinated within.

The principles of sociology

Spencer introduced his three-volume *Principles of Sociology* with the suggestion that superorganic evolution, which is the concern of sociology, arises out of those rudimentary social forms displayed in the animal kingdom at large, by a process analogous to organic evolution. "A social organism, like an individual organism, undergoes modifications until it comes into equilibrium with environing conditions; and thereupon continues without further changes in structure" (ibid.:96). Occasionally a new combination of environmental pressures produces a new type of social organization, which then spreads and replaces inferior types. In both cases, "progressive differentiation of function is accompanied by progressive differentiation of structure" (ibid.:450), and these advances are passed on to future generations. Each social structure comprises interdependent units, and, in each case, *division of labour* is what makes the organism a living whole. The obvious difference is that a society is not a concrete, conscious entity, but one which is widely dispersed and without anything that could be described as a group consciousness. The interdependence of its parts (or units) is maintained in the social organism by communication, and in the other case by the various circulatory systems. Spencer claimed that in both situations size is augmented by two processes: simple multiplication of units and the union of increasingly complex groups of units. This means that increase in size is invariably accompanied by increase in complexity.

The evolutionary origin of institutions

Spencer explained that human societies have evolved a complex of structures that perform certain vital functions for the social group, the most essential being procreation and protection from enemies. In primitive societies enemies included aggressive human neighbours, animal predators and imagined entities such as animal spirits, ancestral ghosts and gods. Around this function there arose the military and religious institutions, which tended to define the entire nature of primitive society, including family forms. Another essential function was the exploitation, protection and distribution of material resources. Progress of this economic function beyond a crude survival level depended upon a relatively peaceful environment, as well as the successful operation of some form of law and education: institutions which, in turn, required, and subsequently enhanced, higher intellectual capacities. This meant that societies defined in terms of their economic institutions tend to be those at a relatively advanced stage of superorganic evolution, as distinct from those emphasizing warfare. Accordingly, Spencer described the entire process of social evolution in terms of a gradual advance from the *military* to the *industrial* stage of organization.

Spencer considered kinship structures to be indicators of the level of social evolution. For example, exogamy and endogamy (the requirement to select wives from either outside or within the home tribe) were rooted in the custom of taking captives as the spoils of war in the early phases of the military society. He traced the evolution of the family from promiscuity through polygamy to monogamy, as societies advanced towards industrialization. Spencer believed monogamy to be most evolved because it is associated with a highly developed conception of property; with the availability of equal numbers of each sex (the result of respite from continuous warfare) and with decreased mortality of offspring. He saw a relationship between the status of women and type of social organization and postulated that monogamy is essential for equality of the sexes. "It is clear," he wrote, "that monogamy has long been growing innate in civilized man" (ibid.:685). He concluded, as well, that "Evolution of the higher types of family, like higher types of society, has gone hand in hand with evolution of human intelligence and feeling" (ibid.:759). He anticipated a strengthening of the moral bond in monogamy as a result of more liberal divorce laws and protection of the rights of women in that marriages founded on the free choice and emotional preferences of *both* parties would reduce the occurence of extra-marital sex.

According to Spencer, the most vital of the institutional structures in modern society, and that which defines it, is the economy. With progress from military to industrial society the principles of voluntary cooperation and contract begin gradually to dominate over ascribed status and coercion. Free labour and limited-liability enterprise evolve together, and in the resulting competition for advantage there are losers as well as winners among both business owners and workers. (Companies go bankrupt and workers lose their jobs.) As in the case of the military society, some members are sacrificed for the sake of the group. "In the earlier stages the sacrifice takes the form of mortality in wars perpetually carried on during the struggle for existence between tribes and nations; in the later stages the sacrifice takes the form of mortality entailed by keen competition in the commercial struggle" (Spencer 1929:525).

Implications for the role of government

Like Martineau, Spencer opposed all government interference in the commercial realm as a matter of principle. However, he also agreed with her that there was a need for labour unions because of the harsh and cruel treatment meted out by employers. He accepted the union movement as an unfortunate and necessarily temporary restriction on competition. But for the more enlightened future he recommended a harnessing of the natural processes of competition and cooperation in a system of piecework combined with employee ownership of business enterprises. This would guarantee a maximum of excellence and productivity while requiring a minimum of supervision.

Spencer claimed that all available scientific evidence argued against the psychological and sociological premises of socialism. Nevertheless, he admitted its appeal. "A state of universal brotherhood is so tempting to the imagination and the existing state of competitive strife is so full of miseries, that endeavours to escape from the last and enter into the first are quite natural — inevitable even" (ibid.:577). He foresaw the failure of all experiments in socialism and predicted as well the failure of its proponents to learn from these failures. He expected them, instead, to claim that errors in application and management were at fault.

In his opinion, the fundamental error of socialists is that they ignore the distinction between the ethics of family life and the ethics of social life. The family's function is to ensure the survival of the *individuals* who ultimately make up society. On the other hand, a strong society is required for the survival of the *group*, which, in the long run, provides the necessary protection and social milieu for the functioning of families. No one individual can function without the group, but, because the reverse is not true, the survival of the group must always have priority over that of any particular individual. "Import into the family the law of society, and let children from infancy upwards have life-sustaining supplies only proportionate to their life-sustaining labours, and society disappears forthwith by the death of all its young. Import into society the law of the family, and let life-sustaining supplies be great in proportion as life-sustaining labours are small, and society decays from increase of its least worthy members, and decrease of its most worthy" (ibid.:580). Spencer spoke compellingly to the prophets of the socialism so popular among the intellectuals of his day. Those societies which abolish the natural relation between merits and benefits, he warned, will ultimately abolish themselves.

He went on to explain that not only is the socialist doctrine evolutionarily fatal in the long run; it is also psychologically and sociologically absurd. The system envisioned by socialism would make conflicting demands on people. While some of the members of the society are expected to be so enduringly *noble* that they willingly sacrifice their entire lives for the common good — happily witnessing most of what they work to produce going to the relatively unproductive — others are presumed to be so *ignoble* that they will just as happily claim their blatantly unearned spoils.

Spencer maintained that the doctrine is naive, as well about the nature of power and social organization. The centralized ownership and control of all property, means of production, transit, communication, education and defence would inevitably result in a powerful and impervious bureaucracy, he said. The managing elite would quickly position themselves as the new ruling class, "which, by being consolidated, would wield a power far beyond that of any present aristocracy" (ibid.:588).

The evolution of ethics

Spencer's ultimate goal was to provide a scientific basis for human ethics, so that it could be freed from a subservience to supernatural beliefs. He believed that humanity was approaching a transition period in which the traditional religious justification of moral rules would gradually be superseded by a more universally valid and workable regulative system based on the experience of the human race. He attempted to trace the evolution of ethics from its roots in the early beginnings of ecclesiastical institutions. These he saw as developing from the primitive belief in shadows that leave the body during sleep; through that of "doubles" which survive death; through clan totems and family cults propitiating dead ancestors; through worship of the tribe's dead rulers as gods; to polytheism resulting from tribal emigration and conquest; and finally, to the condition of a relatively settled kingdom or empire that favours the emergence of monotheism.

Spencer suggested that, during early stages of social evolution, belief in the divine origin of moral laws might be beneficial, and perhaps even necessary. He noted that threats of supernatural punishment are powerful deterrents for simple people psychologically unequipped to connect present behaviour to future consequences. However, "the modified human nature, produced by prolonged social discipline, evolves at length the conception of an independent ethics . . . [and eventually] the authority of the ethical consciousness becomes so high that theological dogmas are submitted to its judgment" (ibid.:154). At this point in evolution there is a gradual transition from supernaturalism to secularism in ethics.

Spencer conceded that there may well be a continuing role for a religious orientation which focuses on the mystery of life's origin, on the future evolutionary direction of human society and on the moral duties of individuals. Such observances and conceptualizations would have to be based on an agnosticism which recognizes the limits of the knowable and on a naturalism acknowledging the authority of scientific knowledge. To those who fear that the capacity for wonder will be destroyed by science he replied that the exact opposite has been amply demonstrated. "From the very beginning the progress of knowledge has been accomplished by an increasing capacity for wonder" (ibid.:173). He noted that it is not the rustic who sees the hatching of a chick or the sight of a fossil as wondrous. It is the biologist and the geologist!

The biological basis of morality

Spencer believed that any highly evolved natural morality would have to be grounded in fundamental biological drives: specifically, the pleasure/pain sensing apparatus which makes possible individual survival; and the urge to coordinate individual ends with those of the group, which facilitates the survival of offspring. In fact, he claimed that conduct becomes ethical only to the degree that it is consistent with mutual aid, or cooperation, in the life-adjustment process. It is that conduct which "simultaneously achieves the greatest totality of life in self, in offspring, and in fellow men" (Spencer 1904:26). He considered it equally true that, assuming that life brings more happiness than misery, and "taking into account immediate and remote effects on all persons, the good is universally the pleasurable" (ibid.:30). No ethical school, said Spencer, has ever avoided taking some combination of this desirable human activity and feeling-state as the ultimate moral aim, whether they use terms like brotherly love, divine blessedness or happiness.

According to Spencer, all current ethical systems have one grave defect. *They neglect causal connections in human behaviour*! They fail to understand that humans do what they do because of their social situation, their psychological equipment and their biological inheritance. They incorporate rules for conduct that ignore all these factors and assume free will or supernatural guidance. Spencer hoped to correct this situation by putting all the strands of his synthetic knowledge into the service of a more appropriate natural ethic.

Moral development in individuals

Spencer set out to show how moral development, at the psychological level, builds upon simple biological sensations and upon the elementary adjustments of acts to biological ends or goals. "The mental process by which adjustment of acts to ends is effected, and which . . . becomes the subject matter of ethical judgments is . . . divisible into feelings constituting the motive and the thoughts through which the motive is shaped and finally issues in action" (ibid.:105). It is a developmental process, culminating, in advanced cases, in "those long deliberations during which, the probabilities of various consequences are estimated, and the promptings of correlative feelings balanced"

(ibid.). Spencer predicted that, for mature people in advanced industrial societies in a peaceful world, moral behaviour will eventually become natural,
for as the judging and weighing process develops into entrenched habit, it will
gradually assume an intuitive "form" capable of being transmitted from generation to generation. Only at that future time, however, would it be even remotely true to say that people are born good!

Ultimate moral principles

Spencer was resigned to the idea that real moral progress must await peaceful
relations among societies. As long as any society is threatened from without,
the norms of militancy will prevail, and these are essentially immoral. However, in his nineteenth-century innocence, Spencer believed that world peace
was immanent, and that the norms of industrial society would soon become
universal. At this stage, he said, the fulfilment of contract becomes the chief
commandment. "So that beyond the primary requirement to harmonious co-
existence in a society, that its units shall not directly aggress one another, there
comes this secondary requirement: that they shall not indirectly aggress by
breaking agreements" (ibid.:146). Spencer declared that the foundation for
the moral principle of *justice* would thus be established at the level of group
relations.

The other necessary and sufficient principle is *beneficence*. In Spencer's
view, efforts to further the welfare of others feed back on the actor to such an
extent that the rational egoism (or enlightened self-interest) fuelling cooperation is really the source of altruism. He saw no discontinuity between the egoism of the infant and the advanced social altruism necessary for the principle
of beneficence to work. Natural egoism, he noted, is required for survival; indeed pure altruism at the biological level would have resulted in extinction for
the species. But if this egoism had not been extended to include offspring, and
thereby to evolve into family altruism, that would have been suicidal as well.
At a more advanced stage of moral development, family altruism becomes extended, in turn, to social altruism, as a more inclusive reciprocity is comprehended.

Spencer explained that all this has to do with the necessary continuity between means and ends. Personal gratification, when selected as an immediate
goal, becomes instead the *means* to a disharmony in relations with others, and
thus carries the *end* of unhappiness in its wake. Conversely, the goal of trying
to achieve happiness for those upon whose reciprocal actions one depends becomes the *means* of increasing the general fund of happiness, and thus
achieves the *end* of greater personal gratification. The principle of beneficence
is grounded on this reciprocity and the continuity of means and ends in social
relations.

Spencer believed that nothing in ethics is absolute except the ultimate principles of justice and beneficence; these being justifiable in terms of species survival. For this reason they must supersede any moral rules or rights logically implied or required by them, as well as cultural-specific ideals and mores — all of which he defined as "lower-order." Because it is impossible to predict with certainty the consequences of daily decisions, most moral judgements must concern courses of action that are either more or less wrong. The "absolute ethics" applicable to all humanity therefore formulates the ideal or ultimate criterion; it establishes that standard from which all individual moral choices ("relative ethics") must diverge to some extent. Spencer thought that this approach would ensure against the establishment of lower-order codes of conduct that are inevitably contradictory when universally applied. He mentioned the example of societies that teach two mutually exclusive sets of rules: the ethics of enmity (towards outsiders) and the ethics of amity (towards insiders).

Ideals and rules for moral behaviour

Spencer noted that all ethical systems throughout history have dealt with the same fundamental social principles of justice and beneficence and the same ideals for moral behaviour. These are: obedience to authority; condemnation of aggression; being guided by the "voice" of conscience; honesty in fulfilling contracts; industry and chastity. His proposed system incorporated all of these, while explaining them in a new way. Moral *authority* in his scheme went far beyond simple obedience to rules. It had to do, instead, with the definition of rights and duties, as in freedom from personal restraint and assault, and from shirked responsibility and broken trust in social and commercial contracts. He considered obedience and generosity to be lower-order virtues than the empathy and reason that make possible assessment of consequences, in terms of persons injured and contracts forsworn. He felt that there is much scope for obedience and generosity under the despotic rule common to military society, but little for justice and beneficence so that the latter tend to function as ethical principles only with the onset of industrial democracy.

Conscience, according to Spencer, is the inner compulsion to recognize "those conditions by fulfilment of which happiness is achieved or misery avoided" (ibid.:335). It is built up through experience and, so far, seems not to have been incorporated into heritable intuitive forms. He conceded that, at least in the current stage of human evolution, "it is impossible to hold that men have in common an innate perception of right and wrong" (ibid.:471).

Concerning *industry*, Spencer was of the opinion that there is little virtue simply in the discipline of labour for its own sake. "The virtue of work consists essentially in the performance of such actions as suffice to meet the cost of maintaining self and dependents and discharging social duties, while the disgracefulness of idleness essentially consists in taking from the common stock the means of living while doing nothing either to add to it or otherwise to further men's happiness" (ibid.:433-34). As for *chastity*, Spencer saw it as a necessary virtue in that it has furthered human evolution in at least three ways: (1) it is conducive to the nurture of offspring; (2) it helps to establish the concept of social limits to *aggression*, as sexual marauding is the most elemental form and motive for assault; and (3) it prevents the severing of the lower from the higher components of the sexual relation, so that a more evolved love becomes possible.

The principle of natural equity

Spencer identified a second-order principle required by his principle of justice: the Principle of Natural Equity. This in turn implies a number of rights, including the right to physical integrity (or freedom and security of person); freedom of movement; access to the resources of nature (such as unpolluted water and land) and to incorporeal property such as one's mental products and unsullied reputation. Also included is the right of free exchange and contract, free industry, open profession of ultimate beliefs, free speech and publication, and freedom to bequeath property (but not to behave so as to restrict how subsequent generations can use the earth).

Spencer believed that it is necessary for society to protect these rights because it is all too easy for the strong or "superior" to oppress the "inferior." It is clear that, in spite (or perhaps because) of his belief in "survival of the fittest," he wanted the struggle to be fair. He opposed the demand, prevalent in the class-ridden England of his day, that those already generously endowed by nature and society be given *more* rights than lesser citizens. He noted that the guarantee of equal rights to inferiors in no way interferes with any legitimate claim by a superior. He pointed out that "in denying to inferior faculty a sphere of action equal to that which superior faculty has is to add an artificial hardship to a natural hardship. . . . Sympathy might contrariwise urge that, by way of compensation for inherited disabilities, they should have extended opportunities" (Spencer 1900:158).

Because the foregoing served as a preamble to Spencer's discussion of the rights of women, one can only assume that at least one example of the "inferior faculty" of which he spoke was the feminine gender. However, he did part company with most of the men of his generation when he argued for equality of the sexes. This was in spite of his reservation about political participation for women *until* they have assumed equal military responsibilities with men. He also believed that women are too carried away by the events of the moment, and by their emotions, to be trustworthy as voters. He noted that there was already too much of this deplorable tendency among lesser men. "Had women votes, this absorption in the proximate and personal to the exclusion of the remote and impersonal would be still greater and the immense mischiefs at present produced would be augmented" (ibid.:195). Also, he concluded that women's marital conditions throughout evolution have predisposed them towards a worship of power and subservience to authority — hence in the direction of conservativism.

If Spencer was torn in applying his theories to women, he had even greater difficulty with the problem of relief to the poor. He was convinced that "each new effort to mitigate the penalties of improvidence has the inevitable effect of adding to the numbers of the improvident" (ibid.:393). Yet he knew that to allow the principle of survival of the fittest to operate "in all its sternness" was impossible, given the evolved level of morality in industrial society. His reluctant conclusion that "the problem is insoluble" no doubt contributed to the depression which plagued the last years of his life.

A profound and lasting influence

The influence of Herbert Spencer on social-scientific thought has been pervasive and long lasting, although few modern social scientists have read his works. In fact, Herbert Spencer is remembered by many not only as a giant of nineteenth-century intellectual history, but as one of the founders of modern social science. His Principle of Natural Equity with its definition of individual rights is echoed to this day by the strong libertarian bias within modern culture and by lovers of freedom everywhere. He was far ahead of his time in his concern for the environment. His ideas on social evolution permeate the works of countless scholars, including Nietzsche, Bergson and Durkheim. His attempt at a comprehensive theory of biological, psychological and sociological functioning, and his resolution of the old dichotomies such as means versus ends — and subjective versus objective — gave new direction to social theory. Much of his "synthetic knowledge" can be seen reflected in the thought of Dewey and Durkheim, the general philosophy of Santayana, the epistemology of Russell, the theories of Julian Huxley and the psychology of Piaget. His powerful concept of equilibrium (coupled with his insight concerning the significance for evolution of the inherent instability of the first rudimentary life forms) provided the foundation for modern systems-theory. Beatrice Webb recalled how he had taught her to approach the study of social institutions as one would aspects of the physical environment, and he may well have done the same for at least two generations of sociology students.

Spencer's weaknesses, however, were as significant as his strengths. Try as he would to operate as an empirical scientist, he was by nature an ideological thinker who began with answers rather than questions. Thomas Huxley said that tragedy for Herbert Spencer was a good deduction ruined by an inconvenient fact. And the one deduction which remained impervious to all conflicting evidence was his belief in the progressive accumulation by the species of favourable characteristics acquired during the life experience of individuals. This is the source of the contradiction concerning the problem of the poor that so depressed him in his last days. It is this that was used by some of his followers to turn an otherwise invaluable contribution to our understanding of human behaviour into a scholarly justification of the ruthless individualism of the American robber barons and the imperialism of Victorian Britain. The destructive legacy of Social Darwinism strikes a discordant note in Spencer's otherwise noble framework, a framework incorporating a remarkably prescient theory of natural ethics into an integrated, evolutionarily based social science.

References for Chapter Eight

Encyclopedia Britannica. 1989. 15th ed., s.v. "Spencer, Herbert."

McGraw-Hill Encyclopedia of World Biography. 1973. s.v. "Herbert Spencer."

Spencer, Herbert. 1885. *The Principles of Sociology*. Vol. 1. London: D. Appleton.

————. 1887. *The Factors of Organic Evolution*. New York: J. Fitzgerald, Humboldt Library.

————. 1898. *The Principles of Biology*. Vol. 1. New York: D. Appleton.

————. 1899a. *The Principles of Biology*. Vol. 2. New York: D. Appleton.

————. 1899b. *The Principles of Psychology*. 2 vols. New York: D. Appleton.

————. 1904. *The Principles of Ethics*. Vols. 1 and 2. London: Williams and Norgate.

————. 1929. *The Principles of Sociology*. Vols. 2 and 3. London: D. Appleton.

Webb, Beatrice. 1926. *My Apprenticeship*. London: Cambridge University Press, p. 31-38 and 294-95.

Nine

What Price Immortality?

The Faustian Tragedy of Sigmund Freud

> Oh God, but Art is long,
> And short is Life! And ever,
> Despite mine uttermost endeavour,
> Will fears my brain and bosom throng.
> To find some method man is ever trying,
> By which to reach the fountainhead —
> And ere one half the weary way is sped,
> Why, a poor devil finds he's dying.
> — Johann Wolfgang von Goethe, *Faust*

Nowhere had there been a more enthusiastic supporter of Darwin than Ernst Haeckel of Germany and Austria. The ideas of this respected scientist, writer and teacher provided a powerful counter-influence in German-speaking universities to the prevailing philosophy of romantic idealism, and to Kant's transcendentalism. However, the naturalistic evolutionary thinker whose ideas may well have been most appealing to the students in those universities during the closing decades of the nineteenth century was neither Haeckel nor Darwin, but a philosopher who charted a very different, and peculiarly iconoclastic, course.

Friedrich Nietzsche (1844-1900) epitomized the ultimate disillusionment with both the rationalism and the empiricism of Enlightenment thinkers. However, there is a direct line to him from Marx. Marx had turned Hegel on his head while accepting the basic ontological grounding of Hegelianism; Nietzsche, in his turn, did the same for Marx. Marx saw history as inherently progressive and humankind as ultimately perfectible. For Nietzsche, the human record was instead a tale of degeneration that began with the death of Socrates. Its characters were merely the most unfortunate species of animal: a race the majority of which was cursed by memory and a culturally induced conscience to forever strive impotently for control of its essentially unpredictable tomorrows.

References for this chapter are on p. 170-71.

Whereas Marx had viewed his "scientific" historicism as the salvation of humankind, Nietzsche (accepting Marx's scientism as legitimate scientific inquiry and Kant's *a priori* reason as the ultimate ground of knowing) indicted science as the enemy of humanity and reason as its slave. For Marx's dialectic of history advancing inexorably toward the goal of human perfection Nietzsche substituted a Lamarckian process of biological evolution with an assumed cosmic moral imperative of ultimate survival of the most powerful and uniquely clear-sighted *Übermensch* (Supermen). Whereas Marx had presented the possibility of "midwifing" a future egalitarian Utopia, Nietzsche saw democracy as a sign of decadence. He looked back to a romanticized Golden Age in which the Hellenic nobility exemplified his concept of the culturally transcendent Superman, and where the masses supposedly had lived in and for the moment — freed in yet another way from the prison of cultural imperatives. Marx saw the evolution of inorganic and organic matter as ordered by natural laws discoverable by scientists. For Nietzsche, all existence was the expression of varying degrees of the "will to power": the attempt of everything to transcend itself by exerting increasing control over its surroundings. Where Marx had updated Rousseau's "General Will" into an inherently civilizing and progressive reflection of the true interests of the proletariat, Nietzsche's "will to power" was essentially a Dionysian impetus imbuing relatively organized entities with increased power to direct the course of change in their own interests.

Nietzsche's theories comprise a mixture of empirically unwarranted and contradictory pronouncements along with a few shrewd (but scarcely original) observations. If one removes the anthropocentric "will" from his analysis of evolution, his claim about the factor of organization makes good sense; but Spencer had expressed it better. The same can be said for Nietzsche's comments on the social source and control-function of conscience — but hardly for his conclusion that conscience is therefore a negative force. However, although he was accused of profound amorality because of his attack on conscience and guilt as well as on all supernatural sources and justifications of morality, he did contribute some useful ideas on the human valuing process.

Surprisingly, given his abhorrence of reason and science, Nietzsche considered values amenable to objective assessment in terms of their observable effects. And his desired "living in the moment" included the concept of "eternal return": the notion that one should live in the present so as not to find oneself in the position of wishing at some future time that one had chosen to act otherwise. All this would seem to demand the type of reasoned, broadly scientific approach to valuing that he rejected out of hand. The other major contradiction in Nietzsche's thought is the one shared with Marx and found in the following century in Karl Mannheim's "sociology of knowledge." It is that, although humankind by definition is a culture-producing animal trapped irretrievably in a culturally shaped perspective on reality, *one uniquely favoured class* of these same humans is nonetheless capable of transcending that entrapment and piercing the mystery to intuit the underlying truth.

Haeckel had differed from Nietzsche in accepting Darwin's central explanation of natural selection as the engine fuelling evolution. Haeckel was also convinced that the implications of this mechanism for the development of human mental processes would someday determine the subject matter for a science of psychology. This idea must have posed a challenge for many ambitious and thoughtful scholars. One who heard it (along with Nietzsche's messages) was a student in the Medical Faculty of the University of Vienna, Sigmund Freud.

Early life and career

Freud was born in Freiberg, Moravia, in 1856, the son of Jacob Freud, a Jewish wool merchant. He was the eldest of a family of eight children born to his father's third wife Amalia Nathanson, the daughter of a wealthy merchant. Sigmund's family seems to have suffered a marginal financial existence, at times living in one room. When he was about three they moved to Vienna. There he was raised as the eldest and his mother's favourite, his three older half-brothers having married and moved away. He was an excellent student, entering university at the age of seventeen with a broad background in both the sciences and classics. He later wrote that he had wanted to specialize in science but discovered that he was emotionally and intellectually unqualified for it. However, throughout a leisurely eight-year stint in the Medical Faculty he was thoroughly immersed in the scientific perspective and became committed to the goal of following in the footsteps of Charles Darwin. He also became familiar with the theories of Schopenhauer and Nietzsche: a fact that was to have a significant impact on his own life's work.

Even before obtaining his M.D. in 1881, Freud had been doing research in neurology at the Brücke Institute. The following year he was given a residency in neurology, and in 1885 became lecturer in neuropathology at the university. This title established him as a specialist in his field. By the end of the 1880s, while still in his early thirties, Freud had achieved considerable success. Besides his post as lecturer, he was Honorary Consultant to the Institute of Children's Diseases and Director of their Neurology Department. In addition, he was married with a rapidly increasing family and a popular private practice dealing with diseases of the nervous system.

The turning point

The decade of the 1890s, when Freud approached and passed the age of forty, seems to have been a watershed for him. He must have felt that if ever he were to have a creative period this would have to be it. A few years earlier he had received a stipend to spend six months in Paris studying under Jean-Martin Charcot, the neuropsychiatrist renowned for his use of hypnosis for the treatment of hysterics. Many of Charcot's highly publicized "cures" for this mysterious disease — witnessed by Freud — were later shown to have been frauds perpetrated by his students, but Freud seems not to have been implicated. Freud's first publication, "On the Psychical Mechanism of Hysterical Phenomena" came out soon after this training period. He retained a strong interest in hysteria from then on and was convinced that it was a culturally induced illness. However, he decided to look for other therapeutic tools in addition to hypnosis. He began to collaborate with his former professor and mentor, Josef Breuer, using the "free association" method whereby patients relate whatever comes to mind in response to selected words or images. The theory was that such intuitive responses would provide clues concerning unresolved problems.

Two other developments in Freud's life initiated in the previous decade became particularly significant in the 1890s. These were his increasing involvement with cocaine and his association with a fellow medical doctor named Wilhelm Fleiss. In the mid-1880s Freud had launched an enthusiastic investigation into the pharmacological properties of cocaine — then a little-known drug. He seems to have been interested only in its potential as a mood alterer and was apparently quite unaware of its addictive properties.

His intimate relationship with Fleiss, who acted as his personal physician and confidant, lasted for more than a decade. Fleiss was obsessed with numerology and astrology and with a bizarre theory concerning the nose as the seat of eroticism, all of which Freud accepted as legitimate scientific speculation. During this period both men seem to have used cocaine regularly, supposedly for the treatment of "nose problems" of increasing frequency and severity. Freud began to suffer as well from severe mood swings and paranoia and eventually from worrying cardiac symptoms. For all of this, the treatment for both men was invariably more cocaine.

A colleague noticed that cocaine killed pain, but Freud seems to have had no interest in ascertaining its value as an anaesthetic. The colleague focused on this and pioneered the use of the drug in eye surgery. Meanwhile Freud, considering himself the discoverer of cocaine, was administering it freely to family and friends. He published a paper in 1885 lauding it as a magic drug and recommending its administration by injection. A much-loved friend, Ernst Fleischl, who was addicted to morphine, came to Freud for help. He was promptly given cocaine in liberal doses and became badly addicted. At the time, Freud was writing, "I take very small doses of it regularly against depression and indigestion with the most brilliant success" (Jones:54). He also seemed to consider it necessary for sexual prowess in his marriage. In the words of his disciple and biographer, Ernest Jones, "To achieve virility and enjoy the bliss of union with the beloved, he had forsaken the straight and narrow path of sober scientific work on brain anatomy, and seized a surreptitious shortcut" (ibid.:57). In 1891 Fleischl died suddenly from an overdose, and Freud struggled for years to convince himself that he was not to blame.

The shortcut that Freud had seized allowed him to avoid entirely the sort of painstaking observation and recording of facts to which his hero, Darwin, had devoted his life. He turned instead to introspection into his own fantasies, fears and frustrated sexual desires and to the testimony of dimly recalled childhood experience. His research methodology became that distinctive form of speculative, abstract theorizing so deeply embedded in the Germanic culture. His considerable writing ability, involving a clever use of mythological and religious metaphor, became a powerful tool which he substituted for the absent factual base. According to Jones, "When Freud found in himself previously unknown attitudes toward his parents he felt immediately they were not peculiar to himself and that he had discovered something about human nature in general . . . and the idea of collecting statistics on the matter was something quite alien to him" (ibid.:66).

Professional success

Freud's first book, *Aphasia*, published in 1891, was the last of his neurological writings. In 1895 he co-authored, with Josef Breuer, *Studies in Hysteria*. This marked the beginning of a long list of speculative publications. It marked, as well, the beginning of a falling-out with Breuer, who apparently was sceptical of Freud's increasing emphasis on sex as causal.

Two years later Freud abandoned his "seduction theory" which had focused on father-child incest as the source of hysteria in girls. He decided, instead, that the childhood sexual abuse reported by his hysterical female patients could not possibly be as widespread as their stories indicated. As he recounted it, he was forced to come to this conclusion when "I was at last obliged to recognize that these scenes of seduction had never taken place, and that they were only phantasies which my patients had made up or *which I myself had perhaps forced on them*" (Freud 1952:65, emphasis added). At the same time he initiated a self-analysis, and his own dreams began to unearth similar fantasies from early childhood. With his propensity to universalize personal experiences (and apparently with an endless supply of troubling dreams) Freud had no shortage of material from which to spin the new theory which he was soon to introduce.

The Freudian era bursts upon the world

The Interpretation of Dreams was published in 1900, followed by *The Psycho-pathology of Everyday Life* in 1904. Both became popular almost overnight. Sometime between these two events Freud's life took another turn. He broke with Fleiss, and probably from cocaine as well. The decade to follow was fruitful and happy. His theories multiplied; he published voluminously and his ideas spread. The first years of the new century saw the beginnings of the Vienna Psychoanalytical Society and the formation of small "Freud groups" throughout Europe. Freud began to attract important converts: Karl Jung, Karl Abraham, Sandor Ferenczi, Hans Sachs, Peter Jones, Otto Rank, Alfred Adler and Wilhelm Stekel. An intimate correspondence with Jung replaced that which he had enjoyed for fifteen years with Fleiss. In fact, throughout the first decade of the new century, Freudianism was considerably influenced by Karl Jung. Freud's Oedipus theory of sons devouring their fathers in the primordial horde is very reminiscent of Jung's mythologically based pantheism. In 1908 the First International Congress of Psychoanalysts was held in Salzburg. In 1909 Freud made a speaking tour of the United States, an experience which he hated because of the lack of respect accorded him by the American academics who were at that time more accustomed than were his German and Austrian colleagues to sharp and open exchange of ideas. However, the following year Freud's ambition for world renown was rewarded by the formation of the International Psychoanalytical Association with Jung as its president.

The end of the first decade of the century marked the apex of Freud's career. Very shortly, dissension began to appear in the ranks of his disciples. First Adler became sceptical of the sexual basis of Freud's theory and the extent of its reliance upon elaborate and unverifiable structures and strivings within the unconscious. Stekel, too, began to doubt some of Freud's cherished doctrines. Then — the bitterest blow of all — Jung departed in 1914, after an extended period of increasing ideological divergence.

Jung had formulated a competing model of the unconscious: one that was material only in its lower reaches and assumed spiritual form at its higher levels through a mysterious incorporation from the "collective unconscious" of "archetypes." Jung believed these to be innate embodiments of the origin and destiny of humanity — accessible in some mysterious way from an inherited non-material "unconscious" and symbolized in myth. Archetypes are presumed to involve a subjective knowledge more valid than the objective kind: the truth of which can be recognized by sensations of "oneness" with the universe. There is little wonder that Freud became angry at what he considered an attempt to construct a loophole for the re-entry of mysticism — especially from the follower to whom he had written in 1909, "I formally adopted you as my oldest son and anointed you successor and crown prince" (Schur 1972:193).

Some time later, Ferenczi recanted, then Rank left. Abraham, the most loyal of all of the followers, died suddenly. Freud and his family suffered through the hardships of wartime. After the war they lost all their savings and insurance in the collapse of the Austrian economy. In 1923, Freud contracted cancer, from which he suffered horribly for the last sixteen years of his life. Through it all he continued his writing, turning toward more broadly sociological, historical and philosophical concerns. Some of these later works, such as *The Future of an Illusion*, *Civilization and its Discontents*, and *Moses and Monotheism*, may well be his most durable. The Nazis allowed him to leave for England in 1938. He died there the following year, mercifully never knowing that most of his family of origin ended their lives in Nazi death camps.

Major premises of Freudianism

What, precisely, *are* the ideas that Freud left behind him? What about their credibility and usefulness? To begin with, all of his original work was based on the following four premises:

- The core aspect of human development, from infancy on, is *sexual* — in fact it is this sexual component which defines and dictates the entire process.
- The key source of human motivation is the *unconscious*: a vast reservoir containing: (a) "race memories" or traces of pivotal events acquired during the cultural evolution of the species; (b) instinctual drives, including repressed sexual desires of a socially destructive nature; (c) fantasies created out of an interaction between (a) and (b) and which have become charged with guilt; and (d) forgotten experiences of actual happenings.
- The contents of the individual's unconscious can be brought to the surface and *the harmful, guilt-ridden fantasies distinguished from the other components* and neutralized: all this through the guidance of a psychoanalyst. This therapist is able to recognize dreams, free-word associations and slips of the tongue and behaviour in everyday life as indices of repressed sexual yearnings — and to explain to the patient the deeper meaning of these.
- The unconscious is the essential psychic reality. In its innermost nature it is as much unknown to us as is the reality of the external world, and it is as incompletely presented by the data of consciousness as is the external world by the communication of our senses. This means that introspection will never lead to knowledge of the psyche. On the other hand, the study of dreams, free-word associations and slips of the tongue *is* a valuable means of achieving "a thorough understanding of the structure and functioning of the mental apparatus" (Freud 1952:613).

In Freud's mind there was no mysticism involved, for he saw the psyche in a strictly naturalistic sense, as the product of biological evolution. He believed that, in time, research in physiology would confirm the structure and function of the unconscious as well as the conscious parts of this natural entity. And he became just as firmly convinced that he could anticipate those answers. So, in a series of speculations based ostensibly on case studies but, in fact, largely on the universalizing of his own conflicts, imaginings, yearnings and dreams, he began to map the unknown country of the human psyche.

Like many philosophers before him, Freud saw the psyche as an amalgam of three parts. These were: (1) the conscious, reasoning, remembering, learning subject (the "I" or "ego"); (2) the objective "it" or "id," representing the "unconscious" or darker Dionysian undercurrent of instinctual drives, incoherent images and emotions carried as unacknowledged baggage by the knowing self; and (3) the conscience (sometimes referred to as the "ego-ideal" or the "super-ego"): a conscious image of the ideal self created out of the values and standards acquired through the disciplinary actions of *loved* parental figures (usually fathers) along with associated guilt feelings embedded in the unconscious, which operate as deterrents to wickedness.

The nature of individual development

Freud posited his theory of sexually defined development based on the foregoing structure and premises. He imagined that, within the psyche, two powerful biological drives struggle for supremacy. One of these is the "libido" (itself the mental representation of the conflicting currents of ego-instinct and sexual instinct) which operates as a push toward extension of life beyond the individual. The other is the aggressive or "death-instinct" which he called *Thanatos*: a drive to complete the individual life span.

For Freud all development is sexual by definition; it follows that child development means the evolution of infant sexuality within the individual. The process moves through (1) the "auto-erotic" stage, (2) the "oral" stage, (3) the "anal-sadistic" stage and (4) the "phallic" stage, which begins at puberty when the Oedipus complex comes into play and culminates when the primacy of the genitals is established.

The Oedipal phase is an important and universal aspect of child sexuality in which the male child and the female react quite differently. The male identifies with the mother and sees the father as a hated and feared rival for the mother's affections. He desires her as his own sexual object and wants to kill his father. He then develops a fear of castration as a result of his conscience imposing guilt for these hateful desires. Freud believed that this Oedipal phase had its origin in a pre-tribal, "primal horde" stage in the evolution of the species, and that traces of it are universally present in the unconscious. With normal development the phase passes, and the male child gradually moves through a bisexual stage to an identification with his father as he achieves puberty.

The female child, on the other hand, identifies at first with the father and suffers from "penis envy" as her clitoris seems a poor substitute for the male appendage. She blames her mother for this deficiency. "Latent homosexuality" in both sexes results from repressed wishes for identification with the opposite-gender parent and is caused by a failure to move beyond the Oedipal phase.

Many other developmental problems arise from the Oedipus complex, which involves the repression (rather than successful sublimation) of the foregoing unacceptable and unacknowledged sexual yearnings and their accompanying guilt feelings. These can result in the creation of fantasies of seductions by the parent which have never actually occurred. It is the most common of the many things that can go wrong in child sexual development. Other potential hazards involve a continuing oral- or anal-fixation, occurring whenever development becomes frozen in one of these early stages. In fact, any undesirable experiences in infancy can stultify or deform the developmental process; therefore nursing, weaning and toilet-training practices are crucial.

Freud recognized the difficulty of distinguishing fantasies caused by arrested or distorted development from forgotten experiences of actual events. Certainly he believed that his patients could not tell the difference. But he based his entire system of therapy on the assumption that this could indeed be accomplished by the therapist.

So far, the hypotheses just described are dealing with effects on the *unconscious* of stimuli both from the outside environment and the innate sexual and aggressive instincts within. Freud's theory also encompassed the *conscious ego*, and the conflict between it and the other two aspects of the personality: "id" and "super-ego." He saw ego-development as resulting from tension between the "pleasure principle" (a striving for the realization and continuation of pleasurable feelings) and the "reality principle" (the need to accommodate to external reality). Here, Freud sounded very much like Hume and Spencer as he claimed that "a given process is always stimulated by an unpleasant state of tension, and then takes a path so that the final result coincides with a relaxation of this tension, that is, with an avoidance of the unpleasant or a production of pleasure" (Rickman:36).

In discussing the substitution of the reality principle for the pleasure principle (the appropriate aim of education) he noted that, "a momentary pleasure, uncertain in its results, is given up, but only to gain in a new way, an assured pleasure coming later" (ibid.). Freud felt that religion, with its illusion of a future life, is a mythical projection of this necessary educational goal. He believed that science represents humanity's best efforts to achieve the desired end of operating in accordance with the reality principle. Art he saw as a rejection of the reality principle due to the artist's inability to come to terms with it. According to Freud, art involves a substitution of created fantasies for real experience. These substituted products then enter the culture as aspects of an inevitably altered reality. Objects of art are subsequently judged on their own merits as more or less helpful and universally significant reflections upon the dilemmas of human existence.

The nature of psychoanalytic therapy

Freud's dream theory was derived from the elaborate structure of ideas summarized above. He explained dreams in terms of unconscious wish-fulfilment. A residue of thoughts resulting from the day's experiences breaks loose from the inhibition of interests that permits sleep and becomes connected with repressed yearnings. These new configurations then emerge into consciousness as dreams. Dream analysis and the technique of free association are the chief tools of psychoanalysis: the royal road to the scientific study of psychic structures and to self-knowledge.

Freud expected this new therapy to be of great value in the treatment of neurotics. According to his theory, neurosis is caused by failure to sublimate an inappropriate desire and the painful guilt associated either with the desire or with the memory of some connected event. Neurotics have driven the memory out of consciousness, in order to save themselves psychic pain, but the wish has merely gone underground to the unconscious. It emerges in a surrogate form to which the same painful sensations attach themselves (the "defence mechanism"). For the neurotic, anything is better than facing up to reality; but it is precisely this agonizing, time-consuming process that the therapist must encourage.

A dialectical "Social Darwinism"

It is impossible to understand Freud's sexual model of human development without an awareness of the philosophical systems that both inspired and limited him. We need to know that he considered his instinct theory to be the only credible extension of Darwinism into the realm of psycho-social and cultural affairs. Above all else, he saw himself as an evolutionary theorist: the one destined to complete the Copernican revolution. As he explained it, Copernicus had destroyed geocentrism, and Darwin had done the same for the illusion that humanity was somehow different from and sovereign over all the rest of creation. Freud believed that his theory had accomplished a similar undermining of the illusion of free will: the belief (still strong in Nietzsche) in the sovereignty of the ego. This was the goal that drove him. This was the challenge that required his theory to remain monist in Haeckel's naturalistic sense, and demanded from him, not the habits of the free-floating speculative philosopher, but those of a scientist.

From the beginning, however, Freud's work was flawed by three serious errors concerning the nature of evolution. Like his contemporary, Herbert Spencer, he never really understood the mechanism of natural selection.

Freud's evolutionary world view was a Nietzschean version of Lamarckism in which the mythological figures dominating early pagan cultures and the emotions driving the primal hordes were somehow passed along the generations by means of a heritable unconscious. A related error involved his captivation with Darwin's notion of sexual selection, and his subsequent distortion of that aspect of evolution. A third had to do with his failure to recognize the implications of the Darwinian revolution for the concept of organic causality.

Few people even today fully comprehend Darwin's crucial insight about the nature of organic causality — as distinct from the push-pull (or "mechanistic") operation of cause and effect at the inorganic level. Darwin had demonstrated how, once life emerged, natural selection operated according to an after-the-fact causality, whereby the *consequences* of the organism's lifetime of environmental forays feed back to shape the species' future by determining which organisms live to reproduce. Freud, intent on applying the rules of Newtonian physics to the contents of the psyche, missed entirely the implications of this revolutionary breakthrough.

He was handicapped as well by the teleological perspective dominant in the culture of his time and argued so convincingly by Arthur Schopenhauer. The older idea of a Great Chain of Being was still prevalent in biology. This involved a belief that separate species emerged intact at each step or link in the chain: all leading to humankind as the ultimate creation. Non-Darwinian evolutionists all assumed that evolution had to be aiming *toward* some predestined goal and inherently *progressive* in its unfolding.

Freud made a second fatal error concerning the key evolutionary concept of sexual selection. He may have been influenced by Schopenhauer on this as well. The latter had claimed that at the root of the "will to live," driving all organic change processes, is the sexual passion. Spencer had also emphasized the priority of the amatory instinct in humans. And Darwin had suggested that, because reproduction is so crucial to the evolution of the species, the process (as well as appendages and behaviours) by which individuals attract potential mates must be of great significance. Freud transferred this idea from the species to the level of the organism. He postulated that, if sex drives species formation it must be the innate force energizing all individual development as well!

The third major mistake followed from Freud's failure to understand the nature of natural selection. He was probably influenced here by Spencer, whose works on biology, psychology, sociology and ethics were widely distributed during the last decade of the nineteenth century. Like Spencer, Freud thought that the characteristics acquired during an individual's lifetime are somehow passed along in the evolutionary process, so that aspects of culture (or civilization) are inherited as biological propensities. Spencer developed an extremely sophisticated explanation concerning this process, which was later taken up and built upon by Jean Piaget. Compared to these theories, Freud's mythologically based model was crude in the extreme. But it had an advantage in its powerful appeal to the imagination.

Freud decided that instincts had to be the repositories of all the past experience of the human race. And, because he saw species reproduction as the "aim" of evolution — and sex its energizing force — he reasoned that experience could only be stored in some sort of sexual form. Only sexually relevant bits of species information would be sufficiently useful to be passed into succeeding human psyches by means of inherited biological instincts.

At this point it was necessary to employ the concept of the "unconscious." Freud believed that the conscious ego has no awareness of much of what actually motivates its actions. He decided that the unconscious layer of the psyche must be a vast storehouse of the earlier defining sexual experience of the human race, and that aspects of this might possibly be revealed to our consciousness through dreams and inadvertent comments and behaviours.

We now understand that there is no possibility for the inheritance of race memory or any messages from an individual's current life experience. Modern biology has demonstrated conclusively that genetic instructions follow a one-way street, through inherited DNA rather than the life experience of the individual. But cherished dogma dies hard, and it seems to take more than scientific knowledge to storm the bulwarks of "true belief," even today. And we must remember that Freud had no such information.

Two characteristics of the social science of Freud's time also helped to lead him astray. Both were attempts to imitate physics. Today, with our more sophisticated understanding of the nature of scientific inquiry, we would call these "scientisms": procedures with the surface *appearance* but neither the appropriate conceptual base and means of measuring, nor the essential rigour and discipline of science. One of these was the widespread tendency to look for universal, immutable *laws* governing individual development and successive forms of society. This was usually combined with the teleological outlook bequeathed by certain of the Enlightenment thinkers and revived by Kant and Schopenhauer. The other was a preference for defining social phenomena as discrete categories or as flows of energy: both assumed to be readily quantifiable.

Marx's theory demonstrated both of these tendencies. So, too, did Freud's. Both thinkers were convinced that, in adopting these approaches, they were being scientific.

There was yet another philosophical premise shared by Marx and Freud. It was the Hegelian dialectic. Only by fitting Freud's theory into a dialectical framework does it begin to assume a sense of inner cohesiveness and logic. In the absence of a recognition of the dialectic as an organizing principle, Freudianism is indeed the confused muddle of discordant ideas referred to by his critics. However, we need to be warned that interpreting Freud's theory in terms of the dialectic does not make it more credible: it merely renders it understandable.

Some critics have seen Freud's propensity for dividing everything in two as an indication of dualism. But a passion for dichotomizing is not dualism. In the usual sense of the term Freud was at least as materialistic as Marx — and less of a dualist. What the famous Freudian dichotomies represent is, instead, the thesis and antithesis of the dialectic. The clue is that, with each of the conflicts of instincts detailed by Freud, there was the expectation of an inevitable synthesis to a more advanced stage.

Freud began in a fairly traditional manner by recognizing two basic biological urges: those for food and love. He eventually came to see these urges as representing the self-preservative or ego instincts on the one hand, and the sexual instinct — functioning to reproduce the species — on the other. He believed both are actually manifested in a force driven by hunger: for nutrition and for sex. The force energizing and synthesizing these drives he called the libido.

Freud saw an inevitable conflict between the ego-instinct and the sexual one. "For, in human beings, it may happen that the demands of the sexual instinct, which of course extend far beyond the individual, seem to the ego to constitute a danger menacing his self-preservation or his self-respect. The ego then takes up the defensive, denies the sexual instincts the satisfaction they claim, and forces them into those by-paths of substitutive gratification which become manifest as symptoms of neurosis" (Freud 1947:15). Neuroses, then, result from the wrong kind of resolution of the conflict — rather than from a healthy synthesis of the two opposing forces.

Indeed, the process of child development begins with a condition of synthesis, according to Freud. In the beginning of its development the sexual instinct is directed toward itself: it *serves* the ego. This is the primitive synthesis of egoism or childhood "narcissism" into which the infant is born. There is a fusion of sensuality and affection as the child satiates both forms of hunger at the mother's breast and through the ministrations of other loving family members. Normal development then leads into the stage in which the infant seeks gratification in its own thumb and other body parts. Gradually, however, the sexual instinct turns away from its own body for sensual pleasure and toward other objects, as the essential conflict between the ego and the sex-drive comes into play.

Freud claimed that, in healthy development, the ego finds it necessary to redirect the operation of the powerful sexual instinct in order to achieve its own goals. It accomplishes this by inhibiting the aim of the sexual instinct and thus directing its energy to other, ego-controlled ends. At the same time another necessary conflict — between the reality principle and the pleasure principle within the ego — operates as a spur to ego growth in this push to achieve a synthesis of effective aim-directed action. Affectional and non-sexual family bonds are constructed, and these are extended to friendships and bonding within successively larger communal groupings. Coincident with this, a new and higher-level synthesis is being formed in terms of an encompassing *mental* form of sexual energy called the libido. The latter comprises both "aim-inhibited" energy and that which is directed toward the original sexual end, in the person of an external sex object.

It is this sublimation of the sexual instinct and the diversion of libido to the service of other goals that makes society and culture possible, according to Freud. All is still not clear sailing, however, for yet another conflict hovers on the horizon, ever ready to assert itself. In later life Freud felt it necessary to make his theory accommodate what appeared to be an instinct for aggression in human beings. So he postulated the existence of an opposition to libido in its task of preserving the organic substance and binding it into ever larger units of organization. He explained this as an antithesis which seeks to dissolve all the organic and social units and reinstate their previous unorganized (or inorganic) condition.

Freud called this the death instinct. He was somewhat ambiguous about its exact nature. Sometimes he seemed to be viewing it as an essential aspect of the process of evolution, because of its function in removing the individual from the scene once the cause of reproduction has been served. At other times he spoke of it only in terms of the eternal conflict between aggression and bonding, or between love and hate within the human psyche.

Freud rehabilitated Plato's concept of Eros in order to posit a higher synthesis of the instinctual forces driving the growth of human civilization: an all-encompassing urge for life. He described cultural evolution as "the particular modification undergone by the life process under the influence of the task set before it by Eros and stimulated by Ananke, eternal necessity; and this task is that of uniting single human beings into a larger entity with libidinal attachments between them" (Freud 1953a:72).

The unscientific approach of the system-builder

Freud admitted that all of the above was conjecture, and that ultimately it would have to be subjected to the test of controlled observation and experiment. But, from that decisive point in his career when his fertile mind turned from scientific inquiry to free-ranging speculation, Freud did not proceed as would be expected of a scientist. His key explanatory constructs (such as Oedipus complex, oral- and anal-fixation, fear of castration, penis envy, wish fulfilment, libido, Eros, sublimation, defence mechanism and *Thanatos*) were very quickly reified and freely granted the authority of an objective reality on a par with observed events. To read the letters written by Freud from that time on (and one can only assume that the responses were similar) is to move into a Land of Looking Glass in which freshly minted fiction has taken on the sober and self-justifying garb of scientific fact.

How have these conjectures stood up, in the decades since their creation, to the kind of scientific scrutiny which Freud claimed to hope for and expect? Incredibly, no effort was made by the master or by his disciples to attempt falsification or confirmation of the testable propositions derivable from the theory. Furthermore, from the very beginning the door was closed to peer criticism as a source of corrective feedback. Early in the 1890s, Freud had written to Fleiss, "A lecture on the etiology of hysteria at the Psychiatric Society met with an icy reception from the asses, and from [one] . . . 'It sounds like a scientific fairy tale' " (Schur:104). The same biographer who recorded the above noted that, soon after, "he had broken off all contact with men in his profession" (ibid.).

As Freud isolated himself from his colleagues it is all too clear that he was isolating himself, as well, from the scientific mode of inquiry. This occurred in spite of the frequent affirmations of the primacy of that very approach which abound in his writings. Apart from the increasingly speculative nature of his work, there are numerous clues as to the direction in which he was heading. In *Beyond the Pleasure Principle* he comments on how little science, following "sober Darwinian lines," has been able to tell us about the origin and evolution of sexuality. His gullibility concerning Charcot's notorious cures and his beloved Fleiss' fantastic ideas and practices indicates a dangerous lack of scepticism. Medical records have since revealed that even routine follow-up observation of his key cases concerning Anna O., Emma, Dora, Wolf Man and Little Hans would have demonstrated conclusively that his diagnoses and explanations were absolutely wrong. They would have shown as well that the misguided treatments rendered not only failed to cure, but often amounted to further cruel abuse of these unfortunate patients.

For example, take the case of Emma. After hearing her familiar story of child abuse, Freud diagnosed her as the typical hysteric, fantasizing a repressed desire for her father. He then sent her to Fleiss for nose surgery. How Freud had become persuaded that an Oedipus complex could best be wrested out through the nose, we will never know! Poor Emma almost died from the infection and hemorrhage caused by a botched operation. In the aftermath, Freud wrote a warm letter to his friend placing the blame, not on Fleiss, but on the specialist who had saved Emma's life by discovering a large surgical dressing festering in her sinus cavity.

Then there was Anna O., upon whose successful treatment Freud's elaborate sexual theory was supposedly based. Recently discovered case records now demonstrate that she was neither hysterical nor cured as a result of her lengthy therapy. In fact, she suffered from a serious physical illness which had been totally overlooked by Freud — tubercular meningitis. It is not surprising that in later life, Anna (an admirable early feminist) had a strong antipathy toward all psychoanalysts.

Freud's arguments against controlled observation and statistical testing of results with a large number of cases are revealing. For example, "humanity is in the highest degree irrational, so that there is no prospect of influencing it by reasonable arguments" (Freud 1952:46). And again, "I cannot put much value on . . . confirmations because the wealth of reliable observations on which these assertions rest makes them independent of experimental verification" (ibid.:149). Also, Freud's habit of destroying his notes and records, even all traces of his 1885 article on cocaine, does not add to one's confidence in the credibility of his work.

It is difficult not to conclude that Freud was a conflict-ridden human being. All of his biographers provide evidence that he was prone to sudden prejudices, jealousies and vindictiveness, yet insatiable for close and lasting friendships; and that he was puritanical in the extreme yet obsessed with sex. He was philosophically opposed to introspection, yet that very approach was the source of most of his theorizing. He was insightfully critical of the "group thought" imposed by church and army, yet devoted to creating an identical type of association among himself and disciples — using similar authoritarian techniques and demands. He was worshipful of science and scornful of supernaturalism and mysticism, yet irresistibly drawn to abstract and empirically unwarranted speculation. He was convinced of his rightful place as heir to Copernicus and Darwin, yet woefully unequipped for the discipline and integrity demanded by science.

The scientific status of the theory

However, the unscientific behaviour of a theorist does not, in itself, invalidate his theories. Certainly, Freud's disregard for facts and belief in his own infallibility would seem to be a poor foundation for the building of knowledge. But it is nonetheless possible for powerful insights to emerge from unlikely sources. The significant question must be: to what degree have Freud's theories been confirmed by the test of scientific observation and general human experience?

In recent years there have been a number of efforts by qualified scholars (some hostile, and others receptive to psychoanalysis) to survey the available research seeking to test the credibility of Freud's theories. Although the methodology of many of the hundreds of studies surveyed sometimes raises questions, certain conclusions now seem incontrovertible. There is considerable support for Freud's conjectures pointing to an environmental origin of at least some instances of homosexuality, and of paranoid schizophrenia and other emotional abnormalities. There is some evidence for the existence of personality complexes in adults that loosely resemble Freud's constructs (but roughly equal support for any number of different patterns of attributes). There is no support for the Oedipus theory — in fact for the entire web of sexually based explanations for normal development. The vast majority of studies attempting to link breast-feeding and toilet-training practices to personality attributes in the developed adult demonstrate no connection whatever. Freud's dreams-as-wish-fulfilment hypothesis has failed all efforts at scientific confirmation, but his idea that dreams have to do with the dreamer's previous experience (rather than future events) is now well supported by research. Finally, the most damning finding of all is the lack of supporting evidence for the effectiveness of Freudian therapy.

Revision and apology in modern psychoanalytic theory

In recent decades, psychoanalysts have been scrambling to salvage something from the wreckage of the theory. Many have drifted into Jungian or Frommian "heresies." Those mystically inclined are attracted to Jung's archetypes, based on the Platonic concept of an ideal reality of generalized ideas behind and above the material and containing many vestiges of the ancient Hellenistic mystery cults. For Freud this had represented an unfortunate reversion to vitalism: the belief (expounded by Schopenhauer) in a mysterious life force directing nature.

Erich Fromm tried to accommodate both Marxism and Freudianism to Rousseau's idea of an essentially good and cooperative human being, corrupted only by society. Fromm gave to love and cooperation the central and innate position that Freud had assigned to lust and aggression. In fact, Freud was scornful of a belief in universal love, either as a defining characteristic or as a goal of human existence. He wrote, "a love that does not discriminate seems to me to forfeit a part of its own value, by doing an injustice to its object; and . . . not all men are worthy of love" (Freud 1961c:102). At any rate, according to Freud, love is never really applied universally by its proponents — only to their own in-group. He suggested that movements claiming love as a motivating force are inherently dangerous, because they inevitably encourage intolerance toward those persisting in error (and hence unloveable). And he would have been appalled at attempts by admirers such as Fromm and Marcuse to reconcile his theory with Marxism. Of the latter, he commented with considerable prescience, "The psychological premises on which the system is based are an untenable illusion. . . . Aggressiveness was not created by property. . . . One only wonders, with concern, what the Soviets will do after they have wiped out their Bourgeois" (ibid.:113-15).

Many modern psychoanalytic thinkers have followed Fromm's lead in attempting to sanitize and rewrite Freud. Unable to refute the rapidly accumulating evidence that the theory is simply wrong, they have done the greatest possible injustice to their founder. They have made two claims: (1) that the English translations distort Freud's ideas so thoroughly as to render all the compelling refutations irrelevant; and (2) that Freud never intended his theory to be validated within the scientific frame of reference. He had access to a different, deeper order of meaning altogether — the subjective, intuitive realm of "understanding" propounded by the romantic idealists: a form of knowledge uncheckable by objective criteria, but no less true.

The first claim is incredibly insulting to a man who read English fluently; who was alive and intellectually alert *after* most of the significant translations were completed; who selected the translators for the *Standard Edition* of his complete works himself; and who put his own daughter, Anna (a famous psychoanalyst in her own right) in charge of the project. The second claim reveals a profound ignorance of Freud's assumptions on the nature of knowledge — spelled out numerous times in his writings. Bruno Bettelheim even went so far as to proclaim that Freud's statements about the depth of his commitment to science cannot be taken at face value. What was he trying to tell us about his intellectual hero?

Freud's intellectual commitment to science

Although it is indeed painfully evident that Freud all too frequently *behaved* in an unscientific manner, it is just as evident from his comments that he *believed* in the primacy of the scientific method and *thought* that he was creating a legitimate science. In his own words, "scientific work is the only road which can lead us to a reality outside ourselves. It is once again merely an illusion to expect anything from intuition and introspection" (Freud 1961a:31). Elsewhere, concerning the untrustworthiness of intuition, he wrote, "people are seldom impartial when they are concerned with ultimate things, the great problems of science and life. My belief is that there everyone is under the sway of preferences deeply rooted within, into the hands of which he unwittingly plays as he pursues his speculation" (Rickman:165).

Freud said that he placed his faith, instead, in scientific inquiry, and in the possibility of anchoring human behaviour in the biological strata. For example,

> The deficiencies in our description would probably vanish if we were already in a position to replace the psychological terms with physiological or chemical ones. . . . Biology is truly a realm of limitless possibilities; we have the most surprising revelations to expect from it and cannot conjecture what answers it will offer. . . . [its findings may] overthrow our whole artificial structure of hypotheses. (Schur:165)

And, again, we find him saying, "If experience should show . . . that we have been mistaken, then we will renounce our expectations" (Gay:31).

Concerning the claim that for some aspects of knowing, the introspective, subjective mode has priority, Freud maintained, " Research regards all domains of human activity as its own and must become pitilessly critical when another power wants to confiscate a part of it for itself" (ibid.:49). He was acutely aware of the transcendentalism and romantic idealism so prevalent in his homeland, which implied access to a different and perhaps superior form of knowledge to that of science. He wrote that proponents of that position liked to accuse the scientifically oriented of intolerance. But, he said, to be tolerant of knowledge claims not amenable to the test of reason and observation is a betrayal of humanity. For, unlike many of the products of introspection, we can be confident that "science is no illusion. But an illusion it would be to believe that we could get anywhere else what it cannot give us" (ibid.:65). Finally, there was his often repeated comment: "There is no court above that of reason" (Freud 1961b:28).

Freud recognized the need to remind his followers that it is "a false assumption that the validity of psychoanalytic theories is definitely established, while actually they are still in their beginning, and need a great deal of development and repeated verification and confirmation" (Bettelheim:83-84). And, most tellingly, he claimed that psychoanalysis "is a branch of science, and can subscribe to the scientific . . . [frame of reference]. It makes no claim to being comprehensive or constituting a system" (Rickman:234).

If Freud is to be granted the respect due any human being who devoted his life to the search for knowledge, two conclusions are imperative. The first is that much of the original part of his theory has now been shown to be that very type of illusion of which he warned us. The second is that if he were alive to see the evidence he would agree that he had been mistaken. Those of his followers who still insist on bolstering and spreading the illusion are doing their master a disservice — not to mention the obvious harm to their students, patients and society at large.

Origins of Freudian concepts

Freud's followers seem also to have been singularly unaware of the historical and cultural sources of his theory. As discussed earlier, he had begun with two premises about the nature of evolution: sexual selection (now supported by modern biology, paleontology and archeology) and the inheritance of acquired characteristics (now discredited by genetics). The first of these was perverted into the psychoanalytic theory of sexually directed individual development. The second, Freud used to justify his theory of a species-inherited Oedipus complex. From Marx and his Enlightenment forebears he had acquired an unfortunate association of scientific method with the deriving of universal, immutable laws from observable phenomena. And from Rousseau (via Bachofen and Engels) came the notion of the primal horde, as well as those of

Freud's ideas about the origin of religion not attributable to Hume, Spencer and Nietzsche.

The concept of the unconscious was a familiar one in Freud's time. In fact, it goes back at least as far as Descartes. A well-known 1868 book by E. von Hartmann, *Philosophy of the Unconscious*, was readily available to students in the late nineteenth century. Freud seems to have been influenced particularly by Schopenhauer's emphasis on the irrational, unconscious "will," and on the idea of a human urge toward death as the ultimate solution to life's burdens. Both the notion of Eros and the threefold structure of the human personality had been a part of classical literature since Plato. And the belief that there is an inherent, growth-producing tension involved in the human need to achieve and maintain pleasure and to accommodate to reality is very reminiscent of Hume and Spencer.

Freud's concept of the relationship between the individual's instinctual drives and the necessarily controlling function of the culture — in the service of social justice — is straight from Thomas Hobbes. His concept of the conscience (or super-ego) as culturally induced and conditioned may have come from Nietzsche — although Freud saw this as an essential factor in civilization, rather than as society's enslavement of the free will of individuals, as Nietzsche would have it. The technique of free-association in therapy was invented by Sir Francis Galton, and published in a journal to which Freud subscribed in the 1880s. And the characteristics of the group mind were described by de Tocqueville, Nietzsche and Le Bon before Freud put the idea to such good use in his work on group (or mob) psychology.

Along with all these specific concepts common to the intellectual world view of the time, there was a current of thought developing in the Germanic culture as a whole from mid-century onward that no doubt distorted Freud's perspective on the evolutionary process. It was the vitalistic *Lebensphilosophic* movement. This represented a tradition that had been steadily gaining ground since the era of Goethe's colourful "primordial image"; and under the spell woven by the powerful works of Wagner it had assumed an increasingly mystical and pseudo-objective mythological form. An admiring study of the Hellenistic mystery cults by Friedrick Creuzer (1771-1858) seems to have been a major source of this irrational but strangely seductive cultural current. It reached its apex in Nietzsche's Dionysian constructs and in Jung's notion of the "collective unconscious" — as well as in the revival of Joachim Herder's concept of the Aryan *Volksgeist* and their mystical connection to the land — all of which helped to plow the ground for Nazism.

Freud came under this influence during the early years of his association with Jung, from whom he claimed to have "caught fire." It was then that he wrote his 1907 study, *Obsession Neurosis and Religious Ritual*, and his subsequent book, *Totem and Taboo*, in which he developed his well-known mythologically oriented Oedipus theory. Although Freud was later to repudiate Jung's tribal mysticism, he failed to root out from his own work those elements which owed their origin to the latter's scientifically unwarranted ideas. This was one of the many ways in which his experience with Jung paralleled that of his earlier relationship with Fleiss.

There was an influence on Freud that went far beyond this complex intellectual legacy, however. It was the general culture from which he had acquired his view of the world. The Hegelian dialectic was so much a part of this that leading theorists seldom even acknowledged it as the foundation of their world view. Equally significant was the fact that Freud's cultural environment was an authoritarian, paternalistic one in which the earlier liberalizing thrust of the revolution of 1848 had been overwhelmed by the spread of a militant nationalism.

The unification of the German states had been furthered by Prussia with Austria's help in 1864, when Schleswig and Holstein were taken from Denmark. The process proceeded at Austria's expense two years later, when it lost those two territories to Otto von Bismarck, and Venetia to Italy, and was forced to agree to the dissolution of the old Germanic Confederation. In Austria as in the new Germany, there was little democratic liberalism and even less demand for it. Freud's theory must be viewed, at least to some extent, as a product of this culture.

The legacy of Freudianism

What can we say about Freud's impact on social science? That he was a naturalist in the tradition of Democritus and Epicurus there is no doubt. He was wholly convinced that theological, metaphysical thinking is incompatible with the search for truth. His intellectual commitment to science as the only reliable road to knowledge is undeniable. He was often clearsighted in his criticism of his own intellectual forebears as well as of mystics and religious believers. Of the "perfectibility of man" he commented, "I see no way of preserving this pleasing illusion. The development of man up to now does not seem to me to need any explanation differing from that of animal development. . . . [Human progress can be better explained in terms of] that repression of instinct upon which what is most valuable in human culture is built" (Rickman:162).

He saw the problems with Marxism, but, unhappily, was not able to recognize similar danger signals in the political nature of the spread of, and support for, his own theories. Marxism, he wrote, "has created a prohibition of thought which is just as ruthless as was that of religion in the past" (Schur:437).

Unfortunately, Freud's penetrating conclusion regarding the experiential source of the individual conscience and its function as an internal brake on socially destructive instinctual behaviour has been underplayed by his followers. And perhaps they should have noted more carefully his wry comment that "a sense of guilt is the necessary price we pay for civilization" (Freud 1961c:

134). Similarly, in his contribution to our understanding of the motivating power of unconsciously retained remnants of previous experience (if not of race memory) Freud made a significant contribution to social science.

His Spencerian insight concerning a parallel between individual development and the evolution of human culture was expanded upon by Henri Bergson and, later, by Julian Huxley and Jean Piaget. His idea that religious figures such as Jesus and Moses functioned as "cultural consciences" in promoting group morality is convincing. Of possible significance, also, is his conclusion that restrictions on sexual life and the institutionalization of the humanitarian ideal together operate in the place of natural selection as determinants of cultural evolution — to be abandoned only at the peril of humanity.

Unfortunately, Freud's worthwhile contributions to social-scientific thought have generally been ignored by his followers and form only a minor part of what we know as Freudianism. It is Freud's original sexual theory and therapy that have been influential. And, ironically, Freudian psychoanalysis and its offshoots must be held at least partly responsible for an obsession with sex which is the source of many of today's psychological and social problems. It is also unfortunate that Freud's emphasis on cause and effect in human behaviour, and on the importance of the joint biological and social history of the individual, have been downplayed by his followers. This was his greatest contribution.

If Freud, the committed evolutionary naturalist, had not to some extent betrayed his own ideals, his contribution to social science would have been invaluable. If he had limited himself to integrating familiar ideas into a theory of the biological and experiential sources of neuroses, his psychoanalytic approach might well have stood the test of time. But he was not satisfied with that. At least twice in his life, while under the influence of certain questionable colleagues, he dispensed with the conscientious research so essential to real progress in knowledge building. The result was that, in place of the fruitful scientific theory for which he had aimed, he created a doctrinaire ideology impervious to the test of reason and experience. This was the "devil's pact" to which he was driven by ambition, and it is on this that posterity will judge him.

References for Chapter Nine

Ackerman, Robert John. 1990. *Nietzsche: A Frenzied Look* Amherst: University of Massachusetts Press.

Bettelheim, Bruno. 1983. *Freud and Man's Soul*. New York: Knopf.

Cioffi, Frank. 1970. Freud and the Idea of Pseudo-Science. In *Explanation in the Behavioral Sciences*. Edited by R. Borger and F. Cioffi. London: Cambridge University Press.

Eysenck, Hans. 1985. *Decline and Fall of the Freudian Empire*. Markham: Penguin.

Fisher, Seymour, and Roger P. Greenberg. 1977. *The Scientific Credibility of Freud's Theories and Therapy*. New York: Basic Books.

Freud, Sigmund. 1947. A Difficulty in Psycho-analysis. In *Freud on War, Sex, and Neurosis*. Edited by Sander Katz. Translated by Joan Riviere et al. New York: Arts and Sciences Press, p. 14-22.

————. 1952. *An Autobiographical Study*. Translated by James Strachey. London: W.W. Norton. (First published in 1925.)

————. 1953a. *Civilization, War and Death*. Edited by John Rickman. London: Hogarth Press.

————. 1953b. *The Interpretation of Dreams*. Translated by James Strachey. New York: Basic Books.

————. 1961a. Totem and Taboo. In *The Standard Edition of the Complete Psychological Works of Sigmund Freud*. Edited by James Strachey. London: Hogarth Press. 13: 1-161.

————. 1961b. Beyond the Pleasure Principle. In *The Standard Edition*. 18: 7-64.

————. 1961c. The Future of an Illusion. In *The Standard Edition*. 21: 5-56.

————. 1961d. Moses and Monotheism. *The Standard Edition*. 23: 1-137.

————. 1975. *Civilization and Its Discontents*. Translated by Joan Riviere and revised by James Strachey. London: Hogarth Press.

Gay, Peter. 1987. *A Godless Jew*. New Haven: Yale University Press.

Grubrich-Simitis, Ilse, ed. 1987. *Sigmund Freud's "Phylogenetic Fantasy."* Cambridge: Harvard University Press.

Jones, Ernest. 1961. *The Life and Work of Sigmund Freud*. New York: Basic Books.

Jung, Karl G. 1969. *The Structure and Dynamics of the Psyche*. Princeton: Princeton University Press.

Kline, Paul. 1981. *Fact and Fantasy in Freudian Theory*. London: Methuen.

Lehman, Hannah. 1986. *A Mote in Freud's Eye*. New York: Springer.

McGuire, William, ed. 1974. *The Freud/Jung Letters*. Princeton: Princeton University Press.

Masson, J. Moussaieff. 1984. *The Assault on Truth: Freud's Suppression of the Seduction Theory*. New York: Farrar, Straus and Giroux.

Miller, Jonathon, ed. 1972. *Freud: The Man, His World, His Influence*. London: Weidenfeld and Nicolson.

Nietzsche, Friedrich Wilhelm. 1908. *Thus Spake Zarathustra: A Book for All or None*. Translated by Alexander Tille. London: Unwin.

————. 1994. *On the Genealogy of Morality*. Edited by Keith Ansell Pearson. Translated by Carol Diethe. New York: Cambridge University Press.

Noll, Richard. 1994. *The Jung Cult: Origins of a Charismatic Movement*. Princeton: Princeton University Press.

Rickman, John, and Charles Brenner. 1957. *A General Selection from the Works of Sigmund Freud*. New York: Liveright.

Rosenbaum, Max, and Melvin Muroff. 1984. Anna O: Her History. In *Anna O*. New York: The Free Press.

Roustang, François. 1982. *Dire Mastery: Discipleship from Freud to Lacan*. Baltimore: The Johns Hopkins University Press.

Schur, Max. 1972. *Freud: Living and Dying*. New York: International Universities Press.

Ten

Ivan Pavlov and the Third Copernican Revolution

Study, son, 'tis science
That teaches us more swiftly than experience,
Our life being so brief.
— Alexander Pushkin, *Boris Godunov*

At the very time that Freud was boldly claiming the mantle of Copernicus and Darwin, a modest Russian researcher named Ivan Pavlov was quietly earning it. Pavlov had been born in St. Petersburg in 1849 — seven years before Freud. He was the son of a priest in the poor country parish of Ryazan, the eldest of only five survivors of the eleven children to which his mother had given birth. Like Freud, he came from a humble, though far from lower-class, background.

A time of hope

Pavlov grew to manhood in what was probably the most liberal period of Russian history. He would have been twelve years old in 1861 when Tsar Alexander II passed legislation to free the serfs, and political and educational reform continued for a few years after that. But, as a result of the Polish Revolt and several attempts on his life, the Tsar began to retreat into conservatism. His reign was followed by those of Alexander III and Nicholas II, who pursued a ruthless Russification policy which involved harassment of the Poles and Finns and pogroms against the Jews. All this contributed to the emergence of the revolutionary movement of 1905, with its dreams of radical change. It was in this social and political context that the young scientist carried out his work.

The youthful Ivan had been extremely fortunate in his role models. His father was a priest with a love of learning and an instinct for research. His godfather (an abbot) taught him the nobility of work and the importance of uniting the labour of the head and hand. An admirable teacher at the Ecclesiastical

---

References for this chapter are on p. 185.

Seminary which Ivan attended after high school advised him to study the natural sciences rather than theology. Probably the same teacher encouraged him to read Charles Darwin, Herbert Spencer and G.H. Lewes' *Practical Physiology*, a book which he treasured all his life. At the University of St. Petersburg he came under the influence of Professor Ilya Cyon, a pioneer of experimental physiology. It was then that Ivan Pavlov discovered his life's work; in fact, he had completed a successful research project on the nerves of the pancreatic gland by the time he graduated in 1875.

Early successes

Cyon offered the promising student an assistantship at the Medico-Cherurgical Academy where he was the head of research. However, upon entering the Academy, Pavlov discovered that Cyon had left unexpectedly for Paris, and his position had been taken by a man of dubious scientific integrity. With the moral strength that was to characterize his behaviour throughout his career, Pavlov turned down the precious assistantship. He worked for two years instead at the nearby Veterinary Institute where he began independent studies on digestion and the physiology of the blood.

This early work was so remarkable that Pavlov was invited, while still a graduate student, to take charge of the Academy's new experimental laboratory. He published his first paper in 1878, and graduated the following year. A professor, travelling out of the country, said of him, "In Russia we have an outstanding physiologist, gifted to the highest degree, who will do something very significant one day" (Babkin:19).

Pavlov continued managing the laboratory, which involved directing the research of numerous fellow candidates while attempting to complete his own dissertation. He received his doctorate in medicine in 1883, and was appointed Lecturer in Physiology the following year. In 1891 he became Director of the Department of Physiology at the Institute of Experimental Medicine. This was the first such department in the world with a physiological laboratory, and it had been carefully planned by Pavlov himself.

He had been married since 1881, and for the ensuing decade the young family had survived on a small monthly stipend. Professional ambition had never been an issue for Pavlov. He was oblivious to monetary or career considerations beyond the requirements of his daily scientific work (which must have made things difficult at home). Before being offered the Directorship at the Institute, he had applied for a Chair at the University of St. Petersburg, but did not get it. As they were suffering real poverty, his wife understandably expressed a degree of disappointment. At that very moment Pavlov, having discovered that some butterflies necessary for an experiment had all died, responded, "Oh leave me alone! A *real* misfortune has occurred. All my butterflies have died and you are bothering me about silly trifles" (ibid.:26).

In 1895 Pavlov was appointed to the Chair of Physiology at the University of St. Petersburg. By this time he was in his forties, with a solid record of accomplishment in research and teaching. His work on the circulatory and digestive systems was known throughout the world. He had revolutionized teaching in his department, incorporating clinical work with research, and building his classes around actual experiments. He had adopted a method of eliciting and responding to questions, rather than lecturing, and his laboratory is said to have been the most democratic of work environments. With his dogs he had introduced a new approach to animal experimentation — using aseptic procedures and replacing "acute" techniques that damaged and traumatized the subjects with methods that allowed painless functioning throughout the experiment.

Sources of a revolutionary world view

We now know that by the end of that decade and the century Pavlov was poised for a radically different pursuit. No ordinary physiologist, he had always viewed his beloved research into the objective indicators of bodily functioning not as an end in itself, but as a means to understanding an infinitely more complex and difficult subject: what it was that governed animal *behaviour*.

The conceptual framework within which Pavlov had chosen to operate as a scientist had been inherited from three sources. One was Charles Darwin, whose evolutionary theory of species adaptation to the environment by means of natural selection seemed to raise the intriguing issue of the possible existence of a mechanism of individual adaptation as well. A second was Herbert Spencer, who grappled, at a theoretical level, with the same problem. The third source was Ivan Sechenov. The latter's 1863 book, *Reflexes of the Brain*, had presented a host of tantalizing and unanswered questions about human mental processes and their possible relation to the interaction of the individual organism with its surroundings.

Through Sechenov, Pavlov was heir to a small but durable strand of Russian naturalism originating with the little circle of Westernized advisers around Peter the Great. Very early, this current of thought had become focused on the need to free the study of human behaviour from the animism and supernaturalism imposed upon it by the strictures of Orthodox religion. Pioneers such as Belinski and Cherniskenski had tried to establish a social science defined in terms of monism, natural causation and evolution. Sechenov built on the work of these men. He maintained that the behaviour of higher animals (including humans) could be explained adequately on the basis of three principles: (1) the organism as inseparable from its environment; (2) Descarte's concept of "the reflex arc" (comprising a receptor, synapse and effector organ capable of receiving energy from the environment and transforming it into activity) and (3) a process of intensification and inhibition of response.

Sechenov was a contemporary of Martineau, Marx, Darwin and Spencer. He lived in exciting times: that brief period when liberal thought was still gaining headway in Tsarist Russia. He was confident that dualism and vitalism were finally in retreat in all branches of science. His hope for social science was that it "will no longer be based on erroneous reasoning prompted by the misleading voice of consciousness; it will rely on positive facts and verifiable propositions. Its generalizations and deductions . . . will no longer depend on the taste and whims of the investigator, which in the past brought [it] to such transcendental absurdities" (McLeish:63).

In an 1878 article, Sechenov described human thought as beginning in the elementary, sensation-bound reflexes of infancy, mainly stimulated by concrete objects. He saw it as gradually progressing to the systematic, suprasensory, abstract mental processes of the intellectually mature adult. He wrote of morality as well, claiming that education and example were its sources, and that the "metaphysical fiction" of free will was irrelevant to the issue. He explained that society must be protected from dangerous offenders regardless of the origin of their inclination to crime. The only difference in approach (if we assumed a genetic-environmental origin) would be in our attitude towards the offender. A justice system no longer based on the premise of free will would likely emphasize rehabilitation rather than retribution. And this, said Sechenov, would surely represent an improved morality on the part of the majority (ibid.:69).

Turning to psychology

The longer Pavlov worked with animal reflex behaviour the more his thoughts kept returning to Sechenov's book. From the turn of the century on, he had come into his own as that rare type of intellectual able to combine a commitment to rigorous practical research with a gift for theorizing. The results of his experiments indicated a need to expand Sechenov's view of the "organism in its environment" to include the model developed by Claude Bernard and Herbert Spencer of a system in dynamic equilibrium with the environment. Like Spencer, Pavlov was compelled to take Darwin's concept of species-descent-with-modification one step further — to the process by which the *individual* survives through adaptive behaviour. His own research had confirmed the opinion of physiologists like Botkin that the cerebral cortex is the ultimate controller of body functions. Sechenov's book had convinced him that the ways in which the cortex works could be investigated objectively by means of the study of reflexes. And, lastly, his work on the salivary glands of dogs provided him with a relatively simple and easily controlled set of reflex mechanisms which could be used as indicators of the functioning of the entire central nervous system.

In 1904, just a year before the political revolution in Russia, Pavlov was awarded the Nobel Prize. The international recognition was well-deserved, for his work on the digestive system remains the foundation for gastroenterology to this day. However, by the time he travelled to Sweden to receive his prize for past triumphs he was already launched on a pioneering attempt to shed similar light on the faltering field of psychology.

His biographer (a former student) says that by nature Pavlov was a pathfinder. He wanted a wide and virgin field to plow for himself. Psychology, with its profusion of conflicting opinions and imaginative but unsupported theoretical constructs, certainly would have posed a sufficient challenge. As Pavlov remarked, "Psychology as the knowledge of the inner world of the human being is still at sea concerning its own essential methods" (Pavlov 1928:121). He could not have guessed that the effort to provide the social sciences with a reliable knowledge base would occupy him and his student researchers for the next thirty-four years. Nor could he have predicted that the results of his research would be far more vehemently resisted than were the strange and unsupported fictions of his contemporary, Sigmund Freud.

Like Freud, Pavlov brought to his physiologically based psychology a scorn for the dualist premises and introspective methods of most of its proponents. But he differed from Freud in that, for him, practice was consistent with proclamation. Always, his research and private life reflected the tenets of scientific integrity that Freud at times so sadly lacked.

Discovering the conditioned reflex

Pavlov was convinced that any fruitful psychology would have to be grounded in sound physiology. He had been noticing for some time that his experimental dogs would begin to salivate, not only when the appropriate food touched their mouths, but at the appearance of any of the events immediately preceding the feeding, such as its odour, approaching footsteps or clatter of dishes. He at first referred to these anticipatory responses as "psychical" (or psychological) reflexes as distinct from inborn ones. But he quickly realized that so-called psychical motivations expressed in terms such as "the dog knows," "the dog expects" or "the dog desires" did not really explain anything. Like most of the psychological explanations of the day, they were merely verbal constructs leading nowhere. They failed utterly to answer the question of "How?"

By the time he accepted his Nobel Prize, Pavlov was already deeply involved in the search for answers to this question. His Stockholm acceptance speech dwelt entirely on the new problem. In explaining his recent research, he noted that "we chose to maintain in our experiments with the so-called psychical phenomena a purely objective position. Above all, we endeavoured to discipline our thoughts and our speech about these phenomena and not concern ourselves with the imaginary mental state of the animal; and we limited our task to exact observation and description of the effect on the secretion of salivary glands of the object acting from a distance" (ibid.:77). The researchers had been able to observe the expected regularities between stimulus and effect and had found they could reproduce and alter them at will.

Pavlov realized that the effects produced on salivary glands from distant or secondary stimuli are indeed reflexes, but of a special kind. The initial reflexes, evoked by stimulation of the mouth cavity, are inborn, constant and unaffected by previous events. They are what most people call instincts. The second type are acquired through experience, subject to fluctuation and dependent on a variety of conditions. In other words, the first type are "unconditioned"; the second, *conditioned* reflexes.

Another difference Pavlov discovered was that, in the case of the unconditioned reflex, the stimuli were those properties of the substance to which the saliva is physiologically adapted. With the conditioned reflex, however, properties having no physiological bearing on the role of saliva (such as colour, form and sound) had acquired the power to act as stimuli. The second group of phenomena had obviously become *signals* for those essential properties which stimulate instinctive responses.

Subsequent research showed that these signalled reflexes could be made more and more discriminating; that is, a dog's saliva system could be made to respond only to very specific stimuli among many in the surroundings (like an exact tone on a bell or a certain tempo on a metronome). All that was necessary was that the animal's sensory organs were physiologically capable of making the necessary distinctions. For example, it was discovered that the hearing of dogs is very acute, but that they are colour blind. It was demonstrated, as well, that the conditioned response could be readily weakened, strengthened or extinguished — depending upon the immediacy, intensity and consistency of the "reinforcement" (or the experienced rewards).

Pavlov was quick to realize the significance of his discovery. Here was the explanation, in objective physiological terms, of the precise nature of the process by which complex organisms learn from experience. As he put it,

> in these conditioned stimuli, looked at from the point of view of biology, we have a most perfect mechanism of adaptation, or . . . a very delicate mechanism for maintaining an equilibrium with the surrounding medium. The body has the capacity to react in a sensitive way to the phenomena of the outside world which are essential to it, because all other phenomena . . . coinciding even temporarily with the essential, become their indicators. (Ibid.:87)

Obtaining food is not the only prerequisite of survival. Avoidance of danger is another. One can think of avoidance reflexes as an example of the role of conditioning. The essential response to the sensation of pain is rapid withdrawal. Inevitably, all aspects of the conditions surrounding the experience of pain will become signalling stimuli, precipitating flight. For an early hunter who had lost a leg to a tiger, the sounds and smells immediately preceding the attack would signal "danger" from that point on.

This simple explanation renders quite irrelevant all the old philosophical arguments about inductive logic not being a valid guide to action — supposedly because the hunter could never *prove* conclusively that the tiger's roar was an inevitable prelude to pain. Pavlov had uncovered the physiological explanation for Hume's prescient conclusion about empirical knowledge. The organism's acquisition of conditioned reflexes, which change continuously with altered circumstances, has nothing whatsoever to do with logical thought — whether inductive or deductive. Those members of any species not open to rapid and finely tuned conditioning simply do not survive to produce progeny.

Pavlov concluded that all activity of the central nervous system must be considered reflex activity, either of the instinctual or the more complex type acquired through experience. According to him, the lower part of the nervous system is devoted to the unconditioned reflexes: definite permanent pathways between the receptors of external phenomena and the organism's biologically determined responses. He came to believe that the highest parts (the cerebral hemispheres) house two important mechanisms. The first is for establishing temporary connections in the conducting paths between external phenomena and the answering reactions of the organism. The second is for the operation of the "analyzers" which discriminate among incoming sensations. He hypothesized that the body's process of ongoing analysis begins with the external receiving apparatus such as the skin or ear (which acts as a transformer of a certain given external energy into a specific nervous process) and ends deep within the connections of the brain.

According to Pavlov's theory, every sensation from the outside world must enter one of the receptor organs through an end point in a centripetal nerve and travel to the receptor cells in the central nervous system. These contain the "reflex arc": a nerve path resembling a chain of three links. The links are the "analyzer," the "connector" or lock, and the "effector" or working part which transforms the received impulses into nervous activity. Initially a wave of excitation travels over the general area of the receptor cells ("irradiation") gradually becoming focused at an exact spot on the cortex, as the conditioning continues. The initial generalized response is gradually inhibited to the extent that the specific one is reinforced ("concentration"). Incoming sensations are continuously exciting and inhibiting the temporary connecting pathways, incessantly correcting them to correspond to reality. It is a functional or "systemic" interaction rather than a three-step linear process. Pavlov explained that this is the means by which the organism learns to adapt to, and thus maintain an ongoing equilibrium with, its surroundings.

> As a part of nature every animal organism represents a very compli-
> cated ... system, the internal forces of which, at any given moment, are in
> equilibrium with the external forces in the environment. The more complex
> the organism the more delicate and manifold are its elements of equilibra-
> tion. The analyzers and connectors establish the precise relations between
> the smallest elements in the environment and the finest reactions of the ani-
> mal. In this way, then, is all life, from that of the simplest to that of the most
> complex organisms, including man, a long series of more and more compli-
> cated equilibrations with the outside world. (Ibid.:129)

Revolutionary implications

Pavlov knew from the beginning that whatever he discovered about the central nervous system of dogs would to a large extent hold for the more highly evolved nervous system of humans. He was aware that his work would arouse a storm of controversy and be subjected to mischievous distortions if he were to point out its implications for the study of humanity. But his commitment to the search for truth permitted no choice in the matter. Darwin had established the fact of evolution: the descent of humans from other animal species. Pavlov's unique discovery was that, built upon the inherited system of *permanent* reflexes of the type that are involved in survival of the species, there exists a second system of *temporary* connections operating according to the same rules; that is, according to the principle of natural selection. This second system allows the individual member of the species to survive and flourish in changing circumstances. Today, with our computer analogy, we would call the first "hard-wired" and the second, "soft-wired."

Pavlov was quick to recognize that this "signalling system" is one which human beings share with other higher animals, just as they share the innate reflexes related to digestion, procreation, orientation to external surroundings and self-defence. For him, the very fact that the conditioned reflex offered both a basic unit of analysis and an objective method for studying hitherto inaccessible mental processes meant that, for the first time ever, an objective science of human behaviour was possible. This was indeed a revolutionary breakthrough equal, in its potential for enlarging human understanding, to those of Copernicus and Darwin!

Language as the second signalling system

Pavlov went on to posit the existence of three reflex systems in the human brain: the subcortical unconditioned one and two cortical signalling systems. The first cortical system comprises the conditioned reflexes studied in dogs:

the means by which all higher animals adapt to their environment. However, Pavlov maintained that there exists a second cortical system which is a uniquely human achievement. He called it "the second signalling system." He was referring to language. The miracle of human speech depends, not on signals of concrete objects and events, but upon *signals of signals*.

As Pavlov explained it:

> Words have built up a second system of signalling reality which is peculiar to us, being a signal of the primary signals. . . . The numerous stimulations by word have, on the one hand, removed us from reality, a fact we should constantly remember so as not to misinterpret our attitude towards reality. On the other hand, it is nothing other than words which have made us human. . . . It is beyond doubt that the essential laws governing the work of the first system of signalling necessarily regulate the second system as well, because it is work done by the same nervous tissue. (Babkin:318)

On the nature of sleep and hypnosis

Besides pointing the way to an objective study of language development, Pavlov's work shed considerable light on a number of other specific psychological issues. For instance, he was interested in the implications of his findings for the study of the hypnotic trance and sleep. His subsequent experiments provided empirical support for Hobbes' insight concerning the cause of dreams and for Martineau's confidence that "mesmerism" would someday be explained naturally. Pavlov discovered that both hypnosis and normal sleep were forms of internal inhibition of response mechanisms. He found that any more or less long-lasting and focused stimulation which produces "inhibition" (a negation of response) on the part of the non-focused areas of the cortex would induce sleep. The sleep would occur, however, only when there was no competing stimulation. This led him to define sleep as an internal inhibition (or negative reflex) which has become diffused continuously, without intervening waves of excitation from without, over the entire cortex, and has descended as well to some of the lower parts of the brain.

He found hypnosis to be somewhat different in that it is based on "imitation" and "suggestion," and involves a partial inhibition only. The long-submerged infantile reflex of imitation (the earliest method of learning by copying) is brought to the surface by the power of suggestion. Pavlov regarded suggestion (intense and repetitive verbal command) as an example of the simplest form of conditioned reflex in humans. It only seems complex because *speech*, rather than concrete objects in the environment, provides the conditioned stimulus. The command of the hypnotist concentrates the excitation of the cortex in some definite narrow region, while at the same time intensifying the inhibition in the rest of the cortex. This command abolishes all competing effects of temporary stimuli and traces of impacts left by previously received ones. It accounts for the almost insurmountable influence of suggestion both during hypnosis and immediately following it. Pavlov explained that hypnotic suggestion and dreams are related, dreams being largely due to traces of previous stimuli (generally of very old ones) while suggestion acts as a powerful immediate stimulus.

On inherited propensity or temperament

Another conclusion reached by Pavlov as a result of his many years of experimenting with reflex behaviour in dogs was the existence of at least three markedly different nervous systems that seem to produce variations in general temperament and are obviously genetically determined. He noticed that in certain animals it was invariably easy to produce positive reflexes, but difficult to produce negative ones (inhibitions). In a second group the opposite obtained, while the third and largest group easily formed both types of reflexes which then remained constant and exact.

In other words, the first group tended to respond rapidly and variably to every environmental input, exhibiting extreme and unpredictable mood-swings as a result. Members of the second group were slow to learn and stubbornly habitual (sometimes even incapable of action) in the face of altered environmental challenges. The majority group readily acquired new behaviours and maintained these in a predictable manner until circumstances changed.

Pavlov found that those in the central, stable group seemed to fall naturally into two categories: a very lively, outgoing one and a quiet, calm one. He was convinced that these categories could be applied to humans as well, and was pleased to discover how closely they matched Hippocrates' four classic types of temperament: the quick-tempered "choleric," then the "sanguine" and "phlegmatic" in the middle or normal range, and finally, the "melancholic" at the other extreme.

In his later years Pavlov studied mentally ill patients to observe how his categories of temperament and the explanations of these in terms of reflex conditioning might point to specific therapies. The theory seemed to explain remarkably well the conditions then known as hysteria (the extreme melancholic) and neurasthenia (the extreme end of the choleric continuum). The appropriate conditioning implied by Pavlov's theory seemed to work well as treatment.

Even more serious mental illnesses such as those loosely described as cyclic psychoses and schizophrenia Pavlov saw as marked manifestations of these two unstable patterns of nervous-system functioning. He considered schizophrenia to be the result of an extreme weakness of the cerebral cortex, to the point where there occurs a splitting of its normally unified function (Pavlov 1928:378). This accords with the older definition of the disease as "a split personality."

On free will

Pavlov, like Sechenov before him, devoted some thought to the concept of free will. He remarked that real freedom of choice for human beings would come in proportion to our knowledge about how the external and internal processes determining our action actually work. In this way only, through scientific knowledge about human functioning, can we hope to attain the control over human nature that we have managed to achieve over external nature. Here he meant control in the sense of becoming masters of our fate, rather than the unknowing victims of circumstances.

On consciousness

Pavlov had no confidence in the ability of subjective psychologies to help us in this quest for understanding, for he believed that their introspective approach was built upon a fatal error concerning the nature and role of consciousness. He contended that simply being the possessor of consciousness does not endow one with the ability to understand how one got that way and what is involved in it, or to what degree it determines one's behaviour — much less that of others. Consciousness contemplating itself from within is futile, said Pavlov, and can only result in fantasies and wishful thinking. For the facts demonstrate that consciousness is not a "given" — distinct from the organic system — but an evolving *product* of the organism's complex inner processes as they respond to external influences. Consciousness or "mind" is in no way the instigator of these processes. In fact, Pavlov's findings provide support for the belief of Freud and others that there is likely to be a vast proportion of human behaviour having little to do with conscious volition.

Pavlov explained that consciousness occurs "in a region of the brain where there is optimal excitability, [where] new connections are easily formed, and differentiation is successfully developed" (McLeish:95). He did not know where it might be housed, guessing that it might not even be fixed at all, but migrate over the area of the hemispheres. He was not at all sure that it even necessarily incorporated all or most of the synthesizing activity. Synthesis might take place beyond the actual sphere of consciousness and enter "as a link already formed, seeming to originate spontaneously" (Pavlov 1960:410). In such instances people given to mystical explanations would imagine that they had experienced a creative flash from the realm of the spirit.

Subsequent support for Pavlov's findings

Later in this century Wilder Penfield's research in Canada confirmed Pavlov's conclusion that the chief task of the cerebral cortex is the analysis of stimuli arriving there from both within and without the body, and the synthesis of their integral parts with the body's organic functions. Interestingly, Penfield discovered that the cerebral cortex is not necessary for the maintenance of consciousness. That state seems, instead, to depend upon the integrity of the region just below the cortex and above the midbrain.

There is also recent evidence from genetics to provide support for Pavlov's hypothesis concerning the heritability of certain personality traits. It now seems that there may be a gene which predisposes some individuals to excitability and a craving for novelty.

The theory of language development implied by Pavlov's work was elaborated and refined by L.S. Vygotsky, A. Luria and A.N. Solokov in Russia. Vygotsky applied Pavlov's systems approach, particularly the principle of language as the second signalling system. He went on to study the gradual development of conceptual thinking in children. He showed how the history of human mental process begins with concretely stimulated conditioned reflexes, then, through interaction with adults, verbalization is gradually acquired by imitation. Ultimately the words become internalized to form concepts of reality that operate as conditioned stimuli for the second signalling system. Thus consciousness is gradually built up as a more or less accurate reflection of reality.

Vygotsky explained that primitive self-consciousness (such as that of the young child) is characterized by a belief in the word as an integral part of the object it denotes. He noted that increased communicative ability is directly related to increased consciousness of the generalizing and abstracting function of symbols. He also pointed out that the communicative function of language preceded its intellectual function: that what first emerged as a tool for sharing the responses of other "selves" became increasingly an instrument for building ever more sophisticated structures of thought.

Luria (a student of Vygotsky) emphasized the importance of internal speech in the development of cognition. He demonstrated in detail how the brain enables the human being to analyze and synthesize information, to create a subjective image of it, to predict the consequences of acting on it and to evaluate the results of that acting. Solokov also saw thought and speech as inseparably bound up with each other at all stages of the individual's development. He explained intuition as "only an after-action of preceding consciously directed observations, experience, and reasoning; it is the fruit of conscious thought" (Solokov:91). All three of these Russian researchers concluded that the seemingly spiritual functions of what we have persisted in calling mind and soul can be clearly explained in terms of the model provided by Pavlov's pioneering work.

Assessing his impact

This seems all the more remarkable when we recall that most of Pavlov's research was conducted under extremely trying circumstances. Much of the time he was isolated from the world scientific community, although he strove mightily to keep in touch. At one time his work was so resented by his colleagues that he was fired from his position as president of the medical association. For years he conducted a solitary battle against a corrupt administrator who filled university positions with his own incompetent students. Pavlov, almost alone among his peers, spoke out against *both* the Tsarist and Bolshevik dictatorships. In 1924 he resigned his professorship because Soviet authorities were not allowing the children of the clergy to have a higher education. He explained that, as the son of a priest himself, he must surely be as unqualified to teach as these young people were to be students. Fortunately for the progress of science, however, Pavlov's prestige had become so great, both in his own country and abroad, that he enjoyed immunity from political reprisals.

Throughout his long career, Pavlov's laboratory was known far and wide as an ideal "school for science." He had little time for writing, but did produce three books of what are, for the most part, collections of public lectures. These demonstrate the true scientist's approach to theory and fact. His biographer says that "to him every new fact that was revealed in the lab was like a link in a chain being pulled out of a dark hold. . . . [For him] research must follow some guiding idea" (Babkin:109). But, he told his students, just as a bird's wings need the air for flight, "facts are the air upon which a scientist leans. Without them you will never fly upward" (ibid.:110).

Pavlov did not seem to consider himself a materialist in the Marxist sense. He was, above all, a naturalist and monist in philosophy. He said, "We are now coming to think of the mind, the soul, and matter as one, and with this view there will be no necessity of a choice between them" (Pavlov 1928:25). He did not attack religion, maintaining that true religious or moral impulses are the highest form of conditioned reflexes. All his life he was able to remain detached from the political and ideological turmoil surrounding him. However, his work was valued by the Communists as it seemed consistent with their assumptions about the human potential for change. In the last decade of his life his research was well supported by the government. He did not have to witness the prostitution of science during the Lysenko period when the Soviet Union outlawed genetics, for he died in 1934. Pavlov would not likely have survived that dark era.

B.F. Skinner tells us that H.G. Wells once compared the contributions to humanity of Ivan Pavlov and George Bernard Shaw. He concluded that if both were drowning and only one life preserver were available, he would throw it to the modest Russian researcher. Elsewhere Wells is reported as saying, "Pavlov is a star that lights the world, shining down a vista hitherto unexplored" (ibid.:31). At the age of seventy-one Pavlov himself wrote what is perhaps the best epitaph for a student of humanity. This was his heartfelt expression of hope for the future of social science: "I am deeply and irrevocably convinced that along this path [the study of conditioned reflexes] will be found the final triumph of the human mind over its uttermost and supreme problem — the knowledge of the mechanism and laws of human nature. . . . Only science, exact science about human nature itself . . . will deliver man from his present gloom and will purge him of his contemporary shame in the sphere of human relations" (Babkin:86).

It seems sadly true that the social-science community, in general, has yet to learn the lesson of Ivan Pavlov's life and legacy. And it is sadder yet that even those who are beginning to explore the path he opened seldom recognize the solid foundation provided by his pioneering work.

References for Chapter Ten

Babkin, B.F. 1949. *Pavlov: A Biography*. Chicago: University of Chicago Press.
Luria, A. 1959. The Directive Function of Speech in Development and Dissolution. *Word* 15: 341-52.
_____. 1971. Towards the Problem of the Historical Nature of Psychological Processes. *International Journal of Psychology* 6(4): 259-72.
McLeish, John. 1981. *The Development of Modern Behavioural Psychology*. Calgary: Detselig Enterprises, p. 43-70, 89-109.
Pavlov, Ivan. 1928. *Lectures on Conditioned Reflexes*. Translated by W.H. Gantt. New York: Liveright.
_____. 1960. *Conditioned Reflexes*. Translated by G.V. Anrep. New York: Dover.
Solokov, A.N. 1971. Internal Speech and Thought. *International Journal of Psychology* 6(1): 79-92.
Vygotsky, L.S. 1962. *Thought and Language*. Cambridge: MIT Press.

Eleven

John Dewey and the Universality of Scientific Inquiry

Logical consequences are the scarecrows of fools
And the beacons of wise men.
— Thomas Henry Huxley, *Animal Automatism*

B y the seventh decade of the nineteenth century, the United States had evolved the world's first successful international immigrant culture. It had been inspired by great naturalists such as Jefferson, Adams, Franklin and Paine; nourished by immigration; forged by revolution; and tested by civil war. It was a vigorous culture that tended to produce an abundance of inquiring minds, technical expertise and entrepreneurial spirit, but few of the truly great whose ideas were destined to change the world. One such, however, was John Dewey, the small-town boy who was to become America's first internationally renowned philosopher.

Early life and times

John Dewey was born in Vermont the year *On the Origin of Species* was published, and died almost a century later. During that period he witnessed and contributed to fundamental changes in human civilization. In his lifetime he became one of the world's greatest educators. He earned a reputation as his country's most original philosopher. He was, in fact, the major contributor to the only authentic American philosophy yet devised. In addition, his published works on the nature of ethics and morality, logic, psychology, art, religion, science and democracy offer us insights surprisingly useful as guides to solving the current crises of humanity.

Dewey was a contemporary of Ivan Pavlov but, unfortunately for the growth of human understanding, the two thinkers seem not to have encountered one another in any meaningful way. Both were deeply influenced by the theories of Herbert Spencer and would have been natural and mutually enriching allies. Dewey's major contribution was the spelling-out of a comprehen-

References for this chapter are on p. 203-204.

sive modern philosophy of science, based upon and growing out of a model for the scientific study of human nature. His work established the philosophical grounding and justification for precisely that naturalistic evolutionary approach to psychology for which Pavlov's research provided the factual underpinnings. Yet neither seems to have been aware of what the other was doing, nor the extent to which the life's work of each paralleled, supported and complemented that of the other. Sadly, the creative imaginations of both men so far outstripped that of their peers that their ideas were misconstrued and distorted by friend and foe alike. It now seems likely that we will have to wait for the twenty-first century to witness the flowering of the seeds planted by these two geniuses.

The young John Dewey attended the University of Vermont. There, he happened to take a course in physiology which used for a text Thomas Huxley's *Lessons in Elementary Physiology*. This gave him both an understanding of human beings as complex natural organisms and a lifelong aversion to dualism. He graduated in 1879 and submitted his first scholarly article that year. Its title was "Metaphysical Assumptions of Materialism." He taught school for two years before entering the graduate program in philosophy at Johns Hopkins.

In graduate school Dewey came under the influence of the Hegelian philosophy so popular at the time. It attracted him temporarily because he saw it as an attack on dualism. There were three powerful counter-influences to Hegel, however, all offering a monism based on a method of knowing nature, rather than on fixed metaphysical assumptions concerning its "essential" rules. In addition to Herbert Spencer's books, Dewey likely encountered Nietzsche's writings, for his subsequent work on values shows some Nietzschean influence. There was also G. Stanley Hall, an early experimental psychologist who encouraged Dewey to transform his vague Hegelian assumptions into a broadly scientific perspective. Another mentor was Charles Peirce, the originator of pragmatism, whose only sustained academic employment happened to bring him to Johns Hopkins for the few years that Dewey studied there. Not surprisingly, the young scholar gradually became attracted less by abstract philosophical systems of a "holistic" nature than by pluralism, and motivated less by the desire to seek immutable laws of cultural development than by a recognition of the open-endedness of human knowledge.

Introduction to pragmatism

Dewey's first teaching appointment was at the University of Michigan. There he worked with George Herbert Mead, a pioneer of social psychology. Mead, along with Peirce and William James, was probably the most significant influence on Dewey during his creative years. All three thinkers were committed to a view of knowledge radically different from that of traditional philosophy.

For them, truth did not represent a fixed structure of absolute, eternal principles available to the human mind, to which any newly discovered facts must conform; but, as Peirce had maintained, "that concordance of an abstract statement with the ideal limit toward which endless investigation would tend to bring scientific belief" (Dewey 1946:157). In other words, truth would be whatever best accorded with the beliefs about the nature of things at which humanity would arrive by means of scientific inquiry, *if that inquiry could be endless*. What best approximates truth in human culture is still only the current way-station on the continuous inquiry process, the practical test for which is contained in the rules of logic and evidence which dictate and determine that very process.

These thinkers believed that there exist no higher principles to be applied from outside this human process of organized intelligence, much as we would like to believe that it could be so. For all that humans *can* experience and have ever experienced is already available to that very process. And that method of intelligence, in turn, can be applied to the entire realm of human experience, past and present, if we would but choose to do so. Dualist philosophies which claim for humans some mysterious kind of access to principles of truth above and beyond human experience are dealing in contradiction and delusion, according to this view.

The epistemology summarized above is called "pragmatism." Peirce took the term from Kant, but used it specifically to mean the primacy of empirical consequences as the ultimate test for truth. Although it now forms much of the basis of modern philosophy of science, pragmatic epistemology was not generally accepted in Dewey's time, even by scientists. The choice of name was perhaps unfortunate (connoting as it does, the "practical" or the "expedient") as was the simple explanation usually given of its central premise: that the test for truth is what "works." What is actually meant is what works to permit dependable expectations of results. A statement expressing an experienced regularity has the status of temporary "truth" or scientific knowledge to the extent that it works to allow us to control the consequences of our acting upon it.

The scientific-inquiry process demands that we study problems in a disciplined and comprehensive way, observing and interpreting the conditions out of which they arise, then imagining a number of possible courses of action and hypothesizing their logical consequences. To the extent that a proposition so derived has been systematically and publicly tested and found reliable as a predictor, it can be considered to "work" and we can depend upon it as a true statement (or as Dewey expressed it, as an "object of knowledge"). This does not mean that it will be true forever, for the problematic conditions out of which it arose may change, or the perceptual and conceptual tools by which we define these conditions (our capacity to observe facts and interpret them within some accepted meaning system) may be vastly improved.

This was the philosophical foundation upon which Dewey stood when he was hired by the University of Chicago in 1894. The appointment launched him on a career in which he rapidly became one of his country's foremost scholars, and the renowned author of dozens of books. He presented countless university lectures, teaching in his last position at Columbia University in New York for over a quarter century from his move there in 1904 until retirement in 1930. It is not easy, therefore, to review his ideas simply and briefly.

On the role of philosophy

Dewey was a radical thinker in both philosophy and education. He disagreed fundamentally with the philosophical establishment, especially the European schools which, he felt, were accepted far too uncritically by Americans. He believed that philosophy is not a technical pursuit for experts but is, instead, for everyone. He did not agree that the purpose of philosophy is to reveal the shape of an eternal reality. Indeed, this goal he considered the ultimate conceit for a humanity constituting merely one small part of that very reality. For him philosophy can never be a quest for certainty of any kind. Only the pretence of certainty is possible, he said, and if philosophers give us that they are doing great harm.

Dewey did not believe that philosophy has any special access to a realm beyond the world of nature in which we think and act. How could it, as a human enterprise arising out of our experience within nature, and bounded as it necessarily is by the limitations of that experience?

The task of philosophy, as John Dewey saw it, is to interpret and assess the cultural epoch from which it springs, and to play an active role in shaping the future direction of that culture. It must forsake the old impossible goal of absolute truth, and seek not knowledge but wisdom. Only science can give us knowledge, he maintained. Art provides us with an intensification of quality in experience: the fuel for imagination and empathy. Philosophy must be a bridge between science and art. For though it is an aesthetic endeavour, like art, it must be founded on and consistent with the most reliable scientific knowledge available. This is quite different from the usual view of a philosophy *competing* with science in attempting to establish alternative roads to knowledge.

Philosophy also has an ethical aspect, according to Dewey. It must begin and end with the problems of humanity within nature. The only instruments available to humans for solving these problems are their thinking and valuing abilities, and it is these that education must develop and science and philosophy put to use.

Dewey believed that a philosophy is only as sound as are the assumptions about human nature on which it is based, and that those psychological assumptions must be firmly grounded in the findings of biology and the history of the species. According to him, none of the problems of human beings, whether classified as educational, moral, economic or political, can be understood apart from their source in and consequences for human nature. As one of the first thoroughly interdisciplinary thinkers of modern times, Dewey dedicated his life to the task of providing a theoretical foundation for this broad study of humanity.

Psychological premises

Understandably, the premises of psychology were tackled first. An article published in 1896, entitled "The Reflex Arc Concept in Psychology," is still considered a classic on this subject. It established Dewey's reputation as an original thinker in both psychology and philosophy. The article explains how the reflex-arc concept (as introduced by Descartes and still applied by the psychologists of Dewey's day) carried with it many of the connotations of the older dualism. Sensation, acting as a stimulus, was being interpreted as a thing existing by itself, outside of experience, just as the resulting motion (the response) was being assigned a separate existence. These two opposite ends of the arc were considered amenable to objective study. To the connection between the two, occurring within, was attributed a different kind of subjective psychic reality, available only to introspection. Dewey said that a *circuit* would be a better analogy than an arc, and a functional, integrated, continuous activity a better description of what was happening when a living organism responded to a stimulus. He explained that the stimulus only functions as such for the organism to the degree that the organism has become sensitized to those features in the environment with the potential for furthering the release of the response.

Dewey viewed the organism's typical transaction with its environment as an organized coordination resulting from a temporary change in the conditions being experienced. This causes something to function as a stimulus which has not done so previously, provoking a corresponding change in the organism in order to meet the challenge. The response is the resulting appropriate adjustment to the problematic situation; it is the key to meeting the altered conditions. The stimulus-response activity is not a linear series of two objective parts with a subjective entity in between that "wills" the connection. The entire "systemic" circuit is of one piece, every aspect of which is as objectively real as any other, just as the relationship among the heavenly bodies — not available to direct measurement — is as real as are their reflected lights in the night sky.

To use the example of Pavlov's dogs we could say that the inherited sensory circuit is interrupted by a new, problematic environmental condition: the sound of a bell accompanying the appearance of food. If the bell's ring were a mere random occurrence in the dog's surroundings, it would still be objectively present (and would be experienced as sound) but would not be a stimulus. It has to become connected with a particular set of organic adjustments, acquire a specific meaning in terms of these, and *thereby* it begins to function as a stimulus. The *consistent* response of saliva is what makes the bell a stimulus. Without such consistency "stimulus" and "response," viewed as linear cause and effect, are meaningless labels. The response of salivation is inevitably tied to the sound of the bell once that sound is *experienced* as a prelude to food. There is no mediating psychic operation which perceives the input, assesses it, then decides to produce energy for the response.

So it is not the bell as an isolated sensation of sound that stimulates a similarly isolated digestive response, but the bell in its gradually acquired function as a predictor of food. First it has to acquire meaning in the organism's adaptive processes — the source of all inference. As such, it begins to serve an integral role in the coordinated activity of digestion, no one aspect of which is less objective than any other — although they may vary in degree of accessibility to direct observation. For Dewey this meant that psychologists who focus on isolated sensations as the basic unit for the study of human behaviour are just as misguided as are those who resort to untestable explanations in terms of the psyche.

It is possible that Pavlov read this article and that it influenced him in his work with conditioned reflexes, for he does seem to have arrived at the same conclusions. Unfortunately, however, it is not clear that Dewey acquainted himself with Pavlov's research in subsequent years. If there is one recurring weakness in the great philosopher's writings it is their abstract nature and lack of a concrete factual base. The body of evidence produced by Pavlov on the functioning of conditioned reflexes would have compensated for that weakness.

On the role of habit

Dewey continued to elaborate on the model of human nature sketched out in the 1896 article. For what he described there (and for what Pavlov referred to as conditioned reflexes) Dewey preferred the ordinary term of "habit." Habits, he maintained, are the basic units of organic behaviour. His aim was to build a psychology based on habits and instincts (which become elements in habits as soon as they are acted upon). He explained: "Habits as organized activities are secondary and acquired, not native and original. They are outgrowths of unlearned activities which are part of man's endowment at birth" (Dewey 1922:89). However, "the *meaning* of native activities . . . is acquired. It depends upon interaction with a matured social medium" (ibid.:90). The infant's native instincts or impulses "are newly starting points for the assimilation of the knowledge and skill of the more matured beings on whom he depends"(ibid.:94).

Dewey wrote that human learning would be impossible "without setting up a mechanism of action, physiologically engrained, which operates 'spontaneously' and automatically whenever a cue is given. . . . All life operates through a mechanism, and the higher the form of life the more complex, sure and flexible the mechanism" (ibid.:70). This mechanism of habit is the way in which the organism incorporates the environment, or learns to adapt to change (ibid.:16). "The medium of habit filters all the material that reaches our perception and thought. . . . The immediate, seemingly instinctive feeling of direction and end of various lines of behaviour is in reality the feeling of habits working below direct consciousness. [This] . . . accounts for the intuitive element in judgments of action" (ibid.:32).

The more numerous our habits the wider is our field of possible action. The more flexible they are, the more finely discriminating and imaginative are our possible responses. Dewey claimed that it is the habits formed originally in, and gradually built upon, the process of instinctive behaviour that are the sole agents of our mature abilities of recollection, foresight and judgement; and "a mind or soul in general which performs these operations is a myth" (ibid.:176).

Habits are essential to intellectual efficiency. However, the more efficient a habit the more unconsciously it tends to operate. It is only where the conditions of experience pose a problem of some kind that habits come into conflict. The resulting release of impulse initiates a conscious search for new connections. Thought is provoked, and to the extent that the thinker has developed problem-solving abilities, the method of intelligence swings into gear.

Action precedes thought, said Dewey, or, more specifically, we must have "a habit before the ability to evoke the thought" (ibid.:30). But the two are not separate. "Thought which does not exist within ordinary habits of action lacks means of execution and . . . [criteria for testing]" (ibid.:67). He explained, "There is no immaculate conception of meanings and purposes. Reason pure of all influence from prior habit is a fiction. But pure sensations out of which ideas can be framed apart from habit are equally fictitious" (ibid.:31). He considered the first of these fictions to represent the rationalist fallacy, and the second, the empiricist fallacy.

Dewey believed that if it were not for the continued operation of habits in every act, there could be no such thing as character. "There would simply be a bundle, an untied bundle at that, of isolated acts" (ibid.:38). This does not mean that everyone achieves the integration of habits necessary for a *stable* character. "A weak, unstable, vacillating character is one in which different habits alternate . . . rather than embody one another" (ibid.).

It is clear that habits are firmly embedded and difficult to change. Dewey noted that people with an understanding of the role of habit in human nature and conduct would not fall for ideologies claiming that rapid and extreme socio-cultural change is possible through violent revolution. But this is not to say that human nature is fixed. New situations *do* elicit alterations in habits of thought and action. These have the potential for developing into the method of intelligence if the conditions of learning are right — but *only* if this is the case.

Habits are the essential mechanisms of thought and action which enable human organisms to achieve balance with the surrounding physical and social environment: "a balance constantly interfered with and as constantly restored" (ibid.:179). Experience is what results from and contributes to the human organism's transactions within nature. This relationship, regardless of the complexity and subtlety of the resulting experience, is perfectly continuous with nature. It is built upon an innate ability to make inferences — or to incorporate as keys to our responses, new connections in our surroundings. Through experience, a genuinely objective world enters into the actions and feelings of people and, in turn, is modified by their responses. Individual persons bring to the ongoing continuum of life experience all their current habits, plans, emotions and ideals, and these shape the momentary transactions with the surrounding objects and living beings, and are at the same time shaped by them. There is nothing we can know outside of this continuum of nature and experience, and even within it there is much of which we are consciously unaware.

This is not to underrate the significance of human consciousness, even though, within the total process, the individual consciousness is "but a small and shifting portion of experience" (Dewey 1916:6). For simpler animals and human infants it is those images, emotions and sensations immediately felt. For a being with language it is much more. It is the perception of actual events *within* their culturally acquired meanings. Consciousness could also be described as "the occasional interception of messages continually transmitted" (Dewey 1958:303). The subconscious, on the other hand, is a record of past experience of which we are currently unaware. It reflects all of the habits previously acquired by the individual, "that is to say, all the organic modifications he has undergone . . . [to the present moment]" (ibid.:300).

On knowing

One experiences many things without being conscious of them, even at the moment of input. However, these may go into the subconscious, along with all that was once "had" and even "known" but is no longer accessible to the consciousness. The above distinction is important. One can be conscious of many things without *knowing* them. We *have* experiences; that is, we continually undergo organic modifications in response to our surroundings, at times being conscious of them as images, urges and fleeting thoughts. But this is not the same as knowing. Central to Dewey's philosophy is the understanding that "having" a datum of experience is not at all the same thing as "knowing" it.

The act of knowing involves reflecting upon the data of our immediate conscious experience in a particular way. We cannot know an immediately felt experience any more than we can know something as an intuitive flash from beyond experience. The intuition is, of course, from the subconscious stratum of our previous experience. It may be the product of previous reflection, or of deeply ingrained habit or of messages from peripheral experience that had never quite made it into consciousness.

Just as knowing is not simply having an experience, it is also not the opposite: observing from without. "It is not the act of an outside spectator but of a participant inside the natural and social scene" (Dewey 1929b:197). We do not *choose* to be inside rather than outside the experience that we are observing; that is the essential condition of human life. Our only contact with the conditions of nature external to us (including social relations) is by means of experience. And we, in turn, are an irrevocable part of the external conditions experienced by other living organisms.

The process of reflection is spurred by the sensation of something problematic in the conditions being experienced. Reflecting amounts to the "determination of the data which define and locate it and which furnish clues as evidence" (ibid.). This involves the sensations being received within the meaning-system which has been built up through previous experience made functional by language. According to Dewey, "The instrumental theory acknowledges the objectivity of *meanings* as well as data. They are referred to and employed in reflective inquiry with the confidence attached to the hard facts of sense" (Dewey 1916:46).

Statements such as the above have often confused people. By "meanings" as employed here, Dewey meant the *explanations* assigned to experienced regularities: explanations that had become public and objective by being shared and tested against the experience of others. It is doubly unfortunate that he chose to refer to internalized "factual" beliefs as "objects of knowledge." This archaic language (traceable to Locke) is no doubt a major source of the widespread misunderstanding of Dewey's theory.

Other requirements for reflection in addition to factual knowledge are the ability to experience the metric properties of data and to employ the logical or symbolic operations that make prediction possible. That is, we must be able to distinguish between more and less, part and whole, additive operations and reversals of these. These operations, like the language that describes them, are acquired through experience from birth onwards, through a continuous adjustment to the demands of our physical and social surroundings.

Armed with a preliminary definition of the problematic conditions encountered (the necessary data with their meanings for us) plus the habits associated with logical operations, we are prepared for reflection. We are able to visualize a number of alternative solutions and to act upon them and experience the consequences of each in the imagination. To the extent that we thereby gain control of the consequences of action, we "know" the object of our reflection. We have gained an object of knowledge when our piece of controlled experience is shared by means of communication and found to "work" in the public domain.

In Dewey's words: "Finally, when these operations, or some combination of them, are used to solve the problems which arise in connection with the things of ordinary preceived and enjoyed objects, the latter, as far as they are consequences of these operations, are truly known" (Dewey 1929b:197).

If this reflective method is beginning to sound very much like the essentials of scientific inquiry, that is as it should be. For what *could* scientific investigation be other than a formalization of that basic human method of intelligence which gradually proved itself superior in solving the problems of human beings throughout the evolution of their species?

For the method of intelligence has indeed proven superior over time. What matters to human beings is not so much the immediate quality of experience as what they have been able to do with it. As Dewey explained: "One mode of experience is as real as any other. But apart from the exercise of intelligence that yields knowledge, the realities of our emotional and practical life have fragmentary and inconsistent meanings and are at the mercy of forces beyond our control" (ibid.:219). He wrote, as well, that "There is no way to know what are the traits of known objects as distinct from imaginary objects or objects of opinion . . . save by referring to the operations of getting, using and testing evidence — the process of knowledge-getting" (Dewey 1916:65).

Knowledge arises and operates, not from within human consciousness or mind, but from human experience of the surrounding *nature*. Indeed, "The exacting conditions imposed by nature, that have to be observed in order that work be carried through to success, are the source of all noting and recording of nature's doings" including those of human nature (ibid.:121). This noting and recording (and hypothesizing and testing — whether in the imagination or laboratory) is the method of intelligence within the individual and scientific inquiry when pursued in a public and disciplined way. Human history demonstrates that reliable knowledge is the fruit of this process *and of no other*. Where the physical conditions of existence are concerned, said Dewey, knowledge built up through the method of organized intelligence has gradually superseded magic and myth. It is only concerning our social relations — equally an aspect of nature —that superstition and mythology continue to prevail, to the detriment of humanity.

In his earlier works Dewey referred to his theory of knowing as "instrumentalism." However, he eventually dropped the more esoteric term in favour of "the method of intelligence." He hoped to discredit once and for all the premises of prevailing dualist epistemologies, whether of the older rationalism and empiricism or of the newer transcendental "phenomenology." All of these, he maintained, either posit the knower as separate in some vital way from what is known, or else attribute to sensation or to reason some prior level of reality. For all of them, he concluded, "The isolation of intellectual disposition from concrete empirical facts of biological impulse and habit-formation entails a denial of the continuity of mind with nature" (Dewey 1922:186).

Dewey considered that one of the most harmful consequences of the various dualisms implied by the prevailing philosophies has been their persistent refusal to apply the method of scientific inquiry to the problems of humanity. He maintained that there is no difference in principle between knowledge of physical facts and that of complex human affairs, even though there is a practical difference (Dewey 1929b:197). The latter may be more vulnerable to the effects of crude attempts at measurement.

Dewey's entire philosophy implied that the process of getting to know experienced objects inevitably alters future events. As he often pointed out, to the degree that we manage to gain control of our actions by applying reliable knowledge of causal connections, we can bring about different consequences from what would have otherwise followed from habitual or impulsive behaviour. Employing knowledge as an instrument as well as measuring effects will inevitably alter subsequent effects. Heisenberg's Principle of Indeterminacy came as no surprise to Dewey. However, as both he and its author pointed out, it has nothing whatever to do with any "essential" nature of reality. Unfortunately, many scientists still believe that their measures provide them with an exact mental picture of reality itself. For these positivist scientists — as well as those scores of lay people who live in a dualist idea world — Heisenberg's principle could only mean that *reality* is essentially random!

As Dewey explained, what Heisenberg had actually discovered was that "the particle observed does not *have* a fixed position or velocity, for it is changing all the time because of interaction: specifically, in this case, interaction with the act of observing, or, more strictly, with the conditions under which observation is possible. . . . [Position and velocity of the particle] . . . belong to our intellectual apparatus for *dealing* with antecedent existence, they are not fixed properties of that existence" (ibid.:202-203).

All this is of little immediate practical consequence where physical conditions are concerned, although the long-term results of great power to alter our physical environment, combined with abysmal ignorance of means of controlling our technology, is frightening enough. But scientific inquiry into such matters as the nature of human sexuality, ethnic differences and the source of religious beliefs does have a potential for altering the objects studied in very apparent ways. However, Dewey was convinced that this fact merely points to the need for increased recognition of the intimate connection between knowing and valuing in *all* aspects of experience. It does not mean that we should refuse the gift of knowledge about human nature and conduct, while applying the technological fruits of our powerful physical knowledge in increasingly haphazard and socially destructive ways.

On valuing

For Dewey, the relationship between knowing and valuing is at the very core of the method of intelligence. And at that same core is the only realm of freedom open to human beings. It resides in the possibility of choice. The necessity for choice arises when there is an excess of preferences. We want things that are incompatible with one another. If that were not the case the flow of habit would not have been interrupted. When we act out of the awareness that emerges from this clash of habits, we make a choice. Choice can be intelligent and reasonable, or merely impulsive. Choosing involves "simply hitting in imagination upon an object which furnishes adequate stimulus to the recovery of overt action" (Dewey 1922:192). Where choice follows deliberation, the chooser visualizes a number of possibilities, predicting the consequences that might flow from each, until "the moment arrives when the imagination pictures an objective consequence of action which supplies an adequate stimulus, and releases definitive action" (ibid.:193).

Imagining and reasoning are involved in the method of intelligent choosing — and feeling too. Reasonableness in choice is "a quality of an effective relationship among desires rather than a thing opposed to desire. . . . Choice is reasonable when it induces us to act reasonably; that is, with regard to the claims of each of the competing habits and impulses" (ibid.:194).

Valuing, however, is not the same as merely feeling or enjoying. It is the *act of judging* which future experiences or "ends-in-view" will be the most desirable. Dewey described it as "the constructing of enjoyable objects [ends] directed by knowledge of consequences . . . a change from looking to the past to looking to the future" (Dewey 1929b:272). Most of human behaviour, regulated by habit, is the result of *past* experience. His main proposition about valuing (or what he called "construction of the good") is that "judgments about values are judgments about the conditions and the results of experienced objects; judgments about that which should regulate the formation of our desires, affections and enjoyments" (ibid.:265).

When one values something one seeks to control the consequences of action by ensuring that what one does is likely to result in the object or event desired. This is where the method of intelligence comes in. Valuing implies choosing, for only by that means can we effect such control. And whenever our choosing involves reasonableness rather than mere impulse, what we are doing is *evaluating* the available alternatives in terms of their probable consequences. It is clear that reasoning and valuing are integral aspects of the method of intelligence, and not at all in opposition to one another, as traditional philosophies would have it. It is, of course, possible to choose without making value judgements, but it is not possible to choose *reasonably* without valuing, nor to value without applying the method of intelligence. For in the absence of intelligent reasoning we can only *feel* various shades of enjoyment or happiness as they occur haphazardly in present circumstances; we cannot control their presence in future experience. Thus do we lose our freedom to shape the future!

In no way did Dewey neglect the significance of emotion. Valuing would be impossible without impulses, feelings and desires as spurs and guides. He pointed out, however, that emotion can be harmful where the imagination becomes obsessed with one particular passion to the exclusion of all others. When this happens, habitual responses serving to maintain this passion take over, and intelligent choosing and valuing cannot occur. But " more passions, not fewer, is the answer. To check the influence of hate there must be sympathy . . . curiosity, caution, respect for the freedom of others. . . . The man who would intelligently cultivate intelligence will widen, not narrow, his life of strong impulses, while aiming at their happy coincidence in operation" (Dewey 1922:196).

On being religious

One of Dewey's least recognized contributions is his influence on American religious thought. His writings offered a sophisticated philosophical foundation for the current of scientific humanism nurtured within the Unitarian denomination. Increasingly, during the latter part of the nineteenth century and the early decades of the twentieth, it was the ideas of John Dewey that lived in the sermons of Unitarian ministers and shaped the religious education programs in their churches. In describing what was happening within American Unitarianism at the time, a historian later described how "Humanism swept through the denomination, becoming its most vital and distinctive theological movement since Transcendentalism. Advocating science against supernaturalism, democracy against tyranny, reason against superstition, experience against revelation, humanists plowed new ground among the Unitarians, eventually achieving parity with the liberal Christian position" (Wright:111-12).

In 1933, the Humanist Manifesto was prepared and signed largely by Unitarians. Among these names is John Dewey's. The Manifesto concluded with the following: "Man is at last becoming aware that he alone is responsible for the realization of the world of his dreams, that he has within himself the power for its achievement" (Kurtz:10). This is the central message of the only one of Dewey's books devoted entirely to the religious issue. In *A Common Faith*, he distinguished between concerns that could be called "religious," and "religions." For him, being religious implied a generalized moral attitude which is applied to all facets of living. He saw religions, on the other hand, as specific institutionalized patterns of behaviour involving ritual and creeds which stress the supernatural.

Dewey, like Bertrand Russell, was often attacked because of his attitude to religion. He claimed that to be religious was to be concerned about the moral implications of one's actions. And because, like Nietzsche, he viewed humans as integral parts of nature, whose every action inevitably affects that nature, he believed that *all* human choices are moral, and therefore religious, although obviously they are not all of equal importance. The sacred/secular dichotomy he saw as just one more harmful result of dualist thinking. He claimed that the ideals for which we strive are rooted in humanity's past experience and that these ideals or "ends-in-view" operate as powerful shapers of future experience because of their crucial role in the human valuing process. It was always Dewey's hope that our species would evolve ultimately beyond the need for a faith in the supernatural phenomena of myth and legend to a faith in these precious human ideals. And he was convinced that only by cultivating human intelligence rather than crippling or subverting it through ritual and dogma could humans learn to be religious in this sense.

On education, science and democracy

Speaking of cultivating intelligence brings us to the role of education in Dewey's scheme of things. He grew up and taught school at a time when schooling was vastly different from what it is today. Children were taught largely by rote and punished often and severely. Only the most privileged were able to attend secondary school. John Dewey's efforts (especially during his tenure at Chicago) contributed to a virtual revolution in North American schooling. By no means were all of the changes in the recommended direction, however, for no aspect of his work was more misunderstood and perverted than his educational theory. Much of what was to become known as "progressive" education was actually in conflict with Dewey's thought.

Dewey believed that all children should be educated, and indeed, must be if we are to have the kind of knowledgeable and intelligent voters necessary to sustain and direct a democratic political system. He did not mean merely that all should be "schooled," nor that education for democracy should be a permissive experience in which children control and direct their own learning process. He taught that the chief goal of education is to cultivate the method of intelligence (the habit of actively choosing in a reasoning and valuing way to experience some consequences and not others). He did not teach that the aim of schooling is to promote *doing* rather than *thinking*. He taught that the educator must begin where the children are, in terms of development and interest, and proceed to enlarge and enrich that present experience by bringing them into contact with selected aspects of the broad culture of humanity. He did *not* mean that the history and content of human culture should be ignored in favour of present fashions and fads.

When Dewey proposed that the public school should operate as society's major agency of social reform he was not advising educators to take advantage of the fact that children are vulnerable to indoctrination and therefore readily shaped into active agents of revolution — as some "social reconstructionists" have thought. He wanted all children to pass through a common public school and have their habits of thinking and valuing developed by it. He believed that the only way to reform and restructure society is to develop the kind of reflective, knowledgeable and moral citizens who are capable of making the necessary decisions at crucial turning points. He *did not* recommend that blueprints for utopian societies favoured by teachers or politicians be employed as goals for an indoctrination process, although his name has been used to lend credence to just such anti-educational endeavours.

Dewey believed passionately in the interdependence of science, education and democracy. It is impossible to understand his philosophy without a firm grasp of this relationship. For him, democracy can exist only insofar as voters have the habits of thought that render them capable of making intelligent judgements. These are the habits of the method of intelligence, or of scientific inquiry into problems. " The very foundation of democratic procedure is dependence upon experimental production of social change" (Dewey 1946: 157). The guarantee of individual freedom by the political system is not enough. Democracy as a moral ideal is irrevocably allied with the scientific spirit. Without the latter the pursuit of freedom is counterproductive. "Unless freedom of individual action has intelligent and informed conviction back of it, its manifestation is almost sure to result in confusion and disorder" (ibid.:61). And there is nothing more likely to ensure authoritarianism in government than the exercise of licence and anarchy!

Dewey was convinced that both science and democracy require, for their sustenance and survival, freedom of inquiry and communication, and tolerance of diverse views. "It is the nature of science . . . to welcome diversity of opinion, while it insists that inquiry brings the evidence of observed facts to bear to effect a consensus of conclusions — and even then to hold the conclusion subject to what is ascertained and made public in further new inquiries" (Dewey 1939:102). But all of these elements are involved in democracy as well! In fact, the glory of democracy, said Dewey, is the ability to admit the existence of problems (rather than to impose a false consensus) coupled with an institutionalized means of resolving problems. Dewey was convinced that "the successful maintenance of democracy demands the utmost in use of the best available methods to procure a social knowledge that is reasonably commensurate with our physical knowledge, and the invention and use of social engineering reasonably commensurate with our technological abilities in physical affairs" (Dewey 1946:33).

Dewey believed that the function of education is to develop in individuals the habits of knowing and valuing that will bring about "realization of the scientific spirit in all phases of human life" (Bernstein 1967:144). Without such people, nothing will guarantee the survival of democracy: no charter of freedoms or free elections or available opposition or even the rule of law. These are the institutions *necessary* for democracy; but they are not *sufficient*. Only if the citizens operate by means of the method of intelligence will democratic institutions long endure. And only through educational experiences carefully designed with that end in mind will such habits of knowing and valuing come about.

Dewey was never satisfied to confine himself to the academic environment. As an educator, he not only wrote numerous books intended as guides for teachers, but visited many classrooms as well. He was particularly involved in organizing the Laboratory School at the University of Chicago, where his educational theories were practised and evaluated. For a period in the 1920s and 1930s he was the most famous educational leader in the world. He spent two years in China at the beginning of the 1920s at the invitation of Sun Yat Sen and went to the Soviet Union when asked by Krupskaya, Lenin's widow, to advise the struggling new nation on how to establish a democratic and scientific school system. Under Stalin, however, Dewey's plans went unrealized. In fact, schooling in the Soviet Union was to proceed in an entirely different direction — authoritarian and elitist.

Dewey had wished the Soviet Union well because he was committed to social reform and believed that the Communists' early attempt to achieve economic equality was a noble one. But he was equally committed to freedom and justice: ideals that he soon came to recognize as being increasingly under threat in the young nation. Any praise of the Soviet Union was unpopular in the United States in those days, but Dewey supported a number of causes that required courage. One of these was the Trotsky Defense Committee formed in the United States after Leon Trotsky had been exiled and sentenced to death in absentia during the infamous Moscow political trials of 1936-38. Dewey chaired this committee of inquiry into the legal status of the charges against Trotsky and published a report of the findings which was extremely critical of the Soviet Union. He made a personal appeal to Stalin, which fell on deaf ears. Then, in Mexico where Trotsky was hiding, his son and secretary were killed. A little later, Trotsky was murdered by a young Spanish Communist and NKVD agent who was subsequently awarded the title of Hero of the Soviet Union by Stalin.

Another unpopular cause in the United States was Dewey's defence of Bertrand Russell, in the matter of a witch hunt against the British philosopher initiated by the City College of New York's offer of an appointment. The governors reneged on their offer to Russell after he had resigned from his previous position to accept it. Dewey used his influence to obtain another post for Russell and led the academic resistance to this shameful episode. He was also joint editor of a book about the case published in 1941. All this is doubly commendable, considering Russell's continuous misrepresentation of Dewey's thought, and Dewey's personal dislike of Russell.

On freedom and responsibility

As the previous stories indicate, Dewey was greatly concerned about human freedom, but he defined it very differently than had John Stuart Mill. His profound belief was that "the road to freedom may be found in that knowledge of facts which enables us to employ them in connection with desires and aims" (Dewey 1922:303). For Dewey, the requirements of human freedom are (1) the efficiency to execute actions, (2) the capacity to change plans and (3) the power of desire and choice to be factors in events. Only reliable knowledge of the regularities or connections among experienced aspects of the social and physical environment can give us the efficiency to execute actions in the pursuit of goals. The capacity to change plans depends on the ability to imagine alternative paths and their predictable consequences. And only by valuing certain consequences over others do we allow our desires and choices to affect the course of future experience. Without the habits of thought and action arising from these abilities we are indeed helpless pawns in an externally determined universe: prisoners of rigid custom on the one hand, and of unrestrained impulse wherever custom does not dictate the rules.

To the extent that we apply the method of intelligence in our daily lives, "we use the foresight of the future to refine and extend present activity. In this use of desire, deliberation and choice, freedom is actualized" (ibid.:313). All the old arguments about free will versus determinism are based on dualist premises which place the experience of humanity outside of nature. Dewey pointed out that freedom has nothing to do with an immaterial will capable of acting *on* nature in order to suspend or alter the natural flow of consequences. It has to do with our ability, through cultivation of the method of intelligence, to select or modify the consequences arising out of a particular situation, by deciding to act in some ways but not in others.

In Dewey's opinion, one of the few harmful legacies of the Enlightenment was the principle of natural law as applied to the social and moral realm. He deplored the endurance within our culture of the notion of a moral or intellectual order apart from the activities of our species, which we can identify and obey, or harmonize with. He believed that this principle (and the various pantheisms and idealisms arising from it) has been a major obstacle to the acceptance by humans of the responsibility to select desirable goals and to build the social institutions necessary for their realization. To refuse to strive for the most moral and appropriate means of achieving our valued ends was, for him, a gross abdication of human responsibility for the life that follows ours.

In this essentially human struggle, means as well as ends are important. Dewey considered the "means-end" problem an extremely significant philosophical issue. All of the twentieth-century rationalizations of violence hinge upon this. Can a moral end justify an immoral means? Dewey's position was unequivocal. Like the great naturalists before him, he maintained that there simply *is* no dichotomy: no dualism of means and ends. They are aspects of the one process; both involve attempts to control the consequences of present actions. "The 'end' is merely a series of acts viewed at a remote stage; and a 'means' is merely the series of acts viewed at an earlier one. . . . To *reach* an end we must . . . attend to the act which is next to be performed" (ibid.:34). If our current act is likely to produce consequences inconsistent with the "end-in-view," then it cannot lead to that end, no matter how we may delude ourselves that it will. No end can remain a good one that requires evil actions in its achievement, for each act alters the habits and character of the actor as well as the surrounding conditions.

It is necessary to assess an end in terms of the course of action to which it commits us, not the other way around, as is commonly supposed. Dewey reminded us that the only means within our power is the habit of knowing and valuing. Ultimately, *all* is means, for we become what we do, choice after irrevocable choice. The role of desirable ideals, or "ends in view" is to make each choice set in motion the best possible chain of consequences.

John Dewey was the most democratic of social philosophers. His was one of the most compelling and sophisticated arguments ever made for the emerging world view of evolutionary naturalism. He laid the foundation for a modern philosophy of science and for a broadly scientific approach to the study of humanity. However, he may be remembered most for his efforts in the service of a goal not yet realized: the heroic attempt to remove the disciplined process of intelligence from the sole jurisdiction of specialists and to place it in the hands of ordinary people, as the one essential tool in our common human search for knowledge and wisdom.

References for Chapter Eleven

Bernstein, Richard J. 1961. John Dewey's Metaphysics of Experience. *Journal of Philosophy* 58(January 5): 5-14.

————. 1967. *John Dewey*. New York: Washington Square Press.

Dewey, John. 1963 [1902]. *The Child and the Curriculum*. Chicago: University of Chicago Press.

————. 1963 [1915]. *The School and Society*. Chicago: University of Chicago Press.

————. 1916. *Essays on Experimental Logic*. Chicago: University of Chicago Press.

————. 1922. *Human Nature and Conduct*. New York: Henry Holt.

————. 1958 [1929a]. *Experience and Nature*. New York: Dover Publications.

————. 1929b. *Individualism Old and New*. New York: Capricorn Books.

————. 1929c. *The Quest for Certainty*. New York: Capricorn Books.

————. 1934. *A Common Faith*. New Haven: Yale University Press.

————. 1938. *Experience and Education*. New York: Collier Books.

————. 1939. *Freedom and Culture*. New York: Capricorn Books.

————. 1946. *Problems of Men*. New York: Philosophical Library.

Kurtz, Paul, ed. 1973. *Humanist Manifestos I and II*. Buffalo: Prometheus Books.

Mills, C. Wright. 1966. *Sociology and Pragmatism*. New York: Oxford University Press.

Ratner, Joseph, ed. 1965. *John Dewey: Philosophy, Psychology and Social Practice*. New York: Capricorn Books.

Wright, Conrad, ed. 1982. *A Stream of Thought*. Boston: Unitarian Universalist Association.

Twelve

From Naturalism to Mysticism

Henri Bergson

> The major task of the twentieth century will be to explore the
> unconscious, to investigate the subsoil of the mind.
> — Henri Bergson, *Le Rêve*

Henri Bergson was born in the same year as John Dewey. Like Dewey he had assimilated the premises of romantic idealism (and of Nietzsche's philosophy) from the university environment along with the very air he breathed. Both men were deeply influenced as well by the moral sentiments and educational ideas of Rousseau. Both became critical of the prevailing idealism and realism of their day and sought a more inclusive and believable third option. They developed somewhat similar philosophies of science based on the new biology and on pragmatism. But Bergson's version contained more of William James than of Peirce, and more of Spencer than of Darwin. And, unlike Dewey, Bergson chose to combine with James' pragmatism and Spencer's evolutionary social science a selection of ideas from Kant, Schopenhauer and Hegel.

Bergson was unwilling to accept the dethronement and demystification of humanity implicit in Darwinism. He preferred to accept Kant's version of a dualism *within* the human being: a dualism which would restrict science to the exploration of inorganic reality. And, whereas Dewey saw human consciousness as co-existent and consistent with nature, Bergson, like Hegel, argued for a consciousness that enveloped and exceeded the physical universe: one that made a divine humanity the focal point of cosmic creation. Finally, where Dewey accepted Darwin's hypotheses concerning evolution, Bergson insisted that something like Schopenhauer's cosmic "will to life" must be the engine driving the process.

Spirit, while thus retained in Bergson's system and imbued with a life of its own, was defined, nonetheless, as an aspect solely of a transcendental human consciousness. It is because of his exclusive focus on, and creative insights into, the *human* origin and limits of this spiritual dimension — as well as his emphasis on our classical heritage and the evolutionary origins of human institu-

---

References for this chapter are on p. 216.

tions — that Bergson can be counted as a pioneer of social-scientific thought. But he never fully accepted the premises of naturalism. While Dewey moved from romantic idealism to a perspective that was essentually monist and scientific, Bergson pushed certain of the ideas of Rousseau and Schopenhauer to their logical culmination in a seductive and extreme form of mysticism.

Life and times

Henri Bergson was born into an upper-middle-class family, and spent his entire life in the cloistered French university environment. He was a privileged child, living in both Paris and London and becoming fluent in both languages. A brilliant scholar, he excelled in mathematics and science as well as in the classics. He was particularly interested in biology and psychology and their interrelations. In 1878 he enrolled in École Normale Supérieure on the classical side, from which he graduated with distinction as a Hellenist. After teaching public school for two years, he was hired by a university in Auvergne. In 1884 he published his first book: a study of the works of Lucretius. During this period he completed his thesis for a doctorate in philosophy, presenting it in both Latin and French. It was published in 1889 as his second book.

During the following decade Bergson became distinguished for the quality and quantity of his scholarly publications. He had a gift of clarity in writing — as uncommon among social theorists then as it is today. He moved steadily upward in the French university system, achieving the apex in 1900 with his appointment to the Chair of Greek Philosophy (later of Modern Philosophy) at Collège de France. In 1907, with the publication of his best-known work, *Creative Evolution*, Bergsonian thought became fashionable throughout Europe and North America. He lectured on both continents during the next few years.

At the outbreak of World War I Bergson was fifty-five years old. The war, and the isolation it imposed, marked a turning point in his influence. He continued to write throughout the next two decades, but became increasingly secluded with the onset of illness and old age. In 1941, just before his death, he made a brave stand against the Vichy government, in defence of that human freedom of choice which his philosophy had declared and celebrated.

The concept of creative evolution

In the end Bergson became the most thoroughgoing of dualists. Not only did his theory posit a difference in *kind* between matter and mind, it expressed a corresponding split between the domain and method of science and that of consciousness; between space and time; between perception and recollection; and between intellect and intuition. As to the genesis of the various human faculties, his knowledge of the biology and psychology of his day had forced him to accept the *fact* of evolution. But he could not go all the way with Darwin's theory, which he mistakenly termed "mechanistic."

Bergson rejected the idea that "evolution must have occurred through a series of accidents added to one another; each new accident being preserved if it is advantageous to that sum of former advantageous accidents which the present form of the living being represents" (Bergson 1975:61). He believed that he had refuted this view of evolution when he cited the emergence of some form of eye in a number of different species. Such parallel development could not have been merely random or contingent, he claimed. However, he considered the teleological explanation equally unsatisfactory. It was impossible for him to believe that a creator had designed evolution for the sole purpose of producing humankind.

Bergson's attempt to resolve the problem was called "creative evolution." He decided that evolution simply could not have been guided from without, either by a "master planner" with a particular goal in mind, or by the contingencies of environmental changes and demands. Adaptation is a *condition* of the process, he claimed; not its guiding force. He preferred to see evolution as guided from within by an *élan vital*: an impulse or force for life that caused the matter in which it moved to continuously reinvent itself in a search for increasing individuality. Usually, in response to his clerical critics, he referred to this inexhaustible source of energy as God.

According to Bergson, there came a moment in that endless repetition of forms in space constituting inorganic matter when the *élan vital* entered and managed to invent forms with the capacity to endure over time. This duration in time was necessary for the beginning of individuality, or rudimentary life. Instead of closed systems with only a spatial dimension, life produced open systems, altering yet enduring over time as they sought perpetuation by establishing equilibrium in action and attempted to reproduce their kind. This was a flashpoint in evolution, said Bergson, resulting in a virtual explosion of life forms.

These first living beings were distinguished from inorganic matter by the "faculty of utilizing a releasing mechanism for the conversion of as much stored up potential energy as possible into 'explosive' action" (ibid.:132). The prerequisite for individualized action was an advanced nervous system, "a veritable *reservoir of indeterminateness*" (ibid.:140). Bergson explained that whereas all change within inorganic matter and simple forms of life is repetitious and therefore determined and theoretically predictable, the animal nervous system allows for time to elapse between sensation and response — and therefore an element of indeterminateness to enter. The development of complexity within the human brain marked a second flashpoint in evolution, as a virtually unlimited choice of possibilities for action became possible, and consciousness emerged.

For the period between the two great discontinuities in the evolutionary process (the advent of *life* and of *consciousness*) Bergson generally accepted the Darwinian theory of descent with modification. He agreed that the essential causes of variation are differences in the germ cells borne by individual members of a species, and not the inheritance of acquired characteristics. His chief disagreement with the scientists lay in his belief that "these differences are due to the development of an impulsion which passes from germ to germ" (ibid.:95) rather than to random mutations.

On consciousness

The crucial breakthrough into human consciousness might never have happened if the particular line of development leading to *Homo sapiens* had been extinguished through inability to adapt to changing external circumstances. Bergson admitted that "The part played by contingency in evolution is therefore great" (ibid.:278). Nevertheless, consciousness did appear, becoming housed in the complex nervous system of the human being. From that point on, humankind forever stood apart, different not only in degree but in kind from other animals. It was located in time, rather than merely in space. No other life form had the capacity to fix "its attention either on its own movement or the matter that it was passing through . . . [thus enabling it to turn] either in the direction of intuition or that of intellect" (ibid.:199).

The recognition of two possible directions for consciousness to pursue is central to Bergson's philosophy. He believed that his presumed dualism of matter and mind necessitated a corresponding separation in approaches to knowing. He recognized the existence of a kind of intelligent functioning that enables the human body to act upon its material surroundings in order to adapt to them. But, like Kant before him, he insisted that there is, as well, a life of the mind which grasps knowledge in the absolute. Bergson claimed that, while the former is the legitimate concern of psychology, the latter belongs to the jurisdiction of metaphysics. "Psychology has for its object the study of the human mind working for practical utility, and . . . metaphysics is but this same mind striving to transcend the conditions of useful action and to come back to itself as pure creative energy" (Bergson 1988:15).

On memory

Having posited the existence of these two dimensions of the human being, Bergson recognized the necessity for explaining their interrelationship. He believed that memory is the key. He envisioned two types of memory: pure recollection and remembered action, incorporated into the body as habit. He seems to have assumed that the other animals possess only the habitual kind of memory, and are therefore destined to function solely in the realm available to science. He claimed that humans, on the other hand, possess a pure form of memory. The brain can condition but cannot create recollections. In Bergson's theory, the brain is an instrument of action upon *present* objects, while pure memory (recollection) is the representation of an *absent* object. The one is therefore material and the other spiritual.

On perception

Bergson founded his theory of perception on yet another heroic assumption. He believed that all of the material universe must be made up of self-existing images. Among these, the human is the only one possessing a consciousness capable of perceiving both its own image and all the others. "My body is an aggregate of the material world, an image which acts like other images, receiving and giving back movements . . . [except that] my body appears to choose, within certain limits, the manner in which it shall restore what it receives" (ibid.:19). The human body is a centre and source of action, not just a reflector of the movements of other images.

For Bergson this meant that the same image must belong to two different systems: "one in which each image varies for itself and in a well-defined measure that is patient of the real action of surrounding images; and another in which all images change for a single image and in the varying measure that they reflect the eventual action of this privileged image" (ibid.:25). Bergson referred to the two systems as science and consciousness. It is the system of science that registers the motion of images in space, and, being the same for all images, is amenable to test. But, he insisted, consciousness is equally real, because we believe in it before all else and because it is our personal confirmation of our existence in time — and of the continuity of past, present and future (ibid.:27). According to Bergson, human consciousness is developed by means of perception. Perception is directed toward certain images on the basis of their relevance to the need of the organism to maintain its equilibrium in space and time. In other words, attention is inevitably fixed on those aspects of the encountered image which have utility for the organism's adaptive functioning. "The bodies we perceive are . . . cut out of the stuff of nature by our *perceptions*, and the scissors follow . . . the marking of lines along which *action* can be taken" (Bergson 1975:15).

The inevitability of distortion in perception

This means that the assimilation of an external image into consciousness is necessarily selective and partial. Affection (feeling or emotion) is another source of distortion. "Affection is the impurity with which perception is alloyed" (Bergson 1988:58). Yet another problem arises from the fact that perception is a learned process: one that is only gradually developed and made meaningful by the lingering echoes of previous perceptions. These memories are either in the pure state of inexpressible recollections, free-floating in the mind, or they constitute the sensorimotor bricks of the habit patterns from which all higher speculative reasoning is ultimately derived. In order for remembered experience to be rendered useful for perception, it must be actualized in "memory-images" whose forms are dictated by and encased within language. "The living thought becomes frigid in the formula that expresses it. The word turns against the idea. The letter kills the spirit" (Bergson 1975: 142). Bergson considered this unfortunate — perhaps even spiritually crippling — but acknowledged it as the necessary price of being human.

The external image, as perceived in the immediacy of contact, is pure sensorimotor, he said: sensation experienced in movement. But memory comes into play instantaneously in its presentation of those memory-images required to define the present moment and connect it to those previously perceived moments in time which have been stored as pure recollections in the mind. In Bergson's model, time is absolute. It is the independent variable. But the purity of the experienced moment is preserved in recollections only when they are undirected towards action, which he viewed as the body's perceptual thrust into space. Once recollections have been made accessible to the *act* of perception, by the intervention of the memory-image, they are already corrupted as sources of truth.

The stream of consciousness

This would seem to represent an irremediable dilemma for the metaphysicist intent on proving the possibility of absolute knowledge. For Bergson explained that the manifestation of pure memory in the culturally conditioned memory-image is as necessary a prelude to action as it is an immediate result of action. The path from perception to pure recollection is a two-way "stream of consciousness" whose currents ebb and flow in flashes of energy, between the present material moment and the spiritual entirety of moments previously known. At midpoint in the current is the memory-image. It is precisely here that Bergson claimed to have found the crucial connecting link between matter and spirit.

All this led him to the following axioms: (1) movements are indivisible, (2) movements are real, (3) division of matter into independent clips is artificial, and (4) real movement is not a thing but a transfer of states. Every act of perception therefore involves a transfer from the state of matter to that of spirit, and *vice versa*. He referred to this as "the continuity of becoming." Within this continuity Bergson believed that we encounter a homogeneity of time and space.

On the contrasting roles of intuition and intelligence

Bergson considered the function of memory to be all-important in other ways as well. For, "by allowing us to grasp in a single intuition, multiple moments of duration, it frees us from . . . the rhythm of necessity" (Bergson 1988:228). This means that we are not totally at the mercy of the demands of the present moment; by recalling the past we can imagine a number of future possibilities. Total subservience to the demands of the spatial dimension was originally lessened with the development of multiple motor-pathways along which the same excitation might proceed. The human became a centre of indeterminateness to the degree that the brain's connections proliferated *and* the spiritual or pure memory component developed.

In Bergson's view, *both* a complex nervous centre and spiritual awareness are required for an element of human freedom and creativity to become possible. "In reality, consciousness does not spring from the brain; but brain and consciousness correspond because equally they measure, the one by the complexity of its structure and the other by the intensity of its awareness, the quantity of *choice* that the living being has at its disposal" (Bergson 1975:286).

Bergson claimed that the existence of our remembered past within us is just as real as is the existence of physical space without. But only if the organism were totally divorced from the context of action within the external world would the previously experienced moments (as intuitions) be available to consciousness. Dreams are a jumbled record of this continued existence of past time. They are recollections floating free of the limitations imposed on memory by the body's waking tasks of willing and acting. In waking hours as well, memories are illuminated as useful memory-images in a totally non-chronological order, appearing only as the requirements of action dictate. For Bergson this is proof that spiritual elements (recollections) exist discontinuously in time.

He noted that when the organism acts on its surroundings, in the process of perceiving external images, consciousness is forced to accommodate itself to the *continuous* determined nature of distances in space. This is the aspect of the spatial dimension that produces regularities in causes and effects, and as the organism operates within this physical context, intelligence is gradually formed. This comes about as a result of the body's ability to coordinate the perspectives gained by its various sensorimotor attacks on the ordered spatial environment. In other words, what we make of the objects of our perception depends on how we fit together the messages from our various senses. However, this act of perception is at the very same time calling forth a non-chronological, *discontinuous* flow of remembered moments from the mind, and consciousness must accommodate to that as well.

For the human, then, "the exigencies of action are the inverse in the one case of what they are in the other" (Bergson 1988:146). Taking in the physical dimensions of the image demands an accommodation to continuity. On the other hand, to give it meaning in terms of past experience, a discontinuity in the content of experience is required. Bergson concluded that humanity, unlike other animals, operates on two planes of existence: the continuous, determined one of external, material space and the discontinuous, indeterminate one of time preserved in consciousness. The first plane is amenable to the "mechanistic" scientist; the second to the artist and mystic. The first responds to the method of intelligence, yielding testable, reliable (but inevitably relative and partial) knowledge; the second — impervious to reason and intellect — yields only to *intuition* which alone can produce an immediate, certain grasp of the "whole."

Contradictions

Bergson's claims about the actual (rather than theoretical) possibility of intuitive knowledge so profoundly contradict the logic and evidential basis of his theory of perception that the reader has the impression of falling off a cliff. One finds him suddenly in the strange position of arguing for the existence of the very thing that his entire theory has shown to be logically and empirically impossible: immediate and total knowledge of reality. How has he leapt from the conclusion that human perception of absolute truth is inevitably prevented by the subjective elements of affectivity and memory (not to mention the organism's need to discriminate among available aspects of its surroundings on the basis of adaptive utility) to the assertion that intuition of immediate reality is possible? How does he get from statements such as "the coincidence of perception with the object perceived exists in theory rather than in fact" (Bergson 1988:66) and "in fact, there is nothing that is instantaneous" (ibid.:69) to "in pure perception we are actually placed outside ourselves; we touch the reality of the object in an immediate intuition" (ibid.:75) and "The great mystic is to be conceived as an individual being, capable of transcending the limitations imposed on the species by its material nature, thus continuing and extending the divine action" (Bergson 1935:209)?

The answer in the myth

There seems to be only one possible explanation for this remarkable lapse in Bergson's otherwise scholarly work. Interestingly, the clue is in his own writings. In examining the social-psychological origins of superstition, he commented that "*Homo-Sapiens* is the only creature to pin its existence to things unreasonable" (ibid.:94). He went on to explain that from the very onset of consciousness within evolution, humanity began to create "counter-factual" structures of certainty wherever what experience revealed was either too puzzling or too frightening to bear. Hence the universal myths that render temporary or obscure the observable fact of death and those surrounding the subjects of fertility and reproduction.

A second function of myth is to protect society, without which humans cannot survive. In the absence of sufficient reliable knowledge to predict long-term consequences of present actions, individual egoism in pleasure-seeking would have imperilled the welfare of the group if necessary moral rules had not been firmly entrenched and invested with an existence apart from humanity. Myths expressing sexual taboos of all kinds fall into this category.

Bergson considered that the myth-making propensity in early humans took on the role of instincts in the other animals and was probably an effective adaptive device without which humanity may not have survived. Religion came to be the greatest repository of myth and, as such, performed an essential function in evolution. "Religion is a defensible reaction of nature against the dissolvent process of intelligence" (ibid.:112). The intellect may have demanded too much individuality, too soon, producing a disintegrative effect on the group.

According to Bergson, in the early stages of evolution, our budding intelligence could have seemed too cruel a master. In a dangerous world it could have forced one to see too much, and perhaps to refuse the self-sacrifice necessary to maintain the group. But, as intelligence and memory developed, providing the means to control nature to some degree, the myth-making propensity began to outlive its usefulness. Indeed, it eventually came to threaten and obstruct the process of knowledge-building and cultural adaptation. Bergson reminded us that myths are essentially security blankets, with the potential to stand in the way of progress. For, he noted, they do not usually express great truths about human relationships. They are rather historical expressions of the fictions that humankind has felt emotionally compelled to create.

It is very possible that Bergson, imbued as he obviously was with a powerful yearning for certainty, could not face the conclusions toward which his own work inexorably pointed. As he grew older, the logic of his own arguments and the evidence of his research may have become too painful to accept. One can trace the gradual ascendancy of the myth-making propensity in Bergson's writings, from middle-age when he completed his more scholarly works to the later decades of his life when he was increasingly debilitated by age and illness. As he himself remarked, when commenting on the prevalent belief in a source of spiritual power *apart from humans*, on which they are able to draw, "Once started on this road, there is hardly any absurdity into which intelligence may not stumble" (ibid.:124).

On morality and religion

The Two Sources of Morality and Religion (1932) demonstrates this change in Bergson. Although much of what he wrote about the biological and social-psychological sources of both phenomena is now generally accepted, that very solid part of his argument seems to have been presented chiefly as a basis for his rejection of traditional religion. He then went on to distinguish between the older "static" religion and his proposed "dynamic" variety. The latter was the approach of mysticism: for him, clearly the hope of the future.

Bergson recognized two categories of morality as well. The morality of obligation he called "social"; the other is "absolute morality." As with all his dualisms, they describe a difference in kind rather than degree. Social morality is inculcated from birth and is necessary for the survival of society. Absolute morality, on the other hand, is — like Kant's moral "autonomy" — internally inspired and requires conscious effort. It is an invention, similar to that of the artist. Moral progress is always the result of *moral creators* who envision a new kind of society and succeed in arousing the emotions and imagination of others. These creative people who personify the good, and with whom the populace comes to identify, are inevitably the mystics of each generation. They are generally found among artists, or the religiously committed. According to Bergson, "it is the mystic souls who draw and will continue to draw civilized societies in their wake" (ibid.:75).

He admitted that true mysticism is rare, but offered neither criteria nor techniques for distinguishing true from false prophets — in an arena where evidence and reason are by definition irrelevant. His description of the heights of mystical ecstasy and the subsequent depths of "darkest night" is remarkably reminiscent of manic depression. Studies indicate that this particular illness occurs more frequently among artistic people and religious fanatics than in the general population: a finding of potential significance for studies of mysticism.

The limitations of mysticism

How can we be sure that the charismatic mystic who has aroused emotional commitment and assumed moral leadership is not mentally unstable or a power-hungry charlatan? Bergson, in a different context, sounded a warning concerning the superstition and magic that have always plagued religion. "Let our attention to science relax one instant and magic will at once come rushing back to civilized society" (ibid.:162). Yet he expressed no similar concern that the rejection of the scientific attitude required for an acceptance of mysticism might allow numerous similar forms of anti-intellectualism to dominate the culture.

Bergson always claimed that he was not opposed to science — as was Nietzsche. Instead, he was merely able to recognize its limitations. But he recognized no such boundaries for mysticism. He saw philosophy as the mystic's tool. And philosophy transcends and incorporates science, he argued, just as consciousness transcends and incorporates matter. Philosophy takes over where science must leave off. It is "a study of becoming in general, it is true evolutionism and consequently a true continuation of science" (Bergson 1975:402) He posited a divine humanity as the ultimate outcome of evolution, within a material universe which is no less than a machine for the making of gods.

This is indeed a romantic mysticism carried to the extreme. The *élan vital*, working within matter in the direction of ever-greater freedom from the bounds of necessity, culminates in the creation of a humanity that is virtually a race of gods! And the precursors of these gods-to-come are the mystics living among us today. No doubt Bergson counted himself as one of the greatest of that elite group.

Bergson's influence on social-scientific thought has been deep and lasting. His major concept bears a strong resemblance to E. von Hartmann's "organic superforce" within nature, and to its subsequent development in Hans Driesch's idea of the "autonomy of life" — or vitalism. Modern Gestalt theory (as formulated from the 1920s to 1950s in psychology by Wolfgang Koehler and Kurt Koffka, and in philosophy by Max Wertheimer) would seem to be the most influential offshoot of Bergsonian philosophy in general. The twentieth-century philosophical movements of phenomenology and existentialism were influenced by his ideas as well.

The relationship between the works of Bergson and Dewey is a fascinating one. Wherever the French philosopher saw himself as operating within the system of science his ideas were very close to those of Dewey. In that mode of operation he contributed some valuable ideas to social-scientific thought. His study of the evolution of religion is insightful. His elaboration of Spencer's model of the organism as a system seeking equilibrium within a dynamic environment by means of sensorimotor activity provided the foundation for the theories of Jean Piaget — as did some of his ideas on moral development. And his insight about the significance of time in the element of indeterminateness required for the evolution of reason had a profound influence on contemporary thinkers such as Dewey and George Herbert Mead. However, that same insight has been viewed by other thinkers as a justification for the "holistic" approach within social science: one which rejects all analysis as "reductionist" and hence inappropriate.

Finally, one could argue that the scientific approach to the study of humanity requires an attitude not apparent in Bergson's writings. It implies a humble and even insignificant role for humans in the scheme of things (at least, before the advent of the relatively powerful scientific method) along with a discarding of the illusions of certainty. Bergson could not accept such conclusions, for they conflicted with his prior commitment to the present possibility of absolute knowledge for a privileged few and to an ultimate reality of humankind as God.

In current jargon, Bergson's "head" pointed in the direction of humility in the universal context, democracy in social relations and the scientific approach to knowing. But his "heart" demanded a central role in the universe for the human ego, along with a social elitism of mystics as moral leaders — with certain knowledge their singular privilege and sole domain. The dualism of his philosophy was perhaps an expression of his own contradictory urges. Like the primitive human that he described, his emotional makeup simply could not accept what his intelligence revealed, and he was convinced that if *he* could not survive such knowledge, much less could society at large. Consequently, and sadly for the progress of social-scientific thought, this man of superb intellect and the gift of eloquence in several languages left an ambiguous message for posterity. In the end, it is for his exalting of the fruits of intuition over those of reason that he is best remembered. And it is his forays into mysticism, rather than his explanations about the nature of perception, that have led critics such as Bertrand Russell and George Santayana to charge him with granting academic legitimation to the tide of anti-intellectualism and irrationalism so characteristic of the twentieth century.

References for Chapter Twelve

Bergson, Henri. 1975 [1907]. *Creative Evolution*. Translated by Arthur Mitchell. Westport, CT: Greenwood Press.

_____. 1988 [1908]. *Matter and Memory*. New York: Zone Books.

_____. 1935 [1932]. *The Two Sources of Morality and Religion*. Translated by R. Ashley, A. and C. Brereton and W.H. Carter. New York: Henry Holt.

Pilkington, A.E. 1976. *Bergson and His Influence*. London: Cambridge University Press.

Ruhe, Algot, and Nancy M. Paul. 1914. *Henri Bergson: An Account of His Life and Philosophy*. London: Macmillan.

Thirteen

The Phenomenology of Edmund Husserl

He was a poet and he hated the approximate.
— Rainer Maria Rilke,
Journal of My Other Self

The incompatibilities within Bergson's philosophy mirror the chasm separating what were to become the two major conflicting currents within twentieth-century social science. One of these was evolutionary naturalism, grounded in Dewey's model of a human consciousness dependent upon and operating within nature, and upon his pragmatic theory of knowledge as an integrated body of inevitably partial and open-ended — but workable and empirically warranted — assertions. The other was a collage of ideas rooted in the *Angst* of a mid-nineteenth-century Danish theologian called Søren Kierkegaard, the mystical transcendentalism of Bergson and the epistemology of Edmund Husserl.

These currents of thought evolved into the various competing modern versions of existentialist phenomenology: "ethnomethodology," "critical theory" and "motivation theory" for example. All share at least some of the assumptions of the movement now known as "postmodernism." This perspective views certain aspects of consciousness as prior to and detached from nature. It offers the possibility of absolute knowledge based on self-evident intuitions, discoverable through a form of knowing that supersedes the "mechanistic limitations" of scientific methodology. By a strange quirk of fate, the man who was to become known as the major architect of the new philosophy was born within a year of Dewey and Bergson.

A philosophical context and commitment

Edmund Husserl's birthplace, like that of Freud, was in Moravia, then part of the Austrian Empire, but now within Slovakia. He was born of middle-class Jewish parents and attended gymnasium in Vienna. He went on to the Univer-

---

References for this chapter are on p. 227.

sity of Leipzig, where he studied mathematics and the physical sciences, and to the University of Berlin for graduate work in mathematics. In 1881 he received his doctorate from the University of Vienna, with a thesis on calculus. After several years of teaching he returned to Vienna to study under Brentano. This experience persuaded him to move into philosophy, and he was hired in that capacity by the University of Halle. He taught at the University of Göttingen from 1901 to 1916, then at Freiburg as Full Professor until his retirement in 1928, at the age of sixty-nine.

Although Husserl believed that he was carrying on the work of David Hume, he was, in fact, very much within the other, more major current of philosophical culture: that which led from Plato through Descartes, Kant, and — most significantly, to Arthur Schopenhauer. However, whereas Bergson was clearly attracted by Schopenhauer's notion of the core evolutionary thrust of "the will to live," Husserl seems to have borrowed primarily from the latter's theories about the nature of knowledge.

Schopenhauer's philosophy was the epitome of rationalistic dualism. He believed that a cosmic "will" and "idea" co-exist within a material reality. Manifestations of "idea" (as in the reasoned understanding of an individual person) are temporal and die with the body; human manifestations of "will," however, merely rejoin the universal "will."

Schopenhauer agreed with Kant's rejection of Descartes' ontological proof of the existence of God, believing, with Kant, that such matters must rest on faith. He was committed to science and to reason. Accordingly, he was utterly scornful of Hegel — that "thoroughly contemptible creature whose whole pseudo-philosophy was really a monstrous application of the ontological proof" (Schopenhauer 1874:16). He was apprehensive about the tide of "anti-reason," in the form of romantic idealism, that Hegel's ideas had encouraged. However, he could not accept Hume's position on causality, offering instead his own "principle of sufficient reason" as a self-evident rational justification for all science. "The law of causality," he said, "relates solely and exclusively to *changes* in material states, and to nothing else whatsoever" (ibid.:53-54). He thought that causality occurs in three different forms: (1) as the *action-reaction* (or mechanism) of the physical sphere; (2) as the response to a *stimulus* in the organic kingdom; and (3) as *motive* in humans. He believed that all intuition is intellectual in nature — the product of an essentially human "understanding."

According to Schopenhauer, "the understanding first creates and produces the external world out of the raw material of a few sensations in the organs of sense" (ibid.:75). These sensations are transformed into objective intuitive perception, and then the understanding operates to construct the *causes* of these. Understanding thus consists of abstract mental representations of causal connections rather than merely the intuitively formed ones of all animals.

Schopenhauer recognized four kinds of truth: (1) *logical* (based on conclusions deduced from *a priori* premises); (2) *empirical* (based on direct experience); (3) *transcendental* (based on judgements resting on intuitive perception of the *a priori* ground of all knowledge, such as innate notions of time and space); and (4) *metalogical* (the logical expression of the conditions of all thought, such as "$a = a$," and "$a - a = 0$").

Schopenhauer provided a number of insights that have reappeared in social-scientific thought in subsequent years. His concept of "mental representations" and his claims about animal knowledge of basic relations of existence (such as "knowing" that "substance is permanent") were adopted by Spencer, and later, by Santayana and Piaget. However, it is his theory of knowledge that seems to have most influenced Edmund Husserl.

Husserl began as a mathematician. Having no background in cultural or historical studies, he approached philosophy with all the preconceptions of a formalist and absolutist. He thought that Descartes had stopped too soon, with his conclusion of "I think, therefore I am," and that Kant had not gone deeply enough into the "essential" structure of consciousness. "Unlike Descartes," he promised, "we shall plunge into the task of laying open the infinite field of transcendental experience ... the ego ... lies ready as a possible field of work" (Husserl 1960:31).

Husserl's goal was to develop a presuppositionless philosophy, stripped down, not to its neurological basis, but to an "egological" structure untainted by any previous experience of surrounding objects. This would be a purely rational, all-encompassing science of consciousness: one which would provide the necessary grounding of absolute knowledge for all the merely partial and relative sciences of fact. Like Schopenhauer, he wanted to demonstrate once and for all *how* and *in what sense* it is possible for humans to know anything at all. He considered his approach different from Bergson's, in that it would be non-metaphysical, and based solely on human reason. Phenomenology would be "a method by which I want to establish, against mysticism and irrationalism, a kind of super-rationalism which transcends the old rationalism as inadequate and yet vindicates its inmost objectives" (Elliston:248). His philosophy was to include no assumptions about the ultimate nature of reality, nor even about the natural facts of our existence in an observable physical and social world. It was Kant's logical *form* of human consciousness that concerned him, emptied of its contents.

Phenomenological reduction

Husserl believed that in this direction only was the true calling of philosophy. But in order for philosophers to embark thence, a radical reorientation of attitude was required. To aid in this he proposed a method of phenomenological reflection that would enable one to peel away the layers upon layers of preconceptions built up through a lifetime of experience in the physical and social world. This would lead the serious practitioner to a bedrock of pure "essence" upon which a founding philosophical science of transcendental phenomenology could be established. In Husserl's words, "Let us reduce till we reach the stream of pure consciousness ... a transcendence in immanence" (Husserl 1962:156). This was not the same as Bergson's "stream of consciousness" which flashes back and forth between "pure memory" and perception. Husserl's idea was to temporarily "bracket off" one's natural attitude of ingrained belief in the reality of the surrounding environment, until consciousness was focused only within a personal "life-world" with its expanding horizons of pure being. This, said Husserl, is the condition of "epochē." The "phenomenological reduction" used to achieve this was to be "a movement from the 'I' as a communally grounded reality to the ego as the source of what is ultimately the individual's own" (ibid.).

At times Husserl used the term "eidetic" to describe what his philosophy was about. "Eidetic phenomenology is restricted to the realm of pure eidetic description, that is, to the realm of the essential structures of transcendental subjectivity immediately transparent to the mind" (ibid.:16). It is through intuition that these structures are apprehended in all their immediacy: an intuition, however, that has nothing to do with either extra-human power or feelings (Natanson:23). Husserl considered intuitions to be instantaneous apprehensions of the essential forms of objects of experience: sources of the essential meaning of the "whole." He thought that these forms, once free of all their physical moorings, assume their own logic: a logic invariably immanent within the the autonomous ego.

Husserl did not equate phenomenological reduction with introspection. Nor did he consider intuitively apprehended truths to be merely subjective; that is, totally dependent upon the ideosyncratic reports of individuals. He was aware that in that direction lay solipsism: a dead-end only slightly less unsatisfactory to him than was the incomplete objectivity of empiricism. He was no doubt expressing a deeply felt need for the certainty of his familiar mathematical logic when he exclaimed, "One cannot abide the relativization of knowledge ... [whereby] truth becomes a function of fact, a variable in the state of mind" (ibid.:50). Clearly, knowledge for Husserl had to be absolute. His phenomenology was to be a philosophical science "of the essential being of things" (Husserl 1962:72).

The primacy of consciousness

Phenomenology, therefore, in no way denies the existence of the external world. Rather, "Its sole task and service is to clarify the meaning of this world, the precise sense in which everyone accepts it ... as really existing" (Husserl 1962:14). But that is possible only if "my own phenomenologically self-contained essence can be posited in an *absolute* sense, as I am the Ego who invests the being of the world which I so constantly speak about with validity. I myself, . . . as the open, infinite field of pure phenomenological data and their inseparable unity, am the transcendental Ego; the absolute positing of which means that the world is no longer 'given' . . . but henceforth it is exclusively my Ego that is 'given' " (ibid.:11).

Husserl maintained that, for the purpose of understanding how it is possible for humans to invest their experience with valid meaning, we are forced to take the ego as primordial and absolute. Ego must be seen as capable of transcending the objects of experience; of rendering them dependent upon it for their meaningful form. The world in which the ego finds itself certainly exists, but, apart from the "intentional I" acting upon it, this external world has no meaning.

Husserl was convinced that naturalism had it all backwards. He declared that it is not true that consciousness is an aspect of nature; nature (insofar as it can ever exist *for us*) is a product of human consciousness. He supported this conclusion by arguing that the world of objective experience has no "essential" logic of its own. "Reality is not in itself something absolute . . . it has no 'absolute essence' whatsoever" (ibid.:139). It exists as a *correlate* but not a *condition* of consciousness. "The existence of what is natural cannot condition the existence of consciousness since it arises as a correlate of consciousness; it *is* only insofar as it constitutes itself within ordered organizations of consciousness" (ibid.:142).

This does not mean, as it seemed to mean for Bergson, that the natural world is actually existing within consciousness, in the form of recollections of pure images. Husserl noted that "neither the world nor any worldly object is a piece of my ego, to be found in my conscious life as a really inherent part of it" (Husserl 1960:26). What consciousness contains, instead, is the "noema": the intentional object, or the perceived thing in the form that it is grasped intuitively as *meant*. The intending act, or "noesis," is there as well, unified with the object grasped. It is not clear from Husserl's writings how one can describe consciousness as autonomous and independent, if it must thus continuously reach beyond itself for its very essence. This is one of the many contradictions that were to plague the philosopher in his later years.

Husserl proceeded to explain — in terms reminiscent of Schopenhauer — that the natural world has no logic of its own. It merely represents, for the ego, a shifting horizon marking the boundaries of potential "phenomena" (objects of the ego's intentional acts). These phenomena assume their being solely in the context of the intentionality of consciousness. They do not exist in the form of observable facts. Granted, he said, the empirically accessible data of nature operate as initiators of phenomena, and as such are not unimportant. Empirical science should not be written off, only understood as necessarily limited. What the surrounding world is actually presenting to consciousness, within these data, is an infinity of possible experience transcending the present moment. However, this transcendent must be, in principle, capable of being experienced by any actual ego (Husserl 1962:136). There is no place in Husserl's theory for other-worldly beings or forces beyond the realm of the natural. Only the "immanent being" of consciousness, transcending but still utilizing the natural world as grist for its mill, is absolute (ibid.:137).

The problem of verifiability

Husserl recognized that his theory of essential meaning had a serious anomaly at its very core: given the private nature of phenomenological reduction, how could it be possible to verify its results? Meaning must be, at least in theory, shareable with other egos, or what is the point of it at all? How can communication of any kind be even remotely possible among autonomously intentional egos? Husserl seemed to be hoist with this petard of his own making. Even his admirers pointed out the obvious fact that he had provided no way for the phenomenologist to check his own work for errors. Nowhere in Husserl's writings can we find a really satisfactory explanation of how verifiable intersubjectivity could be achieved in the context of phenomenology. Yet he claimed priority for the assertions of his philosophy over those of all other human studies. For example: "Perhaps the scientific discipline which the life-world, in its universality, requires is one which is precisely not objective and logical but which, as the ultimately grounding one, is ... superior in value" (Natanson:128).

Husserl, an honest, searching man, was not unaware of this contradiction. He knew the difficulties posed for phenomenology by the intersubjectivity problem and he sought long and hard to overcome them. He began at the beginning, with an attempt to demonstrate a phenomenological explanation for empathy. How can one independent subjectivity share another's feelings, or in any meaningful way experience the egological structure of "the other"?

Husserl concluded that it is indeed possible to account for the obvious existence of empathy without going beyond the phenomenological method. As he explained it, one must first employ a reduction process to return to the sphere of "ownness." Accordingly, "We disregard all constitutive achievements of intentionality which relate either directly or indirectly to another subjectivity" (Husserl 1960:124). He believed that he had indeed accomplished this feat, by reducing his field of experience downward until he had arrived at his own *animate organism*: "the sole object within my abstract world-stratum to which I ascribe fields of sensation ... the only object *in* which I *rule and govern* immediately" (ibid.:128). Husserl was convinced that at that precise point he was aware of an "also there" in addition to "this there." In a unified act of "assimilative apperception" the self accepts the other's thoughts and feelings as analogous to its own. It is intuitive rather than the inferential process that Spencer had claimed it must be. Husserl concluded: "The experienced animate organism of the other continues to prove that it actually exists as an animate organism only in its changing but continuously harmonious *behaviour*" (ibid.:144). Although the inner life of the other can never be "given" to one's consciousness, apprehension of harmony or disharmony among its behaviours, and between them and our own, does occur. This provides the evidence that makes possible a sharing of awareness.

It is impossible not to notice Husserl's reliance on the evidence of observable *behaviour* at this point. This is particularly intriguing in view of the revulsion toward behaviourism expressed by his followers. It is similarly impossible to avoid the conclusion that the type of reduction described here by Husserl — far from transcending the natural world — is actually occurring very much *within* it. According to him, it is "only through the connecting of Consciousness and body into a natural unity that such a thing as mutual understanding between animate natures . . . is possible" (Husserl 1962:149).

He also admitted that this had not, in fact, been a phenomenological reduction at all, the object of the entire exercise having been to reach the bare bones of the ego's organic aspects rather than any "essential' quality of consciousness. Ironically, Husserl's lengthy, convoluted argument intended to establish the mere possibility of intersubjectivity within his theory appears, in the end, to have required the ignoring of phenomenology as a method!

Second thoughts

Not surprisingly, Husserl seemed to have been unable to progress any further in his attempt to discover intersubjectively warranted criteria for assessing the validity of the results of particular applications of phenomenological reduction. The inescapable conclusion that the method had failed to permit navigation of the very first step must have been a bitter blow. How could a sophisticated, rational thinker continue to make the claim that his work had established the "true root of Reason" (Natanson:170)? How could he sustain the belief that he had found the philosophical grounds of certainty, against which all other forms of human knowledge were to be assessed, when his theory had failed to yield even one intersubjective criterion for testing the truth of its revolutionary claims?

Another serious deficiency in phenomenology must have become apparent to Husserl in his later years, for there is evidence that he began to make changes that struck at the very heart of his theory. The ultimate objective of his transcendental reduction was to move from the world which the scientific attitude reveals; in other words, to cordon off all the perceptions and conceptions attesting to the continuity and repetitiveness of sensations flooding in from those everyday surroundings in which we *necessarily* believe. This would supposedly allow us to focus on the primordially given life-world: the world as experienced in the sheer immediacy of the stream of consciousness; the world whose essential meaning could be grasped in its pure rational form; the world as it would exist for us "ideally" in the absence of all cultural pre-conceptions. It seems that Husserl had begun to question not only the efficacy of his method, but the very possibility of this goal.

For he began, belatedly, to acknowledge the necessary role of language in intersubjectivity. This, in turn, seems to have led to a recognition that scientific concepts, disciplined as they are by the rules of mathematical logic and encased as they are within the medium of humanly constructed language, may in some way involve the essential aspects of structures immanent in consciousness. He began to speak of a "horizon of civilization" enclosing the life-world, thus seeming to extend the focus of the egological centre from "things" in the physical environment to certain ideas in the cultural environment: scientific theories, to be exact.

He recognized, however, that scientific knowledge with its internal logic differs from physical "things" in at least one significant way: with the passage of time it alters and accumulates, and, in the process, changes subsequent reality. In fact, Husserl began to suspect that any creation of human consciousness must affect the composition, and perhaps the essence, of what is externally available to the intentional act. He realized that he had failed to deal with the problem of historical change. This led him to wonder whether consciousness could still be considered independent of the cultural sources and consequences of its own constructs.

Husserl was finally forced to acknowledge the significance of the existence of logical constructs in the ego's surroundings. He noted that "these are human formations, essentially related to human actualities and potentialities, and thus belong to this concrete unity of the Life-world, whose concreteness thus extends farther than that of things" (Husserl 1970:130). But this represents a remarkable turn-about for Husserl! In fact, he seems to have contradicted the most central premise of phenomenology. Where is the primordial autonomy of the ego now, when even its innermost recesses — its "objects as intended" — must necessarily comprise not only the essential meanings of unorganized physical data, but the continuously changing conceptual structures of a surrounding culture as well?

The dream is over

At this point Husserl's life began to assume the proportions of a classic tragedy. In 1928 his Chair at the University of Freiburg was taken over by Martin Heidegger, a former student and subsequently a leading light in the existentialist movement. Heidegger became Rector of the university as well. It was almost immediately apparent that he was applying the phenomenological method (along with Nietzsche's notion of the Superman) in the service of Nazism. The first sign of things to come was the change in his attitude toward Husserl, who was known to be a non-practising Jew. The dedication to his former mentor was removed from Heidegger's book, *Being and Time*. Husserl became a non-person, even in his beloved university. Soon after Heidegger's ascension all Jewish professors were quietly removed.

The following quotation from Heidegger's Rector's Address will serve to show how the premises of phenomenology lent themselves all too readily to the support of totalitarianism: "The university's 'essence' must be 'willed' and 'asserted' by a German nation that submits itself to the power of its spiritual-historical 'being.' Mere academic freedom . . . gives rise to meaningless specialized research. Real freedom is achieved only in the discovery of an essence residing in the German student body itself, which is 'on the march'. . . . It is not enough to greet the new order. It is rather a question of choosing one or the other, of deciding to put ourselves under the authority of the new reality or disappear with a world now in decline" (Lilla:43). Elsewhere Heidegger wrote, "The Fuehrer, and he alone, is the sole German reality and law, today and in the future" (ibid.:44). No doubt this "essential meaning" came as an unchallengeable intuition, arrived at by phenomenological reduction!

There were many other students and followers of Husserl intent upon using phenomenology (in combination with the ideas of Kierkegaard and Bergson's "creative evolution") as a foundation for the emerging European existentialism. Husserl himself became increasingly uneasy about the subjectivism and irrationalism which he feared was inherent in the movement, and even challenged its expositors with their use of reason to argue for unreason. Depressed about what the twentieth century was heralding for humanity, and perhaps seeing clearly his own contribution to the approaching deluge, he wrote despairingly, "Philosophy as a science, as serious, rigorous . . . science — *the dream is over*" (Natanson:xvi). He died in 1938, an unsung Jew in a Germany celebrating its mystical unity of "being" in a rush toward the chasm.

One cannot help but wonder whether Husserl's early ideas would have gained any credence whatsoever if he had been able to express them clearly and succinctly. Even his essay on phenomenology for the *Encyclopedia Britannica* was considered too abstruse to publish. Nonetheless, it is an undeniable fact that the writings of Edmund Husserl have been incredibly influential. They have provided a virtually infinite mine of contradictory interpretations for the service of scholars. Perhaps an obscure and turgid writing style is to the academic philosopher what metaphor is to poets: the necessary source of ambiguity that allows their creations to be all things to all people.

However, as Husserl discovered to his great sorrow, ambiguous philosophical assertions can be dangerous for humanity. A careful reading of his works reveals his great respect for science, in spite of his belief that the "essential meaning" of the world cannot be revealed by observable facts. And his commitment to human reason seems unarguable. Yet his theory has been used to justify a pervasive attack on science and rationality, spearheaded by academics and happily spread among the populace by a variety of politically inspired, self-styled mystics. Similarly, his intent throughout was obviously *not* to lend support to a radical subjectivism or idealism, but to maintain the reality of the external world as the necessary context of consciousness. Yet, because his writing contains countless references to Ego as the autonomous source of "being," many of his readers have felt justified in assuming that he meant just what that would seem to mean.

The great tragedy for Husserl is that, in spite of a consuming dedication to logic, his life and work were plagued with contradictions. Foremost among these was his remarkable inability to identify the ontological assumptions of his own world view. For example, there was the hatred of naturalism and positivism and the need for certainty that inevitably directed and shaped his supposedly presuppositionless phenomenological method. Another unrecognized assumption was the one that formed the base of his entire theory: the belief felt by every infant that the ego is primordial and absolute. Then there was his extraordinary lack of awareness of the influence of culture on human thought in general, and on his own way of thinking in particular.

Oblivious to his own conditioning in the protected setting of a middle-class family and privileged schooling (and subsequently, within the "ideal" world of mathematics) he devoted his life to the search for an equivalent logical purity and certainty in the foundations of human knowledge. In the end, he was forced to recognize not only the failure of his quest, but the presence of grievous logical inconsistencies at the very heart of his life work. Committed to human reason as the ultimate ideal, he lived to see his ideas employed by former students as powerful weapons of irrationalism. And, finally, this admirer of science and supporter of the "brotherhood of man" heard his own words used to undermine the scientific attitude and to attack humanity.

Conclusive evidence concerning Husserl's influence on social theory is probably not yet in. Phenomenology's sibling, existentialism, has been of great significance within social science, and will be dealt with in succeeding chapters. A tentative assessment can be made at this point, however. Husserl's work has served as a reminder to cultural scholars everywhere that it is the meaning assigned by humans to experience that is most important; and that private interpretations of experience may not be easily accessible to the observer. His poorly formulated notions about the structuring of categories of meaning have been further developed, as has the concept of intersubjectivity.

Finally, the work of Edmund Husserl is important to our story because various interpretations and misinterpretations of it — along with that of Nietzsche and Bergson — have nourished within the social-science community an "anti-science" current that is influential still. This is ironic, in that he had hoped to be remembered for broadening the scope of *science*.

References for Chapter Thirteen

Carr, David. 1974. *Phenomenology and the Problem of History: A Study of Husserl's Transcendental Philosophy*. Evanston, IL: Northwestern University Press.

Elliston, Frederick A., and Peter McCormick eds. 1977. *Husserl: Expositions and Appraisals*. Notre Dame: University of Notre Dame Press.

Husserl, Edmund. 1960. *Cartesian Meditations: An Introduction to Phenomenology*. Translated by Dorian Cairns. The Hague: Martinus Nijhoff.

_____. 1962 [1913]. *Ideas: General Introduction to Pure Phenomenology*. Translated by W.R. Boyce Gibson. New York: Collier Books.

_____. 1965. *Phenomenology and the Crisis of Philosophy: Phenomenology as Rigorous Science and the Crisis of European Man*. Translated by Quenton Lauer. New York: Harper & Row.

_____. 1969. *Formal and Transcendental Logic*. Translated by Dorian Cairns. The Hague: Martinus Nijhoff.

_____. 1970. *The Crisis of European Science and Transcendental Phenomenology*. Translated by David Carr. Evanston, IL: Northwestern University Press.

Lilla, Mark. 1990. What Heidegger Wrought. *Commentary* 89,1 (January): 41-51.

Natanson, Maurice. 1977. *Edmund Husserl: Philosopher of Infinite Tasks*. Evanston, IL: Northwestern University Press.

Schopenhauer, Arthur. 1896. *The World as Will and Idea*. Vol. 3. Translated by R.B. Haldane and J. Kemp. London: Kegan Paul, Troebner.

_____. 1874 [1818, 1847]. *On the Fourfold Root of the Principle of Sufficient Reason*. Translated by E.F.J. Payne. La Salle, IL: Open Court.

Sokolowski, Robert. 1964. Edmund Husserl and the Principles of Phenomenology. In *Twentieth-Century Thinkers*. Edited by John K. Ryan. New York: Alba House, p. 133-57.

Fourteen

Emile Durkheim and Max Weber
A Matter of Boundaries

> But he sits, and beneath his thoughts his broad wrists almost
> break
> as his mind grows heavier, always heavier.
> — Rainer Maria Rilke, *In the Certosa*

The latter half of the nineteenth century was a time of territorial expansion within universities. No sooner had the natural sciences become firmly established than psychology began to make inroads under Wilhelm Wundt in Germany, Sigmund Freud in Austria, G. Stanley Hall and William James in America and Ivan Pavlov in Russia. Meanwhile Martineau, Comte, Spencer and others had been registering a claim for a separate discipline called "sociology." This was to be a broadly conceived study of the evolution of socio-cultural institutions, which they assumed would involve a scientific search for comprehensive and absolute laws of development comparable to those identified by natural science.

Of those responding to the challenge, two are outstanding in the influence they have wielded — although both have had to yield to Marx in terms of lasting effects on sociology. Emile Durkheim is responsible for establishing the new discipline in France, and Max Weber is generally credited with the same accomplishment in Germany. Both were, to some extent, offering an alternative to Marxism. Both were close in age to Dewey, Bergson and Husserl, and therefore presumably in contact with the original work of those scholars. Both had been influenced in their view of science by Descartes. However, apart from the goal of establishing the academic and scientific credibility of sociology, the two shared little else. The story of their contradictory approaches sheds considerable light on the troubled history of social science to this day.

Max Weber was an admirer of Machiavelli, Kant, Schopenhauer, Fichte and Nietzsche. He had become convinced that the human studies deal with a reality so discontinuous with nature that they require a science equally unique in approach and objective. He also concluded that, within the realm of the hu-

References for this chapter are on p. 255-57.

man, numerous autonomous jurisdictions must be defined and isolated — each with its own distinctive content and appropriate mode of study. Sociology would be concerned only with the study of *culturally significant* and *socially meaningful* phenomena. For inspiration Weber turned to the neo-Kantian and romantic idealist perspectives dominating his familial and educational environment — particularly the ideas of Wilhelm Dilthey and his colleagues, Georg Simmel, Heinrich Rickert and Edmund Husserl. He seldom referred, in his writing, to the work of contemporaries in other intellectual traditions and in other countries.

Durkheim's philosophical premises and objectives for sociology contradicted those of Weber on almost every count. A thoroughgoing interdisciplinary thinker, he developed his own position in the process of an ongoing give-and-take with the world's foremost contributors to the biology, psychology, anthropology and epistemology of his times. His familiarity (and often disagreement) with the works of people like Marx, Spencer, Freud, Toennies, Tylor, Wundt, Bergson, Dewey and James shows clearly in all his writings. And beyond all these are echoes of the profound influence of the Martineau-Comte approach to social science in general.

Durkheim saw the human studies as necessarily connected, simply because their subject matters are connected as a result of their evolutionary origin and their ideational and collective nature. Not only did he chart no boundaries *among* them — where method and objective were concerned — he also refused to draw a firm line between these studies and the natural sciences. It has been the unfortunate fate of sociology to be pulled hither and thither ever since in the wake of the conflicting directives and parameters established, first by the lingering shadow of the early Marx, and then by these two pioneering founders during the dying years of the nineteenth century.

Flickering candles at an era's close

Emile Durkheim was born in 1858 in Épinal in the province of Alsace, and died in 1917. Max Weber's life began in Erfurt, Thuringia, and spanned the years between 1864 and 1920. The formative experiences of the two could scarcely have been more different. Durkheim grew up as the son of an impoverished rabbi at a time and place in which Jewish ghettos were in the process of disintegrating. He was accepted at the École Normale in 1879, on his third try at the entrance exams. Following graduation he taught secondary school from 1882 to 1887, with a year off for study in Germany. While there he studied social science and ethics, under Wilhelm Wundt, and published his first article. It indicated the direction his mature scholarship was to follow. In it he wrote, "Men are attached to one another as naturally as the atoms of a mineral and the cells of an organism. The affinity which they hold for one another is based upon a feeling the germs of which can be found in animal societies; this expands, diversifies and becomes transformed with progress, but is no less natural to man than egoism" (Durkheim 1972:56).

Max Weber lived out his life in an upper-class social environment in Germany. His parents belonged to the powerful elite. His father was a member of both the regional *Landtag* and the central *Reichstag*, and his mother was descended from the aristocratic Fallenstein family. The home of Max's boyhood was a centre of political activity and intellectual discourse. It is not surprising that his first love was politics, and that, throughout his life, he seemed more at ease in that milieu than in the academic environment.

In 1880 Max, already with the reputation of an excellent student, enrolled at the University of Heidelberg to study economics, philosophy and Roman law. Three years later he spent a year in the military. He apparently loved the life — the discipline, duelling and drinking. He then pursued graduate studies at the University of Berlin in 1884 and the University of Göttingen the following year. In 1889 he completed a Ph.D. thesis on medieval trading companies, and two years later qualified as a university lecturer with a thesis on Roman agrarian and legal history. Throughout this period he continued to live at home. In 1892 he was hired to teach law at the University of Berlin. That same year he married a relative, Marianne Schnitzer, who later became known as a leading politician, writer and early feminist in Weimar Germany.

Politics was a passion for Weber all his life. Although he never achieved an elective office, he did become an influential member of the commission which created the Weimar constitution. His first political involvement was with the newly formed National Socialist Association which he initially opposed and later joined. He was a member of the Pan-German Union until he resigned in disgust at their refusal to push for the exclusion of Polish farm workers from Germany's eastern border areas. Weber's first major scholarly study dealt with that subject. His conclusion was that agrarian policy must be determined by the interests of the state, and a border population whose loyalty cannot be assumed concerned him. He wrote, "We wish to arrange external conditions not with a view toward people's wellbeing but . . . to preserve . . . those physical and spiritual qualities that we would like to maintain for the nation" (Marianne Weber:137).

Weber's position here sheds light on what emerges as a persistent ambiguity in his attitude toward Jews. Marianne Weber, writing in 1925, referred (approvingly, it seems) to his concern about the relationship between "Semitic" and Indo-European peoples. "Again and again the intermingling of the two elements seem to him to have led to a 'Semitization,' that is, the defeat of the Aryan culture. . . . He concluded that 'the Indo-Europeans could bear neither an intellectual intermixture nor the despotic forms of government peculiar to the Semites' " (ibid.:47). She also said that he regretted the fact that so many Jews were revolutionary leaders. And yet — she claimed that Weber hated the anti-

Semitism that denied people like Georg Simmel the academic prestige they deserved in Germany. One must believe this, for it is supported by Weber's actions.

Emile Durkheim was hired by the University of Bordeaux to teach the first social-science course in France, and was also married the year of his first appointment. Nine years later, the first Chair and Full Professorship in social science was created for him at Bordeaux. In contrast to Weber, he had little interest in direct political involvement. He was drawn into activism only once, when he felt compelled to take a stand for justice in the Dreyfus affair. In 1902, at the age of forty-four, he was appointed to the Chair of the Science of Education at the Sorbonne, where social science was then still not recognized. It was not until 1913 that the title of the Chair was changed to Science of Education and Sociology.

Meanwhile, Max Weber had become Professor of Political Economy at the University of Freiburg in 1894, and three years later was appointed Chair of Economics at the University of Heidelberg. In 1903, at the age of thirty-nine, after suffering a sustained "nervous breakdown," Weber was placed in semi-retirement at Heidelberg, and taught only sporadically from then until his death from influenza in 1920. Durkheim had died three years before from "a broken heart" after receiving news of the death of his son at the battlefront of World War I.

Weber had done little publishing until his early retirement, and when he died at the age of fifty-six many of his written works were unorganized. He is mainly known for *The Protestant Ethic and the Spirit of Capitalism*. Durkheim seems to have produced steadily until his death at fifty-nine. At least four of his works are considered classics in social science: *The Division of Labour in Society*, *Suicide*, *The Elementary Forms of Religious Life* and *The Rules of Sociological Method*.

In the writings of both men there is a sense of being witness to a watershed of history. It has been said that Weber believed he was living out the death throes of society, while Durkheim thought the turmoil of his times was signalling the birth of a new one. Although neither man personally survived the end of the era marked by the World War I, their ideas lived on — affecting, to a surprising extent, the subsequent course of social science.

Philosophical premises

Every social theorist is forced to come to terms with the nature of reality, if only because some picture of the role of the human species in the scheme of things is a necessary starting point for understanding society. Both Weber and Durkheim claimed that they were not interested in metaphysics, but both operated on the basis of ultimate premises — whether acknowledged or not.

Weber despised naturalistic monism, which he seemed to equate with Nietzsche's version of Social Darwinism. He referred to the "unfortunate" fact that "despite the powerful resistance to the influence of naturalistic dogma due to German idealism since Fichte . . . the naturalistic viewpoint . . . has not yet been overcome" (Weber 1949:86). Weber, like Marx, defined the ideal as an essentially mysterious supernatural realm; unlike Marx, however, he believed in its existence. He defined it as pure rationality — the essential forms of which are, in some mysterious way, immanent in the human mind. In many ways he was the epitome of the nineteenth-century rationalist. However, he disagreed with the premise of his romantic idealist forebears and contemporaries that the ideal necessarily encompasses and shapes the material. For Weber, society assumed an "upstairs-downstairs" aspect with both material substructure and ideal superstructure affecting the course of history. No doubt this is why he sometimes referred to himself as "partly materialistic."

Compared to Durkheim in respect to ontological premises, however, those of Marx and Weber were merely opposite sides of the same coin. Durkheim saw reality very differently. His world view was Hume's naturalistic one of neutral monism. He defined Martineau's concept of "group mind" in naturalistic terms — spelling out its specific function and impact. Like Spencer, he believed that human mental representations of both the real and the good assume an *objectivity* once they are shared through language and thus made collective. These "collective representations" take on an existence of their own because they have a natural origin and cause and similarly natural effects, and because they transcend the individual in both space and time. Durkheim claimed that they become *true* reflections of reality, however, only to the degree that they are built up by individual reason according to the methodology of science.

He drew an analogy between the role of reason in the building of individual representations and that of science as an objective form of collective reason which acts as a source of continuing revitalization for society. But Durkheim's basic categories of reason are not the *a priori* logical constructs of Kant, Schopenhauer and Weber; they are, instead, one with the humanly structured concepts of the positivists that, of necessity, follow nature closely. These "categories are no longer considered as primary and unanalyzable facts," he explained, "but rather they appear as priceless instruments of thought which human groups have laboriously forged through the centuries and where they have accumulated the best of their intellectual capital" (Durkheim 1915:32).

Durkheim's model comes very close to Dewey's at this point. As he expressed it, "Here lies the interest of the Pragmatist enterprise; it is an effort to *understand* truth and reason in themselves, . . . to make them human creations that derive from temporal causes and engender temporal consequences" (Durkheim 1972:251). He added, "All that constitutes reason, its principles and categories, are created in the course of history" (ibid.:252). He was critical of William James' version of pragmatism, however, believing that it opened the door to subjectivism and relativism.

Durkheim's naturalistic philosophy was an attempt to reconcile the older material/ideal dichotomy: one that he hoped would undermine the premise of dualism as the defining aspect of reality. As to the issue that divided Marx and Weber — of whether or not ideal representations affect society — Durkheim considered these to *comprise* that very society, at least in its enduring aspects.

Durkheim explained that individuals construct representations of reality which operate as maps for knowing, and, through language, are shared with the group and thus outlive the individual and the specific situation giving rise to them. There *was* a duality for Durkheim, but it was the duality within human nature involving "an individual being which has its foundation in the organism . . . and a social being which represents the highest reality in the intellectual and moral order that we can know by observation. . . . Insofar as he belongs to society, the individual transcends himself, both when he thinks and when he acts" (Durkheim 1915:29). Also, like Freud, he believed that this representational life extends beyond the individual's awareness of it. Weber, on the other hand, believed that individuals, through their *conscious intent*, transcend society, and that world views (as ultimate complexes of rational intentionality) exert a powerful shaping force on society through the individuals who act in terms of them.

Defining sociology

Weber thought of sociology as "that science which aims at the interpretive understanding of social behaviour in order to gain an explanation of its causes, its courses, and its effects" (Weber 1962a:29). He also explained it as "the science whose objective is to interpret the meaning of social action and thereby give a causal explanation of the way in which the action proceeds and the effects which it produces" (Runciman:7). He seems to have made no distinction between "social action" and "social behaviour" — describing the latter as "activities whose intent is related by the individuals involved to the conduct of others and oriented accordingly" (Weber 1962a:29). Clearly he did not believe that *all* human behaviour is so related and thereby social in nature.

In other words, Weber was attempting — somewhat in the fashion of Husserl — to isolate a conceptually pure type of goal-oriented behaviour for the purpose of scientific analysis. He saw this as the basic unit of sociological research. This unit was not a bite of just any observable human behaviour, however; it was the "meaningful act" which alone defines the social. This was to be conceptualized as the smallest element of behaviour *only* "when and to the extent that the agent or agents see it as subjectively *meaningful*" (Runciman:7). The task of all cultural-historical sciences, he said, is that of "interpreting the meanings which men give to their actions, and so understanding the actions themselves" (ibid.:11).

No doubt realizing that determining the subjective meaningfulness of an act would pose a problem for any external investigator, Weber tried to expand upon his major defining criterion for sociology. He explained that it involves "either (a) the meaning actually intended by an individual agent on a particular historical occasion or by a number of agents in an approximate average in a given set of cases, or (b) the meaning attributed to the agent or agents [presumably by the investigator] as types, in a pure type constructed in the abstract" (ibid.:7). This will be discussed in more detail later in the context of Weber's methodology.

Durkheim, like Martineau, viewed sociology as simply "the science of institutions, of their genesis and functioning" (Durkheim 1938:lvi). He said, "They will be felt as real, living active forces which, because of the way they determine the individual, prove their independence of him" (Durkheim 1951:39). He explained that, because the effects are common to many individuals, they can be observed and regularities among them can be assessed. For Durkheim, it was these *collective* aspects of the beliefs and practices of a group that distinguished social phenomena from the psychological. The *individual* manifestations of these collective factors he considered to be the facts of psychology.

The definition of "social facts" (a term from Comte) is as crucial to an understanding of Durkheim's approach to sociology as is a corresponding understanding of "meaningful acts" to Weber's. "A social fact," wrote Durkheim, "is every way of acting, fixed or not, capable of exercising on the individual an external constraint; or again, every way of acting which is general throughout a given society, while at the same time existing in its own right independent of individual manifestations" (Durkheim 1938:13). Because social facts are both cause and product of individual actions, they are recognizable only by means of those actions and their consequences; but, nonetheless, they are collective things that transcend any specific person in both space and time. In this sense they exist in their own right and have an objective reality of their own.

On the boundaries without

The line between the natural sciences and those which he termed historical-cultural was an unbridgeable one for Weber. This was because "The natural sciences are limited to the formulation of causal uniformities in objects and events, and to explanation of individual facts by applying them" (Weber 1962a:45). On the other hand, "For both sociology and history, the real object of analysis should be the *deeper meaning* of certain behaviours" (ibid.:42). Weber was convinced that, while values determine the content of the latter, they are utterly absent and irrelevant in the former. As he explained it, "This way of being conditioned by 'subjective values' is, however, entirely alien in any case to those natural sciences which take mechanics as a model, and it constitutes, indeed, the distinctive *contrast* between the historical and natural sciences" (ibid.:11).

Nonetheless, Weber did recognize an underlying similarity of *objective*, for he considered both studies to be empirical in approach and to require *certainty* of outcome. His belief that all science, whether natural or historical-cultural, deals with *necessary cause*, is indicated in his comment that "for any empirical science which operates causally, the occurrence of the effect was certain, not from any particular moment, but for all eternity" (Runciman:129). For him, social science differs from the physical in that verification for the former is based on meaningful *as well as* causal adequacy (Weber 1971:97).

Weber seemed torn by conflicting emotions where science was concerned. He advised the sociologist to seek to understand it, for "if one wishes to settle with the devil, one must not take flight before him as so many like to do nowadays. First of all, one has to see the devil's ways in order to realize his power and his limitations" (Wrong:5-6). True to his Kantian groundings, he always referred to the scientific way of thinking as the "rationalization process," and to bureaucratization as the same process at the organizational level. He saw such rationalization as the defining characteristic of modern society, and this was no doubt a contributing factor in his pessimism. For him, the scientific process was, by definition, a matter of the intellect operating in isolation from feelings and values.

Weber claimed that the major reason why his theory was often misunderstood was "The naturalistic prejudice that every conception in the cultural sciences should be similar to those of the exact natural sciences" (Weber 1949: 88). In his divided attitude towards the objective search for knowledge, Weber was closer to Nietzsche than to any other pioneer of social science. But even in this he was torn. Of Freud he once said, "If only he could venture to be *what* he is — and that is to be sure something better than a follower of Nietzsche. And it is not even that part of Nietzsche's work which is of lasting value that he chooses to follow; not the *morality of superiority*; but precisely the *weakest* part of Nietzsche, the biological trimming" (Runciman:387).

No doubt it was Weber's anti-naturalism and his ambivalence about science that caused him to be attracted to the existentialist and phenomenological ideas that were swirling around the tea table at his wife's Sunday gatherings of youthful academics. It was probably here that he got his inspiration for a sociology based on the actor's motivation. He does not seem to have credited Husserl, even though the former published his defining ideas concerning "the intentional act" seven years before Weber came out with his *Basic Concepts*. Weber's later works contain other hints of the newly popular existentialist-phenomenological thought: for example, "Wherever rationally empirical knowledge has consistently achieved the disenchantment of the world, and its transformation into a piece of causal mechanism, there is conclusive estrangement from the claims of the ethical postulate, that the world is ordained by a god, and is therefore somehow an ethically meaningful cosmos" (Stammer: 13).

Weber always insisted that the historical-cultural phenomena which are the subject of sociology are inevitably individual and concrete (and thus irrational in the sense that they are not ordered by general laws). "Social-psychological research," he said, "involves the study of various very disparate *individual* types of cultural elements with reference to their interpretability by our empathic understanding" (Weber 1949:89). He thought that previous knowledge of *individual* institutions would be necessary for such research. In this perspective as well there seems to be a touch of existentialism. And it is Weber's insistence that the actor's intentional *motivation* is the chief object of sociological study that aligns him with the phenomenological tradition. Both these currents of thought — along with Nietzsche's concept of the Superman and "the will to power" — later coalesced in the mind of Martin Heidegger, who was to become the defining influence on German academic thought during the thirties.

Durkheim, feeling no such reservations about the role of human reason and the approach of natural science, was committed to extending these demonstrably powerful instruments of knowing to the moral realm. He called himself a scientific rationalist. Like Martineau, Marx, Comte and Spencer, he believed in the existence of laws of social reality comparable to those discovered by natural science. He hoped that the discovery of these would permit humanity "to direct with more reflection than in the past the course of historical evolution, for we can only change nature, moral or physical, by abiding by its laws" (Lacapra:14). For him, science was a procedure applying equally to all aspects of existence. "Indeed, our principle is to extend scientific rationalism to human conduct in showing that, considered in the past, it is reducible to relations of cause and effect which a no less rational operation can transform into rules for the future" (ibid.:6).

Durkheim's great hope for sociology was that he could help to make it more scientific, and less concerned with abstract philosophical issues. "Our principle, then, implies no metaphysical concepts, no speculation about the fundamental nature of things. What it demands is that the sociologist put himself in the same state of mind as the physicist, chemist or psychologist when he probes into the still unexplored region of the public domain" (Durkheim 1938:xlv). Physical scientists approach the study of individual events by means of some hypothesis concerning the underlying regularities connecting them: of the "fact" they hope to confirm. Durkheim proposed that, in the same way, "When the sociologist undertakes an investigation of some order of social facts he must endeavour to consider them from an aspect that is independent of their individual manifestations" (ibid.:45).

He was critical of the motivational approach being recommended by Weber. In fact, as he pointed out, "When it is simply a matter of our private acts, we know very imperfectly the relatively simple motives that guide us" (ibid.:xlv). He also deplored the attempt to set limits on scientific inquiry on the basis that science cannot be tolerated in the uniquely "human and irrational" historical-cultural realm. "One cannot protest too strongly," he said, "against this mystical doctrine ... [which is] the negation of all science" (ibid.:23).

Durkheim's concern about the growing popularity of this alternative approach to sociology is apparent in comments such as the following: "It therefore seems to us that in these times of renascent mysticism an undertaking such as ours should be regarded quite without apprehension by those who ... share our faith in the future of reason" (ibid.:xi). It was this faith in reason that was the source of Durkheim's optimism regarding science. Not for him Weber's pessimism regarding the "disenchantment" wrought by scientific knowledge!

On the boundaries within

Weber was convinced of the need to establish discrete categories *within* the social sciences as well as *between* them and those dealing with physical phenomena. He thought that each has its own distinctive task, independent of the others. "My view is that the individual sciences lose their point when each fails to perform the specific task which it, alone, can perform" (Runciman:390). But he was somewhat ambiguous as to the empirical source and logical justification for these isolated tasks. He admitted the impossibility of drawing a sharp dividing line between the subject matters of sociology and psychology. Nonetheless, he claimed that "sociology does not have any closer logical relationship to psychology than to any other science" (Weber 1962a: 51). "How mistaken it is," he said, "to regard any kind of psychology as the ultimate foundation of sociological interpretation of human behaviour" (ibid.:50). Elsewhere he claimed that psychological facts are "no more relevant to sociology than inorganic facts" (Runciman:16).

Weber felt the same about biology, as it relates to human activity. Following Schopenhauer, he considered the subject matter in this case to be instinctual response, which he believed has no bearing on *social* behaviour. Similarly, he assigned to anthropology the unique subject matter of traditional and collective behaviour. However, that, along with the claims and concepts of political economy, did pose real problems for him. He admitted that "Sociology cannot afford to ignore the collective concepts of the other disciplines" (ibid.:17). Finally, he tried to resolve the dilemma by conceding that "sociology is not concerned solely with 'social behaviour' but such behaviour provides ... its subject matter" (Weber 1962a:58).

Only history is really relevant in Weber's scheme. "For both sociology and history the real object for analysis should be the deeper meaning of certain behaviour" (ibid.:42). He considered sociology a special kind of *historical* science — the *comparative* form of history. In distinguishing between history and sociology, Weber explained that, while history is inherently interested in individual events, sociology studies the individual in order to arrive at the *typical*. Through the use of "ideal-type" constructs it seeks *universal* understanding of exclusively intentional "social" action.

Durkheim, on the other hand, had the idea that all investigators of social phenomena need to feel that they are collaborating in the same work: that they form an integrated community. "The division of labour presumes that the worker . . . does not lose sight of his collaborators, that he acts upon them and reacts to them" (Durkheim 1933:372). This is clearly what he tried to do throughout his writing as he challenged and responded to Spencer, Freud and William James — and to Weber. He believed that this was not generally occurring in his time. He thought that this sad state of affairs within the social sciences was due to the fact that "they were the last to come into the circle of positive sciences. . . . Scholars installed themselves . . . according to their tastes" (ibid.:370).

Durkheim sought to establish relationships and responsibilities among the social sciences on a more logical basis. Beginning with Spencer's concept of "representations" (conceptual mappings of experience) he distinguished between those which are individual and those which are collective. Following Spencer, he also distinguished between the disorganized state at the inorganic level of existence and the organized "totality" representing life at the organic level of evolution. One cannot explain life in terms of chemical relations, he said, for atoms are not the appropriate unit here: a "synthesis" has occurred creating a new level of organization and therefore a different order of existence. He then applied the same principle to the difference between the "facts" dealt with by psychology and sociology. As he explained it, if "this synthesis constituting every society yields new phenomena differing from . . . those in individual consciousness, we must admit that these facts reside exclusively in the very society itself which produced them and not in its parts, i.e., members. These new phenomena cannot be reduced to their elements" (Durkheim 1938:xlviii). Psychological facts, then, reflecting individual thought and feeling, are relevant to sociology but cannot provide *explanations* of social phenomena. These must rely on the identification of relations among society's members which are manifested in their "collective representations."

Durkheim's definition of sociology included anthropology and history as the necessary sources of subject matter, as well as politics, religion, economics and education as examples of specific institutions to be studied. In addition, he suggested the need for a "social psychology" which would analyze the relationship between individual and collective representations. He foresaw it as "an entirely formal psychology which would be a sort of common ground for individual psychology and sociology" (ibid.:1).

On the methodology of social science

There are three crucial aspects to scientific method. One involves the means employed to *classify* the phenomena under study; the second, the nature of the *explanations* sought; and the third, the *procedures* for achieving these. On all these counts Weber and Durkheim were poles apart. In contrast to Durkheim's focus on collective representations, Weber once wrote in a letter, "If I have become a sociologist . . . it is mainly in order to exorcise the spectre of collective conceptions which still lingers among us . . . sociology itself can only proceed from the actions of one or more separate individuals and must adopt strictly individualistic methods" (Weber 1971:25).

Weber therefore offered an individualistic method of classification based on deduced constructs of rationally related potential means-end connections, which he called "ideal types." These were not intended as reflections of actual social behaviours, but as abstract examples of possibilities against which phenomena to be studied could be assessed. They were to be "genetic" constructs arrived at through a logical process of analysis and synthesis. Weber saw this logical construction as essentially different from "generic" conceptualization which attempts, by means of empirical observation, to isolate certain key criteria and to group phenomena in terms of them. In his view, such generic concepts comprise the "essence" of the mechanistic and valueless reality of the physical world, and constitute the basic facts of the natural sciences. He believed that social reality is so different in its ultimate essence that its concepts must be arrived at quite differently.

Weber thought that he had made a major breakthrough in methodology in deriving the notion of purely abstract concepts capable of distilling the *essential* from the individual manifestations of historical-cultural phenomena. These, he explained — unlike generic concepts — can never correspond exactly to any particular institution or action, but they can be used to understand the value-laden reality being studied in social science. "The more distinct and precise the construction of the ideal-type, the greater its abstract or unrealistic nature and the better it is able to perform its methodological functions in formulating the clarification of terminology, or classification, and of hypotheses" (Weber 1962a:54).

Perhaps because of unfamiliarity with Hume's philosophy — and with the subsequent refinements of pragmatism — Weber seemed unaware that others had grappled before him with the discovery that *all* concepts are necessarily mental abstractions of reality. At any rate, he disagreed vehemently with the new understanding of science as a universal method of inquiry by human observers forever doomed, by their role *within nature*, to the application of abstract concepts to *all* aspects of reality. And he did not discuss the obviously abstract nature of the formulae of physics.

As Durkheim explained it, Weber's problem was not the ideal nature of his concepts, but the fact that they were deduced from *a priori* premises rather than being established through observation. He maintained that "Sociology, to be objective, ought to start, not with concepts formed independent of . . . [sense perceptions] but with these same perceptions" (Durkheim 1938:43).

Durkheim's concepts were representations of functional groupings of phenomena on the basis of some observed similarity. This was not the rule in the social science of his day. As he put it, "Since it has been customary to think of social life as the logical development of ideal concepts, a method which makes social evolution depend on objective conditions defined in space will perhaps be judged crude and possibly be termed 'materialistic' " (ibid.:xxxix).

Durkheim often expressed regret at the tendency in social science to begin in the wrong place, with broad, logically derived categories having no mooring in observed regularities. "In the present state of our knowledge we cannot be certain of the exact nature of the state, sovereignty, political liberty, democracy, socialism, communism, etc. . . . Our method should, then, require an avoidance of all these concepts so long as they have not been scientifically established" (ibid.:22).

Durkheim believed systems of classification should not be drawn from an inventory of all *logically possible* characteristics, but from a small number observed to be the sufficient or *defining* ones. He considered the selection of components for analysis to be crucial, "since the nature of the aggregate depends necessarily on *the nature and number of the components and their mode of combination*" (ibid.:80). He recommended classifying societies according to degree of *organization*, since it is the relations among members that constitute a social group. The basis would thus be the most perfectly *simple* society ever observed both as an isolated segment and as a unit within more complicated forms of society.

The two scholars also differed on the issue of explanation. For Weber, explanation had to incorporate an understanding which reflects self-evident truth. "For once," he is reported to have said, "nothing but the kernel of reality is to be brought out without any illusions" (Marianne Weber:679). Torn, as always, by conflicting imperatives, he strove mightily to compensate for the built-in limitations of his ideal-type approach: the fact that, although it might contribute to the *validity* of his guiding hypotheses, its capacity to ensure *reliability* was questionable. He insisted that his approach was indeed a road to verifiable knowledge. The subjectively intended meaning of an act can be discovered, he claimed, by the method of *Verstehen*. This is Schopenhauer's and Husserl's Kantian idea that the investigator can identify with the subject studied through an intuitive process which produces *understanding* of the underlying *intent* motivating the actor. "For a science dealing with the true meaning of behaviour, explanation requires a grasp of the context of meaning within the actual course of action occurrences" (Weber 1962a:36).

Weber offered his ideal-type methodology as a means of achieving the required understanding. He explained that the latter involves "the interpretive grasp of the meaning present in one of the following contexts: (a) as in the historical approach, the actually intended meaning for concrete individual action; or (b) as in cases of sociological mass phenomena, the average of, or approximation to, the actually intended meaning; or (c) the meaning appropriate to a scientifically formulated pure type (an ideal type) of a common phenomena [*sic*]" (Weber 1962b:94).

It is the ideal type that makes *Verstehen* possible, he said. "When we adopt the kind of scientific procedure which involves the construction of *types*, we can investigate and make fully comprehensible all those irrational, affectively determined patterns of meaning which influence action, by representing them as 'deviations' from a pure type of action as it would be if it proceeded in a rationally purposive way. . . . The constructed model of a fully rational purposive action can be understood by the sociologist with complete certainty and the total clarity which results from its rationality . . . thus enabling him to understand the real action" (Runciman:9).

The *essential* meaning thus arrived at is what Weber meant by *Verstehen*, or "explanatory understanding." He distinguished this from Durkheim's "rational empirical observation of behaviour." However, Weber admitted that, even though the latter is similar in nature to the object of natural science, it may be legitimate as *one* of the goals of sociology. *Verstehen*, on the other hand, although equally rational and empirical, is "an understanding of motivation, i.e., the act as seen as part of an intelligible situation" (Weber 1962a:35). It deals not merely with observed regularities, but "with the 'true meaning' of behaviour" (ibid.:36). By "true meaning" Weber could only have meant the bare bones of Husserl's "intentional act."

Durkheim deplored the fact that explanation in the sociology of his day was generally in terms of either teleological *purpose* or psychological *motivation*. Far from being concerned with the *intentional meaning* of action, Durkheim believed, "The principal object of all sciences of life, whether individual or social, is to define and explore the normal state and distinguish it from its opposite" (Durkheim 1938:14). He considered a social fact "normal" if it is present in the average society at a corresponding phase in social evolution, or if it represents the average pattern of behaviour in a given society. Sociological explanation, for him, required searching for the determining cause of such a pattern "among the social facts preceding it, and not among the states of individual consciousness" (ibid.:110). Discovering its organizational function is an essential part of the task. "We must determine whether there is a correspondence between the fact under consideration and the general needs of the social organism, without occupying ourselves with whether it has been intentional or not" (ibid.:95).

Durkheim's method transferred the focus in social-scientific analysis from *intent* or purpose to *function* or consequence. His procedure was implied by his definition of explanation. His focus on behavioural norms meant that patterns or regularities could be identified among social events in a way similar to the procedures of natural science, and statistics could be applied to the measures of these to allow for comparisons on the basis of degree of deviation from the mean. His comparative study of suicide is a masterful pioneering example of the application of this procedure.

He also emphasized that any social fact can be explained by tracing its evolutionary development. And he believed that his comparative evolutionary method amounted to the closest approximation of the experiment that could be possible for sociology. In the experiment one thing is varied at a time, and the effects assessed. By following a particular social phenomenon through varying stages of historical evolution within one society, or across varying contemporary cultures, Durkheim thought that a somewhat similar result could be achieved.

Weber also recommended what he called a comparative historical approach, and, on the surface, the suggested procedures of the two sociologists might appear to be alike. However, a close look at their actual work reveals a wide gap in methodology. Weber's procedure required the application of an ideal type to the history of a particular society, comparing a specified area of action at varying periods to the rational construct of that same action in order to assess the difference between the actual and ideal (or fully "rational"). In addition, he sought to relate meaningful complexes of action within a society, such as religion and forms of economic organization.

For example, Weber studied the historical development of the dominant religious world view (and its relationship to the economy) in India, China, ancient Israel and Protestant Europe. He began by establishing an ideal type which included every aspect of religion which he had been able to deduce from a reading of theology and moral philosophy. Each religion was then analyzed, at each stage of its development, as to how far it departed from this type. He also assessed its influence on the world view of the social actors in question, and, consequently, on the motivation determining their economic relationships.

This was the context in which Weber framed his famous hypothesis concerning the causal relationship between the Protestant ethic and the spirit of capitalism. It has been said that, for him, "Protestantism was at once sacred history and the wave of the future" (Macrae:38). This was due to his premise that the characteristics most essential to the growth of venture capitalism — specialized expertise, or "the calling," combined with a willingness to defer present gratification for future gain — are the defining aspects of Protestantism.

Durkheim also focused on religion, although he placed it in an evolutionary rather than rationalistic framework. He called his study *The Elementary Forms of Religious Life*. He began by looking for the most primitive form of religion observable: (1) by seeking out the religious practices and beliefs of the society demonstrating the simplest known form of social organization; and (2) by ensuring that the religious institution thus identified could be explained without reference to anything borrowed from any previous religion. By this means he identified totemism as the earliest religion known to humans. By following the increasing complexity of religion over time, he was able to demonstrate its thoroughly natural origin — as a source of explanation, for primitive people, of the world and their place within it. He showed this to be the identical *social* source from which science has evolved. It is said that this work drove Bergson to write his famous book on the *two* sources of religion, in an attempt to refute Durkheim!

On the issue of value neutrality

Value neutrality was an overwhelming problem for Weber because of the subjective nature of his "meaningful act," and the similarly subjective nature of his ideal types. How could one achieve objectivity in the midst of an object of study and investigative procedure that were the very stuff of value judgements? He had hoped that the ideal-type construct would do it for him, in that he had emphasized that the "ideal" in it referred to *rationality* rather than to *value*. But he could not avoid the suspicion that its content was dangerously subject to the presuppositions of the sociologist creating it. And he was also aware that the personal, subjectively held intentions to be investigated by his sociology are by their very nature partial and biased in favour of the actor's desires. Weber decided that the way out lay in the direction of a particular morality to be stipulated for the social scientist: he would have to assume the cloak of value neutrality.

This was rendered even more necessary by Weber's insistence that the very definition of the social sciences was "those disciplines which analyze the phenomena of life in terms of their cultural significance" (Weber 1952:76), and because of his corresponding insistence that it is the researcher's "valuation" or "particular point of view" which distinguishes the significant from the less so (Weber 1949:111). Indeed, to understand Weber's overriding concern with this issue, we must also comprehend the crucial role of values in his entire conceptual scheme. He saw the natural sciences as untainted by value judgements, and believed that all knowledge, to be objective, must be value-free. At the same time he believed that the distinctiveness of the historical-cultural sciences was rooted in the essential value-relatedness and subjective nature of both their object of study and their methodology. He referred to "the hair-line which separates science from faith . . . [because] the *objective* validity of all empirical knowledge rests exclusively upon the ordering of a given reality according to categories which are *subjective* in that they represent the *presuppositions* of our knowledge and . . . [of the value of the truth contained therein]" (ibid.:110). Weber's dualism presented him with an insurmountable obstacle here. It is no wonder that his discussions of the necessity and possibility of value neutrality appear confused and tortured.

Although Weber was at his most ambiguous when dealing with value neutrality in research, he was at his best in his treatment of the inappropriateness of value judgements in teaching. As a youth he had been offended at how his father's friend, Treitschke, had conducted himself in university classrooms. "He politicized his students, filled them with enthusiasm for Bismarck and the Hohenzollern dynasty, and stirred up anti-Semitism among them" (Marianne Weber:119). Weber recommended that, in value-ridden disciplines, each university department should contain representatives of different views. Deliberate attempts by teachers to inculcate their values should be prohibited, he said, adding that "the only specific virtue which they need to inculcate is that of intellectual integrity!" (Runciman:71).

As for academic freedom, Weber believed it should apply only to the teacher's purely specialist qualifications. "There is, however, no specialist qualification in personal prophecy, so it ought not to enjoy that privilege" (ibid.:72). Only when some guarantee is given that all points of view will be represented do teachers have the right to pronounce on value issues, according to him.

Durkheim's position on value neutrality was somewhat different. He thought that education, because of its function in society, is inevitably a moral enterprise. However, he maintained that any ideals taught should, like their conceptual counterparts, be as "true" (or objective) as possible. And where research is concerned, Durkheim was convinced that, in the social as well as the natural sciences, only a rigorously objective methodology can keep the investigator's preconceptions from affecting the results.

One necessary requirement is that "The subject matter of every sociological study should comprise a group of phenomena defined in advance by certain common characteristics and all phenomena so defined should be included within this group" (Durkheim 1938:33). Here he was expanding on Martineau's pioneering idea of an established research design as a means of ensuring replicability — so that findings can be tested by others. Durkheim had little confidence in the common historical method involving the gathering of evidence to support a thesis while ignoring that which disconfirmed it. He also criticized the tendency among social scientists to confuse the *investigation* of social facts with their *evaluation*. So, too, did Weber.

However, Durkheim disagreed with Weber's image of science, in general, as a value-neutral enterprise within society. For him, science was the *only* element in evolution which is thoroughly moral in its objective and function. "Science is ... conscience carried to the highest point of clarity.... An enlightened conscience prepares itself for adaptation" (Durkheim 1933:52). This was the role he saw for social science; it would provide direction for the process of cultural evolution!

Durkheim, unlike Weber, drew no firm line between valuing and knowing. Sounding very much like Dewey, he explained, "There is not one way of thinking and judging for dealing with existence and another for estimating value. All judgement is necessarily based on given fact; even judgements of the future are related materially to the present or to the past ... all judgements bring ideals into play" (Durkheim 1953:95). He thought that the concepts organizing the real and those reflecting the good are equally "ideal" or mental in construction. Consequently, both are social representations in that they are formed through language — a collective thing. This is why the element of judgement is the same in both cases.

As he explained it,

> The function of some is to express the reality to which they adhere. These are properly called concepts. The function of others, on the contrary, is to transfigure the realities to which they relate, and these are the ideals of value. In the first instance the ideal is the symbol of a thing and makes it an object of understanding. In the second, the thing itself symbolizes the ideal and acts as a medium through which the ideal becomes capable of being understood. (Ibid.:95-96)

An example of the ideal as a concept is the word totemism, which symbolizes a system of religious beliefs and rituals. An example of the ideal as a value is the image of the totem which arouses spiritual awareness in the primitive viewer.

On the nature of society

Durkheim defined society very specifically. "Society has for its substratum the mass of associated individuals. The system which they form by uniting together, and which varies according to their geographic disposition and the nature and number of their channels of communication, is the base from which social life is raised. The representations which form the network of social life arise from the relations between the individuals thus combined and the secondary groups that are between the individuals and the total society" (Durkheim 1953:25). One looks in vain through Weber's writings for a similarly pointed definition. His view of society must be inferred from the concepts which he chose to elaborate. The two that are clearly relevant are "status" and "bureaucracy."

Weber expanded fruitfully on Marx's version of society by distinguishing between "class" and "status." He explained that " 'classes' are formed in accordance with the relations of production and the acquisition of wealth, while 'status groups' are formed according to the principles governing the consumption of goods in the context of specific life styles" (Runciman:54). In his view, only during periods of great technological and economic upheaval are naked class interests dominant. As soon as relative stability obtains within the society, status structures emerge and social standing once more assumes major significance.

Weber's analysis of bureaucracy reveals even more about his perspective on society. Durkheim saw the trend in urban society toward specialization as positive because he expected it to increase the potential for organic solidarity due to the impetus provided for the development of reason and the evolution of science. Weber spoke instead of a sort of mechanistic "rationalization" and saw a dehumanizing tendency toward bureaucratization as the defining characteristic of the industrial age.

He recognized the dominance of bureaucracy in modern societies as inevitable, given that "The decisive reason for the advance of bureaucratic organization has always been its purely technical superiority over any other form" (ibid.:350). Its power derives from the fact that "bureaucratization does offer the best chance of putting into power the principle of division of labour in administration according to purely objective criteria" (ibid.:351). But he saw inherent weaknesses in this "rational" form of social organization. "The question is always who controls the existing bureaucratic machinery. And such control is possible only in a very limited degree to persons who are not technical specialists" (Weber 1947:338).

This fear of the rule of the "coldly rational" official pervades Weber's writing, and, no doubt, can be traced to the German culture of his time. He saw no hope for a decrease in such rule if socialism were to replace capitalism. In fact, he feared the precise opposite, for socialism contains no redeeming, rejuvenating "spirit." For him, capitalism was "the manifestation of a spirit, a character; it is much more than a constellation of production, exchange and accounting devices" (Macrae:86). Of socialism he said, "It is the dictatorship of the official, not of the worker" (Stammer:14). He also saw danger in the fact that "If there were no private capitalism, governmental bureaucracies would reign alone. Private and public bureaucracies would then be fused in a single hierarchy" (ibid.:105). He recognized that the significant question to pose concerning any economic system with no role for the entrepreneur is

"Who would then take control and direct this new economy? On this point the *Communist Manifesto* is silent" (Runciman:262).

Except where the economy is concerned, there is little of the social in Weber's work. He seemed to see society only as the necessary framework for his motivational and teleological view of history. Like Kant and Fichte, he believed that the "purpose" of society is to create autonomous individuals. His definition of the state is as close as he comes to explaining the nature of society. He says that when the sociologist "speaks of a state . . . he means . . . nothing more than a specifically structured outcome of the social actions of individuals" (ibid.:17). The collective disappears from view entirely, and the personal act is all. But, for the investigator, the meaningful act becomes a slippery, ephemeral object as well, for what Weber is after is really the actor's *motivation* — not the behaviour which, though momentary, is at least observable.

For Durkheim, on the other hand, society was central. He has sometimes been criticized for making it too central; for visualizing it as a fixed, free-floating entity constraining and shaping individuals in a totalitarian way. His tendency to anthropomorphic metaphor may have contributed to this misunderstanding of his model. But only a cursory reading of Durkheim could lead one to such a conclusion. No one who understands the initiating role he gave to reason (in the creation of individual representations) and to science (as the collective representation of the formalized public reasoning process) could believe that his incipient evolutionary naturalism was a static one-way social determinism.

In terms somewhat reminiscent of Nietzsche, he often defined society as a collective moral force. Nevertheless, as "a force it is not entirely outside of us; it does not act upon us wholly from without, but rather, since society cannot exist except in and through individual consciousnesses, this force must also penetrate us and organize itself within us; it thus becomes an integral part of our being" (Durkheim 1915:240).

There is nothing mystical or mysterious about this, however. "The social realm is the natural realm which differs from others only in its greater complexity" (ibid.:31). Durkheim noted that it is actually this superbly natural society which mythologies have represented in so many "sacred" forms throughout history. It is therefore the source of all religion in the same way that it gives rise to scientific knowledge. "For that which makes a man is the totality of the intellectual property which constitutes civilization, and civilization is the work of society" (ibid.:465).

Durkheim developed an interesting theory on the evolution of human society. He began by rejecting the Enlightenment idea of a social contract "for it has no relation to the facts. . . . Not only are there no societies which have such an origin, but there is none whose structure presents the least trace of a contractual organization" (Durkheim 1933:202). He was just as critical of the Social Darwinism that he considered implicit in Spencer and Nietzsche. "They overlook the essential element of moral life, that is, the moderating influence that society exercises over its members, which tempers and neutralizes the brutal action of the struggle for existence and selection. Wherever there is society there is altruism, because there is solidarity" (ibid.:197).

Durkheim hypothesized that a "mechanical solidarity" emerged very early among human primates, due to the likenesses in the primitive conscience arising from similarity of daily work experience and intimacy of contact caused by simplicity of organization. Some of these consensus-producing forces could have been kinship ties, territorial attachment, ancestor worship and shared habits or routines. "These similarities of consciences give rise to juridical rules which, with the threat of repressive measures, impose uniform beliefs and practices upon all. The more pronounced this is, the more social life is confounded with religious life, and the nearer to communism are the economic institutions" (ibid.:226).

Durkheim expanded upon Spencer's idea that social evolution probably comes about as a result of environmental pressures encouraging a *division of labour*. He thought that, to the extent that this occurs, it "gives rise to juridical rules which determine the nature and relations of divided functions but whose violation calls for only restitutive measures without any expiatory character" (ibid.:226). This is in contrast to the sanctions imposed for infractions of the rules of the earlier, religious or "mechanical" form of society. The increasingly interdependent nature of these functions moves society away from a *consensus* of consciences toward greater "organic solidarity," which Durkheim viewed as a higher stage of social evolution: one that could eventually culminate in a single encompassing society for all humanity. Such a society would be integrated by the need for cooperation among the differing functions required for the ongoing social enterprise. "To be a member of society is to be bound to the social ideal," Durkheim explained, and "when the social ideal is a particular form of the ideal of humanity . . . it is to men as such that we find ourselves bound" (Durkheim 1953:53).

On the nature of morality

One of Weber's earliest references to morality shows the influence of Kant. "Moral judgements cannot be inculcated unless the ability to grasp them, *the faculty for making moral distinctions*, is there, and this, in turn, is based on the antithesis between good and evil. This antithesis, then, must be presupposed to make an education possible and is inherent in man" (Marianne Weber:157). In practical life, Weber seemed to accept an inevitable necessity for the sacrifice of means to ends. For him, rationality is not relevant and prediction is impossible in the realm of morality, where he recognized no operation of cause and effect. In fact, he thought that the realm of morality must be forever shrouded in mystery, and therefore a tolerant polytheism can be the only legitimate stance here. With Hegel, he believed that "it is *not* the case that from good only good, and from bad only bad can come, but that often the opposite holds true" (Runciman:220).

Clearly, Weber belonged to the Machiavellian school of politics. Because, conceptually, he equated political power and violence, he had to believe that violence could beget its opposite. In politics, he was fond of saying, the essential means is violence, and in this "practical" realm, *neither* the ethic of intent nor that of consequence is helpful. "No system of ethics in the world can make it possible to decide when and to what extent the morally good end 'sanctifies' the morally dangerous means and side-effects" (ibid.:218).

Generally, in this realm of practical morality, Weber tended to elevate the Kantian morality of intent over the utilitarian one of consequence. However, he was never fully at ease with this; indeed, it was one of the chief sources of conflict within his world view which seems to have predisposed him to the new existentialism. His only other solution to the contradiction between these two moral principles seems to have been a resort to the Protestantism which he never really relinquished. "Ordinary Protestantism," he concluded, "legitimized the state and therefore violence as a means. . . . Luther took the responsibility for war away from the individual and transferred it to the government, which it could never be a sin to obey in any matter other than a question of faith" (ibid.:221). Prophetic words, given subsequent German history!

For Durkheim, morality was central to all social life and science. In fact, his own preferred sociological specialization was what he called the science of morality. Like Dewey, he saw no way in which ends can be isolated from the means used to achieve them. He explained that, ultimately, science has the potential not only to influence but to *determine* values. For, "by revealing the causes of phenomena, science furnishes the means of producing them. Every means is, from another point of view, an end. In order to put it into operation, it must be willed quite as much as the end whose realization it prepares. There are always several routes that lead to a given goal; a choice must therefore be made between them. If science cannot indicate the best goal for us, how can it inform us about the best means to reach it? . . . If science cannot guide us in the determination of ultimate ends, it is equally powerless in the case of those secondary and subordinate ends called 'means' " (Durkheim 1938:48).

Far from relegating morality to a realm of mystery irrelevant to practical choices, as Weber tended to do, Durkheim saw it as the crucial defining element of human society. "If man conceives ideals," he said, "it is because he is a social being" (Durkheim 1953:92). He explained that every society is constituted in terms of ideals which determine the way its members envision themselves and express their hopes for future development. According to him, "the ideal is not 'cloud cuckoo land'; it is *of* and *in* nature. It is subject to examination like the rest of the moral and physical universe" (ibid.:94). He hoped his proposed science of morality would deal with just that task.

Durkheim considered reason to be the supreme moral faculty in humans, for it "contains, in an immanent state, a moral *ideal* — the *true* ideal which it is able to oppose . . . to that which society follows at each moment in its history" (ibid.:66). For him, this meant that society, as it exists in any moment in evolution, is not a full and accurate reflection of what it could be. It is merely a temporal and situational manifestation of the entire accumulated civilization of humanity which is the source of moral direction. Reason and aesthetic value are for the individual what science and art are at the collective level. Both are the instruments by which "true" ideals can be sought, and both are social things. "It is society that has freed us from nature. . . . The believer bows before his God, because he believes that he holds his being, particularly his mental being, his soul. We have the same reason for experiencing this feeling before the collective" (ibid.:73).

Durkheim's concept of "anomie" is central to an understanding of his view of morality. He began with the proposition that "No living being can be happy or even exist unless his needs are sufficiently proportioned to his means" (Durkheim 1951:246). Desires, by their very nature, are insatiable unless in some way constrained by a force transcending the individual organism. Only the collective (itself created in the course of history by previous members) can establish sanctions, rules and goals for current members. It is these *moral* patterns which give meaning and value to existence. Without them, society disintegrates. The result is that people suffer "anomie": a condition of insufficient or failed socialization which, at the extreme, becomes the amorality of the sociopath. Simply put, there is too little of society in them, and too much of sheer animal lust for momentary pleasure. In the absence of self-discipline and conscience (both of which can only come from "the society within") any imposed discipline seems unbearable. "A thirst arises for novelties, unfamiliar pleasures, nameless sensations, all of which lose their savor once known. Henceforth one has no strength to endure the least reverse" (ibid.:256).

Durkheim concluded that the cause of "anomie" is a too rapid pace of social change, especially when accompanied by a loss of traditional religious beliefs and rites, with no accompanying achievement of a broader social morality to fill the vacuum. He was also convinced that laissez-faire capitalism plays a harmful role in developing insatiable desires for economic goods and financial success, and inculcating the notion that all social restraint is undesirable.

On the nature of the state

Weber referred to the state chiefly in terms of the authority and power exerted by political leadership. "The modern state," he said, "is a compulsory association which organizes domination. It has been successful in tending to monopolize the legitimate use of physical force as a means of domination" (Weber 1965:82-83). One of the problems with his conceptual system is a failure to establish any *moral* limits to the power of the state in exercising this exclusive right to use violence. He claimed that authority is the result of a legitimacy granted by the people, but the source and justification for the state's ultimate power seems to be something else — and undefined.

Weber explained that the granting of legitimacy by the members of a state occurs either from purely *disinterested* motives or in terms of *self-interest* — "through expectations of ulterior consequences" (Weber 1947:127). He specified the following justifications for disinterested forms of loyalty: (a) emotional commitment; (b) rational belief in the abstract validity of the order as an expression of ultimate values; and (c) the promise of religious salvation. One cannot help but note that, while applying abstract principles was considered rational and positive in Weber's scheme, weighing the probable consequences of an action for one's own long-term benefit was something else!

Weber classified the various possible categories of authority according to the kind of claim to legitimacy typical of each. He cited three "pure types" of grounds for authority: rational-legal, traditional, and charismatic. Charismatic authority clearly intrigued him. It rests, he said, on "devotion to the specific and exceptional sanctity, heroism or exemplary character of an individual person, and of the normative patterns or order revealed or ordained by him" (Stammer:328).

Whereas Weber seemed to view the state and society as one and the same thing, Durkheim had a much more restricted notion of the role of the state *within* society. He argued against the two currently popular perspectives on the issue: Spencer's individualistic one and the mystical cult of the Hegelian state that Weber seemed to accept. Like Hobbes, Durkheim also disputed the Enlightenment postulate that the rights of the individual are inherent, and claimed, instead, "that the institution of these rights is precisely the task of the state" (Durkheim 1957:50).

He defined the state as "a special organization whose responsibility it is to work out certain representations which hold good for the collectivity. These representations are distinguished from other collective representations by their higher degree of conscious reflection" (ibid.:50). The state has no mystic aim of any kind. However, Durkheim claimed that its role is not merely to reflect the thought of the masses. Rather, "It is and must be the centre of new and original representations which ought to put the society in a position to conduct

itself with greater intelligence than when it is swayed merely by vague sentiments working on it" (ibid.:92).

For this reason Durkheim was distrustful of plebiscitary democracy. He
believed it necessary to interpose secondary groups of some kind between the
people and government — both to free the people from the heavy hand of the
state and to free the state sufficiently from the short-term demands of the
people to allow for intelligent leadership. He proposed an organization based
on functional complexes in society, each comprising *both* employees and employers, all of whom would have a mandate to keep the welfare of society
uppermost.

Durkheim seems to have been toying with the notion of a responsible par-
liamentary system combined with grassroots political organization involving
some version of technocracy. However, there is no justification for the
charge — sometimes made — that he favoured the anti-government syndical-
ism of Georges Sorel (1847-1922) which recommended complete decentrali-
zation of economic and political affairs. Durkheim's "organic solidarity" was
a very different concept. He thought that politics based either on caste and
class interests or on geographical location are inherently fragmenting. He
wanted secondary groupings based on the division of labour, with all relevant
interests being represented as functioning organs of the whole, and with all
members alert to their interdependence and responsibility to society. He suggested the family as a model for this new type of corporative structure.

Durkheim was overwhelmingly concerned with equality. Although he had
no respect for Marxism as a scientific hypothesis — or as a program for economic reform — he thought it worthy of study as a social fact representing a
commendable passion for justice. A concern for justice was his own major
moral commitment. He was very much the social reformer where social structure and industrial relations were concerned. He believed that "organic solidarity" is thwarted to the degree that inequalities, *external* to the *internally di-
vergent* requirements of specialization, remain significant. "Equality in the
external conditions of conflict is not only necessary to attach each individual
to his function, but also to link functions to each other" (Durkheim 1933:381).
The services exchanged must have a roughly equivalent social value, he
claimed, and this requires relatively equal social positions. He also thought
that an effective and fair capitalism would require an established institutional
framework for regulating property, contracts and banking — and for integrating all citizens into a functioning system of production, distribution and re-
source ownership.

In contrast to Weber, Durkheim always defined social phenomena in terms
of functional and variable relations, rather than as discrete logical categories.
For example, he explained that there is no inherent difference among the various forms of government known to humans; that all can be conceptualized

along a continuum between two contrasting situations. "At one extreme, the government consciousness is as isolated as possible from the rest of society and has minimum range. . . . The closer the communication becomes between the government consciousness and the rest of society, the more this consciousness expands and the more things it takes in, the more democratic the society will be" (Durkheim 1957:84).

Durkheim was committed to freedom and individuality but, unlike Rousseau, he did not see these as in conflict with society. "For man freedom consists in deliverance from blind, unthinking physical forces; this he achieves by opposing against them the great and intelligent force which is society, under whose protection he shelters" (Durkheim 1953:72). He agreed with Weber on the great harm done to society by attempts at political revolution. And they can only ever be failed *attempts*, he claimed, because actual discontinuity in the evolution of collective representations is a chimera! He wrote, "There is no institution where deterioration does not set in at some point in its history. It may be that it fails to adapt itself in time to meet conditions of a new era. . . . This may be a reason for seeking to reform it, but not for declaring it forever useless and doing away with it" (Durkheim 1957:23).

Whereas Durkheim emphasized the restricted, juridical and decision-making function of the state, as compared to society as a whole, Weber seemed to see the former as all-inclusive. Always the state appeared in his writing as coincident with the German nation: a somewhat mystical entity with a unique responsibility to history. In this regard, it is enlightening to compare the inaugural addresses of the two sociologists as they assumed Chairs at their respective universities. At the University of Freiburg Weber said, "The *power* interests of the nation . . . are the ultimate decisive interests that must be served by that nation's economic policy" (Weber:217). The gist of Durkheim's message at the Sorbonne was that "Our society must restore the consciousness of its organic unity. . . . It is necessary to elaborate . . . [these ideas] scientifically at the university" (Lacapra:36).

Weber expressed ambiguous and somewhat contradictory ideas about democracy. He explained that, historically, it emerged as "the transformation of charisma in an anti-authoritarian direction. . . . The introduction of elected officials always involves a radical alteration in the position of the charismatic leader. He becomes the 'servant' of those under his authority" (Weber 1947: 389). However, Weber distinguished between those democratic systems which elect a charismatic leader by direct popular vote (his preference) and those liberal ones which he accused of trying to dispense with leadership altogether. "The latter type," he explained, "is characterized by the attempt to reduce to a minimum the control of some men over others" (Weber 1947:389). He concluded that "It is characteristic of a democracy which makes room for leadership that there should be in general a highly emotional type of devotion to and trust in a leader" (ibid.).

Still, Weber valued democracy as he defined it. He explained that "it means simply that no formal inequality of political rights exists between the individual classes of the population" (Weber 1971:194). He believed that the greatness of modern nations is measured by the degree to which they have become democratic in this sense. He was hampered, however, by his Nietzschean perspective which tended toward an exclusive focus on the greatness of individuals in history, and by his Hegelian tendency to diagnose political situations in terms of extreme opposites. He was hampered, as well, by the fact of his own aristocratic upbringing and outlook. For Weber's ideal-type democracy was a strange invention indeed. He once remarked, when discussing German democracy, "The cardinal fault really is the Greek gift of Bismarck's Caesarism, universal suffrage, the veriest murder of *equal rights for all in the true sense of the word*" (Marianne Weber:147).

In presenting his own ideas for reform, Weber wrote, "In a democracy the people choose a leader they trust. Then the chosen man says,'Now shut your mouth and obey me.' The people and the parties are no longer free to interfere in the leader's business. . . . Later the people can sit in judgement. If the leader has made mistakes — to the gallows with him!" (ibid.:653). He once referred to proponents of the rights of man as "fanatical supporters of extreme rationalism" (Runciman:9).

Significance for social-scientific thought

Although Marx is widely recognized as having indicated the general direction for a scientific sociology, there is no doubt that his untestable ideological doctrines have been obstacles to progress in that field. And it has been said of Weber that he lost himself in the very thickets through which Durkheim staked out clear paths for future sociologists to follow. Yet, inexplicably, it is Marx and Weber who have dominated twentieth-century sociology, while Durkheim's work too often has been either ignored or distorted within his own discipline. Fortunately, however, the echoes of his ideas spread far beyond sociology, reverberating in the theories of George Herbert Mead, George Santayana and Julian Huxley — and, subsequently, in the works of Karl Popper and B.F. Skinner.

From within sociology, Talcott Parsons attempted to reconcile the theories of Durkheim and Weber. However, his rationalistic "structural functionalism" appears to owe more to neo-Kantian premises than to Durkheim's evolutionary naturalism. Reinhard Bendix also lent his considerable skills to this "synthesizing" project during the post-war period, as did Jeffrey Alexander and George Ritzer in the 1970s and 1980s. In the early 1990s, Richard A. Hilbert joined the project in his attempt to trace the philosophical roots of "ethnomethodology." However, these sociological synthesizers all share a tendency to ignore the ontological and epistemological incompatibilities identified in this chapter and to emphasize Weberian ideas rather than those of Durkheim. In fact, among well-known theorists within the discipline, only Robert K. Merton's work can be considered as consistently Durkheimian. Furthermore, even though it might possibly be argued that the use of group statistical procedures in sociology is due largely to Durkheim's continuing influence, it seems that except in the case of a few scholars his name is now mentioned chiefly in connection with the concept of anomie. And, unfortunately, that crucial concept is too often defined by sociologists as the lack of normative constraints *from without* rather than as the lack of conscience ("society within") which Durkheim intended it to represent.

On the other hand, Weber has exerted a pervasive and lasting influence on sociology. Although many university departments are still dominated by Marxist-inspired "conflict theory," Weberian ideas are becoming increasingly significant. In addition to Talcott Parsons' "structural functionalism," both Karl Mannheim's "sociology of knowledge" and the motivation theory of Jurgen Habermas bear his mark, as does the popular 1990s critical theory and much of postmodern thought.

Weber's political theory (particularly the value he placed on charismatic leadership) may have influenced the actual course of history as well. Just before his death in 1920 he wrote, "To restore Germany to her old glory, I would surely ally myself with the devil incarnate" (Marianne Weber:673). The opportunity did indeed present itself to the German people in the following decades, in the person of that most charismatic of leaders — Adolph Hitler. Needless to say, Weber would no more have condoned Nazism than would Marx have claimed Stalinism as a legitimate legacy. But this does serve to remind us of the practical significance of social theory — if only because of its frequent contribution to historical consequences as unintended as they are tragic.

References for Chapter Fourteen

Alexander, Jeffrey. 1982a. *Theoretical Logic in Sociology*. Vol. 1: *Positivism, Presuppositions, and Current Controversies*. Berkeley: University of California Press.

_____. 1982b. *Theoretical Logic in Sociology*. Vol. 2: *The Antimonies of Classical Thought: Marx and Durkheim* Berkeley: University of California Press.

_____. 1983. *Theoretical Logic in Sociology*. Vol. 3: *The Classical Attempt at Theoretical Synthesis: Max Weber*. Berkeley: University of California Press.

_____. 1984. *Theoretical Logic in Sociology*. Vol. 4: *The Modern Reconstruction of Classical Thought*. Berkeley: University of California Press.

Bendix. Reinhard. 1945-46. Max Weber's Interpretation of Conduct and History. *American Journal of Sociology* 51: 518-26.

Dreijmanis, John, ed. 1989. *Karl Jaspers on Max Weber*. Translated by Robert J. Whelan. New York: Paragon House.

Durkheim, Emile. 1915. *The Elementary Forms of Religious Life*. Translated by Joseph Wood Swain. Glencoe, IL: The Free Press.

_____. 1933. *The Division of Labour in Society*. Translated by George Simpson. Glencoe, IL: The Free Press.

_____. 1951. *Suicide*. Translated by John A. Spaulding and George Simpson. Glencoe, IL: The Free Press.

_____. 1953. *Sociology and Philosophy*. Translated by D.F. Pocock. London: Cohen and West.

_____. 1957. *Professional Ethics and Civic Morals*. Translated by Cornelia Brookfield. London: Routledge and Kegan Paul.

_____. 1963. *Incest: The Nature and Origin of the Taboo*. Translated by Edward Sagarin. New York: Lyle Stuart.

_____. 1964 [1938]. *The Rules of Sociological Method*. 8th ed. Translated by Sarah A. Solovay and John H. Mueller, and edited by George E.G. Catlin. Glencoe, IL: The Free Press.

_____. 1972. *Selected Writings*. Translated and edited by Anthony Giddens. Cambridge: Cambridge University Press.

Gane, Mike, ed. 1992. *The Radical Sociology of Durkheim and Mauss*. London: Routledge.

Hilbert, Richard A. 1992. *The Classical Roots of Ethnomethodology: Durkheim, Weber and Garfinkel*. Chapel Hill, NC: University of North Carolina Press.

Lacapra, Dominick. 1974. *Emile Durkheim: Sociologist and Philosopher*. Ithaca: Cornell University Press.

Macrae, Donald G. 1974. *Max Weber*. New York: The Viking Press.

Mestrovic, Stjepan. 1968. *Emile Durkheim and the Reformation of Sociology*. Totowa, NJ: Rowman and Littlefield.

_____. 1992. *Durkheim and Postmodern Culture*. New York: Walter de Gruyter.

Mommsen, Wolfgang J. 1989. *The Political and Social Theory of Max Weber*. Cambridge: Polity Press.

Parsons, Talcott. 1959. General Theory in Sociology. In *Sociology Today: Problems and Prospects*. Edited by Robert K. Merton et al. New York: Harper & Row, p. 3-38.

Ritzer, George. 1983. *Contemporary Sociological Theory*. 2d ed. New York: Alfred A. Knopf.

Runciman, W.G., ed. 1978. *Max Weber: Selections in Translation*. Translated by E. Matthews. Cambridge: Cambridge University Press.

Stammer, Otto, ed. 1971. *Max Weber and Sociology Today*. Translated by Kathleen Morris. Oxford: Basil Blackwell.

Weber, Marianne. 1975. *Max Weber: A Biography*. Translated and edited by Harry Zohn. Toronto: John Wiley and Sons. (First published in 1926.)

Weber, Max. 1947. *The Theory of Social and Economic Organization*. Translated by A.M. Henderson and Talcott Parsons. New York: Oxford University Press.

————. 1949. *The Methodology of the Social Sciences*. Translated and edited by Edward A. Shils and Henry A. Finch. New York: The Free Press.

————. 1951. *The Religion of China: Confucianism and Taoism*. Translated by Hans Gerth. Glencoe IL: The Free Press.

————. 1952. *Ancient Judaism*. Translated by Hans Gerth and Don Martindale. Glencoe, IL: The Free Press.

————. 1958. *The Protestant Ethic and the Spirit of Capitalism*. Translated by Talcott Parsons. New York: Charles Scribner's Sons.

————. 1962a. *Basic Concepts in Sociology*. Translated by H.P. Secher. Westport, CT: Greenwood Press.

————. 1962b. *The City*. Translated and edited Don Martindale and Gertrud Neuwirth. New York: Collier Books.

————. 1965. *Politics as a Vocation*. Translated by H.H. Gerth and C. Wright Mills. Philadelphia: Fortress Press.

————. 1971. *The Interpretation of Social Reality*. Edited by J.E.T. Eldridge. New York: Charles Scribner's Sons.

Wrong, Dennis, ed. 1970. *Max Weber*. Englewood Cliffs, NJ: Prentice-Hall.

Fifteen

The Process of Cultural Evolution

George Herbert Mead

The poets light but
Lamps —
Themselves — go out —
The Wicks they stimulate —
If Vital Light
Inhere as do the Suns —
Each Age a Lens
Disseminating their
Circumference.
— Emily Dickinson,
"No. 883"

There were valuable insights in the works of Bergson and Husserl, in spite of certain paralyzing premises that led both into irresolvable contradiction. Bergson's psychological and anthropological works made a major contribution to the late-nineteenth-century readjustment of philosophical thought from the static transcendentalism of the Aristotelian-Christian tradition (still apparent in Kant) to an evolutionary perspective. No less significant was Husserl's idea that the external world acquires meaning only as humans act upon it. We should also acknowledge Husserl's belated realization of the universality and developmental nature of science, although this is seldom associated with his name.

A more important contribution came from Durkheim, however, in his explanation of the representational nature of human society, and in the path he charted for a future theory of socio-cultural evolution which would necessarily involve the idea of systems of increasing organizational complexity.

An American contemporary, George Herbert Mead, encountered the ideas of these popular European thinkers in his student days, as well as those of Spencer and William James, and later, of A.N. Whitehead and Dewey. He must also have become familiar with Pavlov's research. And, most important, he was a contemporary of Vygotsky, whose work he seems to have studied in depth. It is a reflection of the unique genius of Mead that he was able to dis-

References for this chapter are on p. 275.

card the weaknesses of his mentors while building on their strengths, and to develop out of these seemingly disparate streams of thought a comprehensive theory of cultural evolution. It is perhaps unfortunate that George Herbert Mead's remarkable synthesis emerged a century before its time. Almost his sole continuing impact on twentieth-century social science has been through the sociological model known as symbolic interactionism, which, in fact, merely skims the surface of his evolutionary theory. Only now is that theory beginning to be recognized for what it actually was: an early formulation of the missing conceptual framework essential to progress in social science.

A lifetime of thinking and acting

Mead was born in 1863, in Massachusetts, the son of a Congregationalist pastor. Through his mother, Elizabeth Storrs Billings, he was related to a family distinguished in intellectual accomplishment and public service. When he was seven years old his father became an instructor at the theological seminary at Oberlin, Ohio. In 1879 George entered college there, and became immersed in the classics. He made friends with Henry and Helen Castle, children of a well-travelled and wealthy Protestant mission official. In 1881 the senior Mead died; Elizabeth, now in straitened circumstances, was given a job teaching at the college, and George waited on tables until graduation.

During this college period George and his friend Henry worked their way through to a total refutation of the Christian dogma within which they had been reared, while managing to retain an appreciation of its ethical content and social function. Later, Mead expressed gratitude for this early freeing of his mind from the theological assumptions that might otherwise have blocked the course of his philosophical growth. After graduating he taught school for a time, then spent the next three years tutoring and surveying in what was then considered the Northwestern United States. He was eventually put in charge of surveying the railway route from Minneapolis to Moose Jaw, in what later became Saskatchewan. When the Canadian and American parties of surveyors met, Mead was happy to learn that his computations had been less than four inches out. He read omniverously during these working years. By 1887 he had saved enough money to enter Harvard for graduate studies in philosophy and psychology. He graduated the following year.

The next several years were taken up with studies in Berlin and Leipzig. Here George became interested in the ideas of Bergson and Husserl as well as those of Wundt. It is obvious, by the direction his thinking took later, that he must have been immersed in the ideas of Durkheim as well. He had been well armed against the idealism and subjectivism of the German academic world by William James' insistence that much of what has been located within consciousness by philosophers is instead very much a part of the objective world. From Spencer's works he had gained an evolutionary perspective. This background probably enabled him to read the European masters critically and selectively, and contributed to the fruitfulness of his sojourn in Germany.

In 1891 George married Helen Castle in Berlin, and soon after, he was appointed as an instructor in the Department of Philosophy and Psychology at Ann Arbor, Michigan. He became a colleague of John Dewey and moved with him in 1893 to the newly founded University of Chicago, where he taught until he died in 1931.

A surprising anomaly in the life of George Herbert Mead was his failure to organize and publish his thoughts. He was a brilliant conversationalist and lecturer who obviously spoke more easily than he wrote. He lectured without notes, virtually thinking aloud, and was greatly respected by his students for the power of his ideas. It is only because several of his students arranged for verbatim notes to be recorded during the last years of his life that Mead's theories were preserved in his original wording. This uncommon (and possibly admirable) resistance to the imperatives of academic publishing was no doubt at least partly due to his overwhelming involvement in civic affairs and social issues. The Meads and Deweys were close friends of the social reformer Jane Addams, and they helped to finance Hull House for many years. Hull House was founded in 1889 as part of the Settlement House movement led by Addams. It operated as a place for working people to meet, debate social issues and organize into unions. George served as a trustee of the movement in Chicago, and was an active advocate of women's suffrage. He was also a dedicated outdoorsman, an enthusiastic hiker, jogger and cyclist. Long hours of writing may have lacked appeal for this committed teacher and social activist.

During his later years at Chicago (long after Dewey had departed for Columbia) Mead found himself at odds with President Robert Hutchins. Hutchins was a traditionalist in philosophy, and was pushing an exclusive agenda of his own, in which an integrated psychological-philosophical perspective had no place. Mead's death marked the end of the famous Chicago school of pragmatism, and a turning point in the progress of the human studies in American universities. Henceforth psychology, sociology and anthropology would develop separately from one another and from philosophy and history — and, for the most part, these would become increasingly isolated from the attitude and methodology of science.

On the natural origin of mind

Mead's ideas, as published by former students in four posthumous volumes, are presented in somewhat rambling and repetitious lecture form, rather than as an organized system of thought. This, plus the fact that they were not accessible during his lifetime, meant that his theory did not enter the mainstream of philosophical and social-scientific thought — except indirectly, through the writings of John Dewey. Another factor in the neglect of this seminal thinker may have been the label given to his perspective. He had incorporated Pavlov's theory of conditioning into his thinking, while accepting Dewey's insight concerning the correlativity of stimulus and response. He was accordingly quite willing to refer to himself as a social behaviourist. However, for much of the twentieth century, behaviourism has been out of style. It has been interpreted simplistically by some of its supporters and generally spurned and distorted by its detractors: all this, ironically, in spite of widespread and increasingly fruitful application in practice.

Any attempt to organize Mead's ideas must begin with his naturalistic cosmology. His aim was to follow Darwin's lead in undertaking "to explain how the forms of things arise" (Mead 1956:9). The form with which he was concerned was that of human consciousness, as it had evolved out of the variety of organic life. He started by accepting the concept of evolution as an ongoing process operating within the dynamic flux of a real universe: a universe existing prior to the relatively late emergence of life forms and the much later appearance of human consciousness. And, like Bergson, he recognized the occurrence of life and of consciousness as two uniquely significant developments within the evolutionary process. However, he disagreed fundamentally with Bergson's explanation of how they came about. Mead felt that the two occurrences had not yet been satisfactorily accounted for within the evolutionary framework. He set out to remedy this.

It is important to understand how Mead differed from Bergson. He viewed evolution as a consistent process entirely determined by preceding and obtaining conditions of action within nature. This applied, in his scheme, to the evolution of consciousness as well. "When and how the living process appeared can hardly be conjectured, though there is no reason to assume that it was not a gradual evolution which could be causally described in chemical and physical terms" (Mead 1938:350). And consciousness, in its turn, arose out of nothing more mysterious than organic-environmental interaction. In his opinion, there was no necessity for any unsupportable premise requiring the injection of a mysterious vital impulse marking the human off from other animals at the onset of either life or consciousness. Mead believed, instead, that human consciousness had its beginnings in organic response mechanisms that had become increasingly sensitized to certain aspects of the beckoning surroundings, as "distant stimuli governing immediate responses stretched out the future by their alternative possibilities" (ibid.).

Thoroughly rejecting Bergson's vitalism, as well as Husserl's "transcendental mind" and Wundt's "antecedent self," Mead's formulation, like Durkheim's, maintained the integrity and all-inclusiveness of the evolutionary process within nature. Whereas most previous philosophers and psychologists had assumed that it was the appearance of mind that made social relations possible — or that individuals existed in some anarchic sense prior to the establishment of human society — Mead followed the lead of Marx and Durkheim in maintaining the exact opposite. Expanding on their insight, he explained that sociality came first, and that mind had evolved out of the social process itself. "We are rather forced to conclude that consciousness is an emergent from such behavior; that so far from being a precondition of the social act, the social act is a precondition of it" (Mead 1934:18).

In Mead's view there is no need to posit unexplainable supernatural creative forces or "vital" urges: a perfectly reasonable explanation of the apparently mysterious roots of human consciousness requires only an understanding of the key role of "contingency" and "emergence" within the later phases of evolution.

The concept of emergence

Mead developed the concept of "emergence" to explain the appearance of new forms that were able to maintain themselves over time, and whose structure could be accounted for totally by the conditions of evolution. The first was the living organism which emerged in some crucial accident out of a series of chemical reactions: such reactions being the necessary condition for physical evolution. He suggested that at this point a chain reaction must have occurred and gradually become perpetuated in a pattern of ongoing internal action, rather than consisting merely of entities passing from one state to another. This form was able to endure by reproducing itself and by responding to its environment, and thereby gradually began to function in an entirely new way, altering its environment and in turn itself undergoing alteration. From this watershed onward, a new principle of change (natural selection) operated within evolution, so that the very nature of the process was irreversibly altered by the emergence of the new form — that of life, or the first system of enduring relations.

Mead suggested that consciousness emerged in a similar fashion out of a "sociality" rooted in organic-environmental interaction; such interaction having been established as the necessary condition for the adaptive process that made biological evolution possible. Only by living in groups could individuals survive long enough to reproduce and nurture their young. The emergence of human consciousness initiated another change in the nature of the evolutionary process. Henceforth human language-based communication would provide the necessary condition for reflective thinking. Thus the adaptive capacity of the human process of intelligence became the engine driving the new process of cultural evolution, just as natural selection continued to provide the impetus at the biological level.

The concept of contingency

Contingency, for Mead, referred to the role of organic selectivity at certain crucial points in the process. He thought the chance mutation of a sensitivity to a particular condition in the surroundings must have been the simplest level of contingency as a factor in causation. This would have represented the beginning of sentience in living forms, sentience being "an attitude of the individual in so far as that attitude determines the environment and is determined by it" (Mead 1938:336). In other words, insofar as it is shaped by contingent conditions and, in turn, shapes subsequent conditions. Mead seemed to be saying that, from this point on, contingency became increasingly significant in the process of biological evolution. A sudden alteration of conditions in the surroundings (such as a stone blocking a familiar trail to a food source) would cause an interruption of the mechanical circuit of the act — or an extension of the time between stimulus and response. The organism would take another trail, or go around the rock, or climb over it, or try to push it aside, all the while holding the consummation of the act (eating) in abeyance.

Something in addition to the strict mechanical necessity of spatial relations was operating here, according to Mead. We can see the influence of Bergson in his explanation. "I take it that the indeterminateness of the time dimension of extension introduces the possibility of contingency in nature" (ibid.:341). In other words, once an organism became able to hold on to the response (in this case, the satiation of hunger) over a time duration, while the stimulus continued to beckon in the distance, the experience of a past and a future began to enter the animal's nervous system. From that point on, the spatially related (or physical) conditions of the present moment were no longer the necessary and sufficient causes of action. A type of behaviour was now initiated that was shaped by the contingencies of the organism's past experience and the variety of possible futures which this remembered past made possible. What Mead was outlining here is, in fact, a crucial reversal of causality occurring at the onset of organic evolution, whereby feedback from current behaviours began to shape those of the future.

Natural selection as universal

Mead agreed with Bergson that the emergence of living forms and of human consciousness were the major watersheds in evolution. But he believed that Darwin had successfully identified the principle of change directing the organic level of the process. He agreed that certain alterations occur purely by chance as mutations in the biological form; and organic environmental contingencies then determine which of these will survive to reproduce and thus maintain the altered form. Mead noted that the coincidence of sensitivity to certain stimuli and their occurrence in the immediate environment represents a contingency which makes further changes in the same direction increasingly probable — just as it renders a reversal of direction increasingly unlikely. This is the principle of natural selection in operation, and it accounts for the development of extremely complex organs within living forms as well as the varieties of species, and for the extinction of some and the survival of others.

The emergence of consciousness

Mead explained that in only one of the primate species — the branch leading to humans — a second great emergence occurred. This resulted from the evolution of sociality which had occurred in many animals. "Social conduct presupposes a group of animals whose life processes are determined in considerable part by the actions and consequences of these actions on the part of one another" (ibid.:362). He surmised that at this stage in evolution a large part of the environment affecting the survival and alteration of the species comprised the actions of other animals in the immediate surroundings. In some species, behaviour would have become increasingly selective in terms of particular group patterns — incorporating a network of specialized roles. Successful patterns would have favoured survival of the individuals exhibiting them, and would consequently have been inherited by the progeny of the adapters. Certain of these genetically programmed patterns must have evolved into a complex central nervous system. Others became simple organ-like animals with finely tuned instinctive responses coordinated within a social system. Mead referred to bees and ants as examples of the latter type of social animal, and primates as examples of the former.

In the case of the primate branch leading to humankind, sociality evolved in the direction of increasing openness to the impact of individual experience. Mead maintained that this was due, in large part, to the development of upright posture and the flexible hand. The hand, freed from the need to support the animal, encouraged a prolonged process of feeling and manipulating between the initial encounter of an environmental stimulus (such as a food source) and the ultimate response or consummation (such as eating). This allowed for the onset of a complicated learning process that involved discerning objects and coordinating perspectives of distance and location, as well as those of shape, volume and weight. For the first time it became possible to separate the perceiving subject from the object perceived. Mead explained that the truly momentous postponement of response that had now entered into organic activity began to free the animal from the immediacy of the present moment and to encourage the shadowy beginnings of a sense of past and future. Thus the preconditions for sociality were established, along with a vast increase in the significance of contingency as a causal factor in behaviour.

The evolution of language

The upright posture and flexible hand contributed to a second giant step in the evolution of sociality, according to Mead. Typically, he put to use here the one valid insight from an older psychology. He recalled that Wundt had "isolated a very valuable conception of the gesture as that which later became a symbol, but which is to be found, in its earlier stages, as part of the social act" (Mead 1934:42). Facial expression and bodily posturing is common in most animals, but its impact is limited to close encounters. However, the hand could gesture — and upright primates could see the action from a considerable distance and respond to it. Eventually, the group of primates would have learned to respond to the gesture as the animal making it was responding, even though the original stimulus of approaching danger or food was as yet unperceived by them. Soon the very making of the gesture would bring about, in the animal making it, the response of the others to the gesture. This was a crucial step, for it gave individuals a means of controlling their own behaviour in advance of overt action.

Mead noted that the appearance of the *vocal* gesture was doubly important. "One is more apt to catch himself up and control himself in the vocal gesture than in an expression of the countenance" (ibid.:65). Or even the wave of a hand. Like the manipulations of objects, the vocal gesture encouraged an extension of the time frame of the stimulus-response activity. The individual now had the means to represent more than just a momentary sensation of sight or sound. Eventually images of past sights and sounds and warnings about future possibilities would have been evoked through vocal gestures. At that point the group would have begun to evolve significant symbols. Mind came later. Mead was of the opinion that "the early stages of the development of language must have been prior to the development of mind or thought" (ibid.: 192). According to him, "Gestures become significant symbols when they implicitly arouse in an individual making them, the same response which they explicitly arouse, or are supposed to arouse, in the other individuals. . . . Only in terms of gestures as significant symbols is the existence of mind or intelligence possible" (ibid.:47). Here, Mead was explaining the origin of communication: possible only when there is *meaning* to express and share.

The onset and crucial function of intelligence

This ability to handle significant symbols would have given an obvious advantage to the offspring of those who had developed it and who thereby had the opportunity to pass it on during the necessarily lengthening period of childhood now required for learning. Mead surmised that most early primate learning would have occurred as imitation, in that "In so far as one calls out the attitude in himself that one calls out in others, the response is picked out and strengthened" (ibid.:66). It can be seen how, at this particular stage in the evolution of one of the primate species, the conditions were established for an explosive take-off into complexity and control within the social process. Language appeared, and with it came the great leap forward into human consciousness. A new principle of change had now emerged. From that point on it would be the human potential for reflective thought, operating by means of the instrument of language, that would be the controlling factor in evolution.

One can understand how Mead came to posit "the act" as the basic unit of psychological analysis, rather than the Hobbes' "sensation," or Bergson's "moment," or Husserl's "*intentional* act." For him, thinking rather than feeling was the core of the entire process by which consciousness emerged out of communication. It is the act, in its connection of environmental stimulus with organic response through the medium of symbols, that gradually forms the conscious self. "The essence of the self is cognitive; it lies in the internalized conversation of gestures which constitute thinking" (ibid.:173). This is what Dewey meant when he maintained that action precedes thought, but it is very different from the Husserlian and Weberian idea of *intentionality* or motivation as being the essence of the social.

Taking the role of the other

Mead claimed that these vocalized symbolic gestures enable the thinker to assume the perspective of the intended respondent and to respond internally to the anticipated external response in an unbroken mental circuit: the inevitably social "act." The human being's central nervous system, or brain, with its intricate pathways built up out of repeated organic-environmental acts, is the essential vehicle. It results in an ongoing process whereby the individual develops a self by "taking the role of the other," through a continuous coordination of the perspectives of other members of the surrounding social milieu, or "universe of discourse." "The attitudes of the others constitute the organized ME and then one reacts toward that as an I" (ibid.:176). The I provides the impetus for action, but, contrary to the vain expectations of Husserl, one cannot turn around quickly enough to catch a glimpse of it. As the act moves from the present into the past, the I has become the ME. Mead concluded: "The process of relating one's organism to the others in the interactions that are going on, in so far as it is imported into the conversation of the I and the ME, constitutes the self" (ibid.:179).

Mead believed that there were two distinguishable phases in the emergence of the conscious self. The first was "taking the role of the other," in which an evolving linguistic facility enabled humans to assume and accommodate to a variety of social perspectives. This corresponds to the "play" phase in individual development, during which the hiding child learns to anticipate and respond in advance to the moves of the searcher in the game of hide and seek. In this process the self becomes objectified in the ME and cognition is initiated. The I of the present moment is no longer all there is, as with the cow in the pasture. The I, shared by all sentient animals, is the creature of impulse, "a congenital tendency to react in a specific manner to a certain sort of stimulus, under certain organic conditions" (Mead 1938:336). It is the source of our sense of freedom of choice. But the instant the I assumes the perspectives of the other — or turns back to survey images of past experience — or strains toward the future to consider possible courses of action and their likely consequences — it becomes the ME.

The generalized other

The second phase is the development, within the ME, of a generalized perspective incorporating the joint expectations of the social group. Mead called this the "generalized other." It parallels the game phase in individual development, wherein children carry over into their internal mental functioning the rules governing various daily activities. The rules become part of their real world and, for all practical purposes, unchangeable. They are accepted as universal, and therefore assume an objective reality as powerful in its influence on behaviour as the directly perceived data of the natural environment. Such rules are applied to bring meaning and order to a variety of concrete circumstances, from playground games to moral conduct. In both cases the "generalized other" is the source of social control, but it is a control exerted from within rather than without the self. It is often called conscience.

The "generalized other" represents "the expression of the ME over against the expression of the I" (Mead 1934:210). When an act is inspired and carried through by the I we have behaviour that is either impulsive or habitual. In both cases the act is closed immediately, and is largely the necessary result of either current or past conditions. At the other extreme, when the ME is in full control the behaviour can be extremely predictable as well (in terms of the norms of the social group) and may not be easily adaptable in changing circumstances. It is only when the I and the Me interact in a conscious process of moving from images of the past to those of the future that intelligence has the chance to become operative. The I then responds to the process of reflection, rather than to the direct stimulus of an environmental datum, or to that of the "generalized other," and change is introduced which is contingent upon reasoned choice within the social act.

The social origins of cultural evolution

Mead noted that this "response of the I involves adaptation, but an adaptation which affects not only the self but also the social environment which helps to constitute the self; that is, it implies a view of evolution in which the individual affects its own environment as well as being affected by it" (ibid.:214). This reciprocal adaptation is the source of social change, as well as of whatever indeterminateness there is in evolution, but it has nothing to do with a supernatural creative spirit or force, in Mead's view. He commented that "it is hardly plausible to suppose that this already ongoing and developing process should suddenly, in a particular stage in evolution, become dependent for its continuance upon an entirely extraneous factor, introduced into it, so to speak, from without" (ibid.:225).

For Mead, the existence of human society requires no explanation beyond that of the encompassing and evolving social interaction described above. "Social institutions, like individual selves, are developments within, or particular and formalized manifestations of, the social life process at its human evolutionary level" (ibid.:262). They represent the generalized social attitudes that make an organized self possible. They define patterns of conduct in a general sense, affording plenty of scope for originality, flexibility and variety. But only in terms of the institutions of some relevant social community can individuals act adequately by taking account of the attitudes of others toward their actions.

Mead's theory is interactionist in two senses: it posits a reciprocal relationship between the individual and the socio-cultural environment as well as between physiology and the inorganic surroundings. He emphasized the fact that consciousness itself must refer to both the organism and its environment, and cannot be located simply in one or the other. "The human being's physiological capacity for developing mind or intelligence is a product of biological evolution, just as is his whole organism; but the actual development of mind or intelligence, given that capacity, must proceed in terms of social situations wherein it gets its expression and import: and hence itself is a product of social evolution" (ibid.:226). Biological evolution produced the organic base — the complex central nervous system and the upright posture and flexible hand and tongue of a particular branch of primates — but the emergence in those primates of consciousness or mind required the sociality that gave rise to language.

An evolutionary theory of knowledge

Mead's epistemology, or theory of knowledge, is logically implied by his ontology and psychology. He said that he began by taking *time* seriously, as Bergson advised. He maintained that time becomes a factor in experience only at the point in the evolution of living forms when the response to environmental stimulation is no longer immediate. Previous to that, all behaviour is mechanistically or necessarily determined by prevailing spatial conditions. Causality is linear, or before-the-fact. When the animal begins to become sensitized to certain aspects of the environment and to respond selectively, to some small degree the stimulus-response act is becoming extended over time. This would apply to the animal seeking the food that it smells beyond an obstacle in its path. To this same degree contingency (or "feedback" causality) begins to operate, according to Mead, although at each separate moment in time, all is mechanical necessity, as when the animal hits against the obstacle, or falls into a hole in the path.

As intelligence develops in the context of the conscious self, past experience enters the present act — as remembered meanings associated with presently experienced conditions — and the future enters as well, in terms of imagined goals of action. During the ensuing internal activity (the conversation of reflection) the external response is suspended while a number of possible means to the desired end are run through. Mead said that this is where contingency becomes increasingly significant. Although each possible set of means is subject to mechanical necessity, the specific means selected and the act as then consummated is contingent, not only on obtaining conditions, but upon the choice made. Although the arrived-at end is entirely a product of the interaction of the preceding conditions it is not necessarily determined by the sum of them as identified separately. "There is the necessity which lies in the whole statement of the means, and then there is a sort of selection of means which is fitted for the emergence of some sort of contingent ends or values" (Mead 1938:319). The intended end is actually defining the means selected.

This is contingency with a vengeance! It is important to understand that Mead did not claim that selective organic action is uncaused or scientifically unexplainable. He merely suggested that the concepts of emergence, contingency and probability are better tools and will imply a more appropriate methodology for social science than the the idea of mechanical causality and necessity on which the earlier positivism had been based.

The permanent object

Long before Einstein's discovery, Mead was referring to the notion of differing perspectives being dependent upon one's location in space and time. He maintained that these are located *in nature* and not within the individual, as subjectivists like to believe. The idea of the relativity (and necessity for coordination) of perspectives was central to his entire model of social evolution. Physics came to it later.

According to Mead, the learning human encounters space and time through *experience* which is constructed out of organic-environmental action. The representation of the permanent object (a form in space enduring over time) is not in the mind until action builds it into the pathways of the central nervous system. "It must be remembered that the body of the individual only becomes an object as other objects appear in experience, for they are essential to the delimitation and orientation of the body, and that the content of effective

occupation of space is a common content of the body and other physical objects — it is not projected into other physical objects by the body" (ibid.:327).

He was disagreeing with Bergson here. For Mead it is the adjustments and
adaptations to the changing positions of other objects over time that reflect the
permanent object for the observer. Without this gradual acquisition and coordination of perspectives in the conditions of the permanent object within the
individual's system of action, there would be no conception of space and time
in human experience.

Mead based his theory of knowledge on the premise that, although the
world external to human experience cannot be wholly or absolutely known,
nonetheless it is there! On this issue he was at one with the neo-realists from
Spencer on. Where he and other pragmatists differed from them was in the distinction between information and knowledge. Mead acknowledged that we
obtain information directly from the data of experience. These data "never
lose the actuality of the unquestioned world. . . . They are the solid realities
that can bridge the gap between discredited theories and the discoveries of science" (ibid.:47). However, an observation of a datum of information is a perception, and as such can be illusory and is never entirely free of error. It must
be put into communicable form so that a pool of individual observations can
be formed out of the joint experience of the group and thereby rendered comparable in terms of other individual perceptions. In this way it is informally
tested, and if it proves reliable it will be useful as a guide to the selection of effective means to desired ends in the individual's reflective process.

The hypothetical nature of knowledge

Observations expressed by the perceiving individual in specific common symbols such as words can be assimilated readily and reasonably accurately into
the experience of others. The language of knowledge, to be meaningful to the
recipient, will necessarily reflect the action that precipitated the perception.
This means that it will describe the conditions that held at the time, and then
the move taken and the outcome in terms of altered conditions. The most appropriate form for the communication to take will therefore be an "if-then"
statement, and it will be retained in the individual's internal system of action
in those terms, if it is retained at all. In Mead's view, this was the origin of the
necessarily *hypothetical* form of knowledge. It is a social product, a rendering
of individual observation into communicable form so that it can be shared by
the social group and its reliability ascertained by the receiving individuals
when they repeat the act under similar conditions.

Like Dewey, Mead referred to such group-tested hypotheses as objects of
knowledge. They are ideal objects as distinct from the actuality of permanent
objects. By "ideal" he simply meant what Durkheim meant by his collective
representations. They comprise, not the concrete data of immediate experi-

ence, but *ideas*: "the form in which past objects and future objects, which are not objects in the world that is [presently] there, may exist in the minds of individuals" (ibid.:70).

Knowledge, then, is a system of hypotheses which begins and ends with the data of individual experience. It is initiated by a problem (some restriction of action) presented to one member of the group by the immediate situation; there follows the pursuit of a number of possible means of surmounting the problem, until something works to enable the actor to achieve the desired end. Then, after the successful encounter is shared with others, comes the empirical check by those others, in the course of their own experience. The more useful the hypothesis proves to be, the more solidly it will be embedded in the generalized attitude of the society. That is to say, it will be institutionalized as knowledge.

Observations, and the actual data or information that they present, should therefore not be confused with knowledge, in Mead's opinion. They are the crucial *sources* from which knowledge is inferred, reflectively constructed into hypotheses and subsequently tested. On the other hand, all knowledge — and the science which has evolved out of it — depends upon the assumption that different individuals have had, or would have, the same experience under the same or similar conditions. This is the assumption of the realist as well as the pragmatist. This does not deny the significance of the relativity of perspectives. "To everyone, the world that is there is in varying degrees different from that which is there for any other, because of each one's location and perspective. But it is the location and perspective that are responsible for this. One still looks upon it with a universal eye, and its contacts are those of all men" (ibid.:64).

Mead thus firmly rejected the subjectivist belief shared by transcendentalists and idealists that location and perspective are attributes of the human mind, and that they *determine* reality. For Mead, a reasonably objective and universally applicable knowledge is indeed possible, providing the instruments of observation are capable of compensating for the relativity of perspectives. To the greatest extent possible, all locations and perspectives must be taken into account in the gathering and testing of data, and these must be communicated with the greatest possible precision. To the degree that this is achieved, the knowledge will be increasingly objective, although absolute objectivity is an impossible ideal. This he saw as the promise and the responsibility of science.

For Mead, as for Dewey and Durkheim, the scientific process is simply a social extension and formalization of the individual process of reflection. In reflecting, the thinker begins with the *present* problem, then immediately moves into the *future* by anticipating the preferred outcome or consummation of the current act, and makes use of the remembered *past* to determine the most effective means to achieve that end. Reflection is about selecting means for individual goal-directed action, and that is precisely what science seeks to achieve for the universal human community. This is what pragmatists mean when they refer to knowledge as *instrumental*. It determines means — not ends — and gives great power to the social group acquiring it to pursue whatever goals they favour.

Mead credited Hegel with the insight that "The human animal as an individual could never have achieved control over the environment. It is a control which has arisen through social organization" (ibid.:17). Both Mead and Hegel were, of course, referring to the *degree* of control thus far achievable by science. Mead added, "There is nothing so social as science, nothing so universal" (ibid.:18). It represents the universalization of the process of reflection. It is the one reliable social instrument by which the human community could solve whatever problems the environment reveals, by changing its conduct in an orderly fashion, if the group would but focus on appropriate ends. Unlike mythology, it can never become obsolete, for the objects of knowledge evolve as human capacities for observing the environment (and the environment itself) evolve. "The scientific method is, after all, only the evolutionary process grown self-conscious" (ibid.:23) was the way Mead summed it up in words reminiscent of Durkheim.

On ethics and aesthetics

Mead believed that our species is currently in turbulent transition from a state where individual selves were formed chiefly with reference to tribal and national groupings to one in which the "generalized other" will have become the values and norms of the universal human community. For him the greatest contribution of Christianity was its assumption "that all men should belong to a universal society in which the interests of each would be the interest of all" (ibid.:466). But he was convinced that traditional religious ideas of supernatural ends are no longer adequate nor helpful. There is indeed a need for salvation, he remarked, "not the salvation of the individual but the salvation of the self as a social being . . . that, rather than the mystical attitude, is important" (ibid.:476). What the religious mystic so desperately seeks is a connection with the universe, but "there is no way at the present time that we can with any security connect the history of man and the values that have appeared in society with the history of the physical universe" (ibid.:478).

Mead explained that this is because we function in an entirely different system of organization within the all-encompassing cosmos from that of our inorganic surroundings. The physical universe operates according to mechanical necessity, with the principle of action and reaction holding sway. The system of living organisms operates according to a contingent process of reciprocal adaptive interaction between form and environment, driven from behind by the principle of natural selection. And, finally, the system of human consciousness operates by means of goal-seeking behaviour involving the social organization of perspectives which has given rise to universalized reflection, or science, as the major instrument of change.

Here he was providing an evolutionary explanation for what Schopenhauer had discerned as the three forms of causality. Elsewhere, in an echo of Durkheim, Mead suggested that "The mystical experiences which may be . . . widely felt in terms of excitement, are really a sensing of the relation of man to his society" (ibid.:478). And he added that these are wrongly and wastefully focused on the unknowable universe beyond human experience.

Mead proposed that we accept the fact of our universal social origin and build our systems of morality and art upon that more realistic base. His ideas on ethics and aesthetics flow logically from his model of humans as (potentially) reflective goal-seekers, who, as a universal community, shape their future environment by present actions. To the degree that ever more effective means are constructed, in the form of scientific knowledge, the ends sought by humanity become increasingly important. Mead believed that, whereas knowledge is a matter of means, ethics and aesthetics are concerned with ends — or the consummations of acts. He employed Dewey's explanation of aesthetic experience as a unique phase in the act of reflection: one not routinely present. "What is peculiar to it is its power to catch the enjoyment that belongs to the consummation, the outcome of an undertaking, and to give to the . . . objects that are instrumental in the undertaking, and to the acts that comprise it, something of the joy and satisfaction that suffuse its successful accomplishment" (ibid.:454). The appreciation associated with the desired end flows back into the means, so that means and end are experienced as one harmonious whole. This is quite different from affective states such as the sensation of sexual bliss, fear or pain, and should not be confused with them.

According to Mead, an object of art is an embodiment of value, capable of enriching the experience of the viewer or listener. It is a concrete manifestation of what we can hope for as ends of future action. Morality, or ethics, has to do with the recognition of value as a quality in human experience, and the achievement of it for the individual and the community. It concerns the selection of appropriate goals of action. Mead did not explore this subject very fully, other than to suggest that all relevant social values should be taken into account in establishing ends. "We have no more right to neglect a real value than we have to neglect a fact in a scientific problem" (ibid.:461).

Values must be tested in action, just as knowledge is. Mead advised that where conflicting values are present, we should strive to reconstruct our lives so that all of them can be taken into account, at least to some degree. This is why reflective thinking is as necessary for ethical problems as for technical ones. "The moral question is not one of setting up a right value over against a wrong value; it is the question of finding the possibility of acting so as to take account, as far as possible, of all the values involved" (ibid.:465).

At first glance this seems to indicate that Mead considered all values to be equally worthy of being translated into ends, but this is no more the case than that he believed that all opinions are equally reliable as objects of knowledge. He was not a moral relativist any more than his pragmatism was subjectivist, as many critics claimed. His position was that group goals, developed from individual values and applied in society at large, can be assessed or tested only by the *quality brought to the lives of the individuals living by them*. Do they work over the long term? The very fact of the success of science in providing humans with powerful means has made the wise choice of ends imperative, and Mead was more aware of this than most. Clearly, where evolution is concerned, all possible directions are not equally desirable. Mead's hope was that the human community could, in time, share a social process for developing common goals. This would require the coordination and universalization of value perspectives, just as has been the case for knowledge. He had little confidence in the ability of traditional religion to accomplish this.

Mead recognized the inevitable dilemma faced by humans in their ongoing attempt to construct universally objective and valid means and ends out of the subjectivity of momentary individual experience. Knowers and valuers are inevitably a part of what they strive to know and to evaluate. He tried to sum up the difficulty and the resolution proposed by his pragmatic model as follows: "The epistemological problem is found in the objectivity of that which is subjective. The problem of relativity is found in the subjectivity of that which is objective. The solution of the epistemological problem is found in the recognition of the objectivity of the apparatus by which we reach the subjective. . . . The solution of the relativist's problem is found in the recognition that the emergent value which the individual organism confers on the common world belongs to that world in so far as it leads to its creative reconstruction" (ibid.:613).

It seems that Mead was reminding us that our innermost thoughts are grounded in the actuality of the external objects with which we, as fellow objects, interact. At the same time, we do not merely mirror the raw data of that external world. This is because of the very imperatives of distance in time and location in space that dictate the private perspectives which give to the perceptions of every individual their uniquely subjective character.

As a solution to the first problem Mead suggested that scientific hypotheses, which operate within our minds as guides to action — and which, as ideas, seem so subjective — are in fact objective instruments constructed, shared and tested by the universal human community. Our most powerful subjective insights are actually reflections of these public "objects" of knowledge — rather than the raw data of experience. His solution to the second problem was the understanding that the conditions of the future are, to a considerable extent, determined by the values, perceptions and choices of the individuals living in the world today and in the past. Tomorrow's objective reality is, indirectly, created by today's subjective strivings. Only by understanding the significance of this ultimate process of organic-environmental interaction for the future of humanity within the ecology of our endangered globe can one fully appreciate the potential of the contribution made to the philosophy of social science by George Herbert Mead.

References for Chapter Fifteen

International Encyclopedia of the Social Sciences. 1968. 1st ed., s.v. "Mead, George Herbert."

Mead, George Herbert. 1934. *Mind, Self and Society*. Edited by Charles W. Morris. Chicago: University of Chicago Press.

_____. 1938. *The Philosophy of the Act*. Edited by Charles W. Morris. Chicago: University of Chicago Press.

_____. 1956. *George Herbert Mead on Social Psychology*. Edited by Anselm Strauss. Chicago: University of Chicago Press.

Miller, David L. 1973. *George Herbert Mead: Self, Language, and the World*. Austin: University of Texas Press.

Natanson, Maurice. 1956. *The Social Dynamics of George H. Mead*. Washington, DC: Public Affairs Press.

Sixteen

George Santayana on a Unified Social Theory

Ye whose lost voices echoing in this rhyme,
My tongue usurps, forgive if I have erred.
Not as yet uttered, but as I have heard,
I spell your meanings in an evil time.
— George Santayana, "Invocation"

John Dewey once claimed that George Santayana's commitment to naturalistic premises was half-hearted, and Santayana used the same epithet in criticizing Dewey's position. Neither claim was justified; indeed the two philosophies were very similar in their thoroughgoing naturalism. However, unlike Dewey, Santayana ploughed a lonely road and sometimes found the going difficult. Although solidly grounded in the world view of naturalism, he clung to the terminology of neo-Platonism and to literary metaphor; for his habits of thought and technique were not those of the methodical empiricist, but of the poetic genius. And his aspirations were profoundly religious rather than scientific. He shared Dewey's reverence for truth — insofar as human scientific knowledge can approximate it — but he yearned for yet one further step. From the vantage point of science, he dared to hope for the sense of an eternal harmony resounding from within the flux of existence. This was, for Santayana, the ultimate good.

Such a temperament, if undisciplined, might conceivably have found the mysticism of transcendentalism or romantic idealism more congenial than naturalism. Or, if disciplined in ritual and tradition, it might have been expected to pursue Catholicism. But Santayana's early experience was unique in the effective inoculation it provided against all forms of romanticism on the one hand, and theology on the other. It did something else as well. It made him the epitome of the permanent alien, or the "marginal man" of sociology: a sympathetic but detached observer of the fads and foibles of his fellow humans as they peered and postured from the security of their entrapment within group-

---

References for this chapter are on p. 292.

created caves of illusion. At home nowhere in particular, he was in some ways at home everywhere, for he carried his security within.

The permanent outsider

George Santayana was born in 1864 into what he later called a deeply disunited family. His mother was an American of Spanish descent; his father a well-educated but relatively unsuccessful Spanish artist and official. He was the only child of the union, although his mother had three surviving children from a previous marriage to a member of a Boston merchant family. George was named after the first husband, George Sturgis. His parents had lived together in Madrid for only a few years when the mother suddenly returned to Boston with her three older children to resume her life as a Sturgis, leaving the little George with his father. Then, at the age of eight the child was taken to the United States, and, just as suddenly, deposited with the mother and her family, while the father departed for Spain, never to return.

This fact of virtual desertion by each parent in turn, and the perception of being unwanted that it must have implanted in the young child, was bound to have had lasting effects. Although he had many close friends all his life, Santayana was never to form an enduring intimate relationship except with his older half-sister, Susana. Nurtured in early childhood by a tolerant agnostic in tradition-ridden Spain, his subsequent homesickness would have imbued the world view of that absent father with great value. Resenting his mother, he assessed the Unitarian church, which she forced him to attend, with pitiless eyes. He once wrote of it, "the charm of religious nothingness was probably what drew people to that form of worship; you could feel religious without any intellectual consequences" (Santayana 1986:63).

Slipping away to Catholic mass with Susana became an act of defiance against everything that the Sturgis family stood for. The Catholic environment must also have aroused feelings associated with home in Spain, and fed a need within him for poetry and drama. Yet (probably due to the lasting influence of his father' scepticism) he "never had the least touch of superstition. . . . It never occurred to me to shudder at the doctrine of eternal damnation, as the innocent Unitarians did, or be overawed by it, as were the innocent Calvinists. Hell is set in the bond. . . . Nothing that has ever occurred can be annulled. That is what eternal damnation means" (ibid.:167).

His early experience with Catholicism confirmed it in his mind as a beautiful and comforting pageant, but an imaginary and essentially false one, nonetheless. He says he knew intuitively "there was only one possible play, the actual history of nature and mankind, although there might well be ghosts among the characters and soliloquies among the speeches. Religions, *all* religions, and philosophies, *all* philosophies were the soliloquies and ghosts. They might be excellent reflective criticisms on the play as a whole. Nevertheless . . . their value as criticisms lay in their fidelity to the facts, and to the sentiments which these facts aroused in the critics" (ibid.:169).

Santayana's inoculation against the excesses of romanticism was equally effective. His maternal grandfather had been a follower of Rousseau, and his mother had assumed her father's principles. Merely living with the consequences of his mother's impulsive life-choices was sufficient to convince him that "Rational belief must have other guides than sheer imagination exploring infinite possibilities. Beliefs have an earthly origin and can be sanctioned only by earthly events" (ibid.:171).

Although Santayana's mother, because of her Sturgis connections, was "of" Boston Brahmin society she was never "in" it. Her financial situation was always precarious, and she, like Rousseau, seems to have lacked the gift of sociability. This meant that socially, as well as ideologically, Santayana grew up as an outsider. He attended Boston Latin School, which accepted students from all levels of society on the basis of ability and performance. From there he moved on to Harvard. At university he found a world of ideas in which, finally, he could feel at home. He felt an immediate affinity with such ancients as Thales and Democritus, but not with Socrates. Late in life he expressed the opinion that Socrates had pushed philosophy in the wrong direction. "He was not . . . a sound moralist as he is reputed to be, and really a rogue" (McCormick:467).

Santayana wrote of the thrill of his first encounter with Lucretius. "Even the physiological and biological theories seemed instructive, not as scientific finalities, as if science could be final, but as serving to dispel the notion that anything could be non-natural or miraculous" (Santayana 1986:230). He added a general comment on the ancients. "They were not gaping phenomenologists, but knew that our senses, no less than our poetry and myth, clothe in human images the manifold processes of matter" (ibid.:230). Elsewhere he wrote, "The great master of sympathy with nature, in my education, was Lucretius" (ibid.:538).

Another early intellectual hero was Spinoza. Santayana considered him a complete naturalist, but found him deficient as a humanist. "He had no idea of human greatness and no sympathy for human sorrow" (ibid.:235). Benedict (Baruch) Spinoza was a pre-Enlightenment philosopher who was banished from his Jewish community in Amsterdam because of his beliefs. Discarding Descartes' dualism, he had attempted to reconcile the latter's rationalism and mechanism within a comprehensive pantheism.

Santayana found in Herbert Spencer a more modern source of inspiration, one whose influence on him was to be lifelong. The other thread running through his work is the perspective of Durkheim on the nature of the "ideal." However, it was neither the Hellenic materialists nor Spinoza — nor even Spencer and Durkheim — whose works dominated the philosophical atmosphere at Harvard. As in all universities of that era, Harvard students were immersed by their professors in neo-Platonism and Hegelianism. When Santayana won a fellowship to pursue graduate studies it was to Germany that his mentors sent him. It suited him perfectly, as he was able to see his father once again. So he went to Europe for enlightenment, but remained to become increasingly appalled and repelled by the reigning German romantic idealism. He wrote at that time, "A German professor like Wundt seems to me a survivor of the alchymist" (McCormick:79). Another inoculation!

Frustrations of a career in academia

In 1888 Santayana returned to Harvard to write the thesis for his doctorate. It was a study of the philosophy of Rudolph Hermann Lotze, an admirer of Lucretius who had tried to reconcile idealism with realism (ibid.:82). Although Lotz failed, he did pioneer the idea of replacing formal logic in science by a theory of inquiry. Subsequently this was taken up and developed by John Dewey, but Santayana seems to have been unaware of that fact. Santayana said afterward that he should have worked on revealing the fallacies in Hegel's thought, but that this was not politically possible at Harvard.

The following year Santayana was hired by Harvard as a lecturer in philosophy. He spent the summer at his mother's house in Roxbury, preparing his first lectures. From then on he lived in lodgings in Harvard Yard until, in 1895, he was able to go to King's College in England on a year's leave of absence. He loved the atmosphere at Cambridge, but was not overawed by the dons. "My feeling when I was at King's," he later reminisced, "was that the birds were not worthy of their cage" (Santayana 1986:435).

All his life Santayana seems to have felt more at home in England than anywhere. On that first occasion he visited frequently with Lord Frank Russell and met his younger brother, Bertie. Memories and friendships made that year were to last a lifetime, to be renewed on many subsequent visits. His letters and poetry seem to hint at a youthful proclivity for homosexual attachments, perhaps begun in this period, and this may have contributed to his feeling of social marginality. Another result of the year in England was his first book, *The Sense of Beauty*.

The year following his return to Harvard, Santayana was finally given the rank of Assistant Professor, after having been held at the level of Lecturer for an insultingly long time. President Elliot seems to have disapproved of him. It was not until 1907 that he became a full Professor. Two years before, in 1905, he had published the first volume of *The Life of Reason* — eventually to be followed by four more. In that same year he had accepted an exchange professorship at the Sorbonne. In 1910 came *Three Philosophical Poets: Lucretius, Dante and Goethe*. Santayana believed that these three together illustrated all of European philosophy. He considered Lucretius "the Herbert Spencer of antiquity." Dante interpreted the world in the medieval sense of a moral struggle between grace and sin; while Goethe represented the popular nineteenth-century blend of romanticism and paganism.

Of his later career at Harvard, Santayana once remarked, "I was still disliked, but I was swallowed" (ibid.:395). He was never close to his Harvard colleagues. The leading light was William James, of whom he wrote, "I trusted his heart, but not his judgement. . . . In fact, he got nowhere" (ibid.:401). He concluded that James' "inspiration, even in science, was that of romanticism" (ibid.:405). He distrusted James' pragmatism, believing that it involved "a confusion between the test and the meaning of truth" (McCormick:186).

The life of a professional observer

In 1912, after his mother died, Santayana left Harvard and the United States for what was to be the last time. A small inheritance from his mother and the hope of increasing sums from royalties gave him the courage to resign his professorship. In 1913 he published *Winds of Doctrine*. During World War I he lived in England and wrote *Egotism in German Philosophy*, *Soliloquies in England*, and *Character and Opinion in the United States*.

In 1919 Robert Bridges tried to persuade Santayana to settle permanently in England. He was offered a place to write and think at Corpus Christi College in Oxford. Reluctant to give up his freedom, however, he resumed life on the continent, wintering in Rome from 1920 on, and spending his summers in Spain with Susana until her death in 1928. He returned to England twice, once in 1923 to deliver the Herbert Spencer lectures, and again in 1934, at the age of seventy. After Frank Russell's death there was no longer a friend in England close enough to draw him back.

During those years Santayana was prolific in output. He began his autobiography, *Persons and Places*, and published *Platonism and the Spiritual Life*, *Dialogues in Limbo*, *Skepticism and Animal Faith*, and a best-selling novel, *The Last Puritan*. He found himself trapped in Rome during World War II; out of step, as usual, with his place and time. His sympathies were with England, though he had thought earlier that Mussolini was the right man for depression-ridden Italy. He described both World Wars as the ultimate "adventures in enthusiastic unreason" (Santayana 1986:542). He was never partisan in politics, and was particularly wary of goals and platforms that ignore reliable knowledge of nature and of human nature within it. Of utopian thinking (whether of left or right) he wrote, "This militant method of reforming mankind by misrepresenting their capacities and place in the universe . . . is the official and intolerant method of our most zealous contemporary prophets and reformers. . . . The fanaticism of all parties must be allowed to burn down to ashes, like a fire out of control" (ibid.:546).

In 1940, no longer able to care for himself, he moved into the clinic of the Blue Nuns. Still hard at work during the ensuing years he managed to complete a four-volume distillation of his philosophical system: *Realms of Being*. He resumed his autobiography, completing both it and *Domination and Powers* in 1950, at the age of 86. He died of stomach cancer two years later, steadfastly refusing to be converted to Catholicism by his dear friends, the nuns, and murmuring that his suffering was merely physical — not moral. His poem, "The Poet's Testament," was read at the simple memorial service. The poem began:

> I give back to the earth what the earth gave,
> All to the furrow, nothing to the grave.
> The candle's out, the spirit's vigil spent;
> Sight may not follow where the vision went.

The life of reason

Santayana's philosophy is surely one of the most beautifully expressed of all time. For he was a poet above all else. However, there exists at the core of his work a major source of misunderstanding. He chose to borrow Plato's dramatic verbal vessels and empty them of their supernatural content. But the meanings of words are not that easy to alter. His major categories are the "realms" of matter, essence, truth and spirit. Such terminology suggests a dualism which in fact is not present in Santayana's world view.

The subtitle of the one-volume edition of *The Life of Reason* is "Phases of Human Progress." What Santayana set out to explain in this and subsequent books was the evolution of human culture in terms of the individual's developing thought processes as these occur within, and result from, ongoing organic change. He simply chose to retain the familiar terms of the metaphysics of his day, while seeking to ground them firmly in the bedrock of material existence. He was meticulous in describing the basis of his philosophical naturalism: the assumption "that mankind is a race of animals living in a natural world" (Santayana 1969:229). "All causes are physical," he wrote, "and all values moral" (ibid.:232). "I say that human beings have sprung from the earth. I was not present to observe the event, but it is a general presumption of naturalism that men were not let down ready made by a rope, as Lucretius put it, from heaven" (ibid.:238).

Relentless in his search for truth, he was nevertheless aware of the tendency for humans to crave distorting myths. His response to the claim that illusions are a source of necessary comfort for the human spirit was "he must have a spirit broken already, who would not rather be sobered by truth than tickled by self deception" (ibid.:5). And again, "We gain little by substituting fancy for truth, or heaven for earth" (ibid.:293).

On causality

Santayana rejected any idea of a first cause. For him, existence (or "the realm of matter") is a flux of events or substance: a motion of whatever it is that modern physics attempts to define. "Such motion is impossible if there had to be a static cause for it: it simply exists. And as the most infinitesimal motion is already a transition, so the most elaborate evolution is only one movement; its earlier parts are not the cause, but only the beginning of the later ones" (ibid.:29). The human being evolved out of this motion, as did its psyche. The animal psyche, constructed out of enduring sets of intuitive responses to external change, provides a locus of continuity within the flux of existence. "The *experience* of change requires the continuity of a psyche, preceding and underlying each moment of intuition, and keeping the first term in the offing while the second sails into port, and the *fact* of change requires at least an enduring place where the transformation occurs and an enveloping physical time . . . in whose pulses it may be numbered" (ibid.:41).

Santayana disagreed with the premise of positivism that laws reside in nature, to be discovered. "A law is . . . a device in discourse, not a principle in nature" (ibid.:48). Connections and regularities exist within the flux, to the degree that "similar things under similar circumstances change in the same ways . . . [in fact] a specific manner of reacting under given conditions is the very nature of a specific thing" (ibid.:49). "Nature is not chaos; there is order in it. Knowledge about one part can lead to a true presumption about the character of other parts" (ibid.:115).

On the realm of matter

Here his ideas are very reminiscent of the rational philosophy of Schopenhauer — stripped of its dualism. For Santayana, facts are the universal data of existence. They are experienced merely as signals of "the realm of matter," for "sensation is the index to other things, namely their causes, organic and external" (ibid.:101). Intelligence must be applied to incoming sensations if the essence of experience is to be had. Animal intelligence is "an expression of adaptation in the past and capacity for further adaptation" to the challenge of sensed facts (ibid.:96). It is produced by the psyche as it organizes life in the body from the raw materials of immediate experience. The psyche could be described as "an experiment in domination, an effort to incorporate everything discoverable into the service of a single life" (ibid.:281). He emphasized, however, that "Mere prolongation or variation of immediate experience is not intelligence; it is the helpless condition of infants, idiots and dreamers" (ibid.:104). This understanding is the basis of Santayana's lifelong antipathy to mysticism in all its seductive forms.

Like Mead, Santayana believed that language in humans developed as a set of gestures, functioning to help groups adapt to their surroundings. As more or less clumsy conveyances of the experience of one's fellows, they are necessarily imperfect and secondary signals of nature's data. Nevertheless, in making possible the comparison and assessment of personal intuitions, they have contributed to an incredible refinement and enrichment of the field of human experience. "In the path of knowledge, then, words are perpetual obstacles as well as necessary instruments, at once . . . false masks and true signs" (ibid.:109).

Prior to the onset of intuition and rudimentary language (which make consciousness possible) the animal psyche of the newborn human merely senses external and organic data within the chaos of immediate experience. "Impulses to appropriate and reject first teach us the points of the compass, and space itself, like charity, begins at home" (Santayana 1955:6). These initial impulses to act are checked by experiment, as the infant gropes and flexes; the experiment is in turn judged by impulse, and the process continues in an ever-widening and deepening spiral of psychic growth. "A psyche, the hereditary organ and movements of life in the animal, must first exist and sustain itself by intelligent adaptation to the ambient world; but these adaptations are not conscious until, by virtue of their existence, intuition arises; and intuition arises when the inner life of the animal, or its contact with external things, is expressed in some actual appearance, in some essence given in feeling and thought" (Santayana 1972:9).

By intuition Santayana did not mean a miraculous discovery of that which the sense or intellect cannot discern. Rather, "I mean direct and obvious possession of the apparent" (ibid.:646). It is pre-mental, vital, cumulative and cognitive, . . . a spiritual witness to observe the world and question it" (ibid.:672).

On animal faith

The early impulses are thus gradually organized into intuitions as the process of adapting to material events becomes conscious. Intuitions are the source of the "essences" which come to constitute our animal faith in the order of nature. The active nature of animals "will compel them to regard many of the essences given in intuition as signs for the environment in which they move, modifying this environment and being affected by it" (ibid.:vii).

Santayana's theory of animal faith (based on "the realm of essence") seems to owe much to William James. He noted in a review written in 1891 that James' "natural truths" are "expressions of certain ingrained habits of thought, habits which cannot be revised while human nature remains as it is. That the mind has such a structure and such inevitable ways of thinking is to be accounted for by natural causes, by spontaneous variation, and by selection" (McCormick:87).

As Santayana developed the idea, "These intuitions . . . comprise mental life, are recoverable in memory . . . [They are the building blocks of consciousness] or "the realm of the spirit, whereas the psychical . . . is a part of the realm of matter itself . . . [that part out of which spirit is generated] (Santayana 1969:130). "Consciousness is a spiritual synthesis of organic movements . . . naturally cognitive" (Santayana 1972:349). "It is a commentary on events, in the language of essence, while its light is contemplative, its movement and intent strictly obey the life of the psyche in which it is kindled" (ibid.:350). This results in material competence — an appropriate adjustment by the physical psyche to the realm of matter, and, in the imagination, a suitable picture of same. For intuitions are consciously "imaged" as well as felt.

On the realm of essence

Here, Santayana sought to explain the nature and origin of what Durkheim had termed "ideal representations." Although much of what the consciousness acquires through intuition comprises primary data such as pleasure, pain, hunger and fear, there is also direct acquaintance with "the realm of essence." The physical connection between this ideal realm and that of matter is "found in the mind's initial capacity to frame objects of two sorts: those compacted of sensations that are persistently similar, and those compacted of sensations that are momentarily fused" (Santayana 1955:50). The first type of association (by similarity of events or objects separated in time rather than by contiguity of occurrence) is the source within nature of the human reasoning function. The second type is responsible for images of objects within consciousness. The fatal error of empiricists, according to Santanaya, was that they recognized only this second type of association.

What comes to be possessed by consciousness in the first case is not the image of the *things* of existence, but the form of the *relations* among them. It is the logical or aesthetic aspects of their being. All ideas about how things connect or ideals about their relative worth are "essences," in Santayana's system. They are the elements of reason and of the human spirit. The most fundamental of these is the notion of an independent and permanent world. It is the mind's ideal "used to mark and . . . justify the cohesion in space and the recurrence in time of recognizable groups of sensations. This cohesion and recurrence force the intellect, if it would master experience at all or understand anything to frame the idea of such a reality" (ibid.:25).

Other "essential" ideas are of variation in texture, shape, size sound and colour; and of the passage of time and of motion through space. Santayana claimed that essences are the mind's record of relations and direction (or structure) and in that sense they are universal. But he added that they are not the transcendent abstractions of Kant. They are concrete in that each essence is the direct product of active individual experience. The realm of essence functions as a means of comparing and harmonizing the things perceived. It is controlled by language, as the realm of matter is controlled by action.

All factual knowledge belongs to the realm of essence. It is verbalized belief grounded and confirmed in the realm of matter. It is "animal faith when it describes in suitable symbols . . . the objects encountered in action" (Santayana 1972:4). Belief is always belief *about nature*. "Honest, speculative belief is always speculative physics" (ibid.:198). It is not truth, but a view or expression of it that aids in humanity's vital adjustment to the facts of existence. Truth is the inaccessible standard, forever flickering in the distance.

On the realm of truth

For Santayana, the "realm of truth" is the eternal segment of "the realm of essence." "If views can be more or less correct, and perhaps complementary to one another, it is because they refer to the same system of nature, the complete description of which, covering the whole past and the whole future, would be the absolute truth" (ibid.:xv). It is "the sum of all true propositions, what omniscience would exert" (ibid.:402). It is eternal in that, when an individual life is over, the truth remains that the life *was*. However, logical necessity is not truth. "*True* knowledge . . . should be the cognizance that one existing thing takes of another; and this perforce is a form of faith, though justified in continual physical contacts between the knower and the known: whereas mathematics and theology trace ideal relations for their own sake and end in the air" (ibid.:435).

Mathematics, at least, is justified, for it is a crucial tool "for measuring reliably the footsteps of that stealthy material power that pervades the world" (ibid.:438). Theology, on the other hand, functions as a substitute for truth. Its appeal lies in the fact that nature's truth is "often a nuisance to the slumbering organism" (ibid.:538). It would like to be left in the comfort of the dark. But, Santayana concluded, danger rather than safety lies in darkness, and theology has too often led humanity astray.

Dreams of utopias provide similar false illusions of safety in a problem-ridden world. "A sad waste of spiritual passion comes from looking for truth where, by the nature of things, truth cannot be found: in images, in metaphors, in religion, in moral emotion" (ibid.:539). In Santanaya's opinion, all such misguided commitments by mystics, romantics and religious moralists lead but to fanaticism.

On the realm of spirit

Lastly, Santayana's philosophical system includes a "realm of the spirit." He warns that there is nothing here of tidings from a mysterious world beyond nature. Rather, it represents, within the physical psyche, the total difference between being awake or dreaming, alive or dead. According to him, "the singularity of my belief is that it traces in spiritual things only their spiritual *quality*, while planting them, as far as existence is concerned, unequivocally on natural ground, and showing how they spring out of it" (ibid.:549). Spirit is simply consciousness: "that inner light of actuality or attention which floods all life as men actually live it on earth" (ibid.). He pictures it also as "a product of combustion, a leaping flame, a fountain and a seat of judgement . . . a personal and moral focus of life where the perspectives of nature are reversed as in a mirror" (ibid.:550). It is an entirely natural faculty, with natural movement and goals — yet intellectual and therefore immaterial. It has apparently evolved only in human bodies, as the moral fruition of physical life on earth.

Santayana considered pantheism to be a false doctrine of an animate cosmos. For him there is no fabulous diffusion of spirit (as universal mind or whatever) over infinite space. The human spirit is transcendental only in that it represents "subjectivism in logic united with naturalism in the description of the world" (ibid.:580).

Rousseauian romanticism, as a doctrine of untrammelled freedom of the individual will, is equally false, according to Santayana. He believed, instead, that the free will/determinism issue could be dispensed with by understanding that the will which we feel is no more nor less than "the observable endeavour in things of any sort to develop a specific form and to preserve it" (ibid.:607). An animal's will is free to sustain it in the direction of realization of genetic potential within the exigencies of environmental challenges. Liberation for the spirit is what most people actually seek when they yearn for free will. But spiritual freedom is not to be found by removing oneself from physical reality, as mystics seek to do: an impossible feat at any rate! "Health and knowledge: essentially nothing more is requisite for liberation from distraction by the flesh, the world, and the devil" (ibid.:749).

Santayana always emphasized the fact that "essence, matter, truth and spirit are not, in my view, separate cosmological regions, separately substantial and then juxtaposed. They are summary categories of logic, meant to describe a single, natural, dynamic process and to dismiss from organized reflection all unnecessary objects of faith" (ibid.:831). He was talking about phases of human development, from the perspective of the individual psyche, and the milieu of ideas and ideals that groups of individuals create. He saw the dynamic process involved as one of adaptation to changing external and organic demands — in the latter stages of which memory and reason evolve and begin to act as guides. Memory is the necessary condition for human progress. "When experience is not retained, as among savages, infancy is perpetual. Those who cannot remember the past are condemned to repeat it" (Santayana 1955:82).

Reason is also essential. For Santayana it is no less than the total art of living in harmony with inner and outer nature. Ultimately it depends on emotion: on a feeling that something is of value, or an urge to distinguish excellence, "and that distinction can only be made, in the last analysis, by an irrational impulse" (Santayana 1972:7). In its upper reaches, the "Life of Reason" is "behaviour guided by science and directed towards spiritual goods" (Santayana 1955:70). The test of an ideal "good," according to Santayana, is "that a harmony . . . of impulses should be concerned, leading to the maximum satisfaction possible in the whole community of spirits affected by the action" (ibid.). All ideals operate as "heralds of nature's successes, not always realized" (ibid.:81).

The human animal's ideals are spiritual possessions. Another type of spiritual possession is our system of primary mathematical notions, once their essence has been expressed in symbols. These "are evidence of a successful reactive method attained in the organism and translated in consciousness into a stable grammar which has wide applicability and great persistence, so that it has come to be elaborated ideally into prodigious abstract systems of thought" (ibid.:150). Similarly, he noted, "Every experience of victory, eloquence or beauty is a momentary success of some kind and if repeated and sustained becomes a spiritual possession" (ibid.).

On the fads of philosophy

Santayana apparently decided early in life on a personal goal of liberation from the distractions posed by emotionally charged interpersonal relations and limited material circumstance. This required a simple, non-acquisitive life style and precluded sustained relationships and children. He was thus able to retire at an early age and to speak the truth as he saw it. This he did, spurning personal attacks but sparing the ideas of none of his contemporaries or forebears. He believed that the popular mysticisms, romantic illusions and superstitions of his day posed great dangers to humanity, and was unrelenting in his scorn for them.

He saw superstition as the attempt to subsume the natural order under the moral, and declared it tantamount to establishing a government of the parent by the child. It is the magical in religion. In superstition, "Poetry anticipates science, which it ought to follow, and imagination rushes in to intercept memory, on which it ought to feed" (ibid.:191).

Romanticism he abhorred because of its central doctrine of the primacy of will. He thought that ever since Kant, romanticism had become a transcendentalism turned inward, whereby the natural world is seen as the creation of the human mind. The human being has become God. But, he maintained, that is an inherently contradictory position, for "you cannot identify yourself with God without at once asserting and denying the existence of God and of yourself" (McCormick:230). The most dangerous of all the false prophets of this doctrine was Nietzsche, in Santayana's opinion. For Nietzsche confessed that truth did not interest him: "the bracing atmosphere of falsehood, passion and subjective perspective was the better thing" (ibid.:232).

Mysticism drew Santayana's hottest fire. The mystic seeks "oneness" in immediate experience: pure sensation undistorted by cognition. But, sadly, "This immediate is not God but chaos: its nothingness is pregnant, restless, and brutish; it is that from which all things emerge insofar as they have any permanence or value, so that to lapse into it again is a dull suicide and no salvation" (Santayana 1955:5). Indeed, mysticism "sinks so completely into its subjective commotion as to mistake the suspension of all discriminating and representative faculties for a true union in things and the blur of its own ecstasy for a universal glory" (ibid.:65). However, he noted wryly, mystics do not practise so entire a renunciation of reason, language and objectivity as they preach. The attempt to use reason to justify their point of view as a legitimate general pursuit of religious experience, or as a principle for living, contradicts their assumptions. "Their map leaves out the ground on which they stand" (ibid.:76).

In 1947 Santayana began reading the new existentialist philosophy. In attempting a summation, he referred to it as "a sort of non-religious theory of personal salvation" (McCormick:470), and asked, "Is this really necessary?" (ibid.). He assessed the literary output of Jean-Paul Sartre as clever but nasty. He asked whether the *Angst* of the existentialists is not really "a disease, an emotion produced by Protestant theology after faith in that theology has disappeared" (ibid.:471). Then he added, " And what is this self that feels the *Angst* and leaps heroically for salvation into the unknown?" (ibid.).

On psychology

Santayana, like John Dewey, realized that philosophy must be based upon a sound psychology. This he found sadly lacking in existentialism. He recognized two approaches to psychology: the *literary*, which employs metaphor and analogy to illustrate the reaches of the human spirit; and the *scientific*, which produces knowledge about how the psyche actually operates. "The machinery of growth, instinct and action . . . of speech, is all physical . . . essentially observable . . . the object of biology" (Santayana 1972:332-33). It is a system of habits in matter. "If actual feelings and intuitions have any ground at all, their ground is physical" (ibid.:380). Introspection and psychoanalysis are not helpful in understanding the human psyche, according to him. "Scientific psychology must be behaviouristic; it can discover, not what spirits feel and think, but what people are likely to say and do under specific conditions" (ibid.:836).

Santayana referred to the illegitimate approaches that abound in psychology, as "psychologisms." These have sprung up out of a worthy but exclusive interest in the inner person "forgetful of his origins and of the external forces that sustain his being" (ibid.:358). Such a focus, if not implicitly materialistic, "would be a proclamation of isolation and helplessness in the midst of a presumable chaos" (ibid.:365). To escape this trap, those resorting to psychologisms must take one of the following exits: the subjective, the (allegedly) objective, or that of pan-psychism. Santayana described the first as a transcendental idealism which attributes no existence to the world apart from the subject's idea of it; and the second as a phenomenalism or pictorial physics whereby immediate sensation is the only reality. He concluded that this, of necessity, ends up being completely subjective as well, in spite of its grandiose intentions. (He, too, had recognized Husserl's dilemma.) The third escape Santayana identified with psychoanalysis: the positing of the psyche as a bundle of mental facts within an animate, or essentially mental, external environment. He had no respect for psychologists who were caught up in "the psychological illusion that our ideas and purposes are original facts and forces (instead of expressions of consciousness of facts and forces that are material) and the practical and optical illusion that everything wheels about us in this world." These, he added, "are primitive persuasions which the enemies of naturalism have always been concerned to protect" (Santayana 1957:72).

On religion

Santayana's "realm of the spirit" provided the logical basis for his approach to religion. Religion was his great enthusiasm: religion, not as worship of the supernatural, but as a natural human endeavour and as a worthy social institution. His was probably the world's first integrated philosophy of "natural religion." It was to be a religion based on human reason rather than myths, magic and mysticism. Rather than promising other-worldly rewards, reason "lays before us these possibilities: it points to common objects, political and intellectual, in which an individual may lose what is mortal and accidental in himself and perpetuate what is rational and human; it teaches us how calm and fortunate death may be to those whose spirit can still live in their country and their ideas; it reveals the radiating effects of action and the eternal objects of thought" (Santayana 1955:181).

His was a rational religion that involved contemplation about the nature of things, a striving for ideals, and poetry "in the sense in which poetry includes all images of moral life" (ibid.:198). He recognized a possible need for prayer, as a soliloquy expressing need. For, to him, "The essence of prayer is poetical expression and contemplation, and it grows more and more nonsensical the more people insist on making it a prosaic commercial exchange of views between two interlocutors" (ibid.:197). His religious goal was to "wean the mind from extravagant desires and teach it to find excellence in what life affords, when life is made as worthy as possible" (ibid.:199). As for religious worship, he maintained that "Reverence is something due to . . . the roots or moral supports of existence; it is therefore due really to the realm of matter only" (ibid.:191).

Santayana appreciated the pageantry of Catholic rituals as drama and poetic metaphor. The Catholic tradition he considered an imaginative play about the accumulated strivings and follies of humans — not harmful if it could be cleansed of superstition and fallacious myths. He explained that any particular myth was originally accepted because it seemed to express reality in eloquent metaphor. "It is always by its applicability to things known, not by its revelation of things unknown and irrelevant, that a myth, at its birth, appeals to mankind. When it has lost its symbolic value and sunk to the level of merely false information, only an inert and stupid tradition can keep it above water" (Santayana 1955:202).

Santayana discussed the bitter consequences of most of humankind's religious pursuits. This sad history was due, he claimed, to a "confusion of intelligence and a distraction of sentiment in gratuitous fictions" (ibid.:182). This is to be expected where religion encourages imagination divorced from reason. Such a method proceeds by "intuition and unchecked poetical conceits." (ibid.:183). Eventually these conceits come to pass as truths constituting a logically anterior and morally superior world of faith superimposed upon the world of experience. This is doubly dangerous as it puts obstacles in the way of the psyche's vitally necessary adaptation to the nature of things, and it distorts the focus of human spiritual energy. But nature is ultimately avenged for such transgressions. Humanity pays the price. "Thus religion too often debauches the morality it comes to sanction and impedes the science it ought to fulfil" (ibid.:182).

Santayana maintained that the function of religion is not to provide an alternative to science in the search for truth. "The only truth of religion comes from its interpretation of life, from its symbolic rendering of that aspiration which it springs out of and which it seeks to elucidate" (ibid.:183). Humans in the spiritual phase of development are capable of making moral choices and seeking the sources of moral authority. And here, "just because moral life is inwardly grounded, physical truths are the only guide" (Santayana 1972:478). He believed that the glory of a natural religion would reside in reasoned and knowledgeable retrospection about the nature of human existence within the infinite fields of space and rivers of time. "The stream of animal life leaves behind a little sediment of knowledge, the sand of that auriferous river; a few grains of experience remain to mark the path traversed by the flood" (Santayana 1955:187). For Santayana, ensuring that those precious grains of truth are not buried in the shale of erroneous mythology and ideology was a religious commitment and pursuit superbly worthy of human beings.

Limitations and contributions

Santayana once told a friend that he was happy to be associated with Herbert Spencer in the history of ideas. There were probably several reasons for this. He considered himself an heir to the philosophical tradition of Democritus and Lucretius, and felt that Spencer belonged there too. Like Spencer, he thought in evolutionary and naturalistic terms, and like him, had attempted to trace the implications of evolution for human social-psychic development. However, he was fully aware of Spencer's weaknesses, and one of his telling comments seems to indicate that he suspected they could be his own as well. For he wrote, "Spencer, in his 'principles' was an objective idealist, not a naturalist or scientific man. . . . He meant to be a naturalist, but language and the hypostasized idea of progress turned him into an idealist metaphysician" (Santayana 1986:233). The danger for Santayana lay in the general human temptation to reify logical categories such as reason, essence, truth and spirit. On the whole, his decision to use the terms of neo-Platonism was unfortunate, for, while they did not seduce their author into metaphysical meanderings, they too often had that effect on his readers.

Most serious was the fact that Santayana's terminology made his system vulnerable to the charge of dualism. He always denied this, responding once as follows: "the pint would call the quart a dualist if you tried to pour the quart into him" (McCormick:218). But the criticism of his work persists, in spite of the recent recognition of its relevance for post-Einstein scientific theory. For example, by "essences" he was referring to relations between events as they are experienced and reflected in intuitive beliefs — and subsequently, after being measured and confirmed, in the concepts of physics. In thus discarding the idea of existence as something fixed and absolute, Santayana was ahead of his time.

Santayana was not primarily interested in social science, and this may account for the fact that he did not mention Durkheim, although the ideas of the French sociologist were so compatible with his own. Nor would he have said that he was attempting to construct a conceptual framework for the study of humanity. Neither did he consider himself a humanist, although, when grounded in naturalism and materialism, he found humanism an acceptable description of his approach to life. But he was suspicious of the anti-science strain sometimes found there. "The impulse to reduce science to literature was native to humanism and to the whole Renaissance. . . . Yet, in life, a system of science is always involved; and the system assumed by humanists is probably naturalism" (Santayana 1972:358).

Santayana made two great contributions to social-scientific thought. His theory of essences, dressed in quite different language, was to become one of the sources of Jean Piaget's fruitful model of cognitive development. And his proposal for a resolution of the age-old conflict between religion and science has yet to be given the credit it deserves. He viewed religious endeavours to realize standards of value and harmony, and the scientific search to approximate standards of truth, as twin aspects of the human spiritual enterprise: both firmly grounded in and limited by physical existence. This was not a resolution acceptable in the general philosophical climate in which he worked, however, nor yet in the larger society.

Of Santayana's contemporaries, only Dewey, Durkheim and Mead were close to him in ideas. However, he had adopted Bertrand Russell's view of John Dewey as the philosopher of American industry, and had rejected all intellectual contact with him. This was unfortunate for the scientific study of humanity. It was unfortunate, as well, that Santayana's lifelong prejudice against the American cultural milieu, and his fear of personal distraction, condemned him to the permanent role of outsider. Although rich in the spiritual companionship of the world of ideas, he was nevertheless compelled to write, near the end of his life, "I was *fatally* a stranger, not only in any particular place, but in the world at all" (McCormick:476). If he had been less a stranger, and less inclined to submerge his ideas in prolix and poetic metaphor, social scientists might have known him better and valued him much more.

References for Chapter Sixteen

Lamont, Corliss, ed. 1959. *Dialogue on George Santayana*. New York: Horizon Press.

McCormick, John. 1987. *George Santayana: A Biography*. New York: Alfred A. Knopf.

Santayana, George. 1936. *The Last Puritan*. New York: Charles Scribner's Sons.

————. 1951. Dewey's Naturalistic Metaphysics. In *The Philosophy of John Dewey*. Edited by Paul Arthur Schilpp. New York: Tudor, p. 243-61.

————. 1955. *The Life of Reason*. Rev. one-volume ed. New York: Charles Scribner's Sons.

————. 1957. *Winds of Doctrine* New York: Harper.

————. 1969. *Physical Order and Moral Liberty*. Edited by Daniel Cory. Charlotte, NC: Vanderbilt University Press.

————. 1972. *Realms of Being*. One-volume ed. New York: Cooper Square. (Introduction 1942.)

————. 1979. *The Complete Poems of George Santayana*. Edited by Wm. G. Holtzberger. London: Associated University Presses.

————. 1986. *Persons and Places*. Complete, critical ed. Edited by Wm. G. Holtzberger and Hermann J. Saltkaamp, Jr. Cambridge, MA: The MIT Press.

Seventeen

Bertrand Russell and the Quest for Philosophical Certainty

> When you penned what you thought
> You were cast out and sought
> A retreat oversea
> From aroused enmity;
> So it always will be,
> Yea Xenophanes!
> — Thomas Hardy, "Xenophanes,
>   The Monist of Colophon"

Bertrand Russell was a younger contemporary of Freud, Pavlov, Durkheim, Weber, Dewey, Bergson, Husserl, Mead and Santayana, all of whom he outlived by many years. He was born in 1872 and died in 1970. Unlike Dewey, who, in his life and philosophy achieved a harmonious integration of feeling, thinking and doing, Russell's private and public postures were an ever-changing battleground reflecting the conflicts and contradictions of his times. To study Russell's life and ideas is to trace the roots of, and the wreckage wrought by, most of the powerful ideologies of the twentieth century.

A gifted logician whose early dedication to reason and evidence had forced him to relinquish religious beliefs, Russell sought philosophical certainty with the determination of his aristocratic British forebears in quest of the Holy Grail. Too often his romantic yearnings propelled him precipitously into sexual liaisons and political commitments, each of which he pursued for a time with dogmatic fervour. But the honest empiricist and logician in him allowed no resting place, and always the agnosticism resurfaced, and the search went on.

A life of private passions and public battles

There is probably no other modern life as comprehensively documented as that of Bertrand Russell. Few readers will be unacquainted with at least the outlines of his ultra-Victorian childhood as a fledgling member of England's

References for this chapter are on p. 309.

ruling elite, and of his student days at Cambridge, where he was a leading light of the Apostles: the select few who were later to spawn the famous Blooms- bury group. In Cambridge in the 1890s, as at most Western universities, ideal- ism reigned supreme. Russell became a convert for his first few years as an undergraduate, while concentrating on the study of mathematical logic. Rem- nants of Hegelian — and subsequently Platonic — thinking continued to influ- ence his work until the World War I period. For some years he sought to ac- commodate these to the new realism of his fellow student, G.E. Moore.

He particularly valued Moore's identification of "the naturalistic fallacy": the habit of inferring what "ought" to be from what "is." This is based on the belief (held in varying forms by pantheists, Hegelians and Nietzscheans) in the existence of a moral order in nature — discoverable through science. Russell was similarly alert to the dangers of what could be called "the supernaturalis- tic fallacy": what he considered the equally unwarranted notion that there ex- ists a moral order *beyond* nature — accessible by means of revelation or intui- tion.

In 1894 Russell earned his Honours Degree in Moral Science Tripos. Hav- ing come of age, he married Alys Pearsall Smith against the wishes of the grandmother who had raised him and his older brother, Frank. Alys was older than he and the daughter of wealthy American Quakers.

The honeymooners went to Germany, where Russell worked on his gradu- ate thesis on the foundations of geometry. This he submitted in due course for a Cambridge Fellowship. The following year he was awarded the six-year Fel- lowship, which he accepted just before leaving with Alys for a second trip to Germany. This time the objective was a study of German socialism. The result was his first book, *German Social Democracy*: a starry-eyed version of the Marxist movement marked by an uncritical approach very different from that of his work in mathematics and philosophy. Perhaps he was already showing signs of the fundamental contradiction which was to colour much of his later life and work. Concerning this, a biographer once noted, "Beneath Russell's critical analytical intellect there lay the mind of a romantic *manqué*, forever tempted to look out at events through the rosiest of spectacles and see there not the real landscape but a scene of his own imagining" (Clark:77).

At the turn of the century, Britain's imperialistic involvement in the Boer War must have confirmed Russell in the dislike of war which he shared with his Quaker in-laws. During this time he worked steadily at *Principia Mathe- matica*, which he co-authored with his former professor, Alfred North White- head. This was to become a classic in universities throughout the world. In it he honed the method of philosophical analysis and the emphasis on logical re- lations which were to characterize his ontology and epistemology for the rest of his life. At the same time, the brilliant young philosopher was managing to present a lecture series at the London School of Economics and at Oxford, visit the United States with Alys, work in the Cavendish Laboratory, run unsuccessfully for Parliament as a candidate for woman suffrage, and publish *A Critical Exposition of the Philosophy of Leibniz* (Gottfried Wilhelm Leibniz was the inventor — along with Newton — of the infinitesimal calculus).

During all this, the marriage with Alys was becoming increasingly unhappy, with Russell desperately wanting out, and Alys refusing to admit defeat. In 1911 he began a relationship with the accomplished Lady Ottoline Morrell, the wife of a conveniently obliging M.P. — Phillip Morrell. Lady Ottoline refused to relinquish her husband, daughter and social position, but was discreetly intimate with "Bertie" for a number of years, and a lifelong friend thereafter. She was intensely religious, and succeeded in persuading the agnostic philosopher into a brief flirtation with mysticism, which culminated in his book, *Mysticism and Logic*.

World War I was a watershed for Bertrand Russell. For the first of many times thereafter he forsook the world of philosophy and mathematics and threw himself passionately into social action. Although not a pacifist on philosophical grounds, he vociferously opposed Britain's involvement in the European struggle. During this period he met Colette (an actress — actually Lady Constance — married to the actor, Miles Malleson). Almost immediately the two became lovers, even though Lady Ottoline was still very much in the picture. This development proved to be a lifelong tragedy for Lady Constance, who subsequently divorced her husband. She seems always to have been a "second stringer" for Russell, while remaining a supportive friend and readily available lover for some five decades.

Russell was sentenced to six months in prison for authoring an article deliberately intended to be judged as traitorous in wartime. With the help of his faithful women and other friends, he turned the experience into a welcome opportunity for scholarship, completing the *Introduction to Mathematical Philosophy* while serving the sentence. Soon after his release he met Dora Black, an intelligent and attractive early feminist over twenty-five years his junior. Her acknowledged desire for children intrigued him, as the lack of an heir had been a source of pain ever since his early days with Alys. Now, although approaching fifty and in spite of his continuing desire for Ottoline and passion for Colette, the vision of Dora Black as a willing mother for his children was a powerful magnet.

Second chances and second thoughts

By late 1919 Russell was forced to conclude that Einstein's breakthrough had rendered much of his early philosophical work untenable. "To think," he agonized, "that I have been spending all these years in the muck!" (Wood:133). Then in 1920, while suffering both emotional and intellectual turmoil, he suddenly saw a possibility of visiting the Soviet Union. A labour delegation was to tour the new nation. Still enthusiastic about Marxist ideals, he had written a glowing article in support of Russian Bolshevism for the New York *Liberator*. Perhaps as a consequence of this, he was invited to accompany the group.

After a trip to Europe with Dora Black, Russell set off to see the Russian situation first hand. Quite unexpectedly, he found the experience devastating. As was proving to be habitual with him, an uncritical emotional commitment had fuelled his initial headlong involvement in the situation. However, an equally characteristic respect for facts and a keen intellect could not for long be lulled by slogans — even those he had coined himself! Unlike the other delegation members, he insisted on moving about the country on his own. What he saw and felt during that journey imbued him with a loathing for Communism that alienated him from his socialist friends for many years and even threatened his budding relationship with Dora. Angry at not being included, she had managed to get into the new Bolshevik nation on her own, and returned bubbling with praise and a pro-Communist stance which was never to waver. Russell's experience resulted in *The Practice and Theory of Bolshevism*, the conclusions of which have stood the test of time somewhat better than the political movement with which it dealt.

Immediately upon their reunion in London, Russell and Black set sail for China with the intention of marrying as soon as the now-compliant Alys completed divorce proceedings. Russell was responding to an invitation to teach at the University of Peking, due to Sun Yat Sen's policy, in the last four years of his life, of endeavouring to introduce Western liberalism into the Chinese political culture. John Dewey had arrived the previous year and was to remain throughout Russell's tenure.

Bertie and Dora later remembered their time in China as the happiest of their life together. Both were active, lecturing and writing until Bertie suddenly became seriously ill, hovering on the brink of death for weeks. Dora wrote of the helpfulness of the Deweys, who came forward with necessary funds and other kindnesses. The premature report of his demise at this time by the Japanese press later provided Bertie with the amusing opportunity to read his own obituary notices, including the one in the missionary paper which began: "Missionaries may be pardoned for heaving a sigh of relief at the news of Mr. Bertrand Russell's death" (Russell 1968a:132). As a result of the illness, the couple was forced to return to England in the autumn of 1921, with one recuperating and the other pregnant.

With no job and an expanding family to support, the Russells turned to freelance writing, eventually to be combined with the operation of an experimental school called Beacon Hill. Two children of the marriage, John and Kate, were followed some years later by two more, fathered by another man. From 1927 the couple had tried to put into practice their theories about free love as well as open, democratic education. Russell is reported to have tried to sleep with the teachers — a mixing of business and pleasure of which Dora did *not* approve. When his wife's relationship with an American journalist resulted in her two extramarital pregnancies, Russell's professed belief in open marriage and sexual equality were put to the test.

During this period Russell was writing furiously (producing an American newspaper column as well as books) and making numerous fund-raising lecture tours to the United States. First had come *The Analysis of Mind* and *The Problem of China*, then (with Dora) *The Prospects of Industrial Civilization*. Then, in rapid succession: *Icarus* (or *The Future of Science*), *The ABC of Atoms*, *What I Believe*, *The ABC of Relativity*, *On Education*, a new edition of *Principia Mathematica*, *An Outline of Philosophy*, *The Analysis of Matter*, *Sceptical Essays*, *Marriage and Morals* and, finally, as his second marriage was tottering — *The Conquest of Happiness*.

In 1931 brother Frank died, and the prolific philosopher became a peer of the realm. Perhaps this dealt the final blow to his marriage, for the idea of his wife's second son having the Russell name (and even possibly the title) seems to have become an unacceptable affront. In 1932 Russell left Dora and began a relationship with Patricia (Peter) Spence, a student who had been hired by his wife as the children's governess.

The inheritance had done nothing to lighten the financial burden — in fact, it added the responsibility of yet another monthly alimony payment (to Frank's divorced second wife). Deeply in debt and with two children to keep in school, Russell was now writing almost round the clock. He published *The Scientific Outlook*, *Education and the Social Order* and (with Peter) *Freedom and Organization, 1814-1914*. These were closely followed by *In Praise of Idleness* (no wonder!), *Religion and Science*, *Which Way to Peace* and (again, with Peter) a two-volume history of the family, *The Amberly Papers*. Not surprisingly, he suffered another serious illness in 1935. At this troubling time George Santayana began quietly forwarding monthly payments of $500 to the bankruptcy-threatened household.

New beginnings in America — the third chapter

In 1936 Peter Spence and Russell were married and in 1937 a son, Conrad, was born. In 1938 Lady Ottoline died, and a long and loving correspondence ended. Russell received a one-year appointment to the University of Chicago, and the family sailed to the United States that summer. In 1939 he signed a three-year contract with the University of California. John and Kate arrived for the summer holidays and remained when the war broke out. The following year Russell resigned his position in order to accept an offer from the City College of New York. Some weeks after California had accepted his resignation, the Board of Governors at City College withdrew their offer. They had bowed to the pressure of religious groups, antagonized by the "infamous"

Russell stance on religion and sexual morality. Thus it was that one of the world's most distinguished philosophers found himself, at the age of sixty-eight, penniless and unemployed in a foreign country. He was trapped by war, burdened by debt, and had two offspring in university and a wife and child to support.

Once more into the breach came John Dewey. He led a group of academics who defended Russell's claims against City College and later co-authored a book on the shameful episode. And he helped to arrange for a brief (and also ill-fated) appointment at the Barnes Foundation which kept the impoverished family afloat while Russell wrote *An Inquiry into Meaning and Truth, Let the People Think* and *A History of Western Philosophy.* The publication of the latter finally marked the end of financial stress, as it became a best seller in university bookstores and remained so for years to come.

In 1944, Peter and Conrad left for England, to be followed shortly after by Bertie, who had been invited back to Cambridge. The difficult years in America had doomed the marriage, however. Peter took Conrad with her when she left, and the thrice-divorced father saw little of his younger son until they were reunited many years later. *Physics and Experience* and *An Inquiry into Meaning and Truth,* published in 1948 when he was seventy-six, represented the philosopher's final attempt to sum up his contributions on epistemology.

Chapter four brings acclaim and notoriety

It seems that 1949 marked another turning point in the life of this incredible man. Now, in his seventy-eighth year, came acceptance by the British establishment. He was awarded the Order of Merit, an event that led to a friendly meeting with Alys not long before her death. This was followed by yet another (and this time, final) spurning of the faithful Colette (Lady Constance), and a liaison that led, in 1952, to a fourth and last marriage. The new wife, Edith Finch, was an American academic and a long-time friend who proved to be the perfect companion for Russell in his final decades. During this early period with Edith he became a fixture on the BBC, lecturing on all the great issues of the day. After the age of eighty he went on to produce some three dozen further publications on general topics.

One might have thought that all this would constitute an ample contribution to posterity, even from this unique "man for all seasons." But there was more to come! As the post-war world gave way to the turbulent sixties, Russell's lifelong struggle for a just and lasting peace gained in intensity. He prepared and presented the Russell-Einstein Manifesto on the nuclear threat, helped initiate the Pugwash Conferences, wrote letters to Krushchev and Eisenhower, helped establish the Campaign for Nuclear Disarmament and (for the second time in his life) became a prisoner of conscience.

There was no international crisis in which Russell did not involve himself in the service of peace and freedom for the individual. He chastised both superpowers, writing many letters to Kennedy and Krushchev during the Cuban Missile crisis and later participating in the Who Killed Kennedy Committee. He initiated and funded the Bertrand Russell Peace Foundation and took part in numerous peace marches and sit-ins. He established the International War Crimes Tribunal which sat in judgement on American actions in Viet Nam. Equally distrustful of the Americans and Russians, he longed for a world government capable of controlling both. He criticized Britain and France in the Suez Canal crisis, was strangely silent when the Soviet Union used tanks to put down the Hungarian revolution, but soundly condemned their invasion of Czechoslovakia. And in the midst of all this activity, at the age of ninety-five he began publishing what was to be a three-volume autobiography!

In summing up this remarkable life, one can do no better than to use the words of the writer himself. "Three passions, simple but overwhelming, have governed my life: the longing for love, the search for knowledge, and unbearable pity for the suffering of mankind. These passions, like strong winds, have blown me hither and thither, in a wayward course, over a deep ocean of anguish . . . to the very verge of despair" (Seckel:13).

The reluctant retreat from Pythagoras

It is not only the private liaisons and political commitments resulting from these passions that are well known, but Russell's lifelong intellectual search is likewise an open book — or, more accurately, a large number of them. It was a search compelled by two questions: "Is there any truth to religious beliefs?" and "Is it possible to have *certain* knowledge about *anything* ?" The first question he dispensed with by late adolescence, but the second was to engage him all his life. As he described it, at the end of the nineteenth century he began to undergo a revolution in thought, from the somewhat Platonic "naive realism" of G.E. Moore (which had replaced his earlier Hegelianism) to the perspective of "logical atomism." By the latter he meant the substitution of piecemeal, verifiable results (identified by means of the analytic approach) for the large untested generalities so appealing to philosophers.

It was then that he began to suspect that his beloved mathematics could never provide the certainty which his emotional nature craved; that, instead, the entire edifice was only as true as the premises about reality on which it was based. From that cataclysmic moment on, Russell considered that his world view had undergone a steady evolution. He sometimes referred to the process as a "gradual retreat from Pythagoras" — from the vain hope and inner need for finding a mystical-logical absolute. He never claimed success.

On the role of philosophy

Like Dewey, Russell was convinced that philosophy must be built upon a broad and reliable foundation of knowledge that was not itself philosophical. Such knowledge can only be produced by empirical science. "It is the soil from which the tree of philosophy derives its vigour" (Russell 1959:230). This means that there is no way that philosophy divorced from science can increase understanding or wisdom. Indeed, the philosopher should realize "that science has presented us with a new world, new concepts and new methods not known in earlier times, but proved by experience to be fruitful where the older concepts and methods proved barren" (ibid.:254).

Russell noted that modern philosophy no longer professes to be able to prove great truths of existence, or even to disprove them. "It aims only at clarifying the fundamental ideas of the sciences, and synthesizing the different sciences into a single, comprehensive view of that fragment of the world that science has succeeded in exploring" (ibid.:273). In doing this, the philosopher should be as undistorting a mirror of reality as it is possible to be. Russell realized that some degree of distortion is inevitable. It has its source in the fact that humans are trapped in a particular space-time location. But he pointed out that only by understanding the scientific implications of this fact can we travel a certain distance towards objectivity. "To show the road to this end is the supreme duty of the philosopher," he wrote (ibid.:213).

This belief and commitment ensured that the role and nature of human perception would be the central focus of Russell's philosophical pursuits. It drove him to an early attempt to clarify the relation of perception to the facts of physics; then, of both fact and percept to the language which renders them communicable; and, finally, to the search for a principle (beyond induction) by which asserted percepts could be validated.

A gradual disillusionment with dualism

Russell's changing position on the mind/matter problem is a good example of his philosophical evolution. His rejection of idealism seems to have had something to do with its monism, which at that time he could not abide. The realism which he then grasped allowed for a dualism of physical objects as the sources, and the mind as repository, of sense data. He was committed, as well, to a division of reality between "universals" (abstract essences of things) and "particulars" (their individuated manifestations). In addition, he recognized two ways of knowing: by acquaintance (as in the grasp of sense-data, and in internal feelings and memories) and by description (as in relating external causes to effects).

But by the time Russell wrote *Analysis of Mind* he had moved a considerable distance from Platonic and Cartesian dualism. He was by then maintaining that "the things commonly regarded as mental and the things commonly regarded as physical do not differ in respect of any intrinsic property possessed by one set and not by the other, but differ only in respect to arrangement and context" (Clark:263). And, he was later to add, "in the way in which we acquire knowledge of them" (Russell 1959:254).

As for dualism, he wrote, in later life, "I cannot think of any philosophers who accept it today, except Marxists and Catholic theologians, who are compelled to be old fashioned by the rigidities of their respective creeds" (ibid.: 245). By this time his world view was one of neutral monism. He had come to consider the idea of a non-empirical "essence" (though an intimate part of most philosophies from Aristotle on) as "a hopelessly muddleheaded notion" (Russell 1961:279) and the equally prevalent idea of "substance" as "a metaphysical mistake due to transference to the world-structure of the structure of sentences composed of a subject and a predicate" (ibid.:280).

Russell gave Hume credit for being alone among the great philosophers in denying substance altogether and thus paving the way for a modern perspective on mental and physical events. When finally describing the position to which his journey had led, he was able to write, "I should define a 'mental' occurrence as one which someone knows other than by inference; the distinction between 'mental' and 'physical' therefore belongs to the theory of knowledge, not to metaphysics" (Russell 1948:224).

On the nature of belief

Russell defined a belief as a state of the organism which compels it to act with reference to something not immediately present to the senses. He viewed perception as the initial source of all beliefs, while recognizing it as subjective and therefore unreliable. Because it is, nevertheless, the only source of beliefs about the world available to us, Russell saw the problem for the philosopher of knowledge as "How far the information which we obtain from this tainted source can be purified in the filter of scientific method and emerge resplendently godlike in its impartiality" (ibid.:22).

It is clear that by this time Russell had moved away from the older realism to the extent that he concluded that direct knowledge of reality is not accessible to human perception. He noted that the latter is but "a complex and inaccurate mixture of sensation, habit, and physical causation" (ibid.:448). He had apparently accepted Pavlov's findings concerning the role played by reflexes in perception, and in all habitual behaviour resulting from it. "From unconditioned reflexes, by the law of habit, conditioned reflexes arise and there is every reason to regard habit as physiologically explicable" (ibid.:54). He was therefore forced to conclude that the road from sensation through percept to belief is rocky and indirect at best.

Aiming at the subjectivists, Russell maintained that nothing in the real world *requires* perception for its existence. But perception is necessary if humans are to have beliefs about what exists. He noted, however, that beliefs and facts are not the same. A belief is *felt* and either asserted by means of language or acted upon immediately. What makes it true or false is a fact (regularity reflecting the structure of nature) which exists independently of perception and with which the belief may or may not correspond. To the degree that the belief and the external fact do correspond, *successful* reactions will be initiated by acting upon the belief. He maintained that in such instances we are said to possess knowledge.

Russell followed Pavlov in viewing human cognition as a lifelong process of adapting to the facts of existence, but he saw a problem in that "we cannot say precisely at what point we pass from mere animal behaviour to . . . knowledge" (ibid.:160). He was aware that habits of expectation, gradually developing at a lower level than conscious thought, result in generalizations that we come to hold as implicit beliefs, even though no explicit assessing of evidence has ever occurred. He assumed that this happens as well for the lower animals. A belief, then, said Russell, "is a certain state of the muscles, sense organs and emotions, together perhaps with certain visual images" (ibid.:155). He considered it confirmed as true, for the believer, when followed by a "quite so" feeling. He was convinced that sensation, perception and memory all play a role in such "self-confirming" beliefs. They are pre-verbal experiences of relations in nature shared by all animals to some degree.

On the nature of knowledge

Russell noted that beliefs with knowledge potential, however, require *language*, which "like other acquired ways of behaving, consists of useful habits" (ibid.:112). Although Russell responded emotionally to the seductiveness of the mystic's claim that language separates us from reality, his reason and knowledge told him otherwise. It is the human gift of words, he declared, that allow the knower to organize stimuli on the basis of similarity, and therefore to bring order out of what would otherwise be, not a unity, but a chaos of immediate experience. Furthermore, without language it would be impossible for those beliefs that take the form of habitual expectation (subconscious impulses to action) to be reflected upon and to be expressed in terms of causal laws.

Unlike Hume, Russell never quite reconciled himself to the necessary limits of empiricism (defined by the assertion that all synthetic, or non-tautological, knowledge is rooted in — and confined to — experience). He wanted a guarantee of certainty transcending the possibilities of human experience; Dewey's "warranted assertability" was not enough. Granted, he had relinquished pure rationalism, which maintains that there are certain innate ideas and principles of reality independently known — perhaps inherent in the human mind. But he was still with Kant in many ways. He insisted upon the need for a universal proposition, the truth of which is beyond human verification: the premise of some sort of regularity and permanence in the structure of real events and of an analogy of structure between external events and human percepts and assertions of these. For him, science could not be possible otherwise. Knowledge-seekers must have some ground to stand on, he maintained, and the very success of a science founded on realism would seem to argue for the soundness of the premise. However, he was not satisfied to view this necessary premise as ultimately unprovable by the science which it had made possible.

Russell parted company with most other modern philosophers of science on this issue. He simply could not accept that science could be valid *practically* even though it is impossible to validate it *theoretically*. "Either we know something independently of experience," he was fond of declaring, "or science is moonshine" (ibid.:524). If science lacks even the theoretical possibility of arriving at ultimate truth, it is nothing! And for him such truth had to be known *a priori*: consequences were insufficient, for they were never all in. "We must therefore find grounds for trusting the inference *before* it is verified," he maintained (ibid.:469). He hoped that his method of philosophical analysis could accomplish just this task.

For this and other reasons, the nature of knowledge and of knowing was a difficult issue for Russell. Another problem was that his particular analytic method demanded discrete categories — either of classes or of serial relations — but knowledge did not fit neatly into this framework. He referred to knowledge as a necessarily vague concept because (1) unlike mathematics and logic, it relies for its expression on language (by its very nature an imprecise instrument) and (2) there is no certain knowledge and no categorical way to decide how much uncertainty makes any belief unworthy to be considered knowledge. At times he concluded that knowledge could only be probable opinion; but usually he seemed to want to describe it more discretely as a specific subset of beliefs — those which happen to be true.

Russell identified the conditions that must hold if a belief in a specific causal law is to be considered knowledge. These are (1) the individual has repeatedly experienced that "if A then B"; (2) this has caused the believer to act accordingly; (3) the regularity has been observed and corroborated by relevant others; and (4) A and B are *in fact* so related that the frequency of the observed regularity is evidence of the probability of the event occurring as predicted.

He acknowledged that the fourth requirement exceeds the limits of empiricism. It is, instead, an *a priori* principle which he believed is required in order to justify the privately felt and publicly confirmed inferences made in the first three cases cited above. For Russell, knowledge could only be possible if we are able "to find principles which will make suitable generalizations probable in advance of evidence" (ibid.:454).

Russell claimed that if we can know anything of the external world we must first assume that there exist causal chains proceeding from it to our own nerves and brain. Knowledge must exceed human experience because what we know is actually "the unexperienced cause of experienced events" (Russell 1959:228). While relations and events are directly experienced, causes can only be reached through analysis. They cannot be proved by means of their effects on human knowers. Yet, he said, the existence of more or less self-determined causal processes is one of the fundamental postulates of science.

Russell believed that his original contribution to the philosophy of knowledge was his principle of the constancy and analogy of structure. This solved what was, for him, the paradox of science. He distinguished the *structure* of an event from the quality or *sensation* of it, which is invariably distorted by the conditioning processes underlying perception. This was where his position of "representative realism" differed from what he referred to as "naive" realism. His principle implies that, for the most part, "the structure of a percept is the same as that of each of a series of occurrences leading backward in time to an original occurrence, before which there were no spatio-temporally connected events having the structure in question. This original occurrence is what we are said to 'perceive' when it is held that different people can perceive the same object" (Russell 1948:492). By analogy of structure he meant that evolution has built up, in the human brain, an analogue of the structure of those events within external reality to which humankind has successfully adapted.

On reality and relativity

This brings us to Russell's final position concerning the nature of reality. He saw no problem in reconciling the theory of relativity with his premise of causal laws that exist apart from human experience of them. The basic premise of the older materialism — "substance" as the ultimate constituent of reality — has given way to the idea of "event," he maintained. He accepted the notion that distances in space, like periods of time, are generally not objective physical facts, but are partially dependent upon the observer. They are conceptual devices for measuring periodic physical occurrences. This is really all that Heisenburg's Principle signifies, he noted.

He quoted J.E.Turner on this as follows: "The Principle of Indeterminacy has to do with measurement, not with causation. The velocity and position of a particle are declared by the Principle to be undetermined in the sense that they cannot be accurately measured. . . . Every argument that, since some change cannot be 'determined' in the sense of 'ascertained,' it is therefore not 'determined' in the absolutely different sense of 'caused' is a fallacy of equivocation" (Russell 1931:170).

Russell explained that it is the intervals between events, as well as the events themselves, that are the facts — external to the observer. As long as our measuring devices are recording intervals between events from the same perspective, there is no problem. Until fairly recent times, all our scientific measurements were of this nature. He called such intervals "time-like." From the point of view of the observer location was fixed, and the fact that the measured intervals were relative to it was unacknowledged and irrelevant.

Once scientists began measuring intervals between events far distant in space, however, the fact that the observer is also moving in space relative to the observed becomes extremely relevant. It is no longer physically possible for a body to travel so as to be present at both the measured events. These are "space-like" intervals, Russell claimed. There is clearly no longer any such thing as the "same" time for different observers in the world of space, unless they are at rest relative to each other. So no event in space can be fixed according to a time-like measure. Russell explained that such events must be fixed in "space-time," not merely in space.

What Einstein's revolution in physics taught Russell was that the ultimate facts must be events, rather than bodies in motion. Only events can be measured objectively (unaltered by the movements of the observer). He explained that we have to deal with events whose relative positions in the space-time system are fixed by *four* measures: the usual three giving their location in space (east/west, north/south, up/down) and the fourth locating them in time. The true interval between events can be calculated only when all four of these are taken into account.

"Density" (defined as continuous matter present at any particular point in space and time) when multiplied by a four-dimensional volume of space-time, results in what Eddington called "Action": surely a good candidate for the fundamental constituent of reality, according to Russell. He believed that it is therefore possible to consider events, and the space-time intervals between them, as facts reflecting nature's structure — independent of human experience. He maintained that this is the crucially important implication of the theory of relativity for our philosophical assumptions on the nature of reality.

On the importance of analysis

One constant throughout Russell's philosophical evolution was his confidence in analysis as an approach to understanding. It always seemed evident to him that the approach added knowledge without subtracting any, in the matter of clarifying premises and concepts as well as identifying causal laws. He saw it as a process of prolonged attention, capable of revealing more and more, as when one discerns an object approaching through a thick fog. He suggested that "those who object to analysis would wish us to be content with the initial dark blur" (Russell 1959:133).

Although himself a pioneer of analytic philosophy, Russell became a severe critic of the school of linguistic philosophers who adopted that name. The new movement was based on the ideas of Ludwig Wittgenstein, whom Russell had taught and helped to establish at Cambridge. Wittgenstein contributed to Russell's gradual realization that the laws of logic are not laws of things, but are instead, linguistic formulations expressing relations. The idea that a proposition is an expression of the structure of the facts that it asserts (like a map) Russell found invaluable.

However, when it became clear that Wittgenstein's work implied a purely linguistic philosophy Russell parted company with him. His objection was twofold. First, the idea that ordinary language is sufficient for philosophy seemed a regressive, anti-intellectual move. Russell believed that, on the contrary, "any attempt to be precise and accurate requires modification of common speech both as regards vocabulary and as regards syntax" (ibid.:242). Secondly, there was what he viewed as their concern "not with the world and our relation to it, but only with the different ways in which silly people can say silly things" (ibid.:230). Regarding Wittgenstein's *Philosophical Investigations*, Russell admitted that it was completely unintelligible to him, except for a few positive doctrines that seemed trivial and negative ones that seemed unfounded.

Russell's position was no doubt closest to that of the "logical positivists." However, he strongly rejected their theory that the meaning of a scientific proposition consists in the method of verification; and what he considered their ignoring of causation as a fact of nature external to the knower. For him, seeking the significance of a proposition in its consequences merely incurred an infinite regress, because of the impossibility of "knowing" an infinitely long future. For Russell, science had to depend on assumed factual certainties, not on the verifiability of predictable consequences.

On pragmatism

Although Russell respected Karl Popper (whom he erroneously considered a positivist) as well as linguistic philosophers such as Gilbert Ryle, he seemed to feel nothing but scorn for the founders of pragmatism. His first (and perhaps only?) encounter with the American philosophy was the rather unrepresentative work of William James. He concluded, ironically, that its "pragmatic" consequences were to encourage religious beliefs, which he judged to be pernicious. In a more serious vein, he commented: "Pragmatism holds that a belief is to be judged true if it has certain kinds of *effects*, whereas I hold that an empirical belief is to be judged true if it has certain kinds of *causes*" (Clark: 176). Elsewhere Russell accused the pragmatists of proposing that "a truth is anything which it pays to believe" (Russell 1959:177). He then discussed the pay-off in terms of short-term monetary and power gains for the individual — a deliberate attempt at caricature that one would not expect of such a gifted philosopher.

Russell seems never to have taken Dewey's work seriously enough to read it. For instance, he described it as "holistic." Elsewhere, he remarked that "One important difference between us arises from the fact that Dr. Dewey is mainly concerned with theories and hypotheses, whereas I am mainly concerned with assertions about particular matters of fact" (Dewey:332). As to the vital question of how one is to determine that a proposition is indeed an assertion of fact, if not by framing it as a hypothesis to be tested, he was satisfied to depend on his own method of philosophical analysis.

Russell seemed to have felt a personal antipathy to Dewey in spite (or perhaps because) of all the help the latter had given him in times of need. He persisted in seeing him as an American imperialist bent on foisting industrialization upon a reluctant world. This might also have had something to do with Dewey's rather pointed criticism of Russell's theory of knowledge. According to Dewey, Russell claimed that the event *to be known* is that which operates as the cause of the effect which is its only possible verifier, while at the same time maintaining that causes cannot be known by their effects. How, then, Dewey asked, *are* they to be known? He commented that a doctrine that states that a proposition is true only when it conforms to that which is not known save through itself is truly an epistemological miracle!

Russell's view of pragmatism may also have been coloured by his legitimate fear of the dangers of subjectivism. He had the mistaken impression that Dewey's philosophy was not concerned with questions of truth or falsehood on the basis of correspondence with factual evidence, and that Dewey gave too much credence to feeling. On the other hand, it could be argued that Russell's proposition that there exists a class of private beliefs which are true by virtue of their direct derivation from sense and memory might seem to give more encouragement to subjectivist philosophies than does pragmatism.

First principles

Russell was more than usually aware of the lure of subjectivism and mysticism. As a child he had been powerfully indoctrinated into a comfortable set of Victorian certainties, the content of which could not survive logical scrutiny. But it is likely that a longing for the comfort of some lost "truth" never left him. That longing, combined with a remarkable egocentricity, may well have made him uniquely vulnerable to promises of unity with the absolute. Whenever he was pulled in that direction emotionally, however, reason and logic always forced him back. In *Science and Religion* he was firm in his conclusion that mysticism expresses emotion rather than fact; therefore all assertions of mystics are unwarranted. Still, he was torn, and added, wistfully, that although "the beliefs it inspires are often bad ones, the feelings are good ones"(Russell 1968b:61).

It was Russell's emotional needs that made him struggle to resist the conclusions of humanism in spite of his commitment to its premises. It was only with reluctance that he admitted to a belief that what is of most value in the world is humanity, and to a lesser extent, other animals. "Not the starry heavens, but their effects on human percipients, have excellence; to admire the universe for its size is slavish and absurd; impersonal non-human truth appears to be a delusion. And so my intellect goes with the humanists, though my emotions violently rebel" (ibid.:37).

Although he could be savagely critical of the foibles of his species, he was not without hope for the human condition. He believed fervently in a type of education that would create appropriate mental habits as well as imparting reliable knowledge. He believed in the possibility and necessity of progress in the social sciences, by means of which we might "undo the evils which have resulted from a knowledge of the physical world hastily and superficially acquired by populations unconscious of the changes in themselves that the new knowledge has made imperative" (Russell 1961:724).

Russell consistently opposed the "single cause" ideologies of social reform that have proven so popular (and counter-productive) during the twentieth century. As he noted, "Institutions mould character, and character transforms institutions. Reforms in both must march hand in hand. And . . . diversity is essential in spite of the fact that it precludes universal acceptance of a single gospel" (Russell 1969:222).

He was convinced of the need for a new ethic to accompany necessary advances in social knowledge. He conceded that religion can be helpful when it teaches kindness and social responsibility. He saw these attitudes, not simply as moral duties, but as indispensable for survival. Like Durkheim, he thought that "Human society is becoming . . . more like a single human body, and if we are to continue to exist, we shall have to acquire feelings directed toward the welfare of the whole in the same sort of way in which our feelings of individual welfare concern the whole body and not just this or that portion of it" (Russell 1961:396).

Russell maintained that, of all the virtues, the one of greatest social importance is the habit of deciding vexing questions in accordance with the evidence, and of leaving them undecided where the evidence is inconclusive. This is the principle of agnosticism to which he aspired all his life. And yet — and yet — there was that streak of dogmatism at the very core of his being. His theory of knowledge, although often acclaimed as a logical refinement of Hume, nonetheless retains certain aspects of the Kantian requirement of first principles. And at his emotional centre there was that demand for certainty and ego-transcendence that drove him from Pythagorean mysticism to a restless pursuit of sexual and political passion.

His longtime friend/enemy Beatrice Webb wondered how such a scientific person could be so dogmatic in other realms. Perhaps the answer is simple. He had never fully escaped the limitations of his early conditioning, but, more than most, he tried. No doubt he was reassuring himself as much as anyone when he wrote the following: "Even if the open windows of science at first make us shiver after the cozy indoor warmth of traditional humanizing myths, in the end the fresh air brings vigour, and the great spaces have a splendour of their own" (Russell 1961:370). In these words we find the clearest possible expression of his inner conflict as well as his hope and lifelong commitment. Bertrand Russell may have longed for the warmth of the cave, but he was a man who opened windows.

References for Chapter Seventeen

Clark, Ronald. 1978. *The Life of Bertrand Russell*. Markham, ON: Penguin Books.

Dewey, John. 1946. *The Problems of Men*. New York: Philosophical Library.

Russell, Bertrand. 1971 [1921]. *The Analysis of Mind*. London: Allen and Unwin.

_____. 1925. *ABC of Relativity*. London: Allen and Unwin.

_____. 1931. *The Scientific Outlook*. London: George Allen and Unwin.

_____. 1966 [1940]. *An Inquiry into Meaning and Truth*. London: Allen and Unwin.

_____. 1971 [1946]. *History of Western Philosophy*. London: Allen and Unwin.

_____. 1948. *Human Knowledge: Its Scope and Limits*. London: Allen and Unwin.

_____. 1959. *My Philosophical Development*. London: Allen and Unwin.

_____. 1961. *The Basic Writings of Bertrand Russell, 1903-1959*. London: Allen and Unwin.

_____. 1967-69. *The Autobiography*. 3 vols. Toronto: McClelland & Stewart.

_____. 1968. *The Wisdom of Bertrand Russell*. New York: Philosophical Library.

Russell, Dora. 1977. *The Tamarisk Tree*. London: Virago Press.

Seckel, Al, ed. 1986. *Bertrand Russell on God and Religion*. Buffalo: Prometheus Books.

Wood, A. 1957. *Bertrand Russell: The Passionate Sceptic*. London: Allen and Unwin.

Eighteen

The Evolutionary Social Theory of Julian Huxley

The choice is always ours. Then let me choose
The longest art, the hard Promethean way
Cherishingly to tend and feed and fan
That inward fire, whose precious flame,
Kindled or quenched, creates
The noble or ignoble men we are,
The worlds we live in and the very fates,
Our bright or muddy star.
— Aldous Huxley, quoted in
Julian Huxley, *Memoires*

Darwin's revolution caused an awareness in thinking people that, sooner or later, the world would have to come to terms with the implications of evolutionary theory for individual development and cultural change. Haeckel recognized this at once. Spencer launched a noble attempt to accomplish the task, but a reluctance to accept the principle of natural selection crippled his mammoth project. Pavlov made the first real breakthrough when he showed how the conditioning process in animals operates during the individual's life history in a way parallel to the functioning of natural selection in the species over geological time. Henri Bergson picked up on the significance of this adaptive capacity in the mental processes of the individual organism and tried to extend the idea to the evolution of culture. Unfortunately, he was sadly limited by the mysticism at the core of his world view.

Emile Durkheim provided an important sociological and systems perspective for the idea of social evolution. George Herbert Mead took a giant step, integrating the best of Martineau, Spencer, Dewey, Bergson and Durkheim, but his work remained little known beyond the sociology community in the United States. The insights of Santayana were penetrating, but his psychological knowledge was limited to the concepts of Spencer and James.

References for this chapter are on p. 323.

Finally, however, a truly knowledgeable and comprehensive response to the challenge came from the next generation, in one with impeccable credentials for the task. What could have been more appropriate than that Julian Huxley — like his famous grandfather, Thomas, a distinguished biologist and polymath — should have committed his life to clarifying the meaning of Darwin's theory for the psycho-social realm?

The shaping of an evolutionary theorist

Julian was born in 1887, a product of the union of two remarkable English families. On his mother's side he was related to Matthew Arnold, the great nineteenth-century poet. His maternal grandfather was Tom Arnold, who, along with Matthew, was the son of Dr. Thomas Arnold, the famous founder and headmaster of Rugby. Tom's life had been one long troubled history of alternating bouts of intense religious zeal and equally fervent disillusionment, during which he swung between Catholicism and the Church of England. There is no doubt that Julian was affected by this family background, whether by inheriting the unstable Arnold temperament or through his mother's influence. It is a fact that he suffered all his life from the mental-emotional turmoil that both afflicted and blessed the creative Arnolds. This may have been complicated by his legacy from the paternal side: a large dash of Thomas Huxley's "determination and dedication to scientific truth" (Huxley 1970:preface). Perhaps Julian Huxley's inner conflicts, as well as his accomplishments, were accentuated by the Huxley intellectual integrity and agnosticism doing daily battle with the Arnold mystical and neurotic bent.

Even as a child, Julian was ahead of his times. When, at Eton, he was assigned an essay on the topic, "What I Would Do If I Had a Million Pounds," he suggested buying up as much as possible of the unspoiled British coastline to ensure its survival. He must have been the most imaginative of would-be scientists, for he tells of often being filled with "a magnificent cosmic feeling" and writing a great deal of poetry (ibid.:64). He won a scholarship to Oxford and spent the preceding summer in Germany learning the language. At university he won the coveted Newdigate Prize for poetry.

One day in class Julian experienced what his grandfather Arnold might have termed a "calling." "I thought of my grandfather defending Darwin against Bishop Wilberforce, of the slow acceptance of Darwin's views in the face of religion and prejudice, and realized more fully than ever that Darwin's theory of evolution by natural selection had emerged as one of the great liberating concepts of science, freeing man from cramping myths and dogma, achieving for Life the same sort of illuminating synthesis that Newton had provided for inanimate nature. I resolved that all my scientific studies would be undertaken in the Darwinian spirit, and that my major work would be concerned with evolution, in nature and in man" (ibid.:73).

Following graduation with first class honours in biology, Julian was awarded a research scholarship for work at the marine biology station at Naples. He returned to Britain to lecture at Balliol College in Oxford. At this time he began the scientific bird-watching which he was to pursue for most of his professional life. He published his first journal article on the courtship of grebes.

In 1912 the Rice Institute in Houston, Texas, hired Julian as a professor. After a preliminary visit he was allowed a year in Germany to prepare himself in contemporary biology before assuming the post. While there he suffered a "nervous breakdown," the first of the manic-depressive episodes which were to plague him all his life. He spent some time in a rest home where his brother, Trevor, had also been admitted for the same problem. Just before World War I was declared in 1914, Trevor committed suicide. The third brother, Aldous (later to become a famous writer) had been rendered almost blind from a corneal infection. Julian travelled to America to take up his duties at the Rice Institute and Aldous took a war job as a farmhand at the country estate of Lady Ottoline Morrell.

In 1917 Julian returned to England, enlisting in the Army Service Corps. It was at this time that he wrote "The Captive Shrew," later to become the title poem for a popular book of verse. He was subsequently transferred to Intelligence, but found the work sufficiently undemanding to allow for a heavy program of reading on theology, as well as on the philosophy and anthropology of religion. He "wanted to understand how the religious mind works, and what induces changes in doctrine" (ibid.:113).

During this period Julian made frequent visits to the Morrell farm, first to see Aldous but later to woo and win Juliette Baillot, the family's beautiful, young Swiss governess. After the war's end and marriage to Juliette, Julian obtained a Fellowship to New College, Oxford. Some time later he published the findings of a major research project on the Mexican axolott, an animal previously existing only in tadpole form but which completed its evolution into a salamander-like land creature after having been treated with ground thyroid. This attracted wide attention and probably led to Julian's subsequent role as a respected popularizer of science. Some time later he joined an Arctic expedition and happened to encounter Wegener's theory of continental drift, when it was still largely unknown. Julian wrote that he was immediately captivated by the theory because it explained so many hitherto unresolved issues in biology.

Religion without revelation

In 1925 Julian seemed to have reached the apex of his career. He became Professor of Zoology at King's College, London, a posting which made him the first biologist in Britain to be paid a four-figure salary. He had just finished writing *Religion without Revelation*: the result of intensive religious studies during the war and after. It was in this book that he first spelled out the naturalistic premise that was to provide the crucial connecting link between the two forms of evolution determining the destiny of humankind.

It was, for him, an inescapable fact that "idea-systems play the same sort of role in cultural evolution as do skeletons in biological evolution: they provide the framework for the life that animates and clothes them, and in a large measure determine the way it shall be lived" (Huxley 1925:viii). He intended the book to demonstrate the pressing need for a new integrating idea system concerning the mental and moral aspects of human functioning: one that would eventually succeed in replacing both the current theology of supernaturalism and its mirror opposite, dialectical materialism. The new religious framework would be unitary instead of dualistically split; based on reliable scientific knowledge rather than revealed as *a priori* truths; and continuously capable of incorporating newly confirmed facts and more comprehensive ways of organizing knowledge — rather than being frozen into absolutist doctrine impervious to disconfirming evidence.

This book, published when he was thirty-eight, was Huxley's first organized attempt to apply a broadly scientific approach to the study of religion. Following Dewey, he defined science in terms of its general method of disciplined inquiry into the objects of human experience and its principle of "limited and increasing certitude," rather than by the specific body of knowledge produced or the measuring techniques applied. And, like Martineau, Dewey, Durkheim, Mead, Santayana and Russell, he believed that no realm of experience can be closed to scientific inquiry. Accordingly, he began his study of religion by seeking the common elements underlying all religious experience and belief, hoping thereby to arrive at a comprehensive and scientifically operative definition of the phenomenon.

Huxley suggested that religion is one of the most fundamental of institutions, having its source in the human psyche. It is an organ of culture which performs an integrating function probably necessary for the survival of the group. "It is a way of life which follows necessarily from a man's holding certain things in reverence, from his feeling and believing them to be sacred. . . . [These things or events or symbols] primarily concern human destiny and the forces with which it comes into contact" (ibid.:9-10). By human destiny he meant the genesis, present situation and possible future role of humankind within the cosmos. He concluded that the tendency to revere or value or hold as sacred those artifacts, ideas and rituals that remind us of our joint journey through space and time is as firmly rooted in human nature as are the emotions of fear and anger. For Huxley, the mystical sensation of transcending present experience to which so many religious people attest is simply a poignantly felt awareness of the dimly discerned immensity of which we are all a part.

Like Bergson and Durkheim, Huxley attempted to trace the evolution of religion. He identified four ways in which humans have tended to picture their reality. These are distinctive patterns of thought which, in turn, shape the prevailing religious idea system. The *magic mode* is very close to the infant's view of its surroundings. It encourages "an interpretation of destiny in terms of pervading ... non-material influences ... capable of being humanly controlled by appropriate methods" (ibid.:53). Next comes the *daemonic mode*, characterized by a tendency to personalize events and objects which arouse emotions. The prevailing thought pattern here is projective. The universe is peopled with demons, spirits, devils, ghosts and gods.

Thirdly there is the *mythological mode* whereby, in the absence of the necessary knowledge, attempts are made to explain reality in believable and comforting terms. But since myths are almost always based on false premises, wishful fantasies and emotions, they are usually misleading. At this stage the concept of a hierarchy of gods, leading ultimately to that of one god, makes its appearance. Like the immanent powers and totems and spirits before them, these "gods are creations of man, personalized representations of the forces of destiny, with their unity projected into them by human thought and imagination"(ibid.:49).

Huxley was hopeful that, with the spread of reliable knowledge about nature and humanity's evolution within it, all three of the more primitive thought patterns would gradually be superseded by the *naturalistic mode*. Here gods are viewed in the context of their evolutionary function as interpretive concepts: concepts which can be tested, along with competing hypotheses, in terms of their power to order and explain human experience.

Huxley saw the current phase of religious evolution as one of conflict between two dominant idea systems: the God hypothesis based on mythical thinking and that of naturalism arising out of the scientific attitude. He believed that Communism had engaged the hearts and minds of many of his generation precisely because it was presented as a naturalistic alternative to the God hypothesis. But, he noted, Marxism is only partially free of mythological underpinnings. Its total denial of the reality of products of the human spirit such as ideas, ideals and moral principles was justified, not by the findings of science, but by the myth of dialectical materialism.

All in all, Huxley was confident that the internal contradictions and ecologically destructive consequences of both idea systems would soon render them unattractive to the majority of the world's inhabitants. And, like Martineau, he spoke of the spiritual relief that comes from rejecting the God hypothesis. He said: "The mental life of humanity is no longer a civil war, but a corporate civilization" (ibid.:24). Elsewhere he commented, "Operationally, God is beginning to resemble the last fading smile of a cosmic Cheshire Cat" (ibid.:58). Sadly, he did not live to witness the aptness of his metaphor for the fate of the god of Communism in the 1990s.

Huxley recognized that the process of religious evolution was not one of uninterrupted progress. For example, "The naturalistic type of belief system made a premature appearance in the classical Greek world, . . . and after a limited and primitive flowering, it went through a long period of suppression and subordination" (ibid.:60). He believed that the acceptance of naturalism would solve the current conflict between religion and science. We would finally have a religion that accepted the universal validity of the scientific approach and a science that accepted the psychological basis of religion.

Huxley attempted to show that the striving for religious goals is an integral part of the individual's developmental process. He extended the idea, put forth by the earlier naturalists, that intelligence is adaptive. And he identified three prerequisites of successful adaptation during a human life span. The first is at the level of conditioning — the need to adapt instincts and impulses to environmental actualities. The second is the need to achieve conscious control, within one's physical and psycho-social environment, through the command and use of scientific knowledge. The third is the need to arrive at a continuity and integration of personality (or of mind or consciousness).

Concerning the latter, Huxley had no use for Kant's transcendentalism or for Bergson's mystical concept of "pure" memory representing "spirit." Instead, he accepted Mead's idea that consciousness of self grows gradually and as an aspect of nature, with increasing organization of mental activity. And he concluded that here religion can function to provide the framework for an integrated and unified sense of self and human destiny within the larger picture.

Huxley noted that, while scientific inquiry is beginning to be applied to the first two of the adaptive processes discussed above, very little progress has been made concerning the role of religion in promoting personality integration. Claims regarding the benefits of mysticism and of unquestioning religious faith require more rigorous examination, he felt. He doubted that mysticism represents the ultimate in integration of personality. While conceding that it may *feel* innately and immediately valuable to the one experiencing it, he warned of the dangers involved to morality and intellect. Speaking as one drawn to mysticism himself (and the brother of a convinced and practising mystic) Huxley pointed to its tendency toward spiritual selfishness and distorted mental development. He concluded, "it may be said that the mystic experience is on a lower plane than logical thought or moral effort — for it generally substitutes images for concepts, and is also in many ways a wish-fulfilment rather than a wrestling with fact" (ibid.:151).

Huxley rejected the concept of absolute faith in the prevailing religious belief system, while recognizing that an integrated personality requires that a great many premises be taken for granted. He defined faith as the sum of our beliefs — the more-or-less unconscious bases of our predisposition to act — some of which have their source in evidence and reason, and others, in our human vulnerability to suggestion. He noted that the practical imperatives of living usually make it impossible to wait for sufficient evidence for our every assumption about reality, so for much of the time we act on faith. But this type of faith, being practical, is usually self-correcting. There are consequences that flow from action — from which we learn if we have not been otherwise convinced by dogma. But where the concerns are chiefly theoretical, as with metaphysical ideas, it is our duty to be agnostic. For Huxley, as for Martineau and Russell, unquestioning faith in something that cannot be checked out is almost as crippling to personality development as is faith that is upheld in opposition to reason and evidence.

Huxley's conclusion was that a fulfilled and integrated personality is indeed the appropriate goal of religion, but the preferred means to that end is neither mystic vision nor doctrinal certitude. Rather, it is a proper scale of values with which to confront experience. He suggested that these come from our ideals and moral principles, and are what we should be striving for and applying in any religious quest.

Huxley did not spell out a complete religious belief system. He preferred to identify three aspects of reality with which any satisfactory religious explanation would have to deal. "The first is constituted by the powers of nature; the second by the ideal goals of the human mind; the third by actual living beings, human and other, insofar as they embody such ideals" (ibid.:188). He explained that the first category has to do with the material grounding of life, and the contents will evolve with the findings of the natural sciences. The third, comprising knowledge of the nature of living beings, will evolve with the growth of history and the biological and social sciences.

The second is the moral aspect. For Huxley, as for Durkheim, this is as much a part of nature (and, in theory, as amenable to study) as are the physical organs from which it springs. It provides *direction* for humanity, within the limitations imposed by the other two. In Huxley's words, "Fate is the limiting force of heredity and environment; and freedom is human plasticity — the variety of possible development opening before a man endowed with a definite heredity" (ibid.:193). Such a naturalistic belief system would define for humanity a world and future both determined and free.

A commitment to public life and philosophy

In 1926 Huxley collaborated with H.G. Wells and Wells' zoologist son in producing *The Science of Life*, a comprehensive survey of biological knowledge intended to parallel H.G. Wells' popular *Outline of History*. He resigned his professorship in order to work full-time on the demanding project: a decision that more or less propelled him out of specialized scholarship and into the broader arena of public policy and philosophical writing.

In 1928 Huxley joined the Society for Psychical Research, as he was anxious to know if there was indeed any scientifically valid evidence of parapsychological phenomena. He took part in an investigation of spiritualism, concluding finally that everything he had witnessed could be explained either by natural causes or (more usually) by fraud. He remained open to the possibility of extrasensory perception, however, preferring a stance of agnosticism to one of uncompromising disbelief.

Also in 1928 the Huxleys travelled to East Africa to promote biological education and nature conservation. His resulting book, *Africa View*, sounded the world's first clear warning about the harm being done by humans to the earth's ecology. He expressed an ethical dilemma still unresolved when he referred to the injustice involved in the Kikuyu being driven from their lands by white settlers: "yet it seemed clear that, if not confined to their reserves, they would have cut down all the trees for firewood and reduced the fertile uplands to an eroded desert" (Huxley 1970:183).

In 1930 came another lecture tour of the United States, followed by a trip to the USSR in 1931. The latter was intended as an exchange of scientific information, but Huxley found, to his dismay, that there was little to learn from the officially sanctioned Soviet biologists. The powerful Lysenko "dismissed orthodox Mendelism and Darwin's key idea of natural selection as 'bourgeois' inventions" (ibid.:201). Huxley discussed this at length in his subsequent book, *A Scientist among the Soviets*. During this period he worked as an administrator in the new non-governmental planning agency, Political and Economic Planning. In 1932 came another lecture tour of the United States and the publication of *Relative Growth*, followed by *Principles of Experimental Embryology* and *We Europeans* in 1934 and 1935 (both with collaborators).

Julian's father, Leonard, died in 1933. He had been a man of disciplined energy and placid temperament, perhaps a model for the integrated, fulfilled personality that Julian saw as the appropriate goal of religion. This may have been related to Leonard's upbringing in the cheerfully agnostic and productive T.H. Huxley home: no doubt quite different from the atmosphere fostered by Julian's sensitive and romantic Arnold mother. A former classmate wrote of the deceased, "Leonard was free-born, and had none of the heart searchings incidental to parting with the Old Man Jehovah and his circle!" (ibid.:215). Julian was not free-born, but he was working his troubled way in that direction.

In 1935, Julian Huxley was appointed Secretary of the London Zoological Society. In the years preceding and during World War II he wrote *Evolution: The Modern Synthesis*, the first of a series of books consolidating his views on evolution and naturalism. In the post-war period he became internationally renowned as a member of the BBC "Brains Trust," and as an educator, writer, world traveller and lecturer, scientist, conservationist, philosopher and (appropriately) the first Director-General of UNESCO. Huxley hoped (in vain, as it turned out) to avoid future problems stemming from the tribalism and cultural relativism by grounding UNESCO firmly in the bedrock of a universal evolutionary naturalism. He was instrumental in establishing the International Humanist and Ethical Union at a world congress convened in 1952 in Amsterdam. By 1957 the British rationalists changed the name of their monthly journal to *The Humanist*, largely due to his influence. In 1965 he organized a landmark conference on the Ritualization of Behaviour in Animals and Man.

In 1966 Huxley suffered the last of his debilitating nervous breakdowns and upon recovery, began writing his autobiography. In looking back, he experienced satisfaction at realizing that his "early resolve to be a generalist, instead of a specialist in one of biology's many branches, had led to such comprehensive views on the role of mind in the human or 'psycho-social' phase of evolution" (Huxley 1973:245). He died in 1975 at the age of eighty-seven.

The evolution of culture

Julian Huxley's most significant contribution to social science is surely his remarkable application of evolutionary theory to the evolution of human culture. "All reality," he wrote, "is evolution, in the perfectly proper sense that it is a one-way process in time; unitary; continuous; irreversible; self-transforming; and generating variety and novelty during its transformations" (Huxley 1957a:10). He explained that this comprehensive process occurs in three phases: the inorganic or cosmological; the organic or biological; and the cultural or psycho-social. At each of the two transition points there was a critical barrier that had to be surmounted in order for the next stage to occur. There was nothing predetermined about this; it happened because of the accidental appearance of an extremely successful set of adaptive and reproductive mechanisms.

Huxley explained that the cosmological sector of evolution is spatially all-encompassing, but both its degree of organization and its vehicle of transformation (physical and chemical interaction) are relatively simple. Nowhere in its vastness is there any sign of purpose. "It is impelled from behind by blind physical forces, a gigantic and chaotic jazz dance of particles and radiations" (ibid.:12). On the other hand, the biological sector is restricted to the infinitesimal surface shell of one or a few planets, while the level of organization reached in organic life is infinitely greater than is the case for the inorganic. Nevertheless, he emphasized, it consists of the same matter as lifeless substance. It is made up of complicated self-copying molecules formed from some critical chemical reaction in the cosmological "world stuff": a crucial reaction creating the minute beginning of a stream of life that began flowing down the generations.

Huxley suggested that the earliest living things were the first self-copying units of substance: probably virtually naked genes. Evolutionary transformation happens because of mistakes in the duplicating process of these genes and the differential survival rate of certain of the incomplete copies. The mistakes are called mutations, some of which provide the organism with an advantage in the struggle to respond to environmental demands. In Huxley's words, "reproduction plus mutation produces natural selection" (ibid.:33).

Huxley admitted that, at first sight, the process in this sector seems full of purpose. Surely, to have arrived at *us* it must have been carefully designed and directed! But the purpose is apparent only after the fact, he said. Natural selection results in survival of species in changing environmental circumstances, but not all species do survive. No observer could predict ahead of time which would have been lucky enough to produce the mutation most advantageous at any particular juncture. The evolutionary process is not pulled *toward* anything. Successful adapters live to reproduce, and unsuccessful ones do not, so the adaptive mechanisms of the survivors always *appear as if* they had been designed specifically for the purpose. Huxley maintained that true purpose, in the sense of awareness of a goal, appeared only in the third phase of evolution, and is chiefly notable in the higher animals.

He explained that the psycho-social sector of evolution is even more restricted in space and time. It occurs only in one of over a million species of organisms on this planet, and occupies less than one-twentieth of one percent of the history of life. It is different in quality from the biological, but has its source within it, just as life differs in quality from non-life, but has evolved solely out of the inorganic substance of the cosmos. Huxley emphasized the fact that there is no trace of any special "vital force" at either of the crucial breakthrough points in evolution. "To postulate a divine interference with these exchanges of matter and energy at a particular moment in the earth's history is both unnecessary and illogical" (ibid.:20).

According to him, the advance from organic to psycho-social evolution could not have been possible without the advent of complex mental organization. Mental capacities are able to assimilate and coordinate qualitative differences as well as quantitative ones because the organism's feeling, touching, seeing, hearing and smelling mechanisms register such widely differing sensations. In Huxley's words, mental activities "utilize the raw materials of simple experience and transform them into special systems of organized awareness" (Huxley 1964:53). Eventually the brain, with its capacity for conscious thought, came into being. Huxley explained that what is involved is a process forming an enabling structure which in turn allowed for amplified process: the whole representing twin aspects of a single reality, or "world stuff." "We are simultaneously and indissolubly both matter and mind" (ibid.). The brain made possible an increasingly stable pattern of sensory awareness, which gradually led to discrimination among objects and events by means of perception.

Huxley coined the term "psychometabolism" to describe how the human being "with the aid of its brain, its organ of awareness . . . utilizes the raw material of its selective experience and transforms it into characteristic patterns of awareness which then canalize and help to direct its behaviour" (ibid.:62). Like physical metabolism, this process becomes more intense, varied and organized in each individual during maturation and for the species in general over evolutionary time. According to Huxley, with the build-up of perceptual structures, language became possible and began to operate as the key vehicle of psychometabolism. He guessed that language had its roots in the need for parents to communicate with offspring during the increasingly lengthy period of dependency. The genes of those who had managed to pass on necessary vicarious experience would have had a better chance of surviving.

Although our closest relatives, the apes, have proven able to experience insights, to build crude concepts and to organize their spatial world much as we do, only humankind has made the vital breakthrough into a symbolic world. According to Huxley, this made possible the sharing of experience among individuals widely separated in time and space. "In man's mental organization the two crucial novelties are speech and the creation of a common pool of organized experience for the group" (Huxley 1957a:93). He concluded that the advent of symbolic language changed human beings into creators and transmitters of idea systems with the awesome power to affect the course of their own evolution, and that there could be no turning back.

Once culture entered the picture, a very different type of evolution began to parallel and even supersede the biological process. Huxley explained culture as the total way of life of a society, largely determined by its defining idea systems. It comprises artifacts (material objects); "socifacts" (institutionalized patterns of behaviour and the organizations through which they function); and "mentifacts" (idea systems which provide the psychological frame of reference for the society). Those idea systems, customs and techniques that contribute to successful individual and group responses to environmental challenges tend to survive to be passed on to future generations. The others generally fall by the wayside, appearing intermittently in isolated corners as anachronisms.

Huxley, like Durkheim, recommended that social scientists analyze cultures in functional, rather than simply in structural, terms. Every culture has a material base that limits and conditions, but (regardless of Marx's views) does not determine it. All are embodied in societies comprising sets of structures performing certain functions necessary for the society's members to survive as a group. Just as with the organs of biological evolution, some of these institutions function mainly for pattern-maintenance; others for the reproduction of patterns somewhat altered so as to be better equipped for enabling the group to adapt to changing circumstances.

In Huxley's view, the breakthrough into culture meant that a new kind of environment was created for humanity to inhabit. Somewhat misleadingly, he chose to follow the terminology of Kant, Husserl and Teilhard de Chardin in referring to humankind's psycho-social world as the "nöosphere." He explained that certain aspects of this pool of mental products are transmitted from generation to generation as tradition. Huxley believed that this has placed humanity in a position of incredible power and responsibility in a cosmic sense. He did not assume, as did Teilhard, that a cosmic consciousness is progressing inevitably toward Point Omega. To Huxley it simply meant that human "consciousness, including conscious purpose, can now take a hand in the evolutionary process" (Huxley 1964:50).

Huxley warned that we must face up to our destiny: to the demonstrable fact that there is no help available from outside the stream of earthly life. This does not mean that we are insignificant, however. On the contrary, because humanity is both the creator and potential controller of the cultural process, we have a power unique in the universe. For, wrote Huxley, "man has not been created helpless or as a slave to some external authority, but is the most creative part of the total creative process" (Huxley 1957b:249). Our human destiny is to be the sole agent for the future evolution of the world. Nor does our special situation mean that we are alone in an unfriendly universe. We are firmly rooted in nature, one of many organic species whose destinies we have the power to shape, for good or ill. And we are, as individuals, immersed in a vital sea of human communication: a vast supportive network of knowledge and ideals.

On morality

All this led Huxley to the problem of human morality. He noted that humans have evolved into the only organisms on the planet with a conscience, and he agreed with Freud that its source is the lengthy childhood process of bonding with *loved* authority figures. He added that humans are also alone among animals in their sense of right and wrong in the abstract; in deliberately creating and pursuing beauty; and in expressing awe and a sense of the sacred concerning matters associated with their own origin and destiny.

In Huxley's model the sacred resides not in supernatural powers or beings, but in "particular relations between particular human beings and particular objects and events" (Huxley 1957b:248). For him the ultimate moral criterion is the probable effect of the behaviour in question on the evolutionary process. Is it likely to enhance the possibility of biological survival and opportunities for personality integration over the long term? He considered it imperative that the scientific principle of limited but increasing certitude be applied to the moral realm, so that we can better assess the direction in which our values are propelling the course of biological and cultural evolution. He suggested aiming for "limited but increasing rightness in the field of morality; . . . limited but increasing significance in the field of art; . . . limited but increasing comprehension in the field of religion; . . . [and in all arenas] limited but increasing faith and confidence, checked and validated by experience, in place of the false certitudes of purely subjective feeling" (ibid.:250).

For Huxley, four of the pressing moral or spiritual issues facing humanity overshadowed all the rest. They were the cultural virus of nationalism, world overpopulation, the need for conservation of the variety of organic life forms and the long-term maintenance of quality in the human gene pool. Huxley believed that the establishment of the United Nations was an important initial step in resolving the first problem. Only recently has the world belatedly begun to recognize the significance of his second two concerns.

The fourth idea was controversial when he introduced it and is even more so today. Huxley believed that it is immoral for us not to use available technologies to prevent the transmission of genes causing cruelly disabling illnesses. He also expressed the opinion that more could be done to discourage people of severely limited intellectual capacity from reproducing.

On all of these issues, Julian Huxley was concerned with the long-term consequences for the possibility of individual fulfilment within a successfully adaptive evolutionary process. He knew there were hard choices to be made and he feared that we were poorly prepared by our prevailing religious belief systems for dealing with the tasks ahead. Most of all, he wanted humankind to accept the implications of our unavoidable role in evolution. But he was swimming against a cultural stream that defined humans as atomistic victims of chaos; or as drops of water in the relentless waves of history; or as wayfarers on detour to and from a better world. He must have hoped to reach the generations still unborn when he penned the following message:

> Evolutionary man can no longer take refuge from his loneliness by creeping for shelter into the arms of a divinized father-figure whom he has himself created, nor escape from the responsibility of making decisions by sheltering under the umbrella of Divine Authority, nor absolve himself from the hard task of meeting his present problems and planning his future by relying on the will of an omniscient but unfortunately inscrutable Providence. (Huxley 1964:79)

The worth and significance of Huxley's comprehensive evolutionary framework was generally overlooked by social scientists in spite of the fact that traces of his ideas (along with those of Durkheim and Weber) may be seen in sociology in the form of the overly abstract structural functionalism of Talcott Parsons. However, Huxley was fighting against a powerful tide of antiscience subjectivism that almost engulfed the twentieth century, and has yet to play itself out. The generation whose ideas generated and defined this tide owed their intellectual nourishment not to Huxley's evolutionary naturalism, nor to the pragmatism and neo-realism of his intellectual forebears, but to something more seductive that they had found in romantic idealism, as filtered through the works of Bergson, Husserl and Weber.

Huxley's major contribution to evolutionary naturalism was his compelling model of the evolution of religion, and of the origin and creative role of human intelligence in the process of cultural evolution. But he was out of step with the times. The most vocal of the following generation were existentialists who saw humans as free-floating progeny of the gods, expelled from the cave into a meaningless void.

References for Chapter Eighteen

Huxley, Julian. 1957 [1925]. *Religion without Revelation*. New York: Harper and Brothers.

————. 1957a. *Evolution in Action*. New York: Harper and Brothers (Mentor Books).

————. 1957b. *Knowledge, Morality, and Destiny*. New York: Mentor Books. (Original title: *New Bottles for Old Wine*.)

————. 1964. *Essays of a Humanist*. London: Chatto and Windus.

————. 1970. *Memories*. Vol. 1. London: George Allen and Unwin.

————. 1973. *Memories*. Vol. 2. London: George Allen and Unwin.

Huxley, Juliette. 1986. *Leaves of the Tulip Tree*. London: John Murray.

Lamont, Corliss, 1949. *The Philosophy of Humanism*. New York: Philosophical Library.

Nineteen

The Existential Political Theory
of Hannah Arendt

You must live with your knowledge.
Way back beyond, outside of you are others,
In moonless absences you never heard of,
Who have certainly heard of you,
Beings of unknown number and gender;
And they do not like you.
— W.H. Auden, "There Will
  Be No Peace"

The evolutionary naturalists of the late-nineteenth century had recognized that humanity could not escape its awful responsibility for the future of life on earth. They argued that human destiny was not pre-ordained, but the result of countless individual choices resulting in the evolution of increasingly comprehensive and reliable knowledge and of a variety of religious-ethical systems. It had become somewhat difficult for knowledgeable people to believe that a moral order was embedded in the nature of things. It seemed clear to the turn-of-the-century generation of youth that morality must be a product of the accumulated wisdom of the human group. This meant that better rules than those followed in the past could be derived — and better principles to guide human choices.

But there was a dark side to this recognition of humanity's role in forging the future of the planet. There would no longer be a place to hide. The new generation of intellectuals had seen the enemy, and the face was all too familiar. Even Huxley, who had great faith in the human species, sometimes despaired at the irresponsibility and violence that was beginning to mark the twentieth century.

Inevitably, the reaction came. What if human beings are *incapable* of behaving wisely and humanely, in the absence of an unalterable good beyond the universe of nature? What if our vaunted freedom to define morality is not something long present and only now discerned, but, instead, represents an

---

References for this chapter are on p. 345.

abrupt abandonment of his creation by a dying creator? In that case human-kind would be condemned to meaninglessness and chaos, rather than being released from the fetters of the cave. Such was the conclusion of the disillusioned former believers who came of age in France and Germany during the interwar period. The most influential of these was Jean-Paul Sartre.

Strongly influenced by Marx, Sartre and his followers accepted the atheism of the revolutionary movement while rejecting its optimistic prophecy for the salvation of humanity. Sartre developed a version of existentialism that denigrated reason and glorified both the autonomous subject and violence as its creative vehicle. However, his perspective represents but one extreme of the twentieth-century European revolt against metaphysics. At the other extreme we find the objective existentialism of Hannah Arendt: "the most rational of the anti-reason theorists" (Hill:27). Although these two were born only a year apart in the neighbouring countries of France and Germany, and were thrown into the same cultural milieu in Paris during the thirties, they were never friends. The world views of both had been shaped fundamentally by German romantic idealism (including its offshoot in Hegelian-Marxist dialectical thinking) and by the influence of Husserl and Heidegger. But their mature thought moved in opposite directions. Arendt had experienced compelling counter-influences to her educational conditioning. She had grown up as a Jew in Germany between the two world wars. Whereas for Sartre World War II was an exhilarating game and career opportunity, for Arendt it was, from its beginnings in Hitler's rise to power, a matter of life and death. And — "existentially" speaking — that had made all the difference!

A confusing introduction to a world in turmoil

Hannah Arendt was born in 1906 in Koenigsberg in East Prussia. Her parents were well educated, and socialist in their politics. Her paternal grandfather was a leader of the Jewish community in Koenigsberg; her maternal grandparents, the Cohns, belonged to the city's wealthiest merchant family. But tragedy struck early in Hannah's life. Her father died of syphilis when she was seven years old. She seems to have suffered from continuous illness during her childhood, and there was much concern about the possibility of congenital syphilis.

Hannah had to learn to live with something else as well. Anti-Semitism was a fact of life to her from early childhood on. In spite of all this, with her mother's help she was always able to defend her sense of self-worth. Mother and daughter fled to Berlin at the outbreak of World War I, but were able to return safely ten months later. During the last year of the war Hannah's mother, Martha Arendt, became involved with the social democratic party opposed to the more militant Rosa Luxemburg group — the Spartacists. This was a small revolutionary movement which opposed both Bolshevism and what they saw as the moral decay and permissiveness inherent in the new republican social democracy. They led a successful uprising in 1918 and eventually helped form the German Communist Party. Martha eventually married a widower with two daughters close to Hannah's age.

Hannah was highly intelligent but not always amenable to guidance. At the age of fifteen she was expelled from school for organizing a boycott of a certain teacher's classes. Her mother arranged for an independent study program at the university, where, by a twist of fate that proved to be of great significance, she studied under a Christian existentialist. From him Hannah learned Greek, Latin and Christian theology. In 1924 she passed the entrance exams for university. There, in her first year, she read Kierkegaard, Kant and Jaspers, and wrote romantic and ambiguous poetry.

Arendt's university years coincided with the period of greatest stability in the struggling Weimar Republic. Although the budget deficit and the bankruptcy and unemployment rates were still dangerously high, the worst of the inflation was over. But already, in the University of Berlin, there were alarming signs of things to come. Just before her arrival, the faculty had voted to demand the firing of a young professor who had revealed facts about Germany's illegal build-up of arms.

Arendt soon moved to the University of Marburg, looking for a compatible approach to philosophy. She wrote that she had found it in "the most modern and interesting philosophical tendency, Edmund Husserl's phenomenology, and the perfect teacher, Husserl's protégé Martin Heidegger" (Young-Bruehl:46). She fell immediately and totally under the spell of Heidegger. He was thirty-five years old, married with a family, but given to romancing his female students. He became Arendt's lover and shaped her thinking for years to come. His wife, already a committed National Socialist, resented all Jews, but especially the beautiful young girl infatuated with her husband. Arendt eventually managed to extricate herself from the situation (but not from Heidegger's influence) by moving to the University of Freiburg to study under Husserl himself.

After graduation she went to Heidelberg to do her doctorate under the supervision of Karl Jaspers, another former student of Husserl. Her thesis concerned the concept of neighbourly love in the philosophy of St. Augustine. Jaspers, like Heidegger, was a proponent of the new phenomenological existentialism, although his was a gentler, kinder version. Under Jaspers' wing, she joined a circle expounding German romanticism which met regularly at the salon of Marianne Weber. She smoked a pipe and listened to the flowery German prose expressing ideas that were to be instrumental in digging the grave of the fragile Republic. Perhaps for a time she really believed that she was at the cutting edge of history and in the company of those who would make it.

Her own work on Augustine was not particularly conducive to clarity of thought. It is difficult to see how she could have avoided the conclusion that Augustine had used his great reasoning powers to persuade Christians not to rely on reason, unless it supported their faith. Rather than helping her identify and criticize the contradictions in the philosophy of the Roman philosopher and Christian saint, Jaspers claimed that the fruitfulness of Augustine's system was due to those very contradictions. Arendt seems to have bought the argument, concluding that it was precisely *because* Augustine "encompassed a maximum of contradictions — even in opposition to reason — he was able, within the authority of the Church, to meet its needs so eminently" (ibid.:74).

A rude awakening

By 1930, Arendt had graduated and begun to emerge into the real world. She married Gunther Stern, the son of Clara and William Stern, a pair of gifted psychologists who had, in 1914, published *The Psychology of Early Childhood*. Their book was based on the theories of the young Jean Piaget, who was later to become a major European opponent of the dominant philosophy of phenomenological existentialism. Significantly, Arendt never read the book. Not long after this, she saw Gunther's university career aborted by the reigning faculty group because his philosophy of music was not sufficiently Marxist. The move had been engineered by the psychologist, Adorno, who later became influential in the American university scene. This destroyed some of her illusions about academia.

Arendt had received a grant to study German romanticism — specifically the theme of "autonomous self-transformation" — and her close scrutiny was revealing a dark underbelly to the movement that her teachers had not acknowledged. At the same time she saw the threat of National Socialism mushrooming, while her beloved Professor Jaspers merely continued to pursue the "essence" of the precious German spirit. She came to realize the dangers inherent in the introspection that her entire university experience had encouraged. "Introspection accomplishes two feats," she concluded some years later, "it annihilates the actually existing situation by dissolving it in mood, and at the same time lends everything subjective an aura of objectivity, publicity, extreme interest. In introspection the boundaries between what is intimate and what is public become blurred" (ibid.:87).

Her study of German romanticism changed direction, eventually culminating in a book on the life of Rahel Varnhagen, an assimilated Jew of the late eighteenth century. Her conclusion concerning Rahel's life was that "in a society as a whole hostile to Jews . . . it is possible to assimilate only by assimilating to anti-Semitism also" (ibid.:92). By now Arendt was separating herself from her German upbringing and moving to the support of the imperilled Jewish community. In the words of her biographer, "By way of Fichte, Schelling, and the German romantics Arendt disassimilated, in the direction of Zionism" (ibid.:89). As this happened, she and Gunther drifted apart. In spite of his university experience, he still saw Communism as the more effective response to the dangers posed by Hitler.

Arendt found few intellectuals who shared her conviction of the impending demise of democracy in Germany. Heidegger was now openly espousing National Socialism, while the majority of her peers merely pretended that nothing was happening. There was one person, however, who gained her admiring respect in the early thirties. Raymond Aron was quietly and bravely using his position in the French Institute to aid refugees heading for France. By 1933 Arendt was also heavily involved with the "underground railway" for Jews and Communists escaping persecution, and in documenting anti-Semitic activities by the government. Gunther had already escaped, and she was living in constant fear of betrayal. "The problem . . . was not what our enemies might be doing, but what our friends might be doing. . . . I came to the conclusion that 'cooperation' was the rule among intellectuals, but not among others" (ibid.:108).

Perpetual homelessness

Inevitably, Arendt was arrested, but by sheer chance (and a deliberate and uncharacteristic resort to "feminine wiles") managed to gain a temporary release. She and her mother left at once, making it through to Prague and from there to Geneva, where she worked for a time for the League of Nations, before moving on to France. For the next eighteen years she was a "stateless person": a fact which had a profound effect on her political philosophy. By 1934 Raymond Aron was back in France, on the faculty of the École Normale Supérieure. He introduced Arendt to the intellectual circles of Paris. For the next several years she worked at several jobs in aid of the Jewish cause. In 1936 she began living with a fellow refugee, Heinrich Blucher, a self-educated scholar who had been a Communist organizer in Germany and a member of the Spartacists. In January of 1940 they were married. Both were interned by the French government in May of that year. Her crime was her Jewish ancestry; his was a previous commitment to Communism. Fortunate once more (and prescient too) both managed to escape during the chaos of France's fall. This time luck intervened in the person of Gunther Stern — now in America — who had arranged for emergency visas. Arendt, with her husband and mother, were among the last to escape from France.

Safe in the United States, Arendt began learning English and settling into a life of part-time college teaching and working for Jewish organizations. She had by now parted company with the Zionists, disagreeing with their insistence on a sovereign Jewish state. She favoured a federal Palestine created as part of the British Commonwealth, and incorporating Jews and Arabs on an equal basis. She proposed, as well, a post-war European federalism in which anti-Semitism would be outlawed. In the midst of all the political work and teaching she began, with Blucher's help, to work on an analysis of the genesis and nature of twentieth-century totalitarianism. These two felt a pressing urgency to awaken the world to "the most essential criterion for judging the events of our time: will [they] lead to totalitarian rule?" (ibid.:211).

The origins of totalitarianism

Arendt's first book, entitled *The Origins of Totalitarianism*, established her as an authority on the subject of that new form of terror-based centralized power made possible by twentieth-century technology in the service of nineteenth-century ideology. In introducing the first edition Arendt declared, "The subterranean stream of Western history has finally come to the surface and usurped the dignity of our tradition" (Arendt 1951:xxxi). She saw the stream as a conjunction of two currents, romanticism and race-thinking. She knew all too well, from her study of the romantic movement since Rousseau, and of pan-Germanism (also originating in France) that, far from being new in the world, "Hitler's propaganda spoke a language long familiar and never quite forgotten" (ibid.:93-94).

It had all started, according to Arendt, in revolutionary and Napoleonic times, as a reaction to the threatened disintegration of the nation-state as a source of collective power for its members. The idea of common occupancy of — and responsibility for — a national territory had been gaining headway steadily since the time of Charlemagne. In addition, for many centuries the perception of membership in one human race had been encouraged by the spread of universalizing philosophies. The Enlightenment, with its ideal of empowerment of the individual through the use of reason and the senses, perhaps represented the pinnacle of this evolution away from tribalism. But, with the onset of the terrifying insecurity caused by changing national borders and political liaisons, people turned for comfort and support to the family, clan or tribe. They began to revert to the older notion of blood ties and mystical tribal "oneness" as the criterion for separating groups from one another and as the source of the only collective power that could now be relied upon for protection. And values were changing as well. "The Enlightenment's genuine tolerance and curiosity for everything human was being replaced by a morbid lust for the exotic, abnormal and different as such" (ibid.:68).

Arendt identified two poisonous roots of the tribal nationalism that culminated in twentieth-century totalitarianism: romanticism and the race-thinking which took the form of pan-Germanic and pan-Slavic movements. She noted that both roots were nourished in France as well as Germany. Pan-Germanism as a political movement got its start with a group of alienated French noblemen who claimed an inherited superiority to the masses because of direct descendance from the Germanic conquerors of the Gallo-Roman populace in late-Roman times. In mid-nineteenth century the Comte de Gobineau, enthralled with romanticism, welded the two notions together in his historical doctrine of the "spiritual" superiority of the German race. It was a doctrine that borrowed much from Hegel and romantic idealism in general.

Gobineau believed that he had discovered the "scientific" law governing the fall of civilizations. In his opinion, they fell for one reason only: racial degeneration due to the "intermixing" of blood lines. He was convinced that the original race of "princes" (the Aryans) was in danger of being submerged by inferior non-Aryan races. The greatest threat was posed by Semitic peoples — heretofore, merely a term describing the ancient Hebrew, Ethiopian, Assyrian and Arabic linguistic groups. Gobineau put a new twist to the word, claiming the Semites were the Jewish race who had been bestialized early in human history through intermixing with black Africans: obviously the lowest of all the sub-races in Gobineau's scheme of things!

This focus on "common tribal origin," along with the romantic idealist notions of "innate nobility" and mystical "spirit" welding a people together — reaching its apex in Nietzsche's perverted Social Darwinism — produced a volcano that was to erupt with disastrous consequences for humanity. In Arendt's words: "From the former sprang the organic doctrine of history with its organic laws; from the latter arose at the end of the century the grotesque homunculus of the superman whose destiny is to rule the world" (ibid.:170).

According to Arendt, even this fateful conjunction of erroneous doctrines would not have been sufficient to produce the blatantly destructive form of racism employed by the Nazis. The necessary catalyst was the success of nineteenth-century imperialism in exploiting aboriginal populations. "Imperialism would have necessitated the invention of racism as the only possible 'explanation' and excuse for its deeds, even if no race-thinking had ever existed" (ibid.:183-84). This encouraged the Germans and Russians, with their late start, to invent the only form of the game still available to them: continental imperialism, based on the revival of the "pan" movements.

Arendt saw pan-Germanic Nazism and pan-Slavic Communism as very similar. They had emerged from the same seedbed of German romantic idealism and were based on almost identical pseudo-scientific theories of history. Where Nazism cited race as the defining characteristic of humanity and driving force of history, Communism substituted class. Both declared world conquest necessary and inevitable, and looked forward to the establishment of a new kind of human nature. There was one obvious difference, however. Communism was originally inspired by humanitarian motives and sought international equality, while Nazism aimed at the institutionalization of a system of inherited privilege requiring the enslavement and annihilation of "inferior" races. But Arendt felt that this difference in goals grew increasingly irrelevant the more successful the movements became. She explained that this was because the very nature of totalitarian ideology *guarantees* that the ends will always be overwhelmed by the means employed.

There was another devastating similarity. In both cases "the internal enemy" was readily available. For the Communists, property owners such as the Kulaks were "necessary victims," not through any dissenting acts but simply because the theory had declared them so. At no time in recent history had the Jews been so vulnerable and exposed in their own tribal pretensions and lack of state protection. Arendt's explanation of why this was so involved an original and courageous analysis of the nature of power and leadership. It was subsequently to arouse considerable criticism from the Jewish community when she returned to it in her book on the Eichmann trial.

Once again she looked to European history. It happened, she said, that the threatened decline of the nation-state coincided with the gradual but very real demise of the inter-European role of the Jewish banker. During the state's heyday from the fourteenth to the early nineteenth centuries, successful Jewish businessmen had operated what amounted to an effective central banking system for the European community. They had been encouraged to prosper while maintaining their separateness. Their uncommitted status had suited the interests of all participants in an era of national conflicts. While the laws of their host countries made social acceptance unlikely — and any real political participation impossible — the wealthy Jews were given special privileges and wielded considerable power.

In Arendt's words: "There is no doubt that the nation-state's interest in preserving the Jews as a special group and preventing their assimilation into class society coincided with the Jewish interest in self preservation and group survival" (ibid.:13). Jewish interest as expressed by their spokesmen, that is. In Arendt's opinion, political and social equality in the country of their birth was not an issue for the Jewish leadership. They had special privileges instead, and the assurance of continued distinctiveness. The fact that the majority of their co-religionists had no political protection and little social acceptance was never a major concern.

As time passed an increasingly large proportion of the Jewish community began turning to intellectual pursuits, and to seeking assimilation within their state of residence. In the process they began to shed their commitment to Judaism. Nevertheless, many of these — like Disraeli in England — still wanted to claim a distinction based on their Jewish ancestry. There was only one ground on which such a special status could be claimed. It had to be along blood lines, on the basis of some form of family or tribal nationalism. Arendt referred to this as "race-thinking" and considered that the Jews who upheld it during the nineteenth century played into the hands of the twentieth-century anti-Semites. "Jewish origin, without religious or political connotation, became everywhere a psychological quality, was changed to 'Jewishness' and from then on could be considered only in categories of virtue or vice" (ibid.:83). Whereas, in the pogroms of the past, Jews could always escape from the "crime" of Judaism through conversion to Christianity, "from Jewishness [an inherited vice] there was no escape. A crime, moreover, is met with punishment; a vice can only be exterminated" (ibid.:87).

The European universities, which might have been expected to uphold rational and democratic values, were instead largely hotbeds of irrationalism. They instigated a passion for the "profound," or the "rich essence" beyond "crude appearances"; they mystified and applauded anarchic power at the expense of constitutional authority; and they downgraded the individual in favour of an ambiguous Absolute Unity. "The particular reality of the individual person disappears against the background of a spurious reality of the general and universal; it shrinks into a negligible quantity or is submerged in the stream of dynamic movement. . . . In this stream the difference between means and ends evaporates together with the personality, and the result is the monstrous immorality of ideological politics [wherein] . . . every value has vanished into a welter of pseudo-scientific immanence" (ibid.:249).

Arendt believed that the claim common to all totalitarian movements to have restored the human being to some mystical sort of "wholeness" is irresistibly seductive for intellectuals. In addition, she noted that "The totalitarian movements owed much of their appeal to that vague and embittered anti-Western mood that was especially in vogue in pre-Hitler Germany and Austria, but had seized the general European intelligentsia of the thirties as well" (ibid.:246). All this probably contributed to the disquieting fact that the role played by the university-educated "front generation" was decisive in making possible the rise of totalitarianism during the twenties and thirties.

Arendt noted that, in every country in Europe, these movements were served by a roster of distinguished young intellectuals and artists. She referred to "the anti-humanist, anti-liberal, anti-individualist, and anti-cultural instincts of the front generation, their brilliant and witty praise of violence, power and cruelty. . . . They did not read Darwin but the Marquis de Sade" (ibid.:330). She blamed them more than any other group for destroying the distinction between truth and falsehood and the capacity for moral judgement so necessary for civilization to flourish. They were attracted to activism, regardless of direction, and applauded rebellion against respectable society no matter how cruel or perverted the form it took. *Artists were particularly destructive*. People like Bertolt Brecht felt that it was revolutionary to strike a blow against hypocrisy by applauding amorality. However, in Arendt's view, "the only political result of Brecht's 'revolution' was to encourage everyone to discard the uncomfortable mask of hypocrisy and to openly accept the standards of the mob" (ibid.:325).

The nature of totalitarianism

Arendt concluded that totalitarian movements gain ground most rapidly where the public has taken on that peculiar combination of extreme gullibility concerning conspiracy theories and extreme cynicism about democratic institutions which is characteristic of the mob, and where the interests of the mob and intellectual elites in the promotion of anarchy happen to coincide (ibid.: 246). In the thirties and later, this situation served the goal of the front organizations, which was to provide a protective cover for the movement until it could assume total power. These organizations had a two-way function: "as a façade of the totalitarian movement to the non-totalitarian world, and as a façade of this world to the inner hierarchy of the movement" (ibid.:367). They set out to establish organizations duplicating all existing professional associations and then to destroy the credibility of the latter in the eyes of the unsuspecting public. This ploy became particularly successful in Western universities and labour movements.

Next to the outer layer of the front organizations we find the membership of the totalitarian movement, according to Arendt. "Within the organizational framework of the movement . . . the fanaticized members can be reached by neither experience nor argument; identification with the movement and total conformism seem to have destroyed the very capacity for experience, even if it be as extreme as torture or fear of death" (ibid.:308). Even those attacked by the movement for no reason, such as the accused in Stalin's "treason" trials, will go to their deaths still loyal to the Party.

Arendt claimed that the membership provides a protective mask for the militant groups, and they, in their turn, for the inner, elite corps with their special tool — the secret police. In the centre, like the motor of a giant machine, is the Leader, exercising total, arbitrary control and demanding instant, unquestioning obedience. Layer upon layer, like the body of an onion: all but the deadly core operating as automatons in a monstrous, mindless and malevolent bureaucracy!

Once in absolute control, the defining characteristic of totalitarianism is the use of terror as the chief means of government. Arendt explained that this is where such systems differ completely from mere authoritarian dictatorships. All social and family ties must be destroyed, so "purges are conducted in such a way as to threaten with the same fate the defendant and . . . all his connections" (ibid.:323). Terror within a totalitarian state takes the form of dominating human beings from within. Not only must one avoid expressing one's thoughts; *having* thoughts that do not simply mirror ideological clichés is the ultimate crime. The spouse who overhears one's sleeping murmurs will feel compelled to inform in order to ensure personal safety.

In its early stages the totalitarian regime establishes a volunteer espionage network and begins to ferret out those who had opposed its ascendancy. The second stage involves the definition of the "objective" or "necessary enemy" (one who might be *expected* to oppose the regime according to the governing ideology) and the "possible crime" (what that person *might* have planned to do). After all these are disposed of, the terror becomes purely arbitrary in the third and final stage. In all this, the concentration camp plays a crucial role.

Arendt, writing in the late 1940s, anticipated Krushchev's revelations, and was far more accurate in comprehending the later practices and predicting the dark future of Communism than were most of her contemporaries, whatever their political persuasion. She also pointed out, with devastating prescience, the totalitarian potential in the new revolutionary government of China. She was always at her soundest when discussing political theory. She had lived history first-hand and had found most of the theorizing of her universities sadly out of step with political reality. By 1950, on her first return to Germany, she was able to see Heidegger with vastly different eyes from those of the impressionable student of pre-war days. She reported, perhaps too sanguinely, "What I saw and heard of the Heidegger influence in Heidelberg would be truly disastrous if it weren't so woolly-headed" (Young-Bruehl:306).

On morality and the Holocaust

Arendt never really became part of the university establishment. She claimed that she did not want to be a full-time academic, because of the isolation from reality involved. She admired Eric Hoffer, the self-taught longshoreman philosopher, and had long realized the superiority of her husband's thinking to that of her former teachers. Her ambition was to make a meaningful contribution to a new science of politics. Her interest in current political and moral problems led to her attendance as an observer at the trial of Adolph Eichmann, and this, in turn, precipitated one of the most traumatic periods of her life. Eichmann was a Nazi administrator who ordered the mass murder of Jews during World War II. He was kidnapped in Argentina in 1960 by Israeli agents and taken to Israel where he was tried and found guilty of crimes against humanity. Her book on the trial, entitled *Eichmann in Jerusalem*, created an uproar of hostility from Jews all over the world. She had intended to derive lessons for modern Jewry from the Holocaust. Instead, as a result of pointing out the well-intended but short-sighted complicity of some of the Jewish leadership in the carrying out of the "final solution," she became a virtual pariah to her own people.

Arendt left the Eichmann trial deeply troubled by the utter lack of moral judgement exhibited by the Nazi functionaries and the population that supported them. She felt this to be far more serious than any deficiency in compassion on their part for their Jewish victims. Another worrying observation was the apparent absence of any relationship between firmly held religious convictions and ability to make such judgements. She concluded that "The total moral collapse of respectable society during the Hitler regime may teach us that those who are reliable in such circumstances are not those who ... hold fast to moral norms and standards. ... Much more reliable will be the doubters and sceptics ... because [such people] are used to examining things and making up their own minds" (ibid.:376). These musings led her to the general observation of a widespread reluctance, among otherwise good people secure in their faith in some universal dogma, to make independent moral judgements of particular ideas and behaviours. She used the analogy of the banister to represent the role of a firmly indoctrinated faith. What one gets used to is simply *depending* on a banister. It seems to be frighteningly easy to change any banister for a new one, and to lean on it as trustingly as one did the previous one.

On the glorification of violence

From 1967 on, Arendt was on the faculty of the New School for Social Research in New York. She was also increasingly in demand for seminars and lectures in various universities. Quite often the positions she took on current issues were contrary to the going fashion in academic and media circles. She deplored the undeniable glorification of violence by Western students, and blamed the influence of Sartre and Fanon. She considered it of the utmost importance to maintain meaningful distinctions among the concepts of power, strength, force, violence and authority.

"Power," she said, is the ability to act *in concert* to persuade or coerce others. "Strength" is an individual capacity. "Force" refers to movements in nature or to other humanly uncontrollable circumstances. "Violence" is a destructive instrument by which individuals, or minorities, can impose their will upon a majority. "Authority" represents power that is vested in persons by virtue of their offices. Its exercise depends upon respect and legitimacy, but never on persuasion or coercion. She felt that the current tendency to confuse these terms "not only indicates a certain deafness to linguistic meanings, which would be serious enough, but it also has resulted in a kind of blindness to the realities they correspond to" (Arendt 1969b:43).

Arendt believed that nothing could be more dangerous than "the tradition of organic thought in political matters by which power and violence are interpreted in organic terms ... [and] violence is justified on the grounds of creativity" (ibid.:75). She was appalled by the claim (popularized by Max Weber) that all governments — whether democratic or not — rest on violence against the people. She pointed out that it is not violence but power that is the essence of government. Violence can destroy power, but it can never create it. Violence is therefore a poor basis on which to build a government. "To substitute violence for power can bring victory, but the price is very high; for it is not only paid by the vanquished but it is also paid by the victor" (ibid.:53). She considered this particularly dangerous because "The means ... of destruction now determine the end — with the consequence that the end will be the destruction of all [legitimate] power" (ibid.:54). Only terror is left.

Challenging conventional wisdoms

Other popular ideas challenged by Arendt were those of collective guilt, of the opposition of emotion and reason, and of "just" wars — whether revolutionary or concerned with conflicts over sovereignty. "Where all are guilty no one is; confessions of collective guilt are the best possible safeguard against the discovery of culprits" (ibid.:65). She maintained that the absence of emotion neither causes nor prompts rationality. As for wars and violent revolutions — she believed that they could no longer be justified. She raised the possibility that the only *real* revolution underway in modern society is the process of secularization.

Arendt believed that the concept of sovereignty is obsolete and highly dangerous in the modern world. She recommended a world system of interlocking federal jurisdictions, consisting of "council states" which would be based upon locally elected councils. She felt that humankind has for a long time confused freedom with sovereignty, at both the individual and political levels. The roots of the confusion extend back to ancient times, and are the result of defining freedom in terms of free will. "Politically, this identification of freedom with sovereignty is perhaps the most pernicious and dangerous consequence of the philosophical equation of freedom and free will, for it leads either to a denial of freedom — namely, if it is realized that whatever men may be they can never be sovereign — or to the insight that the freedom of one man or group or body politic can be purchased only at the price of the freedom . . . of others" (Arendt 1961:164).

Freedom and the human condition

For Arendt, freedom is an individual condition that can only be established and protected by the rule of law. It is a feature of the public sphere as opposed to the private, or that of the household. The distinction is between activities related to a common world and those involved with the maintenance of life. Her point was that there are intimacies that need to be hidden or they lose their value, while other matters (such as freedom and equality of opportunity to participate in deciding matters of the common good) must be public if they are to exist at all.

However, with the emergence of a common "social" realm in modern society, the older dichotomy is breaking down. Arendt worried that this heralded the rise of a mass society of alienated carbon copies of media-inspired values: a situation destructive of the plurality necessary for democracy. Tied in with this, she thought, is the "politicization" of society, as the political process is increasingly used to impose a strictly "social equality," or sameness which, if possible, would be highly undesirable.

In her book, *The Human Condition*, Arendt began what was to be a prolonged attempt to draw a firm line between *vita activa* (the life of action) and *vita contemplativa* (the capacity for thinking, willing and judging). She intended this as the culmination of her life's work. The initial book dealt with the first category: what she considered to be the three fundamental human pursuits of "labour," "work" and "action." She saw labour as corresponding to the biological processes required for maintaining life, necessitated by the conditions of *natality* and *mortality*. Work, on the other hand, reflects the unnaturalness of human existence, according to Arendt. It is the means for providing an artificial world of things. She called its necessary condition *worldliness*. The third pursuit, action, is made possible by the condition of *plurality* in human relationships, leading to language and thought. Here she seemed to mean what a sociologist would call "social interaction." These three conditions of human existence (natality-mortality, worldliness and plurality) never condition us absolutely, declared Arendt, in spite of what some social scientists say.

Arendt's focus was on the importance of plurality: acting and speaking together. She explained that this process allows for the sharing and comparing of private sense-impressions resulting in the constructing of a faculty and fund of "common-sense." Here she seems to be harking back to the ideas of the Scottish moral philosophers. "The only feature of the world by which to gauge its reality is its being common to us all," she wrote, "and common sense occupies such a high rank in the hierarchy of political qualities because it is the one sense that fits into reality as a whole our five strictly individual senses and the strictly particular data they perceive" (Arendt 1958:208). Arendt seemed to have recognized plurality as the only possible source of the intersubjectivity sought by Husserl. She considered this phenomenon to be the prerequisite for human freedom. This is why its destruction is invariably the first requirement of a totalitarian movement.

On knowing and thinking

In 1968 Arendt began working on *The Life of the Mind*. She planned a three-stage enterprise, taking the form of three volumes. These were to deal with thinking, willing and judging. She considered these three "faculties" of the mind as distinct but interrelated. Volume 1 dealt with thinking. She began it by declaring that a way of thinking, dominant since Parmenides, has come to an end. It is the belief that "whatever is not given to the senses . . . is more real, more truthful, more meaningful than what appears" (Arendt 1971:10). Not only is the old concept of God dead, but the very idea of an eternal truth, above and beyond mere appearance, is irretrievably gone. She concluded from this that philosophers must recognize that their task is to seek, not truth, but *meaning*. The pursuit of truth must be left to science, although the expectation of *finding* it must be relinquished even there.

Arendt thought that this presents a predicament for science which is no longer present for philosophers, who confine themselves to a focus on meaning. "That modern science, in its relentless search for *the* truth behind *mere* appearances will ever be able to resolve this predicament is highly doubtful, if only because the scientist himself belongs to the world of appearances" (ibid.:26). Here, Arendt, while defining all science in terms of an obsolete philosophy, was also revealing remnants of her own earlier dualism. She indicated that the solution lies not in the claims of positivism, but in reinterpreting science as "an enormously refined prolongation of common-sense reasoning in which sense-illusions are constantly dissipated, just as errors in science are corrected. The criterion in both cases is evidence" (ibid.:54). She concluded that, "The activity of knowing is no less related to our sense of reality and no less a world-building activity than the building of houses" (ibid.:57). The truths of science are "provisional verities": what our senses *compel* us to believe. On this, Arendt seems to have arrived remarkably close to the position of the pragmatists, although obviously she had not read any of the philosophers of naturalism.

Thinking, in Arendt's scheme, is something quite different. Whereas *knowing* depends on involvement in reality, *thinking* requires detachment. Clearly, she was still committed to the Husserlian stance of "epochē": the temporary suspension of common-sense reasoning, and a retreat into privacy and non-action from plurality (and the "intersubjectivity" that plurality makes possible). But she carefully distinguished this from the transcendentalism of Kant. She referred to Kant's declaration that it is necessary to deny knowledge to make room for faith. Arendt argued that all he need have denied was knowledge of things unknowable (such as metaphysical "truths") and what he had actually made room for was *thought about the meaning of* certain unrealized possibilities — not faith in their existence.

Although Arendt admitted that thought arises only from experience, she nevertheless claimed that experience does not condition thought as it does cognition. This seems to be an assumption based solely on Husserl's belief that reality is a correlate but not a condition of consciousness. She believed that thought, in its turn, cannot alter reality as knowing does; it can only clarify the meaning of experienced reality. Only by means of speech does thought take form. Whereas the product of cognition is knowledge, said Arendt, the product of thought is judgement. "The manifestation of the wind of thought is not knowledge; it is the ability to tell right from wrong, beautiful from ugly" (ibid.:192). We develop conscience and taste only if we are able to think. More than anything else, evil is the result of sheer *mindlessness*, according to Arendt.

Arendt went on to explain that, while human cognition, in the form of the scientific endeavour, is instrumental in the quest for truth, thought and reason are concerned only with discovering the meaning of events. She believed that Kant, in rightly insisting on the autonomy of speculative thought, did not intend that its results would have the same validity as those obtained by cognition. It was the romantic idealists, she claimed, who drew this unwarranted conclusion and elevated speculation to the level of scientific "knowing" — with disastrous results.

Arendt hoped that her work on the nature of thinking would succeed in finally putting to rest a number of harmful metaphysical fallacies which had been around for a long time. These were:

- The notion — introduced by Parmenides, and given further credence by Plato and others — *that there exists a superior reality of "pure essential being" behind that of appearances*.
- Descartes' theory *that the thinking ego's subjective consciousness is prior to objective experience and is itself the ultimate proof of existence*. Arendt noted that a subject suspended from birth in an unpeopled desert would be utterly unable to assume any reality whatsoever.
- Kant's *equation of reason with the logic of some supra-human "purpose."*
- The kind of *two-world dualism that equates mind and soul, and isolates both from the body*. In Arendt's scheme the soul is the seat of the emotions, and thus organic in nature and origin, while the mind is merely a means of temporarily suspending the impact of sense impressions.
- The Hegelian idea *that an entity or attribute can turn into its opposite*. This, Arendt considered particularly dangerous because it destroys all possibility of clarity and precision in language and thought.
- The Bergsonian notion *that humankind is God*.

Ironically, however, Arendt's refutation of these principles seems to lend more support to a view of thinking as an activity engaged in by the organism as a whole than to her concept of an isolated faculty of mind. This strange disjunction gives her book a puzzling, unfinished character.

On willing

Volume 2 of *The Life of the Mind* is entitled *Willing*. Arendt began with the premise that free will was "discovered" only *after* the Greek era. "Prior to the rise of Christianity we nowhere find any notion of a mental faculty corresponding to the 'idea' of freedom, as the faculty of the Intellect corresponds to truth and the faculty of Reason to things beyond human knowledge ... to Meaning" (Arendt 1978:6). Arendt declared that if the will exists, it must be the mental capacity that deals with the future, just as memory is that which handles the past. And whereas the intellect is concerned with present and past experiences, and reason with the implications of these matters and their possibilities, the will is concerned with "projects" to be realized in action. Here we can see the continuing influence of existentialism in her thinking.

Arendt acknowledged the modern view that the awareness of being free to will an action is merely a sensation in the consciousness, rather than some faculty existing in the mind. Still, she felt that there is something in Hume's argument that "The touchstone of a free act is always our awareness that we could also have left undone what we actually did" (ibid.:5). And she distrusted the motives of professional thinkers who are more comfortable with the idea of necessity than with that of freedom. Willing may not be a comfortable concept for thinkers, she argued, because it is always aimed at *doing*. However, she concluded that it could involve only a relative, rather than an absolute, spontaneity: one that originates with and is limited by the organic conditions of natality and mortality.

Arendt referred to Augustine's belief that "with man, created in God's own image, a being came into the world that, because it was a beginning running toward an end, could be endowed with the capacity for willing and nilling" (ibid.:109). She seemed to be citing Augustine as the source of the existentialist belief that because humans are *born,* and thus forever newcomers in a world preceding them in time, they must perforce be free spirits. She noted that, on the basis of this rather dubious premise, Augustine had concluded that "the freedom of spontaneity is part and parcel of the human condition" (ibid.:110). Being born, we are doomed to be free.

Arendt's only other favoured authority on the subject of the will was Duns Scotus, the scholastic. She acknowledged that it was he who introduced the notion of "contingency" — meaning, not *uncaused* but, "that which could as well not be ... [given what went before]" (ibid.:136). Scotus taught that the will instigates volitions which then set into motion certain irreversible effects. An element of freedom exists only in the span of time between the will and the volition. Volitions are contingent upon all the possibilities inherent in the situation, but once the will selects one of these, the resulting chain of consequences cannot be willed away.

Arendt considered that Heidegger's concept of will had been dredged up out of the worst of German romantic idealist thought. And that even more disastrous for humanity was Nietzsche's notion of humans being able to *will* immortality. She quoted Machiavelli approvingly on this subject. "People who believe the world is mortal and they themselves are immortal are very dangerous characters, because we want the stability and order of *this* world" (Hill:311). For Arendt, romantic idealism represented the climax of fantastic speculation parading as knowledge. Its "pseudo-kingdom of disembodied spirits [History, Class Struggle and Race] working behind men's backs was built out of homesickness for another world, in which man's spirit could feel at home" (Arendt 1978:157).

For Arendt, on the other hand, there was no such thing as a world where the human mind could or should ever feel at home. Her notion of thinking is really contemplation: a temporary withdrawal from the forces of objective circumstance. Only in such thought can the meaning of experience be comprehended, she claimed. In her thoroughly naturalistic view, the only real spirituality is the process of making moral and aesthetic judgements, in the context of contemplation. As for the will, Arendt seems to have arrived at no logical basis for its existence, other than in the limited sense in which Duns Scotus recognized its operation.

Final judgements

The third book in the intended trilogy was to have focused on judging. Also, one would expect that here Arendt intended to explore the interconnections among her three "faculties" — and between them and the three "organic" pursuits of labour, work and action — as developed in her earlier work. However, because she did not live to write the book on judging, all we know of her ideas on the subject is contained in notes for lectures.

In teaching as in writing she was soundest when she employed common-sense reasoning (Dewey's "method of intelligence"?) in dealing with the current scene. She worried that the growth of meaninglessness in the twentieth century had been accompanied by a corresponding decrease in common sense. For example, she cited the popular argument that we cannot judge anything or anybody unless we have been present and involved ourselves. She commented that, "it seems obvious that if it were true neither the administration of justice nor the writing of history would be possible" (Arendt 1982:98). The exact opposite is nearer the truth, she said. Although impartiality demands taking into account as many perspectives as possible, "only the spectator occupies a position that enables him to see the whole. . . . [This means that] withdrawal from direct involvement . . . is the condition . . . of all judgments" (ibid.:55). For Arendt, the goal of the intellectual is development of this capacity for temporary withdrawal into the life of the mind — not to *avoid* judgement, but to facilitate it.

However, there is nothing in Volumes 1 and 2 to indicate that Arendt was approaching an integrated concept of mind on which to base her social-political theory. Rather, one senses a growing awareness that she had painted herself into a corner from which there was no escape. Could she have begun to suspect that her lifelong pursuit of the "faculties" of the mind had been nothing but a fruitless quest for a chimera? This would explain the contradictory and unfinished quality of the volumes on thinking and willing. And it lends a special poignancy to the fact that, on the night she died of a heart attack in 1975 — seven years after beginning her trilogy — all that could be found of her manuscript for the concluding volume was a blank sheet of paper in the typewriter with the word, "Judging," on the top.

Clearly, Arendt had fallen into the same error that had trapped her mentor, Husserl. In her desire to establish the mind as capable of isolating itself from the knowing process and its "intentional object," she was forced into a denial of what she had previously identified as the inherent human condition of plurality (the crucial prerequisite for a sharing of subjectivities). Consequently, she was forced to reject the very knowledge (findings from the human sciences) that might have lent credence to her work. If thinking, willing and judging are unrelated to knowing, then knowledge — or the lack of it — is irrelevant to contemplation, as well as to acting and to the rendering of judgement. One can scarcely conceive of a premise that would lead to a more anti-intellectual stance, and one less acceptable to a reasonable person such as Arendt.

Husserl's influence during her formative years had convinced Arendt that the "common-sense reasoning" leading to scientific knowledge is of a totally different nature from the type of contemplation that she defined as thinking. At the same time her own unfailing common sense caused her to deplore the fact that "scientific and philosophical truth have parted company" (Arendt 1958:290). She suggested that the gulf between the two perspectives was due to the fact that the traditional philosopher had always started from two premises quite foreign to the scientific thinker. These were: (1) that the natural universe is the creation of a divine maker; and (2) that the human mind is incapable of comprehending what humanity has not itself created. According to Arendt, the inescapable conclusion from such a stance is that people can learn nothing by means of science that is comprehensible in terms of the human condition. Although Arendt obviously did not share this metaphysical perspective, her own work indicates a continuing inability to come to terms with biological and social science.

Denying the universality of science

A real fear of science (especially as applied to the study of humans) pervades the pages of Arendt's book *The Human Condition*. She bemoaned the fact that scientists have developed organizations that make them "one of the most potent power-generating groups in all history" (ibid.:324). She failed to see that, although there is no question that scientists form their own lobby groups, their real power in society comes from their capacity to build organized systems of powerful knowledge. As that knowledge adds to the choices available to all, it seems a strange sort of paranoia to fear the scholars who produce it: scholars usually very much like herself in their dedication to truth.

Arendt's confusion about the objectives and methodology of the social sciences reveals the appallingly one-sided nature of her education. For example: "Economics . . . could achieve a scientific character only when men . . .

unanimously followed certain patterns of behaviour, so that those who did not keep the rules could be considered asocial or abnormal'' (ibid.:42). Does this mean she believed that cultural norms and customs — and the habitual animal behaviour giving rise to them — were *created* by the scientific attempts to identify them?

And on the following page: "Statistical uniformity is by no means a harmless scientific ideal; it is the no longer secret political ideal of a society which ... is at peace with the scientific outlook" (ibid.:43). And yet again: "behavioral sciences aim to reduce man as a whole, in all his activities, to the level and condition of a behaving animal" (ibid.:45). But, surely, the *aim* of all the social sciences (including her own study of politics) is to *identify* and *compare* trends and patterns in group life and individual behaviours — and to *discover* the degree to which we resemble and differ from our animal forebears!

Arendt demonstrated a sadly prevalent misunderstanding of statistics in imagining it to be an all-powerful instrument capable of creating rather than registering regularities and relationships. Later in the same book she wrote, "The trouble with modern theories of behaviorism is not that they are wrong, but that they actually are the best possible conceptualizations of certain obvious trends in modern society" (ibid.:322). This is a *weakness*? And finally, this description from a later book: "The monstrous sameness and pervasive ugliness so highly characteristic of the findings of modern psychology" (Arendt 1971:35). Did she think that "killing the messenger" would solve the problems of society? All this from a person who aimed at developing a "new science of politics," and whose own work in conceptual analysis is a sterling example of the application of the essential first step in a scientific approach to the study of the human condition.

We can only conclude that Arendt tended to lose her sound grasp on experience when she turned from politics to philosophizing about the human condition, possibly because of the one obstacle established by her university indoctrination which she was never able to recognize and overcome. She was locked, emotionally, into a profoundly anti-scientific response pattern where the social studies were concerned. So long as she restricted her conceptual analysis to the field of her own immediate experience, her contribution was of lasting value. Applying common-sense reasoning to what she had witnessed, she was *doing* science without realizing it, by contributing to the theoretical framework so necessary for the development of a pre-scientific social study. But when she turned to problems requiring knowledge already available in the biological and certain of the social sciences, she was obviously floundering. As she struggled with the problem of delineating the various types of mental processes, and of distinguishing these from forms of action, her lack of acquaintance with tested knowledge in the field was all too obvious. Rejecting science in her approach to the study of the human mind, her only resort was to the very type of abstract and unfounded speculation that she had criticized when applied to politics.

Arendt's intellectual dead-end demonstrates the ultimate fruitlessness of a social theory cut off from the wellsprings of reliable scientific knowledge concerning the nature of the human condition. She went as far as she could go in ignorance of the most elementary substantiated findings in biology, psychology and sociology. An understanding of the work of the philosophers of naturalism from Montaigne onward would have given her an intellectually compatible and solid ground on which to stand to launch her analysis of the judging or valuing process in human beings. In spurning social science as a guide, she could only retreat into the contradictions inherent in Husserl's phenomenology.

Still, none of this can detract from the remarkable contribution made by Hannah Arendt to the study of politics. Here she was well served by her Husserlian-inspired phenomenological method: by the conscientious habit of detaching herself mentally from the coercive demands of traditional philosophy and present exigencies. This critical contemplative tendency, combined with her stateless situation, allowed her to view the most pressing problems of the twentieth century from the perspective of the outsider, unencumbered by the "truths" of the older metaphysics and the conventional wisdom that cultural membership endows. In politics, at least, she was able to live her belief that "for the true humanist neither the verities of the scientist nor the truth of the philosopher nor the beauty of the artist are absolutes; the humanist, because he is not a specialist, exerts a faculty of judgment and taste which is beyond the coercion which each specialty imposes on us" (Arendt 1982:106).

In assessing the total impact of this courageous spectator, we are forced to a conclusion fraught with irony. Although burdened by an ideologically fuelled rejection of the scientific-inquiry method as applied to human problems, she was nonetheless following that very method in most of her life's work. Her refinement and elaboration of social/political theory was in fact an invaluable first step in the making of a science. And in spite of the enduring yearning for dualism implanted by her university education, she became profoundly naturalistic and evolutionary in philosophy. Her analysis of the origins and development of totalitarianism demonstrates an acute understanding of cultural evolution in general. All this justifies the conclusion that Hannah Arendt's judgements and clarifications of contemporary political issues are of much more than mere historical interest. They amount, instead, to an extraordinarily significant contribution to the evolution of the naturalistic current in social-scientific thought.

References for Chapter Nineteen

Arendt, Hannah. 1951. *The Origins of Totalitarianism*. New York: Harcourt, Brace and World.

———. 1955. *Men in Dark Times*. New York: Harcourt, Brace and World.

———. 1958. *The Human Condition*. Chicago: University of Chicago Press.

———. 1961. *Between Past and Future: Six Exercises in Political Thought*. New York: Viking Press.

———. 1963a. *On Revolution*. New York: Viking Press.

———. 1963b. *Eichmann in Jerusalem: A Report on the Banality of Evil*. New York: Viking Press.

———. 1969a. *Crises of the Republic*. New York: Harcourt, Brace, Jovanovich.

———. 1969b. *On Violence*. New York: Harcourt, Brace and World.

———. 1971. *The Life of the Mind*. Vol. 1: *Thinking*. New York: Harcourt, Brace, Jovanovich.

———. 1978. *The Life of the Mind*. Vol. 2: *Willing*. New York: Harcourt, Brace, Jovanovich.

———. 1982. *Lectures on Kant's Political Philosophy*. Edited by Ronald Beiner. Chicago: University of Chicago Press.

Ettinger, Elzbieta. 1995. *Hannah Arendt/Martin Heidegger*. New Haven: Yale University Press.

Hill, Melvyn A., ed. 1979. *Hannah Arendt: The Recovery of the Public World*. New York: St. Martin's Press.

Young-Bruehl, Elisabeth. 1982. *Hannah Arendt: For Love of the World*. New Haven: Yale University Press.

Twenty

Erich Fromm and Humanistic Psychology

"In harmony with nature"? Restless fool,
Who with such heat doth preach what were to thee,
When true, the last impossibility;
To be like Nature strong, like Nature cool: —
Know, man hath all which Nature hath, but more,
And in the *more* lies all his hope of good.
Nature is cruel; man is sick of blood:. . . .
Man must begin, know this, where Nature ends;
Nature and man can never be fast friends.
Fool, if thou canst not pass her, rest her slave!
— Matthew Arnold,
"To an Independent Preacher"

Like Arendt, Erich Fromm was a member of the World-War-I generation of European Jews. He had been shaped much more than she, however, by his Judaic heritage. His subsequent lifelong commitment to all three of the popular "isms" of his day (Marxism, Freudianism and existentialism) was always qualified by a deeply embedded love for the Old Testament. This was coupled with respect for the Bible's ancient authors and the scholarly rabbinical tradition stemming from it. The ideas boiling in the mind of this good and caring man at times have proven to be strange bedfellows, and the resolution of logical contradiction was never his strong point. But what emerged over the course of Erich Fromm's long lifetime was a uniquely moral approach to social science: one with a powerful appeal to the Jewish community as well as to a large cross-section of disillusioned twentieth-century youth from other backgrounds.

The life of an existential socialist psychoanalyst

Erich Fromm was born in March of 1900 in Frankfurt, Germany, and died in March of 1980 in Muralto, Switzerland. He was raised in an Orthodox Jewish milieu, the only child of an "anxious, moody" father and a "depression-

---

References for this chapter are on p. 359-60.

prone" mother (Fromm 1957:3). The surrounding community was Christian, and Erich recalled an early dislike for the clannishness of his own people. He considered that World War I had represented a watershed in his intellectual development. Imbued from childhood with a belief in the perfectibility of humankind, yet appalled by such clear evidence of the irrationality of human mass behaviour, the youthful Erich decided to devote his life to understanding "the laws that govern the life of the individual man and the laws of society" (ibid.:9). It is not surprising that he turned to the two theories of the period which were based on the Enlightenment ideas of human perfectibility and essential lawfulness and direction in historical development. These ideas were characteristic of the Hebrew tradition as well. Perhaps it was his Jewish background that allowed him to sense this fundamental philosophical similarity between Marxism and Freudianism which had gone unrecognized by Freud and his followers, and by the Marxists of the time.

After earning a Ph.D. in Heidelberg in 1922, Fromm trained in psychoanalytic methodology in Munich and Berlin. During these years in German academia he encountered the third great influence on his thinking: existentialism, and the notion of humans being forced at birth into a process of becoming free. By 1930 he was a practising "existential" psychoanalyst.

In 1934 Fromm emigrated to the United States, where his future was assured by an academic community enthusiastically receptive to all three of the popular currents of thought which had nourished his own world view. Although understandably grateful for a safe and financially secure haven, Fromm never ceased to feel alienated from the affluent technological society surrounding him. During his American career he taught in a number of universities and founded several institutes of psychoanalysis — all the while continuing to practise as a therapist to those whom he considered the casualties of that society. He authored ten books and edited several more. He was one of the founders of a peace organization known as SANE. He once joined a socialist party, but resigned when he found it insufficiently radical. Fromm always declared that he was temperamentally and intellectually unsuited to political activism. In 1949 he accepted a post at the National University of Mexico, where he remained until his retirement in 1965. From that time until his death he resided in Switzerland.

The dilemma of the human condition

Fromm's efforts to synthesize existentialism, Marxism and Freudianism never included a rigorous assault on their underlying premises. "I have no gift for abstract thought" he admitted (Fromm 1986:106), thus avoiding rather than resolving the glaring inconsistencies so obvious in the writings of Sartre. He saw himself not as a philosopher or scientist, but as a prophet in the Old Testament sense — and a healer. In these roles he had a profound effect on the hearts and minds of several generations of patients and students. He believed that psychoanalysts are literally ministers to the individual soul, and that the unique calling of the modern prophet is to minister to society at large. To this end Erich Fromm dedicated his considerable energies and the remarkable communication skills appreciated by all who ever heard or read his words.

Never one to obfuscate, Fromm spelled out his own understanding of what constitutes the soul with painstaking clarity and honesty. He believed it to be that which distinguishes humans from other animal species: the spiritual aspect resulting from the development of self-awareness. Like Mead and Huxley before him, he was convinced that this occurred not as a mysterious discontinuity in evolution, but as a crucial "emergence" in the process — after that of life and of animal existence. "This birth of man may have lasted hundreds of thousands of years, but what matters is that a new species arose . . . [and from then on] self-awareness, reason and imagination disrupt the 'harmony' that charges animal existence. Their emergence has made man into an anomaly. . . . He is a part of nature, subject to her physical laws, unable to change them, yet he transcends the rest of nature" (Fromm 1968b:307).

Fromm believed this anomaly to be the subconscious motivating force driving cultural evolution as well as individual development. The dilemma of the human condition, he said, is that it can never again be one of harmony with nature; only the animal condition is that. For Fromm, to be human was to be faced with an inescapable tension between the pull towards regression into the cave of infantilism and tribalism and the need to develop reason, objectivity and imagination: between the desire to escape from freedom and the desire to wield in ever more life-enhancing ways the creative power that freedom offers. Clearly, the progressive drive is the spiritual one, representing as it does the strivings of the human soul. The negative drive is the siren's call for harmony with nature; for those "incestuous" ties of blood and soil represented today by tribalism, nationalism and totalitarianism.

In Fromm's model, regression in individual development involves failure to detach oneself emotionally from the concrete, immediately felt "world of the mother" and enter the reasoned and abstractly visualized (cultural) "world of the father." To be human, then, is to live continuously in a series of states of disequilibrium: a situation resulting in that active and creative urge by which we alone, of all the animals, are driven toward transcendence of present circumstances. Fromm summed it up as follows: "Man has to solve a problem, he can never rest in the given situation of a passive adaptation to nature . . . because his inner contradictions drive him to seek for a new equilibrium, for a new harmony, instead of the lost animal harmony with nature" (Fromm 1955a:28).

It is obvious that all this departs from Freudianism on several counts. The concept of equilibrium, for example, was introduced in this context by Spencer — and further developed by Pavlov and Piaget — although Fromm did not acknowledge this. For Fromm, the relationship between humans and society was a dynamic, two-way one, rather than static and one-way, as he believed Freud saw it. It is not merely the satisfaction or frustration of this or that instinct that drives the human being, declared Fromm. "The most beautiful as well as the most ugly inclinations of man are not part of a fixed and biologically given human nature, but result from the social process which creates man" (Fromm 1941:12). Here, Fromm is much closer to Mead in his thinking than to Freud.

The mother-right theory

Although Fromm acknowledged that the unconscious is an important factor in human motivation, he rejected the notion of the libido as the driving force. Instead, he favoured his own idea of an irreconcilable anomaly presented by the human condition itself. He felt that Freud's universalization of the Oedipus complex was a mistake, but he did make use of a non-sexual version of it in his own adaptation of the "mother-right" theory of Bachofen. Johann Jakob Bachofen (1815-87) thought that human history had moved through three phases prior to the establishment of patriarchy: (1) a nomadic, promiscuous period; (2) the lunar phase of matriarchy which gave rise to the Eleusinian mysteries of the Hellenistic world and featured the worship of Demeter; and (3) a transitional Dionysian era. Bachofen's book, published in 1861, was probably also the source of Engel's ideas on the origin of the family. Bachofen had claimed that the seeds of religion found their initial fertile ground in the female psycho-biological structure, which was aptly suited to the early mystery and fertility cults. The dominance of the chthonic religious view coincided with the rule of the matriarchy, according to Bachofen. Like Rousseau, he thought that this system had evolved from a primeval democracy of the herd, where unrestricted sexuality and brotherly love prevailed and where the concept of private property did not exist. Instinctual, "natural," blood-based ties predominated. Nietzsche's "Dionysian" principle may also have had its source in Bachofen's book.

However, Bachofen — unlike many of his romantic followers — did not consider this matriarchal state to be humanity's lost Golden Age. He assumed the inevitability of human progress toward more organized social patterns. He claimed that, as the non-biological creativity instigated by the birth of reason and imagination began to function to produce a surplus and a leisure class, a new spring of immortality came to be worshipped. For Bachofen this was "the male creative principle, in which is bestowed the divinity that was once accorded only to motherhood" (Fromm 1970:88). Gradually the supreme goal of human destiny became "the elevation of earthly existence to the purity of the divine father principle" (ibid.:93) and patriarchal social organization began to replace that of the matriarchy. He concluded that it had reached its apex in nineteenth-century bourgeois society.

Fromm seems to have accepted these speculations as uncritically and enthusiastically as did Engels before him, and with as little awareness of the sexism underlying the theory's premises. His interpretion of the "mother-right theory" in terms of Freudianism and Marxist dialectic was intended as his own original contribution to social science. He broadened Freud's concept of the infantile incestuous Oedipal urge to include all primary ties "of blood and soil," meaning the kind of narcissistic self-identity that has its source in kinship, tribalism and nationalism. As had many of our pioneers before him — from Martineau to Piaget — Fromm recognized a parallel between the long process of cultural evolution and the spiritual and intellectual development of the individual within the biological life span. In both cases Fromm identified an early narcissistic phase of magical omnipotence, evolving into animism and tokenism, through nature worship, then into the beginnings of an effective conscience personified as an authoritarian object of worship. He thought that this evolved into an objectivity concerning self and surroundings and a conscience based on experience of life; and, finally, into a capacity for love for one's fellows in the service of principles of justice and peace.

Fromm saw the present historical era as the one in which the human species would be forced, in order to survive, to achieve a synthesis of the opposing matriarchal and patriarchal psycho-social orientations. For the most part, he considered the matriarchal orientation to be negative and inhibiting to human progress. Its incestuous focus on ties of blood and soil and dependence for self-identity on such ties; its irrationality and lack of vision; its lack of objectivity and tendency to personalize issues; and its inability to handle abstract thought: all these would have to be vanquished from the earth. On the other hand, he said, there are equally destructive aspects of patriarchy: authoritarianism; possessiveness; the tendency to view others as means rather than ends; and arid intellectualism isolated from practice and context. These would have to go as well. The new synthesis would be governed by personal conscience rather than obedience to external rules; self-discipline; non-hierarchical authority structures; a strong sense of identity based on membership in the world community; and on reason and love.

On reason and love

Reason and love were key concepts in Fromm's outlook, and he was careful to define them. Like Schopenhauer, he distinguished between reason and intelligence, noting that the latter is the means by which all animals adapt to their environment. Reason, on the other hand, is a uniquely human attribute — similar to Arendt's "thought." It is "man's faculty for *grasping* the world . . . his instrument for arriving at the truth" (Fromm 1955a:64). Fromm explained that reason allows humans to orient themselves meaningfully within their cultural and physical environment. With the help of imagination it organizes experience to provide them with both an integrated world view and an object of devotion — or ideal end of existence. "Because man is gifted with reason he is life being aware of itself" (Fromm 1957:13). Fromm noted that reason is very different from rationalization, which, like Freud, he explained as the equally human process of giving *irrational* acts the *appearance* of rational motivation.

Fromm's version of love is based on the idea of relatedness, as opposed to narcissism or even simply sentiment. He saw it as a productive activity: "union with somebody, or something, outside oneself under the condition of retaining the separateness and integrity of one's own self" (Fromm 1955a: 31). It involves both rootedness and group-solidarity, rather than the incestuous refusal to detach oneself from the orbit of the mother. The latter is expressed in modern times by narcissism, and by both the authoritarian/submissive and rebellious/anarchic personality structures, and, at the cultural level, by twentieth-century totalitarianisms.

Fromm identified five types of love: brotherly, motherly, erotic, self-love and love of God. He believed that possessiveness is foreign to all of these, but exclusiveness is perhaps necessary for erotic love. "It is exclusive only in the sense that I can fuse myself fully and intensively with one person only" (Fromm 1957:44). And just as exclusiveness is different from possessiveness, so is self-love not to be confused with selfishness. He believed that love of self is the prerequisite for all other forms of love.

Fromm understood love of God as an evolving concept of personal relatedness to the object of worship as defined, by means of reason, in the context of one's world view. He considered that cultures in their early stages, and individuals in their childhood, tend to require first an all-enclosing mother-god figure and then one viewed as "helping father." A step beyond this is mystical theism, in which there is "an assumption of the reality of the spiritual realm as one transcending man, giving meaning and validity to man's spiritual powers and his striving for salvation" (Fromm 1955a:54). All this is very different from the non-theistic frame of reference in which "there exists no spiritual realm outside man or transcending him. The realm of love, reason and justice exists as a reality only because, and inasmuch as, man has been able to develop these powers himself throughout the process of his evolution" (ibid.).

For the non-theist, then, "the concept of God is only a historically conditioned one" (ibid.). In the latter instance, love of God would mean commitment to the principles of love, reason and justice in human affairs. These principles would constitute the objects of devotion within the world view of the "normative humanist" — the label Fromm preferred for himself.

On the evolution of religion

Fromm was always extremely forthright in his religious views. Although religious language abounds in his writings, he made it clear that he was a nontheist. He wrote: "there is no need for the concept of God" (Fromm 1968a: 85). He considered the notion of the "magic helper," unrestrained by nature and history, as an anachronism in the modern world — possibly condoned only as a poetic symbol "for the act of leaving the prison of one's ego and achieving the freedom of openness and relatedness to the world" (ibid.).

Fromm disagreed strongly with the mystical ideology of Carl Jung. He judged that Jung's extreme subjectivism and relativism regarding truth, and his strange view of the unconscious as "a power beyond our control intruding into our minds" (Fromm 1950:17) were subversive of any truly ethical religious stance. "Needless to say," concluded Fromm, "in the logic of Jung's thinking, insanity would have to be called an eminently religious phenomenon" (ibid.:18).

In his analysis of the development of one particular religion, in *The Dogma of Christ*, he traced the alterations over time in the object of worship. He showed how these reflected changes in the culture and society of the worshippers, from the suffering man who was the brother of the powerless living on the fringes of society (and was raised to a god after death) to the god descended to become man: that logically impossible two-in-one divinity created in the image of the absolute monarchy of the Roman Empire. Then came the regression to Catholicism's worship of the Great Mother — reflecting the passive-infantile orientation of the Middle Ages. This was followed by a return to cultural adolescence with the Renaissance and the advent of the Father God of Protestantism, with its growing emphasis on abstraction (seen in its enthusiastic embrace of the Holy Spirit) and its accompanying focus on the individual conscience and reason. Finally, one of his chief criticisms of Christianity was the fact that, since its inception with the death of Jesus, it had tried "to comfort the unhappy individual by promises of life after death" (Fromm 1955a:245) and in the process had made both life and death unreal.

One of Fromm's last books, *You Shall Be as Gods*, was an attempt to similarly incorporate Judaism into the larger picture of the evolution of religion. He loved the Old Testament and saw its message as an essentially revolutionary one. "The Old Testament is a book of many colors, written, edited and re-edited by many writers in the course of the millenium and containing in itself a remarkable evolution from primitive authoritarianism and clannishness to the idea of the radical freedom of man and the brotherhood of man" (Fromm 1966:6). He believed that the history of Judaism demonstrates a constant tension between two opposing trends: nationalism (or tribalism) versus internationalism; fanaticism versus tolerance; and conservatism versus radicalism.

Fromm was convinced that the seeds of a new global spirituality are to be found in the Hebrew Bible. He believed that the Jewish religion is equipped by its history to lead the way toward a new way of being religious: a way in which "man can find oneness with the world, not by regressing to the pre-human state, but by the full development of his specifically human qualities, love and reason" (ibid.:61).

He claimed that the ancient Hebrews were the first to move from the old polytheisms to the concept of a unified god. It was a concept "reflecting the socio-political structure in which the tribal chiefs or kings have supreme power" (ibid.:18). He was able to trace, within the Old Testament, "a growth and evolution of the concept of God that accompanies the growth and evolution of a nation" (ibid.:22). He showed how, with the advent of Abraham and Moses, it is possible to discern primitive beginnings of the rule of law, in the cause of which "God is bound by the norms of justice and love [and] man is no longer his slave . . . above both are principles and norms" (ibid.:28). Eventually the existence of One God becomes the unspoken premise for the practice of the Way: a moral life. Emphasis is no longer on knowledge *about* God, but on *imitation* of him; that is, on the right way of living.

Fromm believed, with Freud, that in the early stages of the evolution of human culture there was probably no other way for the group to liberate itself from the fixation on blood ties and territory than by the requirement to be "obedient to God and his laws" (ibid.:73). The threats of God's punishment were no more nor less than *predictions* of the unavoidable natural consequences associated with certain types of behaviour. Fromm noted that they are as true for today as they were then; they are necessary reminders of the inescapable consequences that attend every human choice. Freedom carries the heavy price of responsibility. Why else would we struggle so hard to escape it?

Fromm saw the war against idolatry as the main religious theme of the Hebrew Bible — an idol being whatever represents the external object of the group's central ruling passion. The stricture against "naming" God was an attempt to do away with the personified object of worship which serves to alienate humans from the self and from human history. An idol worshipper, wrote Fromm, is invariably an alienated person, and *vice versa* "since he has impoverished himself by transferring his living powers into things outside himself which he is forced to worship in order to . . . keep his sense of identity" (ibid.:48).

For Fromm, all authoritarian religions and the ethics they promote are tinged with idolatry. They produce in the human being the infantile authoritarian, "heteronomous" conscience, rather than the mature, humanistic, "autonomous" one. In the former, the conscience reflects only the internalized voice of the external authority, and requires obedience; in the latter, it is the voice of the individual's integrated value system expressing the demands of further life and growth. Here, Fromm seems to be using the two terms in the Piagetian, rather than the original Kantian, sense.

In a radio talk given near the end of his life, Fromm sounded less hopeful in his analysis of the future of religion in general. Until the nineteenth century, he said, religion had possessed two legs: its claim to present a true picture of reality and its claim to present a worthy object of worship. This object of worship (thought to exist beyond nature) defined the ultimate end of moral striving. He claimed that after Darwin there was no longer any justification for the religious world view that presented creation as an unknowable mystery. "In the light of evolution God was reduced to a working hypothesis and the story of the creation of the world and of man to a myth" (Fromm 1986:28). All that was left for religion was morality, but its ingrained attitude of idolatry made the fruitful pursuit of that endeavour impossible. It had no means to fight the new idols of consumption and technology. According to Fromm, " The ethic that dominates modern capitalism has amputated religion's other leg" (ibid.: 29). "Technology," he continued, "is the new God, and the astronauts are the high priests of the new religion" (ibid.:30).

Marxism as a source of morality

Fromm had an abiding faith in socialism and a corresponding hatred of capitalism. As a result, his comparisons of the two systems were never quite objective. His vision of socialism was always that of a future Utopia forever untainted by the failed attempts to apply the theory in the real world. Capitalism, on the other hand, was invariably represented in the equation by only the most distasteful of the features accompanying its actual practice: bureaucratization, consumerism and the misuse of technology. The fact that these features were also present in socialist systems (to the extent that the systems were viable at all) seemed to have escaped his notice. However, in his later years, he did begin to identify bureaucratization and centralization of power as the problem — rather than private saving and investment of capital. He despaired of the communist East as well as the capitalist West, and (in an echo of Weber) prophesied a totally dehumanized mass world society by 2000 AD, in which people would function merely as cogs in the social machine.

The fact was that, as his thinking matured, Fromm had grown increasingly selective in his reliance upon Marx and Freud. He had begun to recognize the inadequacy of Marx's political and economic model and had become uneasy with the authoritarianism that had emerged as a major theme in Marxist thought. However, he continued to value what he saw as the essence of Marx: his concern for economic justice, his belief in human perfectibility and his logic of the dialectic. This "authentic" Marxism represented, for Fromm, the strongest spiritual movement of the nineteenth century. Fromm saw Marxism as "radical and humanistic — radical in the . . . sense of going to the roots, and the roots being man; humanistic in the sense that it is man who is the measure of all things and his full unfolding must be the aim and criterion of all social efforts" (Fromm 1957:142).

Fromm was captivated by the Hegelian-Marxist dialectic: the idea that history evolves according to a predetermined pattern by which conflicting trends eventually synthesize with their opposites to achieve a higher level of integration — within which new opposing forces then begin to form, and the process repeats itself. He tried his best to fit Freudianism into this mould, believing that the failures of applied Marxism must be due to its faulty (or absent) psychological base. Fromm devised the concept of "social character" to provide what he saw as the missing link between the two theories. He thought that Marx's "false consciousness" was due to the "social unconscious," which is in turn "determined by the 'social filter' which does not permit most real human experiences to ascend from unconsciousness to consciousness . . . [such filters being] socially produced and shared fictions" (Fromm 1965:218) which blind people to their real interests. These shared fictions determine how the psychic structure will be moulded in any particular society, by the simple fact of living therein. Fromm argued that this produces a typical "social character" which is overlaid by enculturation upon the core of attributes shared by all humans.

Only when daily experience is encouraged to break through these socially conditioned barriers into consciousness is it open to the onslaught of reason, and the "revolutionary character" thus enabled to break through. "The revolutionary character is the one who is identified with humanity and therefore transcends the narrow limits of his own society, and who is able, because of this, to criticize his or any other society from the standpoint of reason and humanity" (Fromm 1955b:158). There are echoes here of Nietzsche and Karl Mannheim. However, Fromm emphasized that the revolutionary character is neither an authoritarian nor someone who rebels against all authority. It is neither the fanatic nor the violent militant.

On violence

Fromm was concerned that his ideas might be used to justify violence and/or withdrawal into subcultures promoting drugs and promiscuity. Aware that he had become a virtual guru to the youth of the sixties and seventies, he tried not to abuse his power. He was critical of a fellow neo-Marxist for that very reason, and warned against mistaking the romantic conservatism of Herbert Marcuse for authentic radicalism. He wrote: "The ideal of Marcuse's 'non-repressive society' seems to be an infantile paradise where all work is play. . . . He is attracted by infantile regression, perversions and . . . in a more hidden way to destruction and hate" (Fromm 1970:18).

Concerning violent social change, Fromm noted that any real revolution can only proceed one step at a time. "Since there is no miraculous change of heart each generation can only take one step" (Fromm 1966:113). He marvelled that at the very moment in history when violence is losing all its rationale ("in international relations because of the existence of thermonuclear weapons and within a state because of the complexity of its structure") (Fromm 1968a:144) it had become popular with a small but vocal minority of the privileged young. He blamed this on pervasive spiritual despair and on the literature portraying humans as driven by uncontrollable aggressive instincts. He also asked, "Is the fact that we show brutality and cruelty in comic books and movies, because money is to be made from these commodities, not enough of an explanation for the growing barbarism and vandalism of our youth?" (Fromm 1955a:175). This was written before the TV and video market had demonstrated the now-terrifying prostitution of its great power to shape values and behaviour!

On normative humanism

Fromm's concept of "social character" shows that he was very aware of the power of culture to determine human values, in spite of the urge to creativity and action which he considered inherent in the human condition. "All cultures provide for a patterned system in which certain solutions are predominant, hence certain strivings and satisfactions.... The finest, as well as the most barbaric cultures have the same function — the difference is only whether the answer given is better or worse" (Fromm 1968b:312). Similarly, he said, all humans are idealists, in the sense of striving to satisfy other than basic biological needs. "The difference is only that one idealism is a good and adequate solution; the other a bad and destructive one" (ibid.). With these statements, Fromm took up the cudgel against the cultural relativism of much of the anthropology and social philosophy of his day. He called his approach "normative humanism," claiming that it was "based on the assumption that, as in any other problem, there are right and wrong, satisfactory and unsatisfactory solutions to the problem of existence" (Fromm 1955a:14).

Fromm claimed that there *does* exist a hierarchy of values; there are good and there are evil intents and actions, depending on their consequences for the evolution and enhancement of life. " 'Good' for the humanistic conscience is all that furthers life; 'evil' is all that arrests and strangles it" (Fromm 1966: 55). Humans are by nature value-seekers, he claimed. "The structure of our brains allows us to do something quite unique: we are able to define our optimal goals and put our emotions in the service of these goals" (Fromm 1986: 133). This capacity is founded on our elemental urge to survive physically. In this, "we obey the biological impulse, imprinted on us since the birth of living substance and transmitted by millions of years of evolution. The wish to be alive (beyond mere physical survival) is the creation of man in history, his alternative to despair and failure" (Fromm 1968a:86). By this Fromm meant the urge *to* greater freedom and creativity rather than the escape *from* freedom — back into the womb of mother nature.

Thus we are equipped to use our freedom to behave either ethically or unethically. "All ethical behavior is based on the faculty of making moral judgments on the basis of reason; it means deciding between good and evil" (Fromm 1955a:172). As his ultimate criterion of the good, Fromm chose Albert Schweitzer's principle of "reverence for life." He believed that reason, love and imagination could be used to determine those choices most likely to result in the affirmation and enrichment of life; to consequences furthering individual and evolutionary growth rather than destruction and decay. The condition of mental health — for which he aimed as a therapist — he described as the ability to move beyond self-identification in terms of ties of blood and soil to self-orientation within the world through the use of imagination and reason.

Sources of the anti-science bias in humanistic psychology

Fromm's chief weakness as a thinker was his failure to comprehend the nature of modern science. He once remarked on a fundamental difference between Freudianism and Darwinism (to the detriment of the former) but he did not seem clear as to the reason. He claimed that scientific theory and political ideology are similar in that both contain fragments of truth padded with fictions intended to make a more plausible whole. This may well explain his strange abhorrence of behaviourism. Like Arendt, he seemed to see it as a set of perverse and fictitious answers to human problems, twisted into spurious plausibility by a few glimmers of truth, rather than as a way of asking questions about the meaning of certain observed regularities in actual behaviour.

Fromm never seemed quite able to come to terms with modern technology. For example, he often expressed contradictory attitudes toward computers. He warned that humanity was abdicating decision-making to computers. Then, in the same book, he noted that these machines function to allow us to make more accurate predictions of the *consequences* of our own man-made decisions. At times it seemed to be predictability itself that he feared, especially when the behaviourist approach to psychology had had a hand in providing the means for it. Neither behaviourism nor "instinct theory," he claimed, "allows human beings the slightest control over their own lives" (Fromm 1986: 72). The possibility that greater predictability, in terms of the consequences of our choices, might conceivably translate into more, rather than less, control of our lives seems not to have occurred to him!

Fromm's statement is a strange one, revealing more about his own misunderstanding of science than about the theories he condemned. What could he have meant? If the hated theories are not accurate descriptions of the nature of things, how can they have any effect on human lives? And if, on the other hand, they *do* eventually provide reliable propositions about the forces affecting human behaviour, would not the knowledge of such forces *enhance* our potential for choice and possibly increase our awareness of responsibility for the results of our choices? Is that not what psychoanalysts hope for when they claim to have identified similar forces? It is difficult to understand the basis for Fromm's hostility toward what is merely a competing approach to the study of human relations. Could it possibly be that it was the *success* rather than the failure of behaviourism that he feared? And could it be that his attitude is yet another example of that very human urge to "escape from freedom"?

What *is* clear is that Fromm had difficulty applying scientific rigour to his own work. He once described a study which he had conducted in Germany, which supposedly had produced decisive evidence concerning the German "social character." Apparently two thousand questionnaires were administered, but no information is provided as to sampling techniques. Each form listed *hundreds of open-ended questions*, and fewer than half were returned. The very idea that any reliable data could have resulted from such flawed methodology is laughable, yet Fromm attributed political motives to the editors who refused to publish his findings (ibid.:128).

It was Fromm's establishment of a dichotomy between "humanistic psychology" and all the other psychological approaches that has had the most far-reaching and harmful influence on the development of the social sciences. He was convinced that all the allegedly more scientific approaches to the study of humanity are manipulative, mechanistic and positivist: in sum, they are by definition "anti-human."

The indiscriminate application of these pejorative epithets to all attempts at scientific inquiry in the social studies has become widespread since Fromm's time. For this reason the origin of the practice must be discussed. The logical positivism of modern times, as developed by the Vienna Circle of scientific philosophers, was an attempt to adjust the older realism-based empiricism to Einstein's discoveries. It reflected a move from the "mechanistic determinism" of the Newtonian world view to one of "relational determinism." This involved a recognition that scientific laws may reflect — not necessarily the "true" nature of existence, but the logic and linguistic conventions of humans as applied to accessible evidence of that existence. So Fromm was quite out of date in his assumption that the Martineau/Comte version of positivism and the machine-analogy of Newton were representative of the current approach of science.

In addition, Fromm was attributing to all scientists the belief that humans, like inorganic phenomena, are not just analogous to machines in the complexity of their inner workings, but that they are *nothing more* than machines. And that, not only do scientists think that observable regularities are all that we can measure, but that those measures are *all that there is*! The mechanism and positivism that Fromm considered typical were already largely obsolete as guiding paradigms of science. Even so, Fromm's idea of them is a grossly misleading caricature of what they represented at the time of their greatest influence.

Predictably, for Fromm's followers, psychology became a moral pursuit rather than an attempt at objectivity. Their master's emphasis on the importance of reason in human spirituality was completely overlooked in the anti-intellectual fervour of the times — to which his own writings may have contributed. The goal of humanistic social science became, instead, the pursuit of a sentimentalized and sometimes even transcendental sort of love: the antithesis of Fromm's concept of relatedness to humanity and human history.

As one of the generators of the anti-science current within "humanistic" psychology and sociology, it is doubtful that Erich Fromm will be valued by posterity for his contribution to social science or philosophy. He produced little in the way of original thought in those fields, and the integration of popular ideas that he envisioned was sadly bastardized by his followers. His attempted synthesis of Marxist, Freudian and existentialist theory now seems somewhat dated and incoherent. On the other hand, he was always more the moral prophet than sceptical thinker, and it is in that role that he made his lasting contribution to social-scientific thought.

For Fromm did succeed in spelling out a powerful moral vision: one which sometimes has been lacking in social theory. He saw his normative humanism as "a global philosophy which emphasizes the oneness of the human race, the capacity of man to develop his own powers and to arrive at inner harmony and the establishment of a peaceful world" (Fromm 1966:13). Like the existentialists and phenomenologists before him, he really believed that human beings could penetrate their cultural fictions and private illusions to arrive, ultimately, at a "true" grasp of reality itself. Such a grasp, achieved by humanistic social science and communicated to all by humanistic education, would culminate in the salvation of humanity and the arrival of the long-heralded *messianic* era of world history. This would be a salvation accomplished — not by an external God, but by human beings themselves. In this sense, and in this sense only, did Fromm mean that "men" could be as gods.

References for Chapter Twenty

Erich Fromm. 1941. *Escape from Freedom*. New York: Rinehart.
————. 1950. *Psychoanalysis and Religion*. New Haven: Yale University Press.
————. 1955a. *The Sane Society*. Toronto: Clarke, Irwin.
————. 1955b *The Dogma of Christ*. New York: Holt, Rinehart and Winston.
————. 1957. *The Art of Loving*. London: George Allen and Unwin.
————. 1962. *Beyond the Chains of Illusion: My Encounter with Marx and Freud*. New York: Simon and Schuster.

_____. 1965. Introduction, and The Application of Humanist Psychoanalysis to Marx's Theory. In *Socialist Humanism*. Edited by Erich Fromm. Garden City, NY: Doubleday, p. vii-xii and 207-22.

_____. 1966. *You Shall Be as Gods: A Radical Interpretation of the Old Testament and Its Tradition*. New York: Holt, Rinehart and Winston.

_____. 1968a. *The Revolution of Hope: Toward a Humanized Technology*. New York: Harper & Row.

_____. 1968b. On the Nature of Man. In *The Nature of Man*. Edited by Erich Fromm and Ramón Xirau. New York: Macmillan, p. 306-12.

_____. 1970. *The Crisis of Psychoanalysis*. New York: Holt, Rinehart and Winston.

_____. 1986. *For the Love of Life*. Translated by Robert and Rita Kimber. Edited by Hans Jurgen Schultz. New York: The Free Press, Macmillan.

Twenty-One

The Genetic Developmentalism
of Jean Piaget

A Pantheist, not a solipsist, the child cooperates
With a universe of large and noisy feeling-states
Without troubling to place
Them anywhere special, for, to his eyes, Funny Face or Ele-
     phant as yet
Mean nothing. His distinction between Me and Us
Is a matter of taste; his seasons are Dry and Wet;
He thinks as his mouth does.
                    — W.H. Auden, "Mundus et Infans"

There were a number of thoughtful Europeans in the generation following Huxley who tried to make a stand against the twentieth-century tide of irrationalism. A powerful voice in support of the integrity of science was that of Jean Piaget of Switzerland. Building on the insights of Rousseau on education — and consciously following in the footsteps of Spencer, Durkheim, Santayana and Dewey — Jean Piaget set out to create a modern naturalistic philosophy of knowledge based on science rather than introspection and untestable absolutes. And he visualized an interdisciplinary social science, firmly grounded in biology, which would be capable of testing the questions posed by such a philosophy. A true eclectic, Piaget borrowed freely from Kant, Marx and Bergson as well as from the child psychologist J.M. Baldwin, whose work he considered to be a refinement of the insights of Spencer and Dewey. He was also strongly influenced by Einstein's theory of relativity and no doubt hoped to effect a corresponding revolution in the study of humanity.

From this intellectual base Piaget set out on a massive task. He sought to forge an updated Spencerian system of thought concerning (1) the development of the human being as a knowledge-builder; (2) the genetic evolution of the species; and (3) the relationship between the two. One measure of his success is the fact that the theory created by this lifelong effort has functioned as a

References for this chapter are on p. 379.

guiding framework for empirical research in cognitive psychology for over six decades.

The shaping of an empirical systematizer

Jean Piaget was born in 1896 in Neuchâtel, Switzerland, and was something of a child prodigy. By the age of sixteen he had published the results of his biological observations in a number of scientific journals, and was employed part-time in a museum. He credited his father, a local historian and scholar of medieval literature, with his early training in critical thinking and systematic thought. His mother seems to have functioned as a more negative model. In recalling her neuroses, he wrote, "I have always detested any departure from reality . . . [and] have always preferred the study of normality and the workings of the intellect to that of tricks of the unconscious" (Evans:106-107).

The two major crises of the young Jean's adolescence had to do with his emergence from the cocoon of a tradition-defined reality. The process began when he encountered his first formal religious instruction. "Two things struck me at the time: on the one hand, the difficulty of reconciling a number of dogmas with biology, and on the other, the fragility of the 'five proofs' of the Existence of God" (ibid.:110). A book belonging to his father on the evolution of dogmas delighted him at this stage. It must have made him realize, for the first time, that ideas are passed along in the culture somewhat as genes are in the species.

The second crisis of belief was precipitated by an introduction to Bergson's concept of "creative evolution." "The identification of God with life itself was an idea that stirred me almost to ecstasy because it now enabled me to see in biology the explanation of all things" (ibid.:111). From that moment the problem of how humans can come to know about the genesis and functioning of this wonderful life became paramount for Piaget.

He decided to study biology at the University of Neuchâtel. It is probable that he became acquainted at once with the theories of Herbert Spencer, as the *Principles of Biology* would have been required reading in universities of the period. All of Piaget's subsequent theorizing suggests the results of an early immersion in Spencer's thought, as well as that of Bergson, Durkheim and Santayana. He later remembered reading and writing voraciously during the years from 1914 to 1918 — to the point of physical exhaustion. ("I could not think without writing.") He was particularly impressed by a teacher who emphasized the relationship between Aristotelian logic and biological processes. This caused him to reject Bergson's notion of a necessary dualism between the vital and logical aspects of reality. A closer reading of Bergson had already left him disenchanted. "I got the impression of an ingenious construction without an experimental basis. Between biology and the analysis of knowledge I needed something other than philosophy . . . psychology!" (ibid.:

111). So he turned instead to the writings of the American pragmatists, and began to develop Dewey's idea that " action itself admits of logic" (ibid.:113).

Pioneering developmental psychology

In 1918 Piaget obtained a doctorate in science. From 1919 to 1921 he studied at the Sorbonne in Paris, focusing on pathological psychology, logic and the philosophy of science. He also worked at Alfred Binet's laboratory, standardizing Cyril Burt's reasoning tests on Parisian children. Burt of England and Binet of France were the pioneers of IQ testing. Piaget began analyzing the children's *wrong* answers, looking for regularities and noticed that at similar ages they tended to make the very same mistakes. Detailed recording and comparing of observations indicated a definite pattern of development in the way children attacked problems. It seemed as if they were building their own mental tools. When each major concept was completed there was a marked leap forward in the ease with which the child in question could handle similar problems. Piaget's observations seemed to support the proposition that logic is not inborn, as Kant had thought, but develops little by little with appropriate experience.

Piaget's next move was to the Institut J.J. Rousseau at Geneva. In 1923, he married a fellow researcher, Valentine Chatênay. The couple's three children, born from 1925 to 1931, were probably the most minutely and systematically observed infants in history. As Piaget recounted, "I learned in the most direct way how intellectual operations are prepared by sensorimotor action, even before the appearance of language" (ibid.:128). During the next decade he published the results of the couples' research (both at home and at work) in *The Language and Thought of the Child, The Child's Conception of the World, The Child's Conception of Causality, Judgement and Reasoning in the Child* and *The Moral Judgement of the Child*.

We will never know the extent of Valentine Chatênay's contribution to developmental psychology, nor what it might have been had she not married and assumed the role of full-time homemaker. As in the better-known case of the Einsteins, the cultural limitations on opportunities for women ensured that it would be the male partner who became widely acclaimed as an authority on child development.

We do know that Jean — with Valentine's continuing support — was in considerable demand as a lecturer from that time on. He recalled speaking to an audience of psychoanalysts during this period, in the presence of Freud. He noticed with amusement that everyone watched the master and responded only to his responses to the speech. "I was addressing the public, but the public never glanced at the lecturer. . . . When Freud smiled everybody in the room smiled, when Freud looked serious, everybody . . . looked serious" (ibid.:3). So much for critical thinking in the psychology of the period!

On the stages of cognitive development

Piaget had by now identified four stages in the development of a child's reasoning abilities from infancy to adulthood. And he had concluded that, although the sequence of development seems invariant, the rate at which children progress through the stages depends on the nature of their interaction with the physical and social surroundings. He called the stages the "sensorimotor," the "pre-operational," the "concrete operational" and the "formal operational." Understandably, these are reminiscent of Spencer's "presentative," "presentative-representative," "representative" and "re-representative" stages, and of Santayana's four realms in the "life of reason."

Piaget believed that, during the sensorimotor phase, infants are involved in mastering the objects in the surrounding environment. Their behaviour is at first dominated by instinctive nutritional drives. Then motor habits and percepts gradually develop, along with the intuition of object-permanence and the first specific emotions accompanying the newly differentiated spatial context. The child gradually comes to see movements as causal, and to recognize spatial dimensions and the separate identity of surrounding objects.

The pre-operational level is achieved at somewhere around the age of eighteen months to two years. This is the period of spontaneous and specifically differentiated affective responses, during which the child establishes the limits — first, of the self, and subsequently, of the physical and social world. It also marks the appearance of the symbolic function, initially in the form of imitative play and imagery, and then gradually, in language. This makes representational thought possible. Children at this level still cannot perform mental operations; that is, internalized actions that are *reversible* (like adding and subtracting) and *transitive* (like knowing that if A is less than B and B is less than C then C is greater than A). And they still have no concept of time other than an intuition controlled by movement through positions in space. Chiefly, what seems to be involved at this stage is a mastery of symbols.

By the age of seven most children have succeeded in establishing the beginnings of the connected logical operations of transitivity, reversibility and reciprocity; that is, they have mastered relations, number and classes. These involve the comparative notion that is necessary for sequencing and for understanding that seriation can be viewed from both directions, and that groups can be formed on the basis of a number of attributes or dimensions. This marks the onset of logical reasoning, and of a sense of time as duration. It also marks the capacity for empathy and perspective in social relations, and of the notion of the function of rules and therefore the possibility of cooperation.

During the formal operational stage (beginning at about the age of eleven) the child's distinctive personality begins to take recognizable shape. Here we find the emergence of an ability to operate on operations, or to manipulate symbolic relations in logical ways. Algebra is a good example of this. Implications can now be deduced from premises and generalizations inferred from experience. Principles can be identified and applied to various concrete situations. Ideals and future goals can be formulated and theories designed and tested in terms of consequences. Ideas can be separated from the person expressing them and assessed on their merits. Thought itself is finally mastered.

On the transactional nature of intelligence

Piaget saw these four stages as way stations in the process by which the individual structures meaning (or schemes of internal action). Initially these schemes are intuitions which have evolved by means of the organism's thrusts into the environment. What Piaget seems to be discussing here are Russell's implicit or "self-confirming" beliefs — which inevitably reflect ontological structures — or the "animal faith" of Schopenhauer, James and Santayana. They make possible further perception or "taking in" of the surroundings. Whereas both traditional empiricism and Bergsonian Gestalt psychology tried to explain intelligence by means of perception (of either associated sensations or "whole" images) Piaget did the opposite. Unlike Kant, however, he claimed that all perception involves the application or elaboration of intuitive schemes of action, or "a more or less rapid organization of sensorial data as a function of an ensemble of acts or movements" (Piaget 1953:390). Or, in somewhat different terms, "All perception is an accommodation . . . of schemata which have required, for their construction, systematic work of assimilation and organization" (ibid.).

For Piaget, memory is a function of the child's operational capacity as well. He thought that memory could not possibly be "pure" in the Bergsonian sense; nor could it be merely a storing of sensations and images reflecting encountered reality. He agreed, instead, with Pavlov, Dewey and Mead — that memory must constitute a recording within the organs of intelligence established in the nervous system, of coordinated responses to the environment. Therefore childhood memories are not likely to be in strict accordance with the facts as experienced by participating adults. Rather they will reflect the situation as chewed up and digested by the child's primitive cognitive organs.

Piaget expected that his theory would stand or fall on the empirical evidence. Early on, he devised indicators of levels of cognitive development in order to test the model's adequacy. These are measures of conservation and classification abilities. Classification involves sorting objects into groups of increasing abstraction and inclusiveness on the basis of an increasing number of qualities or dimensions. It involves, as well, the quantifying concept of relations: from the ability to orient objects in space and to connect cause and effect in their movements to the ability to order them in series and make comparisons on the basis of different criteria.

Associated with classification is the concept of conservation of matter. This develops from a recognition of object-permanence to the gradual understanding that objects do not gain or diminish in quantity, weight, area or volume at will — or because certain aspects of their appearance such as form and shape happen to change. In other words, a ball of modelling clay does not change quantity when it is divided into a number of variously shaped small pieces, nor when it is formed again into a ball. This recognition requires an ability to coordinate perspectives and to compensate for alterations in the various dimensions of an object.

Piaget identified certain specific skills as indicative of the transition from one stage of intellectual development to another. Research based on standard tasks derived from these began to be carried out all over the world. The objective was to determine whether (1) the *sequential* development posited by the theory holds across varying ages and cultures; (2) the *rate* and *extent* of development through the sequence varies according to cultural milieu; and (3) the *feeling of necessity* concerning logical relations at each stage (indicating closure) is universally experienced with the mastery of the relevant set of action-schemes or concepts. The first hypothesis has been strongly confirmed, in countless studies over many years. As to the second, cross-cultural research seems to indicate that, while the sequence is invariant, the rate and extent of development is highly correlated with degree of technological sophistication in the society. Some groups do not achieve the fourth stage ever. The evidence concerning the third claim is still not at all clear because of the difficulty in distinguishing between a continuous and discontinuous learning process, and therefore of ever falsifying the hypothesis.

Piaget felt sufficiently warranted by the results of ongoing research to continue elaborating his theory. He defined intelligence simply as "the construction of relationships" (ibid.:418): relationships which then serve as tools or incipient organs for the very thinking process which in turn refines and elaborates them. He saw the same kind of process operating from the simple reflex to the most complex conceptualization. He believed that reflexes constitute a utilization by the species of experience somehow stored and passed on in the genes and forming elementary schemes upon which intelligence is built. Like Spencer, he viewed intelligence as the extension of biological evolution, and saw no reason to postulate a mind/body dualism.

On the contingent nature of moral development

Similarly, Piaget recognized no dualism of reason and emotion, nor of intelligence and morality. Emotion fuels the operation of intelligence, he said, while morality cannot exist except in tandem with it. Indeed, in Piaget's model, for every advance in moral functioning, a corresponding level of reasoning ability is a necessary, though not sufficient, concomitant. He saw morality as a system of internally constructed rules, and moral development, like cognitive, as the means by which these rules are established and tested in action. However, he was always careful not to speak of structured stages or even an invariant sequence in the moral sphere. He referred, instead, to two opposite poles of a continuum of development: from "heteronomy," where the adult is seen as an absolute authority (and to be good means to obey), to "autonomy" where goodness is seen in terms of satisfactory ends guided by principles. These terms were taken from Kant, but used very differently in this context.

Piaget claimed that the relationship between the *practice* and *consciousness* of rules is what alters as the child develops in a moral and intellectual sense. The infant begins at the level where behaviour is shaped by impulse and motor habit; rules are not coercive in character, either because they are purely motor or are experienced as unique events not transferrable to other situations. At the next level we find an "egocentrism" where the child imitates the rule-following behaviour of others in idiosyncratic ways, leading to a "moral realism" (recognized much earlier by Martineau, Spencer and Mead) in which rules are felt as sacred and unchangeable elements of nature. Then comes an incipient orientation towards cooperation, as rules are gradually perceived as means for mutual control of behaviour so that group goals are obtainable. Finally, most adolescents arrive at the stage where they begin to develop the ability to codify and evaluate rules, and to apply them hypothetically.

Piaget emphasized that moral development does not just happen. It requires, at each level, certain prerequisite reasoning abilities — the continuing development of which, in turn, depends upon appropriate environmental influences. And it requires, as well, carefully structured social interaction that does not force the child into age-inappropriate response patterns. On this point Piaget departed radically from "innatists" or "maturationists" like Rousseau, and from Noam Chomsky and many "humanistic" psychologists in recent times.

Ultimate goals and assumptions

Piaget's career took a significant turn in 1929 when he became Professor of History of Scientific Thought at the University of Geneva. He also continued as co-director of the Institut J.J.Rousseau, taught experimental psychology one day a week at the University of Lausanne and served as director of the Bureau International Office de l'Éducation. In spite of all these demands, he was able, for the first time, to focus on epistemology. He wrote later, "For ten successive years I studied intensively the emergence and history of the principal concepts of math, physics, and biology. Secondly, I resumed, on a larger scale than before, the research on child psychology" (Evans:132). He was finally in a position to pursue the goal that had beckoned since adolescence, and for which he had considered his psychological research but a preparation. The problem driving him was a daunting one. He wanted to discover the nature of the relationship among three vital processes: growth of cognitive functioning in the individual; historical changes in the content and structure of scientific knowledge; and the biological evolution of the species.

Like Spencer, Piaget was seeking a comprehensive and systematic theory of human knowledge, but he hoped to ground it more solidly than was possible in Spencer's time, in the empirical findings of biology and psychology. He had never studied child psychology as an end in itself. He had seen it as the only means available for understanding how primitive people must have have experienced their world. But he had come to the study powerfully shaped by past experience. The hypotheses that had guided him through his years of observation and experimentation — the very questions he asked — were shaped for good or ill by five fundamental premises concerning the nature of reality. It is necessary to identify these at this point, for Piaget himself reminded us that his theory of psychological development "is impossible to understand if one does not begin by analyzing in detail the biological presuppositions from which it stems and the epistemological consequences in which it ends" (Boden:introduction).

Perhaps the most significant premise influencing Piaget's work was the Hegelian-Marxist principle of the *dialectic* as the necessary pattern of historical change, which he combined with Spencer's biological concept of "equilibration." The second was the notion of *praxis*: the idea of the organism as an essentially active participant in the evolutionary as well as the knowing process. This originated with Rousseau, was interpreted in philosophical and economic terms by Marx, and was justified on psychological and biological grounds by Dewey and the earlier pragmatists. The third was the premise that *construction*, rather than the alternative of either structure or function, is the fundamental process involved in evolution.

The fourth philosophical premise rested on the Spencerian postulate of a continuity between the evolution of life forms and that of intelligence. It was the Durkheimian conviction concerning the essential *unity of science* and of the need for an interdisciplinary focus — especially in those studies dealing with the nature of human life and its social products.

Lastly there was a strictly biological assumption: the one to which Spencer had clung so stubbornly and with such unfortunate consequences for social science. Piaget was similarly committed to an updated version of the belief in *the inheritance of acquired characteristics*: the possibility that improved structural potential is somehow extracted from the adaptive behaviour of individuals and fed back into the genetic code to enrich subsequent generations.

An evolutionary theory of knowledge

Even in his earliest publications on the nature of child development, Piaget was already explaining what he had observed as the adaptation of "self-regulating structures developing by equilibratory processes of assimilation and equilibration" (ibid.:5). Not only did he see cognitive development and biological evolution in terms of such adaptation; it was, for him, the universal pattern by which knowledge evolves as well. He surmised that all mental growth and knowledge-construction develops according to the principle of equilibration, which coordinates the interaction of maturational and environmental effects at progressively higher states of equilibrium. He was convinced that this model satisfactorily resolves the old nature/nurture problem, in that it "presents a dialectical solution halfway between empiricism and innatism" (Piatelli-Palmarini:351).

In each of the disciplines of biology, psychology and philosophy, Piaget viewed his own position as a synthesis transcending previously accepted theses and antitheses. At the most general level he believed that "In each . . . the thesis posits genesis without structure [and] the antithesis posits structuralism without genesis" (Boden:7). Piaget felt that he was offering a synthesis focusing on a genetically based structuring process, which he usually called "constructivism."

In psychology he equated all behaviourist theories with an old-fashioned associationism which he traced to Hume. This was the thesis which he saw in opposition to the antithesis of a Bergsonian-derived Gestalt psychology. He explained that the first theory emphasized the parts and neglected the whole, while the second erred in the opposite direction. Piaget's synthesis viewed the whole, as did Durkheim's, as a *system of relations* holding among the parts. He considered that a similar fruitless conflict had emerged in philosophy between positivism and phenomenology. His suggested synthesis in this case was, in effect, an updated and reformulated version of pragmatism. He was of the opinion that positivism still clung to traditional realism which defined science as the progressive discovery of the "true" nature of an objective reality, while existentialism and phenomenology continued to hark back to the old idealist notion of the subject as the creator of reality.

Piaget's "genetic epistemology" (a term borrowed from J.M. Baldwin) was based, instead, on Dewey's concept of "transaction": the idea that human *knowledge* of reality (not reality itself) is constructed by the knower acting upon, and being acted upon, by the environment. An objective reality external to the knower is assumed but cannot be known other than in terms of its logical relations, the patterning of which is presumably reflected in the regularities encountered in the process of interaction and simultaneously transformed into internal schemes of action. This represents both a recognition and resolution of Russell's epistemological problem. "The theory of knowledge is essentially a theory of adaptation of thoughts to reality, even if this adaptation at last reveals, as does every adaptation, the existence of an inextricable interaction between subject and object" (Piaget 1971b:24).

Piaget was critical of both the modern logical positivism and existential phenomenology for attempting to limit scientific inquiry to the inorganic, or so-called "natural world"; and for denying the behavioural studies the right to be scientific. All reality — including human life and its cultural products — is natural, he claimed. And all aspects of that nature are equally open to disciplined inquiry. Furthermore, he confessed to "a complete aversion with respect to existentialism, which blurs all values and degrades man by reducing freedom to arbitrary choice and thought to self-affirmation" (Boden:106).

Piaget specifically identified the operation of the dialectic where logic is concerned. He claimed that, previously, the only choice has been either to join the modern phenomenologists in viewing logic as the expression of Platonic universals existing pre-formed in some non-natural dimension and mirrored in a similarly non-natural mind; or to agree with the logical positivists in their belief that logic is a mere syntax containing the tautological relations employed in human thought, and having no necessary connection to external reality. He suggested, however, that his own synthesis marked an advance on both positions. He saw logic as the expression, in symbolic form, of the operation of human intelligence as it acts upon external reality and responds to the effects of that action.

Equilibration as the vehicle of evolution

We find another example of Piaget's use of the dialectic in his theory of biological evolution. He liked to claim that he had transcended the conflicting positions of Lamarckism and Darwinism. He believed that it is possible for negative signals from the environment — representing deficiencies in the organism's functioning — to sensitize the genes regulating epigenesis. He saw this as due to a disturbance of the system of equilibrium resulting from the registered dysfunction: a disturbance which would lead, in turn, "to the production of mutations, through its [the system's] inevitable connection with the genes responsible for hereditary transmission" (Piaget 1980:67). The environment, invariably altered by behaviour, thus acts only indirectly on evolutionary selection. For Piaget it is the initial behaviour rather than the environmental response that operates as the motor fuelling the entire process.

In Piaget's hands Spencer's principle of equilibration became a thoroughly dialectical notion: an expression of the dynamic between the internal and external. It became the coordinating process synthesizing ongoing maturation with incoming environmental impact and thereby increasing the viability and comprehensiveness of adaptation. "At each level of development there are two poles of activity: changes in the structure of the organism in response to environmental intrusion (accommodation) and changes in the intruding stimuli due to the existing structure (assimilation)" (Piaget 1967:xii).

Piaget thought that the dialectical synthesis of opposites occurs by means of self-regulating mechanisms operating on the basis of feedback. This process, he explained, is common to biological evolution, psychological development and the growth of scientific knowledge. He saw it as the crucial key for understanding all three, and for any general theory of evolution capable of incorporating them all.

On the organism as an active participant in nature's conditioning

The idea of *praxis*, or of activity as a necessary or given attribute of living organisms, is also central to Piaget's theory. He believed that adaptation, at any of the three levels, begins with explorations or trials into the environment; that is, with behaviour which is actively self-directed rather than passively responsive to external stimuli. "Praxis or action is not [merely] some sort of movement but rather a system of coordinated movements functioning for a result or an intention" (Piaget 1976:64). It is caused by an inner compulsion to re-establish or strengthen equilibrium.

Piaget disagreed with the old empiricist idea that knowledge could be based on either sensation or perception alone, arguing, as had Dewey, that "We can get to know objects only by acting on them" (Piaget 1967:128). He said that Marx "quite rightly went so far as to consider perception itself as an 'activity' of the sense organs" (Piaget 1970:76). The same principle applies to sensation. Knowledge, claimed Piaget, "never stems from sensation alone but from what action adds to this" (Piaget 1971b:64). He noted that "the work of the pragmatists had revealed the role of action in the constitution of all mental operations" (Piaget 1970:147). And he considered Rousseau's great contribution to education to have been the insight that the teacher cannot hope to succeed without utilizing the child's natural urge to action. Piaget's own goal was to build on the ideas of Rousseau, Marx and the pragmatists and to provide tested explanations of the precise nature of this essential human characteristic so that a future educational science could apply his findings.

On the nature of evolution

A final thread connecting and shaping all of Piaget's work is his preference for Spencer's theory of evolution over that of Darwin. Indeed, he could be termed "the last of the Spencerian thinkers." Piaget simply could not believe that chance mutations play the comprehensive role in evolution attributed to them by modern Darwinian biologists. He visualized instead an internal "equilibrating" process mediating between current phenotypic variation and underlying genotypic change. He thought that this was somehow associated with the inheritance of reflex activity and of complex instincts, but he was puzzled about why the latter would have been accomplished so much more successfully for the "lower" than the "higher" animals. He admitted that this is an anomaly with which his progress-oriented theory could not deal.

Like Spencer before him, Piaget believed that his position represented an advance on Lamarckism. He postulated not simply a direct transmission of characteristics acquired by each generation, but a complex feedback mechanism consisting of retroactive repercussions of generational losses of equilibrium. This feedback sensitizes the regulating genes themselves, making certain mutations more likely than others, so that specific variations favouring a return to equilibrium will tend to result for descendants.

Piaget thought that the "phenocopy" (a unique configuration of successfully adapted phenotypic variation) figures largely in the process. His suggestion was that the adaptive behaviours of the successful individual

> occasions an opposition . . . between the requirements of an unaccustomed or altered environment and those of the processes of epigenetic development directed by a hereditary program. The resulting disequilibriums, which will in some cases end up in sensitizing the genes regulating epigenesis, will then trigger off a process of re-equilibration which will take the form of mutations directed at the zone of disequilibrium. These mutations, in turn . . . will ultimately take on forms analogous to those of the . . . [phenocopy]. (Piaget 1980:101)

In all this, Piaget considered himself a follower of well-known early twentieth-century biologists such as C.H. Goldschmidt and Richard Waddington. He believed (somewhat mistakenly) that they were anti-Darwin. He was absolutely convinced that their work supported his conclusion that "in animals, evolutionary transformations of adaptive significance (not, therefore, just any mutation) are closely bound up with new patterns of behaviour" (ibid.:113). He believed that adaptation for the organism and its behaviours is, in effect, a kind of trial-and-error process, and that it is the total *pattern of adaptive behaviours* that is selected or discarded by evolutionary trial and error.

Evolutionary thinkers such as George Herbert Mead and Julian Huxley had disagreed with Spencer's confusion of biological and cultural evolution. Both had pointed out that, in the first case, it is the *genoptype* which evolves by means of the natural selection of favourable phenotypic variations, whereas, in the second case, the human *culture* evolves through the natural selection of favourable behaviours — including verbal ones expressing powerful ideas. Apparently Piaget was returning to Spencer's view that the individual's self-directed trial-and-error forays into the environment (in conjunction with environmental changes wrought thereby) are the causal factors for both levels of evolution, and that it is the sensation of disequilibrium which initiates these forays. He conceded that mutations play a role and that interaction between organism and environment is fundamental. But he insisted that the impetus for evolutionary change is the individual as the *source* of action — not the environmental *consequences* of that action.

In this insistence on the organism as initiator, Piaget seems (uncharacteristically) to have been viewing causality in evolution as linear. He seems to be defining it in terms of the "chicken and egg" question, with himself focusing on the chicken, whereas Darwin had focused on the egg. One would expect that the notion of contingency, or "systems feedback," would render meaningless the old argument of whether organism or environment is the originator of adaptive activity.

Biological evolution and psychological development

Piaget extended his explanation of biological evolution to that of intelligence and to what he saw as the inextricably related process of knowledge-building. At both the biological and psychological levels the adaptive process is one of continuous assimilation of internally mediated consequences of the organism's action on the environment and the resulting accommodation of these action schemes into the previously formed structures. Piaget emphasized two important differences between the two, however. First, while in both instances the *external* influences are encountered as challenges posed by the environment, the *internal* processes involved have different origins. "In the case of the biological phenocopy, they arise from the genome, but in the case of the phenocopy's cognitive equivalents, they arise only from the internal self-regulating mechanisms of the individual subject" (ibid.:89). Although similarly organic in nature, indicators of cognitive disequilibrium (as distinct from the biological) do not extend to the genome and are therefore not hereditary, in Piaget's view.

Here he was clearly parting company with Spencer, whose notion that psycho-social attributes are heritable had turned his theory into a tool for the justification of illusions of racial superiority. If successfully adaptive cognitive behaviours were indeed fed back into the genetic code, evolutionary time would be speeded up incredibly with the advance of civilization, and fortuitously placed members of today's advanced scientific-industrial cultures would be tomorrow's master race. Such a conclusion would have been morally abhorrent to Piaget; it would have been in conflict, as well, with much of the then-available evidence from intelligence testing, of which he was well aware.

In Piaget's model the feedback mechanism, allowing for environmental consequences of current behaviour to prejudice the genome in favour of specific compatible mutations, operates only over the long term of organic evolution and only in very indirect and unpredictable ways. On the other hand, where psychological development is concerned, there is a direct and immediate alteration in cognitive/affective schema resulting from forays into the environment. It is indicated by stage-like leaps in ability to handle the tools of knowing, as the child grows.

This means that *during the individual life span* one would expect that a complex and demanding environment would indeed influence the rate and extent of intellectual and moral development. But, for Piaget, this does not mean that the culturally challenged are *genetically* superior, because cognitive schemes — although built upon an inherited reflex system involving intellectual potential — are not themselves inherited. These elemental intuitions, along with the symbolic function emerging from them and subsequently integrated with them into concepts, are instead constructed as a result of ongoing interaction between organism and environment.

According to Piaget, a second difference between biological evolution and psychological development has to do with the nature of the action involved at the two levels. In the case of biological evolution only one adaptive process occurs: the organically sustaining aspects of external objects are directly assimilated and accommodated by the various digestive and circulatory organs. But with the operation of intelligence the adaptive process involves two kinds of abstraction; that is, it requires a more indirect and complex processing of environmental encounters by the activity of organs of the nervous system.

The first of these is *empirical*. It is derived from the qualities of the encountered objects: their weight, volume, size, texture, etc. The second is *reflexive*: drawn from the coordination of the subject's action upon the objects. Here Piaget is referring to logico-mathematical relations, or reasoning operations such as grouping, sequencing, adding and subtracting. Piaget seems to be refining Santayana's ideas here. He explained that the first type of mental activity contributes to the construction of qualitative logic (that of classes); the second to the quantitative logic of relations. The resulting logical forms provide the internal structuring for all knowledge of reality. "There can be no exogenous knowledge except that which is grasped, as content, by way of forms which are endogenous in origin" (ibid.:91).

Like Russell, Piaget believed that the culmination of all reflection is a pure state of the logical relations holding in nature: a "pure" genotype devoid of the content of the specific phenotypic variations from which it is derived — the ultimate being an algebraic equation expressing the laws of physics. This is what Schopenhauer had named "metalogical truth," and what Santayana referred to as the "realm of essence." Piaget noted that, where biological evolution is concerned, there can be no such content-free representation of the genotype. It can exist only through its various space-and-time-bound manifestations in actual living phenotypes. In the evolution of scientific knowledge the current state of the genotype can be directly assessed, whereas in biological evolution it can only be inferred from the genetic makeup of living organisms.

Cognitive development and the evolution
of scientific knowledge

Piaget hoped that he would be remembered most for his revolutionary contributions to epistemology. His goal had been to establish, once and for all, the connection between the individual's internal process of constructing instruments for knowing and the public process of building scientific knowledge. His studies of the history of knowledge and of child psychology had seemed to reveal an isomorphism between the child's evolving grasp of space, time and causality, and that of early humans as reflected in mythology and the first crude stirrings of scientific thought. He hypothesized that, if we could but comprehend the development of human reasoning from infancy onward, we would be in a position to understand the nature and genesis of human knowledge. At the very least, he hoped to challenge the credibility of any philosophy of knowledge that failed to deal with biological and psycho-social issues.

He explained that, just as science had its Copernican revolution, so too do we find, near the end of the early childhood phase, "a total decentration in relation to the original egocentric space" (Piaget 1976:16). Children no longer experience themselves as the centre of the universe, and objects that move beyond their view can still exist. Just as early humans conceived of surrounding objects as living and endowed with spirits, so too does the young child in the animistic stage see intention in the marble's movement, or in the wall that "hits" them. Just as early primitives saw purpose and design in every occurrence, with human-like gods in total control, so too does the child see no chance or coincidence in nature; "everything is 'made for' man . . . according to a wise plan with a human being at its centre" (Piaget 1967:25). Just as the ancient Greeks advanced a form of causality in which "the whole is explained by the composition of its parts" (ibid.:45), so too does the primary-school child tend to explain melting snow in terms of little balls of water encased in the flakes. And, like Vygotsky before him, Piaget recognized an isomorphism between the "essentialism" of Platonism, and the young child's belief that the word is an integral part of the object it denotes.

Piaget also saw a striking similarity between the development of the child's concept of time and that reflected in the evolution of physics. Before time is grasped operationally by children (at about the age of seven) they comprehend it only in localized terms. Duration is confused with the specific path traversed, and velocity is tied up with overtaking another object in space, regardless of whether the two began at the same place and time. Similarly, with Newtonian mechanics, space and time are absolutes, with velocity being a relationship between them. The concept of velocity as separable from concrete events in space is only possible once a mobile standard of duration such as the regular swinging of a clock pendulum is introduced as a measure, and "lived" intervals between events are rendered comparable. What is involved in the measure of time is "simultaneity": the intuition that when two objects begin and stop moving at the same instant, the one which has gone the farthest has moved the fastest. The child who has acquired a grasp of simultaneity is able to coordinate these two velocities, and thereby compare them. Simultaneity is, of course, always relative to the organic or physical instrument defining it.

Piaget explained that the principle behind Einstein's theory of relativity is really no different. "Einstein's refinements of the concept of time bear solely on non-simultaneity at a distance . . . simultaneity, in the case of great velocities, depends purely on the relative motions of the observer and the phenomena he observes as well as their distance apart . . . the measurement of duration itself will depend on the coordination of these velocities" (Piaget 1971c:306). For Piaget, relativistic time was simply an extension to the case of the velocity of light of a principle that underlies the universal human process of constructing a workable concept of time.

According to Piaget, the very structures of logic stem from connections in the environment reflected by coordinations of action established within the subject in the process of interaction with that environment. Unlike the structuralists within traditional anthropology, sociology and psychology, he was a *constructivist*. He conceived of an active process of construction by the subject, rather than of static structures existing either pre-formed in the mental organs (as implied by Claude Lévi-Strauss and Talcott Parsons and spelled out by Noam Chomsky) or perceived as "wholes" (as in Gestalt psychology). And, for Piaget, what are being constructed are the logico-mathematical forms that function as the very foundations of intelligence and morality.

On the unity of science and the role of philosophy

Piaget suggested that the fact that science becomes more logical in form as it evolves from crude conjecture to the symbolic representations of particle physics is no accident. Why should it not, he asked, given that the knower and the known are aspects of the same underlying conditions of nature? "I, for one, have always maintained that the surprising adaptation of mathematics to physical reality was not only due to the actions that the organism and subject carry out on objects external to them, but to an endogenous source; . . . since the organism is itself also a physiochemical object, its actions and reactions are from the outset transparently dependent on the physical universe, because, through its very inner structure, the organism participates in and obeys the laws of this universe" (Piatelli-Palmarini:283).

This is a compelling statement of Piaget's philosophy of evolutionary naturalism. It is the clearest justification possible for his commitment to the principle of the *unity of science* and for his criticism of those schools of philosophy that continue to refuse to take the social sciences seriously and to base their claims on empirical evidence.

Piaget sometimes mused about the possibility that we are witnessing a strange sort of sociological artifact where modern philosophy is concerned. He was referring to the development, within academia, of a privileged caste of philosophers claiming possession of some mysterious capacity to deal directly with the sum of all reality: all this in the absence of any familiarity whatsoever with the process or results of controlled research in obviously relevant fields. He noted that, whereas the great philosophers of the past all contributed to, or at least learned from, the science of their times, "today we are training specialists in transcendentalism who are then able to leap straight into the world of essences with an ease enormously increased by the fact that they are innocent of any forms of scientific specialization, even in psychology" (Piaget 1970:59).

In opposition to all such pretensions to splendid isolationism, Piaget was a strong proponent of the interdisciplinary approach to biological and human studies. He deplored the trend, clearly accelerating as the century wore on, towards an academic compartmentalization of the social-scientific and philosophical pursuits, and of the various competing schools of thought within these.

Tentative assessments

Most of Piaget's later works deal with either biology or philosophy. The last thirty years of his life brought widespread international recognition. He was awarded honorary degrees from numerous universities, including the Sorbonne, Harvard, Brussels and Brazil. He was appointed to the Executive Council of UNESCO and honoured by the American Psychological Association. He served for many years as Director of the International Centre for Genetic Epistemology, and in 1971 became Professor Emeritus of the University of Geneva. He continued to publish books until he was well into his seventies, and remained intellectually active until his death in 1980.

In assessing Piaget's contributions to social-scientific thought, one must return to his goals. He once wrote that the best theory "always aims at the maximum integration of the . . . previous ones and simply adds . . . such retroactive corrections as may be necessary" (Piaget 1971a:357). His entire life's work can only be understood in the light of his desire to create that one best theory for the study of humanity. He had hoped that his genetic epistemology would provide a philosophical foundation capable of incorporating diverse and conflicting schools of thought within a common conceptual framework. He believed that his model of cognitive development provided that framework and the common terminology that would eventually make possible the replication of hypotheses from a variety of apparently conflicting perspectives within the social sciences.

This may well be happening. Developmental and child psychology seem to be dominated by Piagetian concepts and research designs. And to a considerable extent Piaget's theory influences the questions asked by modern cognitive science, information theory, cybernetics and neuropsychology. His epistemology is, in many ways, a thoughtful elaboration and refinement of pragmatism, and Piagetian research on child development has been a boon to education — whenever it has been understood and used appropriately. His clarification of Vygotsky's and Luria's research in language acquisition and subsequent incorporation of this into cognitive theory has been of great value. And there is widespread recognition of the value of Piaget's pioneering work on the universal sequential nature of cognitive development and its relationship to moral functioning.

But there are critics as well. There seems to be a curious disjunction between the unquestionable breakthrough in child development and the obvious failure of Piagetian research in general to produce a cumulative body of reliable knowledge. The answer to the puzzle may lie in the nature of the model offered by Piaget as the *explanation* of the rich store of documented regularities in cognitive development. His theory of equilibration seems to have proven incapable of generating predictions of future regularities that are clearly refutable.

Even more worrying, for Piagetian researchers, is the fact that one of the key biological premises on which the theory is based seems to have been discredited by genetics and molecular biology. Modern evolutionary theorists maintain that the structural integrity of developmental sequences does indeed cause genetic change to tend to spiral or snowball in certain directions. Nevertheless, this is not because the direction is determined from within the organism, or by the effects of a phenocopy — as an *entity* — on its surroundings. It still seems likely that change occurs through the selection of favourable mutations. One could argue that only the definition of *favourable* is altered as a result of the effect on the total system of the spiral of previous accumulations; that there is no radical change in the nature of the process. We would expect the same to hold for individual development.

However, this in no way diminishes Piaget's monumental contribution to our understanding of individual intellectual, linguistic and moral development, and the relation between the growth of these cognitive operations and the evolution of knowledge. Furthermore, whatever the final verdict on his theory as a whole, one conclusion at least seems warranted. Modern social science would be much less interdisciplinary in organization, less scientific in methodology, and less soundly grounded in the philosophy of evolutionary naturalism if it were not for the work of Jean Piaget.

References for Chapter Twenty-One

Boden, Margaret A. 1979. *Jean Piaget*. New York: Viking Press.

Evans, Richard I. 1973. *Jean Piaget: The Man and His Ideas*. Translated by Eleanor Duckworth. New York: E.P. Dutton.

Piaget, Jean. 1950. *The Moral Judgement of the Child*. London: Routledge and Kegan Paul.

_____. 1953. *The Origins of Intelligence in the Child*. London: Routledge and Kegan Paul.

_____. 1955. *The Language and Thought of the Child*. Translated by Marjorie Gabain. New York: Meridian Books.

_____. 1967. *Six Psychological Studies*. Translated by Anita Tenzer. Edited by David Elkind. New York: Random House.

_____. 1970. *Science of Education and the Psychology of the Child*. Translated by Derik Coltman. New York: Orion Press.

_____. 1971a. *Insights and Illusions of Philosophy*. Translated by Wolfe Mays. New York: World Publishing.

_____. 1971b. *Psychology and Epistemology: Towards a Theory of Knowledge*. Translated by Arnold Rosin. New York: Grossman.

_____. 1971c. *The Child's Conception of Time*. Translated by A.J. Pomerans. New York: Ballantyne Books.

_____. 1976. *The Child and Reality: Problems of Genetic Psychology*. Translated by Arnold Rosin. New York: Penguin Books.

_____. 1978. *Behavior and Evolution*. Trans. Donald Nicholson-Smith. New York: Pantheon Books.

_____. 1980. *Adaptation and Intelligence: Organic Selection and Phenocopy*. Chicago: University of Chicago Press.

Piatelli-Palmarini, Massimo, ed. 1980. *Language and Learning: The Debate between Jean Piaget and Noam Chomsky*. Cambridge, MA: Harvard University Press.

Rotman, Brian. 1977. *Jean Piaget: Psychologist of the Real*. New York: Cornell University Press.

Twenty-Two

Karl Popper and the Evolution of Scientific Knowledge

> The individual appears for an instant,
> joins the community of thought,
> modifies it — and dies;
> but the species, that dies not,
> reaps the fruit of his ephemeral existence.
> — A.S. Byatt, *Possession*

The troubled twentieth century had brought strange eddies into the stream of social-scientific thought. The irrationalism and subjectivism implied by certain of the ideas of Nietzsche, Bergson, Husserl and Sartre — and the authoritarian current in Marxism — seemed to promise either escape or permanent solutions to people who were everywhere in crisis. These ideas threatened to gain ascendancy over the rationality and realism of Durkheim, Santayana, Russell and Huxley, and the liberal-democratic and scientific impulse of Dewey and Mead. During the decades from 1920 to the end of the century it seemed at times that social theory had lost its way in a morass of intellectual nihilism and moral relativism.

However, a few voices remained steadfast in support of the potential of human reason and the ideals of freedom and justice. Arendt and Fromm, from within existentialism, saw the danger to humanity in that movement's essential pessimism and amorality. Piaget spoke up strongly for the universality of science. Another effective voice was that of Karl Popper. He was a courageous proponent of rationality and common sense in an age of intellectual dishonesty; of the open society in an age of totalitarianism; and of a revolutionary perspective on the nature of scientific knowledge in an age when science was increasingly misunderstood and feared.

References for this chapter are on p. 397-98.

The shaping of a critical inquirer

Karl Popper was born in Austria in 1902, the son of a radical liberal barrister who had been knighted by Emperor Francis Joseph. His father, Dr. Simon Siegmund Karl Popper, was the same age as Freud and had been a friend and admirer of the famous psychoanalyst. Karl was reared in an intellectual environment in which socialist ideals were paramount. By 1916 he was convinced of the wrongness of the German and Austrian cause in World War I. While a sixteen-year-old freshman at the University of Vienna he joined the Communist youth group. He was soon forced to question that decision, however. The callous and doctrinaire response of his fellow Communists to the deaths of a few of their number during a deliberately provocative action jolted him awake to the dangers of ideological thinking. He re-examined Marxist dogma and was horrified to realize that he "had accepted a dangerous creed uncritically, dogmatically" (Popper 1974a:26). Socialism held him for a further six years, and even at the end of his career we find him expressing the wistful thought that "if there could be such a thing as socialism combined with individual liberty, I would be a socialist still" (ibid.:27).

After university, Karl worked as a cabinet maker and social worker before being admitted, in 1925, to study at the new Pedagogic Institute. He earned his Ph.D. in 1928 with a thesis on the psychology of thinking. He was hired as a secondary-school teacher of maths and sciences and from there eventually moved into full-time work in philosophy at the University of Vienna.

A specific problem had drawn the young scholar into philosophy. Following his experience with Marxism, he had discovered that Freudian analysis and Alfred Adler's psychology suffered from the same deficiency. It had become apparent to him that they were dogmas rather than scientific theories. Then he had attended a lecture given by Einstein in 1919 and been immediately entranced. There was "the marvelous idea of a new cosmology — a finite but unbounded universe" (ibid.:29). But even more impressive was the great scientist's attitude of openness to refutation. "Einstein was looking for crucial experiments whose agreement with his predictions would by no means establish his theory; while a disagreement, as he was the first to stress, would show his theory to be untenable" (ibid.). Here was an approach to knowledge utterly different from that of Marx and Freud and their followers. Popper became intrigued by the question of the demarcation between ideological, or dogmatic, thinking and that which is critical or scientific.

On the nature of scientific knowledge

This issue led directly to the research that resulted in *The Logic of Scientific Discovery*, in which Popper presented an original solution to the demarcation problem. His ideas so impressed Herbert Feigl (then of the Vienna Circle of logical positivists) that the latter encouraged their publication. The book came out in 1934. By the following year Popper was getting international attention. He was invited to lecture at Bedford College, London, in 1935 and 1936. He had been ready to leave Austria for some time, having predicted totalitarianism in Germany and renewed war as early as 1929. In 1937 an offer came from the University of Canterbury in New Zealand. From there Popper helped to rescue a number of Austrian Jews, while there was still time. His own parents had been Jewish before their conversion to Christianity. Popper explained why he was not tempted, as were some intellectuals of Jewish background, to take up Judaism at that time in a demonstration of loyalty to his ancestry. He felt then, as always, that *all* ethnic pride is stupid, and that *all* nationalism, Jewish included, is evil.

It is not surprising that Popper's first book won acclaim. With the concise writing style that was to characterize his work for the next four decades, he set out to distinguish between science and non-science. He began by establishing the nature of his agreement and disagreement with the prevailing theoretical perspective within the philosophy of science: logical positivism and its more generally applied offshoot of linguistic analysis. He agreed that it is necessary to distinguish between meaningful and meaningless statements, and to substitute words for sensory data as objects of analysis. He appreciated the popular school's support for rationality and clarity of thought. But he believed the "analysts" were wrong in equating philosophical paradoxes with logical ones; that is, in assuming that all metaphysical problems could be reduced to logical and linguistic confusions. He also disagreed with their assumption that logical analysis is the *only* philosophical method and that one should always begin by analyzing "ordinary language."

Popper argued that there are indeed important metaphysical problems, especially epistemological ones having to do with the growth of knowledge and its relation to the nature of things. As for himself, he had chosen the metaphysical premise of realism: a faith in the existence of regularities in a world external to the subject. But he did not believe that the human being could ever *know* that particular assertions about these regularities are accurate "copies" of reality rather than merely the best guesses possible. Popper assumed that there could be no ultimate proof of the truth of assertions concerning the nature of reality. Indeed, for him, the very concept of proof is associated with logical rather than empirical statements. So it is not the *justification* of theories that concerns the scientist, but their *testability* "which is to say, their falsifiability" (Popper 1959:49).

Popper went on to explain that any scientific theory must be in the form of a universal statement capable of being refuted by experience. It has to be possible, by deducing inferences from the theory and attempting to match them against observations, to argue from the singular assertion or description of the observed event to the falsity of the universal statement. This is a strictly deductive inference even though it proceeds in the inductive direction. It is the "hypothetical-deductive" method. It means that although, as Hume had demonstrated, verification is not possible by the test of experience, falsification most certainly is! And it follows that the aim of the empirical method can never be to test for the *truth* of theories, but to corroborate them through failed attempts to prove them false. It must be "not to save the lives of untenable systems, but, on the contrary, to select the one which is by comparison the fittest, by exposing them all to the fiercest struggle for survival" (ibid.:42).

Popper identified the distinguishing characteristic of empirical conjectures, or theories, as their susceptibility to revision. They invite criticism, refutation and supersedence. "Theories are nets to catch what we call 'the world': to rationalize, to explain and to master it. We endeavour to make the mesh ever finer and finer" (ibid.:59). They are systems of causal explanation. As he put it, "To give a *causal explanation* of an event means to deduce a statement which describes it, using as premises of the deduction one or more *universal laws*, together with certain singular statements of the *initial conditions*" (ibid.:59). The explanation, once deduced, becomes a predictor of future events.

For example, he said, suppose the event requiring a causal explanation is the breakage of a thread. We have the universal law in the form of the hypothesis, "*If* a thread is loaded with a weight in excess of its tensile strength, *then* it will break." The singular statements describing initial conditions are "This particular thread can withstand one pound of weight" and "The weight put on this thread was two pounds."

Popper explained that empirical claims are always universal in nature and hypothetical in form. Rather than asserting that something exists in a specific time-space frame, they are expressed in a form that *denies* the possibility of certain occurrences, at *any* time and any place ("Thread cannot withstand a weight greater than its tensile strength"). This is why they are falsifiable. Strictly existential statements or expressions of logical relations ("There are threads" or "Two threads plus two more threads equals four threads") cannot be falsified, and are therefore non-empirical and either metaphysical or tautological.

To sum up Popper's argument: a theory, to be scientific, must clearly rule out certain possible occurrences, so that there will be no question whether or not it is indeed falsified if these events do, in fact, occur. The more a theory survives attempts to refute it, the more highly corroborated it becomes. It is thus increasingly reliable as a means of predicting future events, and one can more confidently hope that to some degree it reflects the regularities that are out there. But there is no guarantee that it is *true*.

Popper's epistemology is somewhat similar to that of pragmatism. This is not surprising, given that he cited Charles Peirce as an intellectual hero. However, like Santayana, he believed that the pragmatists had weakened their position by confusing corroboration with verisimilitude. "They . . . propose to define 'truth' in terms of the success of a theory — and thus its usefulness" (ibid.:275). He agreed that "it is not incorrect to say that science is . . . an 'instrument' whose purpose is . . . to predict from immediate or given experiences, later experiences, and even as far as possible to control them. But I do not think that this talk about experience contributes to clarity" (ibid.:100). In fact, for Popper, scientific theories are not *merely* instruments. "They are genuine conjectures about the world" (Popper 1983:110). For the neo-realist, they can be assumed to *approximate* truth even though the accuracy of that approximation can never be known. Popper was content to operate in the awareness that this is a necessary but unfalsifiable assumption of science, and not a "true" assertion as Russell would have it.

On the poverty of historicism

Very soon after completing this first book on the philosophy of science, Popper launched into a comprehensive and rigorously argued attack on "holistic" and "historicist" theorizing. He called it *The Poverty of Historicism*. He was referring to the approach which takes large-scale historical prophecy as the principal aim of the social studies. He was really trying to discover the reasons for the prevalence of non-scientific and pseudo-scientific thinking in these studies. He began with a statement of the thesis "that the belief in historical destiny is sheer superstition and that there can be no prediction of the course of human history by scientific or any other rational methods" (Popper 1936:v). In the introduction to a later edition Popper presented a logical argument that demolished the claims of the historicists at the very outset. It went as follows:

1. The course of human history is strongly influenced by the growth of scientific knowledge.
2. We cannot predict the future growth of scientific knowledge.
3. We therefore cannot predict the future course of human history.
4. This means that we must reject the very possibility of a scientific theory of historical development.
5. Therefore the fundamental aim of historicist methods is misconceived (ibid.:vii).

Popper pointed out that this argument does not refute the possibility of social *prediction* as such — only long-term *prophesying* of the pattern of history.

On the anti-naturalist bias in historicism

Popper noted that there is a strong anti-naturalist bias among historicists, in that they usually oppose the application of general scientific methodology to the social level. He noted also that the argument on both sides of this issue is sometimes based on a misunderstanding of the nature of science, with pro-naturalists too often proposing a "scientism" involving inappropriate imitation of the measurement and statistical devices of the physical sciences. Popper identified the concerns of the anti-naturalists as being (1) that conditions within the organism are contingent upon previous experience and therefore not subject to "mechanical" causality; and (2) that the observer inevitably affects the observed, and furthermore, any prediction has an influence on the event predicted.

He concluded that their concerns are legitimate, but unwarranted as reasons to reject a scientific approach. This is because (1) science is not restricted to situations where mechanical causality prevails; and (2) as Bohr demonstrated, *every* observation is based on an exchange of energy between observer and observed (usually negligible in physics, however). This means that the difficulty — admittedly more serious in the case of social relations — is one of degree and not of kind.

Popper considered that the anti-naturalist bias of historicists leads them into ideologically based and arbitrary social activism rather than critical analysis of social problems and step-by-step solutions. It is an activism demanding great leaps into the unknown, which in turn require unlimited faith in the promised Utopia. Unlimited faith is not a characteristic of the critical thinker. For committed historicists, however, such faith is warranted by their "intuitive" understanding of the "holistic" quality of a unique event; that is to say, its "essential" historical meaning. Popper viewed Husserl as a good example of this type of methodological essentialist. Like Aristotle, such people teach "that scientific research must penetrate to the essence of things in order to explain them" (ibid.:28). The methodological nominalist, on the other hand, would claim that the task of science is to describe how things behave; and that words — far from having some "pure," *a priori* meaning — are simply instruments for communicating observations and feelings.

Another anti-naturalist bias of the historicist is the denial of the possibility of social uniformities across cultures and across historical periods: regularities based on the common humanity and similar experience of the species. Strangely enough, this is combined with a pro-naturalist, ultra-determinist belief in the irreversible laws of historical development. "Thus the only universally valid laws of society must be laws which link up successive periods" (ibid.:41). Sartrian existentialism represents the epitome of this attitude. This approach implies that it would be useless to try to discover regularities in human behaviour: facts that one would expect to be indispensable for anyone planning improvements in institutions. Clearly, for historicists, rational social reform is impossible! Rather, they are convinced "that society will necessarily change, but along a predetermined path that cannot change, through stages determined by historical necessity" (ibid.:51).

On the dangers of holistic thinking

According to Popper, the "holistic" thinking of the historicist poses a threat to humanity as serious as the anti-naturalist and essentialist one. He considered that such thinking is characteristic of a pre-scientific stage of intellectual operation. He went on to explain that "holistic" literature confuses two usages of "whole." The word denotes "(a) the totality of all the properties of a thing and especially of all the relations holding among its constituent parts, and (b) certain special properties or aspects of a thing . . . namely those which make it appear an organized structure rather than a 'mere heap' " (ibid.:76). Only in the second sense is the entity (as a system) amenable to scientific study. There is simply no way that one can study the "whole" of anything in its immediacy and entirety, as in the first sense of the word. Popper emphasized that "all knowledge, whether intuitive or discursive, must be of abstract aspects . . . [and] we can never grasp the concrete structure of social reality itself" (ibid.:78). The mistaken doctrine that we *can* do so — as well as the clamour for "wholes" — is mystical rather than scientific, and represents a regressive yearning for the lost certainties of tribalism.

In place of historicism, Popper recommended an approach to social change that he called "piecemeal engineering." In this view "there is no clearly marked division between the pre-scientific and the scientific experimental approaches, even though the more and more conscious application of scientific, that is to say, critical methods, is of great importance" (ibid.:87). Scientific progress in the social arena will come about only as a process of learning from carefully evaluated trial and error. "To look out for these mistakes, to find them, to bring them into the open, to analyze them and to learn from them, this is what a scientific politician as well as a political scientist must do. . . . [But] it is very hard to learn from very big mistakes" (ibid.:88). And he could have added that "holistic" social change ensures that humanity will have to deal with very big mistakes.

On the difference between prophecy and prediction

Popper concluded that the problem with historicist causes is that their "laws of development" are not scientific laws, but are, instead, absolute historical trends. And as such, they can only be "the basis of unconditional *prophecies*, rather than conditional scientific *predictions*" (ibid.:129). Historicists fail to understand that scientific prediction is always contingent upon specific initial conditions. Indeed, the poverty of historicism turns out to be a poverty of imagination. Marx, for instance, simply could not imagine a change in the initial conditions of change.

Popper proposed that we substitute for historicism, "a doctrine of the unity of method; that is to say, the view that all theoretical or generalizing sciences make use of the same method, whether they are natural sciences or social sciences" (ibid.:131). In the social sciences, as in the physical, imagination and intuition play an important role, for they provide the guesses or biases with which the scientist initiates the search for a problem-solution. *But*, "science is interested only in the hypotheses which his intuitions may have inspired, and then only if these are rich in consequences, and if they can be properly tested" (ibid.:138).

History, on the other hand, is not a theoretical, generalizing discipline, according to Popper. It deals with causal explanations of a singular event, rather than the application of universal laws to specific initial conditions, in an attempt to identify and predict regularities. Popper recognized two tasks for history, neither of which is scientific in nature: "the disentanglement of causal threads and the description of the 'accidental' manner in which these threads are interwoven" (ibid.:147). Refutation of conjectures is impossible in the study of history. Accordingly, Popper recommended that historians deal with the problem of objectivity in the only way open to them: by consciously and formally introducing a preconceived, selective point of view and gathering as rigorously as possible all the evidence bearing on it.

Because social change is so closely related to the growth of dependable knowledge, Popper believed that we would benefit more from a theory of the evolution of science than from pseudo-scientific theories of social progress. His advice was to begin — not by prophesying an immutable pattern of change in a cosmically predetermined direction — but by imagining the conditions under which the progress of science might be arrested. He suggested one possibility. "There may, for example, be an epidemic of mysticism" (ibid.:156). The reactionary nature of mysticism and the unconscious conservatism of the historicist may both be rooted in fear of an unknowable future, according to Popper. "It almost looks," he concluded, "as if the historicists were trying to compensate themselves for the loss of an unchanging world by clinging to a faith that change can be foreseen because it is ruled by an unchanging law" (ibid.:161).

On Plato as an enemy of the open society

The study of the nature of historicism led Popper to a companion study of its historical roots. In 1943 he completed *The Open Society and Its Enemies*. This is an analysis of the totalitarian impulse in the theories of three influential historicist thinkers: Plato, Hegel and Marx. He considered the project to be his war effort.

Popper was convinced that Plato's influence has been largely destructive of human freedom and democracy. He saw the latter's "holistic" utopianism as an expression of the longing for a return to the lost unity of tribal life, in an age when democracy had begun to seem too much of a burden. It had indeed been an unsettling and chaotic time for Athens, and Plato had blamed the troubles on the democratic heritage of Pericles, rather than on the oligarchy bent on its destruction. Popper believed that Plato set out deliberately to pervert the ideals of justice and individualism that had formed and guided the Greek state. He showed how, with the use of complicated, abstruse argument and twisted logic, Plato managed to equate individualism with egoism; justice with keeping everyone in the proper place in a rigid caste society; and morality with the interest of the state as defined by its (supposedly benign) authoritarian ruler. "Plato's theory of justice . . . is a conscious attempt to get the better of the equalitarian, individualistic, and protectionist tendencies of his time, and to re-establish the claims of tribalism by developing a totalitarian moral theory" (Popper 1962a:119). In the service of this goal, "He successfully enlisted humanitarian sentiments whose strength he knew so well, in the cause of the totalitarian class rule of a superior master race" (ibid.).

Often Plato made Socrates the spokesman for these humanitarian sentiments which were then cleverly twisted into an attack on democratic principles—the attack also being launched by Socrates. Interestingly, Popper demonstrated an uncharacteristic blind spot where Socrates was concerned. He acknowledged that the sole source of the legend of the "great Athenian teacher" is Plato's *Apology*, and that this did not at all accord with the picture of the man as revealed by Aristophanes, another major contemporary source. Yet Popper loved the legendary Socrates and invariably assumed that, where the sentiments reputed to him were noble, they were undoubtedly his own, but where the ideas were clearly subversive of democratic ideals, Plato must be libelling his great mentor. It is equally possible that the original villain was Socrates, and that Plato's totalitarian perspective was the result of a corrupting education at the hands of a master manipulator.

For Popper, even the title of Plato's political treatise, *The Republic*, was a deliberate ploy to harness the democratic beliefs of the populace to a totalitarian cause. Clearly the book describes, not a republic, but an autocratic monarchy, and one which seems peculiarly oriented towards the Athens of Plato's own time. "What a monument to human smallness is this idea of a philosopher king!" exclaimed Popper (ibid.:156). For, in the end, the philosopher king can be none other than Plato himself. In every way he was the only person then living who could have fitted the job description. Popper suggested that this was not an abstract philosophical work directed to posterity, but merely a crude political manifesto written by a power-hungry aspirer who actually thought he might be king. Surely, he said, it is time we broke our habit of deference to such men.

On Hegel as an enemy of the open society

Volume 2 of *The Open Society and Its Enemies* deals with Hegel and Marx. Popper claimed that, although medieval Christianity must be blamed for the harm it did by accepting and perpetuating Plato's distortion of the rational approach of the sophists, it was not until Hegel that the Platonic propaganda campaign against reason and freedom reached full fruition. For Popper, Hegel represented the renaissance of tribalism in Western culture and the missing link between Plato and twentieth-century totalitarianism. He noted that "the Marxist extreme left wing, as well as its conservative centre, and the fascist extreme right, all base their political philosophies on Hegel" (Popper 1962b: 30). While the connection with Communism is indirect, fascism is a direct and logical offshoot of Hegelian thought. Hegel's own words are sufficient evidence: "The State is the march of God through the world. . . . The State is the actually existing, realized moral life" (ibid.:31).

In Popper's opinion, the whole of Hegelianism is nothing more than a mindless apology for Prussianism. Frederick William III appointed Hegel as the official state philosopher with total power over the very definition of philosophy in Prussia. For Popper, it was difficult to believe that Hegel's ideas could have gained credibility without the power of the state behind him. According to Schopenhauer, Hegel's writing was "such stuff as mad men mouth and brain not" (ibid.:32). Popper also quoted the following assessment by Schopenhauer: "Hegel, installed from above by the powers that be, as the certified Great Philosopher, was an . . . illiterate charlatan who reached the pinnacle of audacity in scribbling together and dishing up the craziest mystifying nonsense . . . [which has] been noisily proclaimed as immortal wisdom by mercenary followers and readily accepted as such by all fools" (ibid.:32-33). Sadly, as Schopenhauer also noted, it proved to be precisely the type of mystifying nonsense that confuses and dulls the wits of students to the extent that those engulfed in it for too long are rendered uneducable for life, and fit for nothing but perpetuating the same dogma.

Popper noted Hegel's deliberate distortion of Kant's exposition on the futility of all *metaphysical* conflicts. Kant's point was that one is inevitably led into logical contradiction in such argument, as both a thesis and antithesis can be deduced from the same premise and neither is open to refutation. Hegel turned this legitimate conclusion into the doctrine of the universal *inevitability* and *desirability* of logical contradiction. In Popper's opinion, this may well be the most insidious of all Hegel's harmful ideas, for it renders impossible all learning from criticism and reasonable persuasion. In fact, it must destroy all potential for intellectual and scientific growth (and wherever it has prevailed this has indeed been the result). For, as Popper commented, "if contradictions are unavoidable and desirable there is no need to eliminate them, so all progress must come to an end" (ibid.:39).

Out of this necessarily came the moral doctrine that *might is right*. There are no logical criteria, no rules of evidence applicable; one must only *believe* and wield the political power necessary to impose the "truth." (One can see the echoes of this in Nietzsche and even in Max Weber.) For Hegel the national repository of such power is the state: "The State has . . . to make up its own mind concerning what is to be considered as objective truth," he wrote (ibid.). Whatever *is* is necessarily right, for it has been dictated by the forces of history: admittedly a strange type of history, seen by Hegel as "a kind of huge, dialectical syllogism; reasoned out, as it were, by Providence" (ibid.:47). The phenomena in which the inexorable process is manifested are the Spirits of the various nations, locked in mortal combat for world domination. Individuals, with their "false" morality of personal conscience, get short shrift in Hegel's scheme. The supreme embodiment of the successfully aggressive state is the Great Man — subsequently, Nietzsche's Superman — definer of morality as well as truth for his people.

On Marx as an enemy of the open society

Popper found only one constructive idea in Hegelianism — the recognition that people's thoughts do not simply appear from within, as Rousseau sometimes seemed to assume, but are largely derived from their cultural inheritance and context. Marx took over this insight when he "stood Hegel on his head," and contributed at least two others, according to Popper. He was a forerunner of pragmatism in his recognition of the importance of the *practical consequences* of theories. And he contributed to the notion that social groupings have a significance and identity beyond that of the personalities and motives of their members. Popper also recognized the authenticity of Marx's humanitarianism: a tragic irony, in light of the human cost and counterproductivity of this sad example of one of the really *big* mistakes of historicism!

For Popper, writing during World War II, it was already clear that Marx's errors far outweighed his positive contributions. The central thesis of Marxism — that ideas are invariably the *result* of economic conditions — is only half true at best, he said. The relationship is, rather, one of *interaction*. He concluded that the most harmful aspect of Marxist theory, however, is its justification of the use of violence. Popper's own view on the issue is that violence can be justified *only* against a tyranny, and even then it must have only one aim: the immediate establishment of democratic institutions permitting control and dismissal of the new rulers by the people. He submitted that, from the very first, Marxism had proceeded in the opposite direction by (1) making democracy the scapegoat for the ills of the established society of his time; (2) employing propaganda to convince the ruled that the current rulers and the democratic state were one and the same; and (3) focusing on total *conquest* of power, rather than the development of better checks and balances on power, as the sole road to reform.

On the sociology of knowledge

It was Popper's hope that Marx would be the last of the holistic system-builders: the last influential thinker to confuse historicist prophecy with scientific prediction of piecemeal social changes; the last to substitute mystical faith in utopias for refutable scientific assertions. Nevertheless, he recognized with concern that an intellectual offshoot of Hegelianism and Marxism was rapidly gaining influence in academic circles. This was the surprisingly *un*sociological and *un*knowledgeable "sociology of knowledge" movement. Inspired by Karl Mannheim, its followers argued that modern science is no more warranted as a belief system than any "other" political ideology. They maintained that scientists bring their ideological biases to their work and shape their findings accordingly; that the metaphysical assumptions of science are no more provable than any other set of postulates; that scientists are no more critical of their beliefs and conclusions than are ideologues of any other hue; and that the prevailing scientific consensus at any particular time merely represents that of the group within the scientific community which wields the most political power.

The modern version of the above point of view is "postmodernism" with its preferred method of "deconstruction." In responding to the original source of this challenge, Popper explained that scientific rigour does not depend upon the objectivity of the individual scientists—although one would hope that they would be trained as critical rather than dogmatic thinkers—but on the *intersubjectivity* of the methodology. Ironically, it is just this social aspect of science that the sociologists of knowledge and their postmodern successors have failed to understand. They become stranded on the shoal which has grounded all phenomenologists since Husserl.

As Popper explained it, "In order to avoid speaking at cross-purposes, scientists try to express their theories in such a form that they can be tested, i.e., refuted (or else corroborated) by experience" (ibid.:218). Other types of assertions are unacceptable to scientists, because they do not lend themselves to a replication of the process by which claimants have arrived at their findings, and thereby to the test and possible refutation of their knowledge claims. It is this friendly-hostile cooperation of the universal community of scientists that makes possible the orderly process of hypothesis-testing and theory-building, and the accumulation of *global* knowledge that results. Under these conditions, the theory that wins out and subsequently prevails does so *not* because of the persuasive or political power of its proponents, but because of its power to explain and predict observable regularities while withstanding worldwide attempts to refute it.

Popper admitted that the so-called social sciences have not yet achieved a corresponding publicity of method, but hoped that they would move in that direction rather than the one implied by the sociology of knowledge. He viewed the social studies currently as little more than " 'total ideologies' . . . unable or unwilling to speak a common language" (ibid.:221). If the sociologists of knowledge begin by defining such disciplines as scientific, then their conclusion that science and ideology are identical is not surprising.

On the evolutionary nature of science

After the war Popper moved to England, accepting a professorship at the London School of Economics. He devoted the immediate post-war years to lecturing and writing a lengthy postscript to *The Logic of Scientific Discovery* — in which he hoped to correct misapprehensions and to answer critics. Unfortunately, soon after the galleys arrived in 1957, he suffered a massive detachment of the retinas of both eyes, and was forced to set the task aside for a number of years. In 1963 he published *Conjectures and Refutations*. He received a knighthood in 1965. In 1972, *Objective Knowledge* was completed. This was soon followed by his two-volume autobiography, *Unended Quest* (1974 and 1976). Then came *The Self and Its Brain* in collaboration with John Eccles, the neurophysiologist, in 1977. Among his other works published in this period were *The Open Universe: An Argument for Indeterminism* and *Quantum Theory and the Schism in Physics*. It was not until 1983 that the postscript was finally published, under the title of *Realism and the Aim of Science*.

Although Popper's interests and critical analyses covered the entire range of sociology, psychology and the history of ideas, he is chiefly known as a philosopher of science. His contributions to this field are both comprehensive and revolutionary. He was the first to offer a theory of science that explains the *evolutionary* nature of its progress, although Martineau had hinted at this many years before — as had Spencer, and Piaget had initiated an attempt to do just that. Popper believed that there is a definite connection between Darwinism and his own theory of the evolution of knowledge through the competition and elimination of theories on the basis of their falsifiability. The connection has to do with the fact that "non-physical things like purposes, deliberations, plans, decisions, theories, intentions and values can play a part in bringing about changes in the physical world" (Popper 1979:229).

Popper believed (with Durkheim, Mead and Huxley) that evolution entered a new phase when language emerged. He distinguished two functions of language: the lower (shared with other higher animals) are the expressive and signalling functions. The higher, and specifically human, functions are those of description and argumentation. These higher functions do not replace the lower; they establish over them a control with mechanisms of feedback. This allows for "the evolution of new means of problem solving, by new kinds of trials, and by new methods of error-elimination, that is to say, new methods for controlling the trials" (ibid.:240).

Popper explained that all organisms are constantly engaged in problem-solving by a method of trial and error. "Error-elimination may proceed either by the complete elimination of unsuccessful forms (killing off . . . by natural selection) or by the (tentative) evolution of controls which modify or suppress unsuccessful organs or forms of behaviour, or hypotheses" (ibid.:242). The single organism is itself a tentative solution for the survival problem of its phylum, as it probes available environmental niches, and modifies them. "It is thus related to its phylum almost exactly as the actions of the individual organism are related to the organism: the individual and its behaviour are both trials which may be eliminated . . . as errors" (ibid.:243). The evolution of warning mechanisms, like the eye and the crucial higher functions of language, allows for more and more errors to be eliminated without sacrificing the organism; "it makes it possible, ultimately, for our hypotheses to die in our stead" (ibid.).

For Popper, the growth of human knowledge closely resembled the process of natural selection — *the natural selection of hypotheses* — whether these are the formally expressed conjectures of science or the largely unexpressed guesses of the small child. "Our knowledge consists, at every moment, of those hypotheses which have shown their (comparative) fitness by surviving so far in their struggle for existence; [the idea of] a competitive struggle which eliminates those hypotheses which are unfit . . . can be applied to animal knowledge, pre-scientific knowledge and to scientific knowledge" (ibid.:261).

Popper recognized that a falsification discrediting an entire scientific theory is not necessarily immediately accepted. "It is usually not accepted until the falsified theory is replaced by a proposal for a new and better theory. As Max Planck remarked, one must often wait until a new generation of scientists has grown up" (Popper 1983:xxv). Elsewhere he explained what is demanded of a new hypothesis before its acceptance as a replacement for an earlier one. "(1) It must solve the problems which its predecessor solved at least as well as did its predecessor; [and] (2) it should allow the deduction of predictions which do not follow from the older theory; that is to say, crucial experiments. . . . The two demands together ensure the rationality of scientific progress, that is, an increase in verisimilitude" (Popper 1977:148-49). It is these demands that allow us to distinguish science from ideology; that rescue us from relativism and radical scepticism; and that allow us to assume the general reliability of science without dogmatizing specific results.

Concerns about subjectivism

Thomas Kuhn, as a graduate student, attended a seminar offered by Popper in Princeton in 1950. He built upon the above ideas in his book, *The Structure of Scientific Revolutions*. However, Popper has carefully distinguished his own position from that at which Kuhn ultimately arrived. He felt that Kuhn's work was somewhat coloured by subjectivism and elitism, as well as by "fideism": the idea that scientists are inevitably committed by faith and emotion to their proposed theories. Popper pointed out that, on the contrary, the best scientists (such as Bohr in 1913 and Einstein in 1916) realize the tentative nature of their conjectures and expect that they will be superseded eventually.

In Popper's estimation, Kuhn's wholesale acceptance of "the myth of the framework" is both mistaken and dangerous. He was referring to the notion that, for most operating scientists, the guiding paradigm is accepted as *the truth*, and their research is motivated by the search for confirmation rather than by the spirit of sceptical inquiry. He admitted that this concept of "normal science" is valuable as a warning because it is unfortunately true of some of what occurs in modern science; but it is neither the norm nor is it science. Popper observed that "normal science" has only recently become a significant aspect of the behaviour of some of those who work in the field, and if indeed it should ever represent routine practice, it would signal the *end* of science! Furthermore, he noted that Kuhn's description of the phenomenon obliterates any possible line of demarcation between physics and astrology, for example. Popper concluded that, if Kuhn is right and science is in fact moving in this direction, it will be a major disaster for humanity, for it will mean "the replacement of a rational criterion of science by a sociological one" (Popper 1974b:1147).

Popper always used the word " rational" in a sense which included empiricism as well as logic: he meant an attitude of readiness to listen to critical arguments and to learn from experience. This is the attitude that seeks to solve problems by an appeal to reason and evidence rather than to emotion. He held that those who teach that not reason but love should rule open the way for those who rule by hate. "I see in the irrational and mystical intellectualism which is at present so fashionable the subtle intellectual disease of our time" (Popper 1962b:246). He felt that such theories, although often labelled humanistic, are instead subversive of all that social science must build upon, such as faith in reason and the urge to improve human conditions. The popular twentieth-century slogan — that humans are emotional rather than reasoning beings — says nothing about future possibilities, according to Popper. "We ourselves and our ordinary language are, on the whole, more emotional than rational; but we can try to become a little more rational, and we can train ourselves to use our language as an instrument, not of self expression (as our romantic educationists would say) but of rational communication" (ibid.:278).

On Hume's dilemma

One of Popper's major achievements was his solution of Hume's problem of induction. This was the problem that so dismayed Russell (and Kant before him) because it seemed to imply the impossibility of *proving* any scientific assertion, and therefore of developing a body of verified facts. Popper explained that the entire issue resolves itself once the following is understood: "(a) all scientific or theoretical knowledge is conjectural; and (b) there can be rational preferences for some of the competing conjectures [because] some are better than others in at least two senses: they can be more informative and thus more interesting, more bold; or they can be better in standing up to severe tests" (Popper 1974b:1023). This means that humans *can* have highly corroborated knowledge, even though absolute truth is an impossible goal.

On individual development and cultural evolution

Like many of the evolutionary naturalists before him, Popper was interested in the relation between the learning process in the individual and the evolution of the content of human culture. He saw the roots of totalitarianism in the "naive naturalism" and the "naive conventionalism" characteristic of the early stages of culture. In the first stage, all experienced regularities are thought to be part of an unalterable reality. It is the stage of animistic belief, where humans are viewed as powerless to affect events. In the second stage, that of magic, "both natural and normative regularities are experienced as expressions of, or depend upon, the decisions of man-like gods or demons" (Popper 1962a:60). He noted that the more advanced stage in which all social arrangements are recognized as conventions made by humans did not appear even in Greek philosophy until Protagoras, and was subsequently denied by Plato. Like Piaget, Popper guessed that individuals might recapitulate this evolution in their early childhood development.

He saw the learning process of the individual as somewhat analogous to that of cultural evolution, where false ideas are selected out on the basis of their inability to solve the problems of group survival. As with cultural evolution, he said, learning is an interactive problem-solving activity rather than a one-way conditioning process. Although the cultural and physical environments exist prior to each individual self, they do not merely dictate responses nor pour in sensory data. "I am first of all an organism not fully conscious of myself — a small baby. I have, however, ... dispositions to interpret what reaches me through my senses, and without which the incoming sensory data would never begin to crystalize into perceptual experience" (Popper 1977: 426). By the time the incoming data have become conscious experience, they have already been interpreted by the brain. The very constitution of the infant as a conscious self is the gradual result of an immense amount of active learning: of unconscious interpretation, testing and refuting of expectations.

Roger Sperry's Nobel Prize-winning work on the hemispheres of the human brain was of great interest to Popper. He guessed that the right hemisphere of the human brain corresponds to the functioning of non-human animals, and it is probably the more active in early infancy. It is conscious but not *self*-conscious, while the left hemisphere — developed through language use, and gradually gaining prominence as the child develops — is both. (Recent findings indicating that musical ability is housed in the left hemisphere would seem to support his conjectures.)

Popper's theory is very similar to Mead's, but there is no evidence that he had encountered Mead's ideas directly. For Popper, as with Mead and Huxley, there was no discontinuity in the development of consciousness, from the sentience of the lower animals to the self-conscious human. The onset of the crucial time-delay between stimulus and response was no doubt gradual, according to Popper. He suggested that "we might find that the lower consciousness is also connected with a time-delay though perhaps with a shorter . . . [one] than in higher consciousness. It may be part of the biological function of the lower consciousness to intervene between perception and motor action to somehow delay motor action" (Popper 1977:462). This may have led to increased activity within the brain, making it more and more of an open system of open systems, and producing a left hemisphere capable of incorporating symbols from without.

According to Popper, it is clear that "the human brain and the human mind evolved in interaction with language" (ibid.:11). And sometime during this crucial stage in evolution, as expressions and signals began to be exchanged and interpreted, the human animal transcended the physical limitations of its world and began to function in an internal world created by a remembering, thinking, believing self, as well as in a shared world of abstractions produced by a community of self-conscious selves.

Popper, unlike Santayana, preferred to coin original terms for these simultaneous levels or realms of functioning. He called them "Worlds 1, 2 and 3." He explained that "World 3," or the universal human culture, emerged as a non-physical environment surrounding humans just as significantly and comprehensively as did the air they breathed and the ground on which they stood. For Popper, the difference between humans and other higher animals was this anchorage of the self in "World 3." Humans are not only subjects — like other consciously exploring animals, centres of action — but also "objects of our own critical thoughts, our own critical judgement" (ibid.:144). At this stage cultural evolution incorporates and supersedes genetic evolution by means of "World 3" objects, or ideas. This process is a result of interaction among the open systems of all three realms.

On the nature of human uniqueness

Although Popper rejected nineteenth-century materialism that did not allow for the defining of ideas as real, he was not a dualist. Rather, he was a proponent of naturalism and pluralism in the Dewey, Durkheim, Mead and Santayana sense. He believed that evolutionary theory resolved the old mind/body problem: it simply does not exist in the newer scientific perspective. He did not believe in a realm of the spirit existing parallel to that of nature. And he rejected the idea of a divine spirit beyond the evolutionary process which somehow was injected into life as it broke through into the human stage. Accordingly, he disagreed with his collaborator in *The Self and Its Brain* on the possibility of an immortal soul, and of a genetic break between human and other primate species. In response to Eccles (who *is* a dualist) he said, "I think that human achievements . . . [the contents of] World 3, are unique and that this makes our selves and our minds unique. I don't think that we need . . . a thesis of the genetic uniqueness of man" (ibid.:538).

For Popper, the most unique of all human achievements was the method of problem-solving that grew out of the tension between the human propensity to *describe* or tell stories, and the need to *criticize* the story or description as to its truth or falsity. As he explained it, from this remarkable union of creative imagination and rational critical thought there came the very human endeavour of scientific knowledge-building. Just like the animal learning process from which it evolved, it is based on the continuous modification of previous knowledge; on making guesses and matching them with experience; on trial and error and the elimination of error through feedback. No conjecture is ever proven for certain; no refutation ever finally justified. But at any point in humanity's never-ending struggle for freedom and justice, the results of our admittedly fallible science will be the best means available for avoiding pitfalls in the unknown road ahead.

He believed that science "represents our wish to know, our hope of emancipating ourselves from ignorance and narrow-mindedness, from fear and superstition" (Popper 1983:260) It involves enlightened, disciplined creativity and a vision for humanity. It is nothing less than the remarkable embodiment of that rational vision of evolutionary naturalism to which Karl Popper dedicated his long and fruitful life.

References for Chapter Twenty-Two

Popper, Karl. 1959. *The Logic of Scientific Discovery*. London: Hutchinson. (First published in German in 1934.)

―――――. 1962a. *The Open Society and Its Enemies*. Vol. 1: *The Spell of Plato*. Princeton, NJ: Princeton University Press. (First published in 1943.)

_____. 1962b. *The Open Society and Its Enemies*. Vol. 2: *The High Tide of Prophecy: Hegel, Marx and the Aftermath*. Princeton, NJ: Princeton University Press. (First published in 1943.)

_____. 1964. *The Poverty of Historicism*. New York: Harper & Row. (First published by Routledge and Kegan Paul [London, 1957] and previously presented as a paper in 1936.)

_____. 1974a. The Autobiography of Karl Popper. In *The Philosophy of Karl Popper*. Edited by Paul Arthur Schilpp. La Salle, IL: The Library of Living Philosophers, p. 3-182.

_____. 1974b. "Replies to my Critics." In ibid., p. 949-1180.

_____, and John C. Eccles. 1977. *The Self and Its Brain: An Argument for Interactionism*. London: Springer International.

_____. 1979. *Objective Knowledge: An Evolutionary Approach*. Rev. ed. Oxford: Clarendon Press. (First published in 1972).

_____. 1983. Realism and the Aim of Science. In *Postscript to the Logic of Scientific Discovery*. Totowa, NJ: Rowman and Littlefield. (Written in 1951-52.)

Twenty-Three

The Radical Behaviourism of B.F. Skinner

I shall be telling them with a sigh
Somewhere ages and ages hence:
Two roads diverged in a wood, and I —
I took the one less traveled by,
And that has made all the difference.
— Robert Frost,
"The Road Not Taken"

Like Darwin and Einstein, B.F. Skinner plummeted into his chosen field from the outside. Studying literature as an undergraduate, while practising music and art and writing poetry, might seem an unlikely preparation for a future founder of a science of behaviour. But it so happened that Burrhus Frederic Skinner, after a year of failing to produce good fiction, came to a realization all-too-seldom acknowledged by young writers. He simply did not know enough about the universals of the human condition to capture them for posterity in poetry and prose. So — armed with the guilelessness and vibrant ego typical of the rural American youth of his generation — he set out to resolve his dilemma. He turned to psychology, expecting to discover there the mother-lode of reliable knowledge about why and how humans behave as they do. What he found, instead, was a confused and naked emperor, at war with himself. Undaunted, Skinner promptly determined to devote his life to constructing, if not a complete wardrobe for the overblown emperor, at least a solid platform on which the fledgling social sciences could begin to stand.

Setting out on the road less travelled

For a methodology Skinner went back to the dictums of Francis Bacon on the nature of the scientific enterprise, and to Bertrand Russell on the joint demands of logic and intellectual integrity. With no apparent plan to do so, he

---

References for this chapter are on p. 419.

put these tools to work at sifting through fifty years' accumulation of unsubstantiated constructs on the nature of the human psyche. At some point he must have decided to make a new beginning on the solid ground spelled out by Darwin, Pavlov and Dewey.

Skinner's autobiographical comments indicate no real awareness of the monumental nature of the attack he was launching on the windmills of social science. He simply followed where his research led, step by painstaking step, and published his findings as he made them. It is a fact, however, that he was presented, during these early years, with a sculpture of himself as Don Quixote. What happened to B.F. Skinner and to his theory of human behaviour is a fascinating study of the resistance of the dualist world view entrenched in the larger culture (and either mirrored or accommodated in academia) to the premises and approaches of a thoroughly *scientific* social science.

B.F. Skinner was born in 1904 in a small railroad town on a bend of the Susquehanna River in Pennsylvania. His father was a lawyer from a farming family, his mother the daughter of a carpenter. He recalled that it was in grade eight that he began a lifelong love affair with the ideas of Francis Bacon. In 1922 he entered Hamilton College at Clinton, New York. There he studied Greek, wrote poetry full of "mawkish sentimentality" and planned to become a writer. After being encouraged by Robert Frost, he devoted the year following graduation in 1926 to full-time writing. Nothing happened. He began to suspect that he had been pursuing his interest in human nature in the wrong milieu.

During this period the young would-be writer had discovered Bertrand Russell's *Philosophy*, in which the author addressed "Watson's Behaviourism and Its Epistemological Implications." Russell had commented, "I do not fundamentally agree with this view, but it contains much more truth than most people suppose. I regard it as desirable to develop the behaviourist method to the fullest possible extent" (Skinner 1976:298). After some study of the subject, Skinner also was not sure that Watson was on the right track, but he felt that Pavlov was, and he determined to continue the latter's work. Before departing for Europe with his parents in the spring of 1928, he registered in the department of psychology at Harvard University.

By December of that year Skinner was writing from Harvard, "my fundamental interests lie in ... psychology and I shall probably continue therein, even, if necessary, by making over the entire field to suit myself" (Skinner 1979:38). He was also reading widely in the history of science. He noted particularly the following conclusion of a book by a Harvard professor: "The acquisition and systematization of positive knowledge is the only human activity which is truly cumulative and progressive" (ibid.:57). He found, in Mach and Poincaré, early versions of what was beginning to be called "operationalism," and encountered it as well in the works of the Vienna Circle of Logical Positivists. And Poincaré's definition of science as "a rule of action that succeeds" impressed him.

Skinner was remarkably untainted by preconceptions in the field of psychology. The sole direct influence was that of Thorndike, with his "Law of Effect," and of Pavlov, whose work on reflexes had captivated him. His first published paper was entitled, "The Concept of the Reflex Arc in the Description of Behaviour," and was, in part, an attack on prevailing "mentalistic" explanations of human actions. At that time he was still accepting Pavlov's proposition that the reflex was sufficient to explain all psychological issues. Even this one prejudice almost blinded him to his first real breakthrough.

The major achievement of his doctoral studies was an independent research activity in which he studied the behaviour of rats. He had designed the first known technique for obtaining standard cumulative records and thus was able to obtain data, not merely on whether and how strongly the rat was responding to a stimulus, but on the timing of the response. Nevertheless, he was misinterpreting his findings, for the simple stimulus-response model did not allow for such variations in the learning process. He later wrote, "If I had never heard of Pavlov . . . I should have seen that my basic fact was the *rate* at which an organism engaged in a particular type of behaviour, but because of my exposure to reflex theory I wanted rate to be a measure of reflex strength" (ibid.:81).

The discovery of operant conditioning

After receiving his doctorate in 1931, Skinner was appointed a Research Fellow in General Physiology and was free to pursue his research virtually unhindered. To ease the daily drudgery of caring for his rats, he built an automatic-release cage for food. This precipitated another unexpected breakthrough. He had inadvertently created a situation where "the delivery was for the first time contingent on the response . . . [and] the speed at which the behaviour changed was surprising" (ibid.:88). What he had discovered was a process of conditioning quite different from Pavlov's, and more similar to learning in everyday life. At the same time he had found that a reflex could be conditioned much more rapidly than Pavlov had thought. Depending on how hungry the rat was (the degree of deprivation/satiation), conditioning could occur after only one occasion on which the conditioned and unconditioned stimuli appeared almost simultaneously. Another discovery was that certain types of conditioned responses — those highly rewarded by the environment at the time of acquisition — were extremely resistant to extinction.

When published, these findings referred, for the first time, to the *reinforcement* of a *learned* response, rather than to the mere conditioning of a reflex. Skinner had stumbled on to the mechanism by which vast repertoires of animal behaviour (including the human) are learned and maintained in strength.

He called the process "operant conditioning." By this he meant that all behaviour operates on the environment and produces *effects* which, in turn, contribute to either its extinction or reinforcement. This represented a major extension and refinement of Pavlov's theory, but its significance was not immediately recognized, even by Skinner himself. How could he understand, without having read Mead? What he had discovered was no less than the mechanism by means of which the "after-the-fact" causality of natural selection operates in the most complex forms of human behaviour!

Implications and applications

In 1933, Skinner obtained a two-year extension on his research opportunity by being selected as junior member of the new Harvard Society of Fellows. He had finally reached the point where his evidence justified the conclusion that deprivation and satiation were the operations defining a *drive*. He believed that the drive to satisfy basic survival needs is the motivating factor which impels the organism to operate on the environment and to repeat those responses which have been reinforced; in other words, to learn from the consequences of its actions. He began to consider the implications of his research for the human attributes of learning, speaking, listening and thinking. This launched him upon a treatise on verbal behaviour which occupied him for many years, and was ultimately published under that title.

Skinner landed his first job at the University of Minnesota in 1935, and was married that year as well. He was considered a creative teacher, but commented later, "Much of what was 'original' about me was the fact that I was wholly unprepared for the job" (ibid.:191). By then he was becoming known for his new approach to psychology. "My field was operant rather than respondent [conditioning] and my measure of strength was probability (or at least rate) of responding rather than magnitude of response or latency or after-discharge" (ibid.:201). In 1938 he published his first book, *The Behaviour of Organisms*.

During the war he worked on a project involving the use of pigeons for guiding missiles, but, although the experiment was successful, the Pentagon dropped the plan. This was nonetheless of great significance to Skinner, for it represented an immediate, practical application of his theory. He now realized that his new science would lead rapidly to a technology of behaviour — something no other psychological model had been able to achieve.

Skinner's next move was to the University of Indiana, where he became chair of the Department of Psychology. There, for the first time, he had the services of a secretary. In 1946 he was asked to present the William James Lectures at Harvard. This gave him the incentive to complete his work on verbal behaviour, which he did with the help of a Guggenheim Scholarship. During this period he became famous for his invention of the "baby tender" for his second daughter. (This was a cage-like apparatus provided with a cognitively stimulating environment.) He also wrote the science-fiction novel, *Walden Two*, in which he pictured a utopian society with a culture designed to produce peaceful and fulfilled people. In 1948 he returned to Harvard: a full Professor and nationally recognized as a member of the American Philosophical Society and of the Academy of Science.

Skinner published *Verbal Behaviour* and *Science and Human Behaviour*. He began constructing programs for teaching machines: a project which was to involve him for many years. He found himself working largely in isolation, however. By this time the Harvard Department of Psychology was ignoring behaviourism while focusing on Piagetian-based cognitive psychology, and Skinner felt increasingly alienated. In 1963, as a recipient of a government Career Award, he was able to withdraw from teaching and to concentrate on writing and speaking engagements. In 1969 he spent a term as Overseas Fellow at Cambridge. He published a number of books, including *Contingencies of Reinforcement*, *Beyond Freedom and Dignity*, *About Behaviourism* and a three-volume autobiography, completed in 1983.

Skinner's later books were intended partly as responses to the numerous distortions of his ideas by academics in the humanities and social sciences. It is doubtful that he ever became fully reconciled to the virulence of the attacks on his theory, but this must have been more than balanced by the evidence of its fruitfulness and increasing applicability. He remained actively engaged to the end, satisfied that his work would live beyond him. He planned to speak at the 1990 meeting of the American Free Inquiry Association, but died that summer at the age of eighty-six.

Methodological and radical behaviourism

Skinner was never completely happy with the label of "behaviourist" because he felt that John B. Watson's oversimplified and exaggerated claims may have tarnished the legitimate science of behaviour pioneered by Pavlov. He was aware that most people associated behaviourism with Watson's 1913 publication, *Psychology as a Behaviorist Views It*. They objected to the fact that Watson's research dealt exclusively with animals. They thought that it denied the existence of an "inner person" and implied manipulative control. Nonetheless, Skinner credited Watson with having freed the psychologist to study the behaviour of the "lower" animals, where introspection is not feasible, and thereby to draw comparisons between humans and other species. He appreciated the value of Watson's central thesis ("Study behaviour, not mind!") and used it as a principle to guide his own life's work.

In the end Skinner decided to refer to his own position as "radical behaviourism" to distinguish it from Watson's approach. He claimed that his version "is not a scientific study of behaviour, but a philosophy of science concerned with the subject matter and methods of psychology ... [which, in turn, is viewed as] a science of the behaviour of organisms, human and otherwise ... a part of biology, a natural science for which successful methods are available" (Skinner 1969:221).

Like Piaget, Skinner was chiefly interested in developing a theory of knowledge, but his was one which defined knowing and thinking specifically as forms of behaviour. He recognized, as Watson had not, that any science of behaviour must deal with the problem of privacy, but he pointed out that science is often concerned with things not directly observable. He believed that an adequate science of behaviour must, of course, consider events taking place within the organism. *However*, "it can deal with these events without assuming that they have any special nature or must be known in any special way. The skin is not that important as a boundary. Private and public events have the same kind of physical dimensions" (ibid.:228). On this issue, Skinner was much closer to Dewey and Mead than to Watson. Close, too, to Julian Huxley, although the two misunderstood each other. Skinner thought Huxley was a dualist because he used the term "ideal," and Huxley accused Skinner of "reducing" humans to their observable behaviour.

Skinner explained that Watson's "methodological" behaviourism had limited itself to what can be publicly observed. It acknowledged the existence of mental processes but declared that their private nature ruled them out of scientific consideration except to the extent that physiology could locate their neurological underpinnings. This position appeared to many critics to deny the very existence of consciousness and the possibility of any degree of self-knowledge. On the other hand, according to Skinner's radical behaviourism, the question is not whether humans can in some way know themselves, but *how much* they can actually know when they do so and *how reliable* the result can be. "The difference is not in the stuff of which the private world is composed, but in its accessibility" (Skinner 1971:191). For, he noted, "although privacy may bring the knower closer to what he knows, it interferes with the process through which he comes to know anything" (ibid.).

The problem of where to begin

Skinner thought that his radical behaviourism had restored balance to psychology. He considered that cognitive theory, no less than Freudianism and its offshoots, represented the prevailing mentalistic position. He believed that Piaget had been too concerned with the "inner person," ignoring antecedent events and the consequences of action. Methodological behaviourism had done the opposite, focusing exclusively on the environment and tending to ignore the genetic and historical programming that the individual brings to the situation, and denying the very possibility of self-observation.

In Skinner's model, what is happening inside the skin is inevitably one aspect of the behaviour under study, but it is not the *source* as Piaget seemed to believe. Rather, it is a link between the initiating environmental conditions and their behavioural consequences; it is a difficult-to-get-at, but logical connection between the two sets of observable contingencies. Far from being an autonomous (i.e., mysterious) causal force or entity, it is merely a *drive* representing the middle (and not directly observable) aspect of a functional three-part system of causality. Skinner suggested that we are misled by self-awareness into a belief in the self as an uncaused instigator of action.

Beginning with the link most inaccessible to observation was a suicidal path for psychology to have embarked upon, according to Skinner. For one thing, whenever what a person does is attributed to an unobservable inner structure, all inquiry is brought to an abrupt end. We are left only with the option of accepting the explanation on faith, or rejecting it. He claimed that this is why traditional schools of psychology have inevitably turned into ideologies. Furthermore, "what is felt or introspectively observed is not some non-physical world of consciousness, mind or mental life, but the observer's own body" (Skinner 1974:17). It does not mean that introspection is a special kind of non-physical research *nor* that its imperfectly felt impressions are the causes of behaviour. In fact, said Skinner, the feelings registered by introspection are most likely to be the *consequences* of past and present contingencies.

Skinner believed that a more fruitful approach is to begin, as has all science, with what can be publicly observed. If regular changes in antecedent contingencies result in a corresponding pattern of change in subsequent behaviour, then surely some scientific progress can be made by studying these. Facts (regularities in behaviour) can be documented and the causes of behaviour can be proposed: causes which are actual physical events amenable to alteration and control. He admitted that a scientific analysis which is limited to observable regularities in behaviour represents a simplification of the complexities of the human condition. But every science has to begin at the beginning, by identifying the simplest possible relations among the events under study. Why should the social sciences be any different? When accused of trying to make all psychology dance on the pin of *reinforcement*, Skinner replied, "Try a parallel from another science: . . . the pin of relativity . . . the pin of plate tectonics . . . the pin of genes and chromosomes" (Skinner 1983:387).

The significance of the Pavlovian revolution

Skinner was fully aware that Pavlov's revolutionary extension of Darwin's theory of evolution had been the discovery of the mechanism by which the organism adapts to changing environmental conditions during its lifetime. He saw that survival for the individual can now be understood to be contingent upon certain kinds of behaviour, made possible by the operation of the reflex in static situations and the conditioned reflex where the conditions have altered. In the latter case, a new stimulus has become associated with the old and is now substituting for the former as a reinforcer — as when a new food source brings forth the saliva response. Thus environmental contingencies elicit or *select* appropriate responses. As Skinner put it, "Just as we point to contingencies of survival to explain an unconditioned reflex, so we can point to 'contingencies of reinforcement' to explain a conditioned reflex" (Skinner 1974: 38).

The significance of Pavlov's work had been easily overlooked by psychologists because it could be said to apply only to animal behaviour and not to the complexities of human motivation. Skinner's discovery of operant conditioning was harder to ignore for it claimed to explain the entire range of learned behaviour. As he put it, "a very different process, through which a person comes to deal effectively with a new environment, is operant conditioning. . . . The behaviour is said to be *strengthened* by its consequences and for that reason the consequences themselves are called 'reinforcers' " (ibid.:39). It is no longer merely a matter of substituting a new reinforcing stimulus for the old.

Contingencies of survival and contingencies of reinforcement

Skinner was in fact offering a simple and workable explanation for Popper's contention that the origin of behaviour is comparable to the origin of species. He concluded that "variations, quite possibly random, were selected by their effects" (Skinner 1983:154). As had Mead and Huxley before him, he claimed that selection represents a kind of causality very different from the push-pull mechanisms of the inorganic sciences. Skinner felt that many of the fruitless attempts made by psychology to imitate physics have resulted from a failure to understand Darwin's "organic" or feedback causal principle. Just as a mutation survives because it is selected — rather than *vice versa*: "Behaviour is *followed* by reinforcement: it does not pursue or overtake it. Both the species and the behaviour of the individual develop when they are shaped and maintained by their effects on the world around them. That is the only role of the future" (Skinner 1971:142). In neither case is the process pulled toward a purpose or unfulfilled design; it is, instead, controlled from behind, by the after-the-fact effect of environmental conditions.

Skinner explained that natural selection occurs through the operation of *phylogenic* contingencies; operant conditioning by *ontogenic* ones. "Successful responses are selected in both cases, and the result is adaptation. But the process of selection is very different and we cannot tell from the mere fact that behaviour is adaptive which kind of process has been responsible for it" (Skinner 1969:194). He concluded that most behaviour has resulted, to some degree, from both processes. He saw imprinting as a good example of this. "What the duckling inherits is the capacity to be reinforced by maintaining or reducing the distance between itself and a moving object" (Skinner 1974:41). What it learns through the operant conditioning of experience is to follow *one particular* moving object: the provider of rewarding sustenance and protection. According to Skinner's theory, the old nature/nurture dilemma is resolved totally when understood in terms of the interaction between contingencies of survival and those of reinforcement.

The issue of control

This new definition of the problem implies that any particular instance of behaviour is likely to be a combination of the previous effect of the environment on the evolution of the species and the effect it has exerted during the individual's lifetime. To the extent that either of these can be changed, behaviour can be changed. Clearly, the conditions most amenable to alteration are those impinging on the individual, in the form of effects of current actions. "Behaviour is shaped and maintained by its consequences" (Skinner 1971:18). Desirable behaviour can be reinforced positively (by rewarding it) or negatively (by removing existing aversive effects). Undesirable behaviour can be erased by removing reinforcing contingencies.

Actions can also be punished by imposing unpleasant consequences, but Skinner's research indicated that this is the *least effective* of the possible ways to alter behaviour, and the only one with harmful emotional by-products. Yet, ironically, punishment is the method of control most commonly used in our culture. All this seems to support Skinner's contention that some form of operant conditioning is, in fact, the only means available to any society to socialize or educate its members, and if we do not choose the method knowingly we do it out of ignorance, with unanticipated and often destructive results.

Skinner agreed with Piaget that the child learns to adapt to the physical environment by manoeuvering through the relations of the surrounding space, and by handling objects and being reinforced by regularities in surfaces, dimensions and motions. "If we could not find some uniformity in our world our conduct would remain haphazard and ineffective" (Skinner 1953:13). Adaptation to the social environment is similar. This means that where uniformity in terms of controlling contingencies is absent the child fails to acquire normative behaviour. He noted that punishment becomes the usual means of last resort for correcting what could and should have been established pleasantly by positive control of the learning environment. Those who support punishment argue that it occurs everywhere in the natural world. Skinner admitted this but reminded us that the effort to avoid punishing consequences has led people to work throughout history to build a more comfortable and less dangerous society.

The control of the physical environment achieved through the physical sciences has enabled humanity to make rapid progress to this end. Skinner believed that we are now on the threshold of the same kind of progress where human culture is concerned. For the first time, he said, we have at our disposal a science of behaviour which can provide us with the means of controlling the future direction of human culture in rational ways, and of making it less punishing and more rewarding for all. But we are so terrified of the responsibility involved that we prefer to put our heads in the sand, and, while deploring the power of physical science, follow helplessly in the wake of its technological drift.

The issue of control is responsible for most of the misunderstanding of Skinner's position. To people imbued with the ideology of the "autonomous" inner person born into freedom, any control is anathema. Research demonstrating the powerful shaping role of cultural conditioning is either ignored or attacked with a "kill the messenger" vehemence. The prevalent understanding seems to be that if one's behaviour is being controlled from without, some malevolent *person* must be responsible. The question inevitably posed is "Who is to control?" The answer, of course, is "No one — and everyone." It is the culture that controls through the actions of all of us. As Skinner pointed out, "I did not advocate imposing control; control existed and should be corrected" (Skinner 1980:5).

On the evolution of culture

What most people cannot accept is that all cultures are controlling environments, in which the members provide the reinforcement. Skinner explained that human cultures can be distinguished from one another, not by *whether* they comprise contingencies of reinforcement, but by the nature of those reinforcements, and therefore by the kinds of behaviour they encourage or prevent. (Ironically, Fromm expressed exactly the same idea — in different words — although he would have been appalled to have had this pointed out.) Skinner (again — like Fromm) was scornful of the preachers of permissiveness. "The fundamental mistake made by those who choose weak methods of control is to assume that the balance of control is left to the individual, when in fact it is left to other conditions" (Skinner 1971:99). Elsewhere he wrote, "To refuse control is simply to let control fall into other hands" (Skinner 1983:84).

If people want a more humane and just culture they must build it themselves, Skinner said, in the full realization that they will get the kind of behaviour that they reward. "The practices of a culture, like the characteristics of a species, are carried by its members, who transmit them to other members. . . . A culture, like a species, is selected by its adaptation to an environment; to the extent that it helps its members to get what they need and avoid what is dangerous, it helps them to survive and transmit the culture" (Skinner 1971:129). The two processes are intertwined. "The capacity to undergo the changes in behaviour which make a culture possible was acquired in the evolution of the species, and, reciprocally, the culture determines many of the biological characteristics transmitted" (ibid.). New cultural practices correspond to genetic mutations. However, Skinner noted that, at the point of transmission, the analogy breaks down. Cultural evolution is Lamarckian; *all* cultural practices are acquired and must be transmitted each generation.

According to Skinner, a fatal error in Social Darwinism was that culture was identified with the *people* carrying it rather than their *practices*. Another was the assumption that competition meant a war of all against all, rather than the building of more successful adaptive cultural practices. A third was the idea that cooperation had no adaptive role. Indeed, wrote Skinner, "Practices which induce the individual to work for the good of others presumably further the survival of others and hence the survival of the culture" (ibid.:135). He noted that one of the chief functions of culture is to encourage the deferment of instant gratification and perceived self-interest and develop instead an awareness of the long-term welfare of the group. For every culture, "The practical question ... is how remote consequences can be made effective" (ibid.:173).

Skinner believed that his theory was the first to explain adequately the evolution of complex behaviours such as speaking, listening, thinking and knowing. "The human species had taken a gigantic step forward when, through evolving changes in its nervous system, vocal behaviour came under operant control. Mating calls and cries of alarm had evolved because of their survival value, but vocal behaviour was acquired because of its consequences during the lifetime of the individual" (Skinner 1983:84). The ability to listen to the verbal behaviour of others would have been extremely valuable in avoiding exposure to dangerous contingencies. Skinner echoed Mead in claiming that the evolution of a verbal community is the source of human consciousness. "Verbal behaviour presumably arose under contingencies involving practical social interactions, but the individual who becomes both a speaker and a listener is in possession of a repertoire of extraordinary scope and power, which he may use by himself. Parts of that repertoire are concerned with self knowledge and self control, which ... are social products" (Skinner 1971:122-23).

For the human primates, the achievement of verbal behaviour was important in at least two ways. It provided the means for group coordination and thereby more effective control of the surrounding environment, and it made story-telling possible. Through stories, both speaker and listener could be emotionally aroused in the absence of the original reinforcing contingencies. In addition, the stage was set for a drama in which one person plays several roles. It was this that led to *thinking*. "Verbal behaviour can occur at the covert level because it does not require the presence of a particular physical environment" (Skinner 1953:264).

For Skinner, thought is operant behaviour, but of a very complex variety. In an echo of Marx and Dewey, he noted that it "is not a mystical cause . . . of action, or an inaccessible ritual, but action itself, subject to analysis with the concepts and techniques of the natural sciences and ultimately to be accounted for in terms of controlling variables" (Skinner 1957:449). It is the sum of an individual's responses to living in a complex world, built up over time. In words similar to those of Dewey, he said, "Man Thinking is simply Man Behaving" (ibid.:452). Through thinking we are able to make meaningful the conditions under which our behaviour occurs, and *knowing* becomes a possibility. This is a distinction that probably would have satisfied Arendt, if she had ever deigned to read Skinner.

Putting the theory to work

Skinner reported that there came a time when his theory began to do more for him than he had to do for it. He was finding it useful in "converting mentalistic terms into alternatives which refer to things having physical dimensions" (Skinner 1980:197). For example, it helped him to clarify the basic concept of *self* within the context of verbal behaviour. "The contingencies necessary for self-descriptive behaviour are arranged by the community when it has reason to ask, 'What did you say?' . . . 'Why did you say that?' and so on" (Skinner 1957:314). Elsewhere he referred to the self as an organized system of responses determined by (1) special discriminative stimuli, (2) deprivation and (3) emotional variables.

Emotion, Skinner defined as "the probability of engaging in certain kinds of behaviour, defined by certain kinds of consequences" (Evans:11). They are "by-products of the contingencies and throw no further light on the distinction between public and private" (Skinner 1971:110). They occur just at the right time to give the appearance of serving as causes of behaviour and are often cited as such by mistake. He blamed Freud for the current emphasis on feelings at the expense of true causal variables.

Morality, in Skinner's view, is personal self-management. It involves "how to forego a current reinforcer in order to avoid a future aversive consequence or accept a current aversive consequence for the sake of a future reinforcer" (Skinner 1983:357). A related concept is that of *values* which have to do with the reinforcing effects of things. They are thus central to Skinner's theory of behaviour. "Things are good (positively reinforcing) or bad (negatively reinforcing) presumably because of the contingencies of survival under which the species evolved" (Skinner 1971:104). Humans work to obtain pleasant things and to avoid unpleasant things. This is an echo of Hobbes and Hume, as well as pure Spencer, Dewey and Mead in a simplified form. But it is firmly grounded in tested theory as the ideas of the earlier naturalists were not.

Skinner explained *group behaviour* as social reinforcement. He wrote, "Behaviour reinforced through the mediation of other people will differ in many ways from the behaviour reinforced by the mechanical environment" (Skinner 1953:285). The more people there are manipulating variables having a common effect on an individual's behaviour, the more powerful will be the control. For example, the establishment of institutions of counter-control is the only means by which people can protect themselves from the abuses of control by government.

Creativity, for Skinner, is "one of the shabbiest of fictions and it tends to be used by the least creative people. . . . Just as contingencies of survival replaced an explicit act of creation in the origin of the species, so contingencies of reinforcement replaced the supposed creative acts of artist, composer, writer or scientist" (Skinner 1983:304). He credited Descartes with the original suggestion that creativity is only apparent and that behaviour can be traced, instead, to external conditions. Skinner considered the old notion of creativity an obstacle to the emergence of novel ideas and techniques. As long as the process is defined as a mysterious spontaneity there is no hope of identifying and arranging the conditions that nurture originality.

Skinner maintained that the scientific analysis of *perception* had suffered from the (Bergsonian) idea that somewhere in the brain there must exist a copy of nature and that what must be explained is how that copy differs from reality. He insisted that an organism is responding to nature, not duplicating it — nor even assimilating it — as Piaget thought. Seeing does not require the presence, in the eye, of the things seen. All forms of sensing are actions which involve learning to discriminate on the basis of differential reinforcement of responses. They are not reproductions of reality. Skinner claimed that the traditional concepts of "image" and "sensation" get in the way of scientific analysis. In fact, he said, their use assumes the existence of a subjective world beyond the reach of science. "The behaviourist does not need to support the notion of experience as a form of contact or possession and can therefore leave the environment where it is. The whole organism is then available in analyzing the behaviour of seeing" (Skinner 1969:253). This seems to represent a considerable refinement of the models of both Dewey and Piaget.

On the nature of human nature

Many of Skinner's most hostile critics (such as Arendt and Fromm) felt that his theory somehow belittled human nature. In response, Skinner explained that a change in the theory of human nature cannot change the facts. "Man is not made into a machine by analyzing his behaviour in mechanical terms" (Skinner 1971:202). And, to those who thought that he was "reducing" humans to the "lower" level by generalizing from animal research, he said, "We cannot discover what is 'essentially' human until we have investigated non-human subjects" (ibid.). He emphasized that nothing can take away from humanity's accomplishments. He pointed out that the human being is still the measure of all things, but we must accept human nature as science reveals it, not as we might wish it to be.

Skinner both agreed and disagreed with the comment: "Human beings are the same the world over." He said that it is not true in the sense that the independent variables which determine behaviour are the same. Genetic endowments differ from person to person, and so do environments. This guarantees the uniqueness of each separate human being. He believed the statement to be true, however, in the sense that "behavioural processes are the same wherever they are encountered — that all behaviour varies in the same way with changes in *deprivation* and *reinforcement* — that *discriminations* are formed in the same way — and that *extinction* takes place at the same rate" (Skinner 1953: 421). This is really the same as saying that human respiration, digestion and reproduction are the same the world over. In other words, human nature is such that a science of behaviour is theoretically just as feasible as is a theory of organic functioning.

On education

The theory of operant conditioning has obvious implications for education, and one would have expected it to have been greeted enthusiastically in that field, as Piaget's theory has been. Dewey's ideas had been welcomed also, although sadly misunderstood and distorted. Skinner believed that Dewey had been right in encouraging teachers to discard the old punishment-oriented educational methods, but remiss in failing to provide anything concrete in their place. Skinner's theories did lead to specific and extremely effective teaching procedures and techniques. But they encountered a stubborn resistance — from the public as well as the educational establishment — that puzzled many observers. Skinner himself probably explained it best. "Many people were afraid of programmed instruction just because it worked. They did not fear traditional education because they knew it was ineffective and hence harmless" (Skinner 1983:205).

Learning, in Skinner's model, is a reassortment of responses in a complex situation. There is a continuous demand by the physical and social environment for the individual to discriminate more precisely among reinforcing contingencies. The baby learns to distinguish between the mother's warmth and that of the cradle; between the mother's body with its food source and that of the father; and the process snowballs with each passing day. Nature itself is the source of a myriad of reinforcements, and the largely unplanned contingencies operating in and through the social environment provide the rest.

Teaching, however, implies the identification of desired outcomes and precise planning on the part of the educator. For Skinner it represents "the arrangement of contingencies of reinforcement which expedite learning"

(Skinner 1969:15). The task of the teacher is to prepare the learner for situations not yet arisen by bringing discriminative operants under the control of stimuli expected to occur in those situations. These operants become powerful tools for controlling nature, and their exercise is in itself reinforcing. Because of this, the natural pay-offs inherent in the subject matter are the teacher's chief allies, according to Skinner. If the material is arranged and presented appropriately, artificial reinforcers such as appeals to students' external interests, competition and teacher approbation are unnecessary.

He maintained that all of the educational literature on "motivation" is on the wrong track. "The motives in education are the motives of all human behaviour. . . . We appeal to that drive to control the environment that makes a baby continue to crumple a piece of noisy paper and the scientist to continue to press forward with his predictive analysis of nature" (Skinner 1948:124).

For Skinner, the educator's problem is how to make these natural reinforcements contingent upon desired behaviour. He discovered three conditions under which students learn rapidly: immediate reinforcement; freedom to proceed at their own pace; and a situation where errors are minimized and corrected at once. All of these conditions are satisfied in programmed instruction, and *in no other currently used method.* For a teaching "machine" to be effective, however, it would have to satisfy two demanding requirements. What is necessary is a step-by-step elaboration of extremely complex patterns of behaviour, along with means of maintaining the newly acquired behaviour in strength at each step. With this in mind, Skinner succeeded in designing and testing effective teaching programs to develop a number of basic skills and capacities. Sadly, however, resistance to their use was so great that it was not until the advent of the school computer that his ideas began to gain headway. And, even then, he was not credited for the principles used in computer-based learning programs.

On psychotherapy

It soon became apparent that another area of applicability for behaviourism is psychotherapy. Here what became known as "behaviour modification" has been widely accepted and put to use. Very early on, Skinner had become convinced that a change in contingencies could solve many psychological problems, and could point the way to effective therapy. His theory encouraged reorganization of the patient's *environment* so that the *problem behaviour* could be changed. This was a direct challenge to Freud's focus on feelings, which Skinner considered sadly misleading. "You don't institutionalize a person because of his feelings," he said (Evans:42). It is behaviour that is upsetting or threatening to all concerned.

Skinner gave Freud credit for convincing many people of the operation of cause and effect in human behaviour. But he regretted that, "in filling the gap between the events which he saw as causally related he chose to construct . . . an elaborate set of explanatory fictions" (Skinner 1953:375). Skinner viewed Freud's picture of a mental world inhabited by ego, super-ego and id, and divided into regions of conscious and unconscious mind (and the Jungian notion of the child of our past still being contained within us) "as a form of animism that serves no useful purpose in exploring current behaviour" (Evans:6). These men had merely invented it all, and then persuaded themselves that they had discovered it. Skinner referred to Freud's stated goal of devoting his life to exploring these structures of the psyche. "No matter what the logicians eventually make of this mental apparatus there is little doubt that Freud accepted it as real rather than a scientific construct or theory" (Skinner 1959:186).

Skinner concluded that, although Freud did not himself believe that these inner structures were sources of *spontaneity* (and therefore did not go as far astray as did most of his followers) his theory had four consequences that have proven disastrous for social science. (1) It added weight to the traditional bifurcation of nature into physical and psychical; (2) it encouraged the idea that the therapist is directly engaged in psychic wars within the patient; (3) by its emphasis on misleading mental structures, it obscured the importance of crucial environmental variables; and (4) it caused behavioural change to be ignored as the vital goal of therapy.

Skinner maintained that most of the problems Freud dealt with, and the regularities he observed, can be explained better by operant conditioning than by psychoanalytic theory. Freud's defence mechanisms can be attributed to the prevalence of aversive control in the culture. "They represent ways of avoiding undesirable consequences of one sort or another, and when analyzed in that light, they suggest means of correction" (Evans:41). The non-judgemental, listening role of the therapist is helpful because the patient feels guilty for previously punished behaviours. These have been replaced by psychotic behaviours which have functioned to avert the original punishing consequences. The therapist's role is to arrange for the extinction of the unhealthy behaviours by helping patients to replace the personal histories currently driving them with different ones. The first step is to encourage the previously punished behaviours to appear in the presence of a non-punishing audience. Skinner concluded that "the principal technique of psychotherapy is thus designed to reverse behavioural changes which have come about as a result of punishment" (Skinner 1953:371).

Skinner suggested that what Freud explained by the Oedipus complex would disappear with the advent of equality for women. The asymmetrical relation of the female parent was probably at the root of it all, combined with a culture in which punishment was paramount. "Is it possible," asked Skinner, "that the so-called Oedipal relations to mother and father are simply mythical representations of positive and negative reinforcement? The boy longs, not to sleep with his mother, but to be close to the one who positively reinforces his behaviour. He longs, not to kill his father, but to escape from or destroy one who punishes" (Skinner 1980:353).

Assessing competing schools

Skinner tried to draw precise distinctions between his theory and those of his contemporaries. He was not satisfied with the *operationalism* of methodological behaviourism and logical positivism: the idea that a concept should be defined only in terms of its measurements. He once sent a Christmas card on which a graph showing "number of cards received" plotted against "number of days in the month" was entitled, "An Operational Definition of Christmas"! His position regarding physiological science was that it will likely someday clarify what is actually occurring inside the organism during particular behavioural events, but that should not obscure the need for a corresponding theory of the relevant environmental contingencies. He dismissed modern versions of biological determinism, such as "pop" sociobiology and Chomsky's linguistics, because they seem to conflict with the findings of modern genetics. He had serious doubts, as well, about the widespread use of sophisticated statistical analysis in psychology, given the current crude state of its observations and concepts. And he considered that those schools of psychology devoted to elaborating constructs of "personality types" are little better than superstitions.

Skinner reserved most of his criticism, however, for cognitive psychology. No doubt personal frustration and disappointment fuelled this attitude somewhat, for during his tenure he saw the cognitive approach prevail within the Harvard Department of Psychology, while behaviourism was virtually ignored. He was concerned that mentalism was once more threatening to take over psychology — this time in the guise of Piaget's genetic developmentalism. He saw mentalism as the custom of explaining behaviour in terms of abstract constructs supposedly housed in the human mind. He felt that this had been furthered by the emergence of the computer as the new model for human behaviour, which in itself, he said, would have been sufficient to have opened the door to a flood of such theorizing.

In Skinner's opinion, the cognitive psychologists — with their computer metaphor — had moved the environment back inside the head (where Kant had placed it) in the form of entities of conscious experience representing concepts and rules. And they had constructed an internal simulacrum of the organism to provide for the storage. This simulacrum was then used as the basis for inferring the nature of the nervous system which would be required to generate its search for equilibrium. Skinner noted that his own approach would leave the subject of the nature of the nervous system to those equipped to observe it directly: the physiologists. "Meanwhile the experimental analysis of behaviour would give them a correct assignment, whereas cognitive science sent them looking for things they would never find" (Skinner 1983:367). He concluded that, while adding nothing to our knowledge of the behaviour under study, the hypothetical equilibrating structures of the cognitive psychologists (along with the supposed assimilating and accommodating processes) manage to obscure any possible causal relationships among their observations.

Skinner believed that what these theorists thought to be the contents of the internal computer are instead the effects of contingencies of reinforcement. He considered their theory particularly misleading because of its confusion of the essential distinction between rules and reinforced propensities: the fact that rules are consciously elaborated and learned *descriptions* of contingencies, and that the behaviour governed by them is different from that unknowingly shaped by the contingencies themselves. Skinner explained that people are *conscious* of their own rule-based behaviour, and *unconscious* of their contingency-shaped behaviour. They do not *contain* a consciousness and unconsciousness, as mentalistic psychologists would have it.

On this point Skinner would have done better to have read Piaget more thoroughly. Piaget seems to have viewed the rule-assimilating process somewhat as Dewey saw habit-formation, and as Skinner himself saw contingent reinforcement. Only at a later stage of intellectual functioning is the child able consciously to recognize and apply rules. Piaget saw rules as "contained" within the organism only in the sense of neural connections: connections no doubt assumed by Skinner as well. According to Skinner, however, there is an inevitable conflict between his own approach which "traces human behaviour to its genetic and environmental histories, and the cognitive tradition, which traces the same behaviour to an initiating self" (ibid.:261).

He saw a conflict, as well, between the organism viewed as a storehouse of images and memories — both conscious and unconscious — and the organism seen as operating on the environment and being changed by the process. The conflict may be more apparent than real, however, having to do with the early, relatively simple model of the computer familiar to Skinner, as distinct from the infinitely more complex — and possibly even "open-systems" versions now envisioned by scientists.

For Skinner, it is not good enough to say that humans function by actively sampling and organizing environmental cues into a working model of the world, and by storing all this for later recall. None of this explains or predicts currently observable regularities in behaviour. "Where an organism, exposed to a set of contingencies of reinforcement, is modified by them and as a result behaves in a different way in the future, we do not need to say that it stores the contingencies. . . . What we recall . . . is a response. . . . The conditions which are said to determine the accessibility of stored memories really determine the accessibility of responses" (Skinner 1969:274).

Skinner may have been right to question the computer as a model for learning, for — so far, at least — it represents a closed system requiring pre-programming, rather than an open system operating on its environment and being programmed by the consequences of that action. However, computer programs do provide a helpful analogue for the role of DNA in producing inherited response patterns in humans, and, as Skinner's theory has shown, the actual processes underlying both evolutionary and experiential conditioning are probably the same.

Although some of Skinner's other criticisms of cognitive psychology may be warranted, it is unfortunate that he did not read Piaget's work as carefully as he had read Freud's, and do for Piaget's key concepts what he had done for those of Freud. He might then have noticed what Piaget and his followers (in their similar ignorance of modern behaviourism) also have failed to realize: that the two theories are more complementary than contradictory. It may well be that all of the merely *descriptive* constructs in Piagetian cognitive-systems theory could be *explained* by the simple and powerful principle of reinforcement. For example (as noted above) when Piaget referred to the unconscious assimilation of rules, he seems to have meant exactly what Skinner's theory explains in terms of the reinforcement of effective response patterns.

Skinner claimed that cognitive scientists are confined by their model to verbal reports and instructions that lead nowhere, and that this is why their findings have not been cumulative. What dismayed him most was their persistence in ignoring an available behavioural analysis of verbal behaviour capable of ordering into a science the very facts they have collected. Skinner felt (quite justifiably) that he had provided a comprehensive scientific approach readily compatible with physiology, and one which has already demonstrated its reliability and fruitfulness in providing the essential principles for a working technology of human behaviour. Yet, for ideological reasons, it continues to be ignored by the majority of social scientists.

The power of a theory

Skinner believed that his theory also explained the evolution of logic and science in general within human cultural evolution. Science began to make headway only with "the development of a verbal community especially concerned with verbal behaviour which contributes to successful action" (Skinner 1957: 418). The community is self-policing. It extinguishes or punishes language that is metaphorical, exaggerated, ambiguous or prejudicial, aiming to eliminate all verbal responses which interfere with a logical train of thought. This is essential because the test of scientific prediction is initially in the form of *verbal* confirmation or refutation. "But the behaviour of both logician and scientist leads at last to nonverbal action, and it is here that we must find the ultimate reinforcing contingencies which maintain the logical and scientific community" (Skinner 1957:429).

Skinner observed that an appropriately reinforcing community has not yet emerged in the social sciences. And that as long as this field of study continues to resort to mentalistic structures as causal variables it is still operating in the realm of superstition. But, he declared, that is where every science started! "The fanciful explanation precedes the valid" (Skinner 1953:24). He did not underestimate the difficulties peculiar to his own field, however, for he was constantly reminded of the depth of the cultural resistance to a science of behaviour based on evolutionary naturalism. It has been said that "Skinner may have had the worst press since Darwin" (Skinner 1983:337) and the reasons were similar. His theory challenged centuries of superstition, the remnants of which are still firmly in place.

Because of the clarity and simplicity and sheer *workability* of Skinner's theory, it was immediately recognized by friend and foe alike as the most formidable challenge since Darwin to dualist and mentalistic beliefs. This partly explains the vehement and vicious nature of the attack on radical behaviourism mounted by academics. A general misunderstanding of science came into play as well. Because it explained behaviour in terms of cause and effect, people were easily persuaded that the theory would actually change human nature in some mysterious way. It was as if they thought that scientific explanations *determine* nature in the process of explaining it. But, as Skinner pointed out, "A change in the theory of human nature cannot change the facts. The achievements of man in science, art, literature, music and morals will survive any interpretation we place on them. The uniqueness of the individual is unchallenged in the scientific view" (Skinner 1959:17).

Finally, the theory forced people to acknowledge the power and pervasiveness of operant conditioning as an instrument of individual and cultural change. This in turn required them to face up to the fact that, throughout history, the human group has always been the ultimate source of morality. It alone has always been responsible for the content of individual values and for the direction of cultural evolution. Martineau had shocked her contemporaries by claiming that humans could be so formed by appropriate experience as to produce a happy rather than unhappy society. Dewey and Mead had said the same thing, but their difficult and largely theoretical formulations were easy to ignore. It had been repeated by Durkheim, but the politics of sociology have almost obliterated his insights. Huxley had echoed it, but largely as a future necessity, and his emphasis on eugenics had obscured the central message. Piaget, Arendt, Fromm and Popper had all been committed to educating people on this imperative for humanity. But Skinner's indisputable findings finally forced the issue. Awareness of operant conditioning destroyed, once and for all, the "ghost in the machine." Ignorance and animistic fantasy could no longer be used as excuses for human irresponsibility. And that was the cruellest blow of all!

It remains to be seen whether Skinner will be recognized as the radical philosopher of evolutionary naturalism and the groundbreaking social scientist that he had hoped to be. We do know that his work offered a sound and comprehensive scientific underpinning for the belief in the uniqueness of the individual as a product of biological and personal history. It gave support to Popper's view of the evolutionary process as open-ended, and to the importance of science in building a better future. And, perhaps most important, it may have provided the generalizing principle for a unified approach to the scientific study of humanity.

It may be a long time before Skinner's contribution to social-scientific thought is understood and appreciated. Even Popper, after reading *Walden Two*, thought that its author was a totalitarian Platonist opposed to freedom of the individual. But there should have been no question about Skinner's profound commitment to democracy, humanitarianism and naturalism. He spent a lifetime pointing out the harmful effects of punishment as a technique of social control. And, finally, he expressed the humility of his naturalistic forebears in his approaching death. It was not through a surviving ego, but through the contribution of his work to the continued evolution of human culture that B.F. Skinner dared to hope for immortality.

References for Chapter Twenty-Three

Evans, Richard I., ed. 1981. *Dialogue with B.F. Skinner*. New York: Praeger.

Skinner, B.F. 1948. *Walden Two*. London: Collier-Macmillan.

_____. 1953. *Science and Human Behavior*. New York: Macmillan.

_____. 1957. *Verbal Behavior*. New York: Appleton-Century-Crofts.

_____. 1959. *Cumulative Record*. New York: Appleton-Century-Crofts.

_____. 1969. *Contingencies of Reinforcement*. Englewood Cliffs, NJ: Prentice-Hall.

_____. 1971. *Beyond Freedom and Dignity*. New York: Alfred A. Knopf.

_____. 1974. *About Behaviorism*. New York: Alfred A. Knopf.

_____. 1976. *Particulars of My Life*. New York: Alfred A. Knopf.

_____. 1979. *The Shaping of a Behaviorist*. New York: Alfred A. Knopf.

_____. 1980. *Notebooks*. Edited by Robert Epstein. Englewood Cliffs, NJ: Prentice-Hall.

_____. 1983. *A Matter of Consequences*. New York: Alfred A. Knopf.

Twenty-Four

Modern Evolutionary Theory

Richard Dawkins and Stephen Jay Gould

> The lime in our bones, the salt in our blood,
> Were not from the direct hand of the Craftsman,
> They were, instead, part of our heritage
> From an ancient and forgotten sea.
> — Loren Eiseley, *The Firmament of Time*

Ever since Darwin, many social theorists have recognized the necessity of grounding their world views in evolutionary theory. However, only a few modern thinkers like Durkheim, Mead, Huxley, Popper, Piaget and Skinner — and, more recently, Edward O. Wilson — have tried to spell out the specific implications of that theory for our understanding of human behaviour and culture. Nonetheless, ever since Darwin, there has been a slowly growing acceptance of the idea that questions about the origin and nature of life, and about internal and external constraints upon human existence, are matters to be explored within a biological — rather than a transcendental — frame of reference.

But evolutionary theory is itself evolving. Nothing is more exciting, or more immediately relevant to social science, than recent refinements and elaborations of Darwinism. Fortunately, two of the world's foremost evolutionary biologists just happen to be gifted communicators as well as philosophical naturalists. They also happen to represent two major thrusts at the leading edge of the ongoing knowledge-building process concerned with the nature of evolution. They are Richard Dawkins of Oxford, England, and Stephen Jay Gould of Harvard, USA. A comparative analysis of their ideas is not only an opportunity to examine the state of modern evolutionary theory; it should shed light as well on what Popper described as the evolution of scientific knowledge.

References for this chapter are on p. 443-44.

A shared commitment to Darwinian theory

Both scientists were born in 1941. Dawkins' Ph.D. was earned at Oxford University; Gould's at Columbia. Both were hired as assistant professors in 1967: Gould in Geology at Harvard, and Dawkins in Zoology at Berkeley. Gould was later appointed Professor of Geology at Harvard and Curator of the Invertebrate Paleontology Museum of Comparative Zoology. A true modern Renaissance man, he has been attached, as well, to the Departments of Biology and History of Science. Dawkins became a Reader in Zoology at Oxford, a Fellow at New College and has contributed to science programming on BBC television. Both men have published extensively in academic journals and have received numerous awards and honours. Both are highly respected within the international community of biologists, geologists and paleontologists, and have made notable contributions to a continuing evolution of the conceptual framework that defines and guides that research community. On many grounds they can be counted among the major contributors to current evolutionary theory.

Dawkins and Gould have had their differences, and the cut and thrust of their exchanges make for fascinating reading. But the enlarging area of agreement between them is perhaps the more significant feature of their work. Most important, they share a strong commitment to Darwinian theory: to the idea of natural selection as the key principle of evolution. Dawkins considers the current tentative consensus within biology and related fields to be the latest version of a continuously evolving Darwinian synthesis. Gould views Darwinism as the fruitful core around which new elaborations and refinements coalesce. He has said of it, "no other theme so powerfully encompasses both the particulars that fascinate and the generalities that instruct" (Gould 1985:14). For Dawkins, "natural selection is the blind watchmaker, blind because it does not see ahead, does not plan consequences, has no purpose in view" (Dawkins 1986:21).

Gould and Dawkins agree that evolution is a *non-random*, eons-long, cumulative process by means of which *random* hereditary variation results in far-reaching consequences for living things. It operates through the differential reproductive success of living organisms. The phenotypic variations that give one organism an advantage over its competitors in adapting to changing local environments are the result of mutations, or imperfections in the genetic copying process. Some of the random mutations in genes are fortuitous; they give rise to alterations in bodily architecture that lead to improved adaptability. Most of the resulting design changes are minute. They accumulate in a slow, directional increase in complexity down the generations. Other copying errors affect crucial genetic instructions that alter the embryonic system, with far-reaching and relatively rapid developmental and functional consequences.

422   *Leaving the Cave*

The snowballing effect of successful developmental sequences

Gould was one of the first to make the point, much appreciated by Dawkins, that new designs need not always arise piecemeal, "but in a coordinated way by manipulating the master switches (or regulation) of developmental programs" (Gould 1985:182). Whether the alterations are minute or immediately significant, they build on previously selected survivals, and successful sequences tend to spiral, unless extreme environmental shifts occur. A telling example of just such a successful spiral, with each successive accretion being increasingly useful to its possessor, is the evolution of the eye.

Response to the accusation of tautology

The organisms carrying these successful adaptations live to reproduce in greater numbers than do the carriers of competing variations, so that more adequate designs tend to be perpetuated, while the less adequate gradually disappear from the gene pool (represented by the species). Gould pointed out that survival is the *expression* of this inherited fitness of design — not simply the *definition* of superiority — contrary to the claims of those who accuse Darwin of tautological explanation. Given the previous environmental conditions and the specific nature of the phenotypic change, it would be possible theoretically to predict success or failure *before the fact*, just as does the modern plant breeder when he consciously plans to enhance and accelerate natural selection.

Dawkins claimed that natural selection is the only credible explanation ever discovered for living complexity. The evolution which it effects is irreversible; there is virtually zero probability of life "following exactly the same evolutionary trajectory twice" (Dawkins 1986:94). Gould, in his book, *Wonderful Life*, likewise emphasized the sheer chance involved in any particular evolutionary sequence. Any historical event, he said, has to be an accumulation of improbabilities. If the tape of life could be reversed and played again, and if one small chordate called Pikaia failed to survive in the replay, "we would be wiped out of future history — all of us, from shark to robin to orangutan" (Gould 1989:323).

Sources of public resistance

Both writers have expressed puzzlement concerning continuing public resistance to the principle of natural selection. "How," asked Dawkins," can such a powerful idea go still unabsorbed in the public consciousness?" (Dawkins 1986:xi). He suggested that it is largely because, in everyday life, complexity and elegance of result are invariably associated with meticulously executed design and a purposeful designer. In other words, the "creative God" hypothesis just "feels" intuitively reasonable.

Gould's explanation is somewhat different. His belief is that the stubborn refusal to accept Darwinian theory is due to the extreme radicalism of its philosophical implications. Most people simply find it too difficult to give up the idea that living entities possess some mysterious vital property — some unknowable essence — that makes them forever different *in kind* from other forms of matter and energy. When this type of thinking is applied to efforts to mark off humans from other animals, Gould calls it the "picket fence" syndrome.

All of the recurring criticisms of Darwinism seem rooted in one or the other of these deeply embedded cultural prejudices. Most express, as well, a profound ignorance of the actual theory. What Gould once said of Arthur Koestler (that he was conducting a campaign against his misunderstanding of Darwinism) could be said of countless others. One large and vocal group of critics, the creationists, even continues to deny the very *fact* of evolution. As Gould pointed out, in order to do this they must ignore three types of evidence: (1) readily available scientific reports of direct observation of ongoing evolution as it actually occurs in the field and laboratory; (2) countless signs of transition in the fossil record; and (3) observed imperfections in nature from which we can infer the various stages of unobservable change, such as the flamingo's upside-down bill and the female hyena's remnants of male genitals. He emphasized that "the proof that evolution, and not the fiat of a rational agent, has built organisms lies in the imperfections that record a *history* of descent, and refute creation from nothing. Animals cannot evolve many advantageous forms because inherited architectural patterns preclude them" (Gould 1983:160). Gould also called upon the supporting arguments of logic and common sense. "We know that evolution must underlie the order of life because no other explanation can coordinate the disparate data of embryology, biography, the fossil record, vestigial organs, taxonomic relationships, and so on" (Gould 1989:282).

A shared philosophy of naturalism

Gould and Dawkins have enthusiastically recognized and accepted the naturalistic implications of Darwinian evolution. Gould referred to "Darwin's legacy, a welcome and fruitful retreat from the arrogant idea that some divine power made everything on earth to ease and inform our lives" (Gould 1983: 93). For Dawkins, Darwin's theory of the origin and complexity of life is intellectually satisfying, in that it requires no substitutes for explanation such as a first cause; no mysterious master programmer operating on some spiritual plane; and no design or purpose or ultimate goal directing the workings of nature. Both theorists agree that it is an explanation which forces a radical readjustment of world view. It amounts to the removal of humanity from centre stage to the position of one of the temporarily fortunate players in the emerging drama of geological time.

Dawkins claimed that it is our genes that are the programmers — not the gods that we created in our image — and they are programming for their lives, not ours. He was, of course, speaking metaphorically here. We can think of genes, not as conscious "free will" initiators of a process, but in the sense of having their direction determined by contingent feedback. "Like a river," wrote Dawkins, "natural selection meliorizes its way down successive lines of immediately available least resistance" (Dawkins 1982:46). Gould expressed the same idea somewhat differently: "Life is not a tale of progress; it is, rather, a story of intricate branching and wandering, with momentary survivors adapting to changing local environments, not approaching cosmic or engineering perfection" (Gould 1983:344).

To evolutionists like Dawkins and Gould, the history of natural selection is a tale to inspire awe and delight that we as a species are here at all, and that we as individuals managed to make it on to the stage of life for our brief entrances and exits. Gould reminded us that, because of Darwin, "We can find a message in the animals and plants . . . that enables us to appreciate them, not as disconnected bits of wonder, but as integrated products of a satisfying general theory of life's history" (ibid.:119).

On morality

Both authors have repudiated the romantic idea that we can turn to nature for moral guidance, or that nature expresses some sort of meaningful harmony which we "non-members" must refrain from altering. Gould wrote that nothing angers him more than "the claims of some self-styled 'eco-activists' that large cities are the 'unnatural' harbingers of our impending destruction" (Gould 1979:251). In his view, nature is more nearly "red in tooth and claw" than it is harmonious. And it "contains no moral messages framed in human terms" (Gould 1983:42). It is indifferent to injustice and suffering, as the prevalence of ruthless predation and slow death by parasitic ingestion should make abundantly clear. Gould reminded us that "we must seek the meaning of human life, including the source of morality, in other, more appropriate domains" (Gould 1989:44).

Many people suspect that scientists, when they explain the evolution of life or other similarly mysterious phenomena, are assuming priestly powers of some sort. This is because such questions have for so long been the exclusive domain of the supernatural. Some physicists and astronomers are taking advantage of this public gullibility and are blatantly using their professional status to legitimize their religious views. Some are even offering up new God-substitutes, supposedly based on science. Gould's answer to all this fraudulent clamour is, "If scientists should not play God, they should stop trying to find God as well" (Gould 1987:213).

Our cultural predilection to look for morality in nature tends to create a crippling inability to comprehend biological information. For example, when Dawkins first introduced the idea of the selfish gene, he was thought to be presenting a morality based on the principles of evolution. Many critics assumed that he was actually advocating selfishness as a desirable and necessary way to live. Others understood him to be implying that selfishness and ruthlessness are so deeply ingrained in human nature that we cannot hope to behave morally in any case. He was, of course, saying neither of these things. He was simply contributing to an increasingly reliable knowledge base concerning what we might expect to find in the absence of countervailing influences. "Be warned," he wrote, "that if you wish, as I do, to build a society in which individuals cooperate generously and unselfishly towards a common good, you can expect little help from biological nature. Let us try to *teach* generosity and altruism, because we are born selfish" (Dawkins 1989:3).

On hierarchy in evolution

Another interesting convergence in the ideas of Gould and Dawkins has to do with the concept of hierarchy in living forms. Both probably took their lead from their colleague, George Williams, in downplaying Darwin's exclusive focus on the organism in evolution. But Dawkins was wary of what he called the "sloppily unconscious group selectionism" that has permeated evolutionary theory for decades, and which he saw in the premises of some sociobiologists. He said that there is indeed a hierarchy of levels of biological organization, but the group is not one of them. For him, these levels are: (1) the *gene*, as the fundamental unit of natural selection which functions in the crucial role as copier; (2) the *organism*, as the vehicle carrying the phenotypic manifestation of the genetic recipe; and (3) the *species*, or lineage, representing the current extent and state of the gene pool.

Dawkins emphasized the fact that a species is not a replicator. It is the ultimate indication of the success of the genes as copiers and of the individual members as carriers of those copies. The group, on the other hand, is — for the purposes of biological evolution — no more than a momentary gathering of the current members of a species living in close proximity: a mere swirl of dust arising from the sand dune. It is likely to have an *effect* on the survival of the organism in that it is a significant, and perhaps socially necessary, aspect of the local environment. But natural selection, said Dawkins, is by means of the reproductive success of *individuals*, not of groups. It does not operate *for* the welfare or longevity of the group as it can be said to do for the species and the genes.

Although there is some misunderstanding between Gould and Dawkins on this point, both have recognized the importance of the notion of hierarchy in evolution. Gould asked, "Why should bodies occupy such a central and privileged position in evolutionary theory? . . . Are bodies the only kind of legitimate individual in biology? Might there not be a hierarchy of individuals with legitimate categories both above and below bodies: genes below and species above?" (Gould 1983:173). Gould's special interest was with the species, while Dawkins zeroed in on the gene. He identified the gene as the smallest unit of life — and therefore of the system relevant to biological theory — analogous to the atom in chemistry. Dawkins maintained that "Living matter introduces a whole new level of complexity. . . . At every level the units interact with each other following laws appropriate to that level, laws that are not conveniently reducible to laws at lower levels" (Dawkins 1982:113).

Clearly, this is not reductionism, although Gould and his colleagues did make that charge. For most theorists, reductionism is the *logically unwarranted* use of analysis — not the analytic method itself. Dawkins argued that, as the function to be explained is the evolutionary copying process (with its typical accuracy mixed with occasional imperfections) then surely the fundamental unit of analysis must be the smallest known entity involved in the process: the copier itself. The gene (or at least that aspect of it which can be termed the "active germ-line replicator") is that copier, and it is the regularities governing its interactions that we need to understand.

In this model, the organism and species can be conceptualized as two increasingly comprehensive nesting systems: each with its own units and laws of relationship. At the species level, the units are the organisms. Gould was correct, from his perspective, in viewing them as the fundamental entities involved in *speciation* and in resisting their reduction when studying the process from that angle. But Dawkins was looking at the *organism* as the system, and was seeking to shed light on the evolution of complexity in the design and functioning of individual bodies. Consequently, he was equally entitled to identify the gene as fundamental to increasing understanding at that level of interaction.

There seems no reason for disagreement here. Both theorists believe that, in the long term, what is effected by evolution is the survival of genes, and consequently, of the gene pool, as it is manifested in the state of the species at any given time. There is no logical difference between Gould and Dawkins on this point, and no reductionism is involved in either perspective. If, however, one were to attempt to explain *cultural* evolution in terms of genes (which is what, in effect, the Social Darwinists were doing) or biological evolution in terms of atoms or quarks — that *would* be reductionist! Gould rightly accused Fritjof Capri of being hoist on his own petard on this issue. "The self-styled holist has followed the oldest of reductionist strategies. . . . The very assertion that this lowest level [of inorganic nature] . . . represents the essence of reality, is the ultimate reductionist argument" (Gould 1987:224). Dawkins, who obviously understood the logic of systems theory, would no doubt have agreed wholeheartedly.

Dawkins provides a new perspective

Given Dawkins' particular theoretical interest, it is not surprising that his most important contribution to Darwinism should be the introduction of a profound change in perspective: one that he hoped could "usher in a whole new climate of thinking in which many exciting and testable theories are born and unimagined facts laid bare" (Dawkins 1989:ix). He began by explaining that the basic unit of life is the replicator; that is, anything on earth capable of making copies of itself. They came into existence through a chance jostling of particles, as tiny structures of DNA that somehow acquired stability. Because they were not perfect, errors in copying entered the process, again by chance. Some of these errors survived, along with the accurate copies, by virtue of their effects on their surroundings. At some point in the process, environmental pressures caused a group of mutually compatible replicators to cluster and eventually to form discrete vehicles or "survival machines." These were the forerunners of the complex organisms we see today.

Dawkins explained that another critical mechanism shaping the process of evolution is sexual reproduction, particularly the "bottle-necked" generational cycle in which small pieces of DNA (or bunches of them) are passed from grandparents to grandchildren unchanged by anything that happens to the parents in their lifetimes. This amounts to a one-exit passage into the future for the design specifications of replicators. The sperm and egg of the animal is the ultimate example of this. This mechanism creates recurring opportunities to enter the next generation in increasing numbers, for those replicators associated with "superior" attributes. The more successful are the carriers (or organisms) at surviving and reproducing, the more sustainable is the gene pool which they represent.

According to Dawkins, some copying mistakes, or mutations, have proven to be advantageous in terms of ability to cope with environmental challenges such as climatic change, invasions by new predators and parasites, or the enhanced effectiveness of familiar neighbours. Some have produced changes in design that successfully counter those evolved by competitors. Dawkins referred to this mutually progressive process as an "evolutionary arms race."

Some mutations, accumulating gradually over geological time, have produced behaviours that allowed the body to manipulate its surroundings in very powerful ways, as in the example of beaver dams, ant hills, bird nests and bee hives. Dawkins called this phenomenon "the extended phenotype." The principle behind it is: "An animal's behaviour tends to maximize the survival of genes 'for' that behaviour, whether or not these genes happen to be in the body of the particular animal performing it" (Dawkins 1989:253). He suggested that it is helpful to visualize "the gene as sitting at the centre of a radiating web of extended phenotypic power" (ibid.:265).

This radically new perspective resolves the old anomalies in evolutionary theory around (1) the altruistic/egoistic controversy caused by the *appearance* of selection for the welfare of groups rather than individuals, and (2) the *apparent* selection of learned behaviours that has continued to puzzle theorists for whom Lamarckism has been long discredited. Only the survival of its discrete vehicle (or of those of siblings and other close relatives) is of advantage to the gene. Nonetheless, if certain behaviours of neighbouring vehicles in their transactions with the physical and social surroundings have the indirect effect of ensuring that survival, then genetic variations favouring the entire network of reciprocal behaviours will be selected over the long term. No tenuous assumption of a mysterious hormone for altruism or mechanism for the inheritance of acquired characteristics is necessary.

Selfish genes or selfish DNA?

Many criticisms of the selfish gene theory reveal a widespread incomprehension of the *after-the-fact*, or feedback, nature of causality in evolution. Some even indicate an inability to distinguish metaphor from literal description. Even Gould seemed to have succumbed to this malady to some extent, as when he complained, "I am disturbed by the erroneous idea that genes are discrete and divisible particles, using the traits that they build in organisms as weapons for their personal propagation. An individual is not decomposible into independent bits of genetic coding" (Gould 1979:269). But one might as well object to a medical scientist that a body is not decomposible into its organs! As Dawkins noted, "It is only when we remember that it has many internal parts, all obeying the laws of physics at their own level, that we understand the behaviour of the whole body" (Dawkins 1986:11). And Dawkins was careful to specify as his unit of analysis only the self-replicating aspect of the gene, however that might be defined in the future.

Gould preferred to discuss what he called self-serving DNA. He used, as an argument against Dawkins, the example of that considerable proportion of DNA which is carried along through the generational shuffle without manifesting any phenotypic effects at all. "Dawkins' selfish genes increase in frequency because they have effects on bodies, aiding them in their struggle for existence. Selfish DNA increases in frequency for precisely the opposite reason ... [it is not suppressed because its presence makes no difference to the body's functioning]" (Gould 1983:174). But according to Dawkins, the same principle — that the survival of replicators is determined by the company they keep — is operating in both cases. Where the phenotypic effects are likely to be disadvantageous, "free-loading" genes survive to the degree that circumstances allow them simply to take advantage of the compatible environment in which they have landed by chance.

The punctuated equilibrium theory

Dawkins accepted the likelihood that evolution is not a constantly, nor even exclusively, *gradual* process of change. Gould and and his colleague Niles Eldridge developed the theory of "punctuated equilibrium" to describe this. As Gould explained it, evolution is not just a tale of measured, gradual adaptation within lineages. "Rather, species form rapidly in geological perspective (thousands of years) and tend to remain stable for millions of years thereafter. . . . Whatever accumulates by punctuated equilibrium (or by other processes) in normal times can be broken up, dismantled, reset and dispersed by mass extinction" (Gould 1985:241-42). Furthermore: "Within complex systems, smoothness of input can translate into episodic change in output" (Gould 1980:44). Here Gould was referring to recent findings in molecular biology indicating that living parts are connected in intricate ways and that the ultimate consequences of a minute change of instruction at the gene level can, through embryonic development and subsequent growth, result in relatively large structural changes in organisms.

Interestingly, Dawkins arrived at a similar conclusion before having encountered Gould's theory. In the 1976 edition of *The Selfish Gene* he surmised, "Progressive evolution may be not so much a steady upward climb as a series of discrete steps from stable plateau to stable plateau" (Dawkins 1989:86). When he discovered, somewhat to his embarrassment, that the punctuated equilibrium hypothesis had been published three years earlier, he was concerned that it was being oversold by the press as something revolutionary and anti-Darwinian, which it clearly was not.

In fact, Gould had reminded his readers that Darwin's mechanism of natural selection does not require any postulate about *rates* of change. "All theories of discontinuous change are not anti-Darwinian, as Thomas Huxley pointed out nearly 120 years ago. Suppose a discontinuous change in adult form arises from a small genetic variation. . . . Suppose also that a large change does not produce a perfected form all at once, but rather serves as a 'key' adaptation to shift its possessor towards a new mode of life" (Gould 1980:191). As in the case of giraffes foraging among high-branching trees, the new mode of life would favour those adults with the key adaptation of extended necks. Natural selection is still at work throughout, determining reproductive success on the basis of better environmental fit.

Dawkins admitted that he had benefited from Gould's lead in focusing on embryology. He noted, however, that apparent macroevolutionary changes are only so in terms of adult forms. "If we look at the *procession* of embryonic developments, they turn out to be micromutations in the sense that only a small change in embryonic *instructions* had a large apparent effect on the adult" (Dawkins 1986:236). Both men agreed that the issue is not one of constant-rate gradualism versus large, catastrophic leaps unexplainable by Darwinian theory; credible evolutionists hold neither of these "straw man" positions. Gould merely wanted to compress much of the gradual change occurring in evolution into brief bursts of activity, interspersed with long periods of relative stasis. Dawkins accepted this as a plausible scenario, but could not quite see what all the fuss was about. He acknowledged that Gould was probably describing how speciation occurs, but because in each case it is a one-time event largely effected through accidental circumstance, Dawkins did not consider that process particularly *interesting* in the sense of leading to further refinements of evolutionary theory.

The historical versus the analytic approach

Speciation is, of course, interesting from the historical point of view, in that — like the idea of mass extinctions — it sheds light on momentous singular occurrences in the descent of life. A study of the process traces the causal chains that result in particular events. But Dawkins was suggesting that it usually does not identify regularities, or postulates of great explanatory power likely to provide generalizable knowledge concerning evolution wherever it might occur. However, recent research documenting the phenomenon as an ongoing aspect of within-species selection — even a reversible one — suggests that both Dawkins and Gould may have overstated their cases here.

In the end, the interesting altercation between Dawkins and Gould, as to whether the phenomenon of speciation or within-species evolution is the more interesting, reveals more about the two scholars than about the question at issue. Gould approached his work as a natural historian, open to the possibility that the process is pluralistic as to causality. Dawkins' orientation was that of the theoretical scientist, seeking the key organizing principle for explaining change in living forms wherever it occurs. Each perspective is capable of shedding light on the subject of evolution; each is necessary, if only to compensate for possible weaknesses in the other.

Dawkins was looking for principles of biology that might have similar universal validity to those of physics. He did not expect there to be many, but he did identify one. "This is the law that all life evolves by the differential survival of replicating entities" (Dawkins 1989:192). He viewed this as particularly interesting, in the scientific sense, in that it can be applied to two significant levels of life: the biological and social. He suggested that the gene, or DNA molecule, became, at a very early stage, the principal replicator on this planet, but that — with the appearance of human self-consciousness and culture — another replicator was born. This means that, if his principle holds, *it will for the first time open the way for the extension of a scientifically valid general theory of evolution to the social realm*. It will provide crucial biological support for the premises of thinkers like Durkheim, Mead, Huxley, Popper, Piaget and Skinner concerning individual learning and cultural evolution.

On the nature of evolutionary science

Clearly, Dawkins was influenced by Karl Popper, and was building on his ideas to some extent. Gould, too, had read Popper, and held fast to the criterion of falsifiability — or at least of testability. In fact, one of Gould's greatest contributions was his clarification of the nature of science, in Popper's terms but in language understandable by the public. He underlined the fact that "Science is a procedure for testing and rejecting hypotheses, not a compendium of certain knowledge.... Theories that cannot be tested in principle are not a part of science" (Gould 1985:111). Scientific observation is "a search for a repeated pattern. Laws and regularities underlie the display" (Gould 1987:181). Facts, then, are pervasive patterns in nature that have been observed and "confirmed to such a degree that it would be perverse to withhold provisional assent" (Gould 1983:255). Theories are structures of ideas that explain and interpret facts.

Gould considered the really revolutionary thinkers to be those who weave new theories — or conceptual structures for rendering the familiar more meaningful. For this, he said, they need the right metaphors. On this point, it may be that Dawkins' "selfish gene," "extended phenotype" and "blind watchmaker" (as well as his use of "survival machine" in reference to the organism and "computer" for a crude prototype of the human brain) will help to force the change in world view implied by Darwinism but still so intensely resisted in our culture.

In his own work Gould chose to follow Popper's advice concerning the appropriate historical approach, as distinct from the methods of experimental science. "We must develop criteria for inferring the processes we cannot see from results that have been preserved," he maintained (ibid.:123). For evolutionary science, as a whole, he recommended marrying "the distinctive styles of natural history and reductionist experiment" (Gould 1987:168). His use of "reductionist" here when he was obviously discussing a general experimental approach is dubious, as the two concepts are not the same, nor does the one imply the other. This comment makes sense only in terms of the historicist and/or Gestalt-psychological view that *all* analysis is reductionist. What Gould seemed to be suggesting is the need for his own historical perspective in combination with that represented by Dawkins.

Gould claimed that natural historians like himself, who use the comparative rather than the experimental approach, must convince the scientific community that their explanations are testable by procedures as rigorous as those employed in the usual stereotype of "the scientific method"; and that these explanations can be meaningful and fruitful in the scientific sense. He described his type of scientific endeavour as an attempt to reconstruct history: to identify, through logical inference, the processes that must have led to the results observed. He would probably agree with Edward O. Wilson's explanation of the process: "The evolutionary biologist retrodicts the experiment already performed by Nature; he teases science out of history" (Wilson 1992: 167). Gould was convinced that historical science allows us to rejoice in the causal power of the individual event; of the human choice. "Contingency," he wrote, "is a licence to participate in history, and our psyche responds" (Gould 1989:285).

On contingency

Gould maintained that "life is the product of a contingent past, not the inevitable and predictable result of simple timeless laws of nature" (Gould 1985:15). He viewed contingency as the central principle of all history. It implies "an unpredictable sequence of antecedent states, where any major change in any step of the sequence would have altered the final result. This final result is therefore dependent, or contingent, on everything that came before" (Gould 1989:283).

It is not clear from this whether Gould was referring to Mead's and Skinner's insight concerning after-the-fact causality, or to the concept of indeterminacy in physics; or merely to the operation of something other than simplistic genetic determinism and/or cosmic necessity. After all, what is the principle of natural selection about, if not the role of contingency in evolution — both in the case of chance mutations and the selective demands of environmental effects? Gould did point out that contingency does not mean randomness. He noted that we do not live in the midst of a chaos of circumstance unchanneled by laws of nature such as the physical principles of self-organizing systems. But he recognized that within the genetically determined channels environmental pressures can make a difference.

Clearly Gould wanted to emphasize that it is the external trigger of changing environments that drives history, rather than any internal dynamic of life, and that it is therefore impossible to envisage any predictable order over geological time. His colleague, Richard Lewontin, noted, however, that evolution may be contingent (in Gould's sense) only in a superficial and scientifically *uninteresting* way. According to him, what we in our overwhelming ignorance consider accidental might have been predictable if we had but discerned the rules that operate (Lewontin:7).

A disagreement on determinism?

Dawkins also saw Gould's particular notion of contingency as a reflection of our current lack of knowledge concerning causal connections in nature. This philosophical difference between the two theorists is possibly the source of the controversy between them over the nature/nurture issue. Dawkins, expecting that he would be accused of determinism, made a specific disclaimer in the introduction to *The Selfish Gene*. Elsewhere, he wrote in response to just such an accusation from Gould and a colleague, "I suspect that . . . [they] are determinists in that they believe in a physical and materialistic basis for their actions. So am I. We could also probably all three agree that human nervous systems are so complex in practice that we can forget all about determinism and behave as if we had free will" (Dawkins 1982:11).

Dawkins went on to discuss the strange reluctance of many people to attribute *any* determining role for genes — even in theory. He assumed that they consider such an admission necessarily to imply wholesale genetic determinism. "The belief that genes are somehow super deterministic in comparison to environmental causes is a myth of extraordinary tenacity" (ibid.). He pointed out that *there is in principle no difference between genetic and environmental programming*, except that one occurs before birth and the other after.

In response to Gould's claim that there could not possibly be genes "for" such complex behaviours as general braininess or sexual orientation, Dawkins explained that the difference between two complex chains of circumstances could be caused by very slight variations in some simple thing. He admitted that homosexuality would present a real problem for Darwinism if it were indeed inherited as a fixed genetic entity distinguishing homosexuals from heterosexuals. It is difficult to imagine how it could have been selected on the basis of reproductive survival. However, he noted that, "even if there are genes which, in today's environment, produce a homosexual phenotype, this does not mean that in another environment . . . they would have had the same phenotypic effect" (ibid.:38).

Dawkins saw no reason for what he described as the hysterical opposition to even the suggestion of genetic variation in mental ability. He maintained that genes must exert statistical influence on *any* behaviour pattern that has evolved by natural selection. If we admit, as we must, that the brain evolved, then we must also admit the possibility of significant genetic variation in intellectual capacity within the human population at any given time. He noted that this in no way implies inter*group* differences. Individual differences in inherited braininess, however, must be accepted as fact. But, said Dawkins, "to base any policy on it would be illogical and wicked" (ibid.:26). Dawkins' general position on the subject is that, while genes exert a statistical influence on human behaviour, this influence can most certainly be modified, overridden or reversed by environmental influences of all sorts.

Gould, conscious of widespread misuse of IQ testing to infer genetic differences in braininess among so-called races, was more sympathetic to the opposition. He wrote a book, *The Mismeasure of Man*, with the laudable purpose of exposing the fallacies involved in such practices and claims. In it he deplored the weakness of biologists and social scientists for: (1) *reification* (attributing concrete reality to abstract constructs); (2) *ranking* (ordering complex variation into single scales); and (3) *unwarranted application of the concept of heritability* to comparisons of intergroup mean scores. He also dealt with the unfortunate effects of our continuing obsession with the racial classification of humans. He noted that there is no biological basis for determining subspecies within humankind. Early geographic dispersal (now rapidly reversing) did promote a range of observable variation, but none of the genetic distinctiveness associated with speciation has occurred in the human lineage.

Gould emphasized that it is a mistake to take the behaviours of individuals in particular environments as the only predictable results of their genetic inheritance. The range of genetic potential for any particular set of complex traits is likely much larger than is indicated by the behavioural effects as shaped by specific cultures. He explained that this is because the human species is *neotenous*: we retain into adulthood the originally juvenile features of our evolutionary ancestors. Because of this embryonic stretching-out, the formative stage of development is in a sense extended throughout life. The human is a learning animal, incompletely programmed before birth, and therefore relatively open to environmental influences.

Gould's arguments here were directed not at Dawkins, who would seem to be in complete agreement, but at certain popular "group-selection" sociobiologists, and the racists who distort and misuse their ideas. In fact, he admitted that *knowledgeable* sociobiologists (and one would surely have to include Edward O. Wilson here) "are not genetic determinists in the old eugenical sense of postulating single genes for ... complex behaviours. ... We all recognize that genetic influences can be spread diffusely among many genes and that genes set limits to ranges. In one sense, the debate between sociobiologists and their critics is an argument about the breadth of ranges" (Gould 1981:329). Within these ranges, physical and cultural environmental influences have a powerful determining effect, and Gould and Dawkins seemed to agree that there is little point in attempting to assess the proportion of each factor in any specific trait.

On the evolution of culture

Clearly Gould preferred to avoid making inferences from biological evolution to the sociocultural realm. He did suggest that there must be a potential evolutionary science of behaviour, but his personal priority was to reveal the inadequacies of all current attempts at developing one. Gould implied that the mistake made by many sociobiologists is that they try to explain cultural evolution in terms of natural selection of inherited propensities, rather than as the conditional Lamarckian process that it must surely be. He wanted to remind us of "the necessity of exploring culture with principles different from the laws of evolutionary biology. New levels require an addition of principles [although] they neither deny nor contradict the explanations appropriate to the lower levels" (Gould 1987:69).

Dawkins, on the other hand, was clearly fascinated by the prospect of contributing to a general theory of cultural evolution: one that would be rooted in evolutionary biology. Like Gould, he was aware that, at the level of culture, the process is Lamarckian — and that those (relatively few) sociobiologists who believe that specific behavioural patterns are selected for the welfare of the group have been misled. He identified three key ideas from current evolutionary biology that could form the basis of a fruitful theory of cultural evolution. These are (1) William D. Hamilton's theory of kin selection; (2) John Maynard Smith's concept of Evolutionarily Stable Strategies; and (3) his own hypothesis that all evolution operates by means of the differential survival of self-replicating entities.

Kin selection

Both Gould and Dawkins saw kin selection, and the innate grounding for altruism which it seems to indicate, as extremely important for both biological and social theory. Gould agreed with Dawkins in identifying the phenomenon as a probable early source of social interaction. He claimed that only humans have developed "kinship (the basis of our social structures) by producing an intersection between two fundamental biological relationships . . . [the primary bond of mother and child and the pair bond uniting adult male and female]" (ibid.:70). Elsewhere he said, "the theory of kin selection has extended Darwinian theory fruitfully into the realm of social behaviour" (Gould 1980:14). Edward O. Wilson, who first used the term "sociobiology" in 1956, also recognized kin selection as the key to understanding primate (hence human) behaviour. Neither Wilson, Dawkins nor Gould noted, however, that it was Spencer who first referred to the social consequences of kinship as "family altruism."

Social behaviour as defined by biologists is particularly significant for social theorists. This is because, as Mead recognized, it would seem to provide the necessary precipitating context for self-consciousness — and thus for the possibility of cultural evolution. Gould referred to self-consciousness as "a natural product of evolution integrated within a bodily frame of no special merit [which] has transformed the surface of our planet" (Gould 1983:250). However, the development of this remarkable capacity — and its consequences for human cultural evolution — seem not to interest him as much as the sheer improbability of its emergence, and the mass extinction of the larger dinosaurs that made it possible.

Both Gould and Dawkins have described kin selection as a means by which natural selection preserves the genes of the self-sacrificing relative — rather than in terms of any conscious altruistic concern for the welfare of the group. This accords as well with Wilson's conclusion that such "hard-wired" altruism differs from the "soft-wired" reciprocal variety which evolves culturally if the conditions are favourable (Wilson 1978: 155). And Dawkins agreed with Gould that the principles underlying kin selection (self-serving though they are from the gene's point of view) do have implications for human social behaviour, and, in fact, probably were responsible for establishing elementary social organization in human groups.

Evolutionarily stable strategies

The second theory which Dawkins found significant, and for the same reason, is that of Evolutionarily Stable Strategies. These are genetically programmed ways of relating among animals in geographic proximity that tend to maximize sexual reproduction for the majority of contenders over the long term. They are strategies that, once acquired by most of the population, cannot be bettered by alternative ones. This is why they are stable, for "once an ESS is achieved it will stay; selection will penalize deviation from it" (Dawkins 1989:69). Its stability is not due to the fact that the *groups* practising it will be more successful than others. It is simply the only way of behaving that does not allow huge immediate gains for an individual who makes a sudden change in strategy; in Dawkins' words, it is immune to treachery from within.

Dawkins believed that the theory of Evolutionarily Stable Strategies (ESS) sheds light as well on what Gould had observed as punctuated equilibrium. He thought that the latter is caused by the occurrence of evolutionarily stable gene pools. Because of the mutually rewarding strategies that have evolved, consisting of powerful patterns of co-adaptation, it is difficult for new genes to invade, or to upset the stability if they do manage to survive in the pool. Interestingly, this concept seems very like that of the "self-stabilizing cycles" of general systems theory (Laszlo).

Examples of Evolutionarily Stable Strategies observed in nature are: "Attack opponent; if he flees pursue him; if he retaliates run away" (Dawkins 1989:69) and "If you are resident, attack; if you are intruder, retreat" (ibid.: 78). Once a majority of a population has come to operate in one of these ways, deviants are selected out. Dawkins considered this to be a more satisfying explanation for what has often been considered to be innate aggression and territoriality. With the ESS theory it is no longer necessary to puzzle about the dubious biological adaptibility of much complicated animal behaviour. In each case the advantage is that it *works* to confer survival and reproductive benefits in the particular local situation as established by the behaviour of other animals. That is, it works for most of the individuals most of the time, and those who break the rules are not likely to benefit long enough to reproduce.

Dawkins discussed the possible implications of all this for human social behaviour. He used the example of game theory from the work of Robert Axelrod and Anatol Rapaport on conflict resolution. In the beginning, those moves which could be described as motivated by envy and greed produce the occasional large benefit along with a preponderance of negative returns. But, as the game continues, it becomes apparent that "envious" and "greedy" plays operate to the disadvantage of *all* players over the long term, and the strategy stabilizes into a pattern resulting in consistent but lower-level gains for those who do not try to impose losses on opponents. In games such as the well-known Prisoner's Dilemma, "nice guys really do finish first"! This principle seems to apply wherever the participants have a memory; where the time involved is sufficiently long; and where the game is of the non-zero-sum variety that characterizes most human activities. In such situations the stable strategy is the one which allows for most participants to derive some benefit most of the time, rather than one involving large gains to a few and large aggregate losses to the many.

Dawkins wondered whether the universal incest taboo evolved in human cultures according to an analogous process. The adverse biological and social effects of intermarriage in close-knit tribal communities are sufficiently drastic that they would have been immediately recognizable, even though extraordinarily advantageous combinations of attributes occasionally occur. He suggested that, *although it is cultural*, "selection for active incest avoidance could have been as strong as any selective pressure that has been measured in nature" (ibid.:294).

He also referred to a "Skinner box" experiment featuring a dominant and submissive pig in a room with a feeding trough at one end and at the other, a lever which had to be tripped in order for food to enter the trough. The only possible stable strategy was one that would result in a reward for the worker each time the lever was operated. This was only achieved when the "master" pig did all the lever-pushing, since the "slave" could not get near the full trough except when the other pig was occupied. The very master/slave relationship that led one to expect the submissive partner to do the work guaranteed that, if he did, he would not be rewarded with food, and would therefore not keep working the lever. The dominant pig, on the other hand, could trip the lever and still manage to bully his way back into the trough for his share.

The significance of this experiment for Dawkins was that it indicates an underlying similarity between the slow, cumulative evolution of complex genetic behaviours over geological time and both the development of routines and habits within the individual life-span and the emergence of customs during the course of generations. It appears that *developmentally* and *socially* stable strategies are selected and stabilized by environmental contingencies no less than are the *evolutionarily* stable ones established in the gene pool — and by a parallel process of programming! This is a powerful concept that could be applied fruitfully to many of our institutionalized practices today. And it provides strong support for the behavioural and cultural theories of thinkers like Piaget, Skinner and Popper.

Differential survival of self-replicating entities

The third and most fundamental idea, for Dawkins, was his own proposition that all evolution operates by means of the differential survival of self-replicating entities. He was looking for a basic unit of culture analogous to the gene: the smallest structure of thought that can be learned and stored and acted upon and shared. In a refinement of Huxley's "mentifacts," Dawkins coined his own word "meme" to symbolize these "patterns of information that can thrive only in brains — books — computers" (Dawkins 1986:158). (At the same time, in an intriguing example of convergence in theorizing, Edward O. Wilson began to refer to competing behaviours and mental concepts as "culturgens.")

Understandably, Dawkins was not very clear about the precise nature of the entity or process involved. He suspected that meme-transmission is subject to continuous mutation, and to the blending that sexual reproduction renders impossible for genes. He seemed to recognize that there is no returning to the original recipe with each generation, but did not explore implications of the fact that, from the perspective of the unsocialized infant, *there is no recipe*. What does exist for the infant is infinitely better. It is the potential to *learn* through socialization: to acquire the memes of the group and to create new ones. The process at the level of the culture is thereby immeasurably faster and more all-encompassing than biological evolution in that it accumulates the meme-production of each generation.

Dawkins was guessing that co-adapted meme complexes evolve much as do similarly co-adapted gene complexes. "The meme pool therefore comes to have the attributes of an evolutionarily stable set, which new memes will find it hard to invade" (Dawkins 1989:199). This would explain the perseverence of myths and customs. Dawkins did not believe that the new replicators are subservient to the older ones; his was definitely not a theory of genetic determinism. He seemed, like Huxley before him, to be implying the very opposite: that cultural evolution has the potential for assuming control of its biological antecedent.

The science educator as a shaper of culture

Gould's interest in culture had much more to do with the immediate need to alter what Dawkins would have called the state of the current meme pool. He dedicated himself to battling the rising tide of irrationalism and anti-science sentiment threatening to engulf the pool. He claimed: "No force can be so powerfully destructive, so capable of undoing the patient struggles of centuries with a single blow, as irrationalism (especially when fueled by 'true belief')" (Gould 1987:14). Gould brought two great strengths to this battle: an informed and dynamic world view and the talents of a master teacher and writer. However, in an ironic twist of fate (or "contingency") both these remarkable attributes became at the same time a source of problems that have threatened to undermine his admirable enterprise.

The Hegelian-Marxist dialectic influencing Gould's world view gave him an insight into the cultural-embeddedness of all science, and a resulting awareness of inevitable limitations on the objectivity of the individual scientist. It motivated him in his chosen role as defender of the underdog in evolutionary scholarship, inspiring him to scrutinize respectfully the radical hypotheses of the mavericks of today, and the now-discredited proponents of yesterday's conventional wisdom. It made him sensitive to the larger patterns of historical change; to the play between constraints imposed by internal structure and external environmental pressures; and to the way in which gradual, seemingly quantitative change within a system can suddenly result in the emergence of an apparent difference in quality.

Gould's other defining characteristic has always been his outstanding power as a communicator. His colourful writing style and eloquent use of metaphor, and his ability to make the complex and strange appear simple and familiar by the use of well-chosen examples, have made him one of the world's true master teachers. In assuming this public educating function, Gould has contributed a great deal to science and to human culture in general. His clear expositions on the nature of science and his courageous exposures of popular pseudo-science are a service to us all. Any reader who has had the good fortune to encounter those engaging titles and the captivating detective stories within, about the nature of evolution, has emerged from the experience enthralled by the sheer wonder of it all.

Who but Stephen Jay Gould could so unerringly spot the "Dr. Panglossian" inversion of causality in the religious vision of Freeman Dyson; or Fritjof Capri's promotion of "holistic" irrationalism parading as physics; or Robert Jastrow's wish-fulfilling theology in the guise of astronomy; or Jeremy Rifkin's fallacious logic and twisted facts masquerading as scientific criticism; or the tragedy of Teilhard, the absurdity of Daniken, and the "glorious wrongheadedness" of Velikovsky?

But there is the potential for a dark side to these particular strengths. Dialectical thinking encourages a blurring of the boundaries between ideology and science, so that the naive or ideological reader can too readily interpret Darwin's theory as being not so much *influenced* by his cultural milieu as merely a *reflection* and *legitimation* of it. Similarly, an awareness of the conditioning process shaping the values and perceptions of all humans — including scientists — can too easily translate into the erroneous conclusion that scientific facts are no more reliable or valid than any other set of opinions. This was certainly never Gould's position, as he made clear time and time again, as, for example, when he discussed Lysenko, and when he emphasized the criterion of testability. And yet, far too often, proponents of just such an extreme "postmodern" point of view have somehow been able to cite Stephen Jay Gould in support of their claims.

Another characteristic of dialectical thinking is a rejection of the method of analysis. It is not merely that the whole is seen as more then the sum of its parts, for that is so universally accepted by theorists as to be unworthy of mention. It is rather that the whole is considered somehow so qualitatively different from its parts, and so overwhelmingly determinative in itself, that it cannot be explained at all by examining those parts and the relationships among them. This view stems from a philosophical misunderstanding of Mead's key concepts of "contingency" and "emergence." It implies that *all* analysis is inappropriate, although its proponents are forced to recognize the obvious exceptions of physics and molecular biology, where the method's success cannot be denied. But, as a matter of principle for dialectical thinkers, analysis is the cardinal sin. This is why they use the pejorative label of "reductionism" in ways that are puzzling to theorists who do not share their assumptions. This practice is unfortunate, as it introduces an element of name-calling into what should be a cooperative and mutually respectful search for knowledge. Sadly, Gould was caught up in this, in spite of his frequent acknowledgement of the necessity for both approaches to the study of evolution.

Unlike Marx, many modern dialectical thinkers have existentialist leanings that tend to prejudice them against the very naturalism demanded by a thorough understanding and acceptance of Darwinism. Although Gould could not be accused of this, his interpretation of contingency and emergence as implying some kind of *essential* indeterminacy — and his castigation of "mechanistic" analogies in evolutionary theory — might have inadvertently fed prevalent cultural predilections for this latest version of the "picket-fence syndrome." This could explain the puzzling fact that so many modern vitalists feel justified in claiming him as a supporter.

Gould's power as a communicator has also had its dangers, as he discovered in his altercation with the creationists. All effective public educators have suffered from seeing their provocative enthusiasms, insights and images twisted in unscrupulous hands and made to provide the backup for very different drummers. Gould's remarkable reputation as a science educator was used by such people in the service of a concerted attack upon modern Darwinism. Here, again, his dialectical leanings could be partly to blame, as they may have biased him toward a revolutionary rather than an evolutionary view of scientific progress. In the present climate, any hint that new hypotheses and conclusions are radically different from other aspects of the current Darwinian synthesis seems to encourage a deluge of misleading publicity that can only feed the anti-Darwinian and anti-science ideology that both Gould and Dawkins have fought so hard against.

To his great credit, Gould has struggled mightily to undo the harm caused by the distortion and misuse of his ideas. No modern-day agents of irrationalism should mistake Stephen Jay Gould for a friend! They should heed what he wrote of humanity: "we have become, by the power of the glorious evolutionary accident called intelligence, the stewards of life's continuity on earth. We did not ask for this role but we cannot abjure it" (Gould 1985:431). Not only is this a compelling summary of Dawkins' position as well, but it sounds very much like the central moral message implied by the emerging model of evolutionary naturalism.

That model also owes much to the revolutionary perspective of Wilson, and his groundbreaking work in sociobiology — in spite of the fact that both Gould and Dawkins have raised serious questions about his conjecture that the group might function as a unit in biological evolution. However, this earlier emphasis on group-selection now seems to have given way to a fruitful focus on " 'gene-culture co-evolution' . . . an eternal circle of change in heredity and culture" (Wilson 1994:351). This is similar to Gould's conclusion that "genes and environment interact in a nonadditive way, yielding emergent features in the resulting anatomies, physiologies and behaviors" (Gould 1992:48). By thus emphasizing the *interactive* nature of cultural and biological programming, Wilson and Gould are joining Dawkins in opening the door for sociology to proceed, finally, in a direction that holds out the possibility of real progress for the entire field of studies of which it is a part.

Implications for the study of human behaviour

The recent work of W.G. Runciman contributes further insights for sharpening and expanding the new model. He sees social selection operating at the societal level in a manner analogous to that of natural selection — much as Skinner does in the case of overt and covert behaviours in the process of individual learning. Runciman compares social interaction to the sexual variety, as the means by which new social *practices* (or role relationships) are born. He believes that social evolution selects the groups by whom the institutionalized practices are carried. Those practices that confer an advantage over other social groups in terms of *power* (either coercive, economic or ideological) are favoured by the evolutionary process.

It would seem that Runciman views the evolution of new systems of stable role relationships (or institutions) as corresponding to speciation at the biological level. But it could be argued that the social group in both cases is merely the necessary (although space-and time-bound) context within which practices are pursued and acquired by the young — as Skinner described that process. The *group*, as such, does not evolve. This remains the case whether individuals are grouped in terms of skin pigmentation, territoriality or ethnic origin. Those practices which render a group sufficiently effective to enable individuals to survive to reproduce with relative success will tend to be acquired and maintained by the immediate offspring. But it is the *symbolic aspects* of role relationships — the beliefs and values that justify and define them — which are carried and passed on by the group's members and thus evolve in a cultural sense. And it is the resulting shared *institutions* (ideas and ideals as manifested in reciprocal relations) that define a society. This is an important distinction to keep in mind, lest we once more fall into the errors of Social Darwinism!

These "representations" or "memes" or "culturgens" are carried, not by the group as an isolable entity, but by the tales of the elders in a pre-literate society, and by the books, films and computers of the modern world. Although behaviours are learned and modelled by individuals, only symbolic representations can be self-replicating in the sense that genetic information is carried from generation to generation. Any adequate theory of institutional change would have to take account of this fact. It would also have to incorporate and explain the complex interrelationships between genetic propensities and experiential programming; and among these and the cumulative progress of science, technological expansion and adaptive alterations in social roles.

Gould once wrote that he has three reasons for loving evolutionary theory: it is about life; like its subject it is still evolving; and it stands at the point of intersection between those sciences that deal in timeless generality and those concerned with the particularities of history. He could have added that this applies to the study of human behaviour and cultural evolution as well. A more widespread recognition of this fact could reverse the regrettable tendency for the two fields of study to be pursued in virtual isolation from one another. The present crisis in social science demonstrates the tragic consequences of consistent refusal to base theories in that field on the current consensus in biology and evolutionary theory.

The insights of Dawkins and other leading sociobiologists regarding possible genetic sources of social organization — and the implications of evolution for individual development and cultural change — might well provide both incentive and substance for more valid and fruitful research into human behaviour than has been the case until now. And Gould's perspective can serve to remind us that no approach to the study of humanity can hope to succeed if it ignores either the constraints imposed by our unique biological history or the learning potential of the human being. If evolutionary naturalists like Piaget, Popper, Skinner and Runciman are indeed the harbingers of long-overdue progress in their disciplines, the social science of the twenty-first century will owe much to the clarification and dissemination of current biological knowledge by people such as Dawkins, Gould and Wilson.

References for Chapter Twenty-Four

Australian Broadcasting Corporation. 1989. *Broadcast of Taped Discussion at Oxford between Richard Dawkins and Stephen Jay Gould*. Distributed by Robyn Williams. Sidney, NSW: The Australian Museum, 1989.

Boyd, Robert, and Peter J. Richerson. 1985. *Culture and the Evolutionary Process* Chicago: University of Chicago Press.

Dawkins, Richard. 1976. *The Selfish Gene*. 1st ed. Oxford: Oxford University Press.

_____. 1982. *The Extended Phenotype*. Oxford: W.H. Freeman.

_____. 1986. *The Blind Watchmaker*. New York: W.W. Norton.

_____. 1989. *The Selfish Gene*. 2nd ed. Oxford: Oxford University Press.

_____. 1990. Review of *Wonderful Life* by Stephen Jay Gould. *Sunday Telegraph*, February 25.

_____. 1995. *River Out of Eden: A Darwinian View of Life*. New York: Basic Books.

Degler, Karl N. 1991. *In Search of Human Nature: The Decline and Revival of Darwinism in American Social Thought*. New York: Oxford University Press.

Dennett, Daniel C. 1995. *Darwin's Dangerous Idea: Evolution and the Meaning of Life*. New York: Simon and Schuster.

Dissonayake, Ellen. 1988. *What Is Art For?* Seattle: University of Washington Press.

_____. 1992. *Homo Aestheticus: Where Art Comes From and Why*. Toronto: Macmillan.

Gould, Stephen Jay. 1979. *Ever Since Darwin*. New York: W.W. Norton.

_____. 1980. *The Panda's Thumb*. New York: W.W. Norton.

_____. 1981. *The Mismeasure of Man*. New York: W.W. Norton.

_____. 1983. *Hen's Teeth and Horse's Toes*. New York: W.W. Norton.

_____. 1985. *The Flamingo's Smile*. New York: W.W. Norton.

_____. 1987. *An Urchin in the Storm*. New York: W.W. Norton.

_____. 1989. *Wonderful Life*. New York: W.W. Norton.

_____. 1991. *Bully for Brontosaurus*. New York: W.W. Norton.

_____. 1992. The Confusion over Evolution. *The New York Review*, November 19, p. 47-54.

_____. 1993. *Eight Little Piggies*. New York: W.W. Norton.

_____. 1995. *Dinosaur in a Haystack*. New York: Harmony Books.

Greenwood, Davydd J. 1984. *The Taming of Evolution: The Persistence of Non-evolutionary Views in the Study of Humans*. Ithaca, NY: Cornell University Press.

Laszlo, Ervin. 1991. *The Age of Bifurcation: Understanding the Changing World*. The World Futures General Evolution Studies, 3. Philadelphia: Gordon and Breach.

Lewontin, R.C. 1990. Fallen Angels: Review of *Wonderful Life* by Stephen Jay Gould. *The New York Review*, June 14, p. 3-7.

Lumsden, C.J., and E.O. Wilson. 1981. *Genes, Mind and Culture*. Cambridge, MA: Harvard University Press.

————. 1983. *Promethean Fire*. Cambridge, MA: Harvard University Press.

Runciman, W.G. 1989. *Confessions of a Reluctant Theorist*. London: Harvester-Wheatsheaf.

Thorsen, Thomas Landon. 1970. *Biopolitics*. New York: Holt, Rinehart and Winston.

Wiegele, Thomas C. 1982. *Biology and the Social Sciences: An Emerging Revolution*. Boulder, CO: Westview Press.

Williams, George. 1974. *Adaptation and Natural Selection: A Critique of Some Current Evolutionary Thought*. Princeton, NJ: Princeton University Press.

Wilson, Edward O. 1975. *Sociobiology: The New Synthesis*. Cambridge, MA: Belknap Press of Harvard University Press.

————. 1978. *On Human Nature*. Cambridge, MA: Harvard University Press.

————, ed. 1988. *Biodiversity*. Washington, DC: National Academy Press.

————. 1992. *The Diversity of Life*. Cambridge, MA: Belknap Press of Harvard University.

————. 1994. *Naturalist*. Washington, DC: Island Press/Sheerwater Books.

Wright, Robert. 1994. *The Moral Animal: Evolutionary Psychology and Everyday Life*. New York: Pantheon.

Twenty-Five

Thomas Kuhn and the Crisis
in Social Science

> The curse of modern philosophy is that it has not drawn its in-
> spiration from science; as the misfortune of science is that it
> has not yet saturated the mind of philosophers and recast the
> moral world.
>
> — George Santayana, *The Life of Reason*

W hy is the nature of the prevailing philosophical world view significant
for social science? The obvious answer is that the two are related in the
same sense that a plant is dependent on the seedbed for which it subsequently
provides life-preserving nurture and protection from the wind and sun. It is no
exaggeration to say that the scientific study of humanity and its products can
progress only in the fertile soil of a philosophy of evolutionary naturalism. It is
not merely that the mystical premises of many cultures render social science
difficult; they imply that it is impossible. If humans are distinguished from
other animals by an unknowable essence at their very core, and if this essence
is connected in some mysterious way to a transcendent source of absolute
truth, then the search for cause and effect in individual development and social
relations is a futile endeavour. On the other hand, it is equally clear that any
sound world view depends for its ongoing evolution on the kind of reliable
knowledge base in the psycho-social realm that only science has ever been
able to provide.

The persistence of anti-science sentiments

The influence of the great social philosophers on the larger culture is necessarily indirect and long term, depending as it does on the ultimate effect of their
ideas on social science. It will vary with the degree to which their efforts succeed in rendering this field of study scientific in fact as well as name — and
thereby capable of providing the reliable knowledge base required for the wise

---

References for this chapter are on p. 464-65.

control of technological advance and social change. For many modern thinkers are beginning to realize that, if we fail to take charge of the process of cultural evolution, the process will continue to take charge of us. Here, a valid,
workable and reliable science of psycho-social behaviour and cultural evolution is our only hope. The great philosophers of every century have been those
who managed to shed some new light on this process, and on the nature of human beings who participate in it.

It is sadly true, however, that social theorists have sometimes led us into
detours that proved costly to the progress of social science. For example, the
mythic power of the untestable elements in the works of Rousseau, Marx,
Nietzsche, Freud, Bergson and Sartre has been by no means an unmixed blessing. Karl Popper attempted to clear the field for the wayward would-be science
of humanity when he spelled out the boundaries between the type of ideological perspective that continues to block progress in that field and the procedures
and guiding theories and values that define legitimate science and allow it to
evolve. It happened that a graduate student who heard Popper speak on the
subject in 1950 was wrestling with the same issue. He went on to write a book
on the subject that has sparked a radical revision of the way we understand the
evolution of science. That student was Thomas Kuhn, and the book was *The
Structure of Scientific Revolutions.*

Thomas Kuhn had less direct interest than Popper in improving the validity and reliability of research in the social realm. His concern was solely with
the history and philosophy of science. Nonetheless, his historical account of
the way in which non-scientific studies gradually changed into proto-sciences
and ultimately to mature sciences has important implications for the psycho-
logical/social studies. But that issue was only a minor aspect of Kuhn's book.
The chief message, and the one that gained worldwide attention, was derived
from his analysis of the process by which *established* sciences evolve.

It was one of those strange "contingencies" of history that most of the
practitioners of social disciplines took the wrong message from this seminal
book. Already self-defined as "sciences," and having gained corresponding
political power within the university setting, they failed to recognize themselves in his description of studies at the pre-scientific end of the continuum.
This misunderstanding of Kuhn's paradigm by social "scientists," coupled
with the uncritical enthusiasm with which they expounded and propounded
that misunderstanding, has had devastating results for the progress of the very
disciplines with the most to gain from his ideas.

The conclusion reached by many vocal sociologists who misread Kuhn's
book was that the entire scientific enterprise, in spite of its pretensions of testability, is really relativistic and ideological to its very core; and the current findings of sociology are of equal validity to those of physics and biology! If it is
paradigms that make a study scientific, all is well, they said, for surely the so-

cial disciplines abound with them! No wonder Popper was appalled and angry at this apparent subversion of his life's work. No wonder Kuhn himself was puzzled and alarmed. For this was not what he had intended. With his background in physics he was ill prepared for the massive dimensions of the wave of anti-science sentiment in the public in general, and in the social studies and humanities in particular, that were to characterize the 1960s and following decades. His book hit the crest of that wave, and the popularized distortions of his paradigm did much to nourish its ferocity and durability.

The shaping of a radical thinker

Thomas Kuhn was teaching at Harvard when he first began to organize his ideas on the evolution of science in order to present them in a general education course for non-science majors. He had been born in Cincinnati, Ohio, in 1922, into a highly educated family of German-Jewish background. His parents had emphasized critical thinking rather than religious tradition. In 1940 he enrolled in the physics program at Harvard, and earned a Ph.D. in that subject nine years later. From 1948 to 1951 he was a junior fellow in the Harvard Society of Fellows, then assistant professor until 1956. That year he was appointed to Berkeley University as a Professor in the History of Science. During this period he was influenced by the research of Piaget, particularly that involving children's achievement of the concepts of causality and motion. In 1957 he published *The Copernican Revolution*, a masterful study of the changes in world view initiated by Copernicus and completed by Newton. In it one can find the roots of all the ideas subsequently developed in his second, and more famous book.

Kuhn spent the following year at the Centre for Advanced Studies in the Behavioral Sciences. There he was, for the first time, part of a community of social scientists. He was surprised by the extent of disagreement on fundamentals, and by the proliferation of incommensurable schools of thought in this arena. By incommensurable he meant differences, not only in translatable terminology, but in the very conceptual structures that the terms express and reflect, and the procedures implied for measuring them.

This set him thinking about how this situation paralleled that of astronomy before Copernicus. He remembered that Copernicus had complained specifically about the inconsistent astronomical investigations occurring in his time. In fact he had written, "it is as though an artist were to gather the hands, feet, head and other members for his images from diverse models, each part excellently drawn, but not related to a single body, and since they in no way match each other, the result would be more monster than man" (Kuhn 1970a:83). This recognition no doubt inspired Kuhn to go beyond Popper's separation of science from ideology and to attempt to identify the process by which the one might evolve into the other, and subsequently to progress in the cumulative manner unique to scientific knowledge.

The Structure of Scientific Revolutions was published in 1962, and it gave Thomas Kuhn an international reputation. He moved to Princeton in 1964, and, in 1970, published an enlarged edition of the book in which he responded to his critics. In 1978 he spent a year as a Fellow at the New York Institute for the Humanities, and then became Professor of Philosophy and History of Science at the Massachusetts Institute of Technology in 1979. In 1983 he was named Laurance S. Rockefeller Professor of Philosophy. He has published other books and numerous articles, but none that have commanded the wide readership of his first two remarkable contributions.

The Copernican revolution

If social scientists had read Kuhn's first book they might not have so badly misunderstood his second. In it he traced the development of the earliest roots of science in the tradition of explaining observed phenomena and requiring that the culture's prevailing cosmology be founded on those explanations. He noted it was the Greeks who first established this as a criterion for a psychologically satisfying world view. Primitive cultures made no such demands on their cosmologies; consequently, they had no built-in mechanisms for correction and change.

Kuhn suggested that, in modern culture, explanations are the foundation stones for imaginative conceptual schemes which define not only the pursuit of knowledge, but the very way people perceive and experience reality. Ultimately these schemes stand or fall on the basis of (1) their adequacy as efficient devices for summarizing bits of information, (2) their ability to provide emotional satisfaction and thus to inspire commitment and (3) their fruitfulness for generating predictions of additional observations; that is "their effectiveness as guides to research, and as frameworks for the organization of knowledge" (Kuhn 1957:40).

Kuhn referred to the enduring belief in a two-sphere universe, on which Ptolemy's model was based, as an early example of just such a successful cosmology. Although we now know that the earlier theories of the atomists were much closer to the findings of modern science, they were neither efficient, believable nor fruitful for people whose perspective was firmly earth-bound and who had no technical means for checking the atomist's abstract speculations. From the onset of the fourth century BCE, Greek astronomers and philosophers agreed that the earth was a stationary sphere located at the geometric centre of a much larger rotating sphere which carried the stars. The sun moved in the space between the two spheres, and beyond the outer sphere there was the otherworldly perfection of the heavens. This made sense in terms of the religious and philosophical beliefs of the time, as spelled out in the comprehensive Aristotelian system, and was even more consistent with the premises of Christianity as it spread through the Roman Empire. And still later, when Western Europe was emerging from its Dark Age, the geocentric theory received another boost from a rediscovered Aristotle.

It is true that, throughout this long period, the movement of the planets posed a problem for Ptolemy's model that was never adequately resolved, but that very anomaly fuelled centuries of purposeful study, especially in the early Islamic world. This, in turn, led to the increasingly elaborate theorizing that ultimately resulted in the powerful mathematical formulations of Copernicus — predicting planetary movement — and the gradual recognition of the need for a new cosmology with Newtonian dynamics as the keystone. "That," wrote Kuhn, "is how science advances: each new conceptual scheme embraces the phenomena explained by its predecessors and adds to them. But though the achievements of Copernicus and Newton are permanent the concepts that made those achievements possible are not. It is only the list of explicable phenomena that grows; there is no similar cumulative process for the explanations themselves. As science progresses, its concepts are repeatedly destroyed and replaced" (ibid.:264-65). Here Kuhn was building upon the earlier thesis of Henri Poincaré, which stated that the only invariant aspect of scientific theories is their empirical content.

Kuhn implied that, in relatively minute and self-contained areas of study where the conceptual framework is not intimately connected to the culture's ultimate premises, a single incompatible observation by a scientist would be sufficient to raise grave doubts about a theory's validity, and its "unfitness" would soon be demonstrated. This is entirely consistent with Popper's recognition of falsification as the equivalent of environmental feedback in the process of natural selection among contending hypotheses in scientific evolution.

Kuhn went on to explain that the really culturally significant scientific revolutions like that of Copernicus and Newton — where the very nature of a major aspect of reality is at stake — inevitably necessitate a revolution in theology, philosophy and morality as well. In such cases, the history of science leads us to expect a lengthy period of conflict and instability within the profession following the original scientific breakthrough, and perhaps centuries before the new world view begins to dominate the general culture. He noted that, whenever these comprehensive defining frameworks are involved, the evolution of science and of the cosmology that follows in its wake is no more likely to be tidy and painless than is any other variety. Although Kuhn did not discuss biology, these ideas shed considerable light on the continuing public reluctance to accept Darwinism and the resistance within the social sciences to its implications for human behaviour and cultural evolution.

The structure of scientific revolutions

In his second book, Kuhn introduced the idea that it is the attainment of a common "paradigm" by the community of researchers in a given problem area that distinguishes a science from other forms of study. He used the term in a very specific way to denote four defining characteristics of a uniquely scientific conceptual framework. These are: (1) a set of shared symbolic generalizations; (2) a common model of reality; (3) shared values as to standards and legitimate procedures; and (4) shared exemplars in the form of concrete problem solutions typical of the approach of the relevant scientific community. It is the assimilation of these exemplars, rather than the self-conscious acquisition of formal rules, that is the end result of the socialization process by which the student becomes a member of the community of professional scientists.

Kuhn was referring both to a common language community (as introduced by Skinner) and to the common model or image of the world expressed by and interpreted in terms of that specialized language — as described so presciently by Martineau. The shared values both result from and contribute to consensus on language and world view. Lastly, Kuhn maintained that, in addition to being grounded in a set of taken-for-granted values, the mature science provides many specific examples of how research is to be done. As he put it, "paradigms provide scientists not only with a map but also with some of the directions essential for map-making" (Kuhn 1970a:109).

Subsequently, Kuhn preferred to restrict the term, "paradigm," to the performance standards and sets of examples of appropriate problem-solving procedures of the relevant community, and to refer to the shared conceptual framework with its accompanying symbolic structure as a "disciplinary matrix." In practice, however, the two are not separable, for it is through the shared values and exemplars that would-be scientists acquire an intuitive sense of the conceptual framework of their field and the terms in which it directs inquiry.

The power of an established paradigm

Kuhn emphasized that, after a "disciplinary matrix" has achieved paradigm status, the practitioners of the mature science behave, for all practical purposes, as if that framework were indeed coincident with reality. And the paradigm is initially assimilated by candidates to the field as if it were reality. In fact, science education is often taught as dogma, in courses quite devoid of epistemological sophistication.

For the individuals concerned, this may inhibit the doubt and originality that would seem a prerequisite for scientific progress during revolutionary periods, but it may also be a source of the strength of what Kuhn calls "normal science." For it means that working scientists can dispense with questions of definition, philosophical assumptions and replicability and concentrate directly on puzzle-solving. They are superbly prepared to push the theory as far as it will go and to recognize anomalies in the results. In this process of refining and elaborating the theory, they function as the indispensable knowledge-builders in the cumulative scientific enterprise. They are also armed with considerable resistance to radically different perspectives on the problem, according to Kuhn, and this means that propositions that challenge the established paradigm will not be readily accepted. Only after expectations are consistently violated by the research results will the established paradigm be questioned, and only when a more adequate contender is available will the paradigm be given up.

Popper was concerned that Kuhn's version of "normal science," if it were indeed to become typical, would spell the end of science. His fears may perhaps be warranted, but only to the degree that the norm results in an unnecessarily dogmatic and narrow training program. On the other hand, it is the very fact of the established disciplinary matrix (and the procedures and values dictated by it) that allows and guarantees a scientific approach on the part of the researcher. We are all too aware of the futility of expecting scientists to exhibit a rigorously scientific attitude in matters outside their narrow research interests. Kuhn explained that it is not a generalized attitude, but the built-in mechanism for exact testing — only available in a problem area defined by a shared paradigm — that makes a field of study scientific. This is in accord with Durkheim's argument against Weber's notion of value neutrality as the prerequisite for practising science. It squares, as well, with the general observation that scientists, as individuals, may be as lacking in objectivity as any other people.

It is even possible that many social scientists, precisely *because* of the pre-scientific nature of their field, may be better prepared to examine complex issues with creative scepticism, and respect for logic and evidence, than are their colleagues in the physical sciences. In a field where there is no common paradigm, each honest inquirer has to go back to fundamentals and to operate as a philosopher of science as well as a researcher. Only the practitioners of normal science can afford to live and work as technicians. Even so, the consequences of their tasks of articulating theory, determining relevant facts and matching fact with theory are highly cumulative. Ironically, what Kuhn called the routine puzzle-solving and mopping-up processes of normal science result in additions to the body of reliable knowledge, while the carefully reasoned forays of the individual social scientist do not. This is the real tragedy in the failure of the social sciences to evolve.

The revolutionary phase in an established science

"By focusing attention upon a small range of relatively esoteric problems, the paradigm forces scientists to investigate some part of nature in a detail and depth that would otherwise be unimaginable. And normal science possesses a built-in mechanism that ensures the relaxation of the restrictions that bind research whenever the paradigm from which they derive ceases to function effectively" (ibid.:24). Kuhn concluded that, as long as the tools provided by the paradigm continue to solve the problems it defines, there is rapid progress in knowledge-building in that part of nature. Inevitably, however, there comes a time when anomalies begin to appear in the observations at the leading edge of research, and these result in a series of extraordinary investigations that reveal inconsistencies demanding a different explanation. Evolution of knowledge in the particular area seems to have hit a plateau, while participating scientists scramble to explain their findings. This revolutionary phase is really one of treading water. It is resolved and the accumulation of reliable knowledge begins again, only after someone comes up with a theory that incorporates all the previously observed regularities and accounts for the presently puzzling ones as well. It is possible that standard relativity and quantum theory in physics is in such a phase at the present time.

The current paradigm is never relinquished until a more adequate one becomes available and has been tested thoroughly and adopted by numerous members of the relevant professional community. Even then its universal acceptance is not immediate. Resistance will be great among the professionals, and even more intractable in the public at large, in those cases where the problem area concerned is broad; where the paradigm operates as the ordering principle for an entire discipline or group of disciplines; and especially where there are clear implications for philosophy and morality. However, Kuhn seemed to imply that, in minute problem areas within an established science, revolution and consequent paradigm change may be almost ongoing — requiring only the refutation of one key hypothesis.

Conflict among competing schools in proto-sciences

From the outside, the crisis phase within an established science might appear to be the same thing as the conflict situation typical of pre-scientific fields such as sociology. This is the source of the mistake made by many of the social scientists who became instant "Kuhnians." Understandably, they preferred to define their disciplines as revolutionary, rather than as pre-scientific. But that is not what Kuhn meant at all. As he put it, "there are many fields — I shall call them proto-sciences — in which practice does generate testable conclusions but which nonetheless resemble philosophy and the arts rather than the established sciences in their development patterns. I think, for example of . . . many of the social sciences today" (Kuhn 1970c:244).

Although he admitted that each of the competing schools in such disciplines is guided by something like a paradigm, the crucial issue is the degree to which one particularly compelling, efficient and fruitful school has come to dominate an entire problem area. And Kuhn did not mean domination by political power, whether wielded by academic departments or totalitarian governments — as in the case of Lysenko. This is an important distinction, for a second, and potentially more dangerous, interpretation of Kuhn has allowed certain social scientists to conclude that some sort of politically established consensus (of the type common to ideological thinking) is all that is required for a field to become scientific. Kuhn responded to this as follows: "no part of the argument here or in my book implies that scientists may choose any theory they like so long as they agree in their choice and afterwards enforce it. Most of the puzzles of normal science are directly presented by nature, and all involve nature indirectly. Though different solutions have been perceived as valid at different times, nature cannot be forced into an arbitrary set of conceptual boxes. . . . To suppose . . . that we possess criteria of rationality which are independent of our understanding of the essentials of the scientific process is to open the door to cloud cuckoo land" (ibid.:263-64). By 1991 Kuhn had become even more concerned about the movement among sociologists and political scientists — now called "the strong program" — that claims to have been inspired by his ideas. For these people, he said, all talk of evidence, rationality and degree of probability is merely "the rhetoric behind which the victorious party cloaks its power, what passes for scientific knowledge becomes, then, simply the beliefs of the winners" (Kuhn 1992:9). He referred to this as "deconstruction gone mad" (ibid.).

A common language community as the prerequisite of science

What *should* the social sciences have learned from Kuhn? A good beginning would have been to examine the elements and function of a successful guiding paradigm, and to begin a concerted effort to work in that direction. For Kuhn, as for Skinner before him, the prerequisite is a common language community; that is, one which operates in terms of shared concepts that can be precisely communicated and rendered commensurable.

Social science may finally be at the stage where it is possible to identify those key problem areas that overlap all the artificially separated disciplines — the guiding principles of which must, of necessity, provide the foundation for any future progress in the field as a whole. Once these are identified, social scientists could begin the task of comparing concepts and research procedures and determining the degree to which different terminology is masking similar hypotheses and findings, and is preventing the evaluation of results and replication of research so essential for clearing away the underbrush of invalid, unworkable and unreliable propositions.

It could be argued that the most important phenomenon requiring explanation by the social sciences is the process by which the individual acquires responses to, and beliefs about the nature of, reality — and either behaves habitually or chooses how to act in terms of these. Psychology, sociology and anthropology concern themselves with this process directly, while economics and political science (and even historians of science) build their models on unacknowledged assumptions about its nature. It is studied in terms of concepts such as development, operant conditioning, social learning, socialization and enculturation. Attempts to explain it marshall a host of other incommensurable terms denoting learning, growth, character, enhancement of personality, self-actualization, intelligence, sociability, morality and consciousness. Education, governance, business management, psychotherapy and criminology are forced to operate every day on the basis of a welter of contradictory propositions about this process that are both untested and untestable.

Our continuing failure to begin to work together, as a broadly defined social science profession, on establishing a reliable foundation for the research and policy necessarily grounded in this fundamental problem area is incredible and unforgivable. An appropriate reading of Kuhn might just provide us with the motivation and means for the effort involved. If he is right, a by-product of any successful attempt could well be the comprehensive guiding paradigm that would initiate our long-delayed evolution from proto-science to science.

A survey of psychological theory on development and conditioning, of sociological and political explanations about socialization and of anthropological theory on enculturation indicates that a sort of hit-and-miss process of natural selection has already been occurring. A limited number of competing schools of thought on the subject now extend across current disciplinary lines, and as few as three major perspectives seem to be dominating the field. These are: (1) the Freudian-based psychoanalytic model (favoured by most anthropologists and fused by Jung with mystical transcendentalism and by Fromm with existentialism and Marxism); (2) Piaget's genetic systems model, comprising insights from Rousseau and Bergson combined with the interactionism of Dewey — all incorporated into Spencer's equilibration theory of evolution; and (3) the reflex model initiated by Pavlov, refined and extended by Dewey, Durkheim, Mead and Skinner — and incorporating modern social learning theory. At this point it might be helpful to apply Kuhn's model and assess, for each of these, their economy, fruitfulness and believability.

A Kuhnian assessment of Freudianism

Freud's lasting contribution to social science was his elaboration and promulgation of four insights: (1) that the development of the individual self is consistent with and rooted in the process of biological development; (2) that experience plays a crucial role, not only in forming the conscious self, but the unconscious as well; (3) that most of the programming resulting from experience operates at the unconscious level; and (4) that the development of the human conscience requires an enduring intimate relationship with some respected adult member who reflects the values and norms of the culture. Unfortunately, however, Freud clothed this skeleton of sound propositions in a complex and untestable set of constructs, and drew from them unwarranted conclusions about the possibility and usefulness of therapy based on such a scheme. This original (and less sound) part of his theory was derived from (1) an inappropriate application of Darwin's theory of sexual selection and a distortion of the Greek myth of Oedipus; (2) some of the ideas of Nietzsche and Schopenhauer concerning a trans-human will for life (and death) and for power; and (3) a mistaken belief in the inheritance of acquired characteristics.

Available evidence indicates quite clearly that Freudianism scores appallingly low on economy and fruitfulness, as defined by Kuhn. That is, it has failed to provide a model for summarizing and making sense out of disparate information from a host of social studies and it has failed to demonstrate the capacity to generate testable hypotheses of newly discovered regularities. However, it gets high marks on Kuhn's third criterion. If one is to judge by the strength of professional and lay commitment to it, psychoanalysis continues to operate as a powerful source of emotional satisfaction — and hence, of believability.

This forces us to repeat a question asked by others: How could a theory so manifestly contrary to normal human experience and common sense, and so lacking in empirical support, have achieved the status of revealed truth throughout the entire Western world? The reasons are many and complex, and one can only venture informed guesses. Nonetheless, it is worthwhile to attempt to find the answers, for in the process we may discover something about the cultural obstacles to progress in a proto-science.

One thing can be said at the outset: the Freudian phenomenon could not have happened *without the aura of scientific authority* in which it had its source and in the context of which it was promulgated. And social scientists, in Kuhn's time, were not about to let his paradigm remove that aura from them! Sigmund Freud, with his stature as a researcher and specialist in the medical and academic community, brought the authority of science to whatever he wrote. He proclaimed himself the heir of Copernicus and Darwin and presented his speculations as scientific hypotheses generalized from professional observations.

We have to remember that all this occurred in a culture and an era in which science was held in considerable awe. Darwin's theory of natural selection was being widely acclaimed but little understood. Freud was not the first nor the last who benefited from its reflected glory while distorting and misapplying it. The fledgling social studies, ambitious for the public status and academic power associated with scientific disciplines, had been overwhelmed by Marxism and Social Darwinism. They proved to be fertile ground for yet another ideology clothed in the pretensions of science.

There was also Freud's outstanding gift for literary expression through the use of metaphor. This gave his ideas an ambiguity that made them difficult to tie down, while at the same time endowing them with the echo of classical tradition and long-established truth. From the beginning, his theory had powerful appeal for the literary establishment. His entire superstructure of speculative psychology was taken as axiomatic by a majority of American creative writers. By the late twentieth century, several generations of poets, novelists and dramatists throughout the world had created a vast cultural repertoire of humanity's strivings as reflected in the distorted mirror of Freudian and Jungian assumptions.

Coincident with the establishment of the psychoanalytic metaphor within the literary and social science subcultures, the helping professions began to expand at a rapid rate. Professional schools and faculties for teachers, social workers and nurses proliferated in Western societies. Most of these were staffed by people utterly lacking in the scientific approach to knowing — especially as applied to the study of human motivation and behaviour. Yet that was precisely the sort of study demanded by the situation in which they found themselves. They did not have to look far to encounter esoteric constructs from psychoanalysis. These could be packaged easily and passed on to their students as science, and this was done for decades in countless colleges. The students, most of whom had little background in the social sciences and even less in scientific method, usually encountered this package of constructs as their *sole* introduction to psychology, and accepted it as true. Many of them, in turn, became instructors, and the gospel spread.

One particular type of professional school, the seminary, deserves special mention. Because of Freud's well-known hostility to religion, his theory did not gain much of a foothold in this arena. But, incredibly, psychoanalysis did! The reason for this was Jung, whose appeal to liberal religion was obvious and immediate. Here was a psychology, not merely of the body, but of the spirit! Educated people who had given up a personal God were able to find, in Jungian psychoanalysis, a "scientific" justification for belief in the Holy Spirit. All in all, it seemed to offer a means of accommodating social science to a belief in the supernatural. As with graduates of the other helping professions, candidates for the ministry usually encountered no alternative psychological models. Like the others, their influence on the public was widespread. They joined the ranks of the "hands on" community workers and would-be healers in a society rendered increasingly chaotic by the growing obsession with sex that was beginning to give psychoanalysis the appearance of a self-fulfilling prophecy.

There is also something about the process and the assumptions of psychoanalysis that massages the ego, and is therefore bound to sell. That one's dreams should be, not merely a confused jumble of previous experiences, but the source of profound meaning; that one's unconscious is the repository of the ancient history of the entire race and of mighty forces locked in combat; that one has direct access to the creative spirit of the universe — all this is heady stuff! How could a few mundane regularities about human development, recorded and confirmed scientifically, possibly compete?

Yet another explanation must involve the considerable political acumen of Freud himself. It has been said that he "behaved more like a general marshalling his forces and mapping his movements than a scientist willing to let his ideas carry their own conviction" (Gay:44-45). He tried to leave no paper trail — destroying notes, letters and records of incriminating errors at regular intervals during his long career. He recognized the usefulness of networking, and of organizing his dedicated followers and isolating them from the exchange and testing of ideas so unavoidable in the broader professional arena. The early formation of small "Freud groups," followed by an international association of believers cut off from their fellow labourers in the same protoscientific vineyard; of journals devoted only to the works of the converted; of congresses to which only disciples were invited; and the virtual excommunication of those who expressed doubt or disagreement: all these were shrewd and effective steps in the building of a *political* movement intent on conquering and assaulting the bulwarks of academia. The fact that they are equally effective as obstacles to scientific progress is perhaps the greatest indictment possible of Freud and of those of his followers who have employed the same techniques these many years.

The political success of Freudian and Jungian psychoanalytic theory is an excellent example of the formation of a closed professional group with all the outward trappings of a scientific community as described by Kuhn. How, then, can we maintain that it is not scientific in fact? Certainly Freud took pains to develop a shared disciplinary matrix, complete with standards and exemplars for therapy, if not for research. Why was that not sufficient? For one thing, there were the deliberate attempts to exclude practitioners in the same problem area who happened to disagree or even question the certainties of psychoanalysis. The boundaries of community were drawn on ideological lines — enclosing only one of a number of competing schools of thought concerned with the same phenomena — rather than on the lines defined by the data thrown up by nature. Secondly, there was no clear procedure for identifying anomalies in the results of research or therapy: no way, in fact, ever to enforce acknowledgement of failure. Kuhn pointed out that "In the sciences expectations are ordinarily quite precise. Though practitioners often differ about the significance of some particular anomaly, the existence of a departure from expectation is readily recognized and generally acknowledged" (Kuhn 1980:183).

Clearly, something of crucial importance was missing from Freud's version of science. However, we can be sure that it was not the absence of programs for assimilation of the paradigm by entrants to the community, for both Freud and Jung were far ahead of Kuhn on that requirement. Jurjevich made a detailed study of the brainwashing techniques that he accused psychoanalysts of employing ever since Freud introduced the practice. He claimed that a veiled hypnotic suggestion is the chief tool used to manipulate the patient into accepting the therapist's version of truth. When we consider the popularity of psychoanalysis in the West today, and the fact that a personal program of therapy is required as an initiation rite into the profession, there is little wonder that the movement has spread with all the fervour of a militantly dogmatic religion.

Another reason for the pervasive and lasting influence of psychoanalytic theory is related to the nature of our universities, and this, too, has troublesome implications for Kuhn's concept of the "scientific community." Academic departments, especially in the social sciences, have tended to develop on the basis of political imperatives rather than according to the intellectual integrity of the discipline concerned. In a proto-scientific field such as psychology, the goals of education and the progress of knowledge would seem to be enhanced if, as Weber recommended, all the competing schools of thought are represented within a department. Quite the opposite is usually the case. Departments have tended to become dominated by the belief system of the more powerful members who control the hiring and granting of tenure. Neither professors nor their students read the works of their competitors with respect and thoroughness. Graduate students quickly learn not to question the psychological and philosophical assumptions of those who control assistantships, grants and subsequent publication and job opportunities. In such a setting, those who, through fortuitous accident, have become ensconced in the department are uniquely positioned to shape its ideological direction.

Immediately before and after World War II, large numbers of academics from Germany and Austria emigrated to Britain and North America. Many of these were Freudians or Jungians, and they were welcomed with open arms by the expanding universities of the receiving countries. We have had a long tradition of holding German scholars in uncritical and exaggerated regard. This most certainly contributed to the dominance, within English-speaking academia, of professional communities of psychoanalysts.

It is only fair to concede, however, that there is much in the actual content of Freud's ideas that explains their perseverence. There are the insights (on which he based his model) that ring true, and not only because they appeal to our vanity and desire for melodrama. There are the concepts that, though as yet untestable, seem to be supported by experience, and some that may even operate as useful guides to living. Few of these were original with Freud, but he did arrange them in a new way. And he was so successful in embedding them in his theory that his name is almost universally connected with them.

Nonetheless, when looked at as a total package, psychoanalytic theory closely resembles the ideologies described by Popper, and, like them, it demonstrates only one of Kuhn's three prerequisites of legitimate science. It satisfies deeply felt emotional needs in leader and disciple, in practitioner and client, and in the general public as well.

A Kuhnian assessment of genetic developmentalism

The second school of thought dominating the problem area with which we are concerned is that now associated with the work of Piaget. A survey of the literature on childhood learning indicates that two of Kuhn's criteria can be applied successfully to Piaget's four-stage model of cognitive development, and to some of its implications for moral reasoning and systems theory. The model is highly believable, in that most people who come to understand it feel intuitively that it accords with, and illuminates, their own experience. Anyone who has worked with children is aware of the developmental nature of their intellectual growth and of the revolutionary alterations in reasoning patterns that can be observed at different ages and in different cultural environments.

To a considerable extent the model is fruitful as well, in the testable, scientific sense. It has generated a vast literature of cross-cultural research in developmental psychology, and in disciplines as disparate as cybernetics and neuropsychology. Its findings are being applied in family-systems counselling and education (often in association with techniques for behaviour modification). But Piaget's goal of establishing a common terminology and conceptual framework for the entire field has not been achieved.

What the genetic-developmental model lacks is economy. It is impossible even to refer to it without resorting to a flood of terminology. And, in spite of the sheer volume of research generated by it, there is a dismaying absence of cumulative knowledge. Too many of the findings are non-comparable; too many of the studies are non-replicable. It is not clear just what exact outcomes, in any research situation, would constitute a determining test of the equilibration theory itself, nor what would be recognized as an anomaly. There is no clear ordering principle to cut through the network of abstract constructs and organize the welter of findings. Although grounded in biological evolution, the theory is needlessly complex and ambiguous, due to Piaget's reluctance to part with the notion of the inheritance of acquired characteristics.

This particular perspective fits Kuhn's description of a school which is "guided by something much like a paradigm" (Kuhn 1970a:ix) and whose practitioners operate scientifically, but which has not yet been able to offer the entire relevant community sufficiently compelling answers to the following questions: "What are the fundamental entities of which the universe is composed? How do these interact with each other and with the senses? What questions may legitimately be asked about such entities, and what techniques employed in seeking solutions?" (ibid.:4).

A Kuhnian assessment of behaviourism

The third school is known as behaviourism. Although founded on the work of Pavlov — and containing many of the insights of Dewey, Durkheim and Mead — it is defined today by Skinner's theory of operant conditioning. Perhaps the most recognizable feature of this theory is the way it explains, with exquisite simplicity and clarity, the evolution of complex human behaviours by means of a social process of selection as natural as the biological one. Modes of behaviour (whether covert or overt; whether cognitive, linguistic or moral in nature; and whether group or individual) are either strengthened or weakened by their consequences. Those that are positively reinforced by the environment over time will persevere; those not reinforced will be weeded out. The process is not a conscious one, and its results are not, in practice, separable from those effected by biological programming.

Also noteworthy is the ability of the operant conditioning model to shed new light on the constructs and findings of competing schools of thought, and to simplify, summarize and order these in a more productive way. The model accords, as well, with the propositions of systems theory, and with modern evolutionary theory as proposed by biologists such as Richard Dawkins. Other characteristics are the testability of its propositions and the workability and ready applicability of its findings. Clearly, it is eminently economical and fruitful as a way of ordering experience.

Why, then, has the radical behaviourist model not emerged as the guiding paradigm for the study of human socialization? In many ways the problem area resembles that of evolutionary study before Darwin. The occurrence of some form of evolution had long been established as a fact, although, admittedly, not universally accepted nor clearly comprehended. But it was not until Darwin's simple explanation came along that refutable hypotheses were generated and the rapid accumulation of new facts became possible. Why has the powerful concept of reinforcement not been similarly widely employed?

The issue is believability. Once again Kuhn's explanation of scientific revolution is helpful here. There is indeed an obstacle confronting modern behaviourism. It is a cultural resistance even more massive than that which denied general acceptance to the theories of Copernicus and Darwin. For what concerns us here is not a minor problem area, nor even a single discipline. The conceptual framework defining the process of individual social development will provide the foundation for the entire field of social science — and, ultimately, for our religious and philosophical world views as well. And behaviourism, even more directly than the Darwinian revolution which it promises to complete, attacks the very roots of our prevailing cultural assumptions.

Disagreements between Popper and Kuhn

This comparison of three competing schools of thought in a proto-scientific area can also help us to identify and assess the major points of disagreement between Popper and Kuhn. Popper was more aware than Kuhn of the nature of ideology and the danger it posed for science, particularly to the future of social science and the possibility of scientifically directed social engineering. This had been driven home to him by his study of Plato, and of Hegelianism and Marxism. He had learned that, while scientific knowledge, with the power it gives us, can and does allow humanity to change the world, ideological beliefs have consequences too. By rendering their proponents politically powerful but rationally and *instrumentally* impotent, they throw up insurmountable barriers to reasoned and value-guided social change.

Consequently, Popper drew a clear boundary between the two approaches to reality. Although he was aware that science is a social undertaking, requiring the rigorously defined shared concepts that make precise communication and replication possible, he believed that any distinction relying on sociological rather than logical criteria would harm scientific progress in the long run. Kuhn, less knowledgeable about the ideological tendencies in social science, and more concerned with tracing the actual historical process by which a proto-science evolves into a science, may have inadvertently blurred the crucial *logical* distinction between the two.

In the end, Kuhn's essential criterion was paradigm-consensus among professionals within the relevant specialized problem area. He maintained that, in the case of a science, "the resolution of revolutions is by selection within the scientific community of the fittest way to practice future science" (ibid.:170). But clearly, the critical issue is how such "fitness" is determined. Popper believed it is by means of the uniquely scientific testing process that selects out those hypotheses which fail to survive attempts to refute them. Kuhn said it is by established procedures of verification. "Verification is like natural selection: it picks out the most viable among the actual alternatives in a historical situation" (ibid.:146).

But exactly what did Kuhn mean by verification and how did he see it operating in the selection process? Some modern "Kuhnians" have suggested that it is accomplished by negotiation but Kuhn is rightly critical of this notion. To verify means to confirm the truth of a proposition; that is, the accuracy with which it reflects reality. It is a concept consistent with the older positivist philosophy of science. Yet, Kuhn indicated that "the notion of a match between the ontology of a theory and its 'natural' counterpart in nature now seems to me illusive in principle" (ibid.:206). Like Popper and the pragmatists before him, Kuhn seemed to view scientific knowledge as neither relative nor absolute but rather, the cumulative and increasingly effective product of an irreversible and non-directional evolutionary process.

Kuhn was critical of Popper for denying the existence of verification procedures, but Popper had done this thoughtfully and deliberately. Unless one wishes to claim that scientific evolution is progressing toward a humanly knowable goal of correspondence to the essential nature of reality (and Kuhn agreed with Popper that such a premise is unwarranted) then one must give up the idea of verisimilitude. All that the scientist can ever know about the reliability of a hypothesis is whether it has continued to withstand the test of scientific selection: the unequivocal test of *falsification*!

The test of confirmation simply will not do, for reasons both logical and sociological. Confirming instances can always be found, if the bias is sufficiently strong and the cast of the net sufficiently wide. Every ideology throughout history owes its endurance to the Procrustian warping of evidence that its premises demand and its followers' dogmatic socialization makes possible. The persistent popularity of psychoanalytic theory is a superb example of this. It is possible that Kuhn's model of scientific revolution, with its reliance on confirmation procedures as the trigger of change, helped to blur the line between ideology and science, and thereby to sustain the unwarranted scientific credibility of many proto-sciences.

For shared paradigms (confirmed by selective perception) are characteristic of ideology as well as science, as the social scientists who misused Kuhn's ideas were quick to recognize. The corollary was equally apparent. If Kuhnian epistemology could define certain powerful ideologies as science, then it could also be used to define all science as mere ideology. To a considerable degree this happened in the social sciences. This popular distortion of Kuhn's model became a source of great emotional satisfaction for those who had always prized the appearance and prestige of science more than the reality.

Only one ingredient was missing from Kuhn's powerful organizing principle, but it was an important one, as he himself came to recognize. A paradigm common to all the members of the relevant professional community is the *necessary* condition for science, but it is not a *sufficient* one. Popper's criterion of falsifiability is the crucial link missing from Kuhn's original theory of knowledge. A scientific paradigm is distinguished by the fact that the hypotheses generated by it are amenable to falsification. Science, unlike ideology, has a self-corrective mechanism at its very heart. A conjecture, to be classed as scientific, must be open to refutation. There is a rigorous set of rules according to which hypotheses are formulated and research results are arrived at, reported, replicated and subjected to the possibility of falsification. It is this *process* — not the inquiring attitude or intellectual integrity or value neutrality or negotiating ability of the individual scientist — that ensures the reliability of scientific knowledge.

Kuhn was partially right in maintaining that Popper's description of the scientist, as one who deliberately seeks opportunities for falsifying theory, does not accord with the actual practice of normal science. On the other hand, the record of the universal response of researchers during the 1989-90 fusion debacle in physics would seem to indicate quite the opposite. At any rate, the theory that eventually prevails under the conditions maintained by that same normal science does so not because of its agreement with conventional wisdom. Nor does it succeed because of the political power of its proponents, as is the case with ideology. The survival of a scientific theory such as Darwin's is due, instead, to its power to explain and predict observable regularities in human experience while withstanding worldwide attempts to refute it.

When anomalies do begin to appear as a result of the extensions and elaborations made possible by normal science, they are signalled in the only way possible: predictions have failed to stand up. In Kuhn's words, expectations have been violated. There is only one way that such violations are recognizable. A testable proposition has been refuted, or falsified. It amounts to the sounding of an alert. And, although in one sense this focuses attention on the anomalous circumstance, in another sense it opens up the realm of possibilities, as the search for alternative puzzle-solutions gets under way. Kuhn acknowledged this, as when he wrote, "Clearly the role thus attributed to falsification is much like the one this essay attributes to anomalous experiences" (ibid.:146).

But Kuhn wanted to distinguish between particular falsifying instances (which he recognized) and falsification as a logical principle or determining event resulting in the immediate rejection of an entire theory. Popper made no such distinction, for his model simply identified the crucial mechanism underlying the evolution of science in general, and he was not interested in explaining revolutionary disruptions to an entire field, or tracing the historical course of a specific occurrence. Far from contradicting Popper's theory, Kuhn contributed a major refinement to it when he introduced the idea of a steady accumulation of knowledge punctuated by plateaus — as the guiding framework begins to show signs of inadequacy — followed by wholesale readjustments in the paradigm, and then a great leap forward. This is almost exactly analogous to Gould and Eldridge's "punctuated equilibrium" hypothesis where Darwinism is concerned.

According to Kuhn, for as long as it takes for the prevailing paradigm to be replaced by a more comprehensive and powerful one, the relevant problem area is in a crisis (or revolutionary) situation, with falsifying instances multiplying and scientists searching in new directions to interpret their findings. This is what causes the plateau in the evolutionary process; knowledge will cease to accumulate. This stage in the progress of an established science is not the same as the pre-scientific and ideological phase in which social science is mired, but it may appear so from the outside.

Confirming the distinction between ideology and science

By combining the key elements of the Popper and Kuhn theories, we can get a clearer picture of the difference between ideology and science than either offers on its own. Because ideologies claim to represent truth, they are incapable of generating a means by which they can be corrected as circumstances change. Legitimate science makes no such claim. That is why Popper was right in concluding that scientific tests can never be tests of verisimilitude. Science does not aim for "true" theories purporting to reflect an accurate picture or essence of reality. It leaves such pretensions of infallibility to ideology.

The tests of science, therefore, are in terms of workability and falsifiability, and its propositions are accordingly conjectural and tentative in nature. Kuhn's model shows how a successful scientific theory, while guiding the research in a particular problem area, is continuously elaborated, revised and refined, until it is eventually superseded by the very hypothesis-making and-testing process that it defined and sharpened. An ideology, on the other hand, would be considered a failure under those circumstances, for the truth must be for all time. More than anything, it is this difference that confuses ideological thinkers. Social scientists need to be aware of this difference. They should realize, as well, that the crisis of social science reflects, not the healthy ferment of a science in the process of revolutionary change, but a chaos of conflicting ideologies still rooted in the premises of a cosmology that is no longer adequate.

References for Chapter Twenty-Five

Cioffi, Frank. 1973. *Freud: Modern Judgements*. London: Macmillan.

Eysenck, Hans J., and Glenn D. Wilson. 1973. *The Experimental Study of Freudian Theories*. London: Methuen.

Fisher, Seymour, and Roger P. Greenberg, eds. *The Scientific Evaluation of Freud's Theories and Therapy*. New York: Basic Books.

Gay, Peter. 1987. *A Godless Jew*. New Haven: Yale University Press.

Horwich, Paul, ed. 1993. *World Changes: Thomas Kuhn and the Nature of Science*. Cambridge, MA: MIT Press.

Hutcheon, Pat Duffy. 1976. Socialization: Toward an Interdisciplinary Consensus. Ph.D. diss. Brisbane, University of Queensland.

Jurjevich, R.M. 1974. *The Hoax of Freudism*. Philadelphia: Dorrence.

Kline, Paul. 1981. *Fact and Fancy in Freudian Theory*. London: Methuen.

Kuhn, Thomas S. 1957. *The Copernican Revolution: Planetary Astronomy in the Development of Western Thought*. Cambridge, MA: President and Fellows of Harvard College.

————. 1970a. *The Structure of Scientific Revolutions*. 2d. ed., enlarged. Chicago: University of Chicago Press.

————. 1970b. Logic of Discovery or Psychology of Research? In *Criticism and the Growth of Knowledge*. Edited by I. Lakatos and A. Musgrave. London: Cambridge University Press, p. 1-23.

————. 1970c. Reflections on My Critics. In ibid., p. 231-78.

————. 1974. Second Thoughts on Paradigms. In *The Structure of Scientific Theories*. Edited by Frederick Suppe. Chicago: University of Illinois Press, p. 459-82 and 483-517.

————. 1977. *The Essential Tension: Selected Studies in Scientific Tradition and Change*. Chicago: University of Chicago Press.

————. 1980. The Halt and the Blind: Philosophy and History of Science. *British Journal for the Philosophy of Science* 31: 181-92.

————. 1983. Commensurability, Comparability, Communicability. *PSA 1982*. Vol. 2. East Lansing: Philosophy of Science Association, p. 669-88 and 712-16.

————. 1992. *The Trouble with the Historical Philosophy of Science*. Cambridge, MA: Department of the History of Science, Harvard University.

Popper, Karl. 1959. *The Logic of Scientific Discovery*. London: Hutchinson.

————. 1974. Replies to My Critics. In *The Philosophy of Karl Popper*. Edited by Paul Arthur Schilpp. La Salle, IL: The Library of Living Philosophers, p. 949-1180.

Scott, Peter. 1985. An Occasional Revolutionary. *The Times Higher Education Supplement*. July 12, p. 11.

Twenty-Six

Toward a Unified Social Science

It struck me that an idea is very much like a tune.
It goes through the ages remaining
much the same in itself,
but getting into such very different company.
— George Orwell, *Orwell:*
The Authorized Biography

This study has shown how several interrelated strands of thought have emerged and re-emerged all through history, in spite of consistent resistance from the prevailing culture. They are the foundations of what is suggested as the conceptual framework essential to the growth of social science: that of evolutionary naturalism. This world view stems from the premise that nature is continuous and all-inclusive, and that the human animal, although an integral aspect of the natural world, nonetheless has developed two important claims to distinctiveness. One is the ability to forge reliable knowledge from the chaos of immediate experience. The other is a capacity to imagine and bring to fruition objects of art, and to make both aesthetic and moral judgements.

And finally, behind and within all of these there has appeared the powerful organizing principle of evolution: the process of change common to all levels of existence. It is also a theme that allows us to perceive all these strands of thought as developing over time, along with the evolution of the disciplined approach to knowledge-building that gave them birth and gradually enhanced their meaning.

Naturalism as the foundation

The most necessary aspect of social-scientific thought is surely the premise of naturalism. It is a faith in the existence of some sort of universal natural order extending beyond human experience, and somehow reflected in that experience and made accessible by means of it. It includes a belief that humans and other sentient animals are, at one and the same time, the products and experiencers of nature, and, as such, can never know it in any "holistic" or absolute sense.

466

The universality of cause and effect

Naturalism implies the universality of cause and effect. It was an idea central to early Buddhist thought. It was also not uncommon in Hellenic Greece, from whence it was brought to Rome by Panaetius, in 144 BCE. The early naturalistic thinkers taught that causality is universal in nature: human or otherwise. However, this core belief suffered a devastating setback in the later Hellenistic era with the emergence of powerful currents of dualism and mystical thinking. Only small underground pockets of naturalism managed to endure. Much later, by a fortunate conjunction of circumstance, early Islamic civilization restored an appreciation for the credibility and applicability of cause-and-effect thinking — but in the physical realm only. And, from the Renaissance onwards, what was then called "natural philosophy" flourished. The rebirth of scientific inquiry in Western Europe was led by Jews and Christian monks familiar with Arabic culture. Unfortunately, however, this perspective had been bequeathed in the context of a firm Aristotelian dualism which successfully restricted it to the study of inorganic substances.

Naturalism was rediscovered by Erasmus, and his Renaissance forebears, and was revitalized by the writings of people like Montaigne, Hobbes and Hume, who focused directly on the operation of cause and effect in human actions, and the consequent possibility of discovering reliable knowledge concerning these. Martineau pointed out the causal role of socialization and of a society's institutions. Marx claimed that people's beliefs and values did not have some mysterious source, but resulted from their conditions of life. Freud postulated causal relationships in the development of the psyche. Spencer showed how the same principle must apply to morality. He concluded that all the major ethical systems are crippled by their neglect of causal connections in human behaviour.

Darwin's revolutionary breakthrough in biology provided the ultimate logical and empirical justification for the premise of naturalism, in that he demonstrated the operation of cause and effect in organic life. This process of "after-the-fact" (or contingent) causality was elaborated by George Herbert Mead, and further refined and experimentally supported by B.F. Skinner. Unfortunately, Darwin's theory of evolution by natural selection is still not generally understood and accepted, and much less so are its implications for the social and behavioural studies.

Order or chaos underlying the nature of things

The issue of whether reality is orderly or random has engaged naturalistic thinkers throughout the ages. It has been considered critical because of what the answer might mean for the prospect of discovering ultimate "truth" — or, alternatively, of establishing reliable predictions of cause-and-effect relations in nature. Interestingly, the resolution arrived at by Heisenberg by means of modern physics is very similar to that of Democritus some twenty-five centuries before. Democritus saw the notion of chance as an inevitable correlate of the knower's ability to identify the possibilities surrounding an event, and thereby to predict effects. He said that chance, or randomness, is a useful concept for humans in situations where the causes are likely to remain obscure because of our limited means of registering the multiple and far-reaching conditions of observed occurrences.

Heisenberg's Principle of Indeterminacy makes the same point. He has been misunderstood by people who confuse two common meanings of "determined." In its one sense, the word refers to an inherent order of some kind: in the other, to the capacity to measure. All that we can ever know, even with the aid of modern physics, is derived from what we can, in some way, observe and measure. Heisenberg's work confirmed what the early Greek naturalists had guessed. Because we can measure *either* the velocity or location of events in space — but not both at once — no such event can be assessed according to a single time-like measure. However, this tells us nothing whatsoever about the essential orderliness of existence, or the lack thereof. It merely reflects the limitations of our current conceptual and technical instruments for "knowing": the limitations referred to by Santayana when he reminded us that our measures of cause and effect can reveal no more than a momentary clip in the filmstrip of infinite interconnected movement. But this does not mean, any more than does the Principle of Indeterminacy, that events are uncaused.

References to chaos theory in physics are understandable in similar terms. Modern physicists are operating within a paradigm of quantum mechanics and relativity theory that has served them well, but which may now have been pushed as far as nature's complexity will allow. At this point at the leading edge of scientific knowledge, they are increasingly encountering results not predictable in terms of that paradigm. They are merely resorting to the term "chaos theory" as a way of explaining the (temporarily) unexplainable during what may be a period of treading water as they enter a revolutionary phase in the evolution of science. It just so happens that quantum mechanics and relativity are both based on the premises of calculus. Particle physicists are now discovering that calculus, pursued over infinite time, results in a previously unexpected condition: one which is unexplainable in terms of linear causality.

It is unfortunate that someone chose to label these surprising results "chaos," for the term communicates the dangerously misleading message of some essentially unknowable ontological randomness. What physicists seem to be talking about are the type of complex dynamic systems that biologists and naturalistic thinkers since Darwin have had to deal with, and which natural scientists — in their simpler world of mechanistic relations — have been able to ignore until now. Dynamic systems *evolve* over time through a process of feedback causality, and only if the state of the system at any one time is rigorously known can its state next time be uniquely given by the equations of motion. In the case of most organic, and perhaps all psychological and socio-cultural systems, the totality of the units and relations and impinging contingencies involved in the real dynamics is unlikely to be identified. This means that the best science can do is to determine increasingly reliable *probabilities* of future states. However, most of the evolutionary thinkers discussed in this book were aware of all this long ago.

Chaos theory in physics underlines the need for a comprehensive paradigm of evolutionary naturalism for all of science. Those social scientists and evolutionary theorists who are grasping at the concept of an *essentially* chaotic reality as the basis for a new dialectical model for change have failed to understand both the strengths and limitations of the powerful calculus paradigm in physics. They may also not be sufficiently aware of the proto-scientific nature of their own enterprises, as well as of the inappropriateness of the reductionism involved in looking to physics for some essential truth about the ultimate nature of social reality.

Santayana's premise that knowledge of one part of nature can lead to reliable assumptions about another connected part still stands. So, too, does Russell's claim that the existence of causal processes in nature is one of the most fundamental postulates of all science. Naturalists may rest assured that no discovery in modern physics has challenged the premise of an inherent order in reality, governed by some form of cause and effect. On the contrary, the entire body of knowledge developed within its conceptual framework is founded on just that premise. This means that we are justified in believing that an increasingly reliable knowledge of causal connections in nature is indeed possible. It also means that we are warranted in maintaining a commitment to the idea of the human as both knowing subject and knowable object of study.

The human being as knower and as object of scientific inquiry

Throughout history, social-scientific thinkers have been intrigued by the question of how humans can come to know that nature of which they are a part. Their naturalism predisposes them to a position of neo-realism. Modern evolutionary naturalists tend to be philosophical realists in that they assume an objective reality beyond human consciousness. However, they depart from the older realism in accepting the unattainability of perfect knowledge concerning it. They realize that the fallibility of perception and reason, and the distorting potential of emotion, have always rendered the knowing process a difficult and uncertain undertaking. But history provides ample and convincing evidence that there are no easy shortcuts. Naturalists point out that belief in revelation, divination or transcendental intuition as sources of certainty have always proven to be dangerous delusions, serving to obstruct rather than to open new paths of fruitful inquiry. They are aware that only the discipline of the scientific method has resulted in the progressive accumulation of knowledge. For it, alone, is a method with a self-correcting process at its very heart!

The crucial function of language

If knowledge is produced solely by the efforts of humans, then it must be grounded in the content of experience, and in the means by which the human being takes in that experience, renders it understandable and communicable and tests its consistency and workability. It is not surprising, therefore, that social theorists have focused on such matters as the role of the senses in the process — and of habit, reason and language — and the interdependence of these. One of the enduring themes has involved some sort of sequential conceptual development: the idea that sensing and thinking and using language involve a continuous process in which the organism is altered by contact with the environment and *vice versa*. Another key premise is that reasoning patterns, established within the developing individual by experience, increasingly come to reflect the underlying relations in that encompassing reality of which the human is an interactive aspect. These ideas can be traced through the works of Hume, Mill, Darwin and Spencer to modern thinkers such as Durkheim, Russell and Piaget, from as far back as the Buddha and Democritus.

The recognition of the exclusively human road to knowledge means that what is known can never be total or absolute. Protagoras may have been the first to recognize this. He attributed this limitation to the fact that the matter surrounding and constituting us is in flux and inevitably perceived differently by different people in different situations. Xenophanes expressed it well when he said, "No one has ever known or will know for sure, for even if what he says is exactly right, he does not *know* that it is."

If humans were not thoroughly social animals with an evolved language which has made possible the sharing of experience and the public testing of beliefs, they would, indeed, have an insurmountable problem. However, there is now general consensus in social psychology that, at some point, the human species evolved the capacity to develop mental instruments or patterned responses for ordering experience. These representations, or concepts, emerge in the growing individual through the interaction of a developing reason and language. New members of each generation, through socialization and exchanges with the non-human surroundings, establish neural connections resulting in a conceptual structure that acts as a sieve through which the environment is subsequently experienced.

There is no alternative to this; no way that the "whole" of reality can be taken in directly. There is simply no possibility for human thought except by means of these mental networks that begin as a few crude categories, distinguishing light from dark, hunger from satiation, comfort from discomfort and familiarity from strangeness. Growth in intelligence occurs because the process is a two-way street. While the human animal's concepts shape the environment (both social and physical) into receivable and interpretable patterns, that environment, in turn, challenges and inevitably alters and expands these tools for knowing.

Hobbes was one of the first to point out the significance of language for knowledge-building. He, and others who came after, were called "nominalists" because they demonstrated that meaning does not reside in the "essence" of the objects and events observed, nor yet in the words used to refer to them. Meaning, explained Hobbes, is assigned to things and relations by the humans who experience them, and these meanings are organized and rendered communicable by symbols such as words and numbers. This is why Hobbes felt that it was the lack of precision in the use of language that was largely responsible for the failure of those engaged in the social studies of his day to achieve a grasp of the inevitably imperfect knowledge available to them.

Two centuries later, Durkheim, Mead, Santayana and Russell all contributed to a growing understanding that it is the mental representations created by means of language that both define us as human and make knowing possible. A half-century after that, Popper was able to explain much of the process involved, within the context of the findings of modern neuroscience. During the same period, Skinner's study of the means by which language becomes an increasingly precise instrument of thought culminated in his idea of a unique reinforcing verbal community as characteristic of an established science. This important insight was subsequently expanded upon by Thomas Kuhn.

The conditional nature of knowledge

Hobbes was also the first social theorist to introduce the concept of "conditional" as the essential characteristic of scientific knowledge. Hume went even further, pointing out the inevitability of uncertainty and incompleteness where all human knowledge is concerned. He explained that the deductive logic of Aristotle can prove only the *validity* of conclusions derived from first premises — not their *truth*. It is the premises that describe reality. They are the only part of a closed, logical system that is empirical, and the conclusions derived from them are only as true as are the original descriptive statements.

According to Hume, empirical truth-claims can also never be absolute. They are arrived at by generalizing from experience, through inductive logic, and any conclusive proof of them is beyond our grasp. Only their *reliability* as guides to action can be recognized. Yet, no matter how many confirming instances occur, there is always the possibility of some future refuting evidence. Inductive logic — the logic of scientific inquiry — cannot be expected to reveal truth, said Hume. He then reminded us that humans and other animals have, nonetheless, always learned and acted and lived to act again — not by means of proofs of certainty, but by the intuitive conviction that if the lion's roar had meant danger in all their yesterdays, it would mean the same today.

The pragmatists built upon Hume's ideas. Dewey explained how there developed, over evolutionary time, a more-or-less formal system of warranted assertions describing regularities in the human group's experience of nature. This body of reliable facts was built up by the public process of inquiry made possible by that increasingly precise communication resulting from the emergence of language. Mead also spoke of the essentially hypothetical nature of knowledge. And he explained how, without language, the sharing and joint testing of experience would not have been possible, and the human primate would have remained imprisoned within a chaos of immediate sensation, lacking even a clear consciousness of self.

Durkheim emphasized the social sources of reason as well as language. Santayana saw animal intelligence (and its more advanced language-based counterpart) as primarily an adaptive mechanism. So, too, did Pavlov, Dewey, Russell and Piaget. All these scholars were describing not only the growth of self-awareness, but the birth of scientific inquiry from the womb of everyday trial-and-error behaviour in a social context. Gradually, this behaviour resulted in the evolution of the method of intelligence within the individual, and of its eventual extension to the sphere of group action — as science.

Popper and Kuhn completed the resolution of Xenophanes' dilemma. Popper demonstrated how, once we really grasp the conditional nature of scientific knowledge, the problem resolves itself. Conjectures or hypotheses are generalizations expressing cause-and-effect regularities in the form of "if-then" statements. These statements do not have to be true in any ultimate sense in order to be useful and fruitful. As with any other tool, we need only to have confidence in them; in this case, in their ability to predict the probable effects of our actions. This is possible, said Popper, because there *are* rational criteria for judging competing knowledge claims. Some are more informative than others, and therefore will help us in a wider range of choices. And some are better at standing up to severe tests: that is, we can have confidence in them as guides to choosing because they have been more highly corroborated than their competitors.

Kuhn explained how hypotheses (or the theories of which they are a part) enable inquirers to identify and measure regularities in nature that would not otherwise have been observed. From time to time, these increasingly precise concepts and the more accurate measuring they make possible unearth regularities *not* predicted by the hypothesis, and a flurry of research activity follows in the attempt to resolve the anomaly. This revolutionary situation eventually results in some scientist conceiving a new theory that makes sense of what had previously been observed as contradictory, *in addition to* shedding new light on everything explained by the previous theory. The result is further aggregation of facts.

This is what we mean when we say that science evolves; that it is necessarily progressive. The previously discovered facts (regularities in nature, or descriptions of these) have not changed, even though the explanations have. This means that hypotheses guiding the prediction of future facts have been replaced by new ones, which, in turn, illuminate new facts. The former hypotheses have been eliminated by natural selection, in an ongoing process of attempted falsification that allows only the fit to survive. As with Marx's idea of capitalism, scientific theories contain within their very power to predict new regularities the seeds of their own destruction!

Social-scientific theorists who think in interdisciplinary and evolutionary terms have added greatly to general understanding of the uniquely human process of knowing. One of the ways they have done this is by pointing out what it is that we require from knowledge. In our imaginative flights and emotional depths we may yearn for certainty, but the contingent conditions of life forbid it. And the imperatives of action have never allowed us the luxury of waiting for it. Our private beliefs will tend to reflect either those irrational yearnings or empirically substantiated (albeit ultimately *unprovable*) facts. The first may give us the illusion of certainty, but only the second can provide reliable guidance in the choices that confront us.

The human being as artist and valuer

Once we understand that the knowledge established by humans enables us to achieve a measure of control over the consequences of our actions, we realize the real meaning of the saying, "knowledge is power." In the absence of such knowledge, our actions still affect the scheme of things, but in aimless and conflicting ways. In a state of ignorance it is easy to be blind to the inevitably causal role that we perform. The introspective mystic and the cow in the field are similarly oblivious here, and thus similarly at one with nature. With the real possibility of effective control of circumstances, however, our view of the human condition must undergo a drastic change. The recognition of humanity's power to effect *rational* change in desirable directions forces us, at last, to confront our joint responsibility for all of our blind and *irrational* acts and their destructive consequences. With the awareness of power has come the awareness of responsibility and of the need for us to function as moral beings.

Evolutionary naturalists agree that all of our generalized ends (ideals) and means (actions flowing from choices dictated by our immediate objectives or ethical principles or rules for the good life) have their roots in aesthetic as well as moral values derived from the current experience and past history of humanity, and from the collective wisdom found therein. They have been expressed in various ways, from the pluralism of ancient Hinduism; Buddha's "norm"; the "middle way" and Golden Rule of Confucious and the early Babylonians; the joyful fellowship among equals so dear to Epicurus; and the Ten Commandments of the Jews; to Jesus' teachings on neighbourly love; Mohammed's emphasis on honesty and social obligation; the work ethic of Saint Benedict; the peaceful world citizenship of Erasmus; Guru Nanak's devotion to equality; the justice and benevolence advocated as higher-order principles by Hume and Spencer; Dewey's ideals of democracy and freedom; Huxley's goal of individual fulfilment; Fromm's concept of universal love; and Albert Schweitzer's principles of universal solidarity, respect for truth and reverence for life. Like the ideal of the rule of law bequeathed to us by the ancient Greeks and Romans, they are part of the legacy of our shared human history. And they are often more powerfully communicated by means of the metaphors and imagery of art, music and literature than by the words of moral philosophers.

Evolutionary naturalism has always had strong ties to the arts and humanities, and these were strengthened by the Renaissance in Italy and Spain. The revolution in world view at that time amounted to a revulsion against the obsession with the supernatural which had prevailed in the moral and aesthetic arena for so many centuries. It heralded the return to an appreciation and reverence for the role of the human species in these matters, and for the products of the human imagination, aesthetic sensibilities and conceptual and technical skills. To the extent that it succeeded, it wrested morality and art from the realm of the supernatural and defined them, once again, as the uniquely human endeavours that they had always been.

Morality and art

Modern evolutionary naturalism identifies a close connection between moral and aesthetic sensibilities. Just as meaning and value do not reside in external reality, neither does the quality of excellence sought by artists. It is humans who attribute quality to a work of art, as a result of the responses evoked by it within them. But, whereas morality is represented in the culture in terms of valued human relationships, the arts are objectified as artifacts, and may be widely dispersed over time and space. Those artistic products said to possess lasting quality are appreciated as such because of the consistency of response aroused in those who experience them. These responses may take the form of feelings of fulfilment, or the experience of déjà vu, or heightened understanding of the human condition, or possibly an empathy so intense that the viewer or listener has the sensation of reliving the artist's representation of experience. To the degree that the writer or performer or visual artist has succeeded in accomplishing this end, for people of varying times and cultures, the work is judged to possess quality. Subjective relativism and elitist authoritarianism are no more valid in judgements of aesthetic quality than in those concerning knowledge and morality.

There is another connection between art and morality that is often overlooked. Students of moral development agree that, without empathy, morality is impossible. The arts perform a crucial function in offering a depth and breadth of vicarious experience of suffering and joy that may not be readily acquired elsewhere. They provide an intensification and enrichment of private experience that sensitize people to the potential consequences of their choices for the lives of others. Without this, moral choices lack the essential criterion of concern for something beyond personal gratification.

There is a down side to this relationship between morality and art. Objects need only be defined by their producers as art in order to enter the cultural milieu and to remain indefinitely. Today these objects, regardless of their artistic quality, are communicated to every corner of the globe by mass media fuelled by a tendency to create, and then to feed, a variety of destructive addictions. This means that the most violent and *desensitizing* of such "creative" products are often the most profitable as commodities and therefore the most widely dispersed. These objects then begin to constitute a large part of the culture from which developing individuals extract their values and ideals and rules for living. The process is analogous to that by which individuals use advanced technology to pollute the physical environment for short-term gain, oblivious to the consequences for the health of subsequent generations and the future evolution of all life.

Indeed, it is the reliability of our scientific knowledge of the *inorganic* aspects of nature that has enabled technology to operate as such a formidable instrument for altering the total physical and cultural environment upon which the human species depends for its sustenance, form and survival. Social scientists have been slow to realize the implications of all this. A more comprehensive and knowledge-based paradigm would have forced us to recognize the nature of the power that the evolved capacities of our species have gained for us. It is a power that has rendered us more dangerous, and made moral responsibility — even on the part of artists — more imperative than ever before.

The free will/determinism issue

But is an exclusively human morality possible? Or are moral norms somehow determined by the natural order, like the regularities we observe in the logical relations of things, so that we can achieve harmony with them but are powerless to alter them? Or what if the concept is only meaningful in the context of obedience to precepts ordained by an all-powerful God and revealed occasionally to certain self-proclaimed spiritual leaders, or to mystics, through revelation or transcendental intuition? This question of the possibility of a morality grounded solely in the shared experience of the human race has challenged philosophers throughout history. It has posed a unique problem for evolutionary naturalists, whose premises require a positive answer. At the same time, those premises posit order throughout nature, otherwise how could we assume the universal operation of cause and effect?

The dilemma is resolved, however, by the understanding that traditional determinism implies something quite different from the universality of cause and effect posited by naturalism. The older notion of determinism involves, instead, the concept of a first cause and an unalterable cosmic plan for the realization of an ordained end, either by means of God's will working itself out through the human conscience, or through the imperatives of natural law.

Both traditional versions of determinism would seem to be difficult to reconcile with the idea of moral choosers whose judgement *matters*. Proponents of the first alternative have tried to solve the problem by claiming that the individual conscience is a reflection of God's will, and it is only a crippling moral deafness in individuals (due either to "original sin" or faulty socialization or both) that causes evil to disrupt the pattern temporarily. Those who believe in a natural moral order blame human blindness for the prevailing disharmony. They tend to explain human moral failings in terms of an excessive reliance on thought, which causes a loss of sensibility. The evildoer has simply been obstructed by the inherent limitations of reason and language from that openness to the immediate experience of "oneness" that is necessary for the achievement of harmony with nature.

But the problem remains. For with both views, it is the choosers (relying solely on the admittedly limited human tools for feeling and believing) who must, in the end, decide which available course is the best reflection of God's will, or of natural harmony, as the case may be.

A few twentieth-century social theorists got into even deeper water when they equated the "necessarianism" of these traditional concepts of determinism to the naturalistic idea of the universality of cause and effect — and rejected both! It happened with existentialism. The confusion, in this case, is understandable, as the movement originated with disillusioned Christians such as Kierkegaard, and was greatly influenced by rebels against the older realism and idealism such as Nietzsche. If "God is dead," these people reasoned, *then there is no causality*, no plan but chaos, and no credible conscience as a moral guide. Morality must therefore be meaningless, they preached, except in the awareness of unlimited freedom to choose one's "authentic" pathway, and to accept responsibility for the totality of essentially unknowable consequences that flow from every step.

This is a profoundly frightening position in which to find oneself and one's species. No wonder the existentialists cringed in *Angst* at the prospect. Arendt broke ranks on this when she concluded that freedom or autonomy for the human being could never mean personal sovereignty. She maintained that the concept of freedom is meaningful only in the public sphere, and that it is made possible solely by the rule of law established by humans. This failed to convince the less rational of her generation, who felt, instead, that the only way out was to join the mystics and *celebrate* nature's inherent disorder, secure in a belief that, if only one can feel and will that it be so, one can experience a perfect truth beyond the chaos of unpredictable experience.

Fortunately, from Epicurus on, there have always been a few social philosophers in each era who searched for a more satisfying and intellectually respectable answer to the free will problem: one that would allow a central role for morality in human affairs. The first inkling of a possible solution came from a non-naturalistic source. Duns Scotus, the late-thirteenth-century Scholastic, introduced the idea of *contingency*, to describe the occurrence of effects which — though not uncaused — are, nonetheless, not "necessary," given the preceding conditions. He suggested that any one of a wide range of possible chains of cause and effect could be set in motion by a particular human volition. As a determinist in the traditional dualist sense, he thought that a realm of freedom might possibly reside in the time-lapse between the cosmically determined Will and the influence of contingent conditions on the volition in which the Will found practical expression. The significance of this idea seems to have gone unrecognized, however, for, two centuries later, we find Erasmus expressing a desire to believe in free will, but being unable to explain how it could exist.

Hume claimed that choice *can* be meaningful, because it is always possible to choose *not* to act in a given situation. He maintained that all legal and ethical systems are founded on that premise, and that only philosophers, isolated from the practical world of cause and effect, could find reason to doubt it. Martineau considered it equally obvious that whatever it is that constitutes a person's will is determined by influences beyond the individual. Spencer suggested that what exists is only the *consciousness* of free will within the human thought processes: a virtual necessity for the rational functioning of the self.

Santayana agreed, but added something important. He suggested that the will of an animal — human or otherwise — is free in actuality only to sustain it in the direction of its genetic potential *within the exigencies of environmental challenge*. Huxley emphasized the latter aspect. "Freedom," he said, "is human plasticity." Durkheim saw the evolution of civilized norms and a socially derived conscience as the only source of freedom from momentary sensual urges and environmental pressures. Like Duns Scotus so long before, all three of the above were pointing the way to an answer.

It was not until evolution was fully understood that a truly naturalistic resolution of the free will/determinism issue could begin to take shape. The answer lay in the fact that, once living organisms entered the picture, not only mechanical necessity, but *contingency* determined the operation of cause and effect. The effects of previous actions became the causes of the present, and after consciousness emerged — with the capacity to remember past feeling-states and to construct images of future ones — the role of consequences loomed ever larger.

Bergson explored the evolutionary origin of the element of indeterminateness involved in choice, and found it in the time elapsing between stimulus and response in the animal's nervous system. He saw this as marking the onset of reason, as it allowed for a connecting of past to present events. Dewey took the explanation further, pointing out that the crucial time-lapse which eventually led to reasoned choice in humans is due to habitual behaviour being temporarily suspended by some change in the surroundings. Mead expanded these ideas into an evolutionary theory of the development of human self-consciousness and of intelligence and moral and aesthetic values, based on the work of Pavlov, Bergson, Dewey, Vygotsky and Durkheim.

Pavlov had suggested that we have freedom of choice only in proportion to our knowledge of how the processes determining human actions really work. Durkheim explained that it is the society (or human civilization) within us which frees us from enslavement to our organic natures. In recent decades Skinner's work revealed the precise way in which individual beliefs and values are shaped, for good or ill, by the cultural contingencies produced by the actions of all. This means that every choice (or failure to choose) has moral implications, for every action affects the cultural stream from which all are impelled to drink.

Dewey had previously spent much of his life exploring the implications of this naturalistic perspective for the possibility of a positive morality. His message was that only by applying the method of intelligence to our choices are we able to control the consequences of our actions, and thus have a role in determining our future in humanly fulfilling ways. Only intelligence, and the public knowledge to which it leads, can give us the freedom to affect the ongoing current of cause-and-effect *rationally*, and to move it in directions deemed by us to be desirable. However, this still begs the question of how we distinguish the desirable from the less so, and it is to that problem that we now turn.

Determining the good

If morality is indeed not only possible but imperative for humans, how do we decide what is good? One theme emerges consistently in social-scientific thought on this issue. Just as all knowledge rests ultimately on the animal propensity to experience environmental inputs — and to form memories of the resulting sensations and organize them — so too must morality have its origin in innate capacities of the senses. In the latter case, what is thought to be relevant are the feelings of pain and pleasure, and the desire to prevent the first and to prolong the second — over the long term and the widest possible range of relationships. We owe this insight to Epicurus, and to the work done centuries later by Montaigne, Hobbes, Hume and others.

Spencer pointed out that this innate source of morality corresponds exactly to the capacity to experience cognitive disjunction as painful and meaningful "fit" as pleasurable: the essential capacity that fuels all intellectual development. He proposed a natural morality grounded on this pleasure/pain sensing apparatus (which ensures *individual survival*) along with the urge to coordinate individual ends with those of the kin group, which is necessary for the *survival of offspring*. This is consistent with research and theory on the issue from Dewey to Piaget and Skinner, and makes even more sense today, in terms of recent findings in evolutionary science concerning kin selection.

All this does not mean that morality is therefore relativistic in the subjective sense. A comparison with the process of knowing is enlightening here. Durkheim considered reason, as well as aesthetic and moral value, to be the means by which individuals seek ideals. He saw science as *instrumental* in each case. As with the beautiful and good, the ultimate test of what is real is the evidence of the senses. However, that perceived sensation represents merely the initiation and final test of each brick in the process of knowledge-building. Intelligence, language and imagination are the means by which experienced data are shared with others, connections among them identified and explained, and the explanations subjected to public testing as to their reliability and workability. Only then do we consider the product to be an effective guide to action. The same approach can be applied to the valuing process.

Dewey explained that moral value is not *in* the objects or events experienced (any more than is truth) but in the felt responses of the organism to these: the culminations of its actions on the environment. This is why Bentham's utilitarianism was inadequate. The organism seeks to act so as to maintain a valued response. Memory and language, and the imagination and empathy these generate in the human, make possible the representation of present values in ideal images. The urge to prolong immediate pleasure develops into the goal of ensuring continued survival and achieving fulfilment for one's family and fellows along with oneself — and for the future as well as the present. Ideals such as benevolence and justice and reverence for life symbolize these yearnings; in fact, the concept of God has been used by humans through the centuries as a universal symbol for the highest of humanity's collective ideals. All ideal ends represent the imagined continuation of presently felt value in situations far removed in time and space from the immediate scene, and reason makes the connections between these. Available knowledge suggests appropriate precepts or codes of conduct, which correspond to explanations in the knowledge-building process. The test of these moral precepts is in the consequences of living by them, over time, as assessed by the feeling-states and behavioural patterns which they initiate and maintain in the general population.

Moral development

Piaget's findings drive home the need to understand how children acquire precepts and build values. Evolutionary naturalists realize that this is an important process that cannot be left to chance. Interaction with the *physical* environment provides children with the opportunity to incorporate mentally the connections and limitations in the inorganic realm — and thereby to achieve logical concepts such as conservation. So too, must their *cultural* surroundings encourage them to experience social boundaries, to assimilate rules of conduct and to build in the empathy and habits that not only make social life workable and rewarding, but possible at all. Piaget found that, as children advance intellectually they are increasingly able to make connections between choices and consequences; to identify and understand the social source and function of rules; to acquire perspective; and to apply rules in new situations. Ultimately, with the achievement of the ability for abstract thought, the child is capable of principled ethical behaviour. It must be emphasized, however, that throughout the process of building morality intellectual development is necessary but not sufficient. As Durkheim explained, cultural influences are crucial.

The continuity of means and ends

Moral desires and ideals not connected to effective action accomplish nothing, and lead but to disillusionment and cynicism. And means which initiate a stream of effects that propel the chooser in directions unrelated or even contradictory to desired goals can be morally destructive. Ever since Hume, leading naturalistic thinkers have understood that there is an inevitable continuity of means and ends; without it there could be no workable concept of present responsibility for the future consequences of choice. Certainly Spencer emphasized it, as did Durkheim. But perhaps Dewey put it best when he said each end becomes the means to an end that beckons further on. Means, to be effective, must be shaped by the end we seek, and the end must be logically and knowledgeably predictable in terms of the means. To proceed otherwise is to find the end distorted or forever lost to us, because the paths we chose led elsewhere, and the journey itself shaped our values and turned us into different people. This brings us back once more to the all-important role of knowledge, or reliable belief, in predicting the likely consequences of our choices, and of the means we select to achieve our goals.

The only way we have of judging the effectiveness of those means selected to reach our valued ends — and, ultimately, the worth of our ideals as well — is the very same method humans have devised for the testing of knowledge-claims. Means proposed as solutions for our social problems must be judged as to their moral and logical consistency with the desired goals, and then continuously evaluated under controlled conditions in terms of their consequences. Do they move us toward our goals at an acceptable cost in terms of resources and adverse side-effects? Just as knowledge-building requires a shared, public testing process, so, too, our means of establishing values worth living by must be the responsibility of the social group. And as with knowledge, the scientific approach discourages reckless large-scale innovation in the realm of morality. We do not readily jettison any part of our accumulation of reliable explanations of facts; nor should we too impulsively throw out the ethical principles and precepts that have been found to work throughout the history of the human race.

Morality and politics

The moral perspective of evolutionary naturalism implies that morality and politics are integrally related. Politics is simply the exercise of moral choices at the societal level. It is, above all, about the use (or abuse) of power to achieve group objectives. Perhaps the most unfortunate consequence of our persistent cultural dualism has been its effect on politics. A dualist world view can encourage people to isolate political choices from the moral, to separate the political means chosen from the ends desired, or the "practical" from the "ideal." Machiavelli's exclusive focus on means — although valuable as description of cause-and-effect relations in political behaviour — exemplifies this tendency. For Marx, political means were, by definition, incapable of altering the ends dictated by the laws of history. They might affect the timing of the process, but that was all. Having never quite freed himself from the dualism of his early upbringing, he relegated all moral concerns to the "ideal" realm, the very existence of which his materialism denied. In his view, prevailing moral principles were merely reflections of the most politically powerful of the current society's vested interests. Weber (a committed dualist) also struggled mightily with the issue. He finally decided that neither Kant's morality of *intent*, nor the naturalistic one of *consequence*, is relevant in the political (or "practical") sphere, where he concluded that violence will always be the ultimate arbiter.

Much earlier, Hobbes had attempted to reinstate a positive morality in the political arena by showing that, without it, we are left with the struggle of all against all in a brutish state of nature. Nietzsche also recognized that values have objective consequences and are inevitably interwoven in politics — rather than existing in a separate "ideal" realm of being. However, his model was essentially anti-democratic in that he tended to relegate moral/political responsibility to the Superman, who could discern reality from a loftier height than could the masses. The pragmatists were perhaps the first to identify "the method of intelligence," when employed by ordinary people, as the prerequisite for democracy — and to relate both to the capacity to make reasoned moral choices.

Durkheim, building on pragmatism to some extent, conceptualized all approaches to government on a continuum from democracy to despotism. The more the political process reflects the collective values of the entire society rather than those of the governing elite, he said, the more it will approximate democracy — and *vice versa*. With the advent of twentieth-century totalitarianism, however, the problem became more complex. The work of Popper and Arendt demonstrates that, to the degree that a charismatic leader has managed to gain total control of the socialization process, even individual consciences can be altered and shaped according to the leader's megalomaniac desires. The power that control of the communications media now confers — on either commercial or governmental bureaucracies or the mindlessly self-interested producers of entertainment — makes possible a manipulation of human beliefs and values that could rapidly produce disastrous consequences for civilization. The conclusions of Popper and Arendt imply that both the totalitarian state and its converse — a state of social anarchy — are fed by the absence within the citizenry of the "method of intelligence" and the reasoned morality associated with it.

An understanding of the relationship between politics and morality is essential if we are to accept responsiblity for the use and abuse of power in the world in general. Physical science, and the technology resulting from it, has given us great power to create and alter the physical contingencies controlling our experience. Whether or not we wish it so, humanity, by virtue of the imipact of its cultural products on the surroundings, now intervenes in the course of evolution. This occurs in non-rational and often destructive ways, thus imposing upon us cultural evolutionary paths which we may neither anticipate nor desire. The scientific process can be equally effective, if we would but develop and use it, in creating powerful and *positive* cultural contingencies: selective influences that would direct the stream of cause and effect rationally, in life-affirming and humanly fulfilling directions.

We should be warned that to the degree that our prevailing cultural dualism restricts science to the physical level only, we are deliberately depriving ourselves of our most effective instrument for solving the social problems thrown up by the success of that very process as it continues in its isolated and directionless operation. The result of such a course is becoming clearer with every passing day. The expanding gap between progress in the physical and that in the social sciences ensures that, increasingly, we will find ourselves propelled, crippled and rudderless, into an unmanageable sea of exponentially accelerating technological change. This is bound to occur because the physical sciences and their technological products guarantee a rapid pace of cultural evolution, with or without the consciously reasoned participation of humankind. We will either direct that process by means of morally informed political choices guided by the problem-solving tool of an effective social science, or we will continue to suffer as its helpless victims.

Evolution as the key

One idea, more than any other, has informed the insights of our heroes of naturalistic thought. It is the concept of evolution, as applied to the course of all nature. Through twenty-six centuries of history, various thinkers have seen that we must include within that natural flow the emergence and development of life, of animal forms and sentience and ultimately of a consciousness fuelled by the distinctively human activities of imagining, thinking and valuing. Once the significance of organic evolution was really understood, it became a powerful organizing principle for the study of individual development, social behaviour and human culture in all its aspects. It has led, at last, to a point of demarcation between general reliance on the old dogmatic, mystical and untestable speculations about the human condition, and the real possibility of a social science that can begin to achieve the promise of its name.

In the sixth century BCE, Anaximander of Miletus taught that the world (and countless other worlds) had emerged from a "boundlessness" — representing some sort of orderly progression of existence. He sought to identify a few universal processes governing a continuum within which all is related and coming-to-be. He even guessed that life had emerged from moist conditions in the natural world, and (in a prescient suggestion of mutability of species) that higher forms may have developed from the lower.

The earliest stirrings of the idea of natural selection are found in the works of Lucretius, expanding upon the crude evolutionary concepts of Epicurus. Lucretius explained both the origin of life and the development of civilization within an evolutionary framework. Plants came first, then animals and lastly, humans. Innumerable species were produced by sheer chance, and many died out along the way. Those that survived did so because they possessed qualities superior to those of their neighbours.

These ancient insights were largely ignored for eighteen centuries, due to their incompatibility with the dominant world view. Nonetheless, the vague notion of some sort of developmental process at work in nature had been gaining credence steadily and quietly. The next contribution of note was Rousseau's recognition of the immense *time* that must have been required for human evolution. Also important was his suggestion that humans might possibly be related to the apes. Still, the picture of evolution that became acceptable to educated people during the following century contained few of these powerful concepts from earlier times. It had been accommodated to the conventional wisdom. Evolution was being described as a discontinuous progression of increasingly superior life forms, culminating in humanity as the ultimate creation.

It was this idea of a "Great Chain of Being," designed according to a cosmic purpose and plan, that Darwin's theory undermined. Because of its direct challenge to a deeply entrenched dualism, the theory of natural selection encountered rough going. It was resisted in the scientific community and repudi-ated with great hostility in society at large. Even so, it was not long before some of the best minds of the nineteenth century recognized the soundness of the theory, as well as the light it might someday shed upon individual develop-ment and social change.

The implications of evolution for social behaviour and culture

Three major strands of thought were to dominate social theory in the twentieth century, all concerned with the implications of evolution for the infant social sciences. The first of these was Marxism, with its numerous intellectual de-scendants proposing popular modern variations of "conflict theory." Marxism had retained, in materialistic guise, the Enlightenment idea of an unalterable natural law and cosmic design working through and within history, with indi-viduals as the active agents of that process. The second strand had its begin-nings in Freudian psychoanalytic theory, but has since incorporated aspects of neo-Kantian transcendentalism as well. It now comprises many varieties of neo-Freudianism and Jungian mysticism that have long since forsaken Freud's original emphasis on evolutionary naturalism. It includes, as well, various forms of existential phenomenology and the anti-science, humanistic psychol-ogy of Fromm and others.

The third strand is the only one which has remained consistently within the framework of evolutionary theory. It can be traced through the works of Spencer, Pavlov, Dewey, Durkheim, Mead and Huxley, to its culmination in the Popper and Kuhn versions of the evolution of science, and in the possibili-ty of rapprochement between Piaget's evolutionary systems approach and Skinner's radical behaviourism. To some extent these strands are interwoven, as when we find Marxist and Freudian thought blended with existentialism in humanistic psychology and some forms of "critical theory." Or in the case of the similarity of Marx's and Durkheim's emphasis on culture as a shaper of consciousness to Fromm's "social character" — and the fact that we can find both explained concisely by Skinner's concept of "operant conditioning."

In each instance, however, the feature differentiating the three strands is their approach to cause and effect in human relations. In the end, Marxism and its intellectual offshoots resort to natural law in the form of an inexorable un-folding of history. And neo-Freudians, along with certain of their New Age and "humanistic" counterparts, seem to have rejected altogether the principle of cause and effect as applicable to their methods and conclusions. In this they are, in fact, repudiating Freud's commitment to the biological and experiential sources of effects within the psyche.

The roots of a theory of cultural evolution

It is the third group of thinkers who have made the real breakthrough in discovering the implications of evolution for humanity. Thanks to some of them, we can comprehend, for the first time ever, what natural selection means for the nature of causality at the organic, psycho-social and cultural levels of existence. Because of the work of Spencer, Pavlov, Dewey, Mead, Durkheim, Huxley, Popper, Piaget and Skinner we are now aware that organic functioning, individual development, social behaviour and the growth of culture all differ from inorganic reactions in one fundamental sense. In the first instance, causality is after the fact, with effects being contingent on the environmental conditions as altered by the consequences of previous actions. At the inorganic level, causality is linear and before the fact, or mechanistic.

Support for this comes from another source as well — the chaos theory of modern particle physics, for one, in its recognition of self-organizing systems of disequilibrium, and Roger Sperry's work in neuroscience for another. More directly pertinent, however, is the suggestion of biologists such as Richard Dawkins and Edward O. Wilson that the principle of evolution by differential survival of self-replicating entities must apply not only to genetic change, but to that which shapes behaviour and belief. This has been said before, of course, by social evolutionists from Spencer to Skinner. But Dawkins and Wilson have the authority of modern evolutionary biology to justify their propositions. They recognize the possible origins of human social organization in biological evolution: in the practices of kin selection and Evolutionarily Stable Strategies among animals. The latter are genetically programmed ways of relating that tend to preserve the genes of the self-sacrificing relative in the first case, and, in the second, to maximize sexual reproduction for the majority of the genes' carriers over the long term.

Evolutionarily Stable Strategies are established and maintained by after-the-fact causality. Those who conform to the strategy are rewarded in the sense that their genes are replicated in the bodies of subsequent generations. In other words, the environment — including the activities of neighbours as well as inorganic surroundings — selects out those animals not behaving in ways that work to protect them (or their close relatives) long enough to reproduce. Dawkins thinks it probable that the identical principle determines both the establishment of Evolutionarily Stable Strategies and those learned patterns of behaviour and thought that we call habits, customs and myths.

At this point Dawkins relies on the corroborated findings of Skinnerian research. This compatibility is no accident, for the behaviourists and evolutionary scientists are working from the same conceptual structure. It seems at long last that we have, in this happy conjunction of chaos, evolutionary and behavioural theory, a comprehensive model applicable to the psycho-social-cultural as well as the organic level. This amounts to a major revolution in human knowledge, comparable to those of Copernicus and Darwin. Within sociology, Durkheim's hypothesis of the evolutionary consequences of the division of labour in society may yet bear fruit. The implications of Popper's work for cultural evolution may likewise be recognized. W.G. Runciman is working on a theory conceptualizing social evolution in terms of the selection of practices that shape role relationships within the functional groupings constituting an integrated society. More and more economists, psychologists and anthropologists are joining the sociobiologists and systems theorists in applying an evolutionary perspective to social science.

It is imperative that we begin the task of conceptualizing the fundamental process of socialization within an evolutionary framework. The next stage would be to proceed to analyze other key problem areas, such as those of social organization and institutional change, in terms of an evolutionary perspective. There is a pressing need for a comprehensive interdisciplinary approach to the role of physical science and its technological products — and for that of normative belief systems — in the process of cultural evolution. An evolutionary systems model would make all these steps both feasible and fruitful.

Clearly, the revolution in this field is by no means complete, nor is its eventual success insured. Resistance to a social science with the potential for real reliability and power is still fierce. And, sadly, at this moment in history when we stand at the threshold of a truly scientific approach to the human studies, we are discovering almost as many enemies within the social science camp as without.

Evolutionary dead-ends

It is unfortunately true that students of human behaviour have not been immune to ideas that have proven harmful to social well-being and the survival of life. Fallibility and gullibility are not confined to mystics. For example, the seductive power of ideology continues to cripple the evolution of social-scientific thought. Ideological explanation, as Popper pointed out, comprises claims not amenable to falsification by subsequent experience. These result in unchallengeable doctrines that are supported by emotional yearnings rather than by reason or facts — and are thereby frozen in time.

Occasionally, as well, certain subjectivist currents of thought arise within the social studies: currents placing serious obstacles in the way of scientific progress. This is evident in a common propensity to speculate on untestable entities and urges within the "inner person," to the exclusion of attention to observable conditions and their effects on human actions. To a considerable extent, this particular detour from the mainstream of social-scientific thought enticed influential thinkers such as Rousseau, Freud, Bergson, Husserl, Weber, Sartre, Arendt and Fromm, and has been extremely costly in terms of time consumed and resources wasted.

Subjective relativism and romanticism

Subjectivism has often (though not always) been associated with romantic yearnings. Ever since Rousseau, the belief in a Golden Age of primitive humanity unwarped by civilization has tempted and stroked those who have felt frustrated by authority and burdened by the responsibility of choice. No longer able to blame the gods for the rules we live by, or to depend on Providence or nature for moral direction, many social theorists have retreated into romanticism.

Romantics tend to be moral relativists. Moral relativism is a belief that there are no ethical values applicable to the human species in its entirety. This position seems to confuse objectivity and universal applicability with *absoluteness*. It is the same mistake made by those within the modern social-science community who maintain that, because science cannot yield certainty, it is no more reliable as a source of knowledge than is private intuition.

Marx thought that ethical principles are merely the rules of conduct which work to ensure the survival of the ruling class in any society. A number of other popular approaches similarly equate morality with the norms of the in-group, or else identify it with the imperatives of the immediate situation, as perceived by the participants — or with particular cultures.

At least two generations of anthropologists believed that the customs they observed were so diverse and contradictory from tribe to tribe that it was impossible to discern any ideals, taboos or moral sanctions applicable to humanity at large. The reason for this misunderstanding of the very subject of their studies was the total neglect of biological factors by early twentieth-century anthropologists, and their abysmal ignorance of evolution. This can be explained (although not excused) by the ideological revulsion felt by many anthropologists against the excesses of Social Darwinism. Another reason for the commitment of anthropologists to moral relativism was their flawed methodology. They tended to find whatever they were looking for. They sought exotic differences and indications of harmony within a nature unspoiled by civilization — and they found them. For example, Margaret Mead reported a total absence of sexual restrictions among the youth of New Guinea. We now realize that such findings had more to do with the Rousseauian assumptions of the anthropologists involved than with the actual behaviour of the subjects.

Social scientists who share this perspective should be aware of what a subjective moral relativism really means. It implies a rejection of the existence of any commonalities which would justify ideals and rules of conduct with universal validity: commonalities in either the human developmental process, biologically based needs, imperatives of social organization or environmental limitations. It also demands a rejection of the idea that the human species as a whole may have acquired — by virtue of its evolved power to affect events — a unique and jointly shared responsibility for the future direction of history and the evolution of life.

Ideology as an obstacle to progress

We turn now to idea systems that have survived in social-scientific thought as anachronisms, long after they have ceased to work as explanations for experience. Two of the most pervasive of these are the psychoanalytically inspired and anti-science version of humanistic psychology (also influential within sociology) and Marxist-based socialism. A third is libertarianism — of the economic variety expressed in laissez-faire capitalism and the social libertarianism to which many socialists (in a Hegelian feat of juggling contradictions) are attached as well. All three ideologies are founded on assumptions about human nature and society that are fortified by strong emotions and desires, but belied by the evidence of common sense and scientific inquiry.

We need to rescue from the wreckage of these obsolete belief systems only those ideas that have stood the test of time and disciplined attempts to falsify them. Definitions of our human problems based on erroneous assumptions about human nature will never yield solutions, no matter how good the intentions nor how sustained the effort. Unquestioned assumptions that do not reflect observed regularities in experience are crippling. They are usually exercises in wish-fulfilment, and should be recognized as obstacles to the reasoned pursuit of understanding which has been the major goal of social science throughout its history. What distinguishes ideology from science is the untestability of its assertions, and the fundamentalist commitment fuelling these. The powerful biases of many modern social theorists toward Marxist socialism, economic and/or social libertarianism, and reliance upon anti-scientific approaches in the social disciplines are ideological to the core. They are as impervious to the impact of nature's feedback causality as is the doctrine of creationism, and their practical consequences in today's world may be equally harmful. Like the premises of mysticism, these secular ideologies impede rather than elicit further inquiry. They prevent accurate definition of complex social issues while discouraging flexibility and compromise in attacking them. And they operate as insurmountable obstacles to rigorous evaluation of the changes demanded by their premises.

The anti-science ideology which has emerged within the social-science community is particularly worrisome. Although a general distrust of science is its hallmark, it is characterized specifically by a denial of the possibility of *social* science — by definition, the very pursuit which provides the livelihood of its (apparently suicidal) supporters! This perspective often appears in association with a romantic social libertarianism. Proponents seem to believe that the very process of being subjected to disciplined inquiry will somehow alter and degrade human beings. And that any discovery of cause and effect in human relations will destroy the "autonomy" of choice.

But logic and evidence support a conclusion directly opposite to this. The more reliable knowledge we have about the psycho-social-cultural level, the more we can control the consequences flowing from our actions. Consequently, the more freedom we will have to affect the course of cultural evolution, and thereby, prevailing beliefs and values and behaviours. Without the ability to predict the results of alternative choices, we are forever doomed to be the helpless victims of technological change, or of our insatiable private "needs." Without the kind of warranted assertions that only a *scientific* social science can provide, we can have no confidence that the means selected are, in fact, leading to the ends desired. In sum, without such knowledge our goals are unattainable, and our belief in freedom remains illusory and fraudulent.

Another unfortunate result of the prevalence of the anti-scientific version of humanistic psychology/sociology is that people are prevented from recognizing the cultural origin of *all* values and beliefs. This approach functions as a barrier to understanding the cumulative and inevitably controlling nature of human culture. It thus prevents the disciplined pursuit of knowledgeable, effective and testable ways of redirecting the process. Too often its unintended consequences are an encouragement of anti-intellectualism, and of extremist swings from social passivity to mindless rebellion.

The dominance of both ideology and romantic/subjective moral relativism has had unfortunate consequences for social science. To a large degree we have contributed to the anti-science backlash now aimed in our direction by concerned religious believers, who with some justification, view social science as a threat to a workable moral order. Durkheim understood such worries and explained, by means of his concept of "anomie," how they may indeed be warranted — if a sound, experience-based morality is not available to fill the vacuum left by the loss of traditional mores. A number of today's leading social theorists have claimed that, because of its essential subjectivity and relativity, morality is of no concern to social science. This kind of thinking results in a wholesale lack of any commitment to engage in ethical issues in a disciplined, public way. It ignores our joint responsibility — in the role of scientist as well as artist and citizen — to improve the human condition, and to provide support and direction for the future of all life. It also indicates an appalling ignorance of what Durkheim called the facts of morality: the unavoidable participation of science in the shaping of culture, which, in turn, determines to a large extent, the values and beliefs of succeeding generations.

Social science as an adaptive problem-solving activity

The evidence suggests that today, for the first time in our history, humans are being forced by technology to inhabit one global culture. But we are without the reliable beliefs and values that would enable us to move from a state of international anarchy fuelled by race-thinking to one of world order. The cultural dualism that has subverted and crippled social science has, at the same time, isolated the physical sciences from any possibility of publicly tested and responsible moral direction. Consequently, we are poorly equipped to deal with the problems of environmental degradation, overpopulation and ethnic conflict that are threatening the ongoing course of evolution. If human culture is to evolve in directions necessary for long-term species survival, a radical change of world view is imperative.

Only when we really understand that our future will be determined by surrounding environmental conditions — cultural as well as physical — will we be able to define our problems in terms that render them amenable to solution. And only when we recognize that those environmental conditions shaping and directing us are, in turn, determined by the behaviour of all of us, will we be prepared to solve the problems facing humankind.

These problems are worsening daily. For example, it is impossible to exaggerate the degree to which life on earth is threatened by the current rate of human population growth. We have no choice but to deal with this crisis within the next few decades, for failure here means uncontrollable pollution and devastation of the global conditions required for the support of organic life and human culture. A second general imperative is almost as crucial to the future of humanity as is the need for necessary action to protect our badly threatened physical environment. This has to do with the accelerating corruption of human culture (the context within which all "selves" are shaped) by media portrayals of gratuitous violence and other desensitizing images. A third problem requiring solution is the dilemma of increasing inequality in the way that resources are shared among the world's peoples. Lastly, there are the dangers posed by the social pathology, tribalism and universal brutalization that will be encouraged by our failure to deal with the first three issues: in other words, by our failure to preserve the environmental preconditions for the diversity and enhancement of organic and social life.

Too many of the political means proposed by social theorists for resolving our most complex social problems have been inspired by ideology, or by the unreliable certainties of "scientism," rather than by authentic scientific inquiry. Too often these have involved massive and untestable social innovation with unpredictable consequences — impossible to evaluate until great damage has been done — rather than the careful step-by-step controlled changes required by science.

The most intractable obstacles to progress in social science have been two deeply embedded philosophical assumptions — both consequences of the persistent dualism within human culture. The first of these is the belief in a radical separation between the human species and the rest of nature: an essentially mysterious demarcation which implies a totally unique approach to knowing where the human condition is concerned. This is responsible for the widespread refusal, even by those working in the field, to recognize the universal applicability of scientific inquiry. The second obstacle is the perception of the human being as a repository of discrete defining faculties or functions (such as reason, psyche, spirit, thought, will, emotion, values, individual versus group behaviour, power relations, production, ritual and custom) and the consequent demand for a distinctive conceptual framework and methodology for each. This accounts for the fragmentation of the social disciplines into non-communicating academic specializations — all unaware of concepts and research findings in competing schools and of the biological sources and limitations of their common object of study.

It is time that we faced up to the dead-end nature of our attempts to set limits on scientific inquiry. The same applies to our propensity for establishing sovereign jurisdictions founded on incommensurable theories of isolated aspects of human development and relationships — each of which prides itself on maintaining ignorance of the other jurisdictions. These obsolete practices are doubly inexcusable today when we have available to us — as a result of the evolution of social-scientific thought traced in this book — the perspective of evolutionary naturalism.

This is a perspective based on a recognition of the determining role of the principle of after-the-fact causality — whether the resulting natural selection process involves genes, ideas or habits. And it recognizes the inextricable intertwining of both genetic and environmental programming in any specific behaviour. This key organizing principle has the potential for throwing new light on socio-cultural evolution and the cognitive/moral impact of socialization — and on the crucial function for both, of a scientifically informed education. And, finally, the new world view allows us to conceptualize our object of study, not as something non-natural and essentially unknowable, but in terms of increasingly complex systems of relations in nature: each emerging from, and in turn, encompassing and altering, the preceding system.

This study has shown that, for the first time in human history, we have the broad outlines of a paradigm for social science capable of explaining and organizing all of the available, disparate, documented facts about the human condition — and of generating fruitful hypotheses. Finally, we are being forced to recognize that the organic and interactional nature of the human species necessitates an integrated, interdisciplinary systems approach to social science: one that is soundly grounded in contemporary evolutionary theory and has itself evolved over the course of many centuries. Such an approach is implicit in evolutionary naturalism. Evidence from the history of other sciences indicates that it is only a matter of time before the social-science community begins to define itself in terms of this paradigm, or some related version of it. When this happens, social science will, at long last, be poised for the generation of reliable knowledge about individual learning, social organization, institutional change and the evolution of ideas. It will have emerged as the reasoned instrument for cultural adaptation now so necessary for the continued evolution of the human species. We can only hope that this occurs soon.

All of the current controversies among competing schools of social thought are rooted in the idea systems traced in detail in preceding chapters. This book has demonstrated how the old ideologically fuelled illusions of individual and tribal sovereignty — and the predilection for wholesale leaps into the unknown — have too often led social theorists astray. Humanity can profit from the minute, measurable and retrievable errors inevitable to honest scientific inquiry, but the massive mistakes of ideology could destroy us in the end. Thus far, our lack of progress in the study of human relationships has been due to the failure of our ideologies. Only to the extent that our guiding philosophy can inspire and support a social science with demonstrable reliability as a guide to problem-solving will people in general be willing to leave the imagined security of humanity's culturally created cave. Only then will we replace the comfort of traditional myths and New Age certainties with the satisfaction that real adaptive power can bring.

Appendix

Evolutionary Spiral

by Pat Duffy Hutcheon

P erhaps the Buddha was the first
   to recognize that humankind
emerged from out the stream of life;
was part of one organic pool with nature's order structured in;
that human selves were always more
than isolated spirits floating free,
created out of nothing by some engineering god.

Nothing at all is ever born of nothing by the will of gods, Lucretius said.
And long before the poet wrote,
there was a flowering of thought on Asia Minor's coast.
led by descendants of that great Ionian people who had formed the very heart
    of Greece,
the physical philosophers.
For they it was who pondered long and deep and free from godly fear
upon the nature and beginnings of the world.

T'was Anaximander who maintained that all the early forms of life
emerged from out of earthly moisture and
that higher species grew from out of low
in everlasting spirals of increasingly complex.
Then Alcmaeon of Croton made the claim
that humans with the other species needs must share
their basic nature — even learning through the senses is the same —
to differ only in the power of thought,
which that great man exemplified so well.

Protagoras the sophist taught
that nature's laws are everywhere the same.
with consequences unavoidable;
nor gods nor humans can escape their working out.
The atomist, Leucippus, he it was, they say, who thought
that all reality is matter, ongoing, indivisible, unwrought —

comprising atoms moving constantly,
colliding and combining; then regrouping to compound
in that mad whirl in space that did in time
make up the universe whence all things came.

Democritus of Abdura, Leucippus' student was.
The universe is matter in a constant moving state,
and motion is a given, so he said.
No need to introduce First Cause external to the flux of time,
nor yet transcendent Consciousness nor supernatural Mind.
If gods exist they must as well be governed by necessity
like all things human; and if souls there be,
they must be mortal too;
and with the body merge once more into that long forgotten sea
whence all life grew.

Then Epicurus in a later time
sought to spring wider still the hidden locks
of nature's gates; Lucretius celebrated him
in wondrous verse resounding down
the centuries wherever humans lived to speak and write,
and wonder in the night.
Lucretius wrote of plants appearing, then of animals,
and human species coming forth by merest chance —
with many dying out along the way.

And then the insight almost perished from our sight.
Through many shadowed centuries evolution seemed a dream long past.
'Til Rousseau, living in a light'ning world,
saw the significance of *time* in shaping that which is;
immensity of time enabling humans to evolve —
perhaps from apes.
Then few there were who did not look askance in horror at the thought,
for in his day the popular wisdom was
that a Great Chain of Being did exist,
with species each created whole at every step from out God's mind,
according to His Purpose and His Plan, with humans at the top,
and different in kind.

From Darwin came the spark igniting
all humanity in visions seen but dimly by the Ancient Greeks.
One simple principle at work throughout the aeons long, he said;

one mighty natural engine pulsing down the generations now long dead.
Environmental challenges selecting out; the unadapted ones
surviving not to reproduce their kind,
while random changes proving advantageous endure and thus accumulate.
Directionless, the vehicle of natural selection ran —
no destination fixed ahead; no engineer; no master plan.
Thus awe-inspiring evolution brought us to this unexpected place,
producing finally the human race.

Imagination ne'er conceived a path to life more wondrous than
the story Darwin told; the tale he saw unfold;
in rock and bivalve, limb and organ, all unplanned diversity —
in form and function over time, expanding ever awesomely.
Indeed it was a tale sublime.
"Descent with modification" then, to him, it seemed to be.
Thus nature's process, engineered within,
no blueprint handed down,
nor goal ordained nor Mind at work without, of nature's order free.
All, all is process; yet there works within, a pulsing heart —
reverse causality!

Contingent circumstances feeding back,
determining what forms prevail; what functions fail
to meet confronting challenges of cataclysm or of gradual change.
Those organisms that best fit the niche available survive
to breed and thus their code is carried on
in pool of species' genes.
For adaptation is the key, as nature does select from what by random chance
    is born,
that which can "work" in altered times,
and thus a species, through accumulation, is condemned
to probe alternate paths that work and thus to live,
or to stagnate and die.
For nature never can forgive.

And now the theories build at faster pace.
And now we see the awe-inspiring possibility
that this great principle of natural selection
drives culture too; and science; and the growth of intellect;
and developing behaviours within every living thing.
Like genes that carry information charting out
our organismic form and function as in current strong —

determining the route the species takes,
so too our cultural routines, ideals and norms are passed along
the generations by their individual carriers;
some tossed aside, but others bearing fruit to spare.
And if these work to give us power in changing circumstance,
the cultural spirals in complexity and long endures.
But if they cripple those who carry them, and weigh them down —
those people either change their ways and their beliefs,
or else they die and so, thereby,
the culture disappears.

And finally in scientific process we can see
the path of evolution writ by humankind quite consciously.
Hypotheses created by the minds of those who seek to know
the regularities of that great order all surrounding and immersing and propel-
    ling us to grow.
And in their testing, truths are ferreted with ever finer eye,
and some are found to hold and to withstand attempts to falsify,
and thus give grounds for action with predicted consequence.
But many fail, and thus are cast aside for propositions new
with better fit to circumstance.
And, gradually, by rigorous unforgiving test an edifice of
knowledge builds;
endowing us with power to shape that natural ordering force —
and by this means determine paths whereby the culture will evolve.
Thereby to change for good or ill the future's course,
by our resolve.

But many now recoil in terror at the thought that in our might
we hold potentially the power of heaven's throne.
So too must hominids in dim-lit caves have shuddered at the sight
of fire new-captured and employed as tool —
'til then the instrument of gods alone.
For power gives us choice and choice demands responsibility,
and we are ill prepared by our beliefs in godly wrath
and godly grace;
so it may be that humankind rejects the opportunity
for evolutionary spiral far above the current habits of our race;
the violent depredations of our past —
and by rejecting science may prefer to pave the way that none can stay,
in unremitting spiral down and down;
and into Hell at last!

Index